D1511754

AMERICAN GOVERNMENT:

The

Clash

of

Issues

Edited by

JAMES A. BURKHART
Stephens College

SAMUEL KRISLOV
University of Minnesota

RAYMOND L. LEE
Indiana University of Pennsylvania

PRENTICE-HALL, INC., Englewood Cliffs, New Jersey

AMERICAN GOVERNMENT:

The

Clash

of

Issues

FOURTH EDITION

Library of Congress Catalog Card Number: 76-161456

ISBN: 0-13-026955-7

10 9 8 7 6 5 4 3 2

Printed in the United States of America

Prentice-Hall International, *London*
Prentice-Hall of Australia, Pty. Ltd., *Sydney*
Prentice-Hall of Canada, Ltd., *Toronto*
Prentice-Hall of India Private Limited, *New Delhi*
Prentice-Hall of Japan, Inc., *Tokyo*

CONTENTS

Chapter 3

THE CONSTITUTION: FRAME OR FRAMEWORK?   52

Chapter 4

THE FEDERAL SYSTEM: INSTRUMENT OF LIBERTY OR INEFFICIENCY?   72

Chapter 6

PUBLIC OPINION AND INTEREST GROUPS: WHO SPEAKS FOR ME?   146

PUBLIC OPINION: THE VOICE OF THE PEOPLE OR MANIPULATION BY THE PUBLIC PERSUADERS?

INTEREST GROUP POLITICS: DOMINATION OR BALANCE OF FORCES?

Chapter 7

POLITICAL PARTIES AND POLITICAL PHILOSOPHIES: THE SEARCH FOR PURPOSE AND MEANING   175

DO AMERICAN POLITICAL PARTIES MEAN ANYTHING?

THE NEW POLITICS: NEW FACES IN OLD PLACES

Chapter 8

VOTING BEHAVIOR, NOMINATIONS, AND ELECTIONS: GOVERNMENT BY THE CONSENT OF THE GOVERNED OR THE GOVERNING?

Chapter 9

Chapter 10

Chapter 11

Chapter 16

I am young
and strong
and living
a great
adventure

ANNE FRANK

PREFACE

The success of previous editions of *American Government: The Clash of Issues* together with recent developments in American society and American government reaffirm our original purpose in writing this book. We set out a number of years ago to structure a book which would emphasize and elucidate the significant, controversial, and relevant issues in American government. At that time most if not all of our readers were only potential voters. Today virtually everyone who reads this book is a qualified voter—or should be. Hence, we feel even more strongly that unless the study of American government comes to grips with the issues of the day, it does not, in our opinion, maximize the time and effort expended in preparation and study. As in earlier editions, we are in accord with the late Professor Eugene Burdick who asserted, "The *romantic* part of politics is partisan rather than neutral and deals with issues rather than statistics." We have tried to maintain this heart, while including more technical material relevant to this approach, in accordance with developments in the field of political science.

In previous editions we spelled out our convictions that students must become involved in the political dialogue of our time. We would like to repeat and to reemphasize these objectives:

1. A recognition that controversy and disagreement are natural parts of the democratic process and that their absence rather than their presence should cause alarm.
2. A realization that even though acceptance of political conditions as fixed or "given" can frequently be bad, the opposite—polarized, irreconcilable standing on principle —is equally dangerous.
3. An idea of how emotionally loaded a major issue is, what makes such an issue, and what courses lead to compromise or stalemate.
4. A personal involvement in many of the issues—if not on an action basis, at least an intellectual identification.
5. An awareness that political practices, rights, and liberties are a function of groups of persons and entail a great deal more than the mere passing of a law.

Our debt to the many teachers and students who have used earlier editions is very great. Particularly valuable has been the constructive criticism which we have received on a day-to-day basis from our colleagues, both senior and junior. John F. Ludeman and Gene F. Schmidtlein of Stephens College made many valuable suggestions. Diane Kingsley, a Stephens student in American Government, provided a student's point of view on many selections. She also made several suggestions on the illustrations. Rick Bunin at the University of Minnesota aided in many small and not-so-small ways. We also wish to acknowledge comments and suggestions which have been given to us through the years by various members of the departments of Political Science at the University of Missouri, Indiana University of Pennsylvania, and the University of Minnesota.

THE STATE OF AMERICA:
UPHEAVAL OR REGENERATION?

The unprecedented stirrings, general dissonance, and, on occasion, utter turmoil of recent years have frightened some, disturbed many, and dismayed virtually everyone. Besides being introduced to a whole new lexicon—"cop out," "rap," "paranoia," "generation gap," "lib," "your own trip," "straight"—Americans have seen more flamboyant protest, demonstrations, dissent—constructive and destructive—and confrontation politics than they have witnessed in over a century of political controversy. The complaints were real, the rhetoric was right, but often the means betrayed the ends. A student of contemporary history observed, "The United States has gone through rough times before, but the present crisis has no genuine predecessors." As a consequence, probably not since the Civil War have so many Americans turned their gaze inward and pondered the meaning of the American spirit and the fate of the Republic.

At present, the state of the nation is uncertain. Modern Cassandras bewail an impending crisis and predict radical social disorientation. Many serious observers talk about "a sense of pessimism," "an ailing soul," "a recession of spirit." Others see the discordance and aberrations as transitory styles which will give way to other modes, other patterns. They suggest that the United States has been fighting too many wars, too many crusades, and there is nothing that a few years of peace would not correct. In fact, it is argued that the mood of the country has already changed. The militancy of the late 1960's has evolved into a complex montage of apathy, disillusionment, and empty realism. Yet, for others, now that the voting age has shifted, the era promises opportunities for reform within the system. Hence, we have at least two points of view. According to one analysis, the youth are "turned off" and the country is "cooling." Another view holds that there is an intense sense of outrage lurking beneath the placid surface. A syndicated newspaper column quoted John Viscount Morley, "You have not converted a man because you have silenced him." However, no one is willing to assert that the current mood is permanent or that the problems will disappear. Virtually all observers would agree with Lincoln that, "The dogmas of the quiet past are inadequate to the stormy present." There is also a hope that out of the upheaval and agitation will arise a new movement of renewal and regeneration.

Some of the causes of social disequilibrium are obvious, perhaps the most apparent being the changing generational profile. The input of large numbers of young people in any group, be it a social organization or a nation, will cause repercussions. At present, the number of Americans between the ages of 14 to 24 constitute 20 per cent of the population, and the median age of Americans is 27.6 years. This is an age bristling with unsettling ideas and restless energy. In many ways the category (18–40) is the genius of the country. To quote Sir William Osler, "effective, moving, vitalizing work of the world is done between the ages of 25 and 40." The age bracket also includes the largest number of people who are most likely to plunge in and out of marriage, crack conventions, and open the road to Xanadu. For others, the roads lead only to unfulfillment and eternal searching.

There are additional implications. Young people are currently experiencing longer periods of adolescence than ever before because of the affluent society, educational demands, and the increasing gap between childhood and adulthood. Up until about 75 years ago the long transition between childhood and adulthood, adolescence as a social stage, was virtually unknown, while today the duration of this period seems to be increasing. As a result, teenagers are assigned to a state of limbo until society stamps the badge of adulthood upon them.

If the prolonged probationary period were not enough, the young (as well as others) have experienced hot and cold wars, virtually uncontrolled technical and scientific advance, static social and political institutions, a crisis of belief, and the failure of new and relevant values to emerge. At the same time there has been a revolution against rigid life patterns even before alternate life styles are possible. Optional and multiple ways of living must emerge, for each individual's image of the world is radically changing. The young, as well as many adults, have a new perspective. First, there is increasing recognition that the world is a spaceship with limited environment. Second is the growing awareness that we must bring science and technology under control and humanize the goals of an industrial society. Third, there is a demand from everyone, especially submerged individuals and minority groups, for freer expression and personal involvement in political decisions that matter. Finally, people are developing greater aspirations; there is a revolution of rising expectations at home as well as abroad. People are demanding a wider range of choice in their lives and career opportunities. It is within this framework that we begin a study of American society.

In the first selection, "Revolution by Consciousness," Charles A. Reich affirms that the stage of Consciousness III has arrived and little that we do or say can impede its progress. Herbert Marcuse, "Charles Reich—A

Negative View," has some reservations, as do John Kenneth Galbraith, "Who Minds the Store?" and Daniel Bell, "The Cultural Contradiction." At this point, Robert J. Lifton, "Protean Man and the New History," contends that we are experiencing a revolution in personality as well as culture. The selection "The Cooling of America" suggests that a new mood or perspective may be emerging in the nation. John W. Gardner, "Paralysis of the Will," argues that we need revitalized leadership and the reform of our institutions. James Reston, "Movement to Regain Sovereignty," suggests that the beginnings of such a movement are already under way.

1

Revolution by Consciousness

CHARLES A. REICH

Reich states that "the change to Consciousness III is not, so far as we know, reversible." Would you agree? The author also suggests that there is "loneliness, emptiness and plastic isolation" in our society. Is this a fair characterization? Would Consciousness III be an adequate corrective for the emptiness of the corporate state? Is "the only reality man has . . . the one he makes?" How does the author illustrate the above theme? Can there be a revolution without violence?

. . . Technology may provide a new basis for generating and guiding the energies of man. Instead of summoning man's energies by the lash of hunger, competition, and perpetual dissatisfaction, man can find his sources of energy in the variety, stimulation, and hope that technology can provide. Satisfaction can be a greater stimulant than deprivation. Technology need not sap our energy; it can augment it, amplify it, multiply it, as it has done already with music. And the community that technology makes possible can be a still greater source of energy—the energy of group effort and of Eros. When man is reunited with self and

From Charles A. Reich, The Greening of America *(New York: Random House, Inc., 1970), pp. 390–95. Copyright © 1970 by Charles A. Reich. Reprinted by permission of the publisher.*

with the larger community of nature, all of the cosmos will add to his own sources.

Thus the new age of man can take the best from the ages which preceded it. From the pre-industrial age it can take the integration and balance of life, the sense of God in everything. From the industrial era it can take technology and the steady rise to a higher level of life. From its own age it can take the control and use of technology, and the way of life of satisfaction, community, and love, a way of life that aspires higher and higher, without forgetting its human source. In *Eros and Civilization* Marcuse spoke of releasing man's instincts, but the new age will do more; it will not only release but augment and inspire, and make that the chief end of society. And it will do so within a society that makes the Judeo-Christian ethic not merely an ignored command, but a realistic way of life.

This, then, is the plan for a new society, a workable way of life, a realistic approach to the nineteen seventies and beyond. Many will deny that it is a plan at all, but they are looking for a plan where it can no longer be found. Or it may be called utopian, in the sense that it hopes for what never can be. But man that could build the machines of today, and could learn to live *for* them, can also learn to live *with* them. If "human nature" can teach itself to serve a lifetime in a factory or office, then it can also teach itself the far more rewarding service of self and community that we have described. Some may say we are unduly optimistic— the only answer we can give is that the new way of life is better for man—has been found better by those who have tried it, and will be found better by those who try it hereafter.

What we have said concerning consciousness, technology, the search for wisdom, and community—about the dining halls and the supermarket—is that man must create his own fictions and live by them. Consciousness takes the elements it finds and arranges them to make a life and a society that reflect man's needs and hopes. In Kesey's *Sometimes a Great Notion*, in Vonnegut's *Cat's Cradle,* in Wallace Stevens' poetry, in psychedelic music, man seeks to create for himself an order by which he can live. As Vonnegut says, "Live by the *foma* [harmless untruths] that make you brave and kind and healthy and happy."

To call this order "fiction" is just a way of saying that the only reality man has is the one he makes. The Corporate State cuts man off from his inner sources of meaning and attempts to impose on him an order derived from the State or from the abstract, rational universe. But this imposed order is a fiction too, and it is one that is bad for man. The dining hall and the supermarket, the concept of work as play and of life as a search for wisdom are fictions that are good for man.

For underlying the higher reason of Consciousness III, its search for meaning, for community, for liberation, is an exalted vision of man. Man, it says, is not part of a machine, not a robot, not a being meant to starve, or be killed in war, or driven like a beast, not an enemy to his own kind and to all other kinds, not a creature to be controlled, regulated, administered, trained, clipped, coated, anesthetized. His true nature is expressed in loving and trusting his own kind, being a part of nature and his own nature, developing, growing, living as fully as he can, using to the full his unique gift, perhaps unique in the universe, of conscious life.

Of all the many ways of life known to history, Consciousness III seems the closest to valuing life for its own sake. Almost always, men have lived subject to rigid custom, to religion, to an economic theory or political ideology. Consciousness III seeks freedom from all of these. It declares that *life* is prior to all of them. It does not try to reduce or simplify man's complexity, or the complexity of nature. It values the present, not the past, the future, or some abstract doctrine of mythical heaven. It says that what is meaningful, what endures, is no more nor less than the total experience of life.

It is little more than twenty years since the first members of the new generation were born. And it is only that long since, in Holden Caulfield, the hero of J.D. Salinger's *The Catcher in the Rye,* we heard their first voice. Today Holden Caulfield's dream seems, to most people, further away than ever. A movement exists, a new generation and a new culture have come into being, but repression has grown harsher and the Corporate State has won most of the battles, from People's Park to Harvard. The movement is divided, confused, and deeply depressed, and the forces of death are everywhere. Increasingly, rigid administrators, police, national guard troops, penal laws, prisons, and technological weapons are the dominant realities of today.

But this is a view without perspective. How long ago was it that we first heard of hippies? That we first heard the sounds of acid rock? That we saw the first student demonstration, the first peace march? By the standards of history, the transformation of America has been incredibly, unbelievably swift. And the change to Consciousness III is not, so far as we know, reversible. Once a person reaches Consciousness III, there is no returning to a lower consciousness. And the change of generations is not reversible either. Every evidence we have is that youngsters in high school are potentially more radical, more committed to a new way of life, than their elders in college.

From the perspective of history, change is coming with astonishing speed to the rest of the population as well. The daily newspaper is full of it. More and more people are dissatisfied, are actively protesting something, are drawn into controversies with the State concerning freeways, urban renewal, transportation, or missile systems. More and more groups are resorting to militancy, experiencing repressions, and becoming radical in turn. If young people are in conflict with the State, parents are not immune. Draft refusers have parents. Young people beaten by the police have parents; so do those arrested for possessing drugs. And there are more and more stories of kids turning their parents on—sharing their life-style with them, and gradually, their politics as well. All of the G.I.'s in Vietnam have been exposed to the new consciousness, and a great many are bringing it home with them. (It is almost equally prevalent in domestic army camps.) Perhaps we can look forward to having a million or more young men, army veterans, having a life-style in common with the students and with the new crop of high school students just coming along. The new life-style is no longer just on a few campuses, it is to be found in every region of the country; it is even invading the countryside. And wherever it goes, underground newspapers, free schools, rock music, clashes with the law, rejection of the machine go too. Before long, the sideburns, beards, and long hair will mean votes as well.

Nineteen sixty-eight was the year of Chicago. Nineteen sixty-nine was the year of Woodstock. That speaks of the distance we have come, and the speed with which we are traveling. The new consciousness is sweeping the high schools, it is seen in smiles on the streets. It has begun to transform and humanize the landscape. When, in the fall of 1969, the courtyard of the Yale Law School, that Gothic citadel of the elite, became for a few weeks the site of a commune, with tents, sleeping bags, and outdoor cooking, who could any longer doubt that the clearing wind was coming?

All of these signs might mean little if change had to be produced by the efforts of a minority, working against the power of the State. But the state itself is producing these changes, and its self-destruction has only begun. The people of the Movement may grow tired and discouraged, but time and the force of the machine are on their side. And there is nothing on the other side. There are no enemies. There are no people who would not be better off, none who do not, in the depth of their beings, want what Consciousness III wants.

We have all known the loneliness, the emptiness, the plastic isolation of contemporary America. Our forebears came thousands of miles for the promise of a better life. Now there is a new promise. Shall we not seize it? Shall we not be pioneers once more, since luck and fortune have given us a vision of hope?

The extraordinary thing about this new consciousness is that it has emerged out of the wasteland of the Corporate State, like flowers pushing up through the concrete pavement. Whatever it touches it beautifies and renews: a freeway entrance is festooned with happy hitchhikers, the sidewalk is decorated with street people, the humorless steps of an official building are given warmth by a group of musicians. And every barrier falls before it. We have been dulled and blinded to the injustice and ugliness of slums, but it sees them as just that—injustice and ugliness—as if they had been there to see all along. We have all been persuaded that giant organizations are necessary, but it sees that they are absurd, as if the absurdity had always been obvious and apparent. We have all been induced to give up our dreams of adventure and romance in favor of the escalator of success, but it says that the escalator is a sham and the dream is real. And these things, buried, hidden, and disowned in so many of us, are shouted out loud, believed in, affirmed by a growing multitude of young people who seem too healthy, intelligent, and alive to be wholly insane, who appear, in their collective strength, capable of making it happen. For one almost convinced that it was necessary to accept ugliness and evil, that it was necessary to be a miser of dreams, it is an invitation to cry or laugh. For one who thought the world was irretrievably encased in metal and plastic and sterile stone, it seems a veritable greening of America.

2

Charles Reich — A Negative View

At essentially what point do Herbert Marcuse and Charles Reich part company? What is Marcuse's position on the necessity of violence for inculcating social reform? What aspect of Reich's work does Marcuse consider the best?

HERBERT MARCUSE

If you read a critical essay in The New Yorker, you can be reasonably sure of at least three things: (1) It is beautifully written; (2) it comes very close to the truth; (3) you are satisfied: no reason to get frightened, everything will be all right, or—beyond your (and anybody else's) power.

Take as example the by now classical piece on "Hiroshima": there is to my knowledge no better, no more moving description on what happened, and all this appears like a natural catastrophe, an earthquake, the last day of Pompeii—there is no evidence, no possibility of crime, of guilt, of resistance and refusal.

The most recent example is Charles A. Reich's long piece, "The Greening of America," a condensation of the book with the same title. We should admire the sensitivity and good instincts of the editors: they must have realized immediately the vital importance of the piece. The opening sentences read as follows:

"There is a revolution under way. It is not like the revolutions of the past. It has originated with the individual and with culture, and if it succeeds, it will change the political structure only as its final act. It will not require violence to succeed, and it cannot be succesfully resisted by violence."

So we are advised that we are in the middle of a revolution which is "spreading with amazing rapidity," and at the same time assured that there will be no violence.

If true, this revolution would indeed be very much unlike the revolutions of the past. All that has to happen (and it is al-

Our foreign policy must always be an extension of this nation's domestic policy. Our safest guide to what we do abroad is a good look at what we are doing at home.

LYNDON BAINES JOHNSON

ready happening, according to Reich) is that more and more people develop a new consciousness (Consciousness III as contrasted with Consciousness I, corresponding to the early American tradition, and Consciousness II, corresponding to the "Corporate State"), with new values, new goals, a new sensitivity which reject the values and goals of the Corporate State—and the latter will collapse. There will be, there can be no resistance, for the people will just stop working, buying, selling, and they will have won. For the State is nothing but a machine, controlled by nobody, and if the machine is no longer tended to, it will stop.

Consciousness III is of course that of the young generation in rebellion against the Establishment. What are the new revolutionary values of the rebels? The author formulates them in three "commandments"; the first: "thou shall not do violence to thyself"; the second: "no one judges anyone else"; the third: "be wholly honest with others, use no other person as a means." The astonished reader might ask: What is revolutionary about these commandments which from the *Bible* to Kant and beyond have graced the sermons of the moralists?

In a sense, they are indeed present in "Consciousness III" but in a sense essentially different from the tradition which has professed and "sublimated" them so that they get along well with repression, misery, frustration. For the militant young, they are desublimated so that they are no longer compatible with repression, misery and frustration. They are a little less nonviolent: they presuppose the abolition of the established system of institutions, a new society, a new way of life.

For Reich, this is not really a serious problem. One day in the foreseeable future, men and women, boys and girls from all walks of life will have enough of the old, will quit. And since there is "nobody in control," this will be it.

Nobody in control of the armed forces, the police, the National Guard? Nobody in control of the outer space program, of the budget, the Congressional committees? There is only the machine being tended to? But the machine not only must be tended to, it must be designed, constructed, programed, directed. And there are very definite, identifiable persons, groups, classes, interests which do this controlling job, which direct the technical, economic, political machine for the society as a whole. They, not their machine, decided on life and death, war and peace—they set the priorities. They have all the power to defend it—and it is not the power of the machine but *over* the machine: human power, political power.

Even granted that the dream comes true —is it conceivable that this will come about, all over the nation, spontaneously and at the same time? Without any form of preparation, organization, mobilization?

Violence is ingrained in this society: in its institutions, its language, its experience, its fun—violence of defense and violence of aggression. Nobody in his right mind would "advocate" violence: it is there. The task is to reduce it as much as is humanly and socially possible. But this goal cannot be attained by an ostrich policy.

Reich recognizes that the revolutionary changes to come will have a pattern very different from the preceding historical revolutions, that their scope and depth will be greater, that the traditional concepts do not suffice. His analysis of the hippie subculture is sensitive—although again much too sensitive—sentimental sublimation.

The best part is perhaps his picture of the Corporate State—not its evaluation. But all this is distorted by the false perspective, which transfigures social and political radicalism into moral rearmament. Notwithstanding its insights and critiques, "The Greening of America" is the Establishment version of the great rebellion.

3

Who Minds the Store?

JOHN KENNETH GALBRAITH

According to Galbraith, is Reich's explanation of Consciousness III a justification or rationalization of mere self-indulgent idleness? What is the place of drugs in Consciousness III—expansion or escape? What modifications does Galbraith make to Reich's conception of Consciousness III in order to make it an acceptable life style? In what ways has Reich failed to refine the economics of Consciousness III? What is the meaning of the title, "Who minds the Store?"

Charles Reich has written an enormously interesting book. I am favorably disposed for he draws substantially on "The New Industrial State" (as he is generous in saying) but vanity is not all. His social evidence and interpretation are wide-ranging; his conclusions are well beyond my imagination—or courage. It will have a big audience and his concept of Consciousnesses I, II and III will affect political thinking and behavior.

The core of his idea is that modern large-scale organization in association with the modern state imposes its own truth and discipline on people and persuades them that this is happiness. The discipline compels contrived and barbarous habits of work and leisure and greatly unnecessary, banal and unsatisfying consumption.

The instrument is partly advertising and other organized persuasion; partly it is unexamined pressures to compete and conform. The answer is not to tame and rationalize bureaucratic purpose but to emancipate ourselves from its compulsions—its

standards of achievement, its persuasion and its consumption standards.

Thus, we free ourselves from its power as organization and from the thralldom of its values. And this, precisely, is what he thinks a whole generation is doing. The ability to see one's self as the automaton of a great organization and to see the possibility of being guided instead by one's own thought and feeling is what he calls Consciousness III.

I think Reich is making a most important point. I am greatly impressed by his central idea which is that we can reduce the power of his corporate state (I used the milder phrase, industrial system) only by making it less important in our lives. That means rejecting its persuasion—deciding on our needs for ourselves. If we accept that what General Motors produces is the most important thing in life, we will have to accept what General Motors does.

At the same time, I have some reservations that are not altogether slight. To save space, let me list them:

The rejection of the contrived wants and disciplines of the corporate state—of Consciousness II—could easily become a rejection of all serious mental and artistic purpose. Some recent student revolt has been against the oldest of student grievances which is the need for mental effort. Reich's Consciousness III could become a cover for self-indulgent idleness. On this he is insufficiently alarmed—in this book at least.

In this connection I think especially about drugs—on which Reich is not entirely clear. Perhaps drugs expand consciousness. My Calvinist but clinical view is that they are used mostly to escape it. Hemingway and his people thought they had found self-realization in convivial two-handed consumption of alcohol. I've never believed that either. I think it was just an improved excuse for getting drunk.

Liberals who in some measure designed Reich's corporate state—its welfare system and its Keynesian apparatus—suffer unfairly at his hands. Life is a process; each step builds on the one before. Critics of the earlier steps are not wiser, only later. And while some liberals of the Consciousness II welfare and Keynesian state were profoundly content with their handiwork—and still are—others continued to sustain the critical mood of liberalism. This liberalism paved the way for Reich's Consciousness III. Reich might also be a little less self-flagellant. To be too vehemently critical is to defeat one's critical purpose. Better a bit more cool.

There are, I think, much richer opportunities in the political process for Consciousness III than Reich sees. Something very like this Consciousness sparked the revolt against the Vietnam war and the national security fantasies of the Pentagon, especially of the Air Force. It retired Lyndon Johnson to Texas, denied Humphrey the Presidency, rejected a fair number of corporate sycophants in the recent primaries and at this writing promises to send a sprinkle of its own people to Congress over the anguished mourning of Consciousness II politicians and sages who see the effort as the death of the Democratic party as they have known it. What a good thought.

Most important, Reich has not worked out the economics of the Consciousness III life style. Houses, plumbing, hospitals, schools and universities, policemen, the pill, some clothes will still be necessary. Community consumption—public goods—will, I think, be much more needed. Also there are still the people for whom the whole notion of contrived wants is a distant and bitter myth. Life in Consciousness III cannot be indefinitely the gift of achievement-minded toilers in Consciousnesses I and II.

So however rationally we come to regard consumption—however systematically we reject persuasion and substitute our own judgment—there will have to be work and organization. There will have to be rules for the new game—or the next phase of the old one.

These rules can be devised. And they must be. Our excuse for ever-increasing consumption, arising from ever more elaborately induced wants brought about by an ever more impersonal and massive bureaucracy, cannot be that we don't know how to run any other kind of system. It can't be the case for an increasing GNP that we can't manage a stable or declining one. But if Reich doesn't solve the problem, he at least makes us aware of the task.

4

The Cultural Contradiction

DANIEL BELL

What does Daniel Bell mean by the Protestant Ethic? How has it been betrayed by the growth of capitalism? Would the business community agree that the corporate economy has "no unified value system of its own"? Why will economic growth not solve twentieth century social problems? Has American capitalism lost its traditional legitimacy? What is the cultural contradiction?

The ultimate support for any social system is the acceptance by the population of a moral justification of authority. The older justifications of bourgeois society lay in the defense of private property. But the "new capitalism" of the twentieth century has lacked such moral grounding.

It is in this context that one can see the weakness of corporate capitalism in trying to deal with some of the major political dilemmas of the century. The issues here are not primarily economic but sociocultural. The traditionalist defends fundamentalist religion, censorship, stricter divorce, and anti-abortion laws; the modernist is for secular rationality, freer personal relations, tolerance of sexual deviance, and the like.

Now, the curious fact is that the "new capitalism" of abundance, which emerged in the 1920's, has never been able to define its view of these cultural-political issues. Given its split character, it could not do so. Its values derive from the traditionalist past, and its language is the archaism of the Protestant Ethic.

The fact that the corporate economy has no unified value system of its own, or still mouthed a flaccid version of Protestant virtues, meant that liberalism could go ideologically unchallenged.

But liberalism today is in trouble. Not only in politics, where its pragmatic style has been found wanting, but in an arena where it had joined in support of capitalism—in the economy. The economic philosophy of American liberalism had been rooted in the idea of growth.

The liberal answer to social problems such as poverty was that growth would provide the resources to raise the incomes of the poor. The thesis that growth was necessary to finance public services was the center of John Kenneth Galbraith's book "The Affluent Society."

And yet, paradoxically, it is the very idea of economic growth that is now coming under attack—and from liberals. Affluence is no longer seen as an answer. Growth is held responsible for the spoliation of the environment, the voracious use of natural resources, the crowding in the recreation areas, the densities in the city, and the like. One finds, startlingly, the idea of zero economic growth—or John Stuart Mill's idea of the "stationary state"—now proposed as a serious goal of government policy.

American society faces a number of crises. Yet these crises, I believe, are manageable (not solvable; what problems are?) if the political leadership is intelligent and determined. The resources are present (or will be, once the Vietnam war is ended) to relieve many of the obvious tensions and to finance the public needs of the society. The great need here is *time,* for the social changes which are required (a decent welfare and income maintenance system for the poor, the reorganization of the universities, the control of the environment) can only be handled within the space of a decade or more.

It is the demand for "instant solutions" which, in this respect, is the source of political trouble.

But the deeper and more lasting crisis is the cultural one. Changes in moral temper and culture—the fusion of imagination and life-styles (now so celebrated by Charles Reich of Yale)—are not amenable to "social engineering" or political control. They derive from the value and moral traditions of the society, and these cannot be "designed" by precept. The ultimate sources are the religious conceptions which undergird a society; the proximate sources are the "re-ward systems" and "motivations" (and their legitimacy) which derive from the arena of work (the social structure).

American capitalism has lost its traditional legitimacy which was based on a moral system of reward, rooted in a Protestant sanctification of work. It has substituted a hedonism which promises a material ease and luxury, yet shies away from all the historic implications which a "voluptuary system"—and all its social permissiveness and libertinism—implies.

The characteristic style of an industrial society is based on the principles of economics and economizing: on efficiency, least cost, maximization, optimization, and functional rationality. Yet it is at this point that it comes into sharpest conflict with the cultural trends of the day. The one emphasizes functional rationality, technocratic decision-making, and meritocratic rewards. The other, apocalyptic moods and anti-rational modes of behavior. It is this disjunction which is the historic crisis of Western society. This cultural contradiction, in the long run, is the deepest challenge to the society.

5

Protean Man and the New History

ROBERT JAY LIFTON

Who was Proteus? Why does Lifton consider him an archetype of the contemporary man? What is his new History? And why do the young seek this new heritage? From your own experiences and observations, do you believe that the "spirit of mockery" is a viable characteristic of the young? Is Lifton correct in asserting that the young are rejecting ideological totalism? One reviewer asks, "What is Lifton saying? And how does it square with our own experience of Life?"

Now, we know from Greek mythology that Proteus was able to change his shape with relative ease from wild boar to lion to dragon to fire to flood. What he found difficult, and would not do unless seized and chained, was to commit himself to a single form, a form most his own, and carry out his function of prophecy. We can say the same of Protean man, but we must keep in mind his possibilities as well as his difficulties.

The Protean style of self-process, then, is characterized by an interminable series of experiments and explorations, some shallow, some profound, each of which can readily be abandoned in favor of still new, psychological quests. This pattern resembles, in many ways, what Erik Erikson has called "identity diffusion" or "identity confusion," and the impaired psychological functioning which these terms suggest can be very much present. But I want to stress that this Protean style is by no means pathological as such, and in fact may be one of the functional patterns necessary to life in our times. I would emphasize that it extends to

all areas of human experience—to political as well as to sexual behavior, to the holding and promulgating of ideas, and to the general organization of lives. To grasp this style, then, we must alter our judgments concerning what is psychologically disturbed or pathological, as opposed to adaptive or even innovative.

I would like to suggest a few illustrations of the Protean style, as expressed in America and Europe, drawn both from my own psychotherapeutic work with patients, and from observations on various forms of literature and art.

One patient of mine, a gifted young teacher, referred to himself as "wearing a number of masks" which he could put on or take off. He asked the question, "Is there, or should there be, one face which should be authentic?" He wasn't really sure, and found parallels to this in literature, in which, he noted, there were representations of "every kind of crime, every kind of sin." And then he added: "For me, there's not a single act I cannot imagine myself committing." He went on to compare himself to an actor on the stage, who, as he put it, "performs with a certain kind of polymorphous versatility," and here he was of course referring, somewhat mockingly, to Freud's well-known phrase, "polymorphous perversity" for diffusely inclusive and, in a way also Protean, infantile sexuality. And he went on to ask: "Which is the real person, so far as an actor is concerned? Is he more real when performing on the stage, or when he is at home? I tend to think that for people who have these many, many masks, there is no home. Is it a futile gesture for the actor to try to find his real face?" Here he was asking a very fundamental question, one in fact at issue throughout this chapter. I would add that while he was by no means a happy man, neither was he incapacitated. And although he certainly had considerable strain with his "polymorphous versatility," it could be said that as a teacher and a thinker, and in some ways as a man, he was served rather well by it. In fact, I would claim that polymorphous versatility of one kind or another is becoming increasingly prominent in contemporary life. . . .

There are psychological and historical stirrings of a revolutionary nature throughout the world, especially (but by no means exclusively) among the young. They are influenced by, but at the same time independent of, the Maoist visions described in the last chapter. Indeed they can be understood as part of a vast effort to bring about what we may term a New History.

What is a New History? And why do the young seek one? Let me define a New History as a radical and widely shared recreation of the forms of human culture—biological, experiential, institutional, technological, aesthetic, and interpretative. The newness of these cultural forms derives not from their spontaneous generation but from extension and transformations of existing psychic and physical components, that is, from previously unknown or inadequately known combinations. A New History, then, is both an extension and a resetting of boundaries.

The shapers of a New History can be political revolutionaries, revolutionary thinkers, extreme holocausts, or technological breakthroughs. These and the great events surrounding them, in different ways, cause, reflect, and symbolize historical shifts. I suggested earlier that the combination of Nazi genocide and the American atomic bombings of Hiroshima and Nagasaki terminated man's sense of limits concerning his self-destructive potential, and thereby inaugurated an era in which he is devoid of assurance of living on eternally as a species. It has taken almost twenty-five years for beginning formulations of the significance of these events to emerge—formulations which cannot be separated from the technological developments of the same quarter century, or from the increasing sense of the universal world-society that has accompanied them.

Our own New History, then, is built upon the ultimate paradox of two competing and closely related images: that of technologically induced historical extinction, and that of man's increasingly profound awareness of himself as a single species. It may be more correct to say that this is just one image, extraordinarily divided.

I think we should take seriously the assertion by the young framers of the celebrated 1962 Port Huron Statement of the Students for a Democratic Society, still something of a manifesto for the American New Left, that: "Our work is guided by the sense that we may be the last generation in the experiment with living." What I wish to stress is the overriding significance for every post-Hiroshima generation of precisely this threat of historical extinction. The end of the next era becomes associated, psychologically speaking, with the end of everything. And even those who deny any special concern with this threat share in the general undercurrent of death anxiety.

This anxiety becomes closely associated with other symbolic impairments of our time, with the confusions of the knowledge revolution and the unprecedented dissemination of half-knowledge through media whose psychological impact has barely begun to be discerned.

There is a very real sense in which the world itself has become a 'total environment,' a closed psychic chamber with continuous reverberations bouncing about chaotically and dangerously. The symbolic death perceived, then, is this combination of formlessness and totality, of the inadequacy of existing forms and imprisonment within them. The boundaries of the environment are felt to be in one sense absolute, in another nonexistent. And the young are exquisitely sensitive to this kind of 'historical death,' whatever their capacity for resisting an awareness of the biological kind. They are struck by the fact that most of mankind simply goes about its business, as if these extreme dislocations did not exist —as if there were no such thing as ultimate technological violence or existence rendered absurd. The war in Vietnam did not create these murderous incongruities, but it does exemplify them, and it consumes American youth in them. No wonder, then, that, in their symbolic questions, or (to use Cassirer's phrase), in their "conversations with themselves," the young everywhere ask: "How can we bring the world—and ourselves—back to life?"

Students of revolution and rebellion have recognized the close relationship of both to death symbolism, and to visions of transcending death by achieving an eternal historical imprint. Hannah Arendt speaks of revolution as containing an "all-pervasive preoccupation with permanence, with a 'perpetual state . . . for . . . posterity.'" And Albert Camus describes insurrection, "in its exalted and tragic forms," as "a prolonged protest against death, a violent accusation against the universal death penalty," and as "the desire for immortality." But Camus also stresses the rebel's "appeal to the essence of being," his quest "not . . . for life, but for reasons for living." And this brings us to an an all-important question concerning mental participation in revolution: what is the place of ideology, and of images and ideas, and of the self in relationship to all three?

Most of the revolutionary ideologies of the past have been notable in providing elaborate blueprints for individual and collective immortality, specifications and ultimate cause and ultimate effect, theological in tone and scientific in claim. For present-day revolutionaries to reject these Cartesian litanies is to take seriously some of the important psychological and historical insights of the last few decades. For they are rejecting an oppressive ideological totalism—with its demand for control of all communication in a milieu, its imposed guilt and cult of purity and confession, its loading of the language, its principles of doctrine over person and even of the dispensing of existence itself (in the sense that sharp lines are drawn between those whose right to exist can be recognized and those who possess no such right). This rejection, at its best, represents a quest by the young for a new kind of revolution—one perhaps no less enduring in historical impact, but devoid of the claim to omniscience, and of the catastrophic chain of human manipulations stemming from that claim. In other words, the young resist the suffocating personal boundaries imposed by earlier revolutions.

It is of course possible that their anti-ideological stance could turn out to be a transitory phenomenon, a version of the euphoric denial of dogma that so frequently appears during the early moments of revolution, only to be overwhelmed by absolutist doctrine and suffocating organization in the name of revolutionary discipline. Yet there is reason for believing that the present antipathy to total ideology is something more, that it is an expression of a powerful and highly appropriate contemporary style. The shift we are witnessing from fixed and total forms of ideology to more fluid *ideological fragments* represents, to a considerable degree, the emergence of contemporary or Protean man as rebel. It is an effort to remain open, while in rebellion, to the extraordinarily rich, confusing, liberating, and threatening array of contemporary historical possibilities—and to retain, in the process, a continuing capacity for shape-shifting.

The fluidity of the Protean style greatly enhances tactical leverage. For instance, Daniel Cohn-Bendit, the leader of the French student uprisings of May 1968, in an interesting dialogue with Jean-Paul Sartre, insisted that the classical Marxist-

Leninist principle of the omniscient revolutionary vanguard (the working class as represented by the Communist Party) be replaced with "a much simpler and more honourable one, the theory of an active minority, acting you might say as a permanent ferment, pushing forward without trying to control events." He went on to characterize this process as "uncontrollable spontaneity." In the same spirit are the warnings of Tom Hayden, a key figure in the American New Left, to his SDS colleagues and followers, against what he calls "fixed leaders," and his insistence upon "participatory democracy" as well as upon ideology of a kind that is secondary to, and largely achieved through, revolutionary action. So widespread has this approach been that the American New Left has been characterized as more a process than a program.

I would suggest that the general principle of "uncontrollable spontaneity" represents a meeting ground between tactic and deeper psychological inclination. The underlying inclination consists precisely of the Protean style of multiple identifications, shifting beliefs, and constant search for new combinations that extend both individual-psychological and political boundaries. Whatever its pitfalls, this style of revolutionary behavior is an attempt to mobilize twentieth-century fluidity as a weapon against two kinds of stagnation: the old, unresponsive institutions (universities, governments, families), and the newly-emerging but fixed technological visions (people 'programmed' by computers in a 'technotronic society'). The young thus feel hemmed in by boundaries formed both by legacies of the past and visions of the future.

Throughout the world, the young seek active involvement in the institutional decisions governing their lives, new paths of significance as alternatives to consuming and being consumed, and liberating rhythms of individual and (especially) community existence. Nonspecific and ephemeral as these goals may seem, they are early expressions of a quest for historical rebirth, for re-attachment to the Great Chain of Being, for reassertion of a viable sense of immortality.

The French example is again revealing in its extraordinary flowering of graffiti. Here one must take note of the prominence of the genre—of the informal slogan-on-the-wall virtually replacing formal revolutionary doctrine—no less than the content. But one is struck by the stress of many of the slogans, sometimes to the point of intentional absurdity, upon enlarging the individual life space, on saying yes to more and no to less. Characteristic were such slogans as "Think of your desires as realities," "Prohibiting is forbidden," "Imagination is power," and "Imagination is revolution." Sartre made an apt comment upon both the graffiti and the young revolutionaries themselves when he said, "I would like to describe what you have done as extending the field of possibilities."

Precisely such extending of the field of possibilities is at the heart of the worldwide youth rebellion, for hippies no less than political radicals—and at the heart of the Protean insistence upon continuous psychic re-creation of the self. Around this image of unlimited extension and perpetual re-creation, as projected into a dimly imagined future, the young seek to create a new mode of *revolutionary* immortality.

Of enormous importance for these rebellions is another basic component of the Protean style, the spirit of mockery. While young rebels are by no means immune from the most pedantic and humorless discourse, they come alive to others and themselves only when giving way to—or seizing upon—their very strong inclination toward mockery. The mocking political rebel merges with the hippie and with a variety of exponents of pop culture to 'put on'—that is, mislead or deceive by means of some form of mockery or absurdity—his uncomprehending cohorts, his elders, or anyone in authority. (Despite important differences, there has always been a fundamental unity in the rebellions of hippies and young radicals, which is perhaps just now becoming fully manifest.) In dress, hair, and general social and sexual style, the mocking rebel is not only "extending the field of possibilities," but making telling commentary—teasing, ironic, contemptuous—on the absurd folkways of 'the others.' The mockery can be gentle and even loving, or it can be bitter and provocative in the extreme.

6

The Cooling of America

Is the revolutionary ferment of the sixties dead, or merely in a period of hibernation in which more stirrings are inevitable? While the following article seems to say that the political revolution has been aborted, it also asserts that the cultural implications are very much alive. Is it not possible that a cultural revolution can have more effect than a short-range political revolution?

A beat. A pause. The bomb that arced over the wall lies there unexploded, past its fuse-time, possibly dead. Something has happened in American life—or has failed to happen. In dead winter, 1971, after months of recession, a decade of war abroad and domestic violence, a mood approaching quiet has fallen like a deep snow.

How permanent or transitory is the change remains mysterious. It could be merely temporary calm induced by fatigue or a bit of boredom or even by winter weather. But the change seems more complex than that and therefore more profound. To the extent that an American psychology exists, it has, in nearly all its troubled compartments, undergone numerous and sometimes subtle transformations. . . .

The calm carries little serenity with it, which may be just as well. Instead, it suggests a complex of rather sober fears; of joblessness, of radical violence, of counterviolence from the government. There is a

From Time, "The Cooling of America" (February 22, 1971) Vol. 97, No. 8, 10. Copyright © 1971 by Time, Inc. Reprinted by permission of Time, The Weekly Newsmagazine.

chastened air. A decade of almost amphetamine economic growth culminates in a recession that, although relatively mild in historical terms, has thrown the fear of wolves into the most resolutely buoyant consumer. Simultaneously, even the most heedless slob in a throwaway society begins to understand that his cans and bottles and poisoned gases are piling up in a fatal glut.

As the '60s tested the upper reaches of production and consumption, they opened up new territories of violence. The war would not end. For all the professed incredulity about it, the My Lai massacre has dripped acids onto the nation's conviction of its own innocence. At home, the Sharon Tate murders were so incomprehensible as to excite a stunned awe at what orgies of violence are possible. In the presence of such insanities, many Americans have grown introspective. It is a reaction built on residues of abhorrence going back through sad, internal video tapes to Nov. 22, 1963. Americans seem to be convincingly sick of violence.

Such a weariness—and much more—accounts for the profound hibernation of the radical movement in the U.S. The students who closed down scores of campuses after Kent State and the Cambodian invasion last spring scarcely stirred at the current South Vietnamese expedition into Laos. Only last summer dynamite seemed the shock wave of the future.

Inglorious War

Some argue that "the revolution" in the U.S. is dead. As a cultural influence, however, the movement is still alive and pervasive. The music, language, mores and styles of what used to be known as radical culture have changed and enlivened the country.

The present pause should not, however, obscure the fact that some fundamental assumptions have been altered: the national opinion of a war, the nation's draft policies, attitudes toward pollution and ecology. Today elders as well as the young know that many things are profoundly wrong. Warfare is widely seen as inglorious. There is a growing public, if not yet legal tolerance for marijuana. Still, like England's 19th century Chartists, the radicals are seeing the larger society adopt and subsume much of their revolution. "Co-optation" is an infuriating and unsatisfactory denouement for the revolutionary. The Chief of Naval Operations grows sideburns: the war goes on. Yet drastically changed public attitudes prove that not all of the co-optation has been merely decorative.

Healing Glimpse

Undoubtedly the Nixon Administration has contributed to the new, calmer mood, both by commission and omission. The cautious withdrawal from Viet Nam has largely disarmed the antiwar movement. "Repression," real or imagined, has also stilled a lot of dissent. For all their unfairness, Spiro Agnew's attacks on the press have made many practitioners in journalism and TV a little more cautious about playing up news of dissent. The election results of last fall had a healing effect, for they gave the nation a glimpse of itself, in the kinds of candidates it accepted and rejected, and a notion of its intelligent continuation.

On both sides, there has been a drawing back from anarchy and violence. As much as anything, Americans seem now to be seeking public limits and a private equilibrium, to be answering David Riesman's complaint: "Why are we so evangelical? Why do we not have a happier sense of the ordinary, of dailiness?" Americans have the vanity of thinking that the U.S. must be either the best country or the worst country. There is something reassuring and necessary in the acknowledgment that it is neither.

Many Americans have simply grown more realistic about their own problems. Thus crime is as bad as ever, but the outcry for law and order is not so hysterical as before. The cities, the courts, the welfare systems are still crippling along; yet there now seems to be a broad and pragmatic demand for reform.

The overwhelming response to the new atmosphere must be relief. Yet something will have been lost with yesterday's turbulence if all the urgent pressures for change are allowed to be dissipated. Most of the trouble that breeds violence is still there; the absence of more spectacular political violence can only be considered a period of grace. The great loss will be if nothing is done with that grace, such as it is. The present pause is certainly no reason for thinking that some tranquillity from the middle years of Eisenhower's Administration has magically descended. Rather, it is an opportunity for America to get on with the much-delayed business of rebuilding itself.

7

A Paralysis of the Will

JOHN W. GARDNER

Cite a specific example which might support John W. Gardner's thesis that the United States is suffering a "paralysis of the will." What suggestions does Gardner make to break out of our apparent paralysis? Do you think it is realistic to expect industry to alter its policies in respect to the consumer?

As we enter the 1970s there are many curious aspects of our situation, but none more strange than our state of mind. We are anxious but immobilized.

We see the brooding threat of nuclear warfare. We know our lakes are dying, our rivers growing filthier daily, our atmosphere increasingly polluted. We are aware of racial tensions that could tear the nation apart. We understand that oppressive poverty in the midst of affluence is intolerable. We see that our cities are sliding toward disaster.

But we are seized by a kind of paralysis of the will. It is like a waking nightmare.

I propose that as we enter the new decade we make a heroic effort to alter both our mood and our state of inactivity. The place to begin is with our national leadership in both the Executive branch and the Congress.

We have had failures of leadership before. But rarely before have we had the widespread distrust of our own institutions that we see today. And that distrust is not limited to radicals. If you travel around the country as I do more or less continuously, you will find that there is a deep and

Excerpts from an address by John W. Gardner, St. Louis Post-Dispatch, *March 1, 1970. Reprinted by permission of the St. Louis* Post-Dispatch.

pervasive feeling among all segments of the populace that "things aren't working"—and Washington is given a major share of the blame.

Now let me speak specifically of the President. Any judgment on the President's leadership must take into account that he came into office at a difficult time, must deal with a Congress of the opposing party, and finds his options limited by inflation and the war.

But given all that, he must do more to set a tone of urgency to which we can all respond, and more to exemplify in his own actions a determination to solve our pressing problems.

His greatest test is on the international front. His first task—and one cannot exaggerate its urgency—is to end the war. Even more important in the long run will be steps that must be taken to cope with the threat of nuclear warfare. His recent action with respect to biological warfare was encouraging.

On the domestic front the President must say more explicitly—and with greater urgency—what he conceives to be an appropriate strategy for dealing with the dilemmas of the cities, with equality of opportunity, with the environment and with other problems that are wracking the nation.

Now let's talk about the Congress. This Congress, which has acquired a reputation for lethargy, could dispel that reputation not only by passing needed legislation but by enacting genuinely meaningful congressional reform. Few institutions in our national life are as gravely in need of renewal as is the Congress of the United States. Renewal requires first of all measures to abolish the seniority system and to curb the abuse of power by entrenched committee chairmen.

Congress must also put an end to the hypocrisy of tolerating grave conflicts of interest among its own members while attacking the same fault in others. It should pass a conflict of interest statute with teeth in it.

And what about industry? I would propose that as we enter the 1970s industry address itself to three central issues.

First, it should make an unqualified commitment to equality of opportunity for minority groups. Second, industry should commit itself to end pollution. Some far-sighted business leaders have already done so, but the record of industry as a whole has been deplorable. It has lied to the public and to itself about the seriousness of the problem. Public anger over pollution is rising, and the time for effective action has come.

Third, industry should meet the rising tide of consumerism with constructive measures. Leaders in each industry should set standards of regard for the consumer and should be tough in demanding that the rest of their industry follow suit. If they don't they will be brought under increasingly savage criticism by a bilked and frustrated public.

Labor unions too have their tasks to accomplish—and the one that overshadows all others at the moment is to root out racial discrimination. For more than thirty years the unions have benefited enormously from the fact that America's conscience has been basically on their side. In many of the battles that had to be settled in the public forum, that fact was decisive. Today that advantage is leaking away very rapidly.

Now let's have a look at the person whom practically no one ever attacks, the person who holds the highest title a free society can award; citizen.

In a vital society the citizen has a role that goes far beyond duties at the ballot box. He must man the party machinery, support social and civic reform, provide adequate funds, criticize, demand, expose corruption and honor leaders who lead.

One thing the citizen can do—must do—is to reject fiercely and consistently all politicians who exploit fear and anger and hatred for their own purposes. He cannot rid himself entirely of those emotions. But he can rid himself of politicians who live by manipulating them. Such leaders will not move him toward a better future.

8

Movement to Regain Sovereignty

JAMES RESTON

Can you cite specific examples to support Reston's testimony that people are regaining their sovereignty? How have the earlier activities in the civil rights movement served as models for reform in other areas? To what extent are the professions reflecting the rising concern for revitalization and reform? In your judgment, will the Supreme Court decision on the 18-year old vote be a vital factor in regaining control over seemingly uncontrollable events?

You can hardly pick up a newspaper or turn on your TV these days without coming up against some melancholy character complaining about the helplessness of the individual. The ordinary decent American, according to the current cliches, is numbered, computerized, victimized, and depersonalized by a lot of big institutions and monstrous forces beyond his understanding or control.

Well, it's all too true, and you can get plenty of testimony from the young men caught in the draft, the old pensioners caught in the inflation, the workers laid off by the recession, and the millions who can't even afford to get sick. Even the railroads and the steel companies, and the President of the United States himself are muttering about being trapped by things beyond their influence.

And yet, if you look around, it is hard to avoid a paradox in all this. For here and there the people are stirring, and organizing to regain their sovereignty. Not since the days of the New Deal in America has

Reprinted from James Reston, "Movement to Regain Sovereignty," *The Columbia* Missourian, January 16, 1971, © 1971 by The New York Times Company. Reprinted by permission.

there been so much insistent questioning of the institutions and purposes of America as there is now, and not without evidence of progress either.

These are not mass movements as yet. In fact, they are comparatively small. But slowly, citizens' groups are forming to protect the environment of their communities, to challenge the assumptions and priorities of their elected officials, to defend the average consumer from the commercial gougers and to work in many other ways for the improvement of American life.

What is happening now is that the model for action established during the civil rights battles of the '50s and '60s is beginning to be applied to other fields. To begin with, it was small groups of concerned citizens, working primarily through the courts, that began the great movement for the desegregation of the races.

Likewise, the one-man, one vote principle, which has resulted in the significant reapportionment of the state and federal legislatures, began with individual actions and gradually spread until the political balance of power was measurably changed and improved.

Not only the enfranchisement of the Negro but recently of 11.5 million 18–21 year olds in federal elections came about in much the same way, and despite the cynicism of the old about the casual voting habits of the young, we may very well look back on this 18-year-old vote as the decisive factor in the 1972 presidential election.

It is no accident, for example, that since that 18-year-old vote decision by the Supreme Court, the politicians in Washington are now saying amiable things about the idealistic young, and President Nixon has been stopping off at the University of Nebraska to exhort the students to save the republic.

The young public service lawyers are playing a major role in these rising citizens' movements. Again they are a very small minority, but many of them would rather clean up the local corporations than take them over, and the larger these concerned citizens organizations grow, with the imaginative legal advice they are now getting, the wider will be the attacks on pollution, political corruption and political manipulation.

Just the other day, John Gardner, chairman of the People's Lobby called Common Cause, asked the federal district court here to compel the Democratic and Republican National committees to abide by the unenforced laws limiting campaign spending, and the purpose of this was quite clear: It was not only to enforce present laws, or expose their usefulness, but mainly to prod both the President and the Congress to pass new laws that would put an end to what is widely recognized as the worst scandal in American political life.

Three days later, the National Urban Coalition came out with a five-year-plan to force public scrutiny of the federal budget, and to reorder the allocation of the nation's resources, beginning with a reduction in military spending of $20 billion in the next five years.

"We know," the coalition said, with the support of such men as David Rockefeller, "that the cities are in trouble, that poverty continues in the midst of wealth, that unemployment is high, that malnutrition is widespread, that injustice exists, that tensions endure. In sum, we know that our society is not functioning the way it is supposed to. But if we solve the greatest of our ills—our paralysis of spirit and will—we can narrow the distance between what we have and what we want."

Well, as the committee says, all this has been proposed many times before, but the difference now is that there is a growing segment of concerned and expertly advised people working all over the country on these problems, and in institutions like Common Cause and the Urban Coalition, there is now the start of a potentially powerful political third force in the land.

The tragedy is that Common Cause has only 53,000 members, which is a good beginning but not nearly large enough to be decisive in the basic job of political reconstruction it has taken on. Numbers talk in politics, and if it had a million members it would really be in business. Nevertheless, the situation is not helpless, and the spirit of helplessness may not be quite as justified as the pessimists would have us believe.

YOU HAVE NOT CONVERTED A MAN BECAUSE YOU HAVE SILENCED HIM

(John, Viscount Morley, On Compromise, 1874)

Ben Shahn

Great Ideas of Western Man... one of a series [CCA] Container Corporation of America

DEMOCRACY OR DIRECTION: THEORY AND PRACTICE

The competition between democracy and its rivals takes two forms. On one level it is a contest of ideas, an intellectual disagreement. On the other level it is a confrontation of societies of political and social systems carrying out day-to-day activities, presumably in accordance with the prescriptions of the ideology.

The paradox is that on both of these levels democracy today seems more successful and more vital than a decade ago, certainly than three decades ago; yet the confident mood of democratic thought is gone. Questioning and deprecation are more common than hope and easy affirmation.

The success of democracy as an ideology, the almost universal appeal of its assertions, can be proven by its use as a propaganda device, even by its enemies. Even those who deny majoritarian control try to justify their actions in the name of some purer form of democracy. We get very peculiar arguments about "democratic centralism" and "guided democracy," to name only two of the more prominent variants. No doubt they represent something quite different from what has traditionally been claimed for the democratic philosophy; the important point, though, is that the mantle of democracy is wrapped around their shoulders.

The success of democracy as a system is, perhaps, more open to doubt, yet there are strong indications of its endurance in any race for superiority with other systems. Democracy has proven more capable of change without convulsion than have the structures of Eastern Europe and Communist China. It is more permeable to day-to-day demands as well, as witnessed by the stagnation of personnel and policies that characterizes most of the Eastern European countries.

Why, then, has there been a defensive note in democratic thought of recent years? A small part of the answer can perhaps be found in the ethos of democracy itself. A system devoted to extolling criticism and deprecating absolutes is likely to be self-critical and self-deprecating.

But there are more substantial reasons. By studying American government in a more precise way through real research and conceptual
thought, we have found that the system just doesn't work the way Fourth-
of-July orators say it should. Facing up to the consequences of the less
than perfect division of power in our society and the less than godlike
behavior of our citizens raises problems for democratic theory. The new
efforts to salvage democratic theory have not yet satisfied most thinking
observers of politics.

The second reason is also a consequence of greater experience and
candor. At the turn of the twentieth century and well into it, Americans
and other Westerners believed in the manifest destiny of our form of government as the hope of mankind. Experience has shown that peoples
don't automatically leap up and introduce our type of legal order into
their society, and when they do accept it, they often experience grave
difficulties in making it work.

To some extent the pessimism that was the reaction to the failures of
democracy after World War I persists; to some extent it is mitigated. As
Winston Churchill pointed out, democracy is, indeed, a very bad form of
government, but thus far it seems able to vindicate its superiority over
Brand X. The conviction persists that it is a governmental arrangement
profoundly rooted in the needs of the human personality. Even so skeptical a thinker as Paul Goodman—the spiritual father of the New Left
movement—has recently written: "The question is whether or not our
beautiful libertarian, pluralist and populist experiment is viable in modern conditions. If it's not, I don't know any other acceptable politics, and
I am a man without a country."

Is the Common Man Too Common?

The traditional objection to democracy is aristocratic: the average citizen is incapable of self-control and self-direction. The traditional answer
is as old as the objection. As Aristotle said, the guest can judge at the
banquet better than the chef, though he might not be able to cook the
meal. A suggested variant is that not even scientific machinery can really
determine whether the shoe pinches. But the modern form of this argument against the average man goes further. The modern common man is
even worse than his predecessor. In the past society institutionalized and
rewarded excellence. Today the common man is jealous and self-confi-
dent. In short, it is argued that democratic theory has destroyed the basis
for leadership and thoughtful decision-making. This argument is represented in our readings by the classic statement of Ortega y Gasset, but it
has been argued, for example, on the conduct of foreign policy by Walter
Lippman. It raises the question, too, of whether day-to-day demands of
equality may not extinguish individuality and distinctive excellence in
every field.

What System of Government Best Satisfies Man's Needs?

From the standpoint of "a decent respect for the opinions of mankind," democratic values clearly win the contest. The civilized tone of discussion in even the less well-established democracies must be contrasted to the pronouncements of nondemocratic governments that their critics are worms, jackals, and sometimes less flattering creatures. The humaneness of rotation in office and the congratulatory exchange of telegrams after an election is evident in contrast to the firing squad, the concentration camp, and the mysterious disappearance.

But nondemocratic systems often can generate more excitement, involvement with a charismatic leader, a sense of doing things and going places. It is not even clear—probably the bulk of the evidence suggests the opposite—that people really want to make decisions for themselves, as much as they resent decisions they dislike being made for them.

But the most important argument and deterrent to the spread of democracy has been the claim that tighter systems of control are necessary in economically less advanced countries. The example of the Soviet Union in developing heavy industry has been the model for countries that claim that greater responsiveness to the public will lead to consumer orientation and waste.

Then, too, it has been suggested that democracy is a fragile system not easily exported. It requires, it would appear, unique social and economic underpinnings not usually present in most countries of the world. Where a society is fragmented on religious, ethnic, or even tribal grounds, the charismatic leader can be the only integrating force. Pluralistic expression of views, it is argued, will only lead to disintegration and secession.

Students of comparative government studying developing countries seem to have found confirmation for some of the claims of advantage of tightly knit decision systems in coping with particular stages of development and particular types of decisions. But they have also found that there are times when autocracy is a very bad system, even for economic development. Indeed, the growing emphasis has been not upon which system is more desirable, but upon a statement of under what conditions democracy and direction are most useful.

Is the United States Really Democratic?

In recent years political scientists have developed more precise information on the nature of our political system. Instead of broad assertions and discussions about "the boss system," or vague claims about "sinister interests," we have studies of the exact relative influence of differing groups, and the ways in which different institutions favor specific interests. There have been studies of the decision-making process in various cities to discover just who prevails under what conditions. The scientific posture of these studies is somewhat tainted; most such observors have found in the communities they studied the type of power structure they had expected to find before the study began. Nonetheless, we know considerably more about community power structures, as well as national decision-making, than we did a decade ago. Hand in hand with this information have gone more sophisticated ways of thinking about the processes of power and decision. (Indeed, some of the rhetoric of the civil rights movement—power structure, for example—has been borrowed from such conceptualization.)

The picture that emerges is of a pluralistic organization of power groups, with decisions negotiated largely within the leadership strata. This is not truly a "one man, one vote" operation, and, indeed, in some aspects it makes the American system appear more like some of the systems normally described as oligarchical.

Does this then mean that our democracy is only a pretext? Has there been a change to this system from something pure, more democratic? Have the new institutional arrangements of mass society eroded individual power? Have mass communications reversed the pattern of messages so that the leadership can manipulate people at their will? Or has the opposite happened? Has power now found a new pattern of distribution in which even the formerly powerless have gained a share of control through the weapon of group structure? "If the meek are to inherit the earth, they first have to get organized." Do mass communication and universal education disperse information that allows greater participation? Unfortunately the evidence here is murky, although the answers to these questions seem rather urgent.

1

Dissection of the Mass Man

JOSE ORTEGA Y GASSET

The arguments of Jose Ortega y Gasset are that the rise of the common man in politics has everywhere meant a decline in standards. The common man is a creature of appetites, no more. He is convinced he is perfect. He listens to almost no one. He is like a spoiled child. He is using politics and mass democracy for his own advantages, particularly economic advantages, but he contributes nothing to the further growth and development of democratic politics and government. He recognizes no standards other than his own whims and desires. The more he comes into political power and is wooed and solicited for his biases and whims (called public opinion), the more civilization weakens.

There is one fact which, whether for good or ill, is of utmost importance in the public life of Europe at the present moment. This fact is the accession of the masses to complete social power. . . .

Perhaps the best line of approach to this historical phenomenon may be found in turning our attention to a visual experience, stressing one aspect of our epoch which is plain to our very eyes. This fact is quite simple to enunciate, though not so to analyze. I shall call it the fact of agglomeration, of "plentitude." Towns are full of people, houses full of tenants, hotels full of guests, trains full of travelers, cafés full of customers, parks full of promenaders, consulting-rooms of famous doctors full of patients, theatres full of spectators, and beaches full of bathers. What previously was, in general, no problem, now begins to be an everyday one, namely, to find room. . . .

Jose Ortega y Gasset, The Revolt of the Masses (New York: W. W. Norton & Company, Inc., 1932), pp. 11–15, 17–18, 55, 60–65. Copyright © 1960 by Teresa Carey. Reprinted by permission of the publisher.

What about it? Is this not the ideal state of things? . . .

The concept of the multitude is quantitative and visual. Without changing its nature, let us translate it into terms of sociology. We then meet with the notion of the "social mass." Society is always a dynamic unity of two component factors: minorities and masses. The minorities are individuals or groups of individuals which are specially qualified. The mass is the assemblage of persons not especially qualified. By masses, then, is not to be understood, solely or mainly, "the working masses." The mass is the average man. In this way what was mere quantity—the multitude—is converted into a qualitative determination: it becomes the common social quality, man as undifferentiated from other men, but as repeating in himself a generic type.

The mass is all that which sets no value on itself—good or ill—based on specific grounds, but which feels itself "just like everybody," and nevertheless is not concerned about it; in fact, quite happy to feel itself as one with everybody else. . . .

For there is no doubt that the most radical division that it is possible to make of humanity is that which splits it into two classes of creatures: those who make great demands on themselves, piling up difficulties and duties; and those who demand nothing special of themselves, but for whom to live is to be every moment what they already are, without imposing on themselves any effort towards perfection; mere buoys that float on the waves. . . .

The old democracy was tempered by a generous dose of liberalism and of enthusiasm for law. . . . Today we are witnessing the triumphs of a hyperdemocracy in which the mass acts directly, outside the law, imposing its aspirations and its desires by means of material pressure. It is a false interpretation of the new situation to say that the mass has grown tired of politics and handed over the exercise of it to specialized persons. . . . Now, on the other hand, the mass believes that it has the right to impose and to give force of law to notions born in the café. I doubt whether there have been other periods of history in which the multitude has come to govern more directly than in our own. That is why I speak of hyperdemocracy. . . .

The characteristic of the hour is that the commonplace mind, knowing itself to be commonplace, has the assurance to proclaim the rights of the commonplace and to impose them where it will. . . .

Public authority is in the hands of a representative of the masses. These are so powerful that they have wiped out all opposition. They are in possession of power in such an unassailable manner that it would be difficult to find in history examples of a Government so all-powerful as these. And yet public authority—the Government—exists from hand to mouth, it does not offer itself as a frank solution for the future, it represents no clear announcement of the future, it does not stand out as the beginning of something whose development or evolution is conceivable. In short, it lives without any vital program, any plan of existence. It does not know where it is going, because, strictly speaking, it has no fixed road, no predetermined trajectory before it. When such a public authority attempts to justify itself it makes no reference at all to the future. On the contrary, it shuts itself up in the present, and says with perfect sincerity: "I am an abnormal form of Government imposed by circumstances." Hence its activities are reduced to dodging the difficulties of the hour; not solving them, but escaping from them for the time being, employing any methods whatsoever, even at the cost of accumulating thereby still greater difficulties for the hour which follows. Such has public power always been when exercised directly by the masses: omnipotent and ephemeral. The mass-man is he whose life lacks any purpose, and who simply goes drifting along. Consequently, though his possibilities and his powers be enormous, he constructs nothing. And it is this type of man who decides in our time. . . .

In the schools, which were such a source of pride to the last century, it has been impossible to do more than instruct the masses in the technique of modern life; it has been found impossible to educate them. They have been given tools for an intenser form of existence, but no feeling for their great historic duties; they have been hurriedly inoculated with the pride and power of modern instruments, but not with their spirit. Hence they will have nothing to do with their spirit, and the new generations are getting ready to take over command of the world as if the world were a paradise without trace of former footsteps, without traditional and highly complex problems. . . .

What appearance did life present to that multitudinous man who in ever-increasing abundance the nineteenth century kept producing? To start with, an appearance of universal material ease. Never had the average man been able to solve his economic problem with greater facility. . . .

To this ease and security of economic conditions are to be added the physical ones, comfort and public order. Life runs on smooth rails, and there is no likelihood of anything violent or dangerous breaking in on it. . . . That is to say, in all its primary and decisive aspects, life presented itself to the new man as exempt from restrictions. . . .

But still more evident is the contrast of situations, if we pass from the material to the civil and moral. The average man, from the second half of the nineteenth century on, finds no social barriers raised against him. . . . There are no civil privileges. The ordinary man learns that all men are equal before the law. . . .

Three principles have made possible this new world: liberal democracy, scientific experiment, and industrialism. . . . The world which surrounds the new man from his birth does not compel him to limit himself in any fashion, it sets up no veto in opposition to him; on the contrary, it incites his appetite, which in principle can increase indefinitely. . . . Even today, in spite of some signs which are making a tiny breach in that sturdy faith, even today, there are few men who doubt that motorcars will in five years' time be more comfortable and cheaper than today. They believe in this as they believe that the sun will rise in the morning. The metaphor is an exact one. For, in fact, the common man, finding himself in a world so excellent, technically and socially, believes that it has been produced by nature, and never thinks of the personal efforts of highly endowed individuals which the creation of this new world presupposed. Still less will he admit the notion that all these facilities still require the support of certain difficult human virtues, the least failure of which would cause the rapid disappearance of the whole magnificent edifice. . . .

This leads us to note down in our psychological chart of the mass-man of today two fundamental traits: the free expansion of his vital desires, and therefore, of his personality; and his radical ingratitude towards all that has made possible the ease of his existence. These traits together make up the well-known psychology of the spoilt child. And in fact it would entail no error to use this psychology as a "sight" through which to observe the soul of the masses of today. Heir to an ample and generous past —generous both in ideals and in activities—

the new commonalty has been spoiled by the world around it. To spoil means to put no limit on caprice, to give one the impression that everything is permitted to him and that he has no obligations. The young child exposed to this regime has no experience of its own limits. By reason of the removal of all external restraint, all clashing with other things, he comes actually to believe that he is the only one that exists and gets used to not considering others, especially not considering them as superior to himself. This feeling of another's superiority could only be instilled into him by someone who, being stronger than he is, should force him to give up some desire, to restrict himself, to restrain himself. He would then have learned this fundamental discipline: "Here I end and here begins another more powerful than I am. In the world, apparently, there are two people: I myself and another superior to me." The ordinary man of past times was daily taught this elemental wisdom by the world about him, because it was a world so rudely organized, that catastrophes were frequent, and there was nothing in it certain, abundant, stable. But the new masses find themselves in the presence of a prospect full of possibilities, and furthermore, quite secure, with everything ready to their hands, independent of any previous efforts on their part, just as we find the sun in the heavens without hoisting it up on our shoulders. No human being thanks another for the air he breathes, for no one has produced the air for him; it belongs to the sum total of what "is there," of which we say "it is natural," because it never fails. And these spoiled masses are unintelligent enough to believe that the material and social organization, placed at their disposition like the air, is of the same origin, since apparently it never fails them, and is almost as perfect as the natural scheme of things.

My thesis, therefore, is this: the very perfection with which the nineteenth century gave an organization to certain orders of existence has caused the masses benefited thereby to consider it, not as an organized, but as a natural system. Thus is explained and defined the absurd state of mind revealed by these masses; they are only concerned with their own well-being, and at the same time they remain alien to the cause of that well-being. As they do not see, beyond the benefits of civilization, marvels of invention and construction which can only be maintained by great effort and foresight, they imagine that their role is limited to demanding these benefits peremptorily, as if they were natural rights. . . .

2

American Historians and the Ideal of the Democratic Man

IRVING KRISTOL

Does the notion of the "common man" have to be of a mass, other-directed type? Kristol argues that democratic society can be structured around the notion of the exceptional, growing, learning commoner. Is this reasonable? Practical? Semantics? Would it make any difference for American society if we adopt Ortega's view or Kristol's?

If one were to ask, "What is the most effectively conservative piece of legislation passed by the Federal government in this century?" the answer, I submit, is both obvious and incontestable. It is the Nineteenth Amendment, extending the suffrage to women. The voting habits of the American population are something we know a great deal about, and there is just no question but that women, to the extent that they do more than duplicate their husbands' votes, are to be found disproportionately in the conservative wing of the electorate. Yet in all of our history books the Nineteenth Amendment is regarded as a progressive and liberal action, not at all as a conservative one. . . .

Another example. If one were to ask, "What is the most effectively conservative piece of legislation passed by state legislatures in this century?" the answer—which I again submit is both obvious and incontestable—is the popular referendum. There must be hundreds of American historians alive today who, in their respective localities, have seen more of their most cherished and most liberal ideas—school integration, for instance, or less restrictive zoning laws —buried in a referendum. Yet when they enter their classrooms, or write their books, all this is forgotten and ignored. Almost invariably they regard the advent of the popular referendum as a victory for both democracy and liberalism. They are very upset when you point out that this seems not to be the case. And they get utterly bewildered if you dare to suggest that, on certain other conceptions of democracy or liberty, one need not regard it as a victory for either.

. . . What is involved, it seems to me, is an ideology so powerful as to represent a kind of religious faith. Indeed, we can fairly call this ideology "the democratic faith," since this term is frequently and approv-

From Irving Kristol, "American Historians and the Ideal of the Democratic Man," The American Scholar, 39, No. 1 (Winter 1969–70) 89–104. Copyright © 1970 by Irving Kristol. Reprinted by permission of the publisher.

ingly used by members of the congregation themselves. . . .

First of all, it evidently cares much more about ascertaining the source and origin of political power than it does about analyzing the existential consequences of this power. Which is to say, like all faiths it places much more emphasis on men's "good" intentions—in this case, men's democratic intentions—than on whatever may follow from these intentions. And, of course, like all faiths it ends up grappling with the problem of evil—with the existence of disorder, and decay, and injustice, which ought not to exist in a society constructed on democratic principles, but which patently do. This problem itself is usually resolved in the traditional religious way— that is, by assuming that it flows from the conspiracy of wicked demiurges ("vested interests," in American jargon) or the undue influence of "alien" ideas that frustrate the perfection we are entitled to.

Secondly, and this is but a corollary of my first point, what we are dealing with is obviously *not* a political philosophy. The only reason I go to the trouble of pointing this out is that once upon a time, in this country, the question of democracy *was* a matter for political philosophy, rather than for faith. . . .

The difference between a democratic faith and a democratic political philosophy is basically this: whereas a faith may be attentive to the *problems* of democracy, it has great difficulty perceiving or thinking about the *problematics* of democracy. By "problematics" I mean those kinds of problems that flow from, that are inherent in, that are generated by democracy itself. These problematics change their hue with time and circumstance: the Founding Fathers would have been as bewildered by the current status of the popular referendum as are our progressive historians. But what makes them problematics rather than problems is that they are organically connected with the political system of democracy itself rather than with any external or adventitious factors. . . .

In this respect, the contrast between American historians and the men who created this democracy is a striking one. Although none of the Founding Fathers can be called a political philosopher, most of them were widely read in political philosophy and had given serious thought to the traditional problems of political philosophy. One of these traditional problems was the problematic character of democracies. The Founding Fathers were aware that, in centuries past, democracy—in the sense of the unfettered rule of the *demos,* of the majority—had been one of the least stable and not always the most admirable of political regimes. And this awareness— shared by practically all educated men of the time—caused them to devise a system that was more democratic than the "mixed regimes" that most political philosophers approved of, yet that also possessed at least some of the virtues thought to be associated with a "mixed regime." Such virtues pertained not to the *origins* of government but to its *ends.* In short, the Founding Fathers sought to establish a "popular government" that could be stable, just, free; where there was security of person and property; and whose public leaders would claim legitimacy not only because they were elected officials but also because their character and behavior approximated some accepted models of excellence. The fact that they used the term "popular government" rather than "democracy" is an accident of historical semantics. They were partisans of self-government—of government by the people —who deliberately and with a bold, creative genius "rigged" the machinery of the system so that this government would be one of which they, as thoughtful and civilized men, could be proud.

In establishing such a popular government, the Founding Fathers were certainly under the impression that they were expressing a faith in the common man. But they were sober and worldly men, and they were not about to hand out blank checks to anyone, even if he was a common man. They thought that political institutions had something to do with the shaping of common men, and they took the question, "*What kind of common man does our popular government produce?*" to be as crucial a consideration as any other. They took it for granted that democracy was capable of bringing evil into the world, and they wanted a system of government that made this as unlikely as possible, and that was provided with as strong as possible an inclination toward self-correction. And I should guess that they would have regarded, as a fair test of their labors, the degree to which common men in America could rise to the prospect of choosing uncommon men, speaking for uncommon ideals, as worthy of exercising authority over them.

. . .

In browsing through the literature generated by "the Turner thesis" and "the Beard thesis," I am impressed by the way in which most twentieth-century historians have managed to convert an important ideological debate into a matter of academic opinion. Much of this literature centers around the question as to whether Turner and Beard were right or wrong in the inferences they drew from their evidence. Only rarely will a historian poke around the premises on which Turner and Beard established their historical writings. Yet it is these premises that are the most interesting and important aspects of their work.

In Turner's writings, the various things he has to say about the frontier are really of no great significance compared with the way he uses the term "democracy." After all, no one has ever doubted that the frontier experience had an impact on the American character, that this impact was in the direction of egalitarianism, and that this egalitarianism in turn has had repercussions in all areas of American life. The exact degree of the egalitarian tilt that the frontier, as compared with other influences, did exercise is an issue that may be—and has been—debated. But Turner would hardly have created such fuss, he would hardly be the major historian he is, if all he had done was to call attention in a somewhat exaggerated fashion to the influence of the frontier. To appreciate Turner's impor-

tance, I would argue that one has to see him not so much as a historian as an ideologue; and to understand his work fully, one should regard it as being primarily an ideological enterprise.

The point of this enterprise is indeed to be found in Turner's famous dictum that American democracy was born on the frontier—but that point is not to be found where we have customarily looked at it. Turner was not saying anything terribly novel about the frontier—but he *was* saying something new and important about the way we should use the term "democracy." In effect, he was redefining the democratic idea. . . . He was saying that by "democracy" we ought to mean the Jacksonian-egalitarian-populist transcendental faith in the common man, and he was further explicitly stating that this was something different from, and antithetical to, the kind of democratic political philosophy that the Founding Fathers believed in. . . .

To get a clear notion of what Turner really did, it is useful to turn to an earlier essay on the relation of the frontier to American democracy. I refer to the essay by E.L. Godkin entitled "Aristocratic Opinions of Democracy," which was published in 1865. The fact that this essay is not much read, and only infrequently referred to, even by historians of American democracy, indicates with what success Turner achieved his true intention—which was, precisely, to make essays like Godkin's as unread and unremembered as possible, even by historians of American democracy.

Godkin's essay is a thoughtful rejoinder to what he took to be Tocqueville's excessively pessimistic views of the prospects for American democracy. Whether or not Godkin was correct in his interpretation of Tocqueville is here beside the point. In any case, Godkin—who regarded himself as a perfectly good American democrat—was dismayed by what he took to be Tocqueville's assertion that the many virtues of American democracy were incompatible with a high degree of civilization, an elevated culture, and a noble conception of public life. He conceded that these were not yet to be found in America, but attributed their absence to the special material circumstances of American history—*and especially to the continual, pervasive influence of the frontier.* Although Godkin had many kind words for the frontier, he did allow that it was the aggressive, self-seeking individualism, the public disorderliness, the philistine materialism of the American frontier that prevented American democracy from achieving a more splendid destiny. And he held out the hope that, as the influence of the frontier inevitably declined, the quality of American civilization and of American public life would markedly improve.

Now, it is clear that Godkin's idea of democracy was not Turner's—was, indeed, very much at odds with Turner's. It was what we would today designate as a neo-Federalist idea, which regarded egalitarianism as not only an attribute of democracy but also a problem for it, which was very much concerned with seeing to it that the American democracy was deferential to certain high republican ideals—and, of course, to those republican institutions and those "best men" that represented these ideals. Turner never refuted Godkin; Turner—even in his later years, when his feelings about the frontier were more mixed—never really tried to come to terms with Godkin; he never really argued, in a serious way, with anyone whose conception of democracy differed from his own. He simply did what all successful ideologues do when they establish a new orthodoxy: he ignored, and persuaded everyone else to ignore, the very existence of these different views—and where this was impossible, he blandly excluded these views from the spectrum of democratic opinion, relocating them on another spectrum vaguely called "aristocratic."

I shall not discuss Charles A. Beard in any detail, since his originality, like Turner's, lay in persuading the historical profession to accept the new ideological redefinition of the democratic idea. Aside from imputing crudely self-interested motives to the Founders—a bit of malice that wasn't really crucial to his argument—

Beard, so far as I can see, ended up with the aggressive assertion that the Founding Fathers were not Jacksonian democrats and were men of only partial democratic faith. He was right, of course. The really interesting question is *why* they were not, and whether perhaps they might have had good reason for being what they were. It was not until the end of his life that Beard addressed himself to this question, and in the course of answering it he tacitly abandoned his original thesis. But, by this time, American historians naturally ceased being interested in Beard.

· · ·

It appears to me that there is a great deal of work still to be done in American history. To begin with, one would like to know *why* the political philosophy of the Founding Fathers was so ruthlessly unmanned by American history. Was it the result of inherent flaws in that political philosophy itself? Was it a failure of statesmanship? Was it a consequence of external developments that were unpredictable and uncontrollable? These questions have hardly been asked, let alone answered. And the reason they haven't been asked is, first of all, the dominance of the progressive historian, who sees American history in terms of an ineluctable and providential "Rise of the Common Man". . . . I do not see that the condition of American democracy is such as automatically to call forth my love and honor, although I respect it enough to offer it my obedience. And unlike the so-called "conflict-historians," I get no relief in discovering as many instances as possible of civil strife and mob disorder. Both of these schools of thought, it seems to me, perceive the common man —the one in his potential for merely self-centered activity, the other in his exclusive potential for resisting authority—in terms that remind me of Ortega's definition of the "mass man": the individual who is not capable of assuming responsibility for self-limitation, for a kind of self-definition that is both generous and self-respecting. Interestingly enough, Ortega's definition of the "mass man" is identical with Plato's definition of tyrant. Which in turn suggests that the idea of the tyranny of the majority—whether it be an essentially mindless, self-seeking majority or a simply rancorous one—is capable of more general application than has hitherto been thought to be the case. And this, in its turn, leads me to wonder whether American historians themselves have not too frequently, and all too willingly, fallen victim to what is ultimately a tyrannical vulgarization of the democratic idea.

3

The Case for Control and Direction

MAO TSE-TUNG

How do societies advance? Some argue that only by discarding compromise and enunciating proper principles, ignoring vested interests, can one achieve results. Here Chairman Mao outlines such a case. Where does he find the principles? Whom does he trust to carry them out? Can his argument be adapted by those who rely on different principles or social groups?

"You are dictatorial." My dear sirs, what you say is correct. That is just what we are. All the experiences of the Chinese people, accumulated in the course of many successive decades, tell us to carry out a people's democratic dictatorship. . . .
"You are not benevolent." Exactly. We definitely have no benevolent policies toward the reactionaries or the reactionary deeds of such classes. Our benevolent policy does not apply to such deeds or to such

persons, who are outside the ranks of the people; it applies only to the people. . . .
The job of reforming the reactionary classes can be handled only by a state having a people's . . . dictatorship. . . .
Our party is entirely different from the political parties of the bourgeoisie. They are afraid to speak of the elimination of classes, state power, and parties. We, however, openly declare that we are energetically striving to set up conditions just for the sake of eliminating these things. The Communist Party and the state power of the people's dictatorship constitute such conditions.
. . . Communists everywhere are more competent than the bourgeoisie. They understand the laws governing the existence and development of things. They understand dialectics and can see further ahead. . . .
In this our land of China, the People's Liberation Army has already reversed the counterrevolutionary course. . . . This is a turning point in history. . . . This is a great event. . . .

From Mao Tse-Tung, "On the Present Situation and Our Tasks," report to the Central Committee of the Chinese Communist Party, December 25, 1947; from Report of the Second Plenary Session of the Central Committee of the Seventh Party Congress, Communist Party of China, released in Peking March 23, 1949; and from Mao Tse-Tung, "On People's Democratic Dictatorship," July 1, 1949. The English versions used are from Part IV, "Documents," in Otto B. van der Sprenkel, Robert Guillain, and Michael Lindsay, New China: Three Views *(New York: The John Day Company, Inc., 1951), pp. 154, 156, 165–167, 171, 174–175, 177–178, 180–181, 185–186, 190–192, 197. Reprinted by permission of the publisher.*

The victory of China's New Democratic revolution is impossible without the broadest united front. . . . But this is not all. This united front must also be firmly led by the Chinese Communist Party. Without the firm leadership of the Chinese Communist Party, no revolutionary united front can be victorious. . . .

As long as their reactionary tendencies can still influence the masses, we must expose them among the masses who are open to their influence, and strike at their political influence in order to liberate the masses from it. But political blows are one thing and economic extermination is another. . . . The existence and development of small and middle capitalist elements is not at all dangerous. The same thing applies to the new-rich peasant economy, which, after agrarian revolution, will inevitably come into existence. . . .

Many of China's conditions are identical with or similar to those of Russia before the October Revolution. Both had the same sort of feudal oppression. Economically and culturally they were similarly backward, though China was the more so. . . .

We must take our destinies into our own hands. We must rid our ranks of all flabby and incompetent thinking. . . . We are well aware of the fact that there will still be all kinds of obstacles and difficulties in the path of our advance. . . . We must be up and doing! . . .

. . . they [the business men] have monopolized the economic life of the entire country. . . . This monopoly capitalism, closely combined with foreign imperialism and the native landlord class and old type of rich peasants, becomes comprador-feudal, state-monopoly capitalism. . . . This . . . not only oppresses the workers and peasants but also oppresses the petty bourgeoisie and harms the middle bourgeoisie. . . .

. . . the Party must do its utmost to learn how to lead the urban people . . . and how to administer and build up the cities. . . . The Plenary Session called on all Party comrades to devote all their energies to learning the technique and management of industrial production; and to learning commercial banking and other work closely related to production. . . . if the Party is ignorant in production work . . . the Party . . . will fail. . . .

We must overcome all difficulties and must learn the things we do not understand. We must learn to do economic work from all who know . . . (no matter who they are). We must respect them as teachers, learning from them attentively and earnestly. We must not pretend that we know when we do not know. We must not put on bureaucratic airs. If one bores into a subject for several months, for one year or two years, perhaps three years or four years, it can eventually be mastered. . . .

The war of the People's Liberation Army is of a patriotic, just and revolutionary nature which must of necessity gain the support of the people. . . . the Communist Party seeks earnestly to unite the whole of the working class, the whole of the peasantry and the vast number of the revolutionary intelligentsia as the leading and foundation forces of this dictatorship. . . .

On the basis of the experience of these twenty-eight years, we have reached the same conclusions that Sun Yat-sen, in his will, mentioned gaining from "the experience of forty years." That is, "we must awaken the masses of the people and unite ourselves in a common struggle. . . ."

Internally, the people must be awakened. . . .

Basing itself on the science of Marxism-Leninism, the Chinese Communist Party clearly assessed the international and domestic situation. . . .

4

Comparative Politics—A Developmental Approach?

GABRIEL A. ALMOND / G. BINGHAM POWELL, JR.

The argument for direction emphasizes efficiency and dispatch. The practical record, however, is ambiguous. There are many things that democracies seem to be capable of doing more expeditiously than their rivals—and not just the production of refrigerators. Why should this be so? In this discussion of developmental politics, Almond and Powell point to many of the contradictions and cross-purposes of dictatorial enterprise that may hamper progress.

In part the maintenance of law and order in a society centers around positive orientations toward governmental agencies. Often the citizens of the new nations are oriented only to the benefits of governmental outputs and, perhaps, to the channels through which demands can be made. They have not acquired a positive and supportive subject orientation—that is, they have not learned to obey the laws. Consequently, the political order has little support to draw upon in time of internal crisis. This problem, dramatically illustrated in the Congo, has been encountered in some degree in most of the new nations.

.   .   .

In a comparative study of attitudes in five nations, the difference between attitudes in the United States and in the other nations illustrates this dimension.[1] Only in the United States did a very large propor-

tion of the respondents say that when faced with a local political problem they would form a local political group and seek legitimate means of rectifying their grievances. Such expressions of competence and willingness to work actively through legitimate input channels were striking. All too often, as in Italy, the individual feels that he can have little influence as an individual on government actions. At best, this leads to passive acceptance where dissatisfactions are not overwhelming. At worst, resentments and frustrations will be submerged until the pressure is too great, and then will erupt in violence. Even in societies where interest groups and political parties have begun to develop, the emergence of an appropriate set of individual orientations to them is essential before they can be effectively employed.

It is also important to ascertain the general level of political trust in a society. Are political competitors and opponents viewed with suspicion? Does political interaction and discussion take place on a relatively free and easy basis, or are the channels of communication regarding political matters constricted? In societies such as Italy and Germany the traumatic political experiences of the past half century have made politics a subject to avoid in personal inter-

From *Gabriel A. Almond and G. Bingham Powell, Jr.,* Comparative Politics: A Developmental Approach *(Boston: Little, Brown and Company, 1966). Copyright © 1966 by Little, Brown and Company (Inc.). Reprinted by permission of the publisher.*

[1] Gabriel A. Almond and Sidney Verba, *The Civic Culture* (Princeton: Princeton University Press, 1963), pp. 191 ff.

action. This affects the cohesion of political groups and their willingness to interact with each other.

.   .   .

In considering attitudes toward interpersonal relationships, we may also take note of the level of civility in political interaction—that is, the degree to which more or less formal norms of courtesy tend to dampen the harshness of political disagreement. The formal and informal customs of legislative bodies in Britain and the United States reflect such tendencies. It is perhaps doubly difficult for democratic politics to function in many of the new nations because they lack such moderating norms.

We have devoted considerable attention to the problem of interpersonal relationships because these constitute a crucial problem area in the political culture of the new nations. An ultimate test of a responsive and democratic system is its ability to transfer the power of government from one set of leaders to another. This may occur either between parties or within a single party. But if the level of personal trust is low, if the political process is viewed as a life-and-death conflict, and if little political courtesy mitigates the raw conflict, it will be very difficult for the incumbent elites to relinquish their roles in the political process and step aside for a new group of political actors. The stakes will seem too high; the opposition will seem too dangerous.

. . . The distorting effects of bureaucratic hierarchy may also create considerable problems of information for effective decision making. All large decision-making systems must depend to a considerable degree upon the bureaucracy to obtain and interpret information. In a bureaucracy, hierarchy and discipline are to some degree necessary for coordination of action. But a bureaucratic official is responsible to his superiors and is often dependent upon their favors for advancement. He often develops great sensitivity to the needs and wishes of his superiors. He has an inevitable tendency to tell powerful generals, cabinet ministers, or presidents that which they wish to hear or that which will reflect favorably on his own career. Active and innovating Presidents of the United States, such as Franklin Roosevelt, have been highly sensitive to this danger of distortion and have endeavored to supplement all formal information channels with vast networks of informal contacts with individuals at various points in the hierarchy.[2]

In open political systems, with many autonomous political structures and channels of communication, the elites can also utilize other information sources to help balance distortion by subordinates. Leaders read the newspapers, make personal appearances, and have polls conducted by autonomous organizations, in an effort to get an unbiased understanding of popular attitudes, and various sides of complex issues. However, in matters of security, in complex technological questions, and in times of crisis in particular, these normal channels may cease to operate or to be relevant. The United States' Cuban policy, for example, has tended to be shrouded in secrecy from the beginning, and many observers suggest that political leaders have been dangerously dependent on such secret agencies and information channels as the CIA. Not only the desire to please, but also the special prejudices and orientations of any single agency, may distort information.

Although the differences are easy to exaggerate, the totalitarian systems face these problems of information distortion in a particularly complex fashion. Observers of closed political systems, such as Nazi Germany or Stalin's Russia, have remarked on the constant, but often unsuccessful, efforts made by the ruling elites to obtain information about what is happening throughout the system. The immense scale of government activities and the efforts to accomplish far-reaching goals of economic development and military victory, or simply to maintain top rank within the system in the face of changing and unstable conditions, create an insatiable need for information.

[2] Richard W. Neustadt, *Presidential Power* (New York: John Wiley & Sons, Inc., 1962), pp. 156 ff.; and Deutsch, *Nerves of Government* (New York: The Free Press of Glencoe, 1963), pp. 224–25.

Yet the communications patterns which tend to emerge in these systems are closed, nonautonomous patterns, because the elites wish to prevent the possibility of popular knowledge and activity which might lead to subversion, and because the lower officials are receptive only to pressures from above, and not from below.

These closed communication structures seem to have inherently pathological tendencies, particularly in stress situations. Such tendencies appear as a partial consequence of threats and use of violence and force in order to maintain control over lower officials and citizens. In such cases the lower officials who staff the communications line to the elite are confronted with a difficult set of alternatives. If they deliberately distort information and are discovered, the consequences are likely to be costly. But, reporting unpleasant facts is likely to be nearly as dangerous. The man who dares hint that the leaders may have erred badly in their assessment of a situation is apt to have his career, if not his life, abruptly cut short in favor of those who convey more compatible news. The tendency of tyrants to surround themselves with "yes men," who confirm the existing beliefs of the ruler is well known. Boulding explains this phenomenon in the following terms:

The case is somewhat analogous to that of the schizophrenic or the extreme paranoid. His sense receptors are so much "afraid" of him that they merely confirm the products of his heated imagination. The terrorized information sources of the tyrant likewise tell him only what they think will be pleasing to his ears. Organizations as well as individuals can suffer from hallucinations. It is the peculiar disease of authoritarian structures.[3]

Needless to say, the situation is reinforced by the average citizen's reluctance to tell even the lower officials anything but the formal "party line." Information about popular attitudes is likely to be distorted.

[3] Kenneth Boulding, *The Image* (Ann Arbor: University of Michigan Press, 1956), p. 101.

So are reports of the inefficiency or ineffectiveness of the reporting subordinates. Even general "scientific" information may be heavily slanted, as is apparent in the work of social scientists in the Soviet Union— and which has even been the case in the continuing support (until recently) of biological theories which have been long discredited in the West. It was through such tendencies that Hitler's conduct of the war in the last days become totally divorced from reality.

Barrington Moore has emphasized the strenuous efforts made by totalitarian leaders to lessen their dependency on any single information source.[4] In the Soviet Union, Stalin used the secret police, the party, and the bureaucracy as checks on one another, relying on each separate organization to inform him of errors and deviations of the other two information channels. But, as Apter and others have suggested, in times of stress the multiple channels are apt to reinforce distorted information rather than to correct it.[5] In fact, this is likely even in much more autonomous systems.[6] If it is clear that the leadership is convinced of a set of facts, the information channels will find substantiations rather than denials.

These characteristic problems induced by closed communication systems suggest the limits on the performance of governmental functions in highly controlled authoritarian and totalitarian systems. The increase in control reaches a point of diminishing returns as the distortion of information and the costs of maintaining multiple information channels cut into effectiveness and efficiency.

[4] Barrington Moore, Jr., *Terror and Progress USSR* (Cambridge: Harvard University Press, 1954), pp. 176 ff.

[5] David Apter, *The Politics of Modernization* (Chicago: University of Chicago Press, 1965).

[6] See Ole Holsti, "The 1914 Case," *The American Political Science Review*, June, 1965, pp. 365–78.

5

More Power to Everybody

MAX WAYS

People feel more powerless in America today. Some writers like Goodwin (Chapter Four), Reich (Chapter Three) and Wheeler (this chapter) believe that is because they are powerless. Ways argues the opposite: everyone is sharing power. Is this a reasonable point of view? A con game? What is suggested by your own experience in family life? School life? Your job?

In a world where organization has brought so much impressive achievement —including triumphs of science, art, and philanthropy—the pursuit of independence now carries a note of churlish isolation, of refusal to join heartily in the stirring adventures of one's place and time. As the world recently was reminded in its multinational anxiety, the superlative example of modern organization is the Apollo program. . . . These men are not independent in the old farmer-artisan sense. Although each has a highly individual role, the worth of any man's contribution depends on all the others.

In a society where great organizations—governmental, business, educational—are central to the mode of life, a thrust for greater participation replaces the old drive for independence. To the threat of autocratic power, independence responded with the plea: "Let me alone! Don't tread on me!" Participation, raising a bolder challenge, cries, *"Listen to me!"*

From Max Ways, "More Power to Everybody," Fortune, *(May 1970), pp. 173–175, 290–299. Reprinted by permission of the publisher.*

How Runs the Tide?

For many decades society will be confronted by issues and problems turning upon participation. These will be especially acute—as they are now—in the most advanced countries. As some demands are conceded, they will be translated into policies, and other participatory policies will be adopted without the pressure of demands.

Examples of deliberate policy decisions to spread power include: the numerous experiments in U.S. corporations to increase efficiency by giving groups of employees a greater voice in determining how their work is to be done; the Yugoslav Government's sudden decision in 1950 to turn over control of each economic enterprise to those who worked in it; the broad policies of the German and French governments to increase employee participation in the management of economic enterprises. Outside the economic sphere, participatory policies include: involvement of students in the academic administration of universities, submission of political questions to voter referendums, current plans to lower the voting age. . . .

The central proposition of this article is that the general trend of twentieth-century society, particularly in the U.S., is toward a wider distribution of power, a broadening of participation by individuals in controlling their own lives and work.

Let it be quickly said that this thesis is not subject to hard, statistical proof. Moreover, it is plainly a dissent from the strongly held opinion of the vast majority of American and other intellectuals who assume that "everybody knows" power in modern society is becoming concentrated in fewer and fewer hands.

We had better be right about this matter of the trend. How we assess the broad movement will make a difference in how we assess specific participatory demands and policies. It will also make a difference in the tone and quality of public discussion. Most current demands for more participation are expressly and often angrily linked to an assertion that power is concentrating. Because demanders think they are bucking a mighty tide, they strike a kind of desperate, heroic posture.

The Wrong Vision of History

The situation is very like that of a hundred years ago when it was widely assumed that the rich were getting richer and fewer while the poor became poorer and more numerous. This assumption turned out to be wrong. Today only the most dogmatic Marxists and those members of the New Left who pride themselves on scorning facts still refuse to admit that almost everywhere in the world more people have more goods. Inequalities in the distribution of goods and impatience for faster material progress cause desperate crises in a score of countries—and no small amount of discord in our own. Nevertheless, there is at long last a general agreement that poverty, decade by decade, does diminish. Without that certainty, no society today could cope with the surging material demands of its people.

.   .   .

What is actually happening to the distribution of power in business, politics, the family, and some other key areas of U.S. life?

Let us start in the least likely area, the armed services. Many of the terms, symbols, and concepts we use to describe autocratic power are drawn from the military model of men disciplined to unquestioning obedience of a single will. This will, we say, is transmitted downward through a "chain of command." Along the chain, and especially at the bottom of it, personal judgment is supposed to be subordinated to higher authority. What the troops do is determined by their commander.

This model or ideal of the military structure has endured throughout history. But underneath the conceptual picture of how armies are supposed to work, there have been many shifts and changes through the centuries in how they actually work. In the eighteenth century the commander often had the whole battlefield under his eye. Few if any of his subordinates knew more than he did. Weapon technology was stable and maneuvers were standardized. Years of drill habituated troops to the precise execution of the commander's manipulative will. At that point in history, the facts of military life probably came closest to fulfilling the autocratic model.

By contrast, consider twelfth-century combat. Knights, each providing his own transport, weapons, and maintenance, assembled in loose array. Every knight was an independent fighting unit in a melee of man-to-man contests to which command was functionally superfluous.

Today's military reality is very different from the knight's relative independence of command and from the eighteenth century's almost total subservience. The present organizational structure is, in fact, highly participative. Troops today are dependent on supply, on specialized services, on other members of their combat team. Coordination becomes of paramount importance—but this function can no longer be concentrated, as it was in the eighteenth century, on a top battlefield commander. High command now has plenty to do, but there has been a tremendous distribution of responsibility—and therefore of power—to subordinates. Soldiers at all levels are expected to use their heads, especially in those numerous situations where their knowledge is superior to that of their commanders. Recently, CBS News showed a Vietnam incident where a company of men, suspecting an ambush, had refused to go down a road. Mutiny? A few days later the deputy commander of the brigade of which the unit was a part told CBS News that there would be no punishment. "Thank God, we've got young men who question," he said. The communications that are still called "orders" are frequently initiated from below—where the knowledge is. One of the most important functions of a command post is to serve as a message center where unit A can find out what unit B is doing and intends to do.

· · ·

. . . Clearly, the Israeli Army in action is held together less by a chain of command than by a web of dispersed information that runs up, down, and sidewise. The "will" is not concentrated in the heart of a single top commander but widely distributed among the officers and soldiers. The Israeli Army—man for man and weapon for weapon the most effective force in the world today—is participative in organizational style because it has adapted to the actual trend of twentieth-century personnel, matériel, and combat conditions. But the Israeli Army in this respect is exceptional only in degree. All modern armed forces are trending toward the participative style.

Decisions Are Shaped from Below

In civilian life, as might be expected, the anti-autocratic trend has gone much further than in military organizations. The nineteenth-century mill owner, making a single product with a stable technology, a docile labor force, and a clearly defined market, was in somewhat the same position as the eighteenth-century battlefield commander on his hill. In each case, command could be concentrated because fresh information was of little importance; possible maneuvers were known and standardized; success or failure could realistically be said to rest in decisions made at the only logical place: the top. Neither the old-style boss nor the general had to worry much about the knowledge, the motivations, or the personalities of his subordinates. Nor could he expect much help from the judgment of those he commanded.

By contrast, the corporation chief executive of 1970, like today's military commander, cannot master unaided the hugely expanded body of relevant information. Corporate technologies and tactics have become unstabilized by innovation. Markets now are swampy jungles—fecund, but mysterious and full of the possibilities of ambush.

· · ·

While the unique eminence of the top man was being reduced by his dependence on hundreds of subordinates, the base of the corporate pyramid was also changing drastically. In the period 1900–20, efficiency experts had rationalized many jobs so that men could perform them by mechanical rote. The assembly line seemed to be the ultimate symbol of modern production. But it wasn't.

What Became of the Robots?

In the past fifty years most . . . robot tasks have been taken over by increasingly sophisticated machines. Few Americans pause to wonder what really happened to the millions of workers—and their children—whose jobs have been eliminated by mechanization and automation. The reason they have not formed a huge army of unemployed is that there has been a swelling need for work that requires nonrobots, men who are paid for highly personal qualities such as knowledge, judgment, and the ability to communicate and persuade. The multiplication of professionals and of highly skilled technicians, who typically know more about their jobs than the boss does, is one of the most significant socio-economic changes of the last fifty years. These men and women in their millions have become participators, sharers of responsibility and power.

The deconcentration of power *within* corporations has been paralleled by a deconcentration of power *among* corporations. Hardly any corporate executive today, no matter how big his company, can rest easy in the knowledge that he has a lock on any market. Broader markets and livelier competition give nimble small companies more room for maneuver than they had around the turn of the century. If a giant company tries to browbeat a small supplier, it may find that its intended victim has sidestepped into a different product line—or found other corporate customers here or abroad. The most significant assets in today's economy are special knowledge and managerial skill —qualities that are hard to stockpile and impossible to monopolize.

.   .   .

Our political life has moved a long way from the town meeting, which was an appropriate political form for a community of independent men: farmers, artisans, small merchants. Those who believe that the movement has been in the direction of a greater concentration of power point to enormous budgets at all levels of government, to the multiplication of laws, to huge and fearsome discretionary powers that now rest in the hands of public officials, especially the President of the United States. . . . [T]here are now more than 500,000 *elected* public officials in the U.S. Most, of course, are in local and humble jobs, but each has some power, some area where his judgment carries weight.

Elected officials, including the President of the U.S., can do little or nothing unless they work with and through appointed officials who are protected not only by civil service but by their own indispensable expertise. Bureaucracy has long been notorious for stubborn inflexibility, a condition that arises from a combination of special knowledge, routine, and authority. Everyone from the humblest citizen to the President finds bureaucrats hard to deal with. Yet bureaucrats must be listened to because

they frequently know more than their political superiors—or anyone else—about the subject matter of public affairs. A large part of the job of any mayor or county commissioner or governor or President is trying to bring about some measure of coordination among bureaucratic subordinates who disagree with him—and with one another. He can't, in any literal sense, command them. He can't fire them. He has to "lead"—which usually means a pound of persuasion for every ounce of hierarchical pressure.

.   .   .

The official apparatus of the U.S. bears no resemblance to a machine run from a console of push buttons by a lonely decision-maker in the White House. U.S. officialdom, with several million individual wills in play, is in itself one of the most striking examples of widely distributed power in history. Immense though it is, the official circle does not come close to monopolizing the political power of the country. At the circle's edge hovers the press. The importance of news as a link between government and public is greater than ever, primarily because politicians are now much more sensitive to public reaction than they used to be.

Real People Instead of "The People"

Much of this democratizing trend has been unexpected. In the first third of the twentieth century, when shrewd men began to glimpse the magnitude of technological, economic, and social change, many of them assumed that the appropriate political form for the future would be an authoritarian state which imposed order firmly from above. That was Lenin's intuition and Mussolini's and Hitler's. In the U.S., explicit proposals for political dictatorship have never made much headway. But an assumption that only concentrated political power can deal with the new conditions of life seeps through American opinion.

.   .   .

"Hell is other people" said Jean-Paul

Sartre. Whatever may be his shortcomings as a philosopher, Sartre's ear is exquisitely tuned to the subjective sufferings of his time. Inhabitants of the second half of the twentieth century instantly recognize what his epigram means. In no previous age would "Hell is other people" seem a pithy expression of a universal truth. "Other people" were not hell for the independent farmer of a hundred fifty years ago; his neighbors didn't get in his hair. Nor were "other people" hell for the autocratically ruled man; his scourge was the tyrant, and "other people" were fellow victims.

In our society, where almost everybody has more power than almost anybody had a couple of hundred years ago, people get in one another's way. . . . Political life and home life are full of conflict because what A wants is not necessarily what B wants— and both A and B demand that they be heeded.

No Resting Place Ahead

.   .   .

Nor will the cries for more participation be confined to actually disadvantaged groups: the poor, the ignorant, the black, and the female. Men who deploy quite a lot of power will be stimulated to demand more of it every time their own fields of action or influence collide with somebody else's expanding field of action or influence. . . . There is no denying how difficult it will be to maintain a necessary measure of social cohesion in the face of rising demands for a wider and wider distribution of power. We are more likely to survive this danger if we clearly understand that the demands occur within—and indeed because of—a deep, long-range trend toward participation.

.   .   .

6

Pluralist Democracy in the United States

ROBERT A. DAHL

What is the American system like in practice? How does it truly operate? A leading student of power structures, both at the national and community level, is Robert Dahl, the author of Who Governs?, *a community study of New Haven, and* A Preface to Democratic Theory. *Dahl is the leading exponent of the pluralist model of American democracy. He is also probably the most influencial political scientist of the current generation.*

. . . American political institutions, then, encourage political leaders to respond to

From Robert A. Dahl, Pluralist Democracy in the United States *(Chicago: Rand McNally & Co., 1967), pp. 291–295, 325–326. Reprinted by permission of the publisher.*

severe conflicts in three ways:

1. By forming a new political coalition that can overpower the opposition. But this, as we shall see, is a difficult solution.

2. By incremental measures that postpone comprehensive change.

3. By enduring compromises that remove the issue from serious political conflict.

OVERPOWERING THE OPPOSITION

A severe conflict is sometimes moderated or even terminated when one political coalition gains enough power to overcome the resistance of its opponents. Instead of compromising, the winning coalition enacts its policies despite the opposition of the defeated coalition. If the opposition fights back, as it is likely to do, it finds itself too weak to prevail. Unable to reverse the main direction of policy imposed by the winning coalition, the opposition may in time accept the major policies enacted by the winners and settle down to bargaining for incremental adjustments; thus severe conflict gives way to a period of moderate conflict.

Probably the only effective way in American politics for one coalition significantly to reduce the bargaining power of an enemy coalition is to turn it into a visible and even isolated political minority by defeating it in national elections. However, because of the large number of positions where an embattled minority, unable to win the Presidency or a majority in either house of Congress, can dig in and successfully continue to challenge the policies of the majority coalition, a single electoral victory is ordinarily not necessarily enough, particularly if the contest is close. . . . Why, people often ask, don't elections settle things one way or the other? Why is it so difficult for a President and Congress ostensibly of the same party to terminate a severe conflict by overriding the objections of their opponents, carrying through their legislative program, and letting the country decide at the next election whether it likes the changes or disapproves of them?

By now it must be clear to the reader that American political institutions were never designed to operate in this fashion; nor do they. But in addition to the institutions themselves, several aspects of American beliefs, sentiments, or loyalties reduce still further the likelihood that elections can be decisive. For one thing, party loyalties are, as we have seen, incredibly persistent. It is uncomfortably close to being

true that either of the two major parties could probably win twenty million votes for its presidential candidate even if it nominated Ed the Talking Horse. The overwhelming electoral sweeps in the presidential elections of 1936, 1952, and 1964 left the defeated minority with a substantial share of popular votes (37 per cent in 1936, 44 per cent in 1952, 39 per cent in 1964). In the twenty-six presidential elections from 1864–1964, the defeated party received less than 40 per cent only seven times; it received 45 per cent or more in twelve elections, and from 40–45 per cent seven times. A party overwhelmed by a landslide is far indeed from being in a hopeless situation.

Then, too, the votes of a winning coalition are not uniformly distributed throughout the country; there are sizeable regional variations. A political minority in the nation may be a political majority in a region, as with the New England Federalists in 1800 or the Democrats in the South in every election won by a Republican President from 1860 onward. A defeated minority with a powerful regional base stands a good chance not only of surviving but of keeping most of its senior political leaders in Congress.

Finally, Americans are not agreed on a single, definite, generally accepted rule for legitimate decision-making in government. Although the legitimacy of rule by majorities is frequently invoked, the majority principle is not, among Americans, a clearcut rule of decision-making. This principle invoked to support 'national' majorities (i.e., as revealed in national elections) is also used to support local, state, or regional majorities. . . .

POSTPONING COMPREHENSIVE CHANGES

American political institutions are excellently designed for making incremental changes. But they also foster delay in coming to grips with questions that threaten severe conflict. It is true that delay may provide precious time during which a seemingly severe problem may change its shape, become more manageable, even disappear. But postponement may also inhibit leaders from facing a problem squarely and searching for decisive solutions—solutions that may be forced upon them many years later when they can no longer delay.

. . . In 1948, President Truman, acting on recommendations from his advisory Committee on Civil Rights, recommended federal legislation against lynching, the poll tax, segregation in public transportation, and discrimination in employment. Although mild civil rights legislation was passed in 1957 and 1960, no major legislation on civil rights cleared Congress until 1964, almost two decades after President Truman's recommendations. Passage of American welfare and social security laws has followed the enactment of comparable laws in most European democracies by one to several generations. A national medical care program has been advocated for generations. In 1945, President Truman proposed to a Congress a comprehensive medical insurance program for persons of all ages. The first law establishing a national system of medical insurance, though only for the elderly, was not enacted until 1965.

COMPROMISE

The existence of innumerable fortified positions from which an embattled but well organized minority can fight off and wear down an attack, combined with the absence of any *single* rule for making legitimate decisions on which the political activists are agreed, means that it is difficult to terminate a conflict by the clear-cut victory of one side over another. Hence severe conflicts are sometimes handled by reaching a compromise. Occasionally the result is a long-lasting compromise. . . .

Periods of Moderate Conflict

If you were to pick at random any year in American history since the Constitutional Convention to illustrate the workings of the political system, you would stand a

rather good chance of being able to describe American politics during that year as follows:

Important government policies would be arrived at through negotiation, bargaining, persuasion, and pressure at a considerable number of different sites in the political system—the White House, the bureaucracies, the labyrinth of committees in Congress, the federal and state courts, the state legislatures and executives, the local governments. No single organized political interest, party, class, region, or ethnic group would control all of these sites.

Different individuals and groups would not all exert an equal influence on decisions about government policies. The extent of influence individuals or groups exerted would depend on a complex set of factors: their political skills, how aroused and active they were, their numbers, and their access to such political resources as organization, money, connections, propaganda, etc. People who lacked even suffrage and had no other resources—slaves, for example—would of course be virtually powerless. But because *almost* every group has some political resources—at a minimum, the vote—most people who felt that their interests were significantly affected by a proposed change in policy would have some influence in negotiations.

All the important political forces—particularly all the candidates and elected officials of the two major parties—would accept (or at any rate would not challenge) the legitimacy of the basic social, economic, and political structures of the United States. Organized opposition to these basic structures would be confined to minority movements too feeble to win representation in Congress or a single electoral vote for their presidential candidate.

Political conflict would be moderate.

Changes in policies would be marginal.

.   .   .

Why should this be so? Our paradigm of conflict . . . suggests four reasons:

The political institutions reward moderation and marginal change, and discourage deviant policies and comprehensive changes.

In the United States there is a massive convergence of attitudes on a number of key issues that divide citizens in other countries.

As one result, ways of life are not seriously threatened by the policies of opponents.

On issues over which Americans disagree, overlapping cleavages stimulate conciliation and compromise.

7

The Decline of Liberal Democracy

HARVEY WHEELER

But does the system work as well as Dahl suggests? Harvey Wheeler, of the Center for the Study of Democratic Institutions, presents a critique in many ways typical of writers of the "New Left," finding that our system has degenerated. (This opinion is shared by many Rightists, although their program for the future "Restoration" of our real system of government differs.) Is our system of government today truly a departure from the past? Has participation in a meaningful sense grown or declined? Is it desirable that everybody has to participate fully and equally, whether they want to or not?

What are the theoretical assumptions underlying participational democracy?

1

There were assumptions that the average man was wise; he could find solutions to his and society's problems; he would participate actively in politics; and he was more incorruptible than those in authority.

2

Next was an implicit theory of common goals and how society should realize them. The better statement might be that participational democracy implied a theory of "anti-goals." For it was held that the best way to produce political goals was not through explicit governmental policies but

Harvey Wheeler, The Rise and Fall of Liberal Democracy, pp. 16–20, 25–26. Published by the Center for the Study of Democratic Institutions. Copyright © 1966 by the Fund for the Republic. Reprinted by permission of the Fund for the Republic.

as a cumulative result of the people having been freed to develop, institute, and express goals individually and autonomously. This was the political counterpart of the unseen hand of classical economic theory. It yielded a counterpart of economic competition in the form of pressure-group politics. This was radical pluralism at the deepest level. If society refuses to make explicit its values and goals, the right ones are sure to appear as a result of free men and institutions struggling against each other to achieve their own interests. Every conflicting interest and goal will somehow eventually be harmonized as organized groups battle it out in the legislative chambers and lobbies. Given this view, American political science, like other liberal institutions, reflected instead of prescribing, and its contribution to knowledge was the group theory of politics. The theory still dominates the academy.

3

Participational democracy also implied an assumption about recruitment and employment. The best way to get the public work done was to see that political offices were filled only by average Americans. The wisest governors would spring from and automatically reflect the wisdom of the people. This tenet became enshrined in the folklore of American politics as the Lincoln tradition of log cabin to White House. It was not long ago that politicians finally abandoned their belief that rich men were unsuitable candidates unless they had risen from humble origins.

4

Related to this was a proposition about public administration. It derived from the ongoing struggle against a succession of power élites. The American doctrine was that politics and government were intrinsically simple from an administrative point of view. Nothing would have to be done in government that was above the comprehension or the ability of the average American. This was an attack on the European tradition of a professional civil service or administrative class, which Americans believed to be tainted by aristocratic or élitist principles. It was held that the average American was the most "professional" possible administrator of all governmental functions. Though this first appeared under the Jacksonians as the "spoils system," it persisted as the chief element distinguishing the American civil service from all others that had ever existed in history.

5

This in turn implied a theory about decision-making. Decisions should not be made by government officials except as a last resort and even then subject to severe restrictions. The ideal was that all decisions should be made by the sovereign people organized politically. Every possible governmental decision should be voted upon. Only with the fullest possible popular participation in the decision-making process could government function properly. . . .

8

. . . This also involved an anarchistic assumption about formal education or acculturation. Men should not take collective thought or action for the over-all shape or direction of their culture, their social institutions, or their system of values. Certainly the government should not be concerned with the nature of the family system, the economic order, the religious system, the direction of science, and so on. Everything would be done best if nothing were done about it. The result was a political system that was supposed to produce the common good in an automatic and unguided fashion. It entailed negative government: faith in the operation and efficacy of a kind of residual anarchist harmony. . . . This meant that the automaticity of the system was supposed to produce:

—Children well educated and made into good democratic citizens simply by leaving with each family the responsibility for controlling the acculturation process of its members.

—An economy efficient, equitable, and always tending to the public good.

—An officialdom staff through the rotation of average citizens in and out of office, responsible to the people, and achieving the public good.

—A free flow of information through numerous private channels that would automatically discover the things the people ought to know and see that the appropriate information was available to them when it was needed.

—A country essentially isolated from the rest of the world and able to pursue its own interests without regard to the impact of those interests on others.

—Avoidance of the evils traditionally associated with European cities.

—Avoidance of the evils of aristocracy, oligarchy, and conspiratorial factions not in harmony with the public good.

. . . [D]uring the nineteenth century America made a great commitment to a special, and indeed a historically unique, form of democracy. It backed its gamble with some of the most ingenious governmental and political institutions known to history. Today, these institutions of populism and progressism have been all but dismantled. They appear embarrassingly Victorian in restrospect as intricate gingerbread like those monuments of Victorian architecture we are now busily tearing down.

However, it is harder to eliminate beliefs and institutions than it is buildings. We still carry the participational commitment in two ways. First, a few of the institutional arrangements we developed to facilitate democratic participation are still with us, though often atrophied or modified. The direct primary is the most prominent example. Second and more important is the fact that even though in one part of our minds we realize that our participational experiment has failed, and even though we sometimes ridicule it, nonetheless, as a nation, we still hold to it, myth though it is. Participational democracy is the only really distinctive contribution we have made to politics and we seem fearful of admitting its failure. When we state the basis of our opposition to communism, it is that communism does not provide for democracy as we have understood it and therefore is not a "true" democracy. But the democracy we foist on others is one we ourselves no longer have. Despite our inner knowledge that our own participational forms no longer work, we continue to base our cold war on the claim that the non-Western world should adopt these forms forthwith, and when we look at the political systems of the newer democracies in the underdeveloped areas of the world, one of our chief criticisms is that they are not sufficiently participational in our special Victorian sense.

Participational democracy failed, but nothing was put in its place. We give ourselves numerous reasons for not redesigning our democratic institutions despite how badly they work in comparison with their original purposes. We reiterate defensively that though they may not achieve what they were designed for, what they do accomplish is pretty good; besides, things would be worse if any fundamentally new approach to democracy were attempted. Our immediate, visceral reaction to any current political issue continues to spring from an emotional commitment to participational democracy. We worry about the political apathy of the average voter. We disapprove of any public figure who does not announce his devotion to the innate political wisdom of the common man. We insist that the primary function of our elected representative is to reflect the desires of his constituency, their private interests rather than the dictates of the common good, and when we complain about him as a wheeler-dealer, we do not say that he is applying a corrupt view of democracy or of representation but that he is representing the desires of the wrong groups or is giving too much weight to certain groups over others. We assume that by keeping "his ear to the ground," by "not losing touch with the grass-roots," and by employing the most scientific public-opinion polling devices, our representative can make the original goals of participational democracy realizable.

. . .

We have already seen how the mass media have undercut democratic processes. They have also destroyed the mutuality of communication upon which community depends. What information we get and what communication takes place must come through the channels of the mass media. Yet there is no way of taking organized concern for our total informational needs and comparing them with what we actually produce. It is curious what happens to "communication" in a vast mass-media system. The word communication implies mutuality and reciprocation. But this is precisely what is missing.

We are familiar with the notion that the citizen is not in direct contact with any crucial source of information. This is the nature of a mass medium; in being large enough and extensive enough to cover the mass of people, it must be distant from every person. The individual does not consume information from another "person" directly, but only from mass media "images" which have questionable status as "persons." For each functionary in the mass media must take concern, not for what he is as a person, but for his "image." What we see and hear are constructed "images." . . .

This has been the story of the rise and fall of American liberal democracy. . . . Throughout history democracy has been the most effective device for complex societies to coordinate the actions of masses of people performing a large variety of complex functions. But this quickly produces a dilemma. A complex society requires the participation of the people in the decision-making process, but popular participation in decision-making is possible only at relatively primitive levels of development and complexity. The participational feature of democracy becomes unworkable precisely at the point when complexity calls it forth and affluent masses demand it. The result is that the demand for participational democracy occurs for political reasons just at the time when it has been rendered dysfunctional for technological reasons. This has a further misfortune. The principle of democracy becomes so closely identified with the failings of participational devices that the critics of participational democracy are then able to discredit democracy itself and attribute to it the chief responsibility for the political failings of mass culture.

. . . Our times demand the development of new conceptions of legislation and new processes of deliberation. The theories of Jeremy Bentham and James Madison must be supplanted by new ones appropriate to the conditions of bureaucratic cultures and adequate to the challenges of the scientific revolution.

Are there any signs of such a development? Recently a new doctrine of democracy has appeared. It was developed initially by young people in their twenties but, despite its adamant youth-centered bias, leadership of the movement is exercised by those already in their thirties. The "Port Huron Statement" of the Students for a Democratic Society . . . has already assumed the status of a holy text. Its framers, meaning to turn their backs on the ideological squabbles of the 1930's, seized upon a few simple propositions. Their overriding devotion was given to what they called *participatory* democracy. This not only referred to anti-organization principles for conducting the business of the movement itself but also expressed a new approach to working with the unrepresented or dispossessed members of society. The Establishment, standing in the way of participatory democracy, is the announced enemy. There is no real difference between the Establishment liberals and the Establishment conservatives, between the civil and the corporate élites. Indeed, liberalism's unshakable hold on political and industrial power makes *it* the more formidable adversary. The solution? Organize the unrepresented, activate the poor and the Negroes, reconstitute the discontented, form a new coalition committed to the building of a new society dedicated to democracy, world order, and civil and economic justice.

3

THE CONSTITUTION:
FRAME OR FRAMEWORK?

Forty years of crisis—a depression and a world war plus the cold war—
have produced no major changes in the written American Constitution.
Even the changes in interpretation, custom, and convention that have
occurred have been shifts in relative power rather than differences in the
total structure. The American Constitution, through the centuries, has
proved exceedingly resilient and tough. Classifying the Bill of Rights as
one group of changes and the Civil Rights Amendments as another, there
have been perhaps a half dozen amendments in the entire history of the
nation.

Since it seems fair to assume that the Constitution will continue to be
the basis for American government for the foreseeable future, many of
the grandiose schemes for wholesale change seem unrealistic. There is no
reason to believe that the American people have or will suddenly develop
a genuine desire for parliamentary government or regionalism or, indeed,
a new constitution.

The British writer, Walter Bagehot, suggested in a famous passage
that a government must have two types of agencies—efficient instruments
for carrying out actions and decorative branches for satisfying deep-felt
human needs and emotions. In the British system, of course, this decorative or symbolic function is satisfied by the royal family.

The Constitution: Flexible Symbol or Embodiment of an Ideology?

In the American system most of this symbolism has centered around
the Constitution and the Court. By providing a decorative element, a tie
with the past, and a set of mysteries, the Constitution enriches American
life with a focus for unity.

But if the Constitution is a symbol, the question remains: what does it
symbolize? There have been many interpretations—most, but by no means
all, favorable.

In particular, the debate rages sporadically over the extent *to which* the Constitution should have a fixed symbolic content, or whether it should remain relatively flexible. Ideologues and pragmatists take opposite sides on the degree to which particular religious, economic, or class ideas are, or should be, enshrined in the document.

The Constitution as Instrument: Who Benefits?

The Constitution is not just a symbol, but an operating instrument as well. As such, it is not just the written Constitution that counts but also the customs, patterns, and conventions that have grown around it. For example, the Vice President succeeds on the death of the President and becomes President, although the Constitution does not make clear whether this is the precise intention, or whether he would merely become Acting President. It is, in other words, the Constitution in operation that is the working Constitution.

As an instrument, the Constitution is a source of political power, and is fought over because the wording of the Constitution is a form of strength or weakness for a particular group or program. The Constitution also provides a framework of operation which may accidentally or purposefully determine outcomes. It is also a method of governmental operations which either induces the solution of practical problems, or hinders them.

1

American Society

ROBIN M. WILLIAMS, JR.

How can the Constitution be a symbol of unity? If it is to have a definite symbolic content, wouldn't that divide the country much as political parties or specific measures would? The following reading attempts to show that different groups can read into the Constitution entirely different interpretations. To him, it is the ambiguities of the Constitution that are its strength.

The powers of the government of the United States are set by the somewhat elastic but definitely constricting bounds of

From Robin M. Williams, Jr., American Society *(New York: Alfred A. Knopf, Inc., 1951), pp. 224–225. Copyright © 1951 by Alfred A. Knopf, Inc. Reprinted by permission of the publisher.*

a written constitution. Around that document has gradually accumulated a tremendous number of interpretations and commentaries, of court decisions, of beliefs and myths. The Constitution enjoys a veneration that makes it a substantial barrier against sudden or far-reaching changes in the structure of the states. There is a "psychology of constitutionalism," a widespread conviction that the Constitution is sufficient to cover all emergencies, that deviations from its provisions are unnecessary and dangerous, that a breach of the Constitution would bring down the whole structure of ordered and lawful government.

When it was written, the Constitution was a drastic innovation, not only in its content but in its basic idea that the form of government could be purposively determined. It was radical in the root sense of that word. Yet, in a similar root sense, it has had conservative consequences. During the period of consolidation of authority and partial return to prerevolutionary conditions that always follows the instituting of a new state, the Constitution was one of the few symbols of national scope available to the loose federation of weak and disunited provinces. Furthermore, it has been a rallying point for conserving (maintaining) the political and civil liberties of individuals. But it has been conservative in a more conventional sense, also, for it was actually adopted in a period of what was close to counterrevolution, and a major force in its drafting and adoption was the desire to insure internal stability and the protection of property and trade. (The classical reference is Charles A. Beard: *An Economic Interpretation of the Constitution of the United States*, New York: 1913.) Undoubtedly the Constitution can be interpreted to conform to the interests of the more prosperous and propertied groups, and a stable legal order and venerated symbol of that order is advantageous to those interests.

This dual conservatism partly explains how it is that the Constitution can be defended with equal fervor by individuals whose motivations and interests are in most respects sharply opposed. The document has become almost a symbolic "sponge" that can absorb the allegiances of persons having amazingly diverse interests, values, ideas, political philosophies. Although the process by which this absorption occurs is not well understood (and is a research problem of first interest), its existence is probably of real importance to social stability. As with many other symbols of government, the very indefiniteness of the popularly imputed meanings facilitates a sense of order and integration not derivable from the specific applications of political doctrine. . . .

2

This Is a Republic, Not a Democracy

THE JOHN BIRCH SOCIETY

The ambiguities that seem so valuable to Professor Williams strike others as a vacuum, as a symbol of national decay. Among groups calling for a revitalization of national purpose and for dedication to a defined political program, probably none has attracted the attention given the John Birch Society. This selection, which represents only a portion of a statement of basic beliefs, poses the question and challenge: Isn't there a fundamental form to American government which must be retained? Indirectly it suggests further problems: Just how much of the past must be kept? How do we arrive at such a determination? Who provides the answers?

We believe that a constitutional Republic, such as our Founding Fathers gave us, is probably the best of all forms of government. We believe that a democracy, which they tried hard to obviate, and into which the liberals have been trying for 50 years to convert our Republic, is one of the worst of all forms of government. We call attention to the fact that up to 1928 the U.S. Army Training Manual still gave our men in uniform the following quite accurate definition, which would have been thoroughly approved by the Constitutional Convention that established our Republic. "Democracy: A Government of the masses. Authority derived through mass meeting or any form of direct expression results in mobocracy. Attitude toward property is communistic—negating property rights. Attitude toward law is that the will of the majority shall regulate, whether it be based upon deliberation or governed by passion, prejudice, and impulse, without restraint or regard to consequences. Results in demagogism, license, agitation, discontent, anarchy." It is because all history proves this to be true that we repeat so emphatically: "This is a Republic, not a democracy; let's keep it that way."

We are opposed to collectivism as a political and economic system, even when it does not have the police-state features of communism. We are opposed to it no matter whether the collectivism be called socialism or the welfare state or the New Deal or the Fair Deal or the New Frontier, or advanced under some other semantic disguise. And we are opposed to it no matter what may be the framework or form of government under which collectivism is imposed. We believe that increasing the size of government, increasing the centralization of government, and increasing the functions of government all act as brakes on material progress and as destroyers of personal freedom.

We believe that even where the size and functions of government are properly limited, as much of the power and duties of government as possible should be retained in the hands of as small governmental units as possible, as close to the people served by such units as possible. For the tend-

Statement of the principles of the John Birch Society, Congressional Record, *June 12, 1962, p. A. 4293.*

encies of any governing body to waste, expansion, and despotism all increase with the distance of that body from the people governed; the more closely any governing body can be kept under observation by those who pay its bills and provide its delegated authority, the more honestly responsible it will be. And the diffusion of governmental power and functions is one of the greatest safeguards against tyranny man has yet devised. For this reason it is extremely important in our case to keep our township, city, County and State governments from being bribed and coerced into coming under one direct chain of control from Washington.

We believe that for any people eternal vigilance is the price of liberty far more as against the insidious encroachment of internal tyranny than against the danger of subjugation from the outside or from the prospect of any sharp and decisive revo-

lution. In a republic we must constantly seek to elect and to keep in power a government we can trust, manned by people we can trust, maintaining a currency we can trust, and working for purposes we can trust (none of which we have today). We think it is even more important for the government to obey the laws than for the people to do so. But for 30 years we have had a steady stream of governments which increasingly have regarded our laws and even our Constitution as mere pieces of paper, which should not be allowed to stand in the way of what they, in their omniscient benevolence, considered to be "for the greatest good of the greatest number." (Or in their power-seeking plans pretended so to believe.) We want a restoration of a "government of laws, and not of men" in this country; and if a few impeachments are necessary to bring that about, then we are all for the impeachments. . . .

3

Three-Fifths of a Man

FLOYD McKISSICK

This argument by a leading civil rights figure sees the Constitution as a great weapon for change and rights of minorities. Does it exemplify Williams' notions of the use of constitutions? How does it differ?

Black People have survived three hundred years of slavery in America. They have survived a bloody Civil War in which they were the pawns of white men. Black Men have survived the Reconstruction and its brutal aftermath. They have survived

From Floyd McKissick, Three-Fifths of a Man (London: The Macmillan Co., 1969), pp. 53–57, 84–86. Copyright © by Floyd McKissick, 1969. Reprinted by permission of the publisher.

the Industrial Revolution. And they have survived modern American racism.

The patterns of behavior between the races that were developed during the earliest days of physical enslavement still exist. Every Black-white relationship is in some way affected by the heritage of a master-slave and master-servant tradition. Black-white distrust, Black-white fear, and Black-white tensions are deep rooted and real.

If they are ever to be reconciled, all the

great forces of American revolution must be marshaled to this end. The Declaration of Independence and the Constitution of the United States must be revitalized to include Black Men, for unfortunately the Constitution was not written with the Black Man in mind. It was written by white men, many of whom owned Black slaves. It was written to perpetuate and protect their way of life. It was written to institutionalize racism.

In theory, the Declaration of Independence and the Constitution of the United States provide the means by which to achieve a free nation. *If* they are extended to their full potential, they can become the basis for a new and nonracist society.

The Declaration of Independence is a separatist document. Through that document the thirteen original American colonies declared themselves separate and free from the British empire, separate from the British constitution, separate from British law. The Declaration of Independence was also a revolutionary document. It established the intent and determination of the colonists to fight for their independence by any means, to sacrifice lives, to shoot and kill, to use violence and force to protect their right of freedom.

.   .   .

Whereas the Declaration of Independence articulated the ideology of the American revolution, the Constitution was written to establish a framework through which that ideology could be translated into reality. It was written to provide a basis for the legal structure of a new nation, to provide a means by which to defend the rights and liberties set forth earlier and to make them more explicit.

Although the Constitution was at best imperfect, it created an outline for the impartial administration of justice. Even though it was conceived and developed by racists, the guarantees incorporated, if extended to all men, could be the basis for a truly free society. Most of the ideas included in the Constitution are sound and still viable, for the Constitution is a brilliant document born of a valid revolution. *If*

interpreted justly, in full awareness of today's conditions, and if applied in a consistent fashion, the Constitution can be converted into a document of liberation for Black America.

The severe limitation of the Constitution is that it was written by men incapable of including nonwhites in their concept of revolutionary justice and freedom. In view of the stated purposes of the American Revolution, white Americans should have no difficulty understanding the aspirations of Black Americans today, for they are the same aspirations once expressed by the American colonists. They are the same aspirations for which the American Revolution was fought.

Proper use of the Constitution can be a way to put the full power and resources of the national government into the drive to gain freedom—the drive to achieve Black Power. As Howard Zinn, in *SNCC: The New Abolitionists*, has pointed out, the Constitution provides every possible authorization needed to enforce the Thirteenth and Fourteenth amendments. The legal authority is present; the will is plainly lacking. The Constitution must be enforced—Black People will not and should not have to wait until white America realizes its own evil. The Constitution provides white America with a way for immediate and complete action; it does not presuppose that Blacks have to wait until America somehow undergoes massive self-education to exorcise itself of racism.

Indicative of the white American psyche is the section of the original Constitution that determines the representation and means of taxation for the state. According to Article 1, Section 2(C):

Representatives and direct Taxes shall be apportioned among the several States which may be included in this Union, according to their respective Numbers, which shall be determined by adding to the whole Number of free Persons, including those bound to Service for a Term of Years, and excluding Indians not taxed, three fifths of all other persons.

"All other persons" meant Black People. Taken in context, its implications are staggering. It meant that the slave was considered less than human, a bit more than an animal, perhaps, but less than human. If you were Black, you were only three-fifths of a man in the eyes of Alexander Hamilton, Benjamin Franklin, Roger Sherman, Charles Pickney, James Madison, John Blair, Robert Morris, and the other witnesses in Philadelphia. The Black Man in America has had to live with this stigma of inferiority all his life—a stigma imposed upon him by men who assumed the prerogative of bargaining with his life and destiny.

We must look beyond the immediate reasons why this clause was included in the Constitution—whether it was for acceptance by southern states, whether it was to guarantee the continuation of the plantation economy, or for representation in the new Congress. These are unimportant to the Black Man. Racism had been written into the Constitution. This was the first time in recorded history that such an attitude was officially recognized and sanctioned by a national government.

The hypocrisy of the white slaveholders, evidenced in the Declaration of Independence, was not repeated in the writing of the Constitution; at last true feelings came out. As was written in No. 54 of *The Federalist* (generally attributed to James Madison), "The Federal Constitution, therefore, decides with great propriety on the case of our slaves, when it views them in the mixed character of persons and of property. This is in fact their true character."

.   .   .

A thorough knowledge of the law is valuable to any man forced to deal with a society as complex as modern America. For the Black Man, it is essential. Black Men are daily faced with violations of their rights; they are faced with discrimination and illegality. Without a knowledge of their rights, they cannot possibly defend themselves against exploitation; without a knowledge of their rights, they cannot possibly live as men.

Even poor whites do not have to rely on the law for protection as do Black People.

Their skin color affords them a measure of protection and acceptance Black People lack. Even exploitation of white by white is not as great as Black by white.

The entire legal hierarchy in America—including federal, state, and municipal judges, elected and appointed, as well as the lawyers and law-enforcement officials—all share in the responsibility for bringing about social change in this country. The lesser courts as well as the Supreme Court are charged with equal responsibility. The executive no less than the judicial branch must see to it that court decisions are enacted and legal provisions enforced. We must keep in mind Andrew Jackson's famous retort to the Supreme Court when it commanded him to act. "Justice Marshall has made his decision" he said, "now let him enforce it."

With the cities burning, with America's house burning down, with racism festering in every pocket of American life, men in all branches of the government must become "social engineers."

Those who control the administration of the law control the destiny—individually and collectively—of the entire population. Their control over the Black Community is more absolute than over any other group because that community has the fewest legal resources for its own defense.

In a society in which money is the supreme value, the legal system is irrelevant to the rich, except the use of court decisions in profit-making ventures. By virtue of their expensive lawyers, hearings are guaranteed to the rich for every grievance, and if their wealth is sufficient, they will be above the law. As Cornelius Vanderbilt noted, "What do I care about the law? Hain't I got the power?"

However, in our society the legal system is very relevant to the poor and to the colored. It is the legal system that exercises the authority of freedom and bondage, life and death. The judiciary—and particularly the Constitution—is very important to Black Men. It is their only hope for social justice without chaos.

.   .   .

4

The Greening of America

CHARLES A. REICH

This indictment of the American system by a Yale law professor drew more reader response than any other article in the history of The New Yorker. *Reich sees the vaunted separation of government and society as a fiction and fraud. Is this convincing? Are American liberties less protected today than, say, in 1940?*

1. The Corporate State

There is a revolution under way. It is not like revolutions of the past. It has originated with the individual and with culture, and if it succeeds it will change the political structure only as its final act. It will not require violence to succeed, and it cannot be successfully resisted by violence. It is now spreading with amazing rapidity, and already our laws, institutions, and social structure are changing in consequence. Its ultimate creation could be a higher reason, a more human community, and a new and liberated individual.

This is the revolution of the new generation. It is a transformation that seems both necessary and inevitable, and in time it may turn out to include not only youth but the entire American people. The logic of the new generation's rebellion must be understood in light of the rise of the corporate state and the way in which the state dominates, exploits, and ultimately destroys both nature and man. Americans have lost control of the machinery of their society, and only new values and a new culture can restore control. At the heart of every-

From Charles A. Reich, "The Greening of America," The New Yorker, Vol. XLVI, No. 32 (Sept. 26, 1970), 42–46, 48, 50, 53–54, 60–64.

thing is what must be called a change of consciousness. This means a new way of living—almost a new man. This is what the new generation has been searching for, and what it has started to achieve. Industrialism produced a new man, too—one adapted to the demands of the machine. In contrast, today's emerging consciousness seeks a new knowledge of what it means to be human, in order that the machine, having been built, may now be turned to human ends.

Most of us see the nature of the present American crisis as a collection of problems, not necessarily related to each other, and, although profoundly troubling, nevertheless within the reach of reason and reform. Yet if we list these problems, not according to topic but as elements of larger issues concerning the structure of our society itself, we can see that the present crisis is an organic one, that it arises out of the basic premises by which we live, and that no mere reform can touch it in any way.

(1) *Disorder, corruption, hypocrisy, war.* The front pages of newspapers tell of the disintegration of the social fabric, and of the resulting atmosphere of anxiety and terror in which we all live. Lawlessness is most often associated with crime and riots, but there is lawlessness and corruption in all the major institutions of our society—

matched by an indifference to responsibility and consequences, and a pervasive hypocrisy that refuses to acknowledge the facts that are everywhere visible. Both lawlessness and evasion find their ultimate expression in the Vietnam war, with its unprincipled destruction of everything human, and its random, indifferent, technological cruelty.

(2) *Poverty, distorted priorities, and legislation by power.* America presents a picture of drastic poverty amid affluence. There is a superabundance of some goods and activities, such as defense manufacture, while other needs, such as education and medical care, are at a starvation level for many. These closely related kinds of inequality are not the accidents of a free economy; they are intentionally and rigidly built into the laws and institutions of our society. An example is the tax structure, which subsidizes private wealth and production of luxuries and weapons at the direct expense of impoverished people and impoverished services. The nation has a planned economy, but the planning is done by the exercise of sheer private power, without concern for the general good.

(3) *Uncontrolled technology and the destruction of environment.* Technology and production can be great benefactors of man, but they are mindless instruments, and if undirected they career along with a momentum of their own. In our country, they pulverize everything in their path—the landscape, the natural environment, history and tradition, the amenities and civilities, the privacy and spaciousness of life, much beauty, and the fragile, slow-growing social structures that bind us together. Organization and bureaucracy, which are an application of technology to social institutions, increasingly dictate how we shall live our lives, with the logic of organization taking precedence over any other values.

(4) *Decline of democracy and liberty, powerlessness.* The Constitution and Bill of Rights have steadily been weakened. The nation has gradually become a rigid managerial hierarchy, with a small élite and a great mass of disenfranchised. Democracy has rapidly lost ground as power has been increasingly captured by giant managerial institutions and industrial corporations, and decisions have come to be made by experts, specialists, and professionals safely insulated from the feelings of the people. Most government power has shifted from Congress to administrative agencies, and corporate power is free to ignore both stockholders and consumers. As regulation and administration have grown, liberty has been eroded and bureaucratic discretion has taken the place of the rule of law. The pervasiveness of police, security men, the military, and compulsory military service show the changed character of American liberty.

(5) *The artificiality of work and culture.* Both work and living have become more and more pointless and empty. There is no lack of meaningful things that cry out to be done, but our working days are used up in what lacks meaning: making useless or harmful products, or servicing the bureaucratic structures. For most Americans, work is mindless, exhausting, boring, servile, and hateful—something to be endured—while "life" is confined to "time off." At the same time, our culture has been reduced to the grossly commercial; all cultural values are for sale, and those that fail to make a profit tend to be destroyed. Our life activities have become vicarious and false to our genuine needs—activities fabricated by others and forced upon us.

(6) *Absence of community.* America is one vast, terrifying anti-community. The great organizations to which most people give their working day and the apartments and suburbs to which they return at night are equally places of loneliness and alienation. Modern living has obliterated place, locality, and neighborhood, and given us an anonymous separateness of existence. The family, the most basic social system, has been stripped to its functional essentials. Friendship has been coated over with a layer of impenetrable artificiality as men strive to live roles designed for them. Protocol, competition, hostility, and fear

have replaced the warmth of the circle of affection that might sustain man against a hostile universe.

(7) *Loss of self.* Of all the forms of impoverishment that can be seen or felt in America, loss of self—a sort of death-in-life—is surely the most devastating. It is, even more than the draft and the Vietnam war, the source of discontent and rage in the new generation. Beginning with school, if not before, an individual is systematically stripped of his imagination, his creativity, his heritage, his dreams, and his personal uniqueness, in order to fit him to be a productive unit in a mass technological society. Instinct, feeling, and spontaneity are suppressed by overwhelming forces. As the individual is drawn into the meritocracy, his working life is split from his home life, and both suffer from a lack of wholeness. In the end, people virtually *become* their occupations and their other roles, and are strangers to themselves. Blacks long ago felt their deprivation of identity and potential for life. But white "soul" and blues are just emerging. A segment of our young people are articulately aware that they, too, suffer an enforced loss of self—that they, too, are losing the lives that could be theirs.

We seem to be living in a society that no one created and that no one wants. The feeling of powerlessness extends even to the inhabitants of executive offices. Yet, paradoxically, it is also a fact that we have available to us the means to begin coping with virtually all the problems that beset us. Most people would initially deny this, but reflection shows how true it is. We know what causes crime and social disorder and what can be done to eliminate those causes. We know the steps that can be taken to create greater economic equality. We are in possession of techniques for fashioning and preserving more livable cities and environments. Our problems are vast, but so is our store of techniques. It is simply not being put to use.

The American crisis, then, seems clearly to be related to an inability to act. But what is the cause of this paralysis? Why, in the face of every warning, have we been unable to act? Why have we not used our resources more wisely and justly? We tell ourselves that social failure gets down to individual moral failure: we must have the will to act; we must first find concern and compassion in our hearts. But this diagnosis is not good enough. It is contradicted by the experience of powerlessness that is encountered by so many people. Today, a majority of the people, as moral individuals, certainly want peace, but they cannot turn their individual wills into action by socety. It is not that we do not will action but that we are unable to act, unable to put existing knowledge to use. The machinery of our society apparently no longer works.

The corporate state in which we live is an immensely powerful machine—ordered, legalistic, rational, yet utterly out of human control and indifferent to human values. . . . Other societies have had bad systems, but endured because a part of human enterprise went on outside the system. We have turned over everything to what can be thought of as a single vast corporation. It consists primarily of large industrial organizations, plus non-profit institutions such as foundations and the educational system, all related to the whole as divisions to a business corporation. Government, providing coördination and a variety of needed services, is only a part of this corporate state, which represents a complete reversal of the original American ideal and plan.

· · ·

As for business organizations, their imperative is to grow. They need stability, freedom from outside interference, constantly increasing profits. Everyone in the organization wants more and better personnel, more functions, increased status and prestige—in a word, growth. The medium through which these imperatives operate is law. . . .

The essence of the corporate state is that it is relentlessly single-minded; it has just one value, the value of technology as represented by organization, efficiency, growth, progress. No other value is allowed to interfere with this one—not amenity, not beauty, not community, not even the supreme value of life itself. Thus, the state is essentially mindless; it has only one idea, and it merely rolls along, never stopping to think, consider, balance, judge. Only such single-valued mindlessness would cut the last red-woods, pollute the most beautiful beaches, invent devices to injure and destroy plant and human life. To have just one value is to be a machine.

.   .   .

AMALGAMATION AND INTEGRATION

We normally consider the units of the corporate state—such as the federal govern-ment, an automobile company, a private foundation—as if they were separate from each other. This, however, is not the case. . . .

Let us consider first how government operations are "privately" performed. To a substantial degree, this relationship is for-malized. The government hires private firms to build national-defense systems, to supply the space program, to construct the interstate highway system, and even to do its thinking for it. An enormous portion of the federal budget is spent in simply hiring out government functions. This much is obvious, although many people do not seem to be aware of it. What is less obvious is the "deputizing" system by which a far larger sector of the private economy is en-listed in government service. For example, a college teacher may receive a form from the Civil Service Commission asking him for certain information about an individual who is applying for a government job. When the teacher fills out the form, he is acting as if he had been "deputized" by the government; that is, he is performing a service for the government—one for which he might even feel himself entitled to com-pensation. Now consider a foundation that is granted special non-taxable status. The foundation is in this favored position be-cause it is engaged in activities that are deemed to be of "public benefit." That is, it is the judgment of the government that some types of activity are public services although performed under private auspices. The government itself could do what pri-vate foundations now do—aid education, sponsor research, and carry out other proj-ects that do not command a profit in the commercial sense—but the government has decided that these functions are better per-formed by foundations. This is the same judgment that the government makes when it hires Boeing to build bombers, or a pri-vate construction firm to build an interstate highway. Public utilities—airlines, railroads, truck carriers, taxicabs, oil pipelines, tele-phones—are all "deputized" in this fashion. They carry on *public* functions—functions that in other societies might be taken on by the government itself.

.   .   .

Let us now look at the other side of the coin: government as the servant of the private sector. Once again, the relationship is sometimes formal and obvious. The gov-ernment spends huge amounts for research and development, and private companies are often able to get the benefits of this. Airports are built at public expense for private airlines to use. Highways are built for private trucking firms to use. The gov-ernment pays all sorts of subsidies, direct and indirect, to various industries. It sup-plies credit services and financial aid to homeowners. It grows trees on public forest lands and sells them at cut-rate prices to private lumber companies. It builds roads to aid ski developments.

It is true that government has always existed to serve the society—police and fire departments help business, too, and so do wars that open up new markets. This is what government is and always has been all about. But today governmental activity in aid of the private sector is enormously greater, more pervasive, more immediately felt than ever before. The difference be-tween the local public services provided in 1776 and the expenditure of millions of dollars in subsidies to the shipping industry is not only one of degree. In the difference between a highly autonomous, localized economy and a highly interdependent one, there is a difference of principle as well as one of degree. Government help today is an essential, not a luxury. The airlines could not operate without allocation of routes and regulation of landings and take-offs, nor could the television industry without corresponding regulation. The educational system, elementary school through high school, is necessary for the production of people able to work in today's industry. Thus, it may be said that everyone who operates "privately" really is aided and subsidized, in one degree or another, by the public. The sturdy independent rancher rides off into the sunset on land irrigated by government subsidy, past sheep whose grazing is subsidized and crops whose prices are artificially maintained by government action; he does not look like a welfare client, but he is on the dole nevertheless.

Regulation, originally an instrument of reform, has been remade into a service to industry. State and federal laws enable the oil industry to act as an oligopoly, closely controlling imports, production, and prices that otherwise might be subject to the wishes of consumers and to the other influences of "free enterprise." Without these convenient laws to eliminate competition and the free market, the oil industry might have to go to the trouble and expense of "regulating" itself. Thus, the motion-picture industry and the professional-sports industry have elaborate systems of private regulation, including "commissioners," a corpus of laws, and a scale of fines and other penalties, all designed to place the industry on the best and most united basis to sell its product. Such regulation as is performed by federal agencies like the F.C.C., S.F.C., F.T.C., and C.A.B. is remarkably similar in general effect, but it is a service rendered at taxpayers' expense.

.   .   .

One way to appreciate the true nature of the public-private amalgamated state is to list a few of the kinds of power that can be found in the United States:

Power to make one publication available to airline passengers but not another.

Power to raise bank interest rates.

Power to forbid apartment dwellers to have pets or children.

Power to require peanut-butter eaters to choose either "creamy" or "chunky" peanut butter and to prevent them from buying real, unhydrogenated peanut butter.

Power to force all young people who want to go to college to take examinations requiring a certain standardized kind of mechanical problem-solving.

Power to popularize snowmobiles instead of snowshoes.

Power to dominate public consciousness through the mass media.

Power to induce lung cancer in thousands of persons by promoting the sale of cigarettes.

Power to turn off a man's telephone service.

Power to encourage or discourage various forms of scholarship, educational activity, philanthropy, and research.

Power to construct office buildings with windows that will not open, or without any windows at all.

Power to determine what life styles will not be acceptable for employees.

Power to make relatively large or relatively small investments in the safety of consumer products.

Power to change the culture of a foreign country.

Were we told that all this power was held by a single tyrannical ruler, we would find the prospect frightening indeed. As things are, however, we are likely to take comfort in the thought that although the power may exist, it is divided in many ways, held by many different entities, and subject to all sorts of checks, balances, and controls, and that for the most part it applies only to persons who subject themselves to it voluntarily—by taking a job with a corporation, for instance. But the power of the corporate state is not so easily escaped. The refuge from a job in one corporation will find a choice of other corporations all prepared to subject him to similar control as an employee. The television viewer who tires of one network finds the others even more tiresome. Can railroad passengers do anything about conditions they object to? Do they find alternative means of transportation readily available?

Editorials denouncing students often say that a student who does not like the way a university is run should leave. But society makes it all but mandatory for a young person to complete his education, and in their rules and practices most universities are extraordinarily alike. Moreover, the penalty for many young men who leave is to be drafted. Under these circumstances, it is hardly accurate to say that a student has submitted "voluntarily" to a university's rules. The student's case is the case of the railroad traveller, the peanut-butter eater, the man who wants a bank loan, the corporate employee, the apartment-house dweller who wants to keep a pet. The integration of the corporate state makes inescapable what was formerly voluntary, and powers that once were small and gentle become monstrous and terrifying. The better organized, the more tightly administered, the more rational and inclusive the corporate state becomes, the more every organization turns into a government, and all forms of power take on the aspect of government decrees.

. . .

While the tendency of administration may appear to be benign and peaceful, as opposed to the turbulence of conflict, it is actually violent. For the very idea of imposed order is violent. It demands compliance; nothing less than compliance will do; and it must obtain compliance, by persuasion or management if possible, by repression if necessary. It is convinced that it has "the best way" and that all other ways are wrong; it cannot understand those who do not accept the rightness of its views. A growing tension and anger develop against those who would question what is so carefully designed to be "best" —for them as well as for everybody else. Thus, it is not uncommon for public-school administrators to engage in repression of independent thinking by students, although the ability to think independently is presumably an important objective of education.

At the Del Valle High School in Walnut Creek, California, the students produced a "controversial" yearbook last spring. It included a poem by Robert Danielson, a seventeen-year-old star of the school baseball team, poking fun at school athletes who "don't reason" and "don't ask questions." Because of the poem, young Danielson was told by his coach that he would not receive a team letter and was not welcome at the presentation-awards dinner. The coach sought to mitigate this punishment by telling the faculty, "I like the kid. . . . I think he's pathetic, but I like him. If I hadn't, he wouldn't have played baseball for me for two years." Meanwhile, the principal threatened the faculty adviser of the yearbook, Mrs. Hildegarde Buckette, with dismissal; however, the principal and Mrs. Buckette reached an understanding whereby the yearbook would be subject in the future to "guidelines" established by a faculty committee. Administration wants the best for everybody, and all it asks is that individuals make their lives conform to the framework established by the state.

THE ANATOMY OF THE CORPORATE STATE

We usually make at least three reassuring assumptions about the amalgamated power of the corporate state: (1) power is controlled by the people through the democratic process and pluralism in the case of government and through the market in the case of the "private" sector, (2) power is controlled by the persons who are placed in a position of authority to exercise power, (3) power is subject to the Constitution and the laws. These assumptions stand as a presumed barrier to the state power we have described. Let us deal here with the first two assumptions, leaving a discussion of law until later.

As machinery for translating popular will into political effect, the American system functions very badly. We can hardly say that our political process makes it possible for voters to enforce their will on such subjects as pollution, the supersonic plane, mass transportation, the arms race, and the

Vietnam war. On the contrary, it is usually impossible for popularly held views to be expressed politically; this was demonstrated for all to see in the 1968 Presidential campaign, when both the Republican and the Democratic candidate supported the Vietnam war. And even if the political machinery allowed the electorate to express its views, it would be difficult for citizens to get the information necessary to form an opinion.

. . .

If pure democratic theory fails us in both the public and the private sphere, we must nevertheless consider whether a modified version of democracy makes it possible for large competing interests to achieve a balance that represents a rough approximation of what people want; this is the theory of pluralism. Here again the theory simply does not work out. Robert Paul Wolff has effectively discussed this type of pluralism in his book "The Poverty of Liberalism." (The same essay also appears in a coöperative volume called "A Critique of Pure Tolerance.") The interests that make up the spectrum of political pluralism are highly select; many important interests are entirely omitted. Thus, as Wolff points out, we have recognized the three major religions but no agnostics; we have virtually no representation of the poor, the blacks, or other outsiders, no representation of youth, no radicals, and "pluralism" represents not interests but *organized* interests. Thus, "labor" means large labor organizations, though these do not necessarily represent the real interests of individual employees. "Labor" may support heavy defense expenditures, repressive police measures, and emphasis on economic growth, but this support may not express the true interests of the industrial worker at all. Likewise, the three major religions may fail to represent the spiritual strivings of individual persons, which might take some such form as resistance to the draft. Indeed, at the organizational level there is far more agreement than difference among the "competing interests," so they come to represent the same type of coöperation that conglom-erate mergers produce among interests in the private sphere.

Even if the people had power to give orders, the orders might have little or no effect. Increasingly, the important part of government is found in the executive departments, which are staffed by career men, experts, professional, and civil servants who have specialized knowledge of technical fields. These persons are not elected, nor are they subject to removal on political grounds. They are thus immunized from direct democratic control. Congress and the state legislatures have neither the time nor the specialized knowledge to oversee all these governmental activities. Instead, the legislatures have increasingly resorted to broad delegations of authority. In effect, the legislature abandons any effort to set policy. It is true that Congress makes occasional investigatory forays into agency activities, but these are not in their nature policy-setting. Even if a statute tries to set definite standards—as the Federal Water Power Act, say, lists some factors to be considered in building hydroelectric projects— the standards are simply left to be weighed at the agency's discretion. Thus, in the case of Consolidated Edison's proposal to develop a new power plant at Storm King Mountain, on the Hudson, the Federal Power Commission has continued to show a single-minded devotion to the interests of power development despite mounting public concern about its effect on the environment. What really happens is that government becomes institutionalized in the hands of professionals, experts, managers, whose decisions are governed by the laws of bureaucratic behavior and the laws of professional behavior. . . .

LAW: THE INHUMAN MEDIUM

Law is supposed to be a codification of those lasting human values that a people agree upon. "Thou shalt not kill" is such a law. The corporate state, a distinctively legalistic society, utilizes law for every facet of its activity—there has probably never been a society with so much law, or where law is so important. Thus, it might be expected that law would represent a significant control over the power of the corporate state, and a source of guidelines for it. But law in the corporate state is something very different from a codification of values. The state has transformed it.

During the New Deal period, the law was gradually changed from a medium that carried traditional values of its own into a value-free medium that could be adapted to serve "public policy," which became the "public interest" of the corporate state. This produced law that fell into line with the requirements of organization and technology, and supported the demands of administration instead of protecting the individual. Once law had assumed this role, there began a vast proliferation of laws, statutes, regulations, and decisions. For the law began to be employed to aid all of the work of the corporate state by compelling obedience to the state's constantly increasing demands.

One aspect of this development has been the steady erosion of Constitutional rights and the kind of laws that really do protect our basic values. Thus, despite the vast growth of corporate power, the courts, except in the area of racial discrimination, have failed to hold that corporations are subject to the restrictions of the Bill of Rights. Of course, the drafters of the Constitution did not imagine that corporations would exercise the governmental powers with which the Bill of Rights was concerned. But today private institutions do exercise governmental powers—more, indeed, than "government" itself does. They decide what will not be produced; they do our primary economic planning; they are the chief determinants of how resources are allocated. With respect to their own employees or members or students, they act in an unmistakably governmental fashion; they punish conduct, deprive people of their positions within the organization, and decide on advancement. In a sweeping way, they influence the opinions, expression, associations, and behavior of all of us. Hence the fact that the Bill of Rights is inapplicable is of paramount importance;

it means that these Constitutional safeguards actually apply to only one part—and not the most significant part—of the power of the corporate state. We have two governments in America, then—one under the Constitution, and a much greater one not under the Constitution. Consider a right such as freedom of speech. "Government" is forbidden to interfere with free speech, but corporations can fire employees for free speech, universities can expel students for free speech, and newspapers, television, and magazines can refuse to carry "radical" opinion. In short, the inapplicability of our Bill of Rights is one of the crucial facts of American life today.

Does the Bill of Rights afford protection even where it is still held to apply? The Supreme Court decisions of the last few decades are not reassuring. In its adjudications, the Court gives heavy weight to "the interest of society." The commands of the state are to be overturned only if there is no "rational" basis for them or if they contravene an express provision of the Constitution and that provision is not outweighed by "the interest of society." The result over the years has been that virtually any policy in the field of economics—production, planning, or allocation—has been declared Constitutional; that all sorts of decisions classifying people in different and unequal statuses for tax or benefit purposes have gone unquestioned; that peacetime selective service has been upheld; that free speech has been severely limited.

.   .   .

As the nation has become an increasingly legalistic society, law has become the medium in which private maneuver for power, status, and financial gain takes place. It has provided a huge game board, like Monopoly, on which expert players make intricate moves to positions of advantage. The game of law is played with all of the legal powers of government to provide benefits, subsidies, allocate resources and franchises, and grant special exceptions and favors to the winners. As for the losers, the legal game board embodies almost every inequity, injustice, and irrationality that has become accepted in our society. The tax laws, for example, surely constitute one of the most intricate and remarkable structures of inequity that the human mind has ever devised. There are well-known examples—capital-gains income and oil income taxed at lower rates than other income, deductions for businessmen not available to those in other occupations, distinctions between the person who owns his home and the person who rents one, distinctions between the single person and the married one. A great number of other inequalities and special favors are buried in its endless, complex pages. The draft law is even worse. For it sends some young men off to risk their lives and lose long years that might be spent in ways of their own choosing, while others are privileged to escape any military service. The most recent regulations concerning conscientious objectors continue the inequitable pattern, since they clearly favor the well-to-do and the well-educated. We need not linger here on facts that are well known; the point is that the tax and draft statutes are not unusual examples of how the law works; they are entirely characteristic examples.

From a broader perspective, it can be seen that for each status, class, and position in society there is a different set of laws. There is one set of laws for the government employee, another for the congressman. There is one set of laws for the farmer, another for the writer. The Constitutional right of privacy is not the same for a welfare recipient as it is for a businessman. A person receiving Medicare was required by the original legislation to take a loyalty oath. If "law" means a general rule to govern a community of people, then there is no longer any such concept as "equal protection of the laws."

As administered, the law becomes lawless in an even deeper sense. When the heavyweight boxing champion Muhammad Ali refused to submit to induction into the Army, the New York State Boxing Commission, a public body operating by authority of law, revoked his title. The Commission held no hearing at which Ali could present his case. It did not wait to see whether the courts would convict him of a crime or accept his claim that by reason of his religious views he had a right to refuse induction. In Seattle, the legal authorities initiated action to revoke the license of a coffeehouse because the coffeehouse supposedly encouraged anti-war thinking among young G.I.s; the licensing official said that he did not want such activities around the Seattle area. Through the law, his arbitrary personal view became a governmental act.

When governmental lawlessness is revealed, as in the "police riot" in Chicago or the killings at Kent State, everyone is shocked, as if this were an aberration in our society. But the police have always been brutal and lawless in their treatment of the powerless; we know this from the way blacks were and are treated by the police in the South, and from the way young people, the poor, blacks, and other outcasts are treated in the North. The cry of police lawlessness misses the point. In any large city, all the bureaucracies tend to be lawless—the building inspectors make threats and collect bribes, the liquor-licensing authority is both arbitrary and corrupt, the zoning system is tyrannical but subject to influence.

Misuse of law is not an aberration in our society. It is the inevitable condition of any society that permits a concentration of enough power, of whatever sort, to exercise full control over those within the system. The ideal of the rule of law can be realized only in a political-conflict state that places limits upon official power and permits diversity to exist. Once everything is subject to regulation, the rule of law is inevitably lost, for the rule of law cannot stand as an independent principle of society; it is always tied to the question of power. Recent disclosures concerning the arbitary arrest and jailing of migratory farm workers in New Jersey follow precisely in this pattern: the law is used by those in power as a weapon against those who are powerless. The bitter truth is that despite all our ideals of law and all the talk of law and order, we are today in the most literal sense a lawless society, for our "law" has ceased to be law and become instead its opposite —mere force at the disposal of whoever is at the controls.

5

America's Constitution Looks Greener

HORACE JUDSON

Comparative viewpoints are sometimes helpful. England has long been regarded as the cradle of liberty, yet there are strong suggestions that some things here look better to them than to Reich. Are the issues raised here important? Do they answer Reich in whole? In part?

Over the past two years England has seen a revolution of established opinion that reaches as deep as any this century. At issue is nothing less than the British Constitution, hallowed by generations of political scientists here and in the United States precisely because it is "unwritten," embedded in the statutes and even more in the traditional liberties and restraints of a people with a genius for politics. Future historians will look at these years as the period when British opinion decided it was time to have a written constitution, and took the first parliamentary steps toward that goal. In view is a limitation of the present near-absolute supremacy of Parliament, by means of extensive regionalization, even federalization, of government. To this would be added a bill of rights and an instrument of judicial review surprisingly like what Americans mean by a Supreme Court.

The murmurings for a written constitution began to be audible, on the left and

among theoreticians of the Liberal Party, not much before the beginning of 1968. Within six months, major constitutional reform had become one of the first orders of business for the collective intelligence of the Establishment. Within the year, the idea of a written constitution had advanced from a silly extremist notion to a serious intellectual and political position. By last winter, the subject had commanded a series of lead editorials in the *Times*, had attracted well-placed support from MP's of all parties, and had begun to surface as official government policy, in the form of a commission to study regionalization. In the spring and summer of 1969 the bill of rights began to surface as well, with repeated attempts in Parliament to introduce legislation; the private members' bills recall the pattern by which recent successful reforms—the abortion act, homosexual law reform—have been started.

Fair Play

. . . The claim for the unwritten constitution was put by the nineteenth-century Whig A. V. Dicey:

The general principles of our constitution (as for example the right to personal liberty, or the

From Horace Judson, "The British Constitution," The Atlantic Monthly, 225, No. 2 (February 1970), 18–27. Copyright © 1970, by The Atlantic Monthly Company, Boston, Mass. Reprinted by permission of the publisher.

right of public meeting) are with us the result of judicial decisions determining the rights of private persons in particular cases brought before the courts, whereas under many foreign constitutions the security (such as it is) given to the rights of individuals results, or appears to result, from the general principles of the constitution. . . . Our constitution, in short, is a judge-made constitution. . . . There is in the English constitution an absence of those declarations or definitions of rights so dear to foreign constitutionalists.

.   .   .

Yet it is precisely in the area of individual liberties that alarm about the British Constitution has begun to be felt. Two American visitors were among the first to mobilize the growing unease. Melvin Wulf, legal director of the American Civil Liberties Union, . . . found, in contrast to the unending debate in the United States, that in Britain there is "almost total absence of public discussion of the issues at stake. . . . I suppose the British people also take their liberties for granted—a dangerous frame of mind."

Wulf ticked off several areas of concern. British lawyers: "I find barely any evidence of the legal profession applying its ingenuity to the development of the law affecting personal freedom." The police: "The major criticism is not that they exceed their powers but that the powers given to them by Parliament and the courts enable them to interfere with the privacy of individuals beyond anything which I think is justifiable." Wulf particularly had in mind the powers of arrest and of search and seizure which allow the police to stop and frisk people on the street without objective evidence that they are carrying stolen goods or intending a felony, but with "the free exercise of police intuition." The power to search homes is also exercised, Wulf pointed out, "on grounds that an American court wouldn't tolerate at all."

Despite the famous fair play of the judges' rules, Wulf said, "The whole question of the right to silence is treated so differently here that it makes an American's mind boggle. By and large, the judges' rules only pay lip service to the right to silence." Barristers know Wulf is right. It is a commonplace among them that in criminal cases, upwards of three quarters of convictions secured at trial are the result of confessions or "verbals," alleged admissions by the defendant at time of arrest, put in evidence by the police. Many barristers believe that verbals are all too often invented by the police.

The next American to comment reached a much wider English audience. He was Anthony Lewis, for years Supreme Court reporter for the New York *Times* and . . . that newspaper's chief London correspondent. . . . Lewis wrote a piece for the weekly *Spectator* in which he cited similar and further evidence of erosion in British civil liberties, and explicitly suggested a remedy: "There is undoubtedly a longing in Britain today for some institution that would apply to public questions the kind of ethical standards, focused on the individual, that are relevant in the American Supreme Court."

Get It in Writing

Other cases, other laws, press the indictment further. Some of the most worrisome include:

THE CROWN IN THE COURTS

In 1965, Parliament passed the War Damage Act, which had the specific purpose of overturning a decision of Britain's highest court, the Judicial Committee of the House of Lords. The Burmah Oil Company had sued the government for compensation for damages suffered in the Far East during the Second World War. In 1964 the Law Lords ruled in Burmah Oil's favor. The War Damage Act simply set aside that decision. Parliament's action alarmed many. Lord Devlin, arguably the best legal statesman in Great Britain, called it "a constitutional issue ranking among those which since Magna Carta have settled the balance of power within the state." The act threatened

the fundamental principle that the Crown and its subjects are equal before the law. . . . The independence of the judiciary is not guaranteed by express words. . . . If now we want to preserve some of the few restraints we have left . . . we should do well to get something in writing.

TEN GOOD MEN AND TRUE

In the summer of 1967, a cabal of powerful jurists, including the Lord Chief Justice, Lord Parker, was able to ram through Parliament, as part of a new Criminal Justice Act, a provision which changed the jury system from the unanimous "verdict of you all" to allow majority verdicts by a vote of 10 to 2. As Lord Parker implicitly admitted in a speech to police officers, the motive for the change was the belief, for which he offered fragmentary statistics, that the police were not getting enough convictions. Practicing barristers warned that the change in effect canceled the ancient protection of the defendant by the jury's reasonable doubt of his guilt. The full implication of majority verdicts will perhaps be felt only when a case arises with political content.

THE ONE-MINUTE LIFE SENTENCE

In the spring of 1968, Valentine Sokol, a Yorkshire cloth finisher, was sentenced to life imprisonment for murder—after a trial that lasted one minute, without any statement in open court of the evidence against him. Sokol's case was a bizarre consequence of another thoughtless provision of the 1967 Criminal Justice Act. He had been committed for trial after proceedings in which only written evidence was submitted. In a clause naïvely intended to protect defendants against prejudicial pretrial publicity, the new act forbade press coverage of committal proceedings except with the permission of the defendant. But then, when Sokol came to trial at Leeds Assizes, he pleaded guilty: no evidence needed to be heard, and the judge had no alternative to the mandatory sentence of life imprisonment. When a press uproar followed, the Lord Chief Justice directed that in any similar case the prosecution should detail its evidence at trial. But as the *Daily Telegraph*, among others, pointed out, Lord

Parker's direction "does not at all touch the commoner and potentially more serious disadvantages of forbidding the publication of committal proceedings."

EXPATRIATION BY STATUTE

To all observers the most flagrant recent violation of civil liberties continues to be the law of February, 1968, which deprived a large group of British subjects, the Kenya Asians, of their right as citizens to enter Britain on their British passports. It was this law which moved Anthony Lewis to write his piece in the *Spectator*. "One can say with some confidence," Lewis wrote, "that an American statute of that character would be held unconstitutional. . . . In just such a case . . . [in 1967] Mr. Justice Black said: "The very nature of our free government makes it completely incongruous to have a rule of law under which a group of citizens temporarily in office can deprive another group of citizens of their citizenship. . . .

Breaking Down

. . . Absence of constitutional checks on Parliament has in the past been filled by political checks: balance of opposing interests within the country, opposition of parties, opportunity for lengthy debate in Parliament. But those who believe that the British Constitution is in danger argue that these traditional controls are breaking down.

The evidence of danger to civil liberties has hardly aroused the British public: the total membership of the National Council for Civil Liberties is about 2400, and its total annual budget would not pay the salary of Brock Pemberton, national director of the American Civil Liberties Union. . . .

. . . [T]he modern threat to civil liberties reaches far beyond the previous centuries' conception of a catalogue of basic rights. The vast ad hoc expansion of bureaucracies, both public and private, already represents an unprecedented invasion of the privacy of individuals. . . .

. . . Despite Dicey's confidence, in recent decades judges have been increasingly ineffectual as protectors of the British Constitution. No court has the power to void the merest comma of an act of Parliament, even when the rights of British subjects are fundamentally infringed, and where it is inconceivable that American courts would not act. Further, the lack of judicial review can be generalized to include the first problem, the cancerous growth of bureaucracy. Thus the advocates of constitutional reform are concerned about mechanisms of redress, by appeal to independent authorities with real powers, against acts of trade unions, big corporations, police, the press, local governmental bodies—even, as in one case on the front pages in July, against arbitrary acts of old-age hospitals.

Regionalization, the decentralization of government, is the third problem and the one so far that has most deeply aroused politicians. They had to take serious notice when, in the form of separatism, decentralization began winning elections in Scotland and Wales. Further, decentralization could ease the work loads of MP's, now crushed by routine measures, while allowing them to give major measures proper deliberation. As Tory MP Quentin Hogg points out, in Gladstone's time the second reading of the bill for Irish home rule was debated for three weeks. When Hogg himself first went to Parliament, a major debate was still three days. Now it is one day, which, when opening and closing speches and the administrative machinery are all subtracted, leaves three hours. "Parliament is breaking down under the overload, the ministers are breaking down," Hogg says. "There is one malady but a hundred symptoms."

The idea of regionalization goes far beyond the Scottish and Welsh nationalisms. Eighteen months ago, Hogg mused about a nationwide regional system, "not necessarily on the eighteenth-century model as in the U.S., though even that would be better than what we have. Britain differs from every other country in the world in that there is nothing effectively between the central government and the smallest units of local government."

·   ·   ·

4

THE FEDERAL SYSTEM: INSTRUMENT OF LIBERTY OR INEFFICIENCY?

The federal system is certainly one of the distinguishing characteristics of American government. The existence within the same territory of two sets of governments, both at least theoretically deriving their powers separately, creates problems and puzzles observers. When the former Russian premier, Khrushchev, visited the United States, he was irritated by remarks of state and local officials, being convinced that they really were made at the behest of Washington. The federal system was really quite inexplicable to him, even though the Soviet Union is nominally a federal republic.

The independence of the states in many aspects of their activities has been held up as a bulwark to freedom. It has been described as the product of a people that want "unity without uniformity," and seen as a protection against any tyranny which could not control the diverse states. These separate governments serve as "laboratories for experimentation" and chambers for new programs.

But there are clearly costs as well. The boundaries, sizes, and populations vary tremendously. The existence of 51 different legal systems means that American government is highly legalized. Businesses must deal with elaborate sets of laws. Individuals often are penalized by the existence of different systems of laws, while those who make a study of the complexities can often use them to personal advantage at the expense of the community.

Because of the rapid growth of national economy and dissatisfaction with state government, observers for a long time have been predicting the demise of the states. But events belie these predictions. The states are as strong and active as ever, growing in functions and in expenditures. The federal system seems to take on new patterns and meet new crises, but the American public appears to be satisfied with the system as a whole.

States' Rights: Principle or Pretext?

From the time of Jefferson, the issue of states' rights has been a key slogan in American politics. Many claims have been, and continue to be, made for federalism.

The slogan of states' rights has two aspects. It may be a claim of divisions of power and abstract issues. Maintenance of the federal system is a desire of American public opinion, particularly in the name of freedom or diversity.

The claim that federalism fosters freedom has some very responsible backing. Roscoe Pound has observed that no nation of continental size has been governed except as a federal system or as an autocracy. The American suspicion of power is a source of the support that states' rights can evoke. From Madison to Calhoun to modern writers, the argument is advanced that too much centralism is a threat to human liberty. While Nelson Rockefeller presents the traditional American viewpoint, the late Professor Neumann of Columbia University examines the historical record and suggests that the evidence for the identification of freedom with federalism is shakier than others argue.

States' rights is also often used as an argument in the course of debate to strengthen an issue. While the argument is in terms of abstract states' rights, the real purpose is to advance a particular cause. History seems to suggest that any party long out of power begins to stress states' rights, while the dominant party increasingly finds virtues in greater Federal activity. The classical example is Jefferson's purchase of Louisiana, but the reversal in our times of the positions of the Democratic and Republican parties is also suggestive.

Federal Aid to the States: Help or Hindrance?

This century has seen a shift of power to the national government. This has been a relative matter; all units of government have grown so far as expenditures and personnel are concerned. But the federal government's have grown faster than the states', and those of the states have grown more rapidly than those of the local governmental units. Today money is received from the national government and dispersed to local units or directly to the cities.

Some see these programs as weakening state governments. The states, they argue, have lost their power of independent choice. They follow along in the train of federal grants and aid. Others see these programs not only as socially desirable but as fostering better state government. They recognize the problems of state government—regarded as the weakest link in our current American governmental structure—but find the fault to lie in the states' own internal problems—notably their failure to reapportion and to develop strong leadership in the governor's office and in the legislature. The shift of powers to the federal government then is seen as the result, rather than the cause, of state weakness.

Nation, State, Cities: Partners or Rivals?

Grants-in-aid are only part of a bigger picture. The essential point is the relationship between the two (or three) levels of government. How do they get along in our system? What should be an ideal relationship? Does the existence of the states create rivalries and conflicts that perplex the citizen?

In recent years, there has been an increasing tendency for the national government to deal directly with the cities and eliminate the "middle man" states. Is this a healthy development or an increasing emasculation of the federal system? Does the new prominence of the suburbs mean a new shift back to the states? What of the plight of the cities if new political coalitions develop?

1

Freedom and Federalism

NELSON ROCKEFELLER

Nelson Rockefeller, while a serious candidate for presidential nomination, took time out to develop a series of lectures on the future of federalism. In this extract, he states eloquently the basis for identifying liberty and dispersion of power.

In the ominous spring of 1939, a bright and sunny May 3rd was a day marked by Adolf Hitler with another bellicose speech to the Reichstag calling for a showdown on Poland. On the same day, the League of Nations opened its "peace pavilion" at the World's Fair in New York City. And also on this same day, which seems so remote from the present instant, there was published a vigorous critique of American political life by a visitor from abroad, famed in intellectual and academic circles,

who had just delivered a series of lectures on the American presidency. The visitor was Harold J. Laski. And the obituary he wrote upon an historic American political doctrine bore the title: "The Obsolescence of Federalism."

How did Professor Laski conclude that the age of federalism was languishing near death?

He did concede that "federalism is the appropriate governmental technique for an expanding capitalism." But, he declaimed, a "contracting capitalism cannot afford the luxury of federalism." Leaping from this premise, he insisted that the failure of the federal idea was unmistakably plain not only in the United States but also elsewhere in the world—in Canada, Australia, Ger-

From *Nelson Aldrich Rockefeller*, The Future of Federation *(Cambridge, Mass.: Harvard University Press, 1962), pp. 1–9.* Copyright © 1962 *by The President and Fellows of Harvard College.* Reprinted by permission of the publisher.

many. And he explained this universal failure in these words:

Whether we take the conditions of labor, the level of taxation, the standards of education, or the supply of amenities like housing and recreation, it has become clear that the true source of decision is no longer at the circumference, but at the center of the state. For 48 separate units to seek to compete with the integrated power of giant capitalism is to invite defeat in almost every element of social life where approximate uniformity of condition is the test of the good life.

The two decades since have dealt a harsh retort to Professor Laski's pronouncement on federalism in the United States. It has been proven wrong in economic, social, and political terms. . . .

Private enterprise has become more vigorous, more creative. . . . The grim prognosis of 30 years ago has also been proven wrong in strictly political terms. For federalism—its ideas and its practice—has continued to show itself the adaptable and creative form of self-government that the Founding Fathers of this nation conceived it to be. Decisions vital to national well-being have increasingly been made at the "circumference"—the states—as well as at the national "center," of political power.

These lectures are dedicated to the conviction that these basic political, social, and economic facts of life—and the lessons they carry for us—are crucial to the whole fate of freedom and of free men everywhere in this mid-twentieth century.

I do not use the word "freedom" casually. For nothing less than the historic concept of the free individual's worth and dignity, defined and attested by the whole Judeo-Christian tradition, is at stake in our world. . . .

The Federal Idea

The federal idea: what does this mean?

Let me first make it clear that I do not speak of the federal idea as merely a mechanical or technical or abstract formula for government operations. I refer to the federal idea broadly as a concept of government by which a sovereign people, for their greater progress and protection, yield a portion of their sovereignty to a political system that has more than one center of sovereign power, energy, and creativity. No one of these centers or levels has the power to destroy another. Under the Constitution, for example, there are two principal centers of government power—state and federal. As a practical matter, local government, by delegation of state authority under the principle of "home rule," is a third such key center of power. The federal idea, then, is above all an idea of a shared sovereignty at all times responsive to the needs and will of the people in whom sovereignty ultimately resides.

Our federal idea is complex and subtle. It involves a balance of strengths. It puts into play a sharing of powers not only among different levels of government but —on each level—a separation of powers between the legislative, executive, and judicial branches of government. And it clearly signifies more than mere governmental structure. It demands faith in—and an environment for—the free play of individual initiative, private enterprise, social institutions, political organizations, and voluntary associations—all operating within a framework of laws and principles affirming the dignity and freedom of man.

A federal system, then, seeks stability without rigidity, security without inertia. It encourages innovation and inventiveness —governed by principle, and guided by purpose. It assures responsiveness more thoughtful than mere reflex—and liberty that does not lapse toward anarchy. In short, it seeks to hold the delicately precarious balance between freedom and order upon which depend decisively the liberty, peace, and prosperity of the individual. . . .

By providing several sources of political strength and creativity, a federal system invites inventive leadership—on all levels—to work toward genuine solutions to the problems of a diverse and complex society. These problems—whether they concern civil rights or urban development, industralization or automation, natural resources or transportation—never arise at the same instant and in the same way throughout a great nation. A federal system, however, allows these problems to be met at the time and in the area where they first arise. If local solutions are not forthcoming, it is still possible to bring to bear the influence, the power, and the leadership of either the state or the national government.

2

Federalism and Freedom: A Critique

FRANZ L. NEUMANN

Not all writers find the preceding argument conclusive. Franz Neumann examines the record of history and finds the case not proven. Freedom's link to federalism is vague, but the costs of federalism are clear.

The theoretical argument for federalism revolves around the potential of political power for evil. Federalism is seen as one of the devices to curb the evil use of power by dividing power among a number of competing power-units.

In its most radical form, this sentiment appears in the various anarchist schemes. It has been popular in the anarcho-syndicalist theories and practices of the Latin-speaking countries and with the IWW of the United States.

It is Lord Acton's statement on the corruptive effect of political power which appears to have today the greatest influence: Power tends to corrupt and absolute power corrupts absolutely. Great men are almost always bad men.[1] And Montesquieu[2] said

this even more clearly. According to him[3] power could be checked only by power—a statement that few would be willing to quarrel with. Not ideologies and beliefs but only a counterpower can check power. In this he applies Cartesian principles and stands in the tradition of Spinoza who saw no way of limiting the state's absoluteness (which was a logical consequence of his assumptions and of his geometric method) except by a counterpower.

The Montesquieu generalization is, of course, designed to give his doctrine of the separation of powers an adequate theoretical base. But as little as the theory of separate powers follows from his sociological observation, as little does that of the preferability of the federal state. Bentham[4] rejected the separation of powers not only as incompatible with democracy but also because it could not really maximize freedom if the three organs of government were controlled by the same social group. A quite similar argument can be raised

From Franz L. Neumann, "Federalism and Freedom: A Critique," in Federalism Mature and Emergent, ed. Arthur W. MacMahon (Garden City, N. Y.: Doubleday & Company, Inc., 1955) pp. 45–49, 53–54. Copyright © by the Trustees of Columbia University in the City of New York. Reprinted by permission of the publisher.

[1] Quotations taken from G. Himmelfarb, *Lord Acton, A Study in Conscience and Politics* (Chicago: University of Chicago Press, 1952), p. 161.

[2] My edition of the *Spirit of the Laws* (New York: Hafner Library of Classics, 1949), XI, 4.

[3] See my Introduction, *ibid.*, pp. lvii–lviii.

[4] Bowring, ed., IX, 41 ff.; and Elie Halevy, *The Growth of Philosophical Radicalism*, trans. Mary Morris (New York: The Macmillan Company, 1928), pp. 258–59.

against federalism as a guarantee for liberty. Those who assert that the federal state through the diffusion of *constitutional* powers actually diffuses *political* power often overlook the fact that the real cause for the existence of liberty is the pluralist structure of society and the multi-party (or two-party) system.[5] Federalism is not identical with social pluralism; and neither the two-party nor the multi-party system is the product of the federal state or the condition for its functioning.

Whether the federal state does indeed increase freedom [6] cannot be abstractly determined. We have some evidence that the federal state as such (that is, regardless of the form of government) has not fulfilled this role. The German Imperial Constitution certainly created a federal state but there is little doubt that politically it had a dual purpose: to be a dynastic alliance against the forces of liberalism and democracy,[7] and to secure the hegemony of Prussia.[8]

Perhaps more striking are the respective roles of federalism and centralism in the coming to power of National Socialism. Some believe, indeed, that the centralization under the Weimar Republic is wholly or at least partly responsible for the rise of National Socialism. But there is no evidence for this statement—nor indeed for the opposite one. It is certain that Bavaria, with the strongest states' rights tradition, gave shelter to the National Socialist movement and it is equally certain that the federal character of the Weimar Republic did not, after Hitler's appointment, delay the process of synchronization *(Gleichschaltung)* of the various state governments. Nor is there any definable relation between democratic conviction and federalist (or unitary) sympathies. The National Socialists were both centralists and reactionary, as were the Nationalists. Democrats and Social Democrats were antifederalists and committed to the preservation of political freedom. The Catholic center was not wholeheartedly committed to any position, and the Communists were, in theory, for the unitary state but did not hesitate, during the revolution of 1918, to advocate the secession of Brunswick which they believed they had in their pocket.

The evidence is certainly too slight to be of great value in determining whether the federal system is preferable to the unitary state as an instrument to preserve or enhance civil liberties. Nor is it likely that convincing evidence can be obtained, since other factors—the plurality of the social structure, the functioning of a truly competitive party system, the strength of a favorable tradition, the intellectual level of the population, the attitude of the courts—do far more easily permit the formation of a counterpower against forces hostile to civil liberties than does the federal structure of the government.

If federalism, as such, has nothing in it that automatically guarantees the preservation of political freedom, American federalism may have features that have hindered the solution of pressing economic problems.[9] The impact of the American federal system, of the division of powers, on the condition of this country in the Thirties was not reassuring.

George C.S. Benson, in his book *The New Centralization*,[10] tried to show how federalism worked in the setting of the Great Depression.

First, he found federalism as an "obstruction of social legislation." The states hesitated to enact this legislation not only for fear of placing their manufacturers at a

---

[5] See my Montesquieu Introduction, pp. lvii and lxiv.

[6] Cf. Carl J. Friedrich, *Constitutional Government and Democracy* (Boston: Ginn & Company, 1946), pp. 216–17.

[7] Rudolf Schlesinger, *Federalism in Central and Eastern Europe* (New York: Oxford University Press, Inc., 1945), p. 71.

[8] K.C. Wheare, *Federal Government* (New York: Oxford University Press, Inc., 1947), p. 15.

[9] For a discussion of this situation in Australia, see A. P. Canaway, *The Failure of Federalism in Australia* (London: Oxford University Press, 1930).

[10] New York, Farrar and Rinehart, 1941. On this problem see, in addition, Harold Laski, "The Obsolescence of Federalism," *The New Republic*, Vol. 98 (May 3, 1939), pp. 367–69.

competitive disadvantage with manufacturers of states that did not regulate wages and hours and provide benefits, but also for fear of driving larger industries into these latter states.[11]

Secondly, there was great disparity among the states' financial resources. Not only were most states incapable of financing serious efforts at reform, but "Complete decentralization—complete local responsibility for governmental services—may then result in a 'spread' between the standards of different districts which would shock even the uncritical believer in a national 'American' standard."[12]

Thirdly, Benson found little evidence that the states were really the "experimental laboratories" they were pictured to be.[13]

Fourthly, the ability of the states to put programs into action in an efficient way was seriously questioned.

Lastly, the nature of the economic system is such that its workings were and are obviously not confined to the territory of any given city or state.

As our great business concerns grow more specialized and conduct larger scale operations, government cannot be expected to remain simple and pastoral.[14]

[11] Benson, *op. cit.*, pp. 23–24.
[12] *Ibid.*, p. 30.

[13] *Ibid.*, p. 38.
[14] *Ibid.*, p. 40.

3

There Is No State Point of View

EDWARD W. WEIDNER

States' rights is not just an argument for state power. At its roots the argument stems from the claims and programs of groups seeking to advance some cause. As such, states' rights may be a valid argument or simply a mask for some privileged group.

It is a thesis of the present discussion that in the federal system in the United States there are relatively few direct clashes or compromises between state and national governments on large issues of national do-

From Edward W. Weidner, "Decision-Making in a Federal System," in Federalism Mature and Emergent, ed. Arthur W. MacMahon (Garden City, N. Y.: Doubleday & Company, Inc., 1955), pp. 363, 365–369, 376–377. Copyright © by the Trustees of Columbia University in the City of New York. Reprinted by permission of the publisher.

mestic policy. . . . The disagreements and conflicts that do arise and that may be encouraged by federalism's structural features are not basically clashes between state and national governments. Instead they are clashes between much smaller groups of people, and the opposing groups are located within a single governmental level as often as not. . . .

While differences on public policy or values are to be expected in a country containing as many heterogeneous elements as are to be found in the United States, it does not necessarily follow that officials in the several states will take one policy position and those of the national government another. Indeed, . . . it would seem surprising if this were the case, given the diversity of conditions in the several states and the fact that the union is made up of all states. "States' rights" is only one of numerous values held by state officials, and it is relatively unimportant to many of them. The prime thing that the states have in common is their existence; it is possible that if an issue were presented that threatened the very existence of the states, their political officials might be brought together. In actual fact, a major issue of this kind has not been presented. Consequently, usually national government officials can find many of their state counterparts who support national policy objectives and many others who oppose. And among the states, differences in values are the rule. . . .

The states have been unable to follow a single course even in such comparatively noncontroversial areas as are covered by the so-called uniform state laws. If minimum standards are desired for the nation as a whole in a particular policy area such as health or welfare, it is the central government that must act to assure these ends. To leave the matter exclusively to the states means that there will be a variation in standards from very low to quite high. To set up a system of joint national-state participation means that standards and practices will vary much more than in a system of central action alone. It also means that some disagreement and conflict are inevitable because officials in various states will not all see eye-to-eye with those of the national government in terms of the objectives of the program.

This is not to blame the states in any way for their actions. Rather it is to recognize that public policy is in large part the result of the values that men hold and that these values vary from individual to individual and group to group. It would be unexpected and surprising if the several states followed identical or even similar courses of action on important public issues.

The normal expectancy is that they will differ in greater or lesser degree among themselves in regard to policies they enact and in regard to the policies of the national government. . . .

The values that individuals hold are so diverse that there is no definable "state" point of view in intergovernmental relations as a whole. Even if the 48 governors were considered to be spokesmen for their entire states, there does not emerge a single state approach to intergovernmental relations. Occasionally all the governors will agree on a minor point or two but they have never agreed that a specific general reallocation of activities should take place between national and state governments. This is understandable since some of them are Democrats, some Republicans; some are liberals, others conservatives; some have national political ambitions, others do not; some come from poor states, others from well-to-do areas. These are only a few of the variables that affect the approach governors take on national-state relations. Much of the publicity arising from recent political events, Governors' Conferences, and the Council of State Governments tends to give the impression that all governors demand that certain functions and tax resources of the national government be turned over to the states. The impression is erroneous. It is true that the governors probably defend states' rights as vigorously as any other group of public officials; they tend to stress expediency values relative to state government. In part this is a function of their role as chief executive and chief party leader. Nevertheless, such a set of values may be subordinate to many other considerations, and consequently consensus is not easily forthcoming. . . .

Disagreement or conflict in national-state relations is limited. It is not a matter that normally determines election results or on which there is a clear public opinion. General issues of national-state relations have concerned only a small minority of individuals and groups in recent decades, usually a group of public officials at each level and a few interest groups outside the framework of government. When an important new substantive policy for the national government is under consideration, national-state wide relations may take on a broader significance, as was the case in welfare and labor policy during the Thirties. As a whole, however, interest groups and public opinion have not found states' rights an attractive theme unless by the defense of states' rights they could defend some programmatic value. . . .

Administrative and legislative officials alike are of the opinion that the main clash of values occurs within a unit of government rather than between units. This is true even in regard to the issues arising from intergovernmental programs. . . . This is not to deny that there are some who defend states' rights or local self-government through a genuine concern for decentralism and not on the basis of expediency. . . . However, situations where the programmatic values of professional administrators are overridden by their expediency values are not frequent. . . .

4

Federalism and Political Culture: A View from the States

DANIEL J. ELAZAR

Does the growth of federal aid really mean the emergence of a national attitude, with only the functional disagreements remaining, as argued by Weidner? In this discussion Professor Elazar presents the contrary view. He sees the states as having proven themselves both more resilient and more vital than the federal government. States have been basically successful in altering federal programs to suit their own aims and reflect their own patterns. To develop his analysis, Elazar utilizes the concept of "political culture" developed by Gabriel A. Almond and G. Bingham Powell, Jr. in the study Comparative Politics: A Developmental Approach. *Does such a concept help or interfere with analysis?*

The States as Systems within a System

The 50 American states, located between the powerful federal government and the burgeoning local governments in a metropolitanizing nation, are the keystones of the American governmental arch. This was the case when the Constitution was

From Daniel J. Elazar, American Federalism: A View from the States (*New York: Thomas Y. Crowell Co., 1966*), *pp. 1, 81–85. Copyright © 1966 by Thomas Y. Crowell Company, Inc. Reprinted by permission of the publisher.*

adopted in 1789 and remains true despite the great changes that have taken place in the intervening years.

This assertion runs counter to most contemporary perceptions of American government. If it were based upon an analysis of the present position of the states in light of formal *constitutional* interpretations alone, there would be great difficulty in substantiating it. In fact, the states maintain their central role because of their *political* position in the overall framework of the nation's political system, a position supported by the Constitution but which transcends its formal bounds. Unlike the more or less visible constitutional status of the states, their political position is generally of low visibility, not only to the public at large but often even to those people involved in the day-to-day operations of American government.

.   .   .

Federalism and Political Culture

One of the observations coming out of the several studies of federal-state relations conducted in the 1950's was that the states themselves (or their local subdivisions) could virtually dictate the impact of federal-aided activities within their boundaries.[1] Take the case of the impact of federal aid on the administration of state government. In those states where administration is concentrated at the executive level and the governor is usually strong, federal aid has tended to strengthen executive powers by giving the governor more and better tools to wield. In those states where power is widely diffused among the separate executive departments, federal aid has tended to add to the diffusion by giving the individual departments new sources of funds outside of the normal channels of state control which can even be used to obtain more money and power from the legislature. In those states where earmarked funds reflect legislature or lobby domination over programs, earmarked federal funds have had the same effect. Despite many protestations to the contrary, only in rare situations have federal grant programs served to alter state administrative patterns in ways that did not coincide with already established state policies, though such grants have often sharpened certain tendencies in state administration.

Or, in the case of federal merit system requirements, states dominated by political

[1] Governmental Affairs Institute, *A Survey Report on the Impact of Federal Grants-in-Aid on the Structure and Functions of State and Local Governments,* submitted to the Commission on Intergovernmental Relations (Washington: Government Printing Office, 1956). The statements in this and the following paragraphs are based in large part on the findings in the twenty-five states covered in that report.

attitudes conducive to notions of professionalization and the isolation of certain forms of government activity from the pressures of partisan politics have had little problem adjusting their programs to meet federal standards, since they had either adopted similar standards earlier or were quite in sympathy with the standards when proposed. . . .

A parallel situation exists in regard to the substance of the federal programs. Every state has certain dominant traditions about what constitutes proper government action and every state is generally predisposed toward those federal programs it can accept as consistent with those traditions. Many states have pioneered programs that fit into their traditions before the initiation of similar ones at the federal level or on a nationwide basis through federal aid. This, too, tends to lessen the impact of federal action on the political systems of those states and also to lessen any negative state reaction to federal entrance into particular fields. . . . Today states like California accept federal aid for mental health programs not as an innovative device but as a reenforcement of existing programs. Professional mental health workers in states like New Jersey rely upon the same federal grants to keep their programs free of internally generated political pressures, arguing with the patronage-inclined legislatures that federal regulations demand that professional standards be maintained. Their colleagues in states like Illinois use federal aid to force the hands of their legislatures to expand state activities in new directions. Reformers interested in mental health in states like Mississippi are interested in federal aid to inaugurate new programs. In matters of national defense, the southern states have a long tradition of supporting state militia and National Guard units so that over the years they have taken greater advantage of federal subventions for the maintenance of military reserve units than most of their sisters have.

Many of these and other differences in state responses within the federal system appear to be stimulated by differences in political culture among the states. We have already defined political culture as the particular pattern of orientation to political action in which each political system is imbedded. Political culture, like all culture, is rooted in the cumulative historical experiences of particular groups of people. Indeed, the origins of particular patterns of political culture are often lost in the mists of time. Patterns of political culture frequently overlap several political systems, and two or more political cultures may coexist within the same political system.[2]

2 For a more complete definition of political culture, see Gabriel A. Almond, "Comparative Political Systems," *The Journal of Politics*, XVIII (1956), 391–409. Political culture is directly connected to historical phenomena. Specific elements of political culture frequently have their origins in historical events or situations which cause great and long-lasting changes among those who share

Though little is known about the precise ways in which political culture is influential, it is possible to suggest some ways in which the differences in political culture are likely to be significant.

the experiences they generate. These changes are then transmitted—and often intensified—through the process of acculturation to the descendants of the original group, including both "blood" and "galvanized" (those adopted into the group) descendants. Perhaps because of the close relationship between political culture and historical phenomena, historians have done more to trace the ingredients that combine to create the patterns of political culture than have other social scientists. Though they have not done so to investigate political culture as such, they have provided the raw materials for such an investigation through their studies of other phenomena, such as migration patterns, political alliances and antagonisms, the historical roots of continuing social behavior, and the like. . . .

5

Local and Private Initiative in the Great Society

Norton E. Long

Elazar sees federalism as a benign producer of diversity. Another lifelong observer of the process of American government sees it as a system of buying indulgences and privileges. One lives in communities which impose costs and therefore exclude people from benefits. How would Long's argument affect the plea for community self-government?

Federalism as a Pricing System for Public Goods . . .

. . .

The two most critical events for the future of the states are the implementation

From B. M. Gross, ed., *A Great Society?* (New York: Basic Books, Inc., Publishers, 1968), pp. 81–103. © 1966, 1967, 1968 by Basic Books, Inc., Publishers. Reprinted by permission of the publisher.

of the Supreme Court's one-man, one-vote doctrine and the Heller Plan to transfer to the states without strings some part of the nationally collected revenues. The implementation of the Supreme Court's decision is important both because of its likely alternation of the range, weight, and mix of values involved in the states' decision making process and in the caliber of the states as significant theaters of public action. . . . The quality of people attracted to the public business and the quality and standards of the civic audience they can command are vital to the states' decision making process. . . .

Consideration of our attitude toward the role of the states . . . is particularly relevant to the Heller Plan. Fiscal anemia, stemming in some cases from actual lack of adequate resources and in others from the supposed constraints of interstate competition for the location of wealth and industry, has resulted in a growing tendency for initiatives and power to move to the federal government as the most efficient and politically competent source of tax collection. Any substantial increase in the fiscal blood stream, especially if the transfusion carried no strings, would have the likely effect of increasing the vitality of the states. In the view of some, this would be a tragic mistake. . . . There is certainly a crying need to take a careful look. . . . Our past commitment to what may be an outworn and jerry-built federalism is not necessarily irrevocable. The gradual obsolescence of the states through fiscal anemia may not be the worst way to bring about institutional change.

This view is shared especially by liberals who see the federal bargain as essentially one that allows Southern whites more or less free rein to exploit Negroes. In addition, the gross population and resource differences among the states seem to render them radically incompetent to fulfill their formal potentialities. . . . The pattern of interstate competition between the weak and the strong seems more likely to inhibit the strong than to energize the weak. If the weak are incapable of meeting minimal national standards for the market basket of state public goods, national transfer payments similar to intrastate or intracity transfer payments become in order. With things as they are, despite promising changes in federal need formulas for some education programs, the strong states as well as the weak will insist on proportionate shares in the national largesse. To assist the schools of Maine and Mississippi, California, Illinois, and New York have to make transfer payments via the federal government to

one another as well as to those genuinely in need. The overhead costs of pumping the local taxpayers' money up to Washington and back down the bureaucratic conduits reduce the marginal efficiency of the California, Illinois, and New York federally collected, locally spent tax dollar by a very sizable fraction. Of course, there are those who doubt whether the tax dollars would be collected in comparable magnitudes for education even in California, Illinois, and New York if the more efficient and politically painless federal tax machinery were not invoked. Politically from this point of view the large overhead transfer cost may have its justification.

. . .

The Politics of Metropolitan Distribution

In the Great Depression there was a general feeling that the states failed and verged on bankruptcy. The national government was the only institution capable of meeting the crisis and moving us through it. Major efforts were made to find new and more effective units of regional government than the states. The search for natural regions resulted in a large stock of overlay maps produced in the hope of finding some fit between federal field areas, population, resources, geography, and common problems. The upshot, however, was the sad conclusion that no more greatly compelling arrangement than the existing states shone forth from the data of research. With the waning of the depression, the hunt for new regions of government to replace the states was largely abandoned. Lush war-produced revenues, postwar prosperity, and major new state efforts in the production of education, mental health facilities, and other public goods have given the states renewed vitality. Both those they serve and those interested in the conduct of state government are now powerfully motivated to preserve the going system. It has come a long way since the depths of the depression.

. . . [T]his does not mean that because one accepts the states as having continuing roles . . . one either accepts their present functioning or is precluded from seeking additional structures of local self-government. The major fact that confronts us on the domestic scene is the rise of the metropolitan area to preponderance, and soon perhaps to overwhelming preponderance, in our pattern of settlement. Most of us now live in some two hundred metropolitan areas. Shortly, perhaps the great bulk of the American people will be living in a fraction of these areas. The quality of American life as it is lived will be the quality of the life of these areas, good, bad, or indifferent. . . .

. . . Successful governmental structuring of metropolitan areas not only would mobilize leadership and resources not now mobilized in these areas, it would profoundly alter the balance of political power. In doing so, it could not help altering the mix of values, perspectives, and group influences that determines public policy. . . .

. . . [A] decision to strengthen the states would strengthen bodies which, even if made more representative by the Supreme Court decision, would inevitably be reluctant to see competing metropolitan governments arise. The importance of this probable reluctance needs to be weighed. It is also worth thinking about whether an either/or policy is all that is available to us. In some cases the state government may well make the most sense as the vehicle for metropolitan government. This would obviously be the case in Rhode Island. In other cases, the still large populations outside of metropolitan areas require more than existing local government and may offer no useful possible intermediate layer of government between themselves and the states. We may well be condemned to working our way pragmatically to piecemeal solutions using the governmental institutions and habits we now possess while adding to and altering them wherever possible to further our purposes. Burke's wisdom cautions us to respect the social capital in political institutions and habits that has been painfully accumulated in the course of our history. Society can only be treated as so much formless clay for utopian modeling by those whose vision of the ideal takes no account of the possible and remains untempered by humility or respect for the existing human achievement.

. . . Governments, national, state, and local, are so many devices for mobilizing and allocating resources. Markets, likewise, are devices for mobilizing and allocating resources. Viewed as devices, although these are in reality historically developed institutions, we can look at them objectively in terms of their fitness to achieve the ends in view. National, state, and local governments are obviously quite different in their capacities to mobilize resources and are also different, given effective constituencies, in their allocation of resources mobilized. Equally, if we look at the private sector as opposed to the public, there are significant differences in the kinds of goods produced and the ways in which the goods are allocated. Our policy choices as to how resource mobilization and allocation in the society is to be structured between levels of government and between public and private initiatives depend on the outcomes we value and the most effective mix of governmental and/or private initiatives for producing the desired outcomes.

As noted earlier, the two major values in American society—achievement and equality—are in tension. In the past, the tension has been solved by giving the citizens formal equality in government and accepting actual inequality in the economy as the inevitable and indeed desirable result of differential achievement. This division between the formal equality of government and the actual inequality of the economy led Marxists and many others to characterize bourgeois democracy as a fraud. The seeming emptiness of a political democracy divorced from the workings of the economy has been radically altered by the rapid increase in the production and importance of public goods. Indeed, one of the main problems of a society committed both to an equality norm among citizens and to unequal incomes is how to give effect to this income inequality in the consumption of public goods. As long as the private sector was the overwhelmingly important producer of goods, rationing by price gave full effect to inequalities in income, as it largely does now in the Soviet Union, where the public sector and the private are merged. In addition, differential political power did, and to an important degree still does, serve to differentiate the consumption of public goods in our cities even among formally equal citizens. Variations in quality of schools, garbage collection, police protection, and the like, are still notorious. Nonetheless, the equality norm among citizens coupled with the political activation of submerged groups is bringing about the homogenization of public goods.

To give effect to unequal incomes in the consumption of public goods, the preferred strategy is to achieve territorial segregation of their consumption through suburbanization. The metropolitan area, with its congeries of local governments, provides many competing residential hotels with different qualities of service and different classes of paying guests. It is not surprising that the politics of many local politicians resembles that of hotelkeepers concerned with competing for desired clientele and avoiding undesirable or nonpaying guests. Where local politicians rise a notch above this, property-tax considerations—among others —make their model that of a real estate operator seeking to maximize his revenue from a given tract of land with its inescapable encumbrances. The metropolitan area has become an ecology of governments offering a wide range of public goods and permissible land uses. To some, this seems a perfectly sensible way to reflect the pluralism of the society and to rescue some measure of quality from the menace of homogenized equality. To others, it represents the fragmentation of the community, political absenteeism, social irresponsibility, tax dodging, and the ghettoization of the less fortunate. Both views have their measure of truth and both need some degree of reconciliation if equality, quality, and achievement are to be given appropriate meaning. . . .

At the national level of government, a mix of values and influences has been at work that has made it politically possible and expedient to pass civil rights legislation, utilize national leverage on behalf of equal employment opportunity and open occupancy, and to inaugurate the war on poverty. In its general tendency, this is a politics of role reallocation and equality of opportunity. It means a national purpose to open up improved avenues to housing, education, jobs, and status for deprived minorities. The politics that has made this national purpose achieve both legislative and executive enunciation and some limited degree of realization is supported in many cases by the same people who locally, in practice, support the territorial segregation of public-goods consumption. In effect the local territorial segregation of public-goods consumption powerfully limits any attainment of a national policy of redistribution. Housing has become a key to education, education a key to jobs, and jobs are the key to income, which is the key to housing —at least where the minimal democracy of the dollar is allowed to prevail. For minorities this democracy of the dollar, the free competitive market of the capitalist ideal, is nullified by that other capitalist ideal, the right to discriminate. The existence of fragmented local governments responding to highly unrepresentative samples of populations and problems has reacted back on the federal government to blunt, in the reality of administration, its legislatively expressed goals. Working through local governments, and in some cases through private enterprise as required by law, has meant the accommodation of the expressed federal purpose to the political realities of the status quo of local and private enterprise.

Nowhere has this been more tragically the case than in urban renewal, where the poor have been unhoused with the aid of federal subsidies and banks have been rehoused with the aid of federal subsidies. Given the self-definition of mayors as municipal realtors, it is scarcely surprising that they should, to the extent feasible, use federal aid to maximize the tax yield of their real estate and even on occasion to rid themselves of nonpaying guests. Federal bureaucrats, responding to the survival needs of their agencies, become accomplices in this redirection of national policy. In this they are given support and coercion by congressmen who react to the effectively expressed wishes of those who represent the governments and electorates of the fragmented metropolitan areas. What is frequently viewed with cynicism as the moral failure of politicians and bureaucrats is simply the predictable result of the governmental way interests and values are structured and represented. Given the game and players desiring to win, the effective rules and strategies allow the players no other option unless indeed they decide to change the structure of the game.

This last is what concerns those, who would change the metropolitan area from an ecology of jealous Balkanized principalities surrounding an eviscerated central city fast becoming a ghetto of the Negro, the aged, the poor, and the very rich into a community politically structured to organize its fiscal and leadership resources in a balanced response to the whole range of problems that confront the people of the metropolitan area. Governments can be organized to reflect narrow and selfish interests or they can be set up in such a way as to be able, and even be compelled, to aspire to greatness. Presently, stricken with fiscal anemia, plagued by social absenteeism and the triviality of the country club suburb with its toy government, the nation's metropolises are organized on a necessarily dog-eat-dog, devil-take-the-hindmost basis. Despite the fact that the country's metropolitan areas contain the overwhelming bulk of the nation's financial assets and human talent, they are neither structured, legally empowered, nor possessed of a political and social theory with which to mobilize their spiritual and material wealth behind a meaningful and challenging conception of a common life. A Great Society in an urban age is inconceivable on the basis of the present divisive disorganization of our metropolitan areas which has substituted the competition of municipal realtors for the conduct of responsible politics.

.   .   .

6

The Ghost of Federalism and the Dying States

MARTIN LANDAU

What indeed is happening to the amount of diversity in the system, extolled by Elazar and questioned by Long? Landau suggests a drastic shift to the federal government. Is his argument derived from logic and theory, or from evidence? Does it confirm or conflict with your knowledge of the operations of American politics? How would you test—confirm or refute—his arguments?

I

There are two major viewpoints reflected in discussions of federalism. On the one hand, federalism is taken as an *end* in and of itself. In this context, the problem which emerges is the maintenance of a specified balance of power and jurisdiction between state and nation. To be sure, jurisdictions are subject to modification and the balances to adjustment but as the Commission on Intergovernmental Relations [1] expressed it, "the enduring values of our federal system fully warrant every effort to preserve and strengthen its essence." On the other hand, federalism is deemed to be an *instrument* [2] of social change, a problem-solving device

which possesses utility only for a specified set of conditions. It furnishes the means to "achieve some union where unity is an impossibility"; the goal involved is the development of that "more perfect union" which "federalists" despair of today. The logic of this view leads one to the position that federalism is "a case of political lag which urgently deserves our attention." [3] . . .

III

The classical concept of American federalism specifies a relatively fixed relationship between two domains of autonomous or sovereign authority in the same territorial unit. Each possesses an exclusive jurisdiction, neither is subordinate to the other, neither can be stripped of its authority by the other. The constitutional formulations of this concept present, in Corwin's phrase, a model of two states locked into a "mutually exclusive, reciprocally limiting" power of relationship.

To remark on the inadequacy of this model today is quite superfluous. We have Wilson's description, in 1885, of the "altered

---

Excerpts from "Baker v. Carr and the Ghost of Federalism" by Martin Landau is reprinted by permission of Charles Scribner's Sons from Reapportionment, *pages 241 and 243–248, edited by Glendon Schubert. Copyright © 1965 Charles Scribner's Sons.*

[1] (1955).

[2] See James Bryce, *The American Commonwealth* (1891), Vol. I, p. 342. See also Harvey Manfield, "The States in the American System" in *The Forty-Eight States* (The American Assembly, 1955), p. 13, and see William S. Livingston, "A Note on the Nature of Federalism," *Political Science Quarterly* (March, 1952), pp. 83–84.

[3] Sen. Joseph S. Clark, *Toward National Federalism,* speech of March 28, 1960. Quoted by Robert M. Hutchins, *Two Faces of Federalism* (Center for the Study of Democratic Institutions, 1961), p. 9.

and declining status of the states." A few years later Bryce voiced concern that we are apt to overrate the effects of "mechanical contrivances" in government. The pragmatic Frank Goodnow concludes in 1916 that industrialization has caused the "old distinction" between interstate and intrastate commerce "almost to disappear."[4] And there is Laski's tale of obsolescence[5] and Max Lerner speaking of the ghost of federalism which "haunts a nation in which every force drives toward centralization."[6]

So, we read, the doctrine of dual federalism is dead; if not dead, dying. Our "living Constitution" operates on a new principle, best formulated perhaps by Luther Gulick in 1933: "Nothing effective can be done in the regulation or stabilization of economic affairs unless the area of planning and control has the same boundaries as the economic structure."[7] If the 1930's dramatized this requirement, the decisions of the Roosevelt Court may be taken as the climax—the turning point—of that long, uneven, but inexorable process of transfer—the transfer of authority to the central government.

This is the "crisis of the states." They have had to yield to a "system dominated by the pervasiveness of federal power."[8] They have lost status, prestige, and power. They have lost so much, Leonard White stated, "that competent observers at home and abroad have declared that American federalism is approaching its end." Roscoe Drummond put it more directly: "our federal system no longer exists."[9]

Drummond's conclusion is not sensational.

A system so dominated by central power cannot, by definition, be classified as federalist. If, analytically, we stop the system at various times—ranging from 1800 to the present—and if we examine the state of the system at each of these times, i.e. if we compare the operations of government with the classical or constitutional models, we are bound to find less and less correspondence. As a matter of fact this is what our researches have unquestionably demonstrated. Our findings are of such order that it becomes increasingly difficult to represent our governmental system as federalist. It simply does not possess federal characteristics.

Given, however, the "enduring value" of balance and the "legal habit" of our past, this is not a conclusion we are prone to accept. I do not refer only to embattled senators from the South or to a more or less educated public, or to the bar; I refer as well to professional political scientists, to students of constitutional law, to professional commentators of all sorts. Nor does it matter that many of them have accepted the requirements of a nationally integrated society and of a positive and action-oriented central government. The plain fact appears to be that we cannot lay aside the "ghost of federalism." What we have done is to adjust our vocabulary—but not too far. We now use terms that suggest a modified federalism but federalism nevertheless. Thus, there is substituted for "dual federalism" a "cooperative federalism" or a "centralized federalism." There is a "federalism mature" and there is a "national federalism." These are the synonyms of the "new federalism" which may mean upon analysis "no federalism."

[4] *Principles of Constitutional Government* (1916), pp. 46–47.
[5] "The Obsolescence of Federation," *The New Republic* (May 3, 1939).
[6] "Minority Rule and the Constitutional Tradition," in Conyers Read, editor, *The Constitution Reconsidered* (1938), pp. 196–97.
[7] Quoted in E. S. Corwin, *The Twilight of the Supreme Court* (1934), pp. 45–46.
[8] B. Schwartz, "Recent Developments in American Constitutional Law," in A. Junz, editor, *Present Trends in American National Government* (1961), p. 157.
[9] L. White, *The Crisis of the States* (1954), p. 5. White quotes Drummond. See also White, *The Nation and the States* (1953).

IV

. . . [I]t is inconceivable that a government which reflects the properties and needs of an 18th century environment (society) could be functional, without profound alteration, for a 20th century society. The collection of thirteen autonomous communities standing in relative isolation to one another, the differences in economy, the rural habit, the diversity of norms and behaviors, the multi-centered system of communication, the existence of sharp local loyalties themselves the product of a "local consciousness," the magnitude of distance —these are some of the characteristics of 18th century society. Any attempt at unification required the establishment of a structure which would not, in Bryce's words "extinguish their separate administrations, legislatures, and local patriotisms." For the America of 1787, federalism was the only resource. It was a device designed to solve a social problem—a problem of political organization. It was, as Livingston noted in a brilliant essay, "a response to a definite set of stimuli; . . . consciously adopted as a means of solving the problems represented by these stimuli." [10] Indeed, it may be viewed as a stroke of social genius; at once it protected the federal qualities of 18th century society and provided the means for meeting "the desperate need for a modicum of union where unity is impossible."

From a collection of loose, uncentralized or decentralized units, the United States, as we are prone to speak, has evolved into a highly centralized, integrated community which exhibits symbiotic relationships. It

[10] Livingston, *op. cit.*, p. 84.

no longer possesses federal characteristics. The history (evolution) of the last century is a striking story of vast changes in the structure of society and the needs it generated. That nation concealed under federalism finally emerged. The United States has been for a long time now becoming the United States.

.   .   .

The ultimate effect of this shift will be to weight the party system toward the urban-national side as against the state-local side and this is a necessary condition for the emergence of a national party system. To augment an already developing bypass of the state via direct national-metropolitan relationships with a national party system that is built upon an urban basis must mean a fundamental restructuring of our formal system of government. *Baker v. Carr* is a decision on the functional merits of federalism; it does strike deep into its heart.

Is this such a "massive repudiation of our past"? Or is it a development on our past? Once upon a time this country embarked on a voyage to nationhood. The journey was started by the institution of federalism. Its success in enabling a nation to evolve must by the nature of the instrument signal its own demise.

7

The States Hold the Keys to the Cities

A. JAMES REICHLEY

Writing five years later, Reichley finds Landau's burial of federalism premature. He sights a trend back to state power. Do his arguments join issue with Landau's? Is the coalition between suburbs and state majorities a reality? How do the alignments work in your state? Will such alignments mean certain problems will be neglected or handled improperly?

State government, that old sick man of the federal system, is taking on enhanced authority. Big-city mayors react to this revival with dismay. Potentially, however, state government offers the best available instrument for reversing the urban deterioration that imperils not only core cities but our whole society. "The states are coming alive at last to what needs to be done," says Paul Ylvisaker, . . . New Jersey's first Commissioner of Community Affairs.

New hopes attached to the states, which in the past have generally treated their cities like unwanted foundlings, rise in part from desperation over the apparent limitations of other possible rescuers. The cities themselves, almost everybody from corporate executives to black militants agrees, lack the resources to cope with their most serious problems. The federal government, even if it were not beset by competing military and economic pressures, has proved in twenty years of stabbing involvement that it is simply too awkward a giant to respond intelligently to the needs of cities as

From A. James Reichley, "The States Hold the Keys to the Cities," Fortune (June 1969), pp. 134–136, 152, 154, 158, 162. Reprinted by permission of the publisher.

different as Dallas and Detroit, or Boston and Los Angeles. Private enterprise and the great foundations are entering the action, but by themselves have neither the funds nor the legal authority to achieve more than piecemeal solutions. Only the states remain. Fortunately, state government also possesses positive qualifications to deal with the problems of urban regions. The states, as is sometimes forgotten, are the legal creators of the cities, and possess the basic powers required to repair most urban weaknesses. But do the states have the financial capacity and political will to take on the job?

The tie between the cities and the federal government that developed after World War II was always somewhat unnatural and contrary to the American traditions of government. From the cities' point of view, Washington had two great advantages over the states: more money and greater political sensitivity to urban influences. Now additional federal dollars for the cities are in short supply, and the political facts of life have changed. The new national Administration has both philosophic and pragmatic reason for working through the states rather than dealing directly with the cities. "For a third of a century now," Richard

Nixon told *Fortune* . . . , "we have had a rapid accumulation of power and responsibility by the central government. What we need now is a dispersal of power —so there is not one center of power, but many centers."

Republican doctrine favoring decentralization of government fits neatly with the current distribution of political power. "The governors of most major states are Republicans," Vice President Spiro Agnew points out bluntly, "while the mayors of most cities are Democrats." Besides the Vice President, the Nixon Cabinet contains three former governors and one lieutenant governor, all firm advocates of a large role for the states. At a White House meeting in April with mayors of ten large cities, Agnew emphatically spelled out his view that in most instances federal funds should be channeled through the states. The mayors made it plain that they would prefer direct grants to the cities. They expressed fears that federal money passing through state capitols will be cut up to the cities' disadvantage. Indications are clear, however, that the Nixon Adminstration will insist on state involvement in most programs. "Since coming to Washington," comments George Romney, who left Michigan's statehouse to become Secretary of Housing and Urban Development, "I see more clearly than ever the mistake of bypassing state government."

Although the political tides may shift again in future presidential elections, the underlying trend of national demography is running against restoration of the power of the cities in Washington. Increasingly, population is moving from the central cities to the suburbs. The 1970 census will show more people living in suburbs than in cities for the first time in American history, and projections indicate that by 1985 suburbanites will outnumber city dwellers by almost two to one. The political effects of this transformation are already evident. In the 1952 presidential election, 41 per cent of the total Illinois vote was cast by the city of Chicago, and 19 per cent by the surrounding suburbs. Last year, city and suburbs each accounted for about 30 per cent of the total state vote. Similarly, Philadelphia's share of the Pennsylvania vote dropped from 21 per cent in 1952 to 18 per cent in 1968, while the share of the city's suburban counties was rising from 11 to 16 per cent. Even more dramatically, Detroit during the same sixteen-year period fell from 29 to 18 per cent of the Michigan vote, while the suburbs went from 19 to 30 per cent.

A New Axis Replacing the Old

This change, which has already had a large impact on presidential politics, will affect apportionment of the U.S. House of Representatives. . . . Suburban power will not only exert direct influence on the planning of federal programs, but also enhance the authority of the states, which the suburbs generally feel represent their interests. "The rise of the suburbs is the whole reason for the buildup of the states," says Richard Wade, urban historian at the University of Chicago. "The old axis between the cities and the federal government is being replaced by a new axis between the suburbs and the states."

As the attraction of Washington's financial and political bait for the cities is reduced, primary responsibility for urban problems will return to the states, which should have dealt with them in the first place. The taxing powers, the legislative and administrative authorities, the very boundaries of the cities are derived from state constitutions and statutes. The chief needs of the cities—better education, better courts, more adequate transportation, improved housing, protection against air and water pollution, even more industrial jobs —still fall largely within the province of state governments. Federal interest in most of these problems is obvious, but the states are by nature better suited than either federal or city governments to undertake remedies. Small enough to react sensibly to local needs and realities, the states are at the same time large enough to coordinate programs for entire metropolitan regions.

Buffers Against the Liberal-Labor Coalition

That the states can and should come to the aid of the cities does not, of course, necessarily mean that they will do so. Precedent, indeed, suggests the contrary. For many years a combination of rural squirearchies and business interests held tight control of most state capitols. Rural representatives dominated legislatures partly because apportionment in most states was weighted in favor of sparsely populated counties, but partly, too, because they were generally more able men than the products of city machines. Their values are reflected in the superior highways, land-grant universities, and decentralized public-school systems that until recently were the characteristic achievements of state government. The business lobbies, which maintained the states as buffers against the power of the liberal-labor coalition in Washington and the city halls, devoted most of their attention to holding down taxes and protecting particular industries from regulation. Neither the squires nor the lobbies had much interest in giving help to the cities.

The cities expected that the reapportionment decreed by the Supreme Court's "one-man, one-vote" rulings would increase their power in the state legislatures. But reapportionment, while it diminished the power of the squirearchies, has shifted dominance to the suburbs rather than to the cities. "The chief effect of reapportionment has been to update conservatism," concludes Jesse Unruh. . . . "Instead of the farmer with his conservatism and detachment," says Mayor Carl Stokes of Cleveland, "you now have the man from suburbia, who is as conservative and detached, and sometimes as hostile to the city, as the rural member."

Still, the suburbs do share common concerns with the cities—transportation, environmental control, and land use, among others. Distribution of state subsidies for schools may cause quarrels between suburbs and cities, but both agree on the need for increased investment in education. Many suburban representatives, too, have come to realize that their sheltered communities cannot long remain healthy if the rot of the cities continues. . . .

To Guard Particular Interests

Reapportionment had little or no effect on business influence in the state capitols. While rural legislators cooperated with the business lobbies in return for campaign contributions or support for their favorite bills, suburban representatives are likely to identify their own interests with those of business. The power of business is still to a great extent employed to guard particular economic interests. Retailers fight consumer-protection legislation, mining and manufacturing companies oppose laws to reduce pollution, truckers and petroleum companies insist that gasoline taxes be used only for highways. Companies doing business with the state, like road contractors and suppliers to state institutions, have even more concrete objectives. Licensed industries, like liquor and racetracks, and regulated utilities also have special reasons for seeking the favor of state administrations.

However, the general awakening of business to its stake in peaceful solution of the social problems of cities has had a substantial impact on businessmen's attitudes toward state government. "In the old days," says Senator Edmund Muskie, who . . . has studied the states from outside as a member of the Advisory Commission on Intergovernmental Relations, "the vested business interests would fight federal action on the claim that it violated states' rights, and then would turn around and fight the same action at the state level. Now they are really trying to solve problems through action by the states."

.   .   .

State help for the cities can come through four chief fields of action: increased home rule for city governments; legal provision and encouragement for compacts among cities and suburbs to deal with common regional needs; direct intervention by state government to handle some urban problems; and enlarged financial aid to local government, particularly for education. Many states are already at work in one or more of these areas, but much more needs to be done if the current eruption of urban discontent is to be held short of violence, let alone turned toward creative ends.

The home-rule problem rises out of the fact that the cities derive their legal existence from the states. Provision for local government is nowhere touched upon in the U.S. Constitution, and the states, so long as they do not treat residents of different areas with gross inequality, are free to set up whatever forms of local administration appeal to them. Until recently, most states held their cities on a fairly tight leash. In Massachusetts, for instance, until 1962 state law gave the governor the power to appoint the chief of police for Boston. In Missouri, the St. Louis police department is still under the authority of a board of commissioners appointed by the governor. (This restraint was imposed during the Civil War when rebel sympathizers who controlled the state government wished to curtail the power of the pro-Union city administration.) . . . In forty-six states, local government can exercise only those powers specifically authorized by the state legislature.

.   .   .

Glad to Hold Down the Bosses

The states were slow to grant broad home-rule powers to local governments because of rural distrust of the cities, and also because politicians in the state capitals were not anxious to give up supremacy over their city counterparts, who were frequently of a different party. Municipal reformers, too, were glad to hold down the power of local political bosses. Even now, there is a feeling among many proponents of good government that control of education, at least, should not be entrusted to the voters of big cities. . . . "I'm not sure that Philadelphia is ready for self-government," jokes a local reform leader, explaining why he does not advocate an elected school board for the city.

The general trend, however, runs the other way. Home rule, for one thing, is a reform that costs nothing, and therefore is attractive to political leaders seeking painless change. Recent constitutional revisions in Michigan, Pennsylvania, Connecticut, and Florida all substantially enlarged the powers of local government. . . .

The most important remaining limitations are those that states impose on local revenue-raising authority. Traditionally, local government has derived most of its revenues from taxes on real property. As property owners have been pushed to the limits of their endurance, local governments in general and cities in particular have begun to cast about for other kinds of revenue. They have generally encountered stiff opposition in state legislatures to requests for authority to impose new taxes—especially if these would be levied against suburban commuters as well as city residents. . . .

State governments frequently approve taxes different from those requested by the cities. When the San Francisco Bay Area communities asked for authority to tax gasoline and use bridge tolls to finance a new mass-transit system, the California legislature, under the influence of the powerful "road users" lobby (oil companies, contractors, truckers, auto clubs), granted instead a local tax on retail sales. . . .

The states have not only the right but the responsibility to coordinate the total structure of state and local taxes. Cities cannot be permitted to invade tax resources that the state has reserved for its own needs. But the basic test for local taxes should become the willingness of affected taxpayers to approve them. . . .

Reaching Beyond City Lines

Political freedom alone will not enable the cities to deal with the many serious difficulties that by their nature defy narrow geographic limits. Air and water pollution that originates in the suburbs or the hinterland cannot be prevented by city ordinances. The flow of traffic through metropolitan areas creates difficulties that obviously transcend city lines. Sufficient open space to meet the recreation needs of city residents can never be found within existing city boundaries. The tangled problem of reducing population densities and achieving a better social and economic mix in core cities must be approached through planning for large areas.

Proposals for "metropolitan governments" to deal with these predicaments are common, and a few have actually been set up. Their performance so far has not been impressive. In Florida's Dade County, the best known of these experiments, the suburbs of Miami have kept the metropolitan administration weak by retaining many important functions for themselves. In most states, suburban opposition to metropolitan government is so intense that the idea is not a serious political issue. Suburbanites not only wish to preserve their civic identities, but also are anxious to maintain the relatively high level of administrative services that their communities are able to provide. Most of all, the issue of race hangs over the regional concept. Few suburban parents view with equanimity the possibility of having their children bused into city schools in order to achieve racial balance throughout a regional system.

Really big cities, such as New York, Chicago, Los Angeles, and Philadelphia, are already so large that further extension of their responsibilities and territories would probably not be prudent, even if it were politically feasible. In most of these cities, indeed, the current cry of greatest emotional urgency is for decentralization of vast and impersonal municipal governments.

For these very large metropolitan areas, the most promising approach is organization of various special authorities to deal with particular problems in which city and suburbs have a common interest. Public transportation is the most obvious example. Compacts to operate transit facilities have already been formed for the metropolitan areas of New York, Boston, Philadelphia, and San Francisco. . . . Pollution control, too, requires intercommunity response. Law enforcement is a somewhat more sensitive area, but some county-wide police forces have been set up in metropolitan areas.

Too Urgent to Wait for Evolution

In some places, suburban communities are forming compacts among themselves from which the core city is, at least at first, excluded. The cities would be unwise to oppose this development. The proliferation of government in metropolitan areas—Cook County, for example, contains more than 1,000 separate governing units—greatly hinders efforts at regional cooperation. Compacts among suburban communities should eventually foster joint efforts for entire regions, including cities.

.   .   .

The move toward regional compacts cannot succeed without strong support from the states. State laws in many instances will have to be changed to provide a legal basis for such compacts, and state policies can measurably speed their approval. During the past twenty-five years the states have succeeded, largely through the use of financial incentives, in reducing the number of local school districts from 109,000 to 22,000. Similar methods can be used to encourage compacts and eventual formation of regional councils. While the use of incentives rather than compulsion may slow the process, the results should be more harmonious. In any case, the power of the suburbs in legislatures makes regionalization by fiat in most states politically impossible.

Some urban problems cannot wait for the evolution of regional solutions, and others require a stronger use of executive authority than area councils are ever likely to wield. More industrial jobs for the urban poor, for instance, is a clear and present necessity. Construction of more low- and middle-income housing, and reduction of core-city densities need more push than either cities or regional compacts can be expected to provide. The states, which are closer to the local situation than the federal government, yet free of the day-to-day duties of running schools or collecting garbage, are well equipped to deal directly with some of the most critical of these needs.

·   ·   ·

Unequal Costs of Equal Education

The most important impact of the states on their cities, however, continues to come through financial aid for locally administered programs, particularly education and welfare. In 1967, . . . 48 per cent of all local government expenditures went for education, and 7 per cent for welfare. State subsidies made up 41 per cent of the local cost of education, and 73 per cent of the cost of welfare. These two subsidies amounted to more than ten times what the states spent on health, housing, police protection, and libraries, all together.

·   ·   ·

The states in general have almost tripled their aid to local government in the last ten years, but the extent of their response has been uneven. Per capita expenditures for local aid in 1967 ranged from $170 in New York to $21 in New Hampshire. Nor has it been only the rural and low-income states that have held down on local assistance. While New York in 1967 paid 52 per cent of the cost of local education and the national average was 41 per cent, wealthy industrial states like Connecticut, New Jersey, Ohio, Illinois, and California all paid less than 35 per cent.

Moreover, many states do not distribute their aid in a manner that gives attention to the special needs of cities. Some states, like California, Washington, Louisiana, and Texas, actually give more aid per capita to suburban communities than to the core cities. "Equalization formulas," through which many states distribute subsidies to school districts in inverse proportion to the assessed value of their real property, not only are subject to the vagaries of assessment systems, but also take no account of the extra costs of compensatory programs to meet the educational needs of slum children. As a result, the educational effectiveness of city schools falls further and further behind most other parts of the state. . . .

A few states, notably Pennsylvania and New York, have enacted legislation giving extra subsidies to school districts with particularly high densities or heavy concentrations of poor families. Generally, however, suburbs, which have financial difficulties of their own, insist that the states give them at least as much help as the cities. "You put in a bill to provide remedial education for the ghettos, and by the time it gets through the legislature it is a relief formula for the suburbs," says New Jersey's Ylvisaker. . . .

Some educators, including James Allen, the [former] U.S. Commissioner of Education, have suggested that the best way to handle the equalization problem is to finance education entirely at the state level. This solution, however, not only would undermine the socially valuable institution of the local school district, but also would subject urban minority groups to an administration even more distant and cumbersome than the city bureaucracies against which they now complain.

·   ·   ·

Washington May Come to the Rescue—Later

The needs of the cities cannot be considered in isolation from the over-all fiscal problems of state government. Most state political leaders readily agree that the states should do more to help the cities, but many argue that funds simply are not available at the state level for any major increase in effort. State tax revenues have risen more than 200 per cent in ten years, yet most states are not able to carry on even their current programs out of existing taxes. Of the twenty-five governors who responded to *Fortune*'s survey, only four believe that their present fiscal resources are adequate to meet the needs of the next few years, and seventeen listed the need to find new sources of revenue as the most important problem facing their states.

State officials are strongly disposed to look to the federal government to fill this revenue gap. "There is a fiscal crisis in the whole federal system," says Nelson Rockefeller. "State and local expenditures have been rising much more rapidly than federal expenditures for domestic purposes, but the federal government collects two-thirds of all the taxes." Rockefeller proposes that the federal government come to the rescue. of both the states and the cities by taking over the entire cost of the welfare system, and retaining the present income-tax surcharge to either make block grants for education or provide aid on a per capita basis to state and local governments. The added cost to the federal government would be $30 billion by 1973. . . .

Much though the Nixon Administration may want to secure the fiscal health of the states, there is little prospect that it will soon provide funds on anything like the scale that Rockefeller asks. Unless he is willing to sharply cut military spending or retreat from his promise to slow down inflation, the President cannot now make large increases in domestic expenditures of any kind. Eventually the so-called "fiscal dividend" produced by rising revenues from the federal income tax should make

more money available, but even then it is doubtful that Congress will be in any rush to release huge sums from its control. The most the federal government is likely to do in the near future is pick up a larger share of the cost of welfare—though even here less than the states and cities would like—and perhaps make small block grants to the states to fulfill Nixon's commitment to "revenue sharing." For the next few years, at least, the states will have to pay for any large expansion of effort out of their own resources. There is evidence that most of the major urban and industrial states, at least, are financially—if not politically—able to do so.

.   .   .

A Sort of Reserve to Save the Cities

.   .   .

Raising state taxes will, of course, require real sacrifice by millions of taxpayers who already feel sorely burdened by the costs of government. But the alternative is even more unpleasant. "There's been too much delay, for too long and by too many people," says Richard Ogilvie, chewing on an unlit pipe in the governor's office in Springfield. "State government has ignored its responsibilities."

In a way, the low-tax industrial states, by holding out for so long against additional levies, have created a kind of fiscal reserve. Upon their readiness to tap this reserve now will depend their capacity for vigorous action to save their cities.

8
Sources of the Public Unhappiness

RICHARD GOODWIN

As a speechwriter for Senators Eugene McCarthy and the late Robert Kennedy in their 1968 quests for the Presidency, Richard Goodwin helped raise questions about centralization and power. This extract represents part of the fullest exposition of his views. Do you find the ideal of smaller communities attractive? Practical? Sheer nostalgia? Dangerous? How would Goodwin's article be viewed by Reich? Long? Elazar? Is Reichley's view of what changes we need in governmental units reconcilable with Goodwin's?

It would be hard to overstate the extent to which the malaise of powerlessness has eaten its way into our society, evoking an aimless unease, frustration, and fury. It is probably least pervasive among the poor urban blacks, around whom so much of the surface debate about local control and Black Power now revolves. Their grievances are, for the most part, closer to the classic ills that the New Deal was designed to solve. They want jobs and decent homes, a higher standard of living, and freedom from the welfare bureaucracy. If a beneficent government were to provide these rudimentary components of the just life, it would meet most of the present demands of the black community. Of course, even among America's poor, questions of power are more important than they were thirty years ago. For the poor of today are inevitably caught up in the main currents of our society and partake of the general atmosphere of helplessness and drift, and the resistant nature of racial feelings is forcing

From Richard Goodwin, "Sources of the Public Unhappiness," The New Yorker (Jan. 4, 1969), pp. 38–58. Copyright © 1969 by Richard Goodwin. Reprinted by permission of the Sterling Lord Agency.

black Americans toward a kind of separatism as an alternative to the assimilation that was their initial goal. However, these questions can be seen most acutely among those who are neither poor nor black—the American middle class, or the American majority. Their psychological plight is both worse and more dangerous than that of the black militant leading a slum riot. For he at least has a cause and a purpose, an enemy, and comrades in the struggle. No such outlets and no human connections so satisfying are available to the man who lives in a middle-class suburb or a lower-income city apartment. And his discontents, unlike those of the poor, have real political weight.

. . .

The unexciting and envy-producing tone of the non-poor citizen's private life is heightened by the growing remoteness of public life. The air around him is poisoned, parkland disappears under relentless bulldozers, traffic stalls and jams, airplanes cannot land, and even his own streets are unsafe and, increasingly, streaked with terror. Yet he cannot remember having decided that these things should happen, or even having wished them. He has no sense that there is anything he can do to arrest the tide. He does not know whom to blame.

Somehow, the crucial aspects of his environment seem in the grip of forces that are too huge and impersonal to attack. You cannot vote them out of office or shout them down. Even the speeches of mayors and governors are filled with exculpatory claims that the problems are too big, that there is not enough power or enough money to cope with them, and our commentators sympathize, readily agreeing that this city or that state is really ungovernable. Even when a source of authority can be identified, it seems hopelessly detached from the desires or actions of individual citizens. Thus, the citizens of Boston woke up one day not very long ago to read that two hundred million dollars' worth of anti-missile missiles were scheduled to replace hundreds of acres of nearby woodland. And who could say no? And who was asked?

. . .

This powerlessness, in large measure a product of the complexity and the sheer size of modern society, is a problem in itself. It is a problem in the same way that lack of money or of useful work is a problem. For individuals have a fundamental, instinctive need for a degree of personal mastery over their lives and their environment. The sense of powerlessness is, moreover, greatly aggravated by the failure of our institutions and our social processes to respond to more specific ills. If we were providing good schools, inspiring cities, and safe streets, the degree of public discontent would be far less. If the quality of individual life were being steadily raised, we would be less concerned that we had little share in the process. But that is not the case. The desire to increase our national wealth and distribute it more broadly —a desire that was idealistic in origin and welcome in its consequences—led us to create machinery for both stimulating and regulating the economy. It is not simply that power was withdrawn from private centers and brought to Washington. It is that the use of that power was judged in terms of economic growth, which meant that construction, technology, and expansion were made into self-sufficient virtues.

Build a better mousetrap or a bigger housing development and you not only made money, you were a hero of the Republic. Added to this were the exigencies of the Cold War, which persuaded us of the necessity of a large standing army.

. . .

Unfortunately, the policies and the institutions we evolved to make ourselves wealthy are not appropriate to the needs of a society in which lack of wealth is not the problem either for the country as a whole or for most of the people. It is not simply that we need new values but that our institutions are facing demands they were never shaped to meet. A classic example is the federal housing programs, which were designed to stimulate construction and avoid a postwar depression, and which have failed miserably under the pressure of social demands for slum clearance and the creation of livable neighborhoods. These programs can do a job, but it is not the job we now need done. Moreover, many of our institutions, including our political parties themselves, are led by men who developed their ideas in response to earlier demands, and are therefore unable to understand or cope with a newer set of problems. The worst of these men no longer care for anything except the power and influence they have won, and the best of them are angry because their beneficent and humane intentions are not appreciated. The occasional violence of their response to opposition shows their unawareness that time and change, not particular individuals, have been their remorseless critics.

. . .

The same stiffening of established patterns invades the relationship between private institutions and the public interest. The basic pattern of government regulation of business has hardly changed for decades, although much of it is irrelevant, some is oppressive, and many new abuses are unrestrained. The Internal Revenue Code of 1954, despite its grotesque inequities—some of which are actually harmful to wealth and business—appears to be engraved in marble. We cannot stop incredibly wasteful subsidies to groups like the shipbuilders and large-scale farmers, even though their political power has almost evaporated, while at the same time it is extraordinarily difficult to supplement the income of more needy and numerous groups. No demonology of power and wealth can explain a rigidity that is part of a general resistance to new assertions of what is desirable and good. When we understand the fact that what now seems wrong may once have been right, then we can understand the fierceness of the defense.

·   ·   ·

This phenomenon is not just political. In almost every aspect of life, men are confronted by institutions and processes that seem unresponsive to their needs. There is, for example, no way in which the citizen can even begin to create a community—a place where he can both work and play in some kind of shared fellowship with neighbors. Our society is simply not equipped to deal with such a demand, and our political leaders are not even able to articulate it, since it transcends their own professional assumptions.

Powerlessness is made more acute by the seeming opposite of rigidity—by the swirling inconstancies of modern life. We are like boats tied to a riverbank with the rapid waters constantly seething beneath us while rope after rope breaks away. It is now commonplace to observe the weakening of the ties of family and community. However, it is not merely that we are being deprived of important values. These institutions, and others, gave us a resting spot, an association within which we could have some secure sense of our own value and place regardless of our fate in the world outside. In a more subtle and profound way, the increasing incredibility of religious doctrines and the complexities of science, which have made it impossible to understand the natural world, have deprived us of anchors against the storm of events.

. . . I have no wish to coin a new set of slogans, but certainly the individual must . . . have the freedom to share in those public decisions which affect his private life beyond merely casting a vote in periodic elections. This does not mean a plebiscite on every problem but, rather, a distinct prejudice in favor of community and neighborhood control. We should also be guided by a desire to preserve freedom from isolation, which means, at least, that environmental decisions should be shaped to re-create the possibilities of community and neighborhood life. It is equally important that the individual be given freedom to participate in the important enterprises of our society, from working in the underdeveloped world to improving the life of the ghettos. If citizens are to find a purpose beyond their daily lives, it will come from having a personal share in important public causes, and the causes must be large and worthy enough to tap moral will and energy. Only in this way can we combat the increasing isolation and remoteness that are eroding the moral drive of our society.

Much of this resolves itself into a widening of one of the oldest staples of political language: freedom of choice. For all the talk about our permissive society, that freedom has steadily narrowed. In fact, much of the release of inhibitions on private behavior is surely a reaction to the confinements imposed by our ideology and social structure. (Successful revolutions tend to be puritanical.) When a young man sees no alternative to spending his youth in a classroom and his manhood in a modern suburb, he may want to assert himself by growing a beard. Conversely, the students who turned out to work for McCarthy cut their hair and shaved not because of adult dictates but through self-organization and self-discipline. They were involved in something more important than this kind of assertion. These are trivial things, but they are tokens of the fact that much frantic liberation of private behavior is a futile effort to alter or escape the hardening mold that envelops social man. We virtually demand, for example, that a young man go to college, and beyond, if he is to have a job that uses his abilities. At one time, a boy could go to sea or go West or start working in a factory and still aspire to success in a wide range of demanding tasks. The fact is that a lot of young men would develop more fully outside the regular educational system. The answer is not simply providing more and better schools but making alternative institutions, training, and experience available, and making them acceptable to those who guard the gates to achievement. Similarly, by huddling industry, commerce, and even intellectual life together in great urban areas we have seriously limited the kinds of places in which a man can live. Much of this is a product of the obsessive urge toward system and order, and of the fact that as systems grow larger they swiftly outpace the individual imagination or intelligence and assume a conforming life of their own. It is almost as if our society were afflicted with some kind of compulsive neatness, which it equated with efficiency or high purpose.

The fact is that organizational neatness and central control not only limit human scope but are often inefficient. Government programs break down or prove inadequate not merely because they are badly conceived but because the problems they seek to deal with are far too large for the limited abilities of a few administrators. Even a genius philosopher-king equipped by I.B.M. could not hope to deal with the varied complexities of dozens of American cities. Central direction is inefficient in a more profound way, too. Given human nature in the context of our society, such oppressive structures are bound to breed discontent. This discontent necessarily impairs our ability to solve problems and maintain traditional values. Restless and unhappy people cannot easily be persuaded to join in enterprises of high purpose, especially those involving sacrifice.

. . .

Many of the programs designed to re-create community will concern the physical environment, although the power to act as a community and the consequent sense of shared purpose are also critical. This will require that we concentrate not on the quantity of construction but on assembling the components of daily living within an area that a man can comprehend and easily traverse. Along with housing should go hospitals and government services, recreation and meeting centers, parks, and, to the extent that this is possible, places of work. This does not mean breaking up our cities but restoring the concept of neighborhood under modern conditions—a place where a man can live with other men. Some of this is happening by itself under pressures of growth, as shopping centers move to the suburbs and industry seeks sites outside the city. This beginning can proliferate and expand through program ranging from tax incentives for businesses resettling in residential areas to the construction of new satellite cities. Much can be done, for example, simply by changing and enforcing zoning ordinances, building codes, and tax laws, without a cent of public expenditure. There is a lot more to community than this. Its roots go into the powerful cementing emotions of pride, belonging, friendship, and shared concern, yet these, in turn, depend on the physical possibilities. Not only is it within our power to create those possibilities but it is probably a more practical course than our present unthinking and hopelessly scattered mixture of government programs and private enterprise.

Increasing the individual's power over the conditions of his life involves the blended methods of transferring authority, creating it where it does not exist, and lessening the coercive weight of the state. At other times, I have discussed the need for decentralizing the operations of government—allowing communities, private groups, cities, and states to make public decisions that are now vested in the central government. Although the Constitution contains a prescriptive mandate for a federal system, the actual distribution of authority and responsibility has been worked out over two centuries and is constantly changing. Today, for example, the federal government exerts a power over the economy that would have been inconceivable only a few decades ago. Decentralization is another remodelling of the federal system, and to achieve it will require a patient pragmatism. The state may be the logical unit for dealing with river pollution, the metropolitan area for transportation programs, the neighborhood for schools and even post offices. *The general guide should be to transfer power to the smallest unit consistent with the scale of the problem.* Many conservatives have welcomed the idea of decentralization, hearing in it comforting echoes of old battle cries about states' rights. They are mistaken, for decentralization, if it is to work, will require even larger public programs and even more money for public needs. Otherwise, momentum on which local interest and involvement depend will be lost. Nor does decentralization mean the absence of rigorous national standards for the use of national revenues. For example, money given for education must in fact be used for education open to all. Such standards are necessary to protect citizens against unresponsive government, and local government against the pressures of private interests. Of course, even with decentralization, most people will not actually make decisions. Still, those who do make them will be within reach of their fellow-residents of the community, and thus will be far more familiar and readily accessible than federal officials. This, in itself, will yield at least the potential of influence and effective protest, which may be as close as we can come to the ideal of the town meeting.

Power is conferred in other ways: by a government that feels compelled to explain its policies and intentions with candor, that seeks the counsel of informed private groups and citizens, and that adheres to an honorable observance of the separation of powers. It will also be yielded by increased citizen control over the private institutions and processes that often determine the quality of our private lives. It is incredible, for example, that private builders, acting out of purely economic considerations, should be allowed to determine the shape of our urban environment—that individuals unresponsive to the public will should decide how the public will live. In addition, the expanding machinery of secret police, investigation, bugging, and wiretapping must be halted and dismantled. Fear and suspicion are the most paralyzing agents of all, and the most likely to provoke unrest.

The use of power is also an expression of purpose. All acts have their intention. But you can share in purpose without sharing in power. As a member of a society, the individual's pride and sense of well-being are inevitably enhanced or diminished by the purpose of his nation—what it stands for and where it is going. If money and power, self-indulgence and self-protection are the goals of our society, they will become the goals of its citizens, with damaging consequences. Nothing would do more for our national health than a feeling that we were engaged in enterprises touched with some kind of nobility and grandeur.

.   .   .

9

Fair Game

WALTER GOODMAN

The notion of community control and the breaking up of existing units is seen by many as utopian and nonsense. Here one writer uses sarcasm in an analysis of the notion. Is such a technique fair? Irrelevant? Are there substantive arguments discernible? Are they more or less convincing because of the style of exposition used? How do you feel about the notion after comparing Goodwin and Goodman?

The Heavenly City

In the Heavenly City of Community Control, The People will roll up its sleeves and in a miracle of energy, ability and blinding consensus, it will create schools that educate, hospitals that cure, jails that redeem. The streets will be swept and policemen will smile.

The Sidewalk City

One nagging difficulty in translating men's higher visions of life into reality is that The People turn out to be merely people, with an exasperating array of temperaments, prejudices, quirks, likes and dislikes, loves and hates. These many opinions and eccentricities, usually containable, seem to burst into furious life at the scent of power.

Most of the people in any neighborhood could manage comfortably under a commissar or generalissimo, an emperor or ward boss, as long as he didn't get personal. For them Community Control is a concept of incalculable indifference (Tammany Hall may be regarded as an early

form of Community Control; there was Christmas turkey for the community and boodle all year round for the controllers). Those who do get caught up in it will include the selfless and the self-seeking, the able and the incompetent, reasonable persons and lunatics, honest men and crooks—which is to say, the diverse sorts one finds on any level of political give and take.

One type, however, that is sure to show up in disproportionate numbers in neighborhood politics is the hollerer. It is by the performance of the hollerers, by their ingenuity, daring, persistence, and noise that the neighborhood will be advertised to the outer world. Willy nilly, residents will find themselves being spoken for, most vociferously, by persons who have neglected to ask their opinion on any subject. Moreover, these spokesmen will frequently disagree with one another: Some will be Maoists, others black capitalists; some will demand more police protection while others are demanding that the cops get off their turf. In any case, the hollerers, whether inspired or just cracked, become the stars of the theater of Community Control.

The reason for this is easily grasped. When a group feels that it is in a position to exercise a real influence on the course of things, it does not need to holler. Security breeds courtesy. Recently, a company of responsible Ohio citizens, finding themselves constituted as a proper grand jury with authority to investigate the events at Kent State, indicted a batch of students and teachers who had been shot at and exonerated those who did the shooting. Now, *that* is Community Control. Lacking grand jury status or equivalent credentials, residents of our inner cities—for so long the truly silent minorities—have a way of swinging from pathetic apathy to hit-and-miss activism. The activism naturally features hollering, since it is one of the few privileges of powerlessness. And there is always the chance somebody will listen.

For must the same reason that, we are told, men climb mountains, neighborhood activists set their sights on a hospital, a church, a school. Picketing, blockading, taking-over—such is the stuff of the politics of the street. Conversely, every incident of random violence common to the slums is at once elevated to the status of a political gesture. To establish and maintain their reputations, the sidewalk politicians in one neighborhood must be as adventurous as other fellows from other neighborhoods who make the newspapers. If trash can be burned in the streets of Brooklyn, it can be burned in the streets of the Bronx. In recent weeks, the Puerto Rican Young Lords of East Harlem have been wanly trying to come on like Black Panthers.

The autumn uprisings in several New York City jails may be seen as an episode of Community Control, albeit necessarily of a temporary sort. Despite some internal disagreements between radicals and moderates, the movement's goals were remarkably straightforward: The prisons, abominably overcrowded at present, should be made fit for human habitation, and those who are confined there waiting for the courts to get around to them ought to be let out. The demands of activists outside the prison walls are not always so coherent.

Activist demands bear at least superficial relevance to existing conditions—yet often one is left with the feeling that they are an afterthought of the action. The protests about education, health, police brutality, have plenty of substance—but frequently they appear to be only rationalizations for a flare-up whose cause is obscure. Sometimes the issues seem oddly matched with the passions they arouse. Occasionally, too, the victories are dubious: Not long ago a handful of West Side New Yorkers blocked plans to build a department store that would have given jobs to scores of local people and provided a useful addition to the area. What self-respecting militant could support Alexander's?

Up the Neighborhood

Just as there are many kinds of people within a neighborhood, so there are many different neighborhoods within any city. For years it was an article of the liberal faith that neighborhood control ought not to be vested in neighbors who held unwholesome views. Thus, it was agreed that Jews had a right to move into certain buildings on the East Side of New York no matter what the objections of the residents of those buildings. It was seen as a case of bad neighbors making bad fences, and the problem was taken to city officials, to state officials, to Federal officials, to the legislatures and to the courts, anywhere but to the benighted members of the community. As a rule, civil liberties for outsiders get short shrift from neighborhood folks, wherever the neighborhood. A stimulating form of Community Control in our Southern states, until the Federal government intervened, was the lynch mob.

Even today, when all neighborhood controllers are enlightened, difficulties have a way of arising because the various sections of a city want pretty much the same thing simultaneously. They all want their streets swept and plowed, for example. Nothing unnatural in this—but at a time when the cities are populated so heavily by people who are unable to contribute to the support of public services, the plowing of one neighborhood means that another will be snowed in; if garbage is collected regularly here, it must be collected irregularly there. Community controllers inevitably find themselves in competition with community controllers for the ear of the authorities. (To be sure, residents who can pay their way do tend to make out better in getting their garbage collected.)

The salvation of the nation's neighborhoods, unfortunately, is to be found not in the City Halls, where the hollerers can have some impact, but at the State Capitols and in Washington, where their main impact is to reinforce cherished stereotypes about ill-mannered minorities. City officials try to use the threat of riot as a way of squeezing funds out of state legislators, but few of the latter are likely to miss a night's sleep over a slum block going up in flames. They have by and large evidenced a long-standing aloofness, tinged with distaste for big cities and little people.

Sporadic activism has mostly proven effective in scaring taxpayers and tax-paying companies away from the cities to the outer suburbs, thereby diminishing further the capacity of the municipality to meet the needs of the needy whom the activists ostensibly serve. Yet the activists thrive, because ordinary politicking holds out no popular satisfaction comparable to shutting down a high school. Mr. Stokes is Mayor of Cleveland; Mr. Gibson is Mayor of Newark; but Newark remains Newark and Cleveland remains Cleveland. Against such painful realities, Community Control is the LSD of the masses. The rhetoric alone is sufficient for a short trip.

As for Federal officialdom, it has, to be sure, scarred and eliminated many neighborhoods with its mania for highway-building, and it has not always shown much sensitivity to the feelings of the people whom it has been assigned to assist. Yet it is Washington, with its hung-up experts, niggling accounting procedures and rigamarole of every sort, that has made life easier for millions of people in thousands of communities around the country. Remote Control. Even today, behind all the noise and smoke, the struggle over Community Control has a way of coming down to who will handle the flow or trickle of Federal dollars. As the good Dominican friars used to say when peddling indulgences, "Once you hear the money's ring, the soul from purgatory is free to spring." That's a pretty old form of politics, in a thoroughly democratic tradition.

Still, despite all the foolishness and fraud and cultivation of self-defeating hostilities, the cry for Community Control is an expression of honest yearnings that are felt in suburbs as well as in ghettos. It is a confusing mixture of desires for the material benefits of the system and for a way to beat the system, for a place in the society and for transformation of the society, for personal success, for a say in one's own destiny, and for a shared destiny with others. Which, I suppose, brings us back to the Heavenly City.

CIVIL LIBERTIES:
THE BILL OF RIGHTS

"All declare for liberty," former Justice Reed once suggested, "and proceed to disagree among themselves as to its true meaning." Americans assume that the legacy of the Constitution not only assures freedom but solves all problems with regard to interpretation as well. But each day presents new problems in the field of human freedom. Reconciling liberty and authority, freedom and order, and the rights of the individual with the needs of the community are continuous and demanding tasks.

History helps in understanding some of our civil liberties problems, but no amount of historical knowledge will completely solve such questions as how to treat our giant new mass media—movies, radio, television. Traditional notions of freedom of the press have to be adjusted to deal with these new resources. Domestic tranquillity in the modern world presents problems different at the very least in size and scope from the situations of 1789.

How Free Can We Be Without Chaos?

Americans enjoy remarkable latitude in expression of ideas. Is this a desirable end or is it itself a corruption of thinking and undesirable? In recent years the principal debate has gone beyond expression of ideas into the realm sometimes identified as action. How much latitude should be permitted in dress, personal style, public frankness? Even this is rather outdated.

Now the debate ranges chiefly over individual opting out from societal laws, individual nullification, as it were. When should one obey an unjust law? Can individual conscience be the only guide? What consequences will this have for a viable society?

The Right to Be Let Alone Versus the Need to Organize Society

In the novel *1984*, George Orwell paints a startling picture of life in a society where almost every move is spied upon and controlled by the government. Readers have found this more bloodcurdling and terrifying a story than many a thriller. Instinctively we all feel that there is some corner of our world that is our own and should be untouched by other humans. In recent years an "activist" Court has attempted to protect such individuality. To a large extent this has resulted in a race between the effectiveness of legal procedures and the developments of modern technology. With the perfection of "snooping devices" and methods of recording and analyzing, it is hard to say that technology has been losing any ground.

Another issue that has plagued society through history and over which wars have been fought is the separation of church and state. American society has emphasized the essentially secular nature of government and has left religion largely to operate in its own sphere. But talk of a "wall of separation" between church and state is partly belied by our insistence upon religious ceremonies in connection with government and indirect governmental support. We exempt churches from taxation, and we have chaplains in the army. In recent years, the line of separation has become fuzzy in the area of education. Claims have been pressed for aid to parochial schools on the grounds that it is discriminatory not to help children in religious schools get an education through public funds. At the same time, it is argued whether religious education should be allowed in the schools at all. The Supreme Court has taken the position that a state may not hold religious instruction on school grounds, or require ceremonial prayers, but may release children to go to religious instruction on school time. A number of such questions have caused court rulings and public controversy.

Negroes and Whites: The Challenge of Equal Protection of the Laws

In 1954, the Supreme Court ruled that "in the field of education 'separate but equal' has no place." The Court called for progress with "deliberate speed." Since that time slow and painful progress has been made toward school integration.

Recently, however, the issue of southern school integration has receded to the background. Jobs, housing, and personal respect for the Negro as an individual have now come to the fore. These issues are necessarily raised in the North as well as the South, and have aroused more controversy as the demands involve changes next door rather than in another section of the country.

As progress has been slowed, civil rights leaders have been moved to new tactics—violence, separatism, self-awareness. What will the future look like? Is peaceful progress a reasonable goal or is force the only midwife of change? What type of distinctiveness is a contribution to a multi-ethnic, variegated life, and what constitutes a challenge to its existence? Is race hatred ameliorable or inexorable? These are certainly key—and incendiary—questions for the 1970's.

1

Free Speech and Free Government

ALEXANDER MEIKLEJOHN

Probably the strongest defense of free speech is that made by a little book of about 100 pages by one of the most respected of American philosophers and educators, a man known for maintaining the courage of his convictions where personal sacrifice was involved. Professor Meiklejohn maintains that all speech in the public domain, without exception, is to be allowed, and actions alone proscribed. This he sees not as an individual right, a privilege owed by the community to a citizen, but rather as a social right. When we allow an idea to be expressed we are benefiting ourselves and not the expresser. In recent years Justice Black has openly arrived at a similar form of "absolute" free speech, arguing even that libel laws are unconstitutional.

. . . What do we mean when we say that "Congress shall make no law . . . abridging the freedom of speech . . . ?" . . . Are we, for example, required by the First Amendment to give men freedom to advocate the abolition of the First Amendment? Are we bound to grant freedom of speech to those who, if they had the power, would refuse it to us? The First Amendment, taken literally, seems to answer, "Yes," to those questions. It seems to say that no speech, however dangerous, may, for that reason, be suppressed. But the Federal Bureau of Investigation, the un-American Activities Committee, the Department of Justice, the President, are, at the same time, answering "No" to the same question. Which answer is right? What is the valid American doctrine concerning the freedom of speech? . . .

From *Alexander Meiklejohn*, Free Speech and Its Relation to Self-Government *(New York): Harper & Row, Publishers, 1948), pp. vi–xii, 24–27, 49–50. Copyright © 1948 by Harper & Row, Publishers, Inc. Reprinted by permission of the publisher.*

. . . Here . . . the town meeting suggests an answer. That meeting is called to discuss and, on the basis of such discussion, to decide matters of public policy. For example: Shall there be a school? Where shall it be located? Who shall teach? What shall be taught? The community has agreed that such questions as these shall be freely discussed and that, when the discussion is ended, decision upon them will be made by vote of the citizens. Now, in that method of political self-government, the point of ultimate interest is not the words of the speakers, but the minds of the hearers. The final aim of the meeting is the voting of wise decisions. The voters, therefore, must be made as wise as possible. The welfare of the community requires that those who decide issues shall understand them. They must know what they are voting about. . . .

The First Amendment, then, is not the guardian of unregulated talkativeness. It does not require that, on every occasion, every citizen shall take part in public debate. Nor can it even give assurance that everyone shall have opportunity to do so.

If, for example, at a town meeting, twenty like-minded citizens have become a "party," and if one of them has read to the meeting an argument which they have all approved, it would be ludicrously out of order for each of the others to insist on reading it again. No competent moderator would tolerate that wasting of the time available for free discussion. What is essential is not that everyone shall speak, but that everything worth saying shall be said. To this end, for example, it may be arranged that each of the known conflicting points of view shall have, and shall be limited to, an assigned share of the time available. But however it be arranged, the vital point, as stated negatively, is that no suggestion of policy shall be denied a hearing because it is on one side of the issue rather than another. . . . When men govern themselves, it is they—and no one else—who must pass judgment upon unwisdom and unfairness and danger. And that means that unwise ideas must have a hearing as well as wise ones, unfair as well as fair, dangerous as well as safe, un-American as well as American. Just so far as, at any point, the citizens who are to decide an issue are denied acquaintance with information or opinion or doubt or disbelief or criticism which is relevant to that issue, just so far the result must be ill-considered, ill-balanced planning for the general good. *It is that mutilation of the thinking process of the community against which the First Amendment to the Constitution is directed.* . . .

If, then, on any occasion in the United States it is allowable to say that the Constitution is a good document it is equally allowable, in that situation, to say that the Constitution is a bad document. If a public building may be used in which to say, in time of war, that the war is justified, then the same building may be used in which to say that it is not justified. If it be publicly argued that conscription for armed service is moral and necessary, it may likewise be publicly argued that it is immoral and unnecessary. If it may be said that American political institutions are superior to those of England or Russia or Germany, it may, with equal freedom, be said that those of England or Russia or Germany are superior to ours. These conflicting views may be expressed, must be expressed, not because they are valid, but because they are relevant. If they are responsibly entertained by anyone, we, the voters, need to hear them. When a question of policy is "before the house," free men choose to meet it not with their eyes shut, but with their eyes open. To be afraid of ideas, any idea, is to be unfit for self-government. . . .

. . . Holmes' . . . formula tells us that whenever the expression of a minority opinion involves clear and present danger to the public safety it may be denied the protection of the First Amendment. And that means that whenever crucial and dangerous issues have come upon the nation, free and unhindered discussion of them must stop. . . . Under that ruling, dissenting judges might, in "dangerous" situations, be forbidden to record their dissents. Minority citizens might, in like situations, be required to hold their peace. No one, of course, believes that this is what Mr. Holmes or the court intended to say. But it is what, in plain words, they did say. The "clear and present danger" opinion stands on the record of the court as a peculiarly inept and unsuccessful attempt to formulate an exception to the principle of the freedom of speech. . . .

2

Marcuse Defines His New Left Line

Another point of view assumes there are "correct" and "evil" answers to questions. Here Herbert Marcuse, the most influential spokesman for the student left, explains his views. Similar attitudes are expressed by the Far Right as to the rights of communists—or of Herbert Marcuse. Are these positions on the same level? How would Marcuse distinguish, for purposes of suppression, a "racist" view from differences of opinion on race questions? Which is more "repressive"—Marcuse's view or Meiklejohn's?

What do you hope for from the student unrest but a superficial disorder which only serves to stiffen the repression?

MARCUSE: All militant opposition takes the risk of increasing repression. This has never been a reason to stop the opposition. Otherwise, all progress would be impossible.

No doubt. But don't you think the notion of the "progress" that might result from a revolution deserves to be better defined? You denounce the subtle restraints that weigh upon the citizens of modern societies. Wouldn't a revolution result in exchanging one series of restraints for another?

MARCUSE: Of course. But there are progressive restraints and reactionary restraints. For example, restraints imposed upon the elemental aggressiveness of man, upon the instinct of destruction, the death instinct, the transformation of this elemental aggressiveness into an energy that could be used for the improvement and protection of life—such restraints would be necessary in the freest society. For example, industries would not be permitted to pollute the air, nor would the "White Citizens

Council" be permitted to disseminate racism or to possess firearms, as they are in the United States today. . . . Of course there would be restraints; but they would be progressive ones.

The ones you mention are commonplace enough. The possession of firearms is forbidden in France, and in America it is a survival, not a creation of the affluent society. Let us consider freedom of expression, which means a great deal to us. In the free society which you advocate this freedom disappears, does it not?

MARCUSE: I have written that I believe it is necessary not to extend freedom of the press to movements which are obviously aggressive and destructive, like the Nazi movement. But with the exception of this special case, I am not against freedom of expression. . . .

Even when this means the propagation of racist, nationalist or colonialist ideas?

MARCUSE: Here my answer is no. I am not in favor of granting free expression to racist, anti-Semitic, neo-Nazi movements. Certainly not; because the interval between the word and the act is too brief today. At least in American society, the one with which I am familiar. You know the famous statement of Justice Holmes, that civil rights can be withdrawn in a single case: the case of immediate danger. Today this immediate danger exists everywhere.

Can't this formula be turned against you in connection with students, revolutionaries, or Communists?

MARCUSE: It always is. And my answer is always the same. I do not believe that the Communism conceived by the great Marxist theorists is, by its very nature, aggressive and destructive; quite the contrary.

But has it not become so under certain historical circumstances? Isn't there something aggressive and destructive about the Soviet policy toward Hungary in 1956, or toward Czechoslovakia today?

MARCUSE: Yes. But that isn't Communism, it is Stalinism. I would certainly use all possible restraints to oppose Stalinism, but that is not Communism.

Why do you criticize America more severely for its deviations from the democratic ideal than you do Communism for its deviations from the Communist ideal?

MARCUSE: I am just as critical of these deviations in Communist countries. However, I believe that the institutions and the whole culture of the capitalism of monopolies militate against the development of a democratic socialism.

And you believe that one day we shall see an ideal Communist society?

MARCUSE: Well, at least there is the theory. There is the whole Marxist theory. That exists. And there is also Cuba. There is China. There is the Communist policy during the heroic period of the Bolshevik Revolution.

Do you mean that Communist societies do these reprehensible things in spite of themselves? That the Soviet Union invaded Czechoslovakia in spite of herself?

MARCUSE: In spite of the idea of Communism, not in spite of the Soviet Union. The invasion of Czechoslovakia is one of the most reprehensible acts in the history of Socialism. It is a brutal expression of the policy of power that has long been practiced by the Soviet Union in political and economic competition with capitalism. I believe that many of the reprehensible things that happen in the Communist countries are the result of competitive coexistence with capitalism, while poverty continues to reign in the Communist countries.

Here you are touching upon an important point. It does not seem possible to reduce poverty without an extremely coercive organization. So once again we find that restraint is necessary.

MARCUSE: Certainly. But here, too, there can be progressive restraint. Take a country in which poverty coexists with luxury, waste, and comfort for the privileged. . . . It is necessary to curb this waste to eliminate poverty, misery, and inequality. These are necessary restraints.

The drawback—at least from the viewpoint of revolution—is that the working class is more interested in belonging to the affluent society than in destroying it, although it also hopes to modify certain aspects of it. At least this is the case in France. Is it different in other countries?

MARCUSE: You say that in France the working class is not yet integrated but that it would like to be. . . . In the United States it is integrated and it wants to be. This means that revolution postulates first of all the emergence of a new type of man with needs and aspirations that are qualitatively different from the aggressive and repressive needs and aspirations of established societies. It is true that the working class today shares in large measure the needs and aspirations of the dominant classes, and that without a break with the present content of needs, revolution is inconceivable.

So it will not happen tomorrow, it seems. It is easier to seize power than to change the needs of men. But what do you mean by aggressive needs?

MARCUSE: For example, the need to continue the competitive struggle for existence —the need to buy a new car every two years, the need to buy a new television set, the need to watch television five or six hours a day. This is already a vital need for a very large share of the population, and it is an aggressive and repressive need.

There can be a different use of television.

MARCUSE: Of course. All this is not the fault of television, the fault of the automobile, the fault of technology in general. It is the fault of the miserable use that is made of technological progress. Television could just as well be used to reeducate the population.

In what sense? To persuade people that they do not need cars or television sets or refrigerators or washing machines?

MARCUSE: Yes, if this merchandise prevents the liberation of the serfs from their "voluntary servitude."

Wouldn't this create some problems for the people who work in the factories where they make cars, refrigerators, etc?

MARCUSE: They will shut down for a week or two. Everyone will go to the country. And then the real work will begin, the work of abolishing poverty, the work of abolishing inequality, instead of the work of waste which is performed in the society of consumption. In the United States, for example, General Motors and Ford, instead of producing private cars, will produce cars for public transportation, so that public transportation can become human.

It will take a lot of television programs to persuade the working class to make a revolution that will reduce their wages, do away with their cars, and reduce their consumption. And in the meantime there is reason to fear that things may take a different turn, that all the people affected by the economic difficulties may potentially furnish a fascist mass. Doesn't fascism always come out of an economic crisis?

MARCUSE: That's true. The revolutionary process always begins with and in an economic crisis. But this crisis would offer two possibilities: the so-called neo-fascist possibility, in which the masses turn toward a regime that is much more authoritarian and repressive, and the opposite possibility, that the masses may see an opportunity to construct a free society in which such crises would be avoidable. There are always two possibilities. One cannot, for fear of seeing the first materialize, stop hoping and working for the second through the education of the masses. And not only by words, but by actions.

If freedom of expression no longer exists in the United States, it will no longer exist

anywhere . . . or perhaps in England?

MARCUSE: Yes. England may turn out to be one of the last liberal countries. The democracy of the masses is not favorable to noncomformist intellectuals. . . .

This is the crux of the matter. You have often been criticized for wanting to establish a Platonic dictatorship of the elite. Is this correct?

MARCUSE: There is a very interesting passage in John Stuart Mill, who was not exactly an advocate of dictatorship. He says that in a civilized society educated people must have political prerogatives to oppose the emotions, attitudes and ideas of the uneducated masses.

I have never said that it was necessary to establish a Platonic dictatorship because there is no philosopher who is capable of doing this. But to be perfectly frank, I don't know which is worse: a dictatorship of politicians, managers and generals, or a dictatorship of intellectuals.

Personally, if this is the choice, I would prefer the dictatorship of the intellectuals, if there is no possibility of a genuine free democracy. Unfortunately this alternative does not exist at present.

The dictatorship of the intellectuals must first be established to educate and reform the masses, after which, in a remote future, when people have changed, democracy and freedom will reign. Is that it?

MARCUSE: Not a true dictatorship, but a more important role for intellectuals, yes. I think that the resentment of the worker movement against the intellectuals is one of the reasons why this movement has stopped today.

The dictatorship of the intellectuals is rather disturbing, to the extent that intellectuals often become cruel because they are afraid of action.

MARCUSE: Is that really so? There is only one example in history of a cruel intellectual: Robespierre.

And Saint-Just.

MARCUSE: We must compare the cruelty of Robespierre and Saint-Just with the cruelty and the bureaucratized violence of an Eichmann. Or even with the institutionalized violence of modern societies. Nazi cruelty is cruelty as a technique of administration. The Nazis were not intellectuals. With intellectuals, cruelty and violence are always much more immediate, shorter, less cruel. Robespierre did not use torture. Torture is not an essential aspect of the French Revolution.

You know intellectuals: they are not, or are only slightly, in touch with reality. Can you imagine a society functioning under their direct government? What effect would this have on trains running on time, for example? Or on organizing production?

MARCUSE: If you identify reality with established reality you are right. But intellectuals do not or should not identify reality with established reality. Given the imagination and rationality of true intellectuals, we can expect great things. In any case, the famous dictatorship of the intellectuals has never existed.

3

The Three-Tiered Response to Civil Liberties Questions

SAMUEL KRISLOV

The following summarizes a number of studies on American public opinion and questions of liberty. What does this evidence suggest with respect to Marcuse's ideas on controlled opinion? How much (or little) protection is implied for dissenters?

Over the years, a series of carefully structured studies, surveys, and pools, as well as assorted grab-bag questionnaire arrangements ascertaining the views of groups of questionable representatives, all have probed and examined the attitudes of Americans toward civil liberties. Apparently without exception, these studies record profound antilibertarianism latent throughout our society.

This emerges as a paradox of no mean proportions. In the first instance, when asked to speak in terms of broad values, Americans consistently wrap themselves in the libertarian mantle. Americans overwhelmingly favor civil liberties when asked about their attitudes in highly abstract terms. However, when queried in operational terms, without benefit of shibboleths to guide them, they give antilibertarian responses about rights that are disputed. Many, if not most of these same liberties they support in the abstract. Yet, in practice, Americans seem to provide sufficiently broad general support for such rights to sustain them against attacks on a legal and practical level. This three-tiered pattern of response seems constant, clearcut, and

From *Samuel Krislov*, The Supreme Court and Political Freedom (*New York: The Free Press,* 1968), pp. 43–53. Copyright © by The Free Press, *a Division of The Macmillan Company, 1968.* Reprinted by permission of the publisher.

highly significant in all of its aspects. It would appear to be a fact of American political life that all three levels of response are interdependent and significant.

The contradiction between broad libertarian sloganizing and more concrete antirights attitudes can be taken as a devastating indictment of democracy and as a sign of the irrelevance of the most general articulated values. But this is probably an error; the fact that "all declare for freedom but proceed to disagree as to its application" permits the final outcome or resolution in favor of the disputed rights in practice when the decision emerges, after being channeled through prescribed structures. . . .

The antilibertarian impulse of the general American public, specifically working-class respondents, seems well established, as does the general class bias in libertarian attitudes. Libertarianism emerges largely as a middle- and upper-class luxury. For example, some studies show Republicans more libertarian than Democrats—presumably because of the high working-class components in the latter party—in spite of the fact that the Democrats as a party have taken many more stands favorable to civil liberties. Despite this working-class bias against libertarianism and evidence that education is positively correlated with libertarian views, it is instructive to note that it is on the basis of study of the attitudes of college students—a group strongly skewed on both class and education levels *toward* libertarianism—that some sociologists and political scientists have concluded that the Bill of Rights would be rejected by the populace if it were up for adoption today.[1] Even college students as a group seem lukewarm to liberty.

Some indication of this lack of libertarianism can be gleaned from the results of a group of questions given as part of Stouffer's study of anti-Communist reactions by the public. Public attitudes were tapped in 1954, at a time when repressiveness was at a comparative high point in American history. Although studies show variations between regions in degree of support for the Bill of Rights, with a consistent pattern of much more support in the West and the East—a pattern that is consistent on all kinds of issues—no region emerges with a majority as libertarian as current judicial decisions.[2]

The continued class difference in general tolerance of dissent has also been shown so consistently as to lead to the coining of the expression "working-class authoritarianism" to suggest that liberties are most secure with the upper-class. In recent years, the most conspicuous leaders of American social science have had an anti-working-class and pro-elite orientation in their prescriptions on the export of democracy. The circumstances under which these notions gained ascendancy—the period of McCarthyism, with its concomitant estrangement of intellectuals from mass opinion and the

[1] See, for example, Hanan C. Selvin and Warren O. Hagstrom, "Determinants of Supports for Civil Liberties," *British Journal of Sociology,* LI (March, 1960), 51–73; and Raymond Mack, "Do We Really Believe in the Bill of Rights," *Social Problems,* III (1956), 264.

[2] Some useful summaries of data on these points include, Herbert Hyman and Paul Sheatsley. "Trends in Public Opinion on Civil Liberties," *Journal of Social Issues,* IX (1953), No. 6; Hazel G. Erskine, "The Polls: Some Gauges of Conservatism," *Public Opinion Quarterly,* XXVIII (1964), 154; Hadley Cantril and Mildred Strunk, *Public Opinion 1935–1946* (Princeton, N.J.: Princeton University Press, 1952).

shift in the social standing of intellectuals in an upward mobile fashion—are, of course, suggestive and make such findings somewhat suspect. But even before these elitist notions gained general currency, they constituted the operational code of the American Civil Liberties Union—always a national-office operation viewed as an elite-centered negotiating group—and figured in the analysis of keen observers of our society. Furthermore, the almost unprecedented consistency in the pattern of responses over other eras is also impressive, including years prior to the period in which these notions became fashionable among social scientists.

No different attitude emerges on issues not involving communism: indeed, atheist speech seems the most controversial (see Table 1).

The most interesting and influential finding of the Stouffer study generally cited, confirmed by such efforts as the Selvin-Hagstorm and the McClosky studies, has been the discovery that community leaders were vastly more tolerant than the general population. Even those organizations who were dedicated to repressive programs with regard to civil liberties in the McCarthy era were led by individuals distinctly more libertarian than the mass population. The conclusion is that leadership itself requires or encourages more tolerant attitudes. The difficulty with this finding is that the Stouffer study does not help us to determine whether it is as a result of their activities that leaders appreciate tolerant attitudes or it is the selection process that determines that people with such values are chosen— or that attracts such personality types. It seems clear that the leadership function is associated with more tolerance, even controlling for education and class levels (although even that does not decisively emerge from the Stouffer data). What is not clear is whether it is the selection process or the leadership process that produces such values.

Recent advocates of greater participatory democracy—notably the New Left civil-rights groups—argue that dispersion of

TABLE 1

Attitudes of Community Leaders and General Public
toward Selected Free-Speech Issues

ISSUE: PERMITTING SPEECHES	COMMUNITY LEADERS			NATIONAL CROSS-SECTION		
	YES	NO	UND.	YES	NO	UND.
Advocating government ownership of industry	84	14	2	58	31	11
Against churches and religion	64	43	2	37	60	3
By a person accused of communism who denies it	87	11	2	70	21	9
By an admitted communist	51	47	2	27	68	5

Source: Samuel Stouffer, *Communism, Conformity and Civil Liberties* (New York: Doubleday & Company, Inc., 1955), pp. 29, 33, 36, 41.

leadership functions and encouragement of greater participation on the part of the mass public will lead to more libertarian attitudes, as apparently the process does for community leaders. This would be true, of course, only if it is indeed the process of leadership that produces libertarians and not merely the selection process that finds them.

. . .

The more common reading of the Stouffer study, however, has simply emphasized the importance of heeding authoritative positions in defending civil liberties. Looking about the world, for example, Herbert Hyman has concluded that antilibertarian attitudes tend to be the reflex action of the mass population everywhere. Thus, it is doubtful that the general population in Great Britain has a more favorable attitude toward civil liberties than do Americans, as is sometimes alleged. In Australia, Hyman notes that poll results before and after a referendum on the banning of the Communist Party favored such a ban, but the actual vote was against repression. He suggests that it is likely that there, as in the United States, opinion refined through institutional and leadership structures is more likely to be tolerant than off-hand expression of attitudes in response to casual questions.[3]

[3] Herbert Hyman, "England and America: Climates of Tolerance and Intolerance," in Daniel Bell (ed.), *The Radical Right* (New York: Anchor Books, 1964), pp. 269 ff.

. . . [I]t is argued that, in Great Britain, the general public is more alert and responsive to violations precisely because it does not have a "let Justice George do it" attitude. The late Justice Jackson, for example, suggested that,

In Great Britain, to observe civil liberties is good politics and to transgress the rights of the individual or the minority is bad politics. In the United States, I cannot say that this is so. Whether the political conscience is relieved because the responsibility here is made largely a legal one, I cannot say, but . . . I do not think the American public is enlightened on this subject.[4]

In part, statements about the pre-eminence of politics as defender of British liberty are based on appearances. In his preface to Dicey's authoritative *The Law and the Constitution*, Professor E.C.S. Wade offered the following proposition:

It is only, where constitutional law is concerned, in that small but vital sphere where liberty of person and of speech are guarded that it means the rule of common law. For here alone has Parliament seen fit to leave the law substantially unaltered and to leave the protection of the freedom of individuals to the operation of the common law.[5]

[4] Robert Jackson, *The Supreme Court in the American System of Government* (Cambridge, Mass.: Harvard University Press, 1955), pp. 81–82.

[5] E.C.S. Wade, Preface to A.V. Dicey, *The Law and the Constitution* (9th ed.; London: Macmillan and Co., 1939), p. lxxii.

Nonetheless, the ultimate, even if only occasionally exercised, authority is clearly political, so that the thrust of Justice Jackson's remarks may be deflected but not avoided. In direct response to Jackson, the legal philosopher Edmond Cahn observed that such advocates wanted to import a part of the British system—that part weakening civil liberties—without the supports for liberty implicit in the centralized governmental structure that could control the localities. . . .

Furthermore, as Laurent Frantz reminds us, Frankfurter and his followers have not advocated a system with no judicial review, or even one without review based on the Bill of Rights. (The latter position has been advocated only and sporadically by Learned Hand and perhaps by Henry Steele Commager.) Rather, they speak of minimization of the judicial role, so that the Court would continue to pass on restrictive legislation but virtually never do anything but validate legislation. This, he argues cogently, is the worst of all possible constitutional worlds—the fact of legislative omnipotence would be concealed and the imprimatur of Court evaluation somewhat fraudulently added.[6]

[6] Laurent Frantz, "Is the First Amendment Law? —A Reply to Professor Mendelson," *California Review*, LI (1963), 744.

4

Letter from Birmingham City Jail

MARTIN LUTHER KING, JR.

Nobel Prize winner Martin Luther King composed a rebuttal to white clergymen of Birmingham who protested his leadership of demonstrations while actually imprisoned. This remains the fullest exposition of Reverend King's philosophy of nonviolence, and an eloquent demonstration of why he emerged as the spokesman of the civil rights movement. In recent years, questions have developed as the philosophy has been applied to concrete situations with regard to both civil rights and the Vietnamese war. Are demonstrations which involve force legitimate where Negro political disadvantage is a product of apathy, rather than a consequence of intimidation of legal disability? Does the fact that Negro apathy is a product of discriminatory education and political experience denied them in the past mean that they should have the right to use extraordinary tactics in the present? What if a minority has full access to the political process, but—as in the case of the Vietnamese war—regards the majority policy not just as mistaken but as immoral? And why should minority tactics stop with nonviolence, if indeed immorality is being condoned?

While confined here in the Birmingham City Jail, I came across your recent statement calling our present activities "unwise and untimely." Seldom, if ever, do I pause to answer criticism of my work and ideas. . . . But since I feel that you are men of genuine good will and your criticisms are sincerely set forth, I would like to answer your statement in what I hope will be patient and reasonable terms.

I think I should give the reason for my

From Martin Luther King, Jr., "Letter from Birmingham City Jail," The New Leader, June 24, 1963, pp. 3–11. Reprinted by permission of the publisher.

being in Birmingham, since you have been influenced by the argument of "outsiders coming in." I have the honor of serving as president of the Southern Christian Leadership Conference, an organization operating in every Southern state with headquarters in Atlanta, Georgia. . . .

Moreover, I am cognizant of the interrelatedness of all communities and states. I cannot sit idly by in Atlanta and not be concerned about what happens in Birmingham. Injustice anywhere is a threat to justice everywhere. We are caught in an inescapable network of mutuality tied in a single garment of destiny. . . . Never again can we afford to live with the narrow, provincial "outside agitator" idea. Anyone who lives inside the United States can never be considered an outsider anywhere in this country.

You deplore the demonstrations that are presently taking place in Birmingham. But I am sorry that your statement did not express a smilar concern for the conditions that brought the demonstrations into being. I am sure that each of you would want to go beyond the superficial social analyst who looks merely at effects, and does not grapple with underlying causes. I would not hesitate to say that it is unfortunate that so-called demonstrations are taking place in Birmingham at this time, but I would say in more emphatic terms that it is even more unfortunate that the white power structure of this city left the Negro community with no other alternative.

In any nonviolent campaign there are four basic steps: 1) collection of the facts to determine whether injustices are alive; 2) negotiation; 3) self-purification; and 4) direct action. We have gone through all of these steps in Birmingham. There can be no gainsaying of the fact that racial injustice engulfs this community. Birmingham is probably the most thoroughly segregated city in the United States. Its ugly record of police brutality is known in every section of this country. Its unjust treatment of Negroes in the courts is a notorious reality. There have been more unsolved bombings of Negro homes and churches in Bir-

mingham than any city in this nation. These are the hard, brutal, and unbelievable facts. On the basis of these conditions Negro leaders sought to negotiate with the city fathers. But the political leaders consistently refused to engage in good faith negotiation. . . .

You may well ask, "Why direct action? Why sit-ins, marches, etc.? Isn't negotiation a better path?" You are exactly right in your call for negotiation. Indeed, this is the purpose of direct action. Nonviolent direct action seeks to create such a crisis and establish such creative tension that a community that has constantly refused to negotiate is forced to confront the issue. It seeks so to dramatize the issue that it can no longer be ignored.

I just referred to the creation of tension as a part of the work of the nonviolent resister. This may sound rather shocking. But I must confess that I am not afraid of the word "tension." I have earnestly worked and preached against violent tension, but there is a type of constructive nonviolent tension that is necessary for growth. Just as Socrates felt that it was necessary to create a tension in the mind so that individuals could rise from the bondage of myths and half-truths to the unfettered realm of creative analysis and objective appraisal, we must see the need of having nonviolent gadflies to create the kind of tension in society that will help men rise from the dark depths of prejudice and racism to the majestic heights of understanding and brotherhood. So the purpose of the direct action is to create a situation so crisis-packed that it will inevitably open the door to negotiation. We, therefore, concur with you in your call for negotiation. Too long has our beloved Southland been bogged down in the tragic attempt to live in monologue rather than dialogue.

One of the basic points in your statement is that our acts are untimely. . . . We know through painful experience that freedom is never voluntarily given by the oppressor; it must be demanded by the oppressed. Frankly I have never yet engaged in a direct action movement that was "well timed," according to the timetable of those who have not suffered unduly from the disease of segregation. For years now I have heard the word "Wait!" It rings in the ear of every Negro with a piercing familiarity. This "wait" has almost always meant "never." It has been a tranquilizing Thalidomide, relieving the emotional stress for a moment, only to give birth to an ill-formed infant of frustration. We have waited for more than 340 years for our constitutional and God-given rights. The nations of Asia and Africa are moving with jet-like speed toward the goal of political independence, and we still creep at horse and buggy pace toward the gaining of a cup of coffee at a lunch counter.

I guess it is easy for those who have never felt the stinging darts of segregation to say wait. But when you have seen vicious mobs lynch your mothers and fathers at will and drown your sisters and brothers at whim; when you have seen hate-filled policemen curse, kick, brutalize, and even kill your black brothers and sisters with impunity; when you see the vast majority of your 20-million Negro brothers smothering in an air-tight cage of poverty in the midst of an affluent society; when you suddenly find your tongue twisted and your speech stammering as you seek to explain to your six-year-old daughter why she can't go to the public amusement park that has just been advertised on television . . . and see the depressing clouds of inferiority begin to form in her little mental sky . . . when you take a cross-country drive and find it necessary to sleep night after night in the uncomfortable corners of your automobile because no motel will accept you; when you are humiliated day in and day out by nagging signs reading "white" men and "colored"; when your first name becomes "nigger" and your middle name becomes "boy" (however old you are) and your last name becomes "John," and when your wife and mother are never given the respected title "Mrs."; when you are harried by day and haunted by night by the fact that you are a Negro, living constantly at tiptoe stance never quite knowing what

to expect next, and plagued with inner fears and outer resentments; when you are forever fighting a degenerating sense of "nobodiness"—then you will understand why we find it difficult to wait. . . .

You express a great deal of anxiety over our willingness to break laws. This is certainly a legitimate concern. Since we so diligently urge people to obey the Supreme Court's decision of 1954 outlawing segregation in the public schools, it is rather strange and paradoxical to find us consciously breaking laws. One may well ask, "How can you advocate breaking some laws and obeying others?" The answer is found in the fact that there are two types of laws: There are *just* laws and there are *unjust* laws. One has not only a legal but a moral responsibility to obey just laws. Conversely, one has a moral responsibility to disobey unjust laws. I would agree with Saint Augustine that "An unjust law is no law at all."

Now what is the difference between the two? How does one determine when a law is just or unjust? A just law is a man-made code that squares with the moral law or the law of God. An unjust law is a code that is out of harmony with the moral law. . . .

I hope you can see the distinction I am trying to point out. In no sense do I advocate evading or defying the law as the rabid segregationist would do. This would lead to anarchy. One who breaks an unjust law must do it *openly, lovingly* (not hatefully as the white mothers did in New Orleans when they were seen on television screaming "nigger, nigger, nigger") and with a willingness to accept the penalty. I submit that an individual who breaks a law that conscience tells him is unjust, and willingly accepts the penalty by staying in jail to arouse the conscience of the community over its injustice, is in reality expressing the very highest respect for law. . . .

You spoke of our activity in Birmingham as extreme. At first I was rather disappointed that fellow clergymen would see my nonviolent efforts as those of the extremist. . . . I stand in the middle of two opposing forces in the Negro community. One is a force of complacency made up of Negroes who, as a result of long years of oppression, have been so completely drained of self-respect and a sense of "somebodiness" that they have adjusted to segregation, and of a few Negroes in the middle class who, because of a degree of academic and economic security, and because at points they profit by segregation, have unconsciously become insensitive to the problems of the masses. The other force is one of bitterness and hatred and comes perilously close to advocating violence. It is expressed in the various black nationalist groups that are springing up over the nation, the largest and best known being Elijah Muhammad's Muslim movement. This movement is nourished by the contemporary frustration over the continued existence of racial discrimination. It is made up of people who have lost faith in America, who have absolutely repudiated Christianity, and who have concluded that the white man is an incurable "devil."

I have tried to stand between these two forces saying that we need not follow the "do-nothingism" of the complacent or the hatred and despair of the black nationalist. There is the more excellent way of love and nonviolent protest. I'm grateful to God that, through the Negro church, the dimension of nonviolence entered our struggle. If this philosophy had not emerged I am convinced that by now many streets of the South would be flowing with floods of blood. And I am further convinced that if our white brothers dismiss us . . . and refuse to support our nonviolent efforts, millions of Negroes, out of frustration and despair, will seek solace and security in black nationalist ideologies, a development that will lead inevitably to a frightening racial nightmare. . . .

I must close now. But before closing I am impelled to mention one other point in your statement that troubled me pro-

foundly. You warmly commended the Birmingham police force for keeping "order" and "preventing violence." I don't believe you would have so warmly commended the police force if you had seen its angry, violent dogs literally biting six unarmed, nonviolent Negroes. . . .

I wish you had commended the Negro sit-inners and demonstrators of Birmingham for their sublime courage, their willingness to suffer, and their amazing discipline in the midst of the most inhuman provocation. One day the South will recognize its real heroes. . . . One day the South will know that when these disinherited children of God sat down at lunch counters they were in reality standing up for the best in the American dream and the most sacred values in our Judeo-Christian heritage, and thus carrying our whole nation back to great wells of democracy which were dug deep by the founding fathers in the formulation of the Constitution and the Declaration of Independence. . . .

If I have said anything in this letter that is an overstatement of the truth and is indicative of an unreasonable impatience, I beg you to forgive me. If I have said anything in this letter that is an understatement of the truth and is indicative of my having a patience that makes me patient with anything less than brotherhood, I beg God to forgive me. . . .

Let us all hope that the dark clouds of racial prejudice will soon pass away and the deep fog of misunderstanding will be lifted from our fear-drenched communities and in some not too distant tomorrow the radiant stars of love and brotherhood will shine over our great nation with all of their scintillating beauty.

Yours for the cause of
Peace and Brotherhood

M.L. KING, JR.

5

Democracy and the Student Left

GEORGE F. KENNAN

George Kennan, a leading foreign policy expert, has long been regarded as one of our most independent thinkers. His critique of the student left provoked many replies and counterreplies. Nominally, he is talking about issues different from those discussed by Martin Luther King. Are they really different? Would Kennan agree or disagree with King's main points? How would King regard Kennan's arguments?

These people . . . pose a problem in the quality of their citizenship. One thing they all seem to have in common—the angry ones as well as the quiet ones—is a complete rejection of, or indifference to, the political system of this country. The quiet ones turn their backs upon it, as though it did not concern them. The angry ones reject it by implication, insofar as they refuse to recognize the validity of its workings or to respect the discipline which, as a system of authority, it unavoidably entails.

I think there is a real error or misunderstanding here. If you accept a democratic system, this means that you are prepared to put up with those of its workings, legislative or administrative, with which you do not agree as well as with those that meet with your concurrence. This willingness to accept, in principle, the workings of a system based on the will of the majority, even when you yourself are in the minority, is simply the essence of democracy. Without it there could be no system of representative self-government at all. When you attempt to alter the workings of

the system by means of violence or *civil* disobedience, this, it seems to me, can have only one of two implications: either you do not believe in democracy at all and consider that society ought to be governed by enlightened minorities such as the one to which you, of course, belong; or you consider that the present system is so imperfect that it is not truly representative, that it no longer serves adequately as a vehicle for the will of the majority, and that this leaves to the unsatisfied no adequate means of self-expression other than the primitive one of calling attention to themselves and their emotions by mass demonstrations and mass defiance of established authority. It is surely the latter of these two implications which we must read from the overwhelming majority of the demonstrations that have recently taken place.

I would submit that if you find a system inadequate, it is not enough simply to demonstrate indignation and anger over individual workings of it, such as the persistence of the Vietnam war, or individual situations it tolerates or fails to correct, such as the condition of the Negroes in our great cities. If one finds these conditions intolerable, and if one considers that they reflect no adequate expression either of the will of the majority or of that respect for the rights of minorities which is no less essential to the success of any democratic system, then one places upon one's self, it seems to me, the obligation of saying in what way this political system should be modified, or what should be established in the place of it, to assure that its workings would bear a better relationship to people's needs and people's feelings.

If the student left had a program of constitutional amendment or political reform—if it had proposals for the constructive adaptation of this political system to the needs of our age—if it was *this* that it was agitating for, and if its agitation took the form of reasoned argument and discussion, or even peaceful demonstration accompanied by reasoned argument and discussion—then many of us, I am sure, could view its protests with respect, and we would not shirk the obligation either to speak up in defense of institutions and national practices which we have tolerated all our lives, or to join these young people in the quest for better ones.

But when we are confronted only with violence for violence's sake, and with attempts to frighten or intimidate an administration into doing things for which it can itself see neither the rationale nor the electoral mandate; when we are offered, as the only argument for change, the fact that a number of people are themselves very angry and excited; and when we are presented with a violent objection to what exists, unaccompanied by any constructive concept of what, ideally, ought to exist in its place—then we of my generation can only recognize that such behavior bears a disconcerting resemblance to phenomena we have witnessed within our own time in the origins of totalitarianism in other countries, and then we have no choice but to rally to the defense of a public authority with which we may not be in agreement but which is the only one we've got and with which, in some form or another, we cannot conceivably dispense. People should bear in mind that if this—namely noise, violence and lawlessness—is the way they are going to put their case, then many of us who are

no happier than they are about some of the policies that arouse their indignation will have no choice but to place ourselves on the other side of the barricades.

These observations reflect a serious doubt whether civil disobedience has any place in a democratic society. But there is one objection I know will be offered to this view. Some people, who accept our political system, believe that they have a right to disregard it and to violate the laws that have flowed from it so long as they are prepared, as a matter of conscience, to accept the penalties established for such behavior.

I am sorry; I cannot agree. The violation of law is not, in the moral and philosophic sense, a privilege that lies offered for sale with a given price tag, like an object in a supermarket, available to anyone who has the price and is willing to pay for it. It is not like the privilege of breaking crockery in a tent at the county fair for a quarter a shot. Respect for the law is not an obligation which is exhausted or obliterated by willingness to accept the penalty for breaking it.

To hold otherwise would be to place the privilege of lawbreaking preferentially in the hands of the affluent, to make respect for law a commercial proposition rather than a civic duty and to deny any authority of law independent of the sanctions established against its violation. It would then be all right for a man to create false fire alarms or frivolously to pull the emergency cord on the train, or to do any number of other things that endangered or inconvenienced other people, provided only he was prepared to accept the penalties of so doing. Surely, lawlessness and civil disobedience cannot be condoned or tolerated on this ground. . . .

. . .

. . . [The proposition] . . . that the government in Washington is an oppressive one, along totalitarian lines . . . seems to me not worth serious discussion. I can derive only amusement from the spectacle of students liberally invoking the rights of free speech as a means of arguing that no such thing exists in this country. Several years of residence in both Hitler's Germany and Stalin's Russia qualify me, I think, to say that whoever speaks of the United States government of 1968 as a *totalitarian* government does not know what the word "totalitarian" means. Were it such a government, these student demonstrations and protests would not be taking place at all, and those who are now loudest in their protests would be as still as mice.

One feature of the student outlook that is worth comment is the absence of any visible awareness of the importance of an independent and impartial judiciary in the framework of our political system. This strikes me particularly because it represents so sharp a contrast to my own view of political institutions. Had anyone asked me in recent years which of the foundations of democratic government—the elected executive, the elected legislature, or the independent judiciary—I would least like to part with, or which, if we could have only one of the three, I would most like to retain, I would unhesitatingly have decided for the judiciary. It is better, as I see it, to live under bad laws fairly and impartially administered than to live under good ones for the proper application of which no adequate judicial sanction exists, just as it is better to have narrower rights guaranteed by independent courts than wider ones against the arbitrary denial or curtailment of which there is no judicial recourse. It is not an insignificant fact that during the madness attendant, in the 1940's and early 1950's, on the activities of the late Senator Joseph McCarthy, the only branch of the government that remained substantially unaffected was the judiciary. The Senator's weapon against his victims was the deprivation, or threat of deprivation, of reputation —a punishment which, owing to his own position and the powers generally of con-

gressional committees, he was often able to inflict without involving the law or the courts. Any victim who could contrive to bring his case before a court was, as a rule (there were exceptions), assured of protection. Of all of this, I see . . . no sign of recognition; and I am obliged, once again, to wonder what has been wrong with the teaching of politics in this country, that such a gap in understanding should exist.

. . .

That minorities should have protection from the tyranny of the majority is something nobody would deny. But this does not seem to me to be a danger that is particularly acute in our country, where the traditional system of government rests largely on the veto power of individual minorities and interest groups. It is hard, in fact, to think of any system, unless it be that of the Swiss, which has done better in protecting the interests of minorities. Where American minorities have been oppressed or unjustly treated, it has most often been not the will of the national majority, even as filtered through the corrupting influence of the political machinery, but rather the power of other minorities, social or sectional, that has been at fault. The Southern whites, too, we must remember, are a minority. Are their feelings and interests also to be respected? No, would say the spokesmen of the New Left. Why not? Because they are immoral and unjust. All right, but this then pits the opinion of one minority as to what is just and moral against that of another. If we are to decide these issues on a national, rather than a sectional scale (which I am not, at this point advocating, but which is, surely, the accepted theory of the New Left itself), then who is to strike the balance, if not the national majority?

. . .

6

A Comparative Study of Civil Strife

TED ROBERT GURR

The emergence of large-scale violence in the United States seemed new and danger-ous—perhaps more novel and challenging than facts warranted. Enough concern was generated to have a Presidential Commission examine the phenomenon. The follow-ing is an excerpt from one of the most systematic of the staff reports.

Group protest and violence is episodic in the history of most organized political communities and chronic in many. No coun-try in the modern world has been free of it for as much as a generation. Sorokin analyzed the histories of 11 European states and empires over a 25-century span and found that they averaged only four peace-ful years for each year in which major out-breaks of civil strife were in progress.[1] . . .

Characteristics of American and Foreign Civil Strife

More than 2 million Americans resorted to demonstrations, riots, or terrorism to ex-press their political demands and private antagonisms during the 5 years that ended in May 1968. No more than a fifth of them took part in activities prescribed by law, but their actions reportedly resulted in more than 9,000 casualties, including some 200 deaths, and more than 70,000 arrests. . . . [C]ivil-rights demonstrations mobi-

lized about 1.1 million Americans, antiwar demonstrations about 680,000, and ghetto riots an estimated 200,000. Riots were re-sponsible for most of the consequent human suffering, including 191 deaths, all but a few of them Negroes. Almost all other deaths, an estimated 23, resulted from white terrorism against blacks and civil-rights workers. There is no direct way of determining whether these 5 years were the most tumultuous in American his-tory. . . .

The United States in the mid-1960's ex-perienced relatively more civil strife than the majority of nations in the world, but far less than some. Compared with all other nations, it ranks 24th in total magnitude of strife. When the measures that make up the "magnitude" scores are examined, the United States ranks 27th among nations in the pervasiveness of strife; about 11 out of 1,000 Americans took part in strife, com-pared with an average of 7 per 1,000 in all other countries. The relative intensity of strife in the United States has been con-siderably lower, its proportional casualties ranking 53d among 114 nations; its dura-tion very high, ranking 6th among all na-tions. Most civil strife in the United States was turmoil, in magnitude of which the country ranks 6th among nations. The mag-nitude of conspiracy, which in the United

From Hugh Davis Graham and Ted Robert Gurr, Violence in America, Historical and Comparative Perspectives, *Vol. II (Washington, D.C.: U.S. Gov-ernment Printing Office, 1969), pp. 443–445, 449–452, 481–485.*

[1] *Social and Cultural Dynamics,* Vol. III: *Fluc-tuation of Social Relationships, War, and Revo-lution* (New York: American, 1937), p. 504.

States took the form of interracial terrorism, ranks 38th among all nations.

The most meaningful standard of comparison is provided by the 17 other democratic nations of Western Europe and the British Commonwealth—the nations against which Americans typically judge their cultural, political, and economic progress. In magnitudes of all strife, and of turmoil, the United States ranks first among these nations, though only slightly ahead of France,

Italy, and Belgium; Italy alone had a greater degree of conspiracy in this period. These overall rankings are made more meaningful when the component measures are examined. Strife was more pervasive in six of the European nations than in the United States and more intense in two. Only in the relative duration of strife does the United States markedly surpass all other Western nations.

. . .

TABLE 1

Characteristics and Magnitude of Civil Strife in Selected Nations, 1961–65, Compared with the United States, 1963–68

NATION	PERVASIVENESS (PARTICIPANTS PER 100,000) [a]	DURATION (SUM OF ALL EVENTS) [b]	INTENSITY (CASUALTIES PER 100,0000) [c]	TOTAL MAGNITUDE OF STRIFE
Selected European and Latin nations:				
Sweden	0	0	0	0.0
U.S.S.R.	10	3 months	.5	3.6
Canada	40	5 months	.5	4.9
Mexico	150	1 week	2	4.7
United Kingdom	80	1 year	.5	5.4
Japan	300	2 months	1.0	5.9
Brazil	1,100	4 months	.5	7.4
Belgium	6,700	1 month	6	10.5
France	2,200	2 years	4	12.1
United States	1,100	5 years	5	13.8
Venezuela	1,300	5 years +	120	20.3
Other nations:				
Jamaica	20	1 day	0	1.5
U.A.R. (Egypt)	70	1 month	.5	3.9
Malaya	650	1 day	.5	4.5
Pakistan	200	3 months	1.5	6.3
Ghana	550	1 month	8	7.9
South Africa	600	2 years	3	10.0
Ecuador	1,100	3 months	12	10.1
India	1,600	4 years	1	11.0
Rhodesia	150	2 years	50	16.4
Algeria	900	4 years	150	19.5
Indonesia	1,300	5 years	[d] 4,000	33.7

[a] Total estimated participants in all strife events identified, weighted by population. All figures shown here are rounded to reflect their relative imprecision.

[b] Sum of the duration of all events identified, rounded to reflect the imprecision of the data.

[c] Sum of estimated deaths and injuries in all events identified, weighted by population, rounded to reflect the imprecision of the data.

[d] This figure is probably grossly inflated because it includes an unrealistic estimate of injuries associated with the massacre of several hundred thousand Indonesian Communists. . . .

Differences in Magnitudes of Strife Among World Regions

The forms and magnitudes of civil strife vary greatly among types of nations. . . . The most developed nations have considerably less turmoil and conspiracy than others, and almost never undergo internal wars. The most strife-torn countries are the "developing nations," not the least developed. Differences are equally great among nations grouped by type of political system. The most peaceful nations are the "polyarchic," those which approximate Western democratic forms and processes of government. The centrist countries, those which have autocratic one-party or no-party governments, are only slightly more prone to violence. Strife is likely to be far more pervasive and violent in countries ruled by small, modernizing elites and in nations characterized by unstable, "strongman" rule. It is noteworthy, though, that turmoil is very nearly as great among the democratic nations as it is among all nations; the establishment and survival of democracy are associated with the minimization of conspiracy and internal war, but not of the kinds of demonstrative and riotous protest that have characterized the United States in the past decade.

The countries of Eastern and Western Europe, combined with Israel and the English-settled countries outside of Europe, have had the lowest relative levels of all forms of strife, when compared either with other geocultural regions or the economic and political groupings. When strife does occur in these nations, it is highly likely to take the form of turmoil, internal war almost never. Asian and African nations have the highest levels of internal war and total strife, Latin and Islamic nations somewhat less. Conspiratorial movements are substantially more common in Latin America and tropical Africa than elsewhere.

The final set of comparisons groups nations according to their "racial" homogeneity. Multiracial societies tend to have greater levels of strife of all kinds, not merely turmoil, but the differences are moderate, not great. It is by no means certain that ethnic conflicts are responsible even for these differences. Countries with ethnic diversity also are more likely than others to have regional and political diversities, which also tend to generate internal conflicts.

. . .

Group Participation in Civil Strife

People of almost all walks of life have taken part in civil strife in the United States in the past decade. Civil-rights and peace demonstrations have included tens of thousands of workers, students, and professional people. Ghetto rioters have included relatively large proportions of unskilled workers, but also many of the unemployed, skilled workers, and a few members of the black bourgeoisie.[2] "Backlash" protest and violence have mobilized both working- and middle-class whites. Only public employees have participated relatively little, aside from the tacit support some police have given to white viligante groups and the violent responses of police and soldiers to some riots and some demonstrations.

. . .

A Comparative Interpretation of Civil Strife in the United States

The United States unquestionably has experienced strife of greater intensity and pervasiveness in recent years than all but a very few other Western democracies. It is equally certain that violence in America

[2] For studies of ghetto riot participation, see *Report of the National Advisory Commission on Civil Disorders* (New York: Bantam Books, 1968), pp. 127–35; Governor's Select Commission on Civil Disorder, State of New Jersey, *Report for Action* (Trenton: State of New Jersey, 1968), pp. 129–31; Nathan E. Cohen, "The Los Angeles Riot Study," in Shalom Edleman, ed. *Violence in the Streets* (Chicago: Quadrangle, 1968), pp. 333–46; and Robert M. Fogelson and Robert B. Hill, "Who Riots? A Study of Participation in the 1967 Riots," *Supplemental Studies for the National Advisory Commission on Civil Disorders* (Washington, D.C.: National Advisory Commission on Civil Disorders, 1968), pp. 217–48.

has been less extensive and less disruptive than violence in a substantial number of non-Western nations. Americans have not experienced any strife whose scale or threat to the political order approaches the internal wars of countries like Venezuela, Colombia, the Sudan, or Iraq, much less the grim, nationwide bloodletting of the Congo, Indonesia, South Vietnam, or Yemen. Americans also have had little experience of the chronic revolutionary conspiracy and terrorism that characterizes countries like Algeria, Syria, Guatemala, or any of a dozen other nations. But this is merely to say that conditions in the United States could be worse. They provide little comfort when the tumult of the United States is contrasted with the relative domestic tranquillity of developed democratic nations like Sweden, Great Britain, and Canada, or with the comparable tranquillity of nations as diverse as the Soviet Union, Yugoslavia, Turkey, Malagasy, and Malaya.

Probably the most important general conclusion suggested by the descriptive evidence of the first part of this paper is that civil strife in the United States is different in degree but not in kind from strife in other Western nations. Turmoil is by far the most common form of strife in the United States and in the nations against which we compare ourselves in political, cultural, and economic terms. The antigovernment demonstration and riot, the violent clash of political or ethnic groups, and the student protest are pervasive forms of protest and conflict in modern democracies. Other nations have them in good measure also, but they also are much more likely to have serious conspiratorial and revolutionary movements. Such activities have been no more common in the United States than in other Western nations, despite the lipservice given them. A comparative study of revolutionary movements would suggest that few of the advocates of "revolution" in the United States or most other Western countries have the dedication or skills to organize and sustain an effective revolutionary movement.

. . .

One obvious and distinctive characteristic of civil strife in the United States is the extent to which it is a manifestation of ethnic hostilities. We repeatedly found evidence of parallel problems in other developed, European, and democratic nations. The unsatisfied demands of regional, ethnic, and linguistic groups for greater rights and socioeconomic benefits are more common sources of civil conflict in Western nations than in almost any other group of countries. This is apparent from the relative frequency with which such communal groups initiate strife in Western countries; the frequency with which communal objectives are expressed in strife; and the frequency with which strife includes attacks by members of communal groups on one another. The partial or discriminatory distribution of rights and benefits to minority groups, and the lack of national tolerance for their desires for establishing their own satisfying ways of life, appears to be a pervasive unresolved problem among modern nations. . . .

These findings have some general implications for explaining and resolving civil disorder in the United States. The United States has several of the conditions that in other nations lead directly to civil strife. Persisting deprivation characterizes the lot of most black Americans, whatever lipservice and legal remedies have been given to equality. Repeatedly we found evidence that comparable deprivation is a chronic and all but inevitable source of strife among other nations. If the general relationship holds for the United States, then the country is likely to be afflicted by recurrent racial turmoil as long as ethnic discrimination persists. The United States also has a history of turmoil, which increases the likelihood that all Americans, white and black, will respond to discontent with demonstrative and sometimes violent behavior. Traditions of violence are unalterable in the short run; the discontents whose disruptive effects are magnified by such traditions are susceptible to change.

The United States also has certain characteristics that in other countries tend to minimize the most destructive manifestations of discontent. Most Americans have a high regard for the legitimacy of their political system, however much they may object to some of its policies. If that legitimacy is maintained and reinforced, discontent is unlikely to lead to conspiratorial and revolutionary movements. On the other hand, if policies of government anger enough people badly enough, legitimacy is likely to be undermined. American political and economic institutions are also relatively strong by comparison with most countries of the world, if not by comparison with some Anglo-Nordic nations. Coercive potential also is high: the military and police are numerous and unlikely to support civil violence. Facilitative conditions are low: extremist political organizations have been few and small, and material foreign support for civil strife was and is nonexistent. Such generalizations nonetheless conceal major internal variations. Americans in many cities and regions have been underorganized and underserved by local governments. Police tactics have in many cases been inconsistent and repressive, intensifying rather than minimizing discontent. These conditions can be corrected by strengthening local organizations and improving the quality and training of police. Such policies may reduce levels of violence; if the experience of other nations is a guide, only the resolution of the underlying discontents that give rise to strife will eliminate it.

. . .

7

The First Amendment Has Served Us Well

ROBERT F. DRINAN, S.J.

For years, American schools have emphasized some aspects of religious ceremony in small ways. In a series of Supreme Court decisions, it was held that Bible reading or public prayer in the course of the school day was improper, violating the First Amendment. Protesting this denial of "the prayer throb of the American people," Senator Everett Dirksen of Illinois sought a constitutional amendment to permit "voluntary prayer." In hearings before the Senate Judiciary Committee in 1966, the most effective witness against the proposal was probably Robert Drinan, a Catholic priest, a law school dean, and an authority on constitutional law. Senator Roman Hruska, however, had a few tough questions.

FATHER DRINAN: It is difficult to overstate the significance of the fact that the Bill of Rights has never been amended in all of

From *Statement of Robert F. Drinan, S.J., Dean of the Boston College Law School. School Prayer, Hearings Before the Senate Judiciary Committee, 1967, pp. 7 ff.*

American history. The 10 amendments to the Constitution which spell out the fundamental guarantees have existed there now in a remarkably durable way under the oldest written operative constitution in the world.

The one partially successful attempt in American history to change the first amendment's provisions was the Blaine amendment in 1896, and that proposal, which all but passed the Senate except for one vote, which had been passed by the House of Representatives, would have simultaneously done two things. It would have required Bible reading in the public schools while simultaneously denying any Federal aid or State support for church-related schools. The Blaine amendment reflected the mood at that time and sought somehow to capture the mood and seek the apotheosis of a public school with Bible reading.

Justification therefore for amending the Bill of Rights in the nature of things should be very, very serious. And especially it seems to me, should it be grave when we consider that the 16 words about religion in the first amendment have served us well in this country. . . .

. . .

Let me speak first about the secularization of the public schools.

Since the end of World War II the student population in church-related elementary and secondary schools has more than doubled. These schools—operated by Catholic, Lutheran, Orthodox Jewish, and other groups—now enroll every seventh child who goes to school in America. The unprecedented growth of these institutions in the last 20 years is both the cause and the effect of the secularizing process which has been going on over a long period of time in the public schools.

The private sectarian school seeks to create a religious orientation within its curriculum which will combine with secular learning the essential elements of the Scriptural, sacred, and spiritual values of the Judaeo-Christian culture. The nonpublic church-related school is built on the premise that the orientation of the public school is and must continue to be secular; some advocates of denominational schools would in fact claim that the public school is secularistic—even to the point of unconstitutionally "establishing" a secular or nonreligious philosophy of education.

Whatever one might think about the need or wisdom of private, church-related schools, it is undeniable that the public school has become an institution where religious values may be referred to or taught only in the most general way. It is a school whose only religious orientation is that it has no religious orientation.

The public school has in fact been an institution of this character for a long time; the banning of Bible reading and of prayer by the Supreme Court in 1963 merely stripped away the widespread illusion that the American public school somehow combined piety and learning in an eminently satisfactory way. The various constitutional amendments proposed by Congressmen and Senators to restore to the public schools the last vestiges of their piety—Bible reading and prayer—constitute an almost irrational refusal to surrender one of the most persistent myths in American life—the illusion that the public school can train future citizens in morality and piety.

. . .

Now, as a Catholic and as an educator, I more than most Americans concede and lament the thunderous silence about religion in the public schools. Along with an ever-increasing number of critics of the public schools, I note with regret that virtually all public school administrators have failed to give any leadership or exercise any initiative in establishing courses about religion. . . . And I say categorically that the absence of objective teaching about religion in the public school is one of the most serious educational limitations of public education in this country. Now no one pretends that the structuring of courses about religion or the selection of personnel to teach these courses are easy tasks. But educators would concur that religion should have its place in a public school curriculum which teaches every subject from art to zoology.

There are several feasible and constitutional ways by which the secularization of the public school can be lessened. No one pretends that any of these methods is entirely satisfactory but clearly they offer a more realistic way by which students can actually learn about religion than is offered by the so-called voluntary prayer. Among the clearly available and perfectly constitutional options open to the public school are the following:

1. Released or dismissed time off the school premises, clearly validated in 1952 by the *Zorach* opinion.
2. Teaching about religion. The U.S. Supreme Court went out of its way in the majority and concurring opinions to point out that the Supreme Court in its 1962 and 1963 opinions was not saying anything against the constitutionality of teaching about religion.
3. A study of the Bible. Once again the Court expressly stated that the Bible as literature, the Bible as one of the world's most influential books, certainly can and should be studied.

In view, therefore, of the options that are available to public school educators, which to be sure they have neglected, why is it that anyone can think that a "voluntary" prayer can have any significant effect in neutralizing the impact of 30 hours every week of religionless teaching on the mind and heart of a child? I was requested and strongly urged to testify here today by Catholic, Protestant, and Jewish individuals and organizations, and the overwhelming majority of leaders in all of these three religious bodies is strongly opposed. . . . Why is it then, I ask, that 40 Members of the U.S. Senate introduced in March 1966 a resolution seeking to do that which is directly opposed to the best judgment of virtually all of the religious leaders and denominational groups in the Nation? . . . For what reasons do 40 Senators seek to appear more pious than the churches and more righteous than the Supreme Court?

It is also distressing to me to note that no professional organization of educators, to my knowledge, would endorse an amendment to the Constitution which would permit the recitation of prayers. By what process of reasoning, therefore, do 40 Senators think that they can or should propose an addition to the curriculum of the public schools of this Nation which has not been requested and indeed has been rejected by the vast majority of public school educators in America?

Experts on constitutional law who will support Senate Resolution 148 are as scarce as the religionists and educators who will endorse it. The vast legal literature about the *Engel* and *Schempp* decisions has in general tended to join the consensus among religionists and educators to the effect that an amendment of the Bill of Rights is not the way to bring religion into the public school.

. . .

SENATOR HRUSKA: . . . Would you elaborate on this "truly pathetic desire" of the elected representatives to reflect the thinking and the voices and the desires of those who are responsible for their being in public office?

FATHER DRINAN: It seems to me that Congressmen should decide this on basic constitutional principles, regardless of what the masses or the vast majority or people who write letters say, that they should decide this on educational, religious, constitutional grounds, regardless of how many individuals want more godliness in the schools.

SENATOR HRUSKA: Well, that is an anomaly, really, when you suggest that these elected representatives of the people should decide this on the basis of truly constitutional principles. You see, this is one step of remaking the Constitution. This is not a matter of interpreting the Constitution. This is one of the many steps necessary to change the Constitution.

Now, to what source should these representatives repair in that desire to represent their people? Should they go to the Founding Fathers who said, "Congress shall make no law," should they go back that far or should they go to the present interpretation and say, "No, we will make no change," or should they go to the people? That is the question, should they go to the people they represent?

FATHER DRINAN: You are assuming, Senator, that the people, according to a scientific Gallup poll, are opposed to *Schempp* and

Murray, and I do not think that that is so. That was a 6-to-1 decision, you know, and there was a good deal of controversy about it. But the dust has settled, and I would say that individuals who understand the issues more and more feel that those decisions were correctly decided.

. . .

SENATOR HRUSKA: . . . If there is a substantial difference of opinion, why not let the people decide whether they agree with your view or Senator Dirksen's view as subscribed to by 47 other Senators, and resolve it in that way? Is that an unreasonable request?

FATHER DRINAN: Senator, it can be resolved by litigation. They can bring subsequent cases, as they did in *Stein*—in the *Stein* case in New York. . . .

. . .

SENATOR HRUSKA: Of course, they can litigate and they have litigated, and each time the line gets pushed farther and farther back. But they can also amend the Constitution, can they not?

FATHER DRINAN: Yes, Senator.

8

The President's Crime Commission Meets the Press

MEET THE PRESS

The use of police authority is a peculiarly delicate and vital part of government because it involves thousands of tiny, sensitive decisions. In an increasingly sophisticated society the exercise of authority must also become more sophisticated. But this requires new patterns of thought, and not only on the part of policemen. In 1967 President Johnson's Crime Commission presented the public with new evidence on the nature of crime and social control, new patterns of thinking about dealing with such problems, and some statements concerning old, yet provocative, disagreements. Is crime fundamentally a socially created phenomenon or a reflection of individual failures? Do we "get tough" or work on ameliorating slums? Has there been moral decay in our society?

MR. SPIVAK: Professor Vorenberg, how would you like America to think about crime?

MR. VORENBERG: I think the first step is to move beyond the slogans and the scapegoats that people have used so long to think about crime: claims that police are

From "Meet the Press," The National Broadcasting Company, February 19, 1967. Reprinted by permission of "Meet the Press."

handcuffed or that the young people are going to hell and that all criminals are really sick or misunderstood, that the courts are coddling criminals. These are not only deceiving, they are one of the main reasons so little progress has been made in dealing with the problems of crime, something like a witch doctor chants to avoid facing the fact that the system really needs major surgery or transfusion of money, people and new ideas.

. . .

MR. SPIVAK: Mr. Young, do you conclude that the crime situation in the United States at the present time is a dangerous threat to our society from what you have seen of the Commission report—findings?

MR. YOUNG: I wouldn't say a dangerous threat. I would say it is a serious problem, and I think the great contribution of this Commission is in putting this problem in its proper perspective. I think there has been a tendency to relate crime and Negroes all too often. I think this report really puts it in the proper focus, pointing out as it does with facts and figures, that crime is a phenomenon of socio-economic conditions and not of race, pointing out how the inner-city slums always produce higher crime rates whether they are occupied during a certain period by the Negro or by Italians or by Germans or Poles or Irish, whatever the group might be. In pointing out the implications and the ramifications of poverty and poor housing and its impact upon crime, I think now it puts it in its proper perspective. This is one of the real contributions.

. . .

MR. SPIVAK: Professor Wechsler, a recent article in *The Saturday Evening Post* says, "The American way of dealing with crime, and the people accused of crime, is an unholy and inexcusable mess."

Based on the Commission's findings, will you give us your opinion on that? Do you think it is a mess?

MR. WECHSLER: I think that is a bit of an overstatement, Mr. Spivak. There are good things about it and bad things about it, but insofar as the article points to the general idea that there is one way to deal with crime and that is to hit it hard, with tough prosecution, major penalties, boil the culprits in oil—this general attitude is stupid, ineffective and this report shows why.

. . .

MR. ROWAN: Talking about public attitudes again, do you think the public is prepared to accept this rather broad and compassionate view of crime and criminals?

MR. VORENBERG: I don't think the most optimistic person thinks there will ever be a time when social conditions will eradicate all crime, but I think the combination of trying to deal with the roots of the problem at the same time we are trying to strengthen the operations and the technology of the police and the courts and corrections, I think this is something the people will accept.

MR. ROWAN: But isn't it true that what this report boils down to is a request for massive expenditures for social welfare, for education, for race relations? In short, isn't it a ringing appeal for a greater Great Society?

MR. VORENBERG: I think it is a combination of that, plus an appeal for more resources and ideas in people in the area of law enforcement and corrections themselves. It is both.

. . .

MR. FRANKEL: There is a great debate around the country though on these questions, with many people in law enforcement saying, "We can't do the job if we have to coddle these people and can't even ask a question without a lawyer being around, can't get confessions from people."

Others say, "No, this doesn't really injure the job of the police departments if they were to do it right," and so on. Why didn't the Commission investigate these problems and come up with some studies on whether or not the court has really hampered police enforcement?

MR. CAHILL: Of course I think you have brought up a very good point, Mr. Frankel, because the courts are continually changing our concepts in the field of law enforcement, because of the fact that whether we agree or disagree with the decision, as long as this is the law, we in the field of law enforcement will abide by it. Then we can only change our concepts, elevate our standards and develop new techniques to meet the new challenge.

The Commission actually just did not have the time to go into these particular types of studies in many areas that we would like to. . . .

MR. ROGERS: Mr. Young, as a civil rights leader yourself you are acutely aware that the civil rights movement preaches civil disobedience, sit-ins, lie-ins, refusals to move on and so on.

In your studies with the Commission, did you find that this might have fostered disrespect for the police and thereby add to the rate of crime?

MR. YOUNG: No. I think again one of the great contributions of this Commission was to draw a sharp distinction between legitimate civil rights activity and riots, for example. I think that the attitude of the Negro community which the Commission documented, attitudes of suspicion and hostility in a greater degree than among the white community, was not related to what happened in connection with civil disobedience but was more related to their day-to-day experiences and the fact that the policeman was accessible and a symbol of authority and in many cases many Negroes living in the South, or those who have lived in the South, have suffered at the hand of the policeman who oftentimes was an instrument of maintaining injustice and the status quo.

• • •

MR. SPIVAK: Professor Wechsler, crime, according to the Commission's report, has been increasing at the rate of about 46 per cent during the period, I think, of about five years, while the population itself has increased at a much slower rate. Do you think that this rapid increase of crime compared to the growth of the population is due to a growing disrespect for law? . . .

MR. WECHSLER: As you know, this report presents the most detailed and sophisticated analysis of this problem of increased rates of crime to be presented ever, I think, in the literature of criminology, and there is

nothing in the picture that would lead one to be willing to accept any single simplistic explanation of the sort that you ask about.

The report in great detail shows changes in the percentage of the population represented by people of different age levels. People of different age levels are prone to a greater or lesser degree to commit crimes of particular kinds. It points to factors like the increase in the number of automobiles, for example, which everybody knows about, affects necessarily the number of cars that are stolen.

On the basis of all of this and on the basis of very careful calculations the staff came up with, a conclusion that I think is right, that there has been an appreciable increase in the incidence of crime. Something more than 50 per cent of it is probably mainly attributable to increases in the number of youngsters—relative number of youngsters in the population and the drift to the central cities that has occurred during the period you have in mind. Something less than 50 per cent of the increase is inexplicable in any terms that data can suggest. . . .

MR. SPIVAK: You don't believe then there has been a growing disrespect for law due to the sitdowns, due to the civil rights demonstrations, due to the protest meetings and all the rest? You think that during this past decade there has been no breakdown at all in respect of law?

MR. WECHSLER: This is entirely a personal opinion, but my recollection of the 1920's, when I went to college was that my generation, the class of 1928 in college, hadn't the slightest respect for law indeed. Indeed, we didn't even believe there was a legal system. As a matter of fact, we were almost right about that.

MR. ROWAN: Secretary Katzenbach, let's talk a bit about fighting organized crime.

The Commission says, "The present status of the law with respect to wiretapping and bugging is intolerable. It serves the interests neither of privacy nor of law enforcement. In one way or the other, the present controversy with respect to electronic surveillance must be resolved."

The truth was, the Commission couldn't resolve it, could it?

MR. KATZENBACH: Oh, yes, I think the Commission did resolve it. It said there should be a federal law on this subject, and the Commission unanimously said that federal law should restrict—either abolish or restrict—most rigorously the use of wiretapping or electronic eavesdropping and it should absolutely confine this, if not abolishing it entirely, to the most important category of organized crime-type cases and then in a very limited way with court approval and so forth. So really, there was very little dissension in the Commission in this respect.

The question was whether you cut it out entirely or cut it out almost entirely.

MR. ROWAN: The way I read the report, it says it should be abolished or placed under rigid control when referring to private use. But when talking about fighting crime, it says, "A majority of the members of the Commission believe that legislation should be enacted granting carefully circumscribed authority for electronic surveillance." This implies that a minority didn't feel this way.

MR. KATZENBACH: The minority felt it should be abolished entirely for police officials and for others. The majority felt that police officials might have some occasional use for this, but that should be strictly and rigidly controlled. So the area of difference, Mr. Rowan, between members of the Commission was very, very small, indeed, on this subject.

. . .

MR. STERN: Mr. Young, on page 115 of the report it states, "The Commission does have evidence from its own studies and from police officials themselves that in some cities a significant percentage of policemen assigned to high crime areas do treat citizens with disrespect and sometimes abuse them physically."

. . .

You have indicted all cities though by this general statement. Don't you think it would be fair to those cities not engaged in this practice to indicate which cities do?

MR. YOUNG: No, I think we might have alerted all cities to do a little soul-searching to see whether they were included.

MR. STERN: Chief Cahill, you have sat here silently as Mr. Katzenbach has suggested the recent Supreme Court decisions have not hindered law enforcement. You have sat here silently as Mr. Vorenberg has suggested that the police might stop pointing their fingers at the Supreme Court and get on with the job of law enforcement by themselves.

It is no breach of decorum on this program to disagree with them.

MR. CAHILL: My position has been made very clear on many programs I have appeared on locally in my own city, and my position, I think, is very clear here too. I have made it very clear that progressive police departments, progressive police officers are not going to sit and cry baby shoes. I don't think law enforcement has to make excuses to anybody for the efforts that they have put forth to elevate their standards, to develop the educational background of the persons they are bringing into the field of law enforcement, the proper training, the development of techniques, hardware and all of the uses that we put newfound communications to at the present time.

I still say that I am the one who is closest to the picture. I, as a police officer—I am the man down on the street working with the person. As far as the rulings being handed down by the courts today are concerned, I go back to the same question. I think that in some cases we have forgotten the victim, and the victim also is a member of society. We in law enforcement are attempting to maintain that very delicate balance between the rights of the individual and the rights of society.

If the rights of the individual are so built around, and a fortress of rights are built all around him, then I think society as a whole is going to suffer. . . . [T]he police do have a concern, but again I go back to whatever the law is. We will live with it.

. . .

MR. SPIVAK: Do a large percentage of the poor people, a vast majority of the poor people commit crimes?

MR. YOUNG: No, but most of the crime is committed by poor people. In fact, a study in Washington made by the Stanford University team showed that 90 per cent of the crimes of assault and violence were committed by people making under $5,000.

MR. SPIVAK: But what about the other people who didn't commit crime, did the Commission try to find out why so many people who were poor, decent, self-respecting, hard-working, trying to get out of poverty? Did they look into that at all?

MR. YOUNG: We have to distinguish here between crime. It made quite clear that crimes against property were far greater than crimes against persons, and that in fact crimes of embezzlement and attempts to evade one's tax payments and fraud, that these are crimes that in many cases are much greater in number, and these occur among the very wealthy. But the public reaction is largely to crimes of violence and here again this is greatly overplayed because less than 13 per cent of the crimes in Washington, D.C., for example, are crimes against the person. They are crimes against property.

MR. SPIVAK: Now, I know you are especially interested in the Negro problem. Can you give us any idea why the percentage of crime among the Negroes has been so much higher than among the whites? I think that some of the figures I have seen say that is almost four times as high as among the whites. Thirteen times as high for murder and robbery.

MR. YOUNG: It goes right back to the fact that crime is committed largely by people who are poor, who are circumscribed in their living, who are denied opportunities.

These figures are almost identical with what they were with the Poles, the Irish, the Italian, the German, when they were similarly situated.

But the Negro has had greater difficulty in moving out of the ghetto. I think it is also equally important to point out that the truth of the thing is that much of this crime is directed against the Negro himself. That crime is not inter-racial; it is intra-racial and that the Negro is the greatest victim of that crime, that, actually, in a city like Chicago, the Negro stands six times as much opportunity of being robbed and assaulted as a white person. A Negro who in Chicago has eight times as much chance of being raped as a white person, so the Negro is also the greater victim, and it is very interesting and disturbing to me that all too often we don't get disturbed about the crime among Negroes unless that crime is directed toward white people. Then we get disturbed about it.

. . .

MR. FRANKEL: Professor Wechsler, as I read this material, it seems to me that you were saying something very intriguing that I am not sure the Commission then dealt with explicitly; namely, that although a great deal of the crime in this country is in fact done by the better-off people and they are punished less or able to defend themselves better while committing it, on the other hand, you do have the problem of the attitudes of the poorest of people toward law enforcement, the feeling they are not getting a fair shake at the hands of the law.

Doesn't these two things together cite one of the major problems, namely, that our system of punishment and our system of dealing with criminals is cockeyed, that the embezzler and the tax evader gets a few months in jail, whereas the petty larcenist gets sent up for a few years?

MR. WECHSLER: This is a problem and one of the great needs of the system is to get it looked at afresh and sufficiently objectively so that inequalities and absurdities of this kind are laid on the table and dealt with. I think one of the optimistic features of the present situation is that there is now such a strong disposition to do exactly that. Lawyers who 20 years ago wouldn't soil their hands with criminal law problems are now working at these things. The American Law Institute, the American Bar Association, and judges who handled these matters routinely, 20 or 30 years ago, are really suffering with these problems now, and I sense that we are making progress.

· · ·

MR. ROGERS: Secretary Katzenbach, the Commission surveyed ten thousand households, and you came up with twice as many crimes as the FBI's Uniform Crime Reports, published every year.

Since the FBI report is the best available, how in the world are we going to know what is going on in the world of crime if this is only 50 per cent right?

MR. KATZENBACH: I think the Uniform Crime Reports of the FBI are excellent. They depend on what is reported to them by the police and, of course, the police depend on what is reported to them by the citizens. The significance of that is not so much in the measurement of crime in my judgment as suggesting a new technique which police forces can use to find out whether new measures that they are taking are or are not having any impact within an area. A survey technique, I think we showed, would be feasible in determining this.

MR. ROGERS: Do you think that the public is unduly concerned about crime? There is a note of that in the whole report, that crime is not really bad for you—that you can live with crime.

MR KATZENBACH: No, not at all. I think quite the opposite. I think what we are saying in here is that the public isn't nearly enough concerned about crime and not nearly enough involved in it and, on the other hand, the public is much too much concerned about the wrong kind of crime; that they are concerned about interracial crime that rarely takes place; that they are concerned about what a stranger is going to do to them. Most crimes, at least of violence, are committed by people they know. They have an incorrect picture of crime, but surely they should be concerned about it. I hope this report will help them be more concerned about it.

MR. SPIVAK: Chief Cahill, you are the practical man on this panel of Commission members. I understand that one boy in six is referred to a juvenile court, and that 40 per cent of all male children in the United States will be arrested for non-traffic offenses during their lives. Do you put those figures that high?

MR. CAHILL: I was surprised myself that they were that high. We recognized the fact, because of our statistics in our own department and from the Federal Bureau of Investigation, that it was high. I didn't realize that it was going to be this high, but it certainly does point up to us and to the entire nation that one of the solutions to crime and the area where we are going to have to attack crime in the future is in the area of our youth, because this is a growing segment of our population.

· · ·

MR. SPIVAK: I'd like to ask you one more question on a practical line. Mr. Vorenberg has been reported as saying—and I don't know whether he did, but I will quote it anyhow, "Prison is a lousy place to prepare a guy to live outside a prison."

From your experience would you say that prison, or the fear of prison, plays much of a part in preventing crime?

MR. CAHILL: Again you have to look at the two types of persons we are talking about. You have the hard-core criminal that God above couldn't straighten out. Then you have the other individual who is receptive to proper rehabilitation. These are the persons that we have to work on very, very seriously . . . but then there is the other individual who has to be singled out and recognized, and he is the one who has to be removed from society.

· · ·

MR. ROGERS: Professor Wechsler, the Commission makes a number of sweeping recommendations with respect to the courts, including bringing a lot of sub-rosa practices out in the open like plea bargaining. Do you have any real expectation that the courts will reform themselves along these lines?

MR. WECHSLER: Yes, I have some such expectation. As a matter of fact, there is a very important project going on now in the American Bar Association, the so-called Minimum Standards of Criminal Justice Project, in which committees are examining precisely these types of problems and coming up with standards. These are committees of judges and lawyers, and I have great confidence that these standards, as they get to be approved, will be translated into action.

The one on plea bargaining I think is particularly one where the need for formalization is recognized and where something will happen.

. . .

MR. SPIVAK: One last tough one: If you could only put one recommendation in force, what would it be?

MR. VORENBERG: I think if I could put only one recommendation into effect, it would be the recommendation that the states and cities start tomorrow morning to do the planning that the report talks about.

9

Desegregation: Where Do We Go from Here?

ALEXANDER M. BICKEL

In this arresting article a leading law authority suggests that desegregation has been substantially a failure. Does he view the problem as a moral question? Is he against civil rights? What is the use of solutions that create worse problems? How would he accomplish his suggested modification of Brown v. Board of Education while retaining its moral force?

It will be sixteen years this May since the Supreme Court decreed in *Brown v. Board of Education* that the races may not be segregated by law in the public schools, and six years in July since the doctrine of the *Brown* case was adopted as federal legislative and executive policy in the Civil

From Alexander M. Bickel, "Desegregation: Where Do We Go from Here?" The New Republic, 162, No. 6 (February 7, 1970), 20–22. Reprinted by permission of The New Republic, © 1970, Harrison-Blaine of New Jersey, Inc.

Rights Act of 1964. Yet here we are, apparently struggling still to desegregate schools in Mississippi, Louisiana and elsewhere in the deep South, and still meeting determined resistance, if no longer much violence or rioting.

The best figures available indicate that only some 23 per cent of the nationwide total of more than six million Negro pupils go to integrated public schools. About half the total of more than six million Negro pupils are in the South, and there the percentage of Negroes in school with whites is only 18.

What has gone wrong? The answer is, both less and a great deal more than meets the eye; it is true both that the school desegregation effort has been a considerable success, and that it has not worked.

The measure of the success is simply taken. Sixteen years ago, local law, not only in the 11 Southern states but in border states, in parts of Kansas, in the District of Columbia, forbade the mixing of the races in the schools, and official practice had the same effect in some areas in the North, for example portions of Ohio and New Jersey. Ten years ago, Southern communities were up in arms, often to the point of rioting or closing the public schools altogether, over judicial decrees that ordered the introduction of a dozen or two carefully selected Negro children into a few previously all-white schools. There are counties in the deep South that still must be reckoned as exceptions, but on the whole, the principle of segregation has been effectively denied, those who held it have been made to repudiate it, and the rigid legal structure that embodied it has been destroyed. That is no mean achievement, even though it still needs to be perfected and completed, and it is the achievement of law, which had irresistible moral force, and was able to enlist political energies in its service.

The achievement is essentially Southern. The failure is nationwide. And the failure more than the achievement is coming to the fore in those districts in Mississippi and Louisiana where the Supreme Court and a reluctant Nixon Administration are now enforcing what they still call desegregation on very short deadlines. In brief, the failure is this: To dismantle the official structure of segregation, even with the cooperation in good faith of local authorities, is not to create integrated schools, anymore than integrated schools are produced by the absence of an official structure of school segregation in the North and West. The actual integration of schools on a significant scale is an enormously difficult undertaking, if a possible one at all. Certainly it creates as many problems as it purports to solve, and no one can be sure that even if accomplished, it would yield an educational return.

School desegregation, it will be recalled, began and for more than a decade was carried out under the socalled "deliberate speed" formula. The courts insisted that the principle of segregation and, gradually, all its manifestations in the system of law and administration be abandoned; and they required visible proof of the abandonment, namely, the presence of black children in school with whites. The expectation was that a school district which had been brought to give up the objective of segregation would gradually reorganize itself along other nonracial lines, and end by transforming itself from a dual into a unitary system.

All too often, that expectation was not met. The objective of segregation was not abandoned in good faith. School authorities would accept a limited Negro presence in white schools, and would desist from making overt moves to coerce the separation of the races, but would manage nevertheless to continue operating a dual system consisting of all black schools for the vast majority of Negro children, and of white and a handful of nearly white schools for all the white children. This was sham compliance —tokenism it was contemptuously called, and justly so—and in the past few years, the Supreme Court, and HEW acting under the Civil Rights Act of 1964, determined to tolerate it no longer.

HEW and some lower federal courts first raised the ante on tokenism, requiring stated percentages of black children in school with whites. Finally they demanded that no school in a given system be allowed to retain its previous character as a white or black school. Faculties and administrators had to be shuffled about so that an entirely or almost entirely black or white faculty would no longer characterize a school as black or white. If a formerly all-Negro school was badly substandard, it had to be closed. For the rest, residential zoning, pairing of schools by grades, some busing and majority-to-minority transfers were employed to ensure distribution of both races through the school system. In areas where blacks were in a majority, whites were necessarily assigned to schools in which they could form a minority. All this has by no means happened in every school district in the South, but it constitutes the current practice of desegregation. Thus among the decrees recently enforced in Mississippi, the one applicable in Canton called for drawing an East-West attendance line through the city so that each school became about 70 per cent black and 30 per cent white. Elsewhere schools were paired to the same end.

It bears repeating that such measures were put into effect because the good faith of school authorities was in doubt, to say the least, and satisfactory evidence that the structure of legally enforced segregation had been eliminated was lacking. But whatever, and however legitimate, the reasons for imposing such requirements, the consequences have been perverse. Integration soon reaches a tipping point. If whites are sent to constitute a minority in a school that is largely black, or if blacks are sent to constitute something near half the population of a school that was formerly white or nearly all-white, the whites flee, and the school becomes all or nearly all-black; re-segregation sets in, blacks simply changing places with whites. The whites move, within a city or out of it into suburbs, so that under a system of zoning they are in white schools because the schools reflect residential segregation; or else they flee the public school system altogether, into private and parochial schools.

It is not very fruitful to ask whether the whites behave as they do because they are racists, or because everybody seeks in the schools some sense of social, economic, cultural group identity. Whatever one's answer, the whites do flee, or try to, whether in a Black Belt county where desegregation has been resisted for 16 years in the worst of faith and for the most blatant of racist reasons, or in Atlanta, where in recent years, at any rate, desegregation has been implemented in the best of faith, or in border cities such as Louisville, St. Louis, Baltimore or Washington, D.C., where it

was implemented in good faith 15 years ago, or in Northern cities where legal segregation has not existed in over half a century. It is feckless to ask whether this should happen. The questions to ask are whether there is any way to prevent the whites' fleeing, or whether there are gains sufficient to offset the flight of the whites in continuing to press the process of integration.

To start with the second question, a negative answer seems obvious. What is the use of a process of racial integration in the schools that very often produces, in absolute numbers, more black and white children attending segregated schools than before the process was put into motion? The credible disestablishment of a legally enforced system of segregation is essential, but it ought to be possible to achieve it without driving school systems past the tipping point of resegregation. . . .

. . .

. . . It is relatively simple to make flight so difficult as to be just about impossible for relatively poor whites in rural areas in the South. There is little residential segregation in these areas, and there is no place to move to except private schools. State and local governments can be forbidden to aid such private schools with tuition grants paid to individual pupils, and the Supreme Court has so forbidden them. Private schools can also be deprived of federal tax exemption unless they are integrated, and a federal court in the District of Columbia has at least temporarily so deprived them. They can be deprived of state and local tax aid as well. Lacking any state support, however indirect, for private schools, all but well-to-do or Catholic whites in the rural and small-town South will be forced back into the public schools, although in the longer run, we may possibly find that what we have really done is to build in an incentive to residential segregation, and even perhaps to substantial population movement into cities.

On a normative level, is it right to require a small, rural and relatively poor segment of the national population to submit to a kind of schooling that is disagreeable to them (for whatever reasons, more or less unworthy), when we do not impose such schooling on people, in cities and in other regions, who would also dislike it (for not dissimilar reasons, more or less equally worthy or unworthy)? This normative issue arises because the feasibility question takes on a very different aspect in the cities. Here movement to residentially segregated neighborhoods or suburbs is possible for all but the poorest whites, and is proceeding at a rapid pace. Pursuit of a policy of integration would require, therefore, pursuit of the whites with busloads of inner-city Negro children, or even perhaps with trainloads or helicopter-loads, as distances lengthen. Very substantial resources would thus be needed. They have so far nowhere been committed, in any city.

. . .

Polls asking abstract questions may show what they will about continued acceptance of the goal of integration, but the vanguard of black opinion, among intellectuals and political activists alike, is oriented more toward the achievement of group identity and some group autonomy than toward the use of public schools as assimilationist agencies. And so, while the courts and HEW are rezoning and pairing Southern schools in the effort to integrate them, Negro leaders in Northern cities are trying to decentralize them, accepting their racial character and attempting to bring them under community control. While the courts and HEW are reassigning faculties in Atlanta to reflect the racial composition of the schools and to bring white teachers to black pupils and black teachers to white ones, Negro leaders in the North are asking for black principals and black teachers for black schools.

. . .

Can we any longer fail to acknowledge that the federal government is attempting to create in the rural South conditions that cannot in the forseeable future be attained in large or medium urban centers in the South or in the rest of the country? The government is thus seen as applying its law unequally and unjustly, and is, therefore, fueling the politics of George Wallace. At the same time, the government is also putting itself on a collision course with the aspirations of an articulate and vigorous segment of national Negro leadership. Even if we succeed at whatever cost, in forcing and maintaining massively integrated school systems in parts of the rural South, may we not find ourselves eventually dismantling them again at the behest of blacks seeking decentralized community control?

. . .

. . . The involvement of cohesive communities of parents with the schools is obviously desired by many leaders of Negro opinion. It may bear educational fruit, and is arguably an inalienable right of parenthood anyway. Even the growth of varieties of private schools, hardly integrated, but also not segregated, and enjoying state support through tuition grants for blacks and whites alike, should not be stifled, but encouraged in the spirit of an unlimited experimental search for more effective education. Massive school integration is not going to be attained in this country very soon, in good part because no one is certain that it is worth the cost. Let us, therefore, try to proceed with education.

10

The Failure of Black Separatism

BAYARD RUSTIN

Bayard Rustin was the organizer of the famous March on Washington, perhaps the high point of the civil rights movement. A leading Black intellectual, he is also the spokesman for coalition politics for minorities, particularly with the labor movement. Can an alliance such as the proposed one between blacks and the labor movement be stable? Is separatism desirable as an end in itself, or as an alternative because of the failure of integration? Is Rustin or Bickel closer to reality? Are they both right? Have all courses failed, making open strife the only future?

. . .

. . . There is a new assertion of pride in the Negro race and its cultural heritage, and although the past summer was marked by the lack of any major disruptions, there is among blacks a tendency more pronounced than at any time in Negro history to engage in violence and the rhetoric of violence. Yet if we look closely at the situation of Negroes today, we find that there has been not the least revolutionary reallocation of political or economic power. There is, to be sure, an increase in the number of black elected officials throughout the United States and particularly in the South, but this has largely been the result of the 1965 Voting Rights Act, which was passed before the "revolution" reached its height. . . .

There has been, it is true, some moderate improvement in the economic condition of Negroes, but by no stretch of the imagination could it be called revolutionary. According to Andrew Brimmer of the Federal

From Bayard Rustin, "The Failure of Black Separatism," Harper's, 240, No. 1436 (January, 1970), 25–34. Reprinted by permission of the publisher.

Reserve System, the median family income of Negroes between 1965 and 1967 rose from 54 per cent to 59 per cent of that for white families. Much of that gain reflected a decrease in the rate of Negro unemployment. But between February and June of 1969, Negro unemployment rose again by 1.3 per cent and should continue to rise as Nixon presses his crusade against inflation. The Council of Economic Advisers reports that in the past eight years the federal government has spent $10.3 billion on metropolitan problems while it has spent $39.9 billion on agriculture, not to mention, of course, $507.2 billion for defense. . . .

Any appearance that we are in the grip of a black revolution, then, is deceptive. The problem is not whether black aspirations are outpacing America's ability to respond but whether they have outpaced her willingness to do so. Lately it has been taken almost as axiomatic that with every increase in Negro demands, there must be a corresponding intensification of white resistance. This proposition implies that only black complacency can prevent racial polarization, that any political action by Negroes must of necessity produce a reaction. But such a notion ignores entirely the question of what *kind* of political action, guided by what *kind* of political strategy. One can almost assert as a law of American politics that if Negroes engage in violence as a tactic they will be met with repression, that if they follow a strategy of racial separatism they will be isolated, and that if they engage in anti-democratic activity, out of the deluded wish to skirt the democratic process, they will provoke a reaction. To the misguided, violence, separatism, and minority ultimatums may seem revolutionary, but in reality they issue only from the desperate strivings of the impotent. . . .

The irony of the revolutionary rhetoric uttered in behalf of Negroes is that it has helped in fact to promote conservatism. On the other hand, of course, the reverse is also true: the failure of America to respond to the demands of Negroes has fostered in the minds of the latter a sense of futility and has thus seemed to legitimize a strategy of withdrawal and violence. Other things have been operating as well. The fifteen years since *Brown vs. Topeka* have been for Negroes a period of enormous dislocation. The modernization of farming in the South forced hundreds of thousands of Negroes to migrate to the North where they were confronted by a second technological affliction, automation. Without jobs, living in cities equipped to serve neither their material nor spiritual needs, these modern-day immigrants responded to their brutal new world with despair and hostility. The civil-rights movement created an even more fundamental social dislocation, for it destroyed not simply the legal structure of segregation but also the psychological assumptions of racism. Young Negroes who matured during this period witnessed a basic challenge to the system of values and social relations which had presumed the inferiority of the Negro. They have totally rejected this system, but in doing so have often substituted for it an exaggerated and distorted perception both of themselves and of the society. As if to obliterate the trace of racial shame that might be lurking

in their souls they have embraced racial chauvinism. And as if in reply to past exclusions (and often in response to present insecurities), they have created their own patterns of exclusiveness.

The various frustrations and upheavals experienced recently by the Negro community account in large part for the present political orientation of some of its most vocal members: seeing their immediate self-interest more in the terms of emotional release than in those of economic and political advancement. One is supposed to think black, dress black, eat black, and buy black without reference to the question of what such a program actually contributes to advancing the cause of social justice. Since real victories are thought to be unattainable, issues become important in so far as they can provide symbolic victories. . . . So that, for instance, members of the black community are mobilized to pursue the "victory" of halting construction of a state office building in Harlem, even though it is hard to see what actual economic or social benefit will be conferred on the impoverished residents of that community by their success in doing so.

. . . Deracinated liberals may romanticize this politics, nihilistic New Leftists may imitate it, but it is ordinary Negroes who will be the victims of its powerlessness to work any genuine change in their condition.

The call for Black Power is now over three years old, yet to this day no one knows what Black Power is supposed to mean and therefore how its proponents are to unite and rally behind it. If one is a member of CORE, Black Power posits the need for a separate black economy based upon traditional forms of capitalist relations. For SNCC the term refers to a politically united black community. US would emphasize the unity of black culture, while the Black Panthers wish to impose upon black nationalism the philosophies of Marx, Lenin, Stalin, and Chairman Mao. Nor do these exhaust all the possible shades and gradations of meaning. If there is one common theme uniting the various demands for Black Power, it is simply that blacks must be guided in their actions by a consciousness of themselves as a separate race.

Now, philosophies of racial solidarity have never been unduly concerned with the realities that operate outside the category of race. The adherents of these philosophies are generally romantics, steeped in the traditions of their own particular clans and preoccupied with the simple biological verities of blood and racial survival. Almost invariably their rallying cry is racial self-determination, and they tend to ignore those aspects of the material world which point up divisions within the racially defined group.

But the world of black Americans is full of divisions. Only the most supine of optimists would dream of building a political movement without reference to them. Indeed, nothing better illustrates the existence of such divisions within the black community than the fact that the separatists themselves represent a distinct minority among Negroes. No reliable poll has ever identified more than 15 per cent of Negroes as separatists; usually the percentage is a good deal lower. Nor, as I have already indicated, are the separatists unified among themselves, the differences among them at times being so intense as to lead to violent conflict. The notion of the undifferentiated black community is the intellectual creation of both whites—liberals as well as racists to whom all Negroes are the same—and of certain small groups of blacks who illegitimately claim to speak for the majority.

The fact is that like every other racial or ethnic group in America, Negroes are divided by age, class, and geography. Young Negroes are at least as hostile toward their elders as white New Leftists are toward their liberal parents. They are in addition separated by vast gaps in experience, Northern from Southern, urban from rural. And even more profound are the disparities in

wealth among them. In contrast to the white community, where the spread of income has in recent years remained unchanged or has narrowed slightly, economic differentials among blacks have increased. . . . This trend probably reflects the new opportunities which are available to black professionals in industry, government, and academia, but have not touched the condition of lower-class and lower-middle-class Negroes.

.   .   .

James Forman's *Black Manifesto* . . . provides a nearly perfect sample of . . . bombast combined with positive delusions of grandeur. "We shall liberate all the people in the U.S.," the introduction to the *Manifesto* declares, "and we will be instrumental in the liberation of colored people the world around. . . . We are the most humane people within the U.S. . . . Racism in the U.S. is so pervasive in the mentality of whites that only an armed, well-disciplined, black-controlled government can insure the stamping out of racism in this country. . . . We say think in terms of the total control of the U.S."

One might never imagine from reading the *Manifesto* that Forman's organization, the National Black Economic Development Conference, is politically powerless, or that the institution it has chosen for assault is not the government or the corporations, but the church. Indeed, the exaggeration of language in the *Black Manifesto* is directly proportional to the isolation and impotence of those who drafted it. And their actual achievements provide an accurate measure of their strength. Three billion dollars in reparations was demanded—and $20,000 received. More important, the effect of this demand upon the Protestant churches has been to precipitate among them a conservative reaction against the activities of the liberal national denominations and the National Council of Churches. Forman's failure, of course, was to be expected: the only effect of an attack upon so organizationally diffuse and nonpolitical an institution as the church can be the deflection of pressure away from the society's major political and economic institutions and, consequently, the weakening of the black movement for equality.[1]

The possibility that his *Manifesto* might have exactly the opposite effect from that intended, however, was clearly not a problem to Forman, because the demands he was making upon white people were more moral than political or economic. His concern was to purge white guilt far more than to seek social justice for Negroes. It was in part for this reason that he chose to direct his attack at the church, which, as the institutional embodiment of our society's religious pretensions, is vulnerable to moral condemnation.

. . .

The response of guilt and pity to social problems is by no means new. . . . Two hundred years ago, Samuel Johnson, in an exchange with Boswell, analyzed the phenomenon of sentimentality:

Boswell: "I have often blamed myself, Sir, for not feeling for others, as sensibly as many say they do."
Johnson: "Sir, don't be duped by them any more. You will find these very feeling people are not very ready to do you good. They *pay* you by *feeling*."

Today, payments from the rich to the poor take the form of "Giving a Damn" or some other kind of moral philanthropy. At the same time, of course, some of those who so passionately "Give a Damn" are likely to argue that full employment is inflationary.

We are living in a time of great social confusion—not only about the strategies we must adopt but about the very goals these strategies are to bring us to. Only recently

whites and Negroes of good will were pretty much in agreement that racial and economic justice required an end to segregation and the expansion of the role of the federal government. Now it is a mark of "advancement," not only among "progressive" whites but among the black militants as well, to believe that integration is passé. Unintentionally (or as the Marxists used to say, objectively), they are lending aid and comfort to traditional segregationists like Senators Eastland and Thurmond. Another "advanced" idea is the notion that government has gotten too big and that what is needed to make the society more humane and livable is an enormous new move toward local participation and decentralization. One cannot question the value or importance of democratic participation in the government, but just as misplaced sympathy for Negroes is being put to use by segregationists, the liberal preoccupation with localism is serving the cause of conservatism. Two years of liberal encomiums to decentralization have intellectually legitimized the concept, if not the name, of states' rights and have set the stage for the widespread acceptance of Nixon's "New Federalism."

The new anti-integrationism and localism may have been motivated by sincere moral conviction, but hardly by intelligent political thinking. It should be obvious that what is needed today more than ever is a political strategy that offers the real possibility of economically uplifting millions of impoverished individuals, black and white. Such a strategy must of necessity give low priority to the various forms of economic and psychological experimentation that I have discussed, which at best deal with issues peripheral to the central problem and at worst embody a frenetic escapism. These experiments are based on the assumption that the black community can be transformed from within when, in fact, any such transformation must depend on structural changes in the entire society. Negro poverty, for example, will not be eliminated in the absence of a total war on poverty.

[1] Forman is not the only militant today who fancies that his essentially reformist program is revolutionary. Eldridge Cleaver has written that capitalists regard the Black Panther Breakfast for Children program (which the Panthers claim feeds 10,000 children) "as a threat, as cutting into the goods that are under their control." He also noted that it "liberates" black children from going to school hungry each morning. I wonder if he would also find public-school lunch programs liberating.

We need, therefore, a new national economic policy. We also need new policies in housing, education, and health care which can deal with these problems as they relate to Negroes within the context of a national solution. A successful strategy, therefore, must rest upon an identification of those central institutions which, if altered sufficiently, would transform the social and economic relations in our society; and it must provide a politically viable means of achieving such an alteration.

Surely the church is not a central institution in this sense. . . .

. . .

While the church, private enterprise, and other institutions can, if properly motivated, play an important role, finally it is the trade-union movement and the Democratic party which offer the greatest leverage to the black struggle. The serious objective of Negroes must be to strengthen and liberalize these. The trade-union movement is essential to the black struggle because it is the only institution in the society capable of organizing the working poor, so many of whom are Negroes. It is only through an organized movement that these workers, who are now condemned to the margin of the economy, can achieve a measure of dignity and economic security. I must confess I find it difficult to understand the prejudice against the labor movement currently fashionable among so many liberals. These people, somehow for reasons of their own, seem to believe that white workers are affluent members of the Establishment (a rather questionable belief, to put it mildly, especially when held by people earning over $25,000 a year) and are now trying to keep the Negroes down. The only grain of truth here is that there *is* competition between black and white workers which derives from a scarcity of jobs and resources. But rather than propose an expansion of those resources, our stylish liberals underwrite that competition by endorsing the myth that the unions are the worst enemy of the Negro.

In fact it is the program of the labor movement that represents a genuine means for reducing racial competition and hostility. Not out of a greater tenderness of feeling for black suffering—but that is just the point. Unions organize workers on the basis of common economic interests, not by virtue of racial affinity. Labor's legislative program for full employment, housing, urban reconstruction, tax reform, improved health care, and expanded educational opportunities is designed specifically to aid both whites and blacks in the lower- and lower-middle classes where the potential for racial polarization is most severe. And only a program of this kind can deal simultaneously and creatively with the interrelated problems of black rage and white fear. It does not placate black rage at the expense of whites, thereby increasing white fear and political reaction. Nor does it exploit white fear by repressing blacks. Either of these courses strengthens the demagogues among both races who prey upon frustration and racial antagonism. Both of them help to strengthen conservative forces—the forces that stand to benefit from the fact that hostility between black and white workers keeps them from uniting effectively around issues of common economic interest.

. . .

The bitterness of many young Negroes today has led them to be unsympathetic to a program based on the principles of trade unionism and electoral politics. Their protest represents a refusal to accept the condition of inequality, and in that sense, it is part of the long, and I think, magnificent black struggle for freedom. But with no comprehensive strategy to replace the one I have suggested, their protest, though militant in rhetoric and intention, may be reactionary in effect.

. . . My strategy is not meant to appeal to the fears of threatened whites, though it would calm those fears and increase the likelihood that some day we shall have a truly integrated society. It is not meant to serve as an outlet for the terrible frustrations of Negroes, though it would reduce those frustrations and point a way to dignity for an oppressed people. It is simply a vehicle by which the wealth of this nation can be redistributed and some of its more grievous social problems solved. . . . In fact, if I may risk a slight exaggeration, by normal standards of human society I think it would constitute a revolution.

6

PUBLIC OPINION AND
INTEREST GROUPS:
WHO SPEAKS FOR ME?

Few concepts in democracy are more widely held and more fluently expressed than the belief in the validity of public opinion. The American literary tradition is full of lyrical references to "the sovereignty of the people," and our everyday language contains such aphorisms as "You can't fool all of the people all of the time," or "Know the truth and the truth shall make you free."

In the middle of the nineteenth century, Abraham Lincoln said, "Public sentiment is everything," and a few years later James Bryce referred to our political system as "government by popular opinion." This idealistic appraisal of public opinion was rudely shattered after World War I by the opinion theorists who, using the tools and findings of some of the new social sciences, tended to discount or deglamorize the earlier exaltations. New concepts of mass and individual psychology, many emphasizing the irrational and emotional bases of opinion, refuted or at least modified some of the previous assumptions.

Walter Lippmann published *Public Opinion* and *The Phantom Public* in the 1920's. Both of these books reappraised the nature of public opinion and the role of the average man in the process of self-government. In the 1950's there were alarming concerns that the passive persuasiveness of mass media and the "engineering of consent" would do serious damage to the integrity and critical power of public opinion. Today there is still great solicitude regarding the impact of mass media and the danger of manipulation by public opinion experts. However, there may be a trend toward more confidence in public opinion, or at least a greater feeling of the importance of public opinion. As V.O. Key, Jr., points out, "Unless mass views have some place in the shaping of public policy, all the talk about democracy is nonsense."

From a consideration of public opinion it is just one short step to a discussion of lobbying activity and interest groups. Public opinion, like all forms of social interaction, has a group basis. Groups meet, have opinions, and take public positions. Their views are frequently expressed with great skill and great effectiveness.

The following chapter discusses the role of public opinion and lobbying activity in representative government. The material is presented in the framework of two issues—"Public Opinion: The Voice of the People or Manipulation by the Public Persuaders?" and "Interest Group Politics: Domination or Balance of Forces?"

Public Opinion: The Voice of the People or Manipulation by the Public Persuaders?

Do the people have the same opportunity to be heard as they had a century ago? Is public opinion becoming merchandized and manipulated? How powerful is the public relations industry? Some students of contemporary trends see great danger in the combination of electronic communication and "the engineering of consent." Other writers take a more relaxed view of the present scene, pointing out that there are protections built into the system. For example, there are many publics and subpublics, and we know the things that sway one public will alienate another. We also know there is a difference between the "attentive" public and the public at large, and that public opinion may be silent as well as active. The latent public serves as a check upon irresponsible and unrestrained leadership. Finally, there is a system of interaction between democratic leadership and the mass, and in this interaction public opinion rules an area within which permissive governmental discussion and action may occur.

The classic role of public opinion in democratic theory assumed open and effective channels of communication. What happens when these channels become less open and tend to be dominated by the few? What is the consequence of new and persuasive media and the rise of a skilled group of public persuaders who can use the media for particular purposes? Television is a case in point. We are rapidly moving into a "television environment" and its effect upon our traditional democratic institutions is not yet known. Will we make television serve the communication and election processes, or will the medium become controlled by the affluent who will hire proficient public persuaders to manipulate our consent?

The first part of this chapter deals with several problems arising from the use of television in the political process. Joe McGinniss writes on "The Breaking, Making, and Selling of a President" with special references to the 1968 presidential election. Vice President Spiro Agnew discusses "The Bias in the Media," while Federal Communications Commissioner Nicholas Johnson addresses himself to the topic of "Government By Television."

Interest Group Politics: Domination or Balance of Forces?

Every individual is born into a group, and unless a person becomes a Robinson Crusoe or a recluse in Death Valley, he maintains his natural group identity. The individual must inevitably pay a price for his group membership. Yet, the rewards of self-identity and societal identity more than compensate for the limitations imposed upon unfettered individuality. It is through the group and associational interaction that a person exerts political influence and affects the formation of public policy. David B. Truman states, "The process of government cannot be adequately understood. . . . Apart from the groups . . . which are operative at any point in time." In the broadest sense, all groups are political (as agents of socialization or structures of authority). However, some groups are more political than others. A ladies' bridge group is usually less political (although it may talk more) than a woman's county political committee. The importance of groups in political action should not make us overlook the individual. Groups are simply collections of individuals more or less in concert. Furthermore, leadership is almost always an individual matter.

Groups are more effective than individuals in making demands upon the government and in bargaining with other groups and with the agents of government. Obviously some groups are more effective than others. The political power of any group depends upon interest and participation of members, speed in mobilization for action, degree of cohesiveness, ability to apply sanctions and to pledge members, leadership, and skill or finesse in operation. Perhaps even more important in determining the strength of a group is the matter of numbers, their concentration in key areas, and, at the same time, their spread throughout the United States. Farmers and postal workers have considerable political influence because of their dispersal over wide geographic areas.

The old concepts of lobbying and interest group action are virtually obsolete. It was formerly thought interest groups were smaller and narrower in focus than political parties. Today some interest groups are larger than some minor parties (AFL-CIO vs. Socialist party) and are broader in scope and exert greater influence in their demands upon the government (AFL-CIO vs. Prohibition party). In a similar manner, most of our checks on lobbyists are ineffective. The techniques of passive persuasion far outrun our capacity to understand or control.

It was thought at one time that a rough balance of power formula permitted groups to equalize each other in influence. We now know that this is not necessarily true, and instead of balance we may get a situation analogous to an "elephant dancing around in a chicken coop and shouting 'every man for himself.'" [1] Furthermore, we seem to be moving to a situation in which huge numbers of interest groups (the Military-indus-

[1] U.S. Congress, House Select Committee on Lobbying Activities, *General Interim Report* (Washington, D.C.: U.S. Government Printing Office, 1950), p. 9.

trial complex) combine with other groups and command unprecedented power. Some observers believe that the entire system (corporate liberalism) is stacked against certain minority and powerless groups. Criticism of interest group liberalism asserts: 1) interest groups are not representative; 2) the canceling-out character of interest groups may demand too many compromises and thus frustrate necessary emergency programs; 3) government planning and overall government programs are often sidetracked by narrow interest groups.

James Deakin discusses lobbying from the vantage point of a Washington correspondent; Lester W. Milbrath analyzes it from the perspective of a political scientist. Theodore J. Lowi makes a case against interest group liberalism, while John W. Gardner reasserts his faith in the lobby of the people.

1

The Breaking, Making, and Selling of a President

JOE MCGINNISS

In the process of making political choices, do you think the individual is helped or hindered by television? What recommendations would you make to prevent the medium from becoming the message, i.e., the dominant factor, in political campaigns? What specific restrictions should be placed upon the use of television in order to close the gap between the image and reality of a candidate? Should the open market and the dollar be the sole restraints upon the use of television in campaigning?

Politics, in a sense, has always been a con game.

The American voter, insisting upon his belief in a higher order, clings to his religion, which promises another, better life; and defends passionately the illusion that the men he chooses to lead him are of finer nature than he.

It has been traditional that the successful politician honor this illusion. To succeed today, he must embellish it. Particularly if he wants to be President.

"Potential presidents are measured against an ideal that's a combination of leading man, God, father, hero, pope, king, with maybe just a touch of the avenging Furies thrown in," an adviser to Richard Nixon wrote in a memorandum late in 1967. Then, perhaps aware that Nixon qualified only as father, he discussed improvements that would have to be made—not upon Nixon himself, but upon the image of him which was received by the voter.

That there is a difference between the individual and his image is human nature. Or American nature, at least. That the difference is exaggerated and exploited electronically is the reason for this book.

Advertising, in many ways, is a con game, too. Human beings do not need new automobiles every third year; a color television set brings little enrichment of the human experience; a higher or lower hemline no expansion of consciousness, no increase in the capacity to love.

It is not surprising, then, that politicians and advertising men should have discovered one another. And, once they recognized that the citizen did not so much vote for a candidate as make a psychological purchase of him, not surprising that they began to work together.

The voter, as reluctant to face political reality as any other kind, was hardly an unwilling victim. "The deeper problems connected with advertising," Daniel Boorstin has written in *The Image*, "come less from the unscrupulousness of our 'deceivers' than from our pleasure in being deceived, less from the desire to seduce than from the desire to be seduced. . . .

"In the last half-century we have misled ourselves . . . about men . . . and how much greatness can be found among them. . . . We have become so accustomed to our illusions that we mistake them for reality. We demand them. And we demand that there be always more of them, bigger and better and more vivid."

The Presidency seems the ultimate extension of our error.

Advertising agencies have tried openly to sell Presidents since 1952. When Dwight Eisenhower ran for reelection in 1956, the agency of Batton, Barton, Durstine and Osborn, which had been on a retainer throughout his first four years, accepted his campaign as a regular account. Leonard Hall, national Republican chairman, said: "You sell your candidates and your programs the way a business sells its products."

The only change over the past twelve years has been that, as technical sophistication has increased, so has circumspection. The ad men were removed from the parlor but were given a suite upstairs.

What Boorstin says of advertising: "It has meant a reshaping of our very concept of truth," is particularly true of advertising on TV.

With the coming of television, and the knowledge of how it could be used to seduce voters, the old political values disappeared. Something new, murky, undefined started to rise from the mists. "In all countries," Marshall McLuhan writes, "the party system has folded like the organization chart. Policies and issues are useless for election purposes, since they are too specialized and hot. The shaping of a candidate's integral image has taken the place of discussing conflicting points of view."

Americans have never quite digested television. The mystique which should fade grows stronger. We make celebrities not only of the men who cause events but of the men who read reports of them aloud.

The televised image can become as real to the housewife as her husband, and much more attractive. Hugh Downs is a better breakfast companion, Merv Griffin cozier to snuggle with on the couch.

Television, in fact, has given status to the "celebrity" which few real men attain. And the "celebrity" here is the one described by Boorstin: "Neither good nor bad, great nor petty . . . the human pseudo-event . . . fabricated on purpose to satisfy our exaggerated expectations of human greatness."

This is, perhaps, where the twentieth century and its pursuit of illusion have been leading us. "In the last half-century," Boorstin writes, "the old heroic human mold has been broken. A new mold has been made, so that marketable human models—modern 'heroes'—could be mass-produced, to satisfy the market, and without any hitches. The qualities which now commonly make a man or woman into a 'nationally advertised' brand are in fact a new category of human emptiness."

The television celebrity is a vessel. An

inoffensive container in which someone else's knowledge, insight, compassion, or wit can be presented. And we respond like the child on Christmas morning who ignores the gift to play with the wrapping paper.

Television seems particularly useful to the politician who can be charming but lacks ideas. Print is for ideas. Newspapermen write not about people but policies; the paragraphs can be slid around like blocks. Everyone is colored gray. Columnists—and commentators in the more polysyllabic magazines—concentrate on ideology. They do not care what a man sounds like; only how he thinks. For the candidate who does not, such exposure can be embarrassing. He needs another way to reach the people.

On television it matters less that he does not have ideas. His personality is what the viewers want to share. He need be neither statesman nor crusader; he must only show up on time. Success and failure are easily measured: How often is he invited back? Often enough and he reaches his goal—to advance from "politician" to "celebrity," a status jump bestowed by grateful viewers who feel that finally they have been given the basis for making a choice.

The TV candidate, then, is measured not against his predecessors—not against a standard of performance established by two centuries of democracy—but against Mike Douglas. How well does he handle himself? Does he mumble, does he twitch, does he make me laugh? Do I feel warm inside?

Style becomes substance. The medium is the massage and the masseur gets the votes.

In office, too, the ability to project electronically is essential. We were willing to forgive John Kennedy his Bay of Pigs; we followed without question the perilous course on which he led us when missiles were found in Cuba; we even tolerated his calling of reserves for the sake of a bluff about Berlin.

We forgave, followed, and accepted because we liked the way he looked. And he had a pretty wife. Camelot was fun, even

for the peasants, as long as it was televised to their huts.

Then came Lyndon Johnson, heavy and gross, and he was forgiven nothing. He might have survived the sniping of the displaced intellectuals had he only been able to charm. But no one taught him how. Johnson was syrupy. He stuck to the lens. There was no place for him in our culture.

"The success of any TV performer depends on his achieving a low-pressure style of presentation," McLuhan has written. The harder a man tries, the better he must hide it. Television demands gentle wit, irony, understatement: the qualities of Eugene McCarthy. The TV politician cannot make a speech; he must engage in intimate conversation. He must never press. He should suggest, not state; request, not demand. Nonchalance is the key word. Carefully studied nonchalance.

Warmth and sincerity are desirable but must be handled with care. Unfiltered, they can be fatal. Television did great harm to Hubert Humphrey. His excesses—talking too long and too fervently, which were merely annoying in an auditorium—became lethal in a television studio. The performer must talk to one person at a time. He is brought into the living room. He is a guest. It is improper for him to shout. Humphrey vomited on the rug.

It would be extremely unwise for the TV politician to admit such knowledge of his medium. The necessary nonchalance should carry beyond his appearance while *on* the show; it should rule his attitude *toward* it. He should express distaste for television; suspicion that there is something "phony" about it. This guarantees him good press, because newspaper reporters, bitter over their loss of prestige to the television men, are certain to stress anti-television remarks. Thus, the sophisticated candidate, while analyzing his own on-the-air technique as carefully as a golf pro studies his swing, will state frequently that there is no place for "public relations gimmicks" or "those show business guys" in his campaign. Most of the television men working for him will be unbothered by such remarks.

They are willing to accept anonymity, even scorn, as long as the pay is good.

Into this milieu came Richard Nixon: grumpy, cold, and aloof. He would claim privately that he lost elections because the American voter was an adolescent whom he tried to treat as an adult. Perhaps. But if he treated the voter as an adult, it was as an adult he did not want for a neighbor.

This might have been excused had he been a man of genuine vision. An explorer of the spirit. Martin Luther King, for instance, got by without being one of the boys. But Richard Nixon did not strike people that way. He had, in Richard Rovere's words, "an advertising man's approach to his work," acting as if he believed "policies [were] products to be sold the public—this one today, that one tomorrow, depending on the discounts and the state of the market."

So his enemies had him on two counts: his personality, and the convictions—or lack of such—which lay behind. They worked him over heavily on both.

Norman Mailer remembered him as "a church usher, of the variety who would twist a boy's ear after removing him from church."

McLuhan watched him debate Kennedy and thought he resembled "the railway lawyer who signs leases that are not in the best interests of the folks in the little town."

But Nixon survived, despite his flaws, because he was tough and smart, and—some said—dirty when he had to be. Also, because there was nothing else he knew. A man to whom politics is all there is in life will almost always beat one to whom it is only an occupation.

He nearly became President in 1960, and that year it would not have been by default. He failed because he was too few of the things a President had to be—and because he had no press to lie for him and did not know how to use television to lie about himself.

It was just Nixon and John Kennedy and they sat down together in a television studio and a little red light began to glow and Richard Nixon was finished. Television would be blamed but for all the wrong reasons.

They would say it was makeup and lighting, but Nixon's problem went deeper than that. His problem was himself. Not what he said but the man he was. The camera portrayed him clearly. America took its Richard Nixon straight and did not like the taste.

The content of the programs made little difference. Except for startling lapses, content seldom does. What mattered was the image the viewers received, though few observers at the time caught the point.

McLuhan read Theodore White's *The Making of The President* book and was appalled at the section on the debates. "White offers statistics on the number of sets in American homes and the number of hours of daily use of these sets, but not one clue as to the nature of the TV image or its effects on candidates or viewers. White considers the 'content' of the debates and the deportment of the debaters, but it never occurs to him to ask why TV would inevitably be a disaster for a sharp intense image like Nixon's and a boon for the blurry, shaggy texture of Kennedy." In McLuhan's opinion: "Without TV, Nixon had it made."

What the camera showed was Richard Nixon's hunger. He lost, and bitter, confused, he blamed it on his beard.

. . .

Image-builder Harry Treleaven, advertising creative writer hired in 1967.

[Nixon's lack of humour] can be corrected to a degree but let's not be too obvious about it. Romney's cornball attempts have hurt him. If we're going to be witty let a pro write the words. [On lack of warmth. . . .] He can be helped greatly in this respect by how he is handled . . . give him words that will show his *emotional* involvement in the issues . . . he should be presented in some kind of situation rather than cold in a studio. The situation should look unstaged even if it's not.

Image-builder Raymond K. Price, campaign speech-writer.

[Rational arguments will] only be effective if we can get people to make the emotional leap or what the theologians call "leap of faith." [And on personal factors involving low opinion of Nixon. . . .] These tend to be more a gut reaction, unarticulated, non-analytical, a product of the particular chemistry between the voter and the image of the candidate. We have to be very clear on this point; that the response is to the image, not to the man. . . .

Image-builder Jim Howard, Chicago public relations man on campaign team.

Never let a candidate wear a hat he does not feel comfortable wearing. You can't sell the candidate like a product. A product, all you want to do is to get attention. You only need two per cent additional buyers to make the campaign worthwhile. In politics you need a flat 51 per cent. of the market, and you can't get that through gimmicks.

Nixon's campaigners pick a Jewish psychiatrist for a TV confrontation.

"You're not going to believe this but Nixon hates psychiatrists."

"What?"

"Nixon hates psychiatrists. He's got this thing, apparently. They make him very nervous. You should have heard Len on the phone when I told him I had one on the panel. Did you hear him? If I ever heard a guy's voice turn white, that was it."

"Why?"

"He said he didn't want to go into it. But apparently Nixon won't even let one in the same room."

Image-builder Roger Ailes, producer, in charge of Nixon's TV appearances.

Let's face it, a lot of people think Nixon is dull. Think he's a bore, a pain in the ass. They look at him as a kind of kid who always carried a book bag. Who was forty-two years old the day he was born. They figure other kids got footballs for Christmas, Nixon got briefcases and loved it. He'd always have his homework done and he'd never let you copy. Now you put him on television and you've got a problem right away. He's a funny-looking guy. He looks like somebody hung him in a closet overnight and he jumps out in the morning with his suit all bunched up and starts running around saying "I want to be President." I mean this is how he strikes some people. That's why these shows are important. To make them forget all that.

Image-builder William Gavin, 31-year-old teacher hired in 1967.

[I recommend] saturation with a film in which the candidate can be shown better than he can be shown in person because it can be edited so only the best moments are shown . . . [Nixon] has to come across as a person larger than life, the stuff of legend. People are stirred by legend, including the living legend, not by the man himself. It's the aura that surrounds the charismatic figure more than it is the figure itself that draws the followers. Our task is to build that aura. . . .

. . .

Scripts

On the pages that follow are the complete scripts of a representative sampling of the spot commercials made by E.S.J. Productions, Inc., for Richard Nixon.

TWO VERSIONS:

:60 seconds
:40 seconds

E.S.J. #2
"ORDER"

VIDEO	*AUDIO*
1. OPENING NETWORK DISCLAIMER: "A POLITICAL ANNOUNCEMENT."	
2. FADEUP ON RAPIDLY MOVING SEQUENCE OF RIOTING, URBAN MOB MOTIVATING TO CROWDS TAUNTING POLICE AUTHORITIES.	SFX UP FULL. SFX UNDER.
3. FLAMING APT. HOUSE DISSOLVING TO POLICE PATROLLING DESERTED STREETS IN AFTERMATH OF VIOLENCE.	R.N. It is time for some honest talk about the problem of order in the United States.
4. PERPLEXED FACES OF AMERICANS.	R.N. Dissent is a necessary ingredient of change. But in a system of government that provides for peaceful change—
5. SEQUENCE OF SHOTS OF PEOPLE MOVING THROUGH BATTERED STREETS BORDERED BY DESTROYED SHOPS AND HOMES.	—there is no cause that justifies resort to violence. There is no cause that justifies rule by mob instead of by reason.
6. ELOQUENT FACES OF AMERICANS WHO HAVE LIVED THROUGH SUCH EXPERIENCES, CLIMAXED BY SINGLE SHOT OF CHARRED CROSSBEAMS FRAMING A RIOT RUIN. IN CENTER OF PICTURE IS BATTERED MACHINE ON WHICH CAN STILL BE SEEN IN RED LETTERS THE WORD "CHANGE." FADEOUT.	MUSIC UP AND OUT.
7. FADEUP TITLE: "THIS TIME VOTE LIKE YOUR WHOLE WORLD DEPENDED ON IT."	
8. DISSOLVE TO TITLE WORD "NIXON." ZOOM TO CU. HOLD. FADEOUT.	
9. CLOSING NETWORK DISCLAIMER: "THE PRECEDING PRE-RECORDED POLITICAL BROADCAST WAS PAID FOR BY THE NIXON-AGNEW CAMPAIGN COMMITTEE."	

2

Bias in the Media

VICE PRESIDENT SPIRO AGNEW

Vice President Agnew's attack on the news media has been widely publicized. In your opinion, did the news media overrespond to his remarks? Or is the implied danger of government pressure on the integrity of the news media too great a threat to ignore? How do you reconcile Mr. Agnew's assertion that news commentators have a liberal bias and do not give a Republican President's remarks a fair analysis with Senator Fulbright's contention that the President has unmatched access to television? What responsibility does the government have in preventing or modifying the concentration of channels of communication? How would you evaluate Mr. Agnew's suggestion that the TV networks should follow the example of the newspapers in separating news stories from editorials?

Tonight I want to discuss the importance of the television news media to the American people. No nation depends more on the intelligent judgment of its citizens. No medium has a more profound influence over public opinion. Nowhere in our system are there fewer checks on vast power. So, nowhere should there be more conscientious responsibility exercised than by the news media. The question is are we demanding enough of our television news presentations? And are the men of this medium demanding enough of themselves?

Monday night a week ago, President Nixon delivered the most important address of his Administration, one of the most important of our decade. His subject was Vietnam. His hope was to rally the American to see the conflict through to a lasting and just peace in the Pacific. For 32 minutes, he reasoned with a nation that

---

From speech by Vice President Spiro Agnew to the Mid-West Regional Republican Committee, Des Moines, Iowa, November 13, 1969, as recorded by The New York Times, *November 14, 1969, p. 24.*

has suffered almost a third of a million casualties in the longest war in its history.

Weeks of Preparation

When the President completed his address—address, incidentally, that he spent weeks in the preparation of—his words and policies were subjected to instant analysis and querulous criticism. The audience of 70 million Americans gathered to hear the President of the United States was inherited by a small band of network commentators and self-appointed analysts, the majority of whom expressed in one way or another their hostility to what he had to say.

It was obvious that their minds were made up in advance. Those who recall the funbling and groping that followed President Johnson's dramatic disclosure of his intention not to seek another term have seen these men in a genuine state of nonpreparedness. This was not it.

One commentator twice contradicted the President's statement about the exchange of correspondence with Ho Chi Minh. Another challenged the President's abilities as a politician. A third asserted that the President was following a Pentagon line. Others, by the expression on their faces, the tone of their questions and the sarcasm of their responses made clear their sharp disapproval.

To guarantee in advance that the President's plea for national unity would be challenged, one network trotted out Averell Harriman for the occasion. Throughout the President's message, he waited in the wings. When the President concluded, Mr. Harriman recited perfectly. He attacked the Thieu Government as unrepresentative; he criticized the President's speech for various deficiencies; he twice issued a call to the Senate Foreign Relations Committee to debate Vietnam once again; he stated his belief that the Vietcong or North Vietnamese did not really want a military takeover of South Vietnam; and he told a little anecdote about a "very, very responsible" fellow he had met in the North Vietnamese delegation.

All in all, Mr. Harriman offered a broad range of gratuitous advice—challenging and contradicting the policies outlined by the President of the United States. Where the President had issued a call for unity, Mr. Harriman was encouraging the country not to listen to him.

About Mr. Harriman

A word about Mr. Harriman. For 10 months he was America's chief negotiator at the Paris peace talks—a period in which the United States swapped some of the greatest military concessions in the history of warfare for an enemy agreement on the shape of the bargaining table. Like Coleridge's Ancient Mariner, Mr. Harriman seems to be under some compulsion to justify his failure to anyone who will listen. And the networks have shown themselves willing to give him all the air time he desires.

Now every American has a right to disagree with the President of the United States and to express publicly that disagree-

ment. But the President of the United States has a right to communicate directly with the people who elected him, and the people of this country have the right to make up their own minds and form their own opinions about a Presidential address without having a President's words and thoughts characterized through the prejudices of hostile critics before they can even be digested.

When Winston Churchill rallied public opinion to stay the course against Hilter's Germany, he didn't have to contend with a gaggle of commentators raising doubts about whether he was reading public opinion right, or whether Britain had the stamina to see the war through.

When President Kennedy rallied the nation in the Cuban missile crisis, his address to the people was not chewed over by a roundtable of critics who disparaged the course of action he'd asked America to follow.

The purpose of my remarks tonight is to focus your attention on this little group of men who not only enjoy a right of instant rebuttal to every Presidential address, but, more importantly, wield a free hand in selecting, presenting and interpreting the great issues in our nation.

First, let's define that power. At least 40 million Americans every night, it's estimated, watch the network news. Seven million of them view A.B.C., the remainder being divided between N.B.C. and C.B.S.

A Sole Source of News

According to Harris polls and other studies, for millions of Americans the networks are the sole source of national and world news. In Will Rogers' observation, what you knew was what you read in the newspapers. Today for growing millions of Americans, it's what they see and hear on their television sets.

Now how is this network news determined? A small group of men, numbering perhaps no more than a dozen anchormen, commentators and executive producers, settle upon the 20 minutes or so of film and commentary that's to reach the public. This selection is made from the 90 to 180 minutes that may be available. Their powers of choice are broad.

They decide what 40 to 50 million Americans will learn of the day's events in the nation and in the world.

We cannot measure this power and influence by the traditional democratic standards, for these men can create national issues overnight. They can make or break by their coverage and commentary a moratorium on the war.

They can elevate men from obscurity to national prominence within a week. They can reward some politicians with national exposure and ignore others.

For millions of Americans the network reporter who covers a continuing issue—like the ABM or civil rights—becomes, in effect, the presiding judge in a national trial by jury.

It must be recognized that the networks have made important contributions to the national knowledge—for news, documentaries and specials. They have often used their power constructively and creatively to awaken the public conscience to critical problems. The networks made hunger and black lung disease national issues overnight. The TV networks have done what no other medium could have done in terms of dramatizing the horrors of war. The networks have tackled our most difficult social problems with a directness and an immediacy that's the gift of their medium. They focus the nation's attention on its environmental abuses—on pollution in the Great Lakes and the threatened ecology of the Everglades.

But it was also the networks that elevated Stokely Carmichael and George Lincoln Rockwell from obscurity to national prominence.

Nor is their power confined to the substantive. A raised eyebrow, an inflection of the voice, a caustic remark dropped in the middle of a broadcast can raise doubts in a million minds about the veracity of a public official or the wisdom of a Government policy.

One Federal Communications Commissioner considers the powers of the networks equal to that of local, state and Federal Governments all combined. Certainly it represents a concentration of power over American public opinion unknown in history.

Now what do Americans know of the men who wield this power? Of the men who produce and direct the network news, the nation knows practically nothing. Of the commentators, most Americans know little other than that they reflect an urbane and assured presence seemingly well-informed on every important matter.

We do know that to a man these commentators and producers live and work in the geographical and intellectual confines of Washington, D.C., of New York City, the latter of which James Reston terms the most unrepresentative community in the entire United States.

Provincialism Charged

Both communities bask in their own provincialism, their own parochialism.

We can deduce that these men read the same newspapers. They draw their political and social views from the same sources. Worse, they talk constantly to one another, thereby providing artificial reinforcement to their shared viewpoints.

Do they allow their biases to influence the selection and presentation of the news? David Brinkley states objectivity is impossible to normal behavior. Rather, he says, we should strive for fairness.

Another anchorman on a network news show contends, and I quote: "You can't expunge all your private convictions just because you sit in a seat like this and a camera starts to stare at you. I think your program has to reflect what your basic feelings are. I'll plead guilty to that."

Less than a week before the 1968 election, this same commentator charged that President Nixon's campaign commitments were no more durable than campaign balloons. He claimed that, were it not for the fear of hostile reaction, Richard Nixon

would be giving into, and I quote him exactly, "his natural instinct to smash the
enemy with a club or go after him with a
meat axe."

Had this slander been made by one political candidate about another, it would
have been dismissed by most commentators
as a partisan attack. But this attack ema-
nated from the privileged sanctuary of a
network studio and therefore had the apparent dignity of an objective statement.

The American people would rightly not
tolerate this concentration of power in Government.

Fair and Relevant

Is it not fair and relevant to question its
concentration in the hands of a tiny, en-
closed fraternity of privileged men elected
by no one and enjoying a monopoly sanctioned and licensed by Government?

The views of the majority of this fraternity do not—and I repeat, not—represent
the views of America.

That is why such a great gulf existed between how the nation received the President's address and how the networks received it.

Not only did the country receive the
President's address more warmly than the
networks, but so also did the Congress of
the United States.

Yesterday, the President was notified that
300 individual Congressmen and 50 Senators of both parties had endorsed his efforts
for peace.

As with other American institutions, perhaps it is time that the networks were made
more responsive to the views of the nation
and more responsible to the people they
serve.

Now I want to make myself perfectly
clear. I'm not asking for Government censorship or any other kind of censorship. I'm
asking whether a form of censorship already
exists when the news that 40 million Americans receive each night is determined by
a handful of men responsible only to their
corporate employers and is filtered through
a handful of commentators who admit to
their own set of biases.

The questions I'm raising here tonight
should have been raised by others long
ago. They should have been raised by those
Americans who have traditionally considered the preservation of freedom of speech
and freedom of the press their special provinces of responsibility.

They should have been raised by those
Americans who share the view of the late
Justice Learned Hand that right conclusions
are more likely to be gathered out of a
multitude of tongues than through any kind
of authoritative selection.

Advocates for the networks have claimed
a First Amendment right to the same unlimited freedoms held by the great newspapers of America.

Situations Not Identical

But the situations are not identical. Where
The New York Times reaches 800,000 people, N.B.C. reaches 20 times that number
on its evening news.

The average weekday circulation of The
Times in October was 1,012,367; the average Sunday circulation was 1,523,558.

Nor can tremendous impact of seeing
television film and hearing commentary be
compared with reading the printed page.

A decade ago before the network news
acquired such dominance over public opinion, Walter Lippmann spoke to the issue.
He said there's an essential and radical difference between television and printing.
The three or four competing television stations control virtually all that can be received over the air by ordinary television
sets. But besides the mass circulation dai-
lies, there are weeklies, monthlies, out-of-
town newspapers and books. If a man
doesn't like his newspaper, he can read another from out of town or wait for a weekly
news magazine. It's not ideal, but it's infinitely better than the situation in television.

House Report Cited

There if a man doesn't like what the
networks are showing, all he can do is turn

them off and listen to a phonograph. Networks he stated which are few in number have a virtual monopoly of a whole media of communications.

The newspapers of mass circulation have no monopoly on the medium of print.

Now a virtual monopoly of a whole medium of communication is not something that democratic people should blindly ignore. And we are not going to cut off our television sets and listen to the phonograph just because the airways belong to the networks. They don't. They belong to the people.

As Justice Byron White wrote in his landmark opinion six months ago, it's the right of the viewers and listeners, not the right of the broadcasters, which is paramount.

Now it's argued that this power presents no danger in the hands of those who have used it responsibly. But as to whether or not the networks have abused the power they enjoy let us call as our first witness former Vice President Humphrey and the city of Chicago. According to Theodore White, television's intercutting of the film from the streets of Chicago with the current proceedings on the floor of the convention created the most striking and false political picture of 1968—the nomination of a man for the American Presidency by the brutality and violence of merciless police.

If we are to believe a recent report of the House of Representatives Commerce Committee, then television's presentation of the violence in the streets worked an injustice on the reputation of the Chicago police. According to the committee findings, one network in particular presented, and I quote, a one-sided picture which in large measure exonerates the demonstrators and protesters. Film of provocations of police that was available never saw the light of day while the film of a police response which the protesters provoked was shown to millions.

Another network showed virtually the same scene of violence from three separate angles without making clear it was the same scene. And, while the full report is reticent in drawing conclusions, it is not a document to inspire confidence in the fairness of the network news.

Serious Questions Raised

Our knowledge of the impact of network news on the national mind is far from complete, but some early returns are available. Again, we have enough information to raise serious questions about its effect on a democratic society. Several years ago Fred Friendly, one of the pioneers of network news, wrote that its missing ingredients were conviction, controversy and a point of view—the networks have compensated with a vengeance.

And in the networks' endless pursuit of controversy, we should ask: What is the end value—to enlighten or to profit? What is the end result—to inform or to confuse? How does the ongoing exploration for more action, more excitement, more drama serve our national search for internal peace and stability?

Gresham's Law seems to be operating in the network news. Bad news drives out good news. The irrational is more controversial than the rational. Concurrents can no longer compete with dissent.

One minute of Eldridge Cleaver is worth 10 minutes of Roy Wilkins. The labor crisis settled at the negotiating table is nothing compared to the confrontation that results in a strike—or better yet, violence along the picket lines.

Normality has become the nemesis of the network news. Now the upshot of all this controversy is that a narrow and distorted picture of America often emerges from the televised news.

A single dramatic piece of the mosaic becomes in the minds of millions the entire picture. And the American who relies upon television for his news might conclude that the majority of Americans feel no regard for their country. That violence and lawlessness are the rule rather than the exception on the American campus.

We know that none of these conclusions is true.

Perhaps the place to start looking for a

credibility gap is not in the offices of the Government in Washington but in the studios of the networks in New York.

Quiet Men Less Known

Television may have destroyed the old stereotypes but has it not created new ones in their places?

What has this passionate pursuit of controversy done to the politics of progress through local compromise essential to the functioning of a democratic society?

The members of Congress of the Senate who follow their principles and philosophy quietly in a spirit of compromise are unknown to many Americans, while the loudest and most extreme dissenters on every issue are known to every man in the street.

How many marches and demonstrators would we have if the marchers did not know that the ever-faithful TV cameras would be there to record their antics for the next news show.

We've heard demands that Senators and Congressmen and judges make known all their financial connections so that the public will know who and what influences their decisions and their votes. Strong arguments can be made for that view.

But when a single commentator or producer, night after night, determines for millions of people how much of each side of a great issue they are going to see and hear, should he not first disclose his personal views on the issue as well?

In this search for excitement and controversy, has more than equal time gone to the minority of Americans who specialize in attacking the United States—its institutions and its citizens?

Tonight I've raised questions. I've made no attempt to suggest the answers. The answers must come from the media men. They are challenged to turn their critical powers on themselves, to direct their energy, their talent and their conviction toward improving the quality and objectivity of news presentation.

They are challenged to structure their own civic ethics to relate their great feeling with the great responsibilities they hold.

And the people of America are challenged, too, challenged to press for responsible news presentations. The people can let the networks know that they want their news straight and objective. The people can register their complaints on bias through mail to the networks and phone calls to local stations. This is one case where the people must defend themselves; where the citizen, not the Government, must be the reformer; where the consumer can be the most effective crusader.

Dependent on Media

By way of conclusion, let me say that every elected leader in the United States depends on these men of the media. Whether what I've said to you tonight will be heard and seen at all by the nation is not my decision, it's not your decision, its their decision.

In tomorrow's edition of *The Des Moines Register*, you'll be able to read a news story detailing what I've said tonight. Editorial comment will be reserved for the editorial page where it belongs.

Should not the same wall of separation exist between news and comment on the nation's networks?

Now, my friends, we'd never trust such power, as I've described, over public opinion in the hands of an elected Government. It's time we questioned it in the hands of a small and unelected elite.

The great networks have dominated America's airwaves for decades. The people are entitled to a full accounting of their stewardship.

3

Government by Television

NICHOLAS JOHNSON

FCC Commissioner Nicholas Johnson quotes Senator Fulbright: ". . . the President's power to use television . . . has done as much to expand the powers of his office as would a constitutional amendment formally abolishing the co-equality of the three branches of Government." Can you cite examples to support Senator Fulbright's assertion? What would be the effects of giving the opposition party equal time for every Presidential speech? Would it be practical/possible to do this? Why do you suppose Nicholas Johnson recommends that "candidates should be forbidden to use time in less than five-minute segments"?

. . . This is really only a superficial beginning to a project which I believe should occupy some of the best minds in the U.S. and elsewhere for some time: the examination and close study of television as a power phenomenon in American politics. As Senator J. W. Fulbright recently testified:

Communication is power and exclusive access to it is a dangerous, unchecked power. . . . As matters now stand, the President's power to use television in the service of his policies and opinions has done as much to expand the powers of his office as would a constitutional amendment formally abolishing the co-equality of the three branches of Government.

Self-evident as that statement appears to me, we are only beginning to grapple with its implications. We, all of us, FCC Commissioners, political consultants, citizens of the world, have a vital interest in collecting data, and simply informing ourselves, about this phenomenon.

The press bears a special opportunity and

responsibility in this regard. It must investigate and expose the charades and facades. And it must develop its own traditions, including firm positions on pressure it will not tolerate—such as subpoenas and calls from Directors of Communications. The public must be educated about the uses of, and pressures upon, the media.

There is a precedent for this in the British tradition. Although the Prime Minister has the authority to ask that a certain program not be shown on the BBC, that power has not been exercised, for one simple reason: can you imagine the public reaction to the simple announcement that "the program originally scheduled for this time segment has been censored by the Prime Minister." Suppose ABC had said: "In deference to President Nixon's wishes, we have decided not to broadcast the Buffalo University Band's peace program."

We need ground rules as to when the President can command TV time, and when, if ever, he is entitled to all three networks rather than just one.

We need ground rules as to when the opposition party is entitled to reply to the President. Perhaps we can benefit from the British concept of a "loyal opposition"

From speech by Commissioner Nicholas Johnson to the International Convention of Political Consultants, London, England, December 13, 1970.

which is entitled to regular access to television as a means of informing the electorate.

One response of the party out of power may be the selection of Presidential candidates much earlier than the present nominating conventions. There is no way a 535-man Congress (or even the Democratic "leadership") can effectively rebut the President in the personality-oriented medium of television. There simply has to be but one opposition spokesman. We may see the day when the party out of power nominates its next presidential candidate two years before the President's term expires in order to permit him to play his role and build up a following before the election. Indeed, there are those who believe the supporters of Senator Muskie have already pulled off precisely that result when he was "nominated" to be the Democratic spokesman to answer President Nixon this last election eve.

We need ground rules on television advertising, particularly with respect to "spot" television ads. You gentlemen have a vital interest in this subject, because those spots have tarnished your own image and made a disparaging epithet of the word "image-maker."

Members of your fraternity have told me that they would often prefer to show longer portraits of their candidates but are unable to do so because the networks simply refuse to jeopardize their ratings. If this is so, it is in your interest, and the Nation's interest, for you to speak out and work to change this situation.

I would predict that there will be longer time periods used in the future, either because the Courts, Congress or FCC will require it, or the broadcasters will permit it under threat of such a ruling. I would also predict that there will be an increasing emphasis on "reality"—candidates who come across as their honest-as-possible selves. So many viewers are by now so hardened to the commercial slick sell that, as some of you observed this past election, the political commercials themselves are becoming issues in the campaigns. This is based upon nothing but feel. But, as the American musician/poet Mason Williams has said, "In the process of selling to America, business has created an America that will no longer buy its products. Their how blew their what." I think you gentlemen may find yourselves the victims of the same phenomenon. I suspect that a great deal of the cynicism on the part of many of the young and old alike about politics can be traced to the TV commercials backlash: if it's on TV it's probably not true, not good for you, overpriced, and of questionable moral and ethical value. (Polls reveal that 20 per cent of those Americans who watched the moon landing—"Brought to you by the Gulf Oil Company"—refuse to believe that it wasn't just another phony commercial television program.) Television communicates a lot more about a candidate than his words—especially when the setting, his dress, or his expressions and gestures communicate that the words are untrue or hollow. I believe the increasing demand for real live human beings in politics is going to continue, whether in spite of or because of you. Indeed, the disappointment and disgust over the lack of responsiveness of both major political parties to other than military and corporate demands now raises the very real possibility of at least a "stand by" fourth party, ready to spring into action in all 50 states if the major parties do not adequately reform themselves by 1972. But you can be helpful in choosing your candidates, and their programs, and I hope you will be.

Finally, I want to present a series of proposals for your consideration; I would like to receive your comments and suggestions on these proposals, as well as on the subject I have discussed with you today.

1. Television time should be made available free to all candidates for public office.
2. This time should be equally apportioned among all major party candidates, and made available to others based upon the votes received in prior elections or the number of signatures on petitions.
3. The purchase of any additional political time on television should be prohibited.

4. Candidates should be forbidden to use time in less than five-minute segments.
5. When political propaganda films and advertising techniques are used, such presentations should be followed immediately by time during which the candidate is shown by the station in a setting over which he has no control, such as a debate, press conference or news interview.

4

A Washington Correspondent Looks at Lobbying

JAMES DEAKIN

Why is the popular image of lobbying misleading? Is it true that "he who pays the piper calls the tune" in American politics? How does the author justify his contention that if there were no Washington lobbyists we would have to create some?

Politicians come and politicians go, as the public chooses. But the lobbyist—the hardy, resourceful agent of the non-public interest—goes on forever.

Lobbyists have been called a secret, invisible arm of government. Washington's lobbying corps has been nicknamed "the third house of Congress" and "the fourth branch of government." Both labels attest to the intimate relationship between lobbying and government. Often the nicknames have been less complimentary: "influence peddlers," "fixers," "five percenters" and, in an earlier day, "boodlers."

To apply these epithets indiscriminately to all lobbyists today is both inaccurate and unfair. The modern lobbyist is more likely to be a technician, competent and well informed in his field. He performs a vital function in furnishing Congress with facts and information. But he is more than a technician of facts. He is a technician of pressure. He exerts pressure on those who make the laws.

From James Deakin, The Lobbyists *(Washington, D.C.: Public Affairs Press, 1966), pp. 1–8, 12–15. Reprinted by permission of the publisher.*

Washington swarms with lobbyists. It always has and probably always will. More than 1,100 individuals and organizations are currently registered as lobbyists, which means that, on the face of things, they outnumber the 535 members of Congress by two to one. But the real ratio is much higher than that. Because the law regulating lobbying is virtually a dead letter, a horde of company representatives, public relations men, lawyers and organizations engaged in influencing government in one way or another do not register as lobbyists. There are at least 8 to 10 lobbyists for every member of Congress.

No group in Washington is more controversial than these gentlemen. Their operations are scrutinized occasionally—and usually unfavorably—by Congress, the President and the press. But remarkably little is known about the lobbyists themselves and what they do.

They are an immensely diverse crew.

A lady named Margo Cairns has been gently pressuring Congress for years to adopt the corn tassel as the national floral emblem. She is a lobbyist.

Attorney Charles Patrick Clark represents

Franco Spain and various well-heeled clients to the tune of $200,000 a year, about twice the salary of the President of the United States. He is a lobbyist.

A group of Washington teen-agers organized a campaign to persuade Congress to vote more money for the capital's dilapidated schools. Several of the students registered under the lobbying law. They were lobbyists.

Frank Ikard, a former Texas Congressman, registered as a lobbyist shortly after he became executive vice president of the American Petroleum Institute at a salary of $50,000 a year. While in Congress Ikard was a member of the House Ways and Means Committee, which has jurisdiction over such matters as oil depletion allowances. At the present time he is president of the institute.

A "retired" couple, Harry and Ruth Kingman, pound the marble corridors of Congress in unceasing, selfless pursuit of votes for public interest legislation, including civil rights and federal aid to education. Kingman, a former Y.M.C.A. executive in his seventies, and his wife, in her sixties, are the entire staff of the Citizens' Lobby for Freedom and Fair Play. Their organization has an annual budget of just over $8,000, most of which comes from Kingman's pension. They are lobbyists.

Stephen G. Slipher, an assistant vice president of the powerful United States Savings and Loan League, is in the $40,000 to $50,000-a-year bracket. His assistant, Glenwood S. Troop, makes more than $25,000 a year. So does Sidney Zagri, legislative counsel for the International Brotherhood of Teamsters. Former Congressman Andrew Biemiller, head of the AFL-CIO's legislative department, draws about $20,000 per year. All these men are lobbyists. . . .

If there were no lobbyists, as Voltaire said of God, we would have to invent some. In effect the founding fathers authorized lobbying. As a result of some frustrating experiences with George the Third, they decided the American people must have a guaranteed right of access to their new government. Lobbying followed, inevitably.

Today lobbying is so inextricably bound up with the governmental process that it is often hard to tell where the legislator leaves off and the lobbyist begins.

Lobbyists draft much of the legislation introduced in Congress. Some lobbyists estimate that fully half of the bills dropped in the hopper are written in whole or part by pressure groups. Lobbyists write and present much of the testimony heard by Congressional committees. Lobbyists and special interest spokesmen ghostwrite many of the speeches given in Congress.

The public relations firm of Selvage and Lee, Inc., representing the Overseas Companies of Portugal, admitted writing speeches on Portuguese policy in Angola for 14 legislators. One of them was Representative Joseph W. Martin Jr., Massachusetts Republican and former Speaker. Selvage and Lee boasted that Martin "used [our] stuff without change, apart from abbreviation."

Lobbyists have been known to use Congressmen's offices as their own, sometimes with long-distance telephone calls and stenographic help thrown in, all at the taxpayers' expense.

Lobbyists take an intimate part in the continual wheeling and dealing, the conferring, negotiating and compromising that go on in the formation of laws.

Not surprisingly, there are some distasteful connotations to the word lobbyist. In the minds of a good many Americans it conjures up disreputable images. It suggests a sinister character slinking through the halls of Congress, trailing behind the faint aroma of thousand-dollar bills. To the cringing Congressman, desperately in need of ready cash to meet his alimony, the overhead on his yacht and the demands of his Lolita, this crafty traducer dispenses the long green from a handy little black bag. In return for which the fawning legislator cheerfully sells the Republic down the river. After the vote, of course, there is the nightly orgy at the palatial manse of the beautiful Washington hostess who is having an illicit affair with this or that prominent Senator, and all clink glasses in a toast to another good day's work.

Bribes, blondes and booze—these are the durable ingredients in the popular image of lobbying and an everlasting boon to writers for slick magazines and Sunday supplements. The changing nature of American politics, however, has reduced the importance of all three as elements in pressure and power.

There are no reliable statistics on cash bribery and outright corruption, since the participants seldom advertise and cannot be depended upon to answer questionnaires truthfully. But students of government agree that the direct bribe—once a standard lobbying technique—is not a major factor today. The campaign contribution, perfectly legal and absolutely vital to most members of Congress, is another matter. The campaign donation, not the out-and-out bribe, is an important weapon in modern lobbying. But even it is far from being the only way in which money is used to influence the course of government.

Some authorities caution that the campaign contribution can be overrated as a means of gaining influence and exerting pressure. Professor Alexander Heard, who made a thorough study of money in American politics, concluded that "he who pays the piper does not always call the tune, at least not in politics. Politicians prize votes more than dollars."

Nevertheless, many Washington lobbyists are heavy contributors to the national party committees and to individual Congressmen. Furthermore, their contributions frequently go to members of Congressional committees which handle legislation directly affecting the interests of their clients. To interpret all campaign gifts by lobbyists as altruistic donations, as contributions given purely out of desire for good government, would be risky. But to view them only as bribes is to ignore the realities of government. They fall somewhere in between.

Sex is, if anything, a more dubious factor in lobbying today than the bribe. Sex is nice, but it doesn't necessarily swing votes.

There are several reasons for this. Extramarital dalliance is politically dangerous for the married Congressman. And if he is a chaser despite his vows, he does not have to depend on the lobbyist as a source of supply. Washington is freshly furnished each year with a new stock of callipygian young things eager to work on Capitol Hill. The amateurs always outnumber the pros.

This is not to say that Washington is sexless. The amatory proclivities of some lawmakers are an endless source of gossip at the equally endless cocktail parties. But the lobbyist who uses girls in his work is more likely to find himself obtaining them for his out-of-town clients and employers on their trips to Washington than for Congressmen. There are exceptions, but generally speaking, bedroom gymnastics have little real impact on the business of making laws. For one thing, the older legislators who dominate Congress, and who are the objects of the lobbyist's tenderest concern, are not easily swayed by women. They have other vices, other rheums. Their main and enduring vice is power.

There are differences of opinion about the third item in the popular lobbying trilogy—entertainment (including, of course, liquor). When political scientist Lester W. Milbrath interviewed 100 Washington lobbyists, he found that they gave entertaining a very low rating. On an effectiveness scale of 0 to 10, entertainment scored a median of 1.17. The lobbyists explained that members of Congress and other top officials are deluged with invitations, that some of these are "required" social events which they feel they must attend, and that they are under such pressure to go to parties that an evening spent at home with the family "seems like a gift."

Nevertheless, the lobbyists do a lot of entertaining. It has been estimated that 1,500 large cocktail parties complete with receiving line and music—"alcoholic mass meetings," one reporter has called them—take place in Washington each year. Besides these are numberless at-home dinners and parties, large and small. Not all of these affairs are given by lobbyists. The diplomatic corps, the military and the Mmes. Mesta and Cafritz are unflagging. But lobbyists are among the most indefatigable partygivers.

A veteran staff member of a Senate subcommittee subject to intense lobbying pressures advised:

"Don't leave out the parties. They're damned important, especially with the new Congressmen. . . ."

Washington is a very practical town, and money and votes mean more than liquor. In the final analysis, this is why bribes, blondes and booze don't rank as high as they once did in the lobbyist's scheme of things. They just aren't as important to the Congressman (to his political survival, which is his first law) as votes, and the money with which to get votes. The legislator may accept the lobbyist's entertainment, and gladly, but he is far more likely to do what the lobbyist wants if votes are involved.

Entertainment remains an important lobbying technique, but its principal function is to create and maintain good will. It is not usually a major determining factor in the legislative process. Some lobbyists explain that they wine and dine the lawmakers primarily because their clients expect them to, not because they believe it will have a direct impact on legislation. Many businessmen, they say, assume that what works corporately will work governmentally. The experienced lobbyist may consider this naive, but to tell the client would be to jeopardize the expense account, so the partying goes on.

There are always, of course, the sleazy, fly-by-night operators, holding forth over drinks in the crowded hotel bars on Capitol Hill, talking big, and willing, for a price, to try to "reach" a Congressman with a thinly-veiled campaign contribution, a drinking bout or a party girl. These are the shady, not-so-clever gentry who end up in the headlines. It makes spicy reading, but the point to remember is that this kind of thing seldom affects the course of government in any significant degree.

After an extensive investigation of lobby-ing, a House committee headed by the late Representative Frank Buchanan of Pennsylvania discussed the changed character of lobbying. "In the 1870's and 1880's, 'lobbying' meant direct, individual solicitation of legislators, with a strong presumption of corruption attached," the committee said. But in the middle of the twentieth century, the Buchanan report went on, it means something quite different.

"Modern pressure on legislative bodies is rarely corrupt . . . it is increasingly indirect, and [it is] largely the product of group rather than individual effort," said the committee. The key words are "indirect" and "group."

Indirect pressure consists of campaigns to whip up public opinion for or against a piece of legislation. These campaigns almost always are organized and directed by lobbyists or lobbying groups. Indirect pressure, also known as grassroots lobbying, is one of the prime techniques of modern lobbying. In terms of the money spent and the impact on the public interest, it is the most important technique. It has the greatest effect on the legislator simply because it involves a large number of actual or potential votes.

Group pressure, as the Buchanan committee pointed out, means that large organizations, possessing the financial resources required to organize grassroots pressure, and commanding substantial blocs of votes, are the most significant factor in lobbying today. The massive, heavily-financed grassroots campaign is the trademark of modern lobbying, not the cash-under-the-table, babes-in-the-bedroom approach of the nineteenth century entrepreneur.

The individual lobbyist is, of course, still with us and always will be. He is as important as ever, but these days he usually operates with a big corporation, a trade association or a labor union behind him. He regularly combines direct lobbying and persuasion of Congressmen with organized indirect pressure from the legislators' constituents back home. . . .

. . .

The conventional image of lobbying unfortunately misses both the good and the bad sides of the subject. Conceiving of the lobbyist only as tempter and corrupter, it ignores his very real contribution to the process of making laws. The Congressman confronted with an annual mountain of complicated legislation and distracted by the problems of his constituents, must rely on the lobbyist for facts, statistics and information. This is the informational side of lobbying, and it is essential.

The immense complexities of the American economy make it impossible for Congress to legislate without informed, expert assistance. It must know, as accurately as possible, how a law will affect the diverse elements of the economy. One means of transmitting this information is the lobbyist.

In the case of federal highway legislation, for example, the late Senator Richard L. Neuberger of Oregon commented that three substantial segments of the economy felt that their interests were directly at stake: the truck lines, the railroads because the truck lines are their principal competitors for freight, and the American Automobile Association because the motorist pays most of the cost of building the highways.

"Lobbyists for these groups paraded to my office constantly," Neuberger reported.

"They presented vast quantities of facts and figures—some of which I challenged, but a lot of which were accurate and impressive. No improper inducement ever was ventured. Without the data made available by railroads and truckers and the A.A.A., I doubt if I would have felt fully qualified to reach a decision on the kind of highway bill which was best for the nation."

From the founding days of the Republic it has been recognized that special interest groups must be represented in some way in the councils of government. . . .

. . . Professor Heard has observed that "no popular government in history has yet survived that did not in some way permit such interests to exercise effective means of petition."

The interplay of special interests in the formation of laws is considered one of the strengths of democracy. It is vital to the survival of the democratic system that groups with well-defined interests—business and industry, labor, farmers, veterans, teachers, professional men, women's groups and so on—have a way of communicating with the legislature. Many devices are used to make this communication possible. The lobbyist is one of them. He is an agent of the special interest group, the nonpublic interest.

5

A Political Scientist Looks at Lobbying

LESTER W. MILBRATH

How does the author support the position that "the overall impact of lobbying is relatively minor"? What are the best safeguards against irresponsibility and possible corruption in lobbying activity? What positive contribution does lobbying make to the political process?

The weight of the evidence that this study brings to bear suggests that there is relatively little influence or power in lobbying per se. There are many forces in addition to lobbying which influence public policy; in most cases these other forces clearly outweigh the impact of lobbying. Voters set the broad trends of public policy which all the other influences on policy must follow. It is for this reason that so many forces battle to manipulate public opinion. Public opinion is a factor which sets the boundaries for the policy struggle. On certain questions the boundaries are closely restricted, and the policy decisions of officials must closely follow public demands. On other questions, the boundaries may be broader, leaving wider discretion to decision-making and more possibility for lobbyists to influence their decisions. Questions of large public attention and import are chiefly determined by considerations of political success and winning the next election. The chief executive, through his political leadership, his ability to mold public opinion, and his command of the resources and imagination of the executive bureauc-

From *Lester W. Milbrath*, The Washington Lobbyists *(Chicago: Rand McNally & Co., 1963), pp. 354–358. Reprinted by permission of the publisher.*

racy, has the greatest single impact on the shape of public policy. Questions of small technical nature, which attract little public attention, are more subject to lobbying influence. The growth of one lobby group or coalition generally stimulates the development of an opposing group. Most careful observers of governmental decision-making have concluded that the overall impact of lobbying is relatively minor. This point was made by both lobbyist and congressional respondents and agrees with the observation of other writers on the subject.[1]

If the conclusion that lobbying has a relatively weak impact on policy is added to the conclusions that system controls and legal controls are adequate, that public decisions cannot be bought or stolen, and that the lobbying process is relatively clean, the result is clear: lobbying as we see it today in Washington presents little or no danger to the system. This does not mean that a dangerous situation could not arise or that

[1] William S. White, *Citadel: The Story of the U.S. Senate* (New York: Harper & Row, Publishers, 1956), pp. 145, 149; Donald R. Mathews, *U.S. Senators and Their World* (Chapel Hill: University of North Carolina Press, 1960), pp. 195–96; V. O. Key, Jr., *Public Opinion and American Democracy* (New York: Alfred A. Knopf, Inc., 1961), chap. xx.

lobbyists would not engage in unethical or unfair tactics if they believed these would be to their special advantage. The best insurance against danger and corruption in the process is an alert citizenry which elects responsible officials to public office. A wide-open communications system and viable and responsible public media are important preconditions to maintaining public alertness.

. . .

Eckstein raises the most fundamental question about lobbying and pressure groups: "What contributions do pressure groups make to the political system as a whole, and do these contributions tend to make the system more or less viable (stable and effective)? Are their consequences 'dysfunctional' or 'eufunctional' for the larger systems in which they operate?" [2] Though this study focuses on lobbying rather than pressure groups, the question is essentially the same; however, the contribution of these data to an answer is relatively limited.

In this context it is relevant to point out again that lobbying is inevitable and is likely to grow in scope. One lobbyist says it is analogous to automobile drivers: there are a few bad drivers, but people continue to drive, and more cars are added to the road each year. Lobbying is protected by the First Amendment to the Constitution, and government officials are not disposed to hamper its growth or activities.

Granted the inevitability of lobbying, what are its positive contributions to the political process? Lobbyists provide information and other services which are welcomed by governmental decision-makers. These services are costly and somewhat wasteful; the public or the consumer pays for them ultimately; congressional officials even claim they could function quite adequately without them. In another sense, however, they are indispensable. If information from lobbyists and lobby groups was, for some reason, unavailable to government officials, they would be largely dependent on their own staff for information and ideas. Since the Congress is reluctant to staff itself adequately, it would have to turn primarily to the Executive for information. This would create an even further imbalance between Congress and the Executive in policy-making.[3] More important, cutting off lobbying communications would eliminate a valuable, even indispensable, source of creativity. There is no assurance that government institutions can turn up all the possible alternative solutions to policy problems. A decision-maker who has his mind made up may well have to have new points of view forcefully thrust upon him before he can perceive and accept them. The clash of viewpoints between contesting groups is not only informative; it also is creative. Formerly unperceived alternatives may arise from the challenge to previously accepted possibilities.

Eckstein (1960, p. 162) suggests that *lobby groups perform* two other indispensable functions in the political system: *integration* and *disjunction*. Officials must know very specifically what the effects of a given policy will be and how citizens will react to that policy. Lobby groups and lobbyists define opinion for government with a sense of reality and specificity which political parties, the mass media, opinion polls, and staff assistants seldom, if ever, can achieve. Aggregating and defining specialized opinions have both integrative and disjunctive aspects. The function is integrative in that persons with special interests or problems need group action to aggregate their views and communicate the positions to officials. The aggregation process requires some compromise on the part of group members and therefore is integrative. Group opinion is a more manageable consideration for officials than scattered individual opinions.

Specialized opinion is disjunctive as well, in that it encourages multiple group demands. Political parties (especially in a two-party system) strive for a very broad

[2] Harry Eckstein, *Pressure Group Politics: The Case of the British Medical Association* (London: George Allen & Unwin, 1960), p. 152.

[3] The author is indebted to James A. Robinson for suggesting this point.

integration in order to win elections. That kind of integration can be achieved only by reaching a very low and vague denominator which may not be very functional for making policy. If special interests were confined to vague representation through political parties, they might begin to feel alienated from a political system which persistently distorts their goals.[4] Affording disparate interests special representation

through their own lobby group probably contributes to the stability of the system. There is reason to suppose, then, that the policy-making system produces wiser or more intelligent decisions and functions with more stability than might be the case if lobby groups and lobbyists were not present. If we had no lobby groups and lobbyists we would probably have to invent them to improve the functioning of the system.

[4] The Washington representatives at the Brookings round table all represented corporations. They expressed dissatisfaction with general business organizations such as the National Association of Manufacturers and the National Chamber of Commerce and even with their own trade associations for compromising too much on policy, being too

vague, and being too slow to take action. Paul W. Cherington and Ralph L. Gillen, *The Business Representatives in Washington* (Washington, D.C.: The Brookings Institution, 1962).

6

The Case Against Interest Group Liberalism

THEODORE J. LOWI

In your judgment, is Professor Lowi's account of the role of interest groups in our society fair minded? Overly critical? Why? In what ways does our system of interest group representation work poorly? What groups are advantaged? Which are disadvantaged?

. . . Interest-group liberals have the pluralist paradigm [frame of reference] in common, and its influence on liberal policy and liberal methods of organization has obviously been very large and very consistent. Discrediting the pluralist component of interest-group liberalism has been one of the central purposes of this volume, in the hopes that a change of theory can have

From Theodore J. Lowi, The End of Liberalism (New York: W. W. Norton & Company, Inc., 1969), pp. 294–297. Copyright © 1969 by W. W. Norton & Company, Inc. Reprinted by permission of the publisher.

some small impact on history. Nothing seems to be more evident than the observation that present theory is inappropriate for this epoch. Among the many charges made against pluralism, the following three seem relevant to a final effort at discrediting the entire theoretical apparatus.

(1) The pluralist component has badly served interest-group liberalism by propagating and perpetuating the faith that a system built primarily upon groups and bargaining is perfectly self-corrective. This is based upon assumptions which are clearly not often, if ever, fulfilled—assumptions that groups always have other groups to con-

front them, that "overlapping memberships" will both insure competition and keep competition from becoming too intense, that "membership in potential groups" or "consensus" about the "rules of the game" are natural and inevitable, scientifically verifiable phenomena that channel competition naturally toward a public interest. It is also based on an impossible assumption that when competition does take place it yields ideal results. As has already been observed, this is as absurd as a similar assumption of laissez-faire economists about the ideal results of economic competition. One of the major Keynesian criticisms of market theory is that even if pure competition among factors of supply and demand did yield an equilibrium, the equilibrium could be at something far less than the ideal of full employment. Pure pluralist competition, similarly, might produce political equilibrium, but the experience of recent years shows that it occurs at something far below an acceptable level of legitimacy and at a price too large to pay —exclusion of Negroes from most of the benefits of society.

(2) Pluralist theory is outmoded and unrealistic in still another way comparable to the rise and decline of laissez-faire economics. Pluralism has failed to grapple with the problem of oligopoly or imperfect competition as it expresses itself in the political system. When a program is set up in a specialized agency, the number of organized interest groups surrounding it tends to be reduced. Generally it tends to be reduced precisely to those groups and factions to whom the specialization is most salient. That in turn tends to reduce the situation from one of potential competition to potential oligopoly. That is to say, one can observe numerous groups in some kind of competition for agency favors. But competition tends to last only until each group learns the goals of the few other groups. Each adjusts to the others. Real confrontation leads to net loss for all rather than gain for any. Rather than countervailing power there will more than likely be accommodating power.

Galbraith has assumed that each oligopoly will be checked by an oligopsony—an interest from the opposite side of the market rather than a competitor for a share in the same market. This notion of countervailing power—competition between big labor and big industry, big buyers against big sellers, etc.—was to explain economic and political phenomena. But not only is this new kind of confrontation an unfounded assumption. It was to be created by public policy: ". . . the support of countervailing power has become in modern times perhaps the major peacetime function of the Federal government." [1] Countervailing power, in old or new form, can hardly be much of a theory of the way the industrial state naturally works if it requires central government support. And it hardly warrants government support if its consequences, as already proposed, do not produce the felicitous results claimed for them.

(3) Finally, the pluralist paradigm depends upon an idealized and almost totally miscast conception of *the group*. Laissez-faire economics may have idealized the firm and the economic man but never to the degree to which the pluralist thinkers today sentimentalize the group, the group member, and the interests. Note the contrast between the traditional American notion of the group and the modern pluralist definition. Madison in Federalist 10 defined the group ("faction") as "a number of citizens, whether amounting to a majority or minority of the whole, who are united and actuated by some common impulse of passion, or of interest, *adverse to the right of other citizens, or to the permanent and aggregate interests of the community.*" [Emphasis added.] David Truman uses Madison's definition but cuts the quotation just before the emphasized part.[2]

[1] Galbraith, *American Capitalism, op. cit.*, p. 136. *Cf.* Anshen and Wormuth, *op. cit.*, p. 18 and p. 132. For the best case of accommodation, see any study of the cigarette industry, especially Chapter 10 of *The Structure of American Industry*, ed. Walter Adams (New York: Macmillan, 1961).

[2] Truman, *op. cit.*, p. 4.

In such a manner pluralist theory became the complete handmaiden of interest-group liberalism, in a sense much more than laissez-faire economics was ever a handmaiden to big capitalism. To the Madisonian, and also to the early twentieth-century progressive, groups were necessary evils much in need of regulation. To the modern pluralist, groups are good; they require accommodation. Immediately following his definition in Federalist 10, Madison went on to say: "The regulation of these various interfering interests forms the principal task of modern legislation. . . ." This is a far cry from Galbraith's "support of countervailing power," or Schlesinger's "hope of harnessing government, business and labor in a rational partnership . . . ," or the sheer sentimentality behind the notion of "maximum feasible participation," and "group representation in the interior processes of. . . ."

A revived feeling of distrust toward interests and groups would not destroy pluralist theory but would only prevent its remaining a servant of a completely outmoded system of public endeavor. Once sentimentality toward the group is destroyed, it will be possible to see how group interactions might fall short of creating an ideal equilibrium. Such distrust of prevailing theory might then lead to discomfort with the jurisprudence of delegation of power, for it too rests mightily upon an idealized view of how groups make law today. In such a manner the theoretical foundations for interest-group liberalism can be discredited. Some progress will then have been made toward restoration of an independent and legitimate government in the United States. Until that occurs, liberalism will continue to be the enemy rather than the friend of democracy. . . .

7

A Lobby of the People

JOHN W. GARDNER

In view of the massive and impersonal character of American government, is a citizen's lobby possible or practical? Assuming that you are a member of Common Cause, what specific recommendations would you make for positive action—issues, institutions, reforms? Toward what level of government would you direct your program—local, state, national? Why? Would you urge a friend to join?

Since we announced the formation of Common Cause as a citizens' lobby we have heard various doubts expressed about lobbying and the effectiveness of the citizen's voice. One kind of inquiry reflects the

From John W. Gardner, "Let Us Act," Common Cause Report from Washington, 1, No. 3 (February 1971).

view that *all* lobbies are bad, even well-motivated ones.

Some who hold this view even believe that all lobbies should be abolished by law. But everyone's right to attempt to influence governmental decisions is constitutionally protected (by the "right to petition" clause of the First Amendment).

From the beginning of the Republic both

special interest groups and more broadly based citizen movements have sought to influence government. And today all experts on government accept lobbying as a legitimate part of the political process. Lobbying activities in Washington are carried out not only by commercial interests but by groups representing the unions, the cities, the universities, the various professions, religious groups and so on.

Then there are those who accept the idea of lobbying but say in effect that it must be left to the special interests. The theory is that each special group pursues its own selfish concerns but taken all together they balance one another out and the public interest is served.

The only trouble is it isn't true.

First, the public interest is neglected. All the special interests clashing in the urban setting have not somehow balanced out to produce wise and far-seeing urban solutions. The public interest in clean air and water has not been automatically served by the clash of special interests in the environmental field.

Second, the quality of life for individual Americans is affected. Most of the things individual Americans want come to them through the mediation of large institutions —industrial companies, government agencies, school systems and so on. And large-scale organizations tend to ignore the individual's right to have his say, ignore the fact that he isn't a statistic.

We must design our institutions so that they do not affront the self-respect of individual Americans.

The voices of special interests are legitimate—but so is a strong voice for the public interest. If the system were working perfectly, established political and governmental institutions would be that strong voice. When they fail to function as such, in our free society, groups of citizens make themselves heard directly. It's a tradition as old as the nation.

If one grants the legitimacy of citizen action, one must still answer the question concerning its efficacy. There is a folk cynicism about the impact of citizen movements, but the record does not bear out the cynicism. Citizens' movements brought the vote for women, abolished child labor, foisted Prohibition on the nation (and later repealed it), launched the civil rights movement, made the environment a national issue, placed family planning on the national agenda and so on. Citizen movements have proven, over and over, that they are among the hard political realities of American life.

It is a mistake to view such citizen action as outside politics. *It is an integral part of the political process.* I have heard observers describe Common Cause as being "above politics." It is nonpartisan, but it is most decidedly *not* above politics.

Skeptics ask how a well-meaning citizens' lobby can possibly compete with powerful vested interests that spend millions in the down-to-earth business of supporting candidates. The answer is that citizens have beaten the vested interests on more than one occasion in the past, and will again.

But too often citizen lobbying has been plagued by amateurishness, hit-and-run enthusiasms, and an unwillingness to bother with the dull, grimy details of the political process. These defects can be cured. Citizen action has its own strengths and its own weapons.

Many people today are interested in new strategies for citizen action; and so are we —but first things first. As Vince Lombardi said, "First learn to block and tackle." A citizen must understand the processes of self-government. His capacity to make his views felt at the federal level is particularly important. The public interest can be benefited or butchered by the day-to-day decisions of federal agencies or actions of Congress.

Of course many observers believe that "the people," i.e., individual Americans, are powerless before the great interlocking machinery of our society. Such observers believe that we have to accomplish a shift of power. But power is the capacity to influence the course of events. The reason citizens have lost that capacity is that they have allowed *their* instruments of power—

the instruments of self-government—to fall into disrepair.

So when they turn to government for effective pollution control or consumer protection legislation, government fails them. When they seek excellent candidates for public office, the parties fail them.

It is *only* by regaining command of the instruments of self-government and making those instruments effective that the people will regain command of their situation. To help accomplish just that is one of the chief aims of Common Cause.

7

POLITICAL PARTIES AND POLITICAL PHILOSOPHIES: THE SEARCH FOR PURPOSE AND MEANING

American political parties are anything but ideological in their orientation, and they are not highly organized (except on paper) or tightly disciplined. They are, in effect, loose coalitions of diverse but like-minded people organized largely to win elections and thereby to staff and control the government. Perhaps the two factors which have most influenced American political parties are the federal system and the single elector district. The federal system tends to discourage strong national parties and favor parties oriented to state and local issues. (In a sense we have 100 major parties, two for each state.) The single elector districts and the single executive dictate that the "winner take all." This system discourages minor parties and tends to promote two-party competition. In addition to these elements, there is also a historic factor. A flexible two-party system helped to contain rising sectionalism and (according to its advocates) helped preserve the Union.

Political parties are a hallmark of virtually every modern government, democratic and totalitarian. In fact, their ability to provide alternatives is considered an essential characteristic of democracy. Some more obvious functions of political parties are: (1) to facilitate the transfer of power; (2) to educate the citizenry (critics claim that parties do a poor job in this area); (3) to personalize and humanize big bureaucratic government; (4) to legitimatize power; (5) to provide identification and response for the individual and access to pressure on government; (6) to serve as a clearing house for the recruitment of government personnel. In addition, parties in America are characterized by wide diversity of membership, broad disagreements within each party (often as great as those between the parties), and slogans and programs aimed to appeal to all and alienate few.

Advocates of the present two-party system contend that the compromising character of the two major parties is good. As William C. Carleton states, "In the coming struggle to save America's heritage of freedom, it is not too much to say that the traditional party system in America, the system which does not divide people along ideological lines and which keeps lovers of freedom in both parties, is America's best bulwark against totalitarianism." It is claimed that the moderation and compromising character of American political parties constitute the real genius of American politics. On the other hand, critics assert that unless political parties become more responsive, responsible, and programmatic, they and the country are in trouble. Finally, critics and supporters of the two-party system would agree that political parties and the politics of America are already changing.

The first section of this chapter focuses on the perennial question, "Do American Political Parties Mean Anything?" This section brings together several different viewpoints on the social and psychological aspects of political parties and the growing erosion of party identification.

The second section discusses "The New Politics: New Styles or New Programs?" It is a rather well-documented observation that political parties in America are changing; but are they changing in a meaningful way? Are new forces and new recruits going to restyle and restructure American political parties, or is the new politics all mood and no movement, all shadow and no substance?

Finally, in the third issue, "Which Way America—Left, Right—Center?" we turn to a discussion of liberalism and conservatism, the new left and the radical right.

Do American Political Parties Mean Anything?

Political parties are nowhere mentioned in the Constitution, and if a straw vote had been taken on the subject at the Constitutional Convention, the majority of delegates would probably have voted against the idea. Both Madison and Washington felt that parties contributed to factionalism and consequently were to be discouraged; Washington devoted almost two-thirds of his farewell address to the dangers of factionalism and political parties. In that sense, political parties are extra-constitutional, since they have evolved outside the constitutional structure. Today, however, political parties are commonly regarded as a necessary adjunct to both democratic and totalitarian government.

Supporters of the American party system suggest that the greatness of American parties is their ability to compromise and hence to avoid divisive and highly polarized issues which might divide the country. It is frequently pointed out that American parties compromise before the election, while in a multiparty system compromise occurs after the election. Critics, of course, argue that this practice of consensus politics tends to cause serious and important issues to be swept under the rug. It is also possible, they argue, that disadvantaged minority groups can end up with little or no representation, since there is little to protect them from self-serving elites and interest groups.

The first three selections in this chapter deal with these questions. We begin with a humorous article by Will Stanton, "How to Tell a Democrat from a Republican." Walter Dean Burnham, "The Erosion of Parties," discusses shifting trends in party support. In the final reading, "Democrats or Republicans: What Difference Does It Make?" Clinton Rossiter makes a case for the present two-party system.

The New Politics: New Styles or New Programs?

The phrase "New Politics" came into political currency during the early 1960's and has acquired increasing, if ambiguous, usage ever since. In 1962 Carey McWilliams, editor of *The Nation*, asserted that the United States was careening into a postindustrial era, a special period in which new conditions were creating unprecedented opportunities and at the same time emphasizing dissatisfaction with old problems. Many of these old problems were previously considered insolvable. Simultaneously, new groups were pushing new demands into the political channels.

Affluence and extended periods of leisure time are two characteristics of our postindustrial society. Problems arise and tensions increase when these benefits are unobtainable, for some our so-called "affluent society" is merely a Madison Avenue caption. Many individuals and groups are realizing the failure of the American dream. The promising aspect of this new awakening is the mobilization of groups which had previously been denied economic support and political representation. The helpless are becoming more hopeful. Women, Indians, Chicanos, Blacks, the poor, are all demanding the correction of obvious inequities. They are beginning to insist that our public officials respond to pressing issues and deal with critical problems effectively. Furthermore, spokesmen for these groups urge that the solutions be found now.

There are other moods and stirrings in the new politics. Perhaps the most noticeable feature is the special emphasis on, and in some cases exploitation of, youthful styles. Television and other mass media are replacing political machines and political bosses. As a consequence, candidates strive to appear younger, more colorful, more photogenic. These are the winning qualities in a modern campaign.

Perhaps the most important goal of the new politics is the redirection of our national priorities toward the achievement of a more equitable, humanistic society.

The new politics has its critics as well as its advocates. Critics assert that the new politics is more emotional than realistic, that the base of support is not broad enough to maintain the movement, and the youthful activists not sufficiently pragmatic. In fact the recruits often are charged with being too romantic, a bit anti-intellectual, oversimplistic in their analysis of contemporary problems, and not sufficiently clear in their identification of goals and alternative solutions. Whether the new politics movement can overcome some of its apparent weaknesses and implement a pragmatic program with social goals is a question which only time can answer.

In selections 4, 5, and 6, Senators George McGovern and Adlai Stevenson III comment on the new politics, and Jack Newfield offers a critical evaluation of the movement.

Which Way America—Left, Right—Center?

There is a fairly widespread assumption that political parties in America have no discernible differences, but that the terms "conservative" and "liberal" are solid words with fixed dictionary meanings. This may be true to some extent in the abstract. However, it is confusing and sometimes utterly misleading to apply the conservative and liberal label to individuals and groups on the contemporary political scene. Here one finds a range of views, a complexity of loyalties, and a whole spectrum of personal convictions.

In his book, *Conservatism in America: The Thankless Persuasion*, Clinton Rossiter classifies American conservatives into three main groups —ultra-conservatives, middling conservatives, and liberal conservatives. He dramatizes the difficulties of definition by distinguishing between "conservative" (a generic heading for those who believe in a philosophy based upon order and tradition) and "Conservative" (a precise term for those who hold a philosophy reaching back to Edmund Burke). Nor is the problem of the conservatives a singular one. Liberals face the same dilemma in attempting to encompass the views of all who march under their banner. In fact, liberalism has been referred to as a "wild deuce" that can fit in any hand.

All of this makes categorical statements hazardous. As an alternative to definitive explanations, in selections 7 and 8 we present the views of two distinguished Americans, one a noted conservative, the other an eloquent liberal. Barry Goldwater states his views in "The Conscience of a Conservative" and Eugene McCarthy of Minnesota sets forth his convictions in "The Conscience of a Liberal." To add to the picture, a noted scholar, Daniel Bell, comments in selection 9 on the radical right and the politically dispossessed, while Jack Newfield discusses "The New Left" in the final reading.

1

How to Tell a Democrat from a Republican

WILL STANTON

Are there real differences between Democrats and Republicans, or does everything depend upon picking the right kind of parents, choice of residence, occupational status, educational attainment, and financial position? How many of the social and psychological characteristics between the two parties do you regard as valid?

To the casual observer of turtles, it is pretty hard to tell the difference between a male and a female. Fortunately, this doesn't present any problem to turtles. So it is in politics.

It takes no more than a glance for a Republican to spot a Democrat and vice versa, although to the outsider they may appear to be almost indistinguishable. It is true that their platforms and points of view do overlap—to about the extent that a dime covers a penny. However, there does remain this narrow border of difference, and this is the area I should like to explore.

The Democrats tend to think of themselves as the more openhanded party. Surprisingly, the Republicans agree. You have to have an open hand, they say, in order to reach into somebody else's pockets. They, in turn, think of themselves as more tightfisted. Again there is agreement. They already have theirs, the Democrats point out, and they're not going to let anyone take it away.

Although Republicans are traditionally the party of wealth, some extremely rich families are Democrats. A similar situation exists in England, where a few families are so unbelievably ancient that they don't have to send their children to the proper schools. Here, these people are so loaded they don't have to be Republicans. When one of them runs for high office, the argument is that he is so rich he can afford to run the country as a sort of hobby. The Republicans are more likely to represent their candidate as a sober sort of chap who could use the job.

This brings up a curious facet of our economy. Bankers, being Republican, would prefer to lend their money to other Republicans. The catch here is that other Republicans already have money. So bankers must daily undergo the traumatic experience of handing over money to people they consider irresponsible and untrustworthy at best.

During a recent survey in an Eastern university, it was discovered that whereas the faculty were predominantly Democrats, the students were, for the most part, Republicans. The only significant exception to this pattern was the football team, whose members had been recruited mainly from Democratic families. It was felt that these athletes would not change their political views until their bowling alleys had started paying off.

Republicans are often pictured as solemn or even pompous—Democrats are more friv-

From Will Stanton, "The View from the Fence, or How to Tell a Democrat From a Republican," Ladies' Home Journal, *November 1962, pp. 58–59. Reprinted by permission of the author.*

olous. That is to say, Democrats are the sort who go around pushing one another into swimming pools on which a Republican holds the first mortgage.

In general, Democrats are people trying to get someplace—Republicans are people trying to stay where they are. Both feel the Government should help them do it. It may help to picture them as Jack Sprat and his wife, with the country being represented by the platter.

Critical observers are fond of referring to the Democrats as the War Party and to the Republicans as the Depression Party. No one has ever explained who started all the wars and depressions before there were Republicans and Democrats. It is as though the Russians should accuse the United States of having started athlete's foot. It wouldn't do anyone any harm and might have a therapeutic effect on the Russians —helping them to relieve tension and anxieties.

Perhaps if we pay a visit to an imaginary small town, the differences between the two factions can be noted more specifically. The first things we notice as we approach are the signs erected by the chamber of commerce and the various service and business organizations. These will be manned mostly by Republicans. Perhaps the town has a little-theater group; here you will find nothing but Democrats—at least on the stage. There are two explanations for this. The Democrats maintain that Republicans make poor actors. The other viewpoint is that actors make poor Republicans.

At any rate, all the Republicans you will find in a little-theater group will be in the box office or on the board of directors. Then when the actors demand fancier costumes or more greasepaint, the board says, "No, you can't have it." Most people feel that is the natural order of things.

Incidentally, the plays they put on will be written by Democrats. Republicans do their share of writing, but not plays. They write letters to the editor. Democrats circulate more petitions and carry more signs. Republicans do biographies of other Republicans. They feel these are the only fit subjects for a literary work. Republican women usually write about their grandfathers.

It has been suggested that a man best reveals himself by the things he throws away. Let us suppose, for example, that in exploring our imaginary small town we come upon a trash can containing an empty sourmash whiskey bottle and some sprigs of sodden mint. A Democrat lives here. Moving on, we find a bottle that has contained a fine brand of Scotch. A Republican this time. But now we find not one but several empty Scotch bottles of various brands. This one is tricky. Not, as you might first suppose, a number of Republicans sharing a common trash can. This would be greatly out of character. Much more likely, I think, a Democrat wishing to impress the trashman.

Continuing our exploratory walk along a tree-shaded street we see a house. It is two and a half stories high, painted tan with brown trim.

In front there are matching bay windows and on either side of the door are panels of stained glass. In the center of the door is a bell with a handle that turns. At one corner is a hexagonal tower with a cupola. There is a lilac bush in front of this, somewhat root-bound, and along the side is a row of peonies.

In the backyard is a grape arbor with built-in seats, a bed of rhubarb, and by the back door a trumpet vine. The garage was formerly a carriage house. In it is a three-year-old dark-blue sedan of the medium-price field. If you examine the inside of the rear window, you will discover the remains of a Nixon sticker.

A month later we pass the house again. There is a red-and-cream station wagon in the driveway with one door open. It is last year's model, but looks considerably older. Directly in back of one rear wheel is a toy steam shovel. In the backyard a badminton net trails from a single, listing pole. There is a case of empty tonic bottles beside the front door. From the hi-fi in the living room comes the voice of Dylan Thomas. A family of Democrats has moved in. The former owners have gone to Pasadena.

In this account I have attempted to feel my way along, stepping on the same number of toes on either side of the fence. I have tried to avoid singling out any one person or group as an object of ridicule. The only fair and just way—indeed the American way in my opinion—is to offend everybody equally.

To Be Read Aloud by a Democrat To a Republican or by a Republican to a Democrat

Although to the casual glance Republicans and Democrats may appear to be almost indistinguishable, here are some hints which should result in positive identification:

Democrats seldom make good polo players. They would rather listen to Béla Bartók.

The people you see coming out of white wooden churches are Republicans.

Democrats buy most of the books that have been banned somewhere. Republicans form censorship committees and read them as a group.

Republicans are likely to have fewer but larger debts that cause them no concern.

Democrats owe a lot of small bills. They don't worry either.

Republicans consume three fourths of all the rutabaga produced in this country. The remainder is thrown out. Republicans usually wear hats and almost always clean their paintbrushes.

Democrats give their worn-out clothes to those less fortunate. Republicans wear theirs.

Republicans post all the signs saying NO TRESPASSING and THESE DEER ARE PRIVATE PROPERTY and so on. Democrats bring picnic baskets and start their bonfires with the signs.

Republicans employ exterminators. Democrats step on the bugs.

Republicans have governesses for their children. Democrats have grandmothers.

Democrats name their children after currently popular sports figures, politicians and entertainers. Republican children are named after their parents or grandparents, according to where the most money is.

Large cities such as New York are filled with Republicans—up until 5 P.M. At this point there is a phenomenon much like an automatic washer starting the spin cycle. People begin pouring out of every exit of the city. These are Republicans going home.

Democrats keep trying to cut down on smoking, but are not successful. Neither are Republicans.

Republicans tend to keep their shades drawn, although there is seldom any reason why they should. Democrats ought to, but don't.

Republicans fish from the stern of a chartered boat. Democrats sit on the dock and let the fish come to them.

Republicans study the financial pages of the newspaper. Democrats put them in the bottom of the bird cage.

Most of the stuff you see alongside the road has been thrown out of car windows by Democrats.

On Saturday, Republicans head for the hunting lodge or the yacht club. Democrats wash the car and get a haircut.

Republicans raise dahlias, Dalmatians and eyebrows. Democrats raise Airedales, kids and taxes.

Democrats eat the fish they catch. Republicans hang them on the wall.

Democrats watch TV crime and Western shows that make them clench their fists and become red in the face. Republicans get the same effect from the presidential press conferences.

Christmas cards that Democrats send are filled with reindeer and chimneys and long messages. Republicans select cards containing a spray of holly, or a single candle.

Democrats are continually saying, "This Christmas we're going to be sensible." Republicans consider this highly unlikely.

Republicans smoke cigars on weekdays.

Republicans have guest rooms. Democrats have spare rooms filled with old baby furniture.

Republican boys date Democratic girls. They plan to marry Republican girls, but feel they're entitled to a little fun first.

Democrats make up plans and then do something else. Republicans follow the plans their grandfathers made.

Democrats purchase all the tools—the power saws and mowers. A Republican probably wouldn't know how to use a screwdriver.

Democrats suffer from chapped hands and headaches. Republicans have tennis elbow and gout.

Republicans sleep in twin beds—some even in separate rooms. That is why there are more Democrats.

2

The Erosion of Parties

Walter Dean Burnham

What are likely to be the consequences of an increase in nonpartisan voting trends? Would more conservatives get elected? Does the independent voter lack commitment and information? In what ways could stronger parties act as a shield against unwarranted pressure group activity?

. . .

Both in presidential and off years, a persistent trend toward the erosion of party in shaping voting choices has developed since 1900. This trend toward "non-partisan" electoral politics, exemplified by split-ticket voting, first peaked in the 1920s but was reversed in the 1932–50 era. It subsequently resumed an upward movement which has rapidly accelerated during the 1960s. This trend has been most pervasive in the last two of our off-year elections, 1966 and 1970. Its end is not yet in sight.

There are serious implications in all this for our entire political system. Without party, the many who are individually powerless are left with little or no influence of even the broadest kind over the nature of the policy divisions which our elites make. More than that, the cumulative erosion of party links between voters and candidates calls into serious question the future possibility of critical realignments favoring any party or ideology. Such realignments require two things: their electoral effects must be durable, and they must penetrate

From a statement by Walter Dean Burnham, "The Erosion of Parties," St. Louis Post-Dispatch, December 2, 1970. Reprinted by permission of the publishers.

to all levels of election from presidency to state house. But for these conditions to be met, a certain minimum level of stable support for party as such must exist among most voters. Otherwise, critical realignments cannot occur no matter what battle plan political leaders follow.

As party erodes, voters increasingly turn to cues for their choice wherever cues can be found. This in turn reinforces two powerful contemporary election trends. First, incumbency as such becomes ever more important in determining election outcomes. Second, election results become increasingly stratified—or fragmented—according to the level of election. Both trends were conspicuous in 1970.

Senate races, which are highly visible to voters, were very largely decided by a combination of incumbency and candidate-image factors. Losses by incumbents were dramatic, but they were few. Congressional elections have much lower visibility. Sitting incumbents have thus developed an immense advantage: 95 per cent of those seeking a new term this year won it, though Republicans suffered a marginal disadvantage. Congressional election outcomes are gradually becoming more actuarial and less political. Finally, the state races of today are conflicts between the desire of the public for more governmental services and its unwillingness to pay for them. Here the very visibility of incumbent governors works increasingly to their disadvantage. The 1970 Democratic statehouse sweep is an unusually striking example of this.

The Administration is acting rationally in attempting to link Democrats with a "side" of the law and order issue which has almost no public support. In present conditions, it is nearly the only way conservative ideologies can overcome a tenacious majority coalition which stands between them and durable power. But, questions of political morality apart, it is just possible that the erosion of party has already gone far enough to destroy the chances for this or any other realignment strategy.

For many decades the two-party system has been one of America's chief symbols of government. The paradox of our time is that Americans are increasingly voting that system out, as though they were disillusioned not only with the parties but with politics and government themselves. This is part of the profound legitimacy crisis which now grips the United States.

President Nixon's efforts to "spoil" the Democrats with the social issue, rather than inaugurating a conservative millennium, may simply intensify the legitimacy problem for the entire political system by feeding a widespread public cynicism about politics and politicians. In any case, we can expect electoral fragmentation and some startling election results until this crisis is somehow resolved. One of the latter may even be increasingly frequent defeats of incumbent Presidents who seek re-election.

3

Democrats or Republicans: What Difference Does It Make?

CLINTON ROSSITER

Does the author assert that there are strong differences between Democrats and Republicans? What generalizations does he make regarding the character of the two parties? Where would Professor Rossiter place the heart of each party?

. . . My answer, I fear, will prove unsatisfactory to many, because in some important respects there is and can be no real difference between the Democrats and the Republicans, because the unwritten laws of American politics demand that the par-

From Clinton Rossiter, Parties and Politics in America (Ithaca, N.Y.: Cornell University Press, 1960), pp. 108–118, 148–149. Copyright © 1960 by Cornell University. Reprinted by permission of the publisher.

ties overlap substantially in principle, policy, character, appeal, and purpose—or cease to be parties with any hope of winning a national election. Yet if there are necessary similarities between the Democrats and the Republicans, there are also necessary differences, and we must have them clearly in mind before we can say that we understand the politics of American democracy. [The classic statement of the point of view that there is no real difference between the parties was made by

Bryce in *The American Commonwealth:*

There are now two great and several minor parties in the United States. The great parties are the Republicans and the Democrats. What are their principles, their distinctive tenets, their tendencies? Which of them is for free trade, for civil service reform, for a spirited foreign policy, for the regulation of telegraphs by legislation, for a national bankrupt law, for changes in the currency, for any other of the twenty issues which one hears discussed in the country as seriously involving its welfare?

This is what a European is always asking of intelligent Republicans and intelligent Democrats. He is always asking because he never gets an answer. The replies leave him in deeper perplexity. After some months the truth begins to dawn upon him. Neither party has anything definite to say on these issues; neither party has any principles, any distinctive tenets. Both have traditions. Both claim to have tendencies. Both have certainly war cries, organizations, interests enlisted in their support. But those interests are in the main the interests of getting or keeping the patronage of the government. Tenets and policies, points of political doctrine and points of political practice, have all but vanished. They have not been thrown away but have been stripped away by Time and the progress of events, fulfilling some policies, blotting out others. All has been lost, except office or the hope of it.[1][2]

The parties themselves—the leaders, organizers, propagandists, and "card carriers" of our two enduring coalitions—seem to have a number of differences clearly in their minds, or should I say firmly in their viscera? Emotion, after all, is a vital ingredient of politics, and our parties are about as divided on emotional grounds as we would want them to be. Scratch a real Republican and you will find a man with a deep suspicion of the Democrats. Scratch a real Democrat and you will find a man at least as ready to assault the Republicans as he is to bicker with his own colleagues. Perhaps the best way to measure the emotional gap between the two parties is to talk in terms of images. What image does each party have of itself? What image does it have of the other party? These are ad-

mittedly vague questions to which one can give only vague answers that are derived largely from a process best described as "intuitive empiricism." Yet the questions are important; they deal with some of the essential considerations of party allegiance and party division in this country. We must answer them as best we can.

Certainly the Democrats have a fairly clear self-image of themselves, and one need not read far at all in their platforms, speeches, and appeals to learn that the image is, altogether naturally, colorful and flattering. Those Democrats who raise their eyes occasionally above the consuming, two-act spectable of the struggle for victory and the division of its spoils make much, perhaps too much, of their fabulous past. They celebrate the achievements of the party, paying special attention to its domestic and diplomatic leadership in the twentieth century and, in addition, insisting that it is preeminently "the party of the most liberty and opportunity for the most people." They salute its heroes, of whom four—Jefferson, Jackson, Wilson, and Roosevelt—loom over the landscape of memory like giants, which they were. They delight in the whole sweep of American history, certain that they have been the "movers and shakers" and their opponents, whether Federalists or Whigs or Republicans, the "stick-in-the-muds." Sometimes their enthusiasm gets the better of their sense of proportion, as when they, having laid claim to Jefferson, lay claim to the Declaration of Independence; but for the most part they have spun their self-congratulatory myths out of the substance of fact—spun nylon out of coal, as it were.

The Democrats, being primarily a party and only incidentally a lodge, are really much more concerned with the present and future than with the past. It is the image of themselves they project into the American future that moves them to their best efforts. They pride themselves as "the party of progress," as the men most willing to experiment boldly with new methods for achieving welfare, security, and prosperity. They pride themselves as "the party of the

[1] James Bryce, *The American Commonwealth*, II, 20.   [2] Footnote Rossiter.

people," as the men most concerned to scatter the fruits of progress widely among all ranks and classes. They are beginning to pride themselves as "the party of the world," as the men best fitted to carry forward the work of Wilson, Roosevelt, and Truman and to negotiate benevolently and prudently with men of all nations. And deep down inside, where feelings are cherished but not openly flaunted, they pride themselves as "the party of the professionals." They are the men who have brought order to politics; they are the men who have taught the nation its lessons in meaningful compromise. Amateurism is all very well in its place, which is on the fringes of the Democratic party or at the core of the Republican party; but professionalism, be it the professionalism of Southern county bosses or Northern precinct bosses, is the essence of the kind of politics that most Democrats like to practice. The Democrats, in their own opinion, are the "old pros" of American politics. . . .

To the Republicans this self-molded image of achievement, heroism, liberty, progress, democracy, worldliness, and professional competence appears as a caricature of reality. Even when we make allowance for the natural mistrust of one band of politicians for the other band across the street we are struck by the intensity of the Republican image of Democratic weakness, wickedness, and false counsel. Republicans usually begin their assessment of the Democratic party by throwing out everything that took place before the Civil War. Jackson is only a name out of a misty past; Jefferson would be happier with the Republicans today than with the Democrats. Whatever services the Democrats performed before the Republicans came upon the scene in 1856, their record ever since has been one of which modern Democrats, if they would ever look up from the anxious toil of keeping a brawling family from breaking up completely, would hardly choose to boast.

The plain fact is that the Republicans, for all the friendly contacts they keep with their counterparts in the Democratic party, look upon that party as a vehicle of dema-goguery, radicalism, plunder, socialism, unsound economics, bossism, corruption, subversion, and ill repute. Even the stanchest Republican will boast that some of his "best friends" are Democrats, but even the mildest finds something off-color in the party as a whole. There have been too many patrician demagogues like Roosevelt and too many vulgar ones like Huey Long, too many addlepated "pinks" like Henry Wallace and dangerous ones like R. G. Tugwell, too many big spenders like Harry Truman and big lenders like Dean Acheson and big plunderers like Frank Hague. It is a party much too willing to hazard inflation in the interest of false prosperity and real votes. It is a party racked since time out of mind by big and little bosses who have no principles save that of victory and no interest in victory save that of the spoils. The morals of party politics are never exactly dainty, the Republicans admit, but the morals of Democratic politics are downright shoddy.

Worse than all this, it is a party that cannot be trusted to maintain a patriotic front against the assaults of the nation's acknowledged enemies and the blandishments of its self-styled friends. It has harbored a shocking number of heretics, subversives, and traitors; it has surrendered our freedom of maneuver to the leaders of a dozen other countries, some of them not even friendly; it has squandered American lives and treasure in a vain search for peace and world order. As it was the party of Clement Vallandigham in the 1860's, it was the party of Alger Hiss in the 1940's. "Not all Democrats were rebels," Republican orators shouted as they "waved the bloody shirt" after the Civil War, "but all rebels were Democrats." "Not all Democrats were pinks and subversives," I heard a Republican remark just the other day, "but all pinks and subversives were Democrats—and they still are."

And as it was the party of the Boston Irish in the 1850's, it is the party of the New York Puerto Ricans in the 1960's. This is the last and most repelling element in the total image of the Democratic party held by many good Republicans: it speaks with an accent; it is not quite American; it is just not respectable. And if the accent of the Pole or the Jew or the Puerto Rican is music to the friendly ears of other, perhaps more broad-minded Republicans, there is always the accent of the Southern racist to remind them to stay put in the ranks behind Lincoln and McKinley.

This is, admittedly, a harsh image, not all of whose harshness can be explained as a simple, corrective reaction to the pretensions of the Democrats themselves. It is not an image, fortunately, on which many Republicans dwell obsessively or most Republicans are prepared to act. In the real world of politics, lawmaking, and administration it presents no insurmountable barrier to the bipartisan jockeying and cooperation that makes our system livable and workable. The image is there, nonetheless, carried sturdily in millions of Republican bosoms, and it is perhaps a more important force in the total pattern of our politics than the positive image carried by the Democrats themselves. The latter does not forbid loyal Democrats to go off the reservation; the former makes it an act of heresy for loyal Republicans to embrace the sweaty Democrats.

Let that be the essential image of the Democratic party in which both Democrats and Republicans put stock. It is indeed a sweaty army—heavy with the sweet sweat of toil for the American people, according to the Democrats themselves; reeking with the sour sweat of corruption and "80 per cent Americanism," according to the Republicans.

Democrats will say angrily that, in my review of the achievements and failures of the Republicans . . . , I was much too kind to the Grand Old Party. Republicans will say even more angrily that I was much too cruel. They, too, carry a flattering self-image in their minds, which, because of their fewer years and less motley composition, is a good deal sharper than the self-image of the Democrats. They, too, celebrate their historic achievements, painting them in far brighter colors than the schol-

arly pastels I have used. Consider these claims in the *Republican Fact-Book* of 1948:

The Republican Party has a long and honorable history of majority control of this country during the most expansive period of its development. Between 1861 and 1933, Republican Presidents were in office three-fourths of the time. They shaped governmental policy which encouraged the development of the country's vast resources; built up its defenses; created its national banking system; established a currency which circulated throughout the world on a par with gold; made the credit of the country the most stable in the world; formulated economic policies which made this country the leader among all nations in agriculture, mining, and manufacturing—in short, made the United States first among the nations.

Having broken the slave bonds of the Negro and made him a free man; having bound up the deep wounds of a nation divided against itself; the Republican Party continued to proceed on a program of adherence to the principles of Constitutional Government which the genius of the founding fathers had laid down. Within the framework of justice and law, the Republican Party built up the confidence of the people in the American Way of Life.[3]

They, too, salute their heroes joyfully. If the Democrats have four giants, they have one, Abraham Lincoln, who is more than a match all by himself for these four and all others the opposition can muster. Lincoln belongs to all Americans, indeed to all men of good will everywhere in the world, but he belongs first of all to the Republicans. He is an essential myth without whom no Republican orator or organizer or platform writer would know just how to proceed. It is possible that Dwight D. Eisenhower is a similar myth in the making.

The *Fact-Book* makes this short, happy statement of "Republican Principles," and catches almost perfectly the feeling millions of Republicans have about their party:

The Republican Party was originated in 1854 as the political group dedicated to the freedom of the individual and the safeguard of his inalienable rights. It has since remained steadfastly devoted

3 *Republican Fact-Book* (Washington, 1948), 5.

to these basic American principles—free initiative, free enterprise, and the dignity of the average man. More than ever the deep significance of the Republican stand for Constitutionalism, States' Rights, encouragement of American enterprise and a minimum of Government interference with freedom of opportunity becomes apparent today when the extent to which these principles have been whittled down by the Democratic Party is realized.

Here is the essence of true Republicanism, even in these days of the modern, domesticated, politely New Dealish party: individualism as opposed to collectivism, free enterprise as opposed to "socialistic meddling," constitutionalism as opposed to "one-man rule," states' rights as opposed to centralization. It is, indeed, the party of "the American Way of Life." It took the lead in building the Way; it has defended it patriotically against subversion and radicalism; it is, in a real sense, the Way Incarnate. I do not mean this at all facetiously when I say that the average Republican is much readier than the average Democrat to identify his own party with the nation and its household gods—home, mother, the flag, and free enterprise.

A final ingredient in the Republican self-image is the warm feeling of respectability that characterizes the record, principles, operations, and tone of the party. It is businesslike without being coldly professional, sound without being callous, steady without being stale. It is "100 per cent American," not only in the stout fight it puts up for American principles, but in the mood in which it thinks, the temper in which it acts, the accent in which it speaks. Here, in particular, the image the Republicans have of themselves needs the image they have of the Democrats to bring it into sharp focus. The Democrats are plainly a disreputable crowd; the Republicans, by contrast, are men of standing and sobriety. Many a middle-class American in many a small town has had to explain painfully why he chose to be a Democrat. No middle-class American need feel uneasy as a Republican. Even when he is a minority—for example, among the heathen on a college campus—he can, like any white, Anglo-Saxon Protestant, warm himself before his little fire of self-esteem. [The situation described by Brand Whitlock in the Ohio of his youth still exists in many parts of America:

In such an atmosphere as that in the Ohio of those days it was natural to be a Republican; it was more than that, it was inevitable that one should be a Republican; it was not a matter of intellectual choice, it was a process of biological selection. The Republican party was not a faction, not a group, not a wing, it was an institution like those Emerson speaks of in his essay on Politics, rooted like oak trees in the center around which men group themselves as best they can. It was a fundamental and self-evident thing, like life, and liberty, and the pursuit of happiness, or like the flag or the federal judiciary. It was elemental like gravity, the sun, the stars, the ocean. It was merely a synonym for patriotism, another name for the nation. One became, in Urbana and in Ohio for many years, a Republican just as the Eskimo dons fur clothes. It was inconceivable that any self-respecting man should be a Democrat. There were, perhaps, Democrats in Lighttown; but then there were rebels in Alabama, and in the Ku Klux Klan, about which we read in the evening, in the Cincinnati *Gazette*.[4]][5]

The Democrats find all this talk of the American Way of Life a sham and a bore. The Republican party with which they have to contend is a pompous, superpatriotic, self-centered, hypocritical band of hard-minded men with a unique penchant for serving themselves while insisting that they are serving all America. Who are they, ask the Democrats, to shout about individualism when they fought so bitterly against all attempts to rescue helpless individuals in the 1930's? Who are they to wave the bloody shirt of treason against the administrations of Roosevelt and Truman when they yapped and snarled at almost every constructive step toward leadership of the free world? Who are they to shout the glories of free enterprise when they have always banked so heavily on the government for friendly support of

4 *Forty Years of It* (New York, 1914), 27.
5 Footnote Rossiter.

their schemes? Who are they to strike a posture of purity and wag their finger at the corruption of the city machines when they took favors from this government— protective tariffs, subsidies, land grants— that were worth billions rather than millions? The Republicans may rejoice in the memory of Lincoln, but if Lincoln were here today he would have a hard time warming to a single man in Eisenhower's Cabinet.

The essence of the Democratic image of the Republican party is the certain knowledge that, for all its protestations about liberty and justice for every American, it is the party of the few, of the rich, of the interests, of the upper classes. It is constitutionally incapable of looking out over the whole of America and, in the skillful, purposeful manner of the Democrats, of caring for the legitimate needs of all ranks and callings. It takes no broad view; it thinks no big thoughts; it has no warm heart. It is not creative in domestic affairs, for the best it has been able to do throughout a generation of Democratic innovation and progress is first to shout "Good God! No!" and then "Me, too!" It is not reliable in foreign affairs, for it has repeatedly confused our friends and neighbors with its threats and boasts and changes of mind. It is not even what a conservative party is supposed to be: sound and prudent and steady. The Republicans, not the Democrats, produced the wildest demagogue in American history and backed him with zeal. The Republican party is indeed a minority, the Democrats conclude, in the range of its interests as well as in numbers. It is a minority, that is to say, because it deserves to be a minority.

If we can discount the natural excesses of admiration and abuse that are present in these pairs of images, we can come up with some fairly useful generalizations about the character of our two parties. To speak of the character of a group of human beings as numerous and formless as an American party is an exercise in illusion, for it is to personalize the impersonal and individualize the collective. Yet one cannot

spend much time in the clubhouses and convention halls in which the parties do their political business without becoming aware of certain vague but substantial differences in character or, as I prefer, style. A gathering of Democrats *is* more sweaty, disorderly, offhand, and rowdy than a gathering of Republicans; it is also likely to be more cheerful, imaginative, tolerant of dissent, and skillful at the game of give-and-take. A gathering of Republicans *is* more respectable, sober, purposeful, and businesslike than a gathering of Democrats; it is also likely to be more self-righteous, pompous, cut-and-dried, and just plain boring. In a Republican office one hears much talk of programs and policies; at a Republican convention the color and excitement, such as they are, seem labored and staged. In a Democratic clubhouse one hears much talk of votes and voters; at a Democratic convention the color and excitement are generated by the delegates themselves. Republicans seem to lean to the ideological side of politics, Democrats to the practical. The most famous of all "smoke-filled rooms" (Colonel Harvey's at the Blackstone in Chicago in 1920) was, to be sure, inhabited by Republicans, but I have the distinct impression—distinct as only the impressions of a nonsmoker can be—that the air is bluer and thicker and yet somehow softer in any room where Democrats have gathered to do their immemorial business.

Taken all-in-all, the two parties show two of the familiar faces of America, much alike in respects that would catch the attention of the foreign observer, somewhat different in those for which an American with a sharp sociological eye would be looking. A writer who has been, in his time, to many political conventions and to even more business luncheons once summed it up for me by remarking, "The Republicans look to me like Rotarians at the speakers' table, the Democrats like Rotarians at table 16, back near the entrance to the kitchen." Those at the speakers' table, we agreed, are just a little bit stiff, correct, falsely hearty, and conscious of their eminence.

No angry voice is raised to mar their unity of principle and purpose. They all wear vests, they all smile brightly, they all sing the familiar songs with fervor. They are leaders of the community, and they know it. Meanwhile, back at table 16, things are more relaxed and less self-conscious. Arguments are aired with abandon and settled (or forgotten) with a shrug. Dress is more casual, salutes are more boisterous, jokes are more earthy. They may be leaders, too, but at the moment they are just the boys at table 16. The respectable Republicans who delight in their polite unity, the relaxed Democrats who cherish their rowdy variety —they are all good Americans together, but there is a difference in their styles. That difference is caught vividly in the choice of beastly emblems that was made for all of us long ago: the slightly ridiculous but tough and long-lived Donkey—the perfect symbol of the rowdy Democrats; the majestic but ponderous Elephant—the perfect symbol of the respectable Republicans. Can anyone imagine the Donkey as a Republican or the Elephant as a Democrat? . . .

Where, then, is the heart of each party, and what is the distance between dead-center Republicanism and dead-center Democracy? The answer, I think, is that the heart of the Republican party is that position where Senator Taft pitched his famous camp—halfway between the standpattism of "the unreconstructed Old Guard" and the me-tooism of "the disguised New Dealers." The heart of the Democratic party, at least in thirty-nine states of the Union, is that position where Adlai Stevenson raised his famous standard—halfway between the aggressive reformism of "the laboristic liberals" and the moderate opportunism of "the Texas brokers." Neither of these notable men could win through to the Presidency and thus put his mark indelibly on his party. Taft, indeed, was too good a Republican even to win the nomination. Yet each in his own way and at his best moments came as close to being the beau ideal of his party as did any man in the postwar years.

The distance between the well-known positions of these two men on domestic and international affairs is a pretty accurate measure of the distance between the two parties and as reasonable an answer as one can make to those who still demand to know "the difference between the Democrats and the Republicans." The difference, I repeat, is one of tendencies rather than principles. In most parts of this country it comes down to a difference between an urban, working-class, new-stock, union-oriented party with a penchant for reform and spending, and a rural-suburban, middle-class, old-stock, business-oriented party with a penchant for the status quo and saving. Look deep into the soul of a Democrat and you will find plans to build 400,000 units of public housing and to ship 300 tractors to Ghana (whether Ghana wants them or not); look deep into the soul of a Republican and you will find hopes for a reduction in taxes and for a balanced budget.

There are those who will insist that this is not enough of a difference. Each of the parties is a permissive coalition within which the basic urges of the heart are too often sacrificed on the altar of a specious unity. Each overlaps the other excessively in principle, aspiration, and appeal; each abandons its alleged identity in the scramble for votes. And in each may be found, even in states where the Republican-Democratic split is sharpest, important men who seem to vote more often with the other party than with their own, for example, Senator Lausche of Ohio and Senator Javits of New York. To persons who complain on all these scores I can say only that those are the facts of life in a two-party system that operates under a constitution of divided authority. A party that presumes to be a majority must of necessity be a coalition; two parties that are locked in equal struggle must of necessity overlap. Let the critics of the American parties go to any other country with two-party politics, even to relatively homogeneous Britain, and there, too, they will hear complaints about the lack of clear-cut differences between the parties. This is the burden of the citizen of such a country, and epescially of the United States: never to be sure of the "real difference" between the two parties, never to be certain that his vote will "count," always to be on the alert for maverick candidates, always to look beneath party labels at the men who wear them. . . .

4

The New Politics

GEORGE McGOVERN

Has liberalism in America been handicapped by a lack of realism and pragmatism? Is idealism incompatible with pragmatic politics? Cite some examples in American history where idealism has elevated both the party and the country. Can you also point out periods or events in American history which were hampered by excessive idealism? How do you respond to Senator McGovern's comment on national priorities?

The need for a new approach to politics and political problems is as obvious as it is urgent. Everywhere we see irrefutable evidence of the failure of conventional politics, the tragic results of politics as usual and the consequence of "benign neglect" toward particular groups, issues and problems. If we really believe, and I do believe, that our political system can work, we must make it work and work now.

In addition to making the political system work, I think we must introduce into American politics a new emphasis upon sincerity. It is time that we brought honesty, integrity and personal commitment back into politics, and this is what the new politics is attempting to do. We must say what we believe, and believe what we say. We must close the credibility gap between the people and their elected officials. The place to begin is on the national level, since this is the

focal point of the nation. We must say less and do more. Certainly there should be much less stress on rhetoric and much more positive action. Nowhere is this gap between rhetoric action more striking than in the realm of foreign affairs. Here we must trim our pronouncements to our resources; our promises to our ability to fulfill them; and our commitments to priorities here at home.

This leads into the second characteristic of the new politics, and that is the pressing need for a new list of national priorities. Currently we are spending over $70 billion for arms and armaments, while at the same time 10 million people in this country are hungry and malnourished. The idea of spending $4 billion on a supersonic air transport which will permit a few people to travel to Paris two hours quicker than they can today is almost unthinkable when one considers the problems of our cities, our schools, and our poor. We need to put first things first in our country—to create a national agenda of our problems and to enact programs for solving these problems.

From Senator George McGovern, "The New Politics," amplified telephone interview with six colleges, January 8, 1969.

We need then, both to examine the pressing issues of our society and to reexamine our present foreign and domestic policies in terms of what is most urgent and what is realistically possible to achieve.

Finally, we need to open up the political process to large numbers of submerged individuals in our society. The disadvantaged minorities need to be brought into the policymaking process. At the present time there are large, relatively unorganized groups which are without their proper share of representation in the government and without political influence. Youth, blacks, Indians, Chicanos, women; these groups are not participating fully in decision-making, particularly in the making of those decisions which vitally affect their fate and fortune. We must restore the confidence and the competence of these groups by increasing their participatory role in the governmental process.

5

Politics: The Old and the New

ADLAI STEVENSON III

How far and how fast can or should a new political movement break with older traditions and older programs? Are there any procedures or methods of the old politics which the new politics could profitably adopt? On what specific attitudes and procedures should the new politics break with the old? To what extent are the views of Senator Stevenson a bridge between the old and the new politics?

I think some things are rather obvious. I don't think that the old politics is going to work very well any more for a variety of reasons. The patronage system, the paid political worker, the person who is on the public payroll in return for working in the precincts—this system doesn't seem to be productive any more. The plain unvarnished fact is that there are too many more attractive alternatives to political patronage. It is not the same as it was back in the days of the 19th century when there were waves of immigrants who were terribly dependent on the local political boss for jobs, for turkeys at Christmas and for all sorts of hand-

outs. Consequently, these people became indebted to the precinct captain and the machine. They helped the party and the party helped them. Many worked their way up in the party.

Today, of course, we have immigrants—both from the South and from rural areas. Generally, these new arrivals are Blacks and Puerto Ricans, and concentrate in the cities. They are frequently unskilled and forced to live in the ghettoes and do not have the opportunity to work up the ladder in or out of the party. The "older immigrants" of the 19th century climbed their way up the ladder and when they reached the top they often drew up the ladder and closed the doors behind them. In many urban communities, economic, political, and social injustices have incited a great deal of unrest among black people. However, the same conditions apply to Puerto

From Adlai Stevenson III, "Politics: The Old and the New," amplified telephone interview with seven colleges, January 10, 1969. Senator Stevenson's comments were spontaneous and unrehearsed.

Ricans, Latin Americans, and other disadvantaged groups who live in the larger cities. What I am saying, I suppose, is that one aspect of the old politics was reliance on massive ethnic voting blocs. Well, you cannot rely on these coalitions to quite the same extent. They are becoming a little more shaky all of the time. Moreover, the groups which formed the basis of the Democratic party from 1932 to 1964 are not the same—labor, the social reform groups, the intellectuals. The cities are not the same. People are continuously moving not only to cities from the rural areas, and from the South into the North, but also from the cities to the suburbs. We find so many cities like Chicago where the traditional Democratic base in the central city is remaining pretty static; but this citadel of power is not getting any larger. On the other hand, the Republican base in the suburbs is expanding continuously. Added to all of this, we have the news media, especially TV, which provides new opportunities for the candidate to reach the people directly, to bypass the middleman, the power broker, the organized political leader, the local county boss, the ethnic leader who used to ply back and forth between his people, and the politicians. These individuals are becoming less important. The citizens are exercising judgments for themselves. They do it through public opinion polls, as well as election polls. They see the candidates on TV.

All of this is changing politics and changing it very rapidly. It is making it very hard for the old politics and the old political leaders to survive. The problem is, as I see it, that we really haven't come up with the right answers, the alternatives to the old politics. This means institutional reform, reforming the electoral process, direct election perhaps of all party officials. It means all kinds of structural reforms. These reforms take time. Right now, it seems to me, that we're caught in the middle—between the old politics and the new politics.

In this time of transition, there is tension between the individuals who have come up through the old politics and the individuals who are trying to come up through the new politics; the public figures who are reaching out directly to the people, who not only understand the techniques of the new politics but who are also aware of the new issues, the new problems of urban America; the environmental problems of air and water pollution, the regional problems, the problems of mass transportation.

All of these problems have many dimensions. For example, crime is not so much a local problem as it is a metropolitan problem, or perhaps a regional and national problem. The cost of financing the technical equipment and expertise which the police departments so desperately need [is] almost prohibitive. Since we are much more mobile than we used to be, the criminal will live in one place and commit a crime in another place. He may then move to still another area. We need more efficient and more flexible law enforcement to cope with new conditions.

The old politicians have failed to grasp many of the new issues. Right now we're in a real period of conflict between the old and the new. The "new" forces are going to win, but there may be a period of agonizing conflict in the immediate future. Certainly there can be a great deal of self-destructiveness and demoralization for young people who become involved in a purely negative way. If young people participate constructively they can really help the country get through this transitional period.

As soon as you engage in the language of violence and coercion, and self-righteousness, you invite the same kind of response from the other side and your efforts can become counterproductive. Violence is not the language of a free society. We are just not going to make this transition without citizen participation. I think it's really going to take very painstaking, patient, hard work in the precincts and at every level. It is going to require good will, the putting aside of violence, and recriminations and abuse, and all the rest.

6

New Politics: More Mood than Movement

JACK NEWFIELD

From your own observations of political trends and events, would you say that the New Politics is a valid analysis? Do advocates of the new politics have more to gain or to lose in identifying themselves with the Democratic party? In what ways is this tactic advantageous? In what ways is it a liability? How do you explain Newfield's assertion that the new politics has been unable to win the trust of college activists?

The new technology or the new politics—call it what you will—has arrived.

　　　　　—James M. Perry, *The New Politics*

　　The New Politics is becoming a huckster's phrase, invoked by plastic politicians, to con what they think is a gullible electorate. It is as much a cliché as the New Journalism or the New Theatre. It has become like Silly Putty, bent and twisted into dozens of distorted and unnatural shapes by careerists trying to redefine it to their particular advantage.

　　Jacob Javits, who campaigned last autumn for Richard Nixon, proclaims himself a partisan of the New Politics because "it means problem solving." Theodore Sorensen, who tried to convince Robert Kennedy not to speak out against the war in Vietnam, says he is for it because it "means participation, like giving 18-year-olds the vote." Organization men like Jesse Unruh and Stanley Steingut claim to be part of the New Politics. James Perry and Penn Kimball have written whole books defining the New Politics exclusively in terms of manipulative technology, computers and mass

From Jack Newfield, "New Politics: More Mood than Movement," The Nation, July 28, 1969, pp. 70–73. Copyright © 1969 by Nation Associates, Inc. Reprinted by permission of the publisher.

communications. Hubert Humphrey and Fred Harris say they are "for" the New Politics. But then Albert Shanker *says* he is for decentralization and Mayor Richard Daley *says* he is for civil liberties. It all makes one recall George Orwell's prophetic quote:

> In our time, political speech and writings are largely the defense of the indefensible. . . . Political language has come to consist largely of euphemism, question-begging and sheer cloudy vagueness. . . . The inflated style is itself a kind of euphemism. A mass of Latin words falls upon the facts like soft snow, blurring the outlines and covering up all the details.

　　The sociologist Daniel Boorstin has written perceptively about "pseudo events" and "pseudo personalities," but the New Politics just might be the first pseudo movement. It has no program, no money, no leadership, no power, a weak national organization and almost nothing for its citizen supporters to do. An Albany meeting of the cannibalistic New York group in May broke up in petty bickering. Candidates running in the name of the New Politics—Tom Bradley, Henry Helstoski and Herman Badillo—all lost important elections within the last month. Instead of an issues convention, the New Democratic Coalition

(NDC) spent its energies last spring organizing a fundraising dinner in Washington.

At this point, the New Politics is still more mood than movement, more desire than reality, more label than program. I hope in this exploratory and fraternal article to suggest a few reasons why the New Politics groups have been ineffective, and why, since the Chicago convention, they have lost the political initiative to the Nixon Administration, and to the old politics, machine Democrats, corporate managers, union bureaucrats and senior Southern Congressmen.

One reason is that most of the organizational leaders of the New Politics seem wedded to the notion that incremental change should come exclusively through electoral politics. . . . At their conferences they talk at length about taking over irrelevant, hollow shells like the Young Democrats and the Democratic National Committee. This parochial electoral vision has tended to flood the local organizations with anal technicans and power-tripping hustlers, while turning off the younger activists, who prize ideas and confrontations more than candidates and campaigns.

Up to now, the orators of the New Politics have sounded much too optimistic and impatient. They recall 1968 in shades of victory, and see the Democratic convention of 1972 as a final vision of Armageddon. They are not mentally preparing for a movement that will span a decade or more of hard work in local communities. They have a furtive eye fixed on a short cut. And they see the Democratic Party as the only possible vehicle for reform, even though it was the Democratic Party that involved us in fighting the Vietnamese, ruined the poverty program and sanctioned the police violence during the Democratic convention.

Although I shall speak here primarily of cooperation with grass-roots movements to the left of the Democrats, I also believe that an excessive preoccupation with the Democratic Party is causing the New Politics to ignore the progressive wing of the

Republican Party: the Ripon Society, Senators Goodell, Aiken and Percy and Mayor Lindsay.

The Democratic Party still houses the worst institutionalized elements in our national politics: the Meany-Lovestone-CIA complex; the Dixiecrats, the missile contractors and the Mafia. We should try to think of the New Politics as historically ten minutes old, and still view the idea of a new political party, including Ripon Republicans, as an open option. The endless talk of "capturing" the Democratic Party is both elitist and delusional. And much harder than folks think.

This narrow electoral bias seems based on a bad misreading of the history of this decade in America. Since the sit-ins of 1960, history has been pushed forward by insurgent movements rather than by political candidates. The black movement, the student movement, the anti-war movement and the dump LBJ movement should be the models of a new participatory politics. These were—and are—long-term, issue-oriented movements, on the margins of parliamentary politics, that engage thousands of ordinary citizens. At the necessary moment these movements invented their own leader—Eugene McCarthy—and entered the electoral process. By emphasizing infighting over nominations and positions within the Democratic Party now, the New Politics groups are cutting themselves off from the generators of energy and imagination on the campuses and in the ghettos. If the New Politics becomes a broad enough movement, it will once more have the power to create its own leaders at the right time.

The electoral strategy also neglects two of the most significant lessons to be extracted from the events of 1968. One is that *the basic institutions of liberal politics—the unions, the convention system, the mass media and the Democratic Party itself—are undemocratic.* Only by exposing and reforming these institutions—and by building alternatives to them—can citizen politics be made to work. One must remember that Vice President Humphrey lost every primary where his name was on the ballot, and was still nominated because of the power of three men—Mayor Daley, Governor Connally and George Meany. And the convention adopted a hawkish Vietnam plank, even though the policy had been repudiated by 80 per cent of the primary voters.

The other lesson of 1968 is that you can no longer base mass movements on charismatic heroes in this country, because those heroes get assassinated. Any American insurgent movement must be anchored on participation and commitment in order to survive the gunmen.

The New Politics will have to root itself in issues that move masses of people: an end to the endless war in Vietnam, a drastic reduction in military spending; community control, citizen participation, and opposition to the general over-centralization of American life; reform of the draft; democratization of the rules and structures of the Democratic Party; a guaranteed annual income, socialized medicine and the closing of tax loopholes for corporations and the very rich. And possibly most urgently, it must devise a program that addresses the legitimate needs and frustrations of the powerless white working class. Robert Kennedy won the votes of the steelworkers, farmers and cops in Indiana, Nebraska and California, and they can be won again by men who speak in plain Populist language against remote experts and bureaucracy; against big business and the war; and against the casual hypocrisy of programmed politicians.

This should be the agenda of a New Politics, not the small maneuvers for small positions within the existing Democratic hierarchy.

Another shortcoming of the New Politics has been its inability to win the trust—or even the curiosity—of the high school and college activists, a group of about 3 million. I don't mean to suggest that this is an easy thing to do these days. The young today quite properly believe in no adult authority in the country. With Dylan they sing, "I've got nothin', ma, to live up to." But if there is any New Politics, in the sense of ideas and constituency, it is the radical, activist students, from McCarthy volunteers to draft resisters. They are the one authentically new element in the body politic of the country since the union movement of the 1930s.

No current national political leader now expresses the feelings or demands of the students. Worse, none even adequately defends them against the swelling backlash of repression. Yet, they all covet the students as volunteers in their future campaigns to climb the greasy pole.

Rep. Edith Green, who was Robert Kennedy's Oregon campaign manager, is emerging as the major draftsman of the vicious new and anti-student bill in the House Committee on Education and Labor. Eugene McCarthy, the man for one inning, refused to testify on behalf of his own delegates when they were on trial in Chicago last spring. Theodore Sorensen tells the National Book Association that the enemy is equally Herbert Marcuse and Ronald Reagan, neglecting to mention John Mitchell, Melvin Laird and Richard Nixon, who hold actual raw power, but whose names lack the same symmetry of the two cited. No Senator as yet has called illegal the indictments of the eight New Left leaders in Chicago, or dared suggest that Mayor Daley should have been indicted instead, if the grand jury had only read the Walker Report. What Senator has spoken out against the systematic roundups of Black Panthers, or the Congressional probe into SDS? There is a new McCarthyism in the land, and the New Politics has hardly noticed it, much less fought back.

One thing the liberal politicians can do is understand the cultural root of the generational alienation. The kids hate the environment most of them grew up in—impersonal split-level suburbs, homogenized religion, dull 9-to-5 jobs, sex by the marriage manuals, a mass media that promotes banality and suppresses the Smothers Brothers. The young just can't live in that world.

They are in revolt against the most traditional values of the middle class—God, money, status and the family. One small way in which the New Politics can begin to relate to these kids would be to develop a cultural analysis of America that takes the adversary culture of the young seriously.

To summarize: the New Politics seems too committed to the Democratic Party as the one historical agency of renewal. It seems too remote from the para-political movements at the base of the society: blacks, students, the poor, women. It has not begun to raise the idea of redistribution of wealth and income. It is white and elite.

The New Politics should be more activist, more radically concerned with institutions, more concerned with cultural issues, more like a social movement than a political campaign. For example, it should now be leading the opposition to the war in Vietnam, organizing a new March on Washington, or perhaps a national strike. It should lend its support to the basic demands of the campus movements, and not contribute further to the paranoid backlash against the young. It should try to strike alliances with low-income whites on issues of economic self-interest, possibly through the new Alliance for Labor Action. It should be able to grasp the enormity of the present crisis, and realize that the business-as-usual ritual of making good speeches and nominating assemblymen is insufficient as long as 350 Americans are dying each week in Vietnam.

Right now the New Politics hardly exists, except as a simplistic slogan easily appropriated by hacks and hucksters. What we do have, out of the ashes of 1968, are some *excellent new politicians:* Sam Brown, Adam Walinsky, Paul Schrade, Don Peterson, Julian Bond, Channing Phillips, Representatives Chisholm, Koch and Lowenstein. But we do not yet begin to have a *new politics* that can generate a new majority for radical reform. I will end by quoting the candid and passionate speech

Adam Walinsky delivered to the founding meeting of the National Democratic Coalition in Minneapolis last October:

We are a rump faction of a party which is sliding—indeed, rolling—into an abyss of ruin.

It would be easy and comforting to attribute this failure to the sins of Humphrey, Richard Daley, or John Connally, to a killer five years ago or a killer more recent. It would be easy—and it would be self-deluding and self-defeating and wildly, catastrophically wrong. . . .

These men, the current villains in the liberal demonology, have played their full part in these events . . . [*but*] there is no hope for this coalition, no hope for a regeneration of our politics, unless we are prepared to learn from the errors and illusions that have brought us to our present pass; not the errors of others, though they have been more than plentiful, but our own. It is time to face our truth. . . .

This is not only a matter of the war in Vietnam—where we promised peace in 1964 and then stood silent for too long as that pledge was broken and our Administration went to war. It is a matter, sadly, of almost all the great social legislation of the last four years.

We promised education—but our education programs have not taught the children. We promised new cities—but our housing programs have gone far toward destroying the ones we have. We promised health—and our vaunted medicare program has shot the cost of medical care up while doing little or nothing to improve the quality of care for which we now pay so much. We promised help to the farm—and nearly eliminated the farmer.

We promised blacks that patience would bring justice. We promised whites that justice would bring order. We have achieved neither. We promised and promised, passed laws and appropriation bills, taxed and spent. And when it was all over, who is there to say that life is truly better than it was before?

7

The Conscience of a Conservative

BARRY GOLDWATER

The most interesting phenomenon in recent American politics has been the rise of a very articulate conservative movement, and the most noted of the political conservative spokesmen is Barry Goldwater of Arizona. In the following paragraphs Mr. Goldwater sets forth his beliefs on the meaning of conservatism and the steps that should be taken to translate these beliefs into action.

I have been much concerned that so many people today with conservative instincts feel compelled to apologize for them. Or if not to apologize directly, to qualify their commitments in a way that amounts to breast-beating. "Republican candidates," Vice-President Nixon has said, "should be economic conservatives, but conservatives with a heart." President Eisenhower announced during his first term, "I am conservative when it comes to economic problems but liberal when it comes to human problems." Still other Republican leaders have insisted on calling themselves "progressive" conservatives.[1] These formulations are tantamount to an admission that conservatism is a narrow, mechanistic economic theory that may work very well as a bookkeeper's guide, but cannot be relied upon as a comprehensive political philosophy.

The same judgment, though in the form of an attack rather than an admission, is advanced by the radical camp. "We liberals," they say, "are interested in people. Our concern is with human beings, while you conservatives are preoccupied with the preservation of economic privilege and status." Take them a step further, and the liberals will turn the accusations into a class argument: it is the little people that concern us, not the "malefactors of great wealth."

Such statements, from friend and foe alike, do great injustice to the conservative point of view. Conservatism is not an economic theory, though it has economic implications. The shoe is precisely on the other foot: it is socialism that subordinates all other considerations to man's material well-being. It is conservatism that puts material things in their proper place—that has a structured view of the human being and of human society, in which economics plays only a subsidiary role.

The root difference between the conservatives and the liberals of today is that conservatives take account of the whole man, while the liberals tend to look only at the material side of man's nature. The conservative believes that man is, in part, an economic, an animal creature; but that

---

From Barry Goldwater, The Conscience of a Conservative *(Shepherdsville, Kentucky: Victor Publishing Company, 1960), pp. 9–14. Reprinted by permission of the publisher.*

[1] This is a strange label indeed: it implies that "ordinary" conservatism is opposed to progress. Have we forgotten that America made its greatest progress when conservative principles were honored and preserved?

he is also a spiritual creature with spiritual needs and spiritual desires. What is more, these needs and desires reflect the superior side of man's nature, and thus take precedence over his economic wants. Conservatism therefore looks upon the enhancement of man's spiritual nature as the primary concern of political philosophy. Liberals, on the other hand—in the name of a concern for "human beings"—regard the satisfaction of economic wants as the dominant mission of society. They are, moreover, in a hurry. So that their characteristic approach is to harness the society's political and economic forces into a collective effort to compel "progress." In this approach, I believe they fight against nature.

Surely the first obligation of a political thinker is to understand the nature of man. The conservative does not claim special powers of perception on this point, but he does claim a familiarity with the accumulated wisdom and experience of history, and he is not too proud to learn from the great minds of the past.

The first thing he has learned about man is that each member of the species is a unique creature. Man's most sacred possession is his individual soul—which has an immortal side, but also a mortal one. The mortal side establishes his absolute differentness from every other human being. Only a philosophy that takes into account the essential differences between men, and, accordingly, makes provision for developing the different potentialities of each man can claim to be in accord with nature. We have heard much in our time about "the common man." It is a concept that pays little attention to the history of a nation that grew great through the initiative and ambition of uncommon men. The conserva-

tive knows that to regard man as part of an undifferentiated mass is to consign him to ultimate slavery.

Secondly, the conservative has learned that the economic and spiritual aspects of man's nature are inextricably intertwined. He cannot be economically free, or even economically efficient, if he is enslaved politically; conversely, man's political freedom is illusory if he is dependent for his economic needs on the state.

The conservative realizes, thirdly, that man's development, in both its spiritual and material aspects, is not something that can be directed by outside forces. Every man, for his individual good and for the good of his society, is responsible for his own development. The choices that govern his life are choices that he must make: they cannot be made by any other human being, or by a collectivity of human beings. If the conservative is less anxious than his liberal brethren to increase social security "benefits," it is because he is more anxious than his liberal brethren that people be free throughout their lives to spend their earnings when and as they see fit.

So it is that conservatism, throughout history, has regarded man neither as a potential pawn of other men, nor as a part of a general collectivity in which the sacredness and the separate identity of individual human beings are ignored. Throughout history, true conservatism has been at war equally with autocrats and with "democratic" Jacobins. The true conservative was sympathetic with the plight of the hapless peasant under the tyranny of the French monarchy. And he was equally revolted at the attempt to solve that problem by a mob tyranny that paraded under the banner of egalitarianism. . . .

8

The Conscience of a Liberal

EUGENE J. McCARTHY

Senator McCarthy examines the term "liberalism" and points out what it is and what it is not. He shows some of the strengths and some of the pitfalls into which liberals are prone to fall, but most of all Senator McCarthy explains what it means to be a liberal at this point in the twentieth century.

Politics in the United States is nondoctrinaire and nonideological. Two terms, however, applied to politics seem to have doctrinal or ideological content for those who use them. These are the words "liberal" and "conservative." In states which do not have party designation for legislators—like my own state, Minnesota—it is a practice to hold organizing caucuses of "liberals" and of "conservatives." Americans for Democratic Action, a "liberal" organization, regularly calls for the purification of the Democratic party by the elimination of the "conservative" members. The Conservative Citizens Committee, in companionship with a new organization called simply the New Party, is trying to purge the Republican party of its "liberal" tendencies.

The clarification of the terms liberal and conservative, at least as they are applied to politics, is made more difficult because many explanations and definitions of liberals and liberalism have been offered by conservatives, and on the other hand, many explanations and definitions of conserva-

tives and of conservatism have been offered by liberals.

In line with this practice William F. Buckley, Jr., admitted conservative and editor of the *National Review*, makes his case against the liberals by saying that "there is an enormous area in which the liberal does not know how to think. More specifically," says Buckley, "he is illogical, he is inconsistent, and he cannot assess evidence."

Liberals on the other hand are inclined to be less direct and harsh, but rather given to more subtle or sophisticated explanations of their conservative opponents. Witness Arthur Schlesinger, Jr.'s analysis of the new conservatism as having strong interior tendencies toward schizophrenia.[1] He asserts that it is out of touch with reality. There are less sophisticated liberals, I admit, who are satisfied to call conservatives "medieval" or "Neanderthal."

Life would certainly be made much easier for liberals if it were possible to define carefully the word "liberalism" and limit its use according to this restricted definition. Until such a definition can be worked out, it would be helpful if the word "liberal" were used only as a modifier. If this were general

From Eugene J. McCarthy, Frontiers in American Democracy *(New York: World Publishing Company, 1960), pp. 63–70. Copyright © 1960 by Eugene J. McCarthy. Reprinted by permission of the publisher.*

[1] "The New Conservatism: Politics of Nostalgia," *The Reporter*, June 16, 1955, p. 11

agreement, no one would be merely a liberal, or a "pseudo-liberal" in the terminology of J. Edgar Hoover. Anyone to whom the word was applied would have to be a liberal something. In politics he would not be merely a liberal, but a liberal Republican, a liberal Democrat, or a liberal Vegetarian, or a liberal something else. There no longer would be religious liberals, but liberal Methodists, liberal Presbyterians, liberal Catholics, and so on. The word "intellectual" and the word "liberal" would no longer be considered synonymous. There would henceforth be liberal intellectuals and illiberal intellectuals, and when *Time* magazine's phrenological distinctions were applied, liberal eggheads and illiberal eggheads—or turnip-heads, if you prefer.

The truth is that American liberalism is not a twentieth-century manifestation of nineteenth-century liberalism. It is not even a development from that earlier liberalism.

Liberalism in the United States is not a system of philosophy, or a religion, or a school of political, economic, or social thought. It is not a way of life, as some of its proponents claim and as some of its opponents charge. It is not a "demanding faith" as Americans for Democratic Action say; nor is it on the contrary an "undemanding faith" as Professor William Leuchtenburg of Harvard University critically described it; nor is it without faith, or at least without a home for "faith," as Frederich K. Wilhelmsen of Santa Clara University wrote in *Commonweal*.

I believe it fair to say that American liberalism is no more materialistic in its metaphysics than is American conservatism. It is no more rationalistic in its psychology than is American conservatism. It cannot be described as more utilitarian, more positivistic, or relativistic in its ethics and in its value judgments than can conservatism. Nor can it be described as more opportunistic or Machiavellian in its politics.

To the extent that the liberal movement in the United States in this century can be given historical position and positive content, it must be identified and associated with the New Deal of the first two Roose-

velt administrations. The New Deal involved political and economic changes which were the results of a response to urgent practical demands, rather than a fulfillment or an advancement of an ideology or a doctrinaire theory of political, economic, or social organization.

The total program provided for the pooling of social risks, as in the case of the social security program, and the pooling of economic risks, as in the case of the Federal Deposit Insurance program. It included such projects as the Tennessee Valley Authority and the hydroelectric developments in the Far West. In each case, the decision to include the specific program or project was based on practical considerations—the development and distribution of power, for example, or the related problems of navigation and flood control, rather than to an ideological demand for social ownership or collectivization. At the same time that the above-mentioned programs were advanced, or projects begun, along with others providing for greater control by government over such things as the investment market and the wages and hours of workingmen, efforts were made to protect the small independent business and the independent family-size farm.

As the general economic well-being of the people of the United States improved, the positive content of the liberal movement narrowed and popular support fell away. When there is a call for volunteers to make and carry the bricks of domestic economic reform, the liberal response is strong. The Marshall Plan and Point IV programs too—foreign-aid programs closely akin in spirit to our domestic programs—were strongly endorsed by liberal groups.

In short, if American liberalism has one mark it is its economic emphasis. Yet few if any liberal thinkers really believe the "belly" communist argument, or believe that communism can be overcome by dropping Montgomery Ward catalogues from airplanes flying over communist countries.

The lack of ideological unity among American liberals, beyond agreement on economic programs and civil rights, explains in part their attachment to individual leaders manifest in their enthusiasm for President Roosevelt, their short-lived courtship of General Eisenhower in the Eisenhower-and/or-Douglas campaign of 1948, and since then their enthusiastic support of Adlai Stevenson. The attachment to one person eliminates or at least moderates the division, reduces the uncertainties and conflicts, and provides in the person a unity of cause.

If the bond among American liberals today is not one of ideas or even of program, how can we distinguish them? The common trait, I believe, is one of method or manner of approach to human problems. It is this manner of approach that distinguishes the liberal from the illiberal and establishes the characteristics of modern liberalism and the modern liberal.

The liberal is ideally and characteristically an optimist, not blindly so as one who fails to understand or to comprehend the reality of the times, but rather as one who, with full awareness of the difficulties of a situation and with full awareness also of the potentiality for failure of man and his institutions, remains hopefully confident that improvement and progress can be accomplished. This does not mean that he believes that things are necessarily getting better and better, nor does it require any belief in the inevitability of progress.

The ideal liberal is normally progressive, willing both to advocate and to accept change—really a safe general position since no individual person or human institution can ever claim perfection. But he need not always advocate something wholly new; he can support elements of the status quo, or he may even advocate a return to conditions known in the past. He does not necessarily believe in change for the sake of change or, as some critics of liberals insist, in historical determinism and the inevitability of collectivization.

The liberal is normally tolerant of the opinions and actions of others, yet he exercises this tolerance without abjectly denying the certainty of his own position, without conceding that another's position may be right, without agreeing to disagree, and certainly without accepting that one man's opinion is as good as that of another. The basis for his tolerance must be a genuine humility arising from the awareness of the limitations of the human person and from a sense of the dignity of every man.

There are, of course, dangers in the liberal approach. Optimism can become self-delusion, change an obsession. Because the future is not the past, the liberal may be led, as Vincent McNabb points out, to think that it must be something entirely different from the past. He may therefore neglect or take lightly the lesson of history and underestimate the value of custom and of tradition. He may accept that there must be an absolute break between past and present, and again between present and future. His tolerance gone too far may lead him to accept unsound positions of religious indifferentism, of intellectual pluralism, and of subjective morality. However, such excesses are not inherent in liberalism.

In his concern for freedom, the liberal is in danger of forgetting the obligations and restraints that are the price of freedom and of discounting the importance of institutions and their function in the perfecting of individual persons.

The liberal of today cannot be satisfied in the belief that his approach to human problems is the better one, but must clarify his ideas as to the nature of man and the meaning and goal of human existence. The liberal of today must do more than "feel free." He must concern himself not only with claiming freedom, but with understanding it, since time has worked significant changes in the meaning of this word.

The liberal who speaks much of freedom must stop to consider its meaning. He should recall that the free man of the Greek philosophers is the man who has achieved freedom, who has overcome ignorance and acquired a measure of self-mastery. In this classical philosophical tradition, the concept of freedom is applied principally to the state of being, rather than to the conditions under which man lives and works in order to attain that state. In our time the emphasis has been upon the condition of the striving, rather than upon the status which might be reached. The meaning which we give to the term "freedom," either in the static sense or as it relates to the condition of man's living and seeking for fulfillment, depends basically upon our concept of the nature of man and the purpose of his existence.

It is not enough to want freedom for its own sake. Freedom is not baseless or relative, but desired and pursued to make man more responsible, more in control of his life and his time. Thus freedom from want makes a man more surely free to choose poverty if he wishes. Freedom from oppression or domination leaves a man more truly free to choose the object of his allegiance, or to whom he will give obedience.

The complexity of modern problems, the quickened pace of historical change, the involvement with people of other races and cultures—all call for a liberal response.

American liberalism as a force bearing on American politics can be a positive force for good only if it clarifies its positive content and becomes something more than the liberalism of the immediate past. Optimism, generosity, tolerance, and even humility, good and necessary as they are, are of little use unless there can be some agreement as to what is good.

American liberals today are faced with the pluralistic society they once only dreamed and talked about. There is no longer a dominant group in our American culture, although it will take time for the popular mind to cast off the image of the American prototype, to whose loyalties and mores all other groups conformed and were American in so far as they conformed. The liberal's task is to secure this individualistic society with his tolerance and generosity and at the same time in the words of Woodrow Wilson, "to make sure of the things which unite."

9

Our Radical Right—The Dispossessed

Daniel Bell

A phenomenon of the 1960's has been the rise throughout the country of various radical-right groups—the John Birch Society, Christian Crusade, and White Citizen Councils, to name a few. Although they may differ in detail, on many points these disparate groups are united. Most political, social, military, and economic trends are viewed with alarm. They also exhibit something of a nostalgia for an earlier age. What groups are a fertile recruiting ground for the radical right? Why do these people feel dispossessed? Is this rebellion a transitory movement, or does it have deep roots?

Most of the political changes that have transformed American life, the changes

From Daniel Bell, "The Dispossessed—1962," Columbia University Forum, Fall 1962, pp. 4–12. Reprinted by permission of the author.

that have aroused such notable right-wing rancor today, originated in legislative measures passed thirty years ago and before—the income tax, social security, welfare measures, and the like. In many instances, the changes have been irrevocably built into the structure of American society. Why then have the consequences of these changes become manifest only at this very late date? And what is the nature of the right-wing rancor? . . .

Over the years since 1932, then, there has been a steady erosion of conservative influence. The expansion of the executive agencies of government in the past three decades, drawing key personnel largely from the major universities, has given the middle and (later) top echelons of government a predominantly liberal coloration; and this is one of the factors that accounts for the tension between the Executive and the Congress which has been so marked in the last decade and a half. More slowly, the personnel of the life-time federal judiciary began to change through appointments by Democratic presidents.

The right-wing Republicans hoped that the election of Dwight Eisenhower would reverse this massive trend. But it did not—perhaps could not. Eisenhower's Labor Secretary courted the unions; social security benefits increased; during the 1957–59 recession, unemployment benefits were extended; and to reverse the economic slowdown, the government, in good Keynesian style, ran a $12,000,000,000 budgetary deficit. Only Congress, reflecting the disproportionate power of the small-town areas and the established seniority system, has remained, practically speaking, under conservative control. For the Radical Right, then, eight years of "moderation" proved as frustrating as twenty years of New Dealism.

To this extent, the meaning of the Kennedy victory for the members of the Radical Right was the gnawing realization that as a social group they were becoming dispossessed of their power in American society. But more than a generational change has taken place. Until thirty years ago, the source of "visible" political and social power in American life was predominantly the small-town leaders: lawyers, real estate dealers, bankers, merchants, and small manufacturers. Their political hegemony in the states was virtually complete; nation-ally, the values of the society reflected the influence of the business community.

The first challenges to this dominance came from the ethnic groups in the large urban centers and from the trade union movement. Only after considerable friction were these challenges absorbed; power became more diffused. But the newer threat does not arise from any direct political competition, as was true in the case of the urban political machines. It arises from the fact that the complex problems of contemporary economic and political and military management require a technical expertise which is far beyond the understanding of the dispossessed groups for whom the "simple virtues" and the "traditional moralities" were the only guides that were felt to be necessary to the formulation of public policy. It arises from the fact that social change now has to be directed and planned. For the ramifications of many major changes —whether it be space exploration, counterforce military strategy, urban renewal, or medicare—are widespread and produce a whole series of secondary effects whose consequences have to be anticipated lest chaos result. (The passage of medicare, for example, would require a widespread hospital-building program and a stepped-up recruitment of nurses to meet the shortages that would certainly ensue.) As a corollary to these general conditions, it is a new "technocratic" elite—scientists, mathematicians, economists, sociologists, with their new techniques of decision-making: input-output matrices, systems analysis, linear programming—that now becomes essential if not to the wielding of power, then to the formulations and analyses on which political judgments have to be made. It is these complexities and the rise of the new skill groups which pose the real threat of dispossession to those who once held power by virtue of their wealth or property or gerrymandered political control.

The Small-Town Mind

In identifying "the dispossessed" it would be misleading to apply economic labels. It is not economic interest alone that elicits their anxieties. A small businessman may have made considerable amounts of money in the last decade (in part, because he has wider scope in masking profits than a large corporation), and yet . . . strongly resent the regulations in Washington, the high income tax, or, more to the point, the erosion of his own political status. Indeed, to the extent that any such economic location is possible, one can say that the social group most threatened by the structural changes in society is the "old" middle class: the independent physician, farm owner, small-town lawyer, real estate promoter, home builder, automobile dealer, small businessman, and the like. But the common denominator of such groups is the life-style and value of Protestant Fundamentalism—the nativist nationalism, the good-and-evil moralism through which they see the world. Theirs are the values of the dominant thought of the nineteenth century; and they have been defending these values—in what is now a rear-guard action—for the last forty years.

The present upsurge of American nativism on the Radical Right is most directly paralleled, in fact, in the virulent assaults on teachers' loyalty which were levied in the 1920's by fundamentalist churchmen in the name of God and by patriotic organizations like the American Legion in the name of country. Such conflicts—most vividly the Scopes trial and the bellicose efforts of Mayor "Big Bill" Thompson in Chicago to expunge favorable references to Great Britain from the school textbooks—were between "fundamentalists" and "modernists," between "patriots" and "internationalists." These skirmishes in the 1920's were the first defensive reactions of the nativist and the old middle-class elements to the entry into society of formerly "disenfranchised" elements, particularly the children of immigrants and members of minority ethnic groups—an entry made through the only major route open to them, the urban political machines. In short, theirs was a reaction to the rise of a mass society. . . .

The social ideas of fundamentalism are quite familiar—a return to the "simple" virtues of individual initiative and self-reliance. In political terms, this means a dismantling of much of the social security program, the elimination of the income tax, the reduction of the role of the federal government in economic life, and the return to the state and local governments of the major responsibilities for welfare, labor, and similar legislation. Now from any realistic political view, the dismantling of social security, income tax, etc., is quite hopeless, as elections since 1936 have proved. But what gives the fundamentalist Right its political momentum today is its effort to hitch these attacks on "collectivism" to a high-powered anticommunist crusade, which identifies any extension of government power as communism. What in effect it seeks to do is identify the welfare state with socialism and equate liberalism with communism. In this respect, it represents a crude but powerful effort to resist all social change, to use the emotions generated by foreign policy conflicts to confuse domestic issues.

Until now, much of the political strength of the small-town right wing has stemmed from its ability to block the reapportionment of seats in the state legislatures and to gerrymander seats for Congress; the result is a heavily disproportionate representation of the small towns and rural areas in both assemblies. In the U.S. House of Representatives, for example, 260 of the 435 seats—or almost 60 per cent of all the seats—are in districts dominated by small towns and rural areas. In thirteen states, fewer than a third of the voters—and these are primarily in small towns—can elect a majority of the state legislators; in forty-four states, less than 40 per cent can elect a majority. The Supreme Court decision of April, 1962, ordering a redistricting of seats in the Tennessee legislature (which had blocked all reapportionment since 1901) may be the most important political act of the decade. Certainly it will break the hold of the small town on many state legislatures and reduce its influence in Congress—but how soon remains to be seen.

The Managerial Dispossessed

To list the managerial executive class as among "the dispossessed" seems strange, especially in the light of the argument that a revolution which is undermining property as the basis of power is enfranchising a new class of technical personnel, among whom are the business executives. Yet the managerial class has been under immense strain all through this period, a strain arising, in part from the discrepancy between their large power and prestige within a particular enterprise and their lesser power and esteem in the nation as a whole.

The modern corporation, even though it holds its legitimation from the institution of private property, is vastly different from the family firm which it has succeeded. The family firm of old was securely rooted in the legal and moral tradition of private property. The enterprise "belonged to" the owner, and was sanctioned, depending on one's theological tastes, by God or by Natural Right. The modern manager clearly lacks the inherited family justification: increasingly he is recruited from the amorphous middle class. He receives a salary, bonus, options, expense accounts, and "perks" (perquisites, like the use of company planes [and] memberships in country clubs), but his power is transitory and he cannot pass on his position; the manager needs an ideology. In no other capitalist order but the American—not in England, or Germany, or France—has this drive for ideology been so compulsive. . . .

Already in 1960, the efforts of a number of corporations led by General Electric, to go "directly" into politics by sending out vast amounts of propaganda to their employees and to the public, by encouraging right-to-work referendums in the states—indicated the mood of political dispossession in many corporations. Since then, a significant number of corporations have been contributing financially to the seminars of the Radical Right evangelists. The National Education Program, at Harding College in Arkansas, which prepares films on communism and materials on free enterprise, has been used extensively by General Electric, U.S. Steel, Olin Mathieson Chemical, Monsanto Chemical, Swift & Co., and others. Boeing Aviation and the Richfield Oil Co. has [sic] sponsored many of the anticommunism seminars on the West Coast. The Jones and Laughlin Steel Company has a widespread propaganda program for its employees. One of the most politically active companies is the Allen Bradley Co. of Milwaukee, which makes machine tools and electrical equipment. The Allen Bradley Co. advertises in the John Birch Society magazine and reprinted the testimony before the House Un-American Activities Committee on Fred Schwarz, a reprint which Schwarz claims had "wider distribution than any other government document in the history of the United States, with the possible exception of the Bill of Rights, the Declaration of Independence, and the Constitution." Ironically, the Allen Bradley Co., which continually extols the virtue of free enterprise, was one of the electrical companies convicted of collusive bidding and illegal price-rigging.

Despite the failure of the corporations to affect significantly the 1960 elections—their failure on the right-to-work issue being one key indicator—it is likely that the Kennedy-Blough imbroglio of 1962 will provide an even greater impetus for corporations to finance right-wing political activity in the coming years.

The Military Dispossessed

The irony for the American military establishment is that at a time when the military in the new states overseas has emerged as one of the ruling forces of those states (often because it is the one organized group in an amorphous society), and while at this time in United States history the amount of money spent for military purposes (roughly 50 per cent of the federal budget) is the highest in peacetime history, the U.S. military is subject to grave challenges in its very own bailiwick. The problems of national security, like those of the national economy, have become so staggeringly complex that they can no longer be settled simply by military common sense or past experience. . . .

In the last decade, most of the thinking on strategic problems, political and economic, has been done in the universities or in government-financed but autonomous bodies like the RAND Corporation. A new profession, that of the "military intellectual" has emerged, and men like Kahn, Wohlstetter, Brodie, Hitch, Kissinger, Bokie, Schelling "move freely through the corridors of the Pentagon and the State Department," as the TLS writer observed, "rather as the Jesuits through the courts of Madrid and Vienna three centuries ago."

In structural terms, the military establishment may be one of the tripods of a "power elite," but in sociological fact the military officers feel dispossessed because they often lack the necessary technical skills or knowledge to answer the new problems confronting them. Since the end of World War II, the military has been involved in a number of battles to defend its elite position, beginning in 1945 with the young physicists and nuclear scientists, down to the present action against the "technipols" (the military's derisive term for technicians and political theorists) whom Secretary McNamara has brought into the Department of Defense. For in present-day decision-making the nature of strategy involves a kind of analysis for which experience alone is insufficient. Consider the complex problem of choosing a "weapons system": the long lead time that is necessary in planning and testing—let alone producing—such weapons compels an analyst to construct mathematical models as almost the only means of making rational choices. The recent controversy over the desirability of the RS-70 bomber is a case in point. The systems analysts in the office of the Secretary of Defense, led by Charles Hitch, an economist from RAND who has become the comptroller in the Pentagon, decided on the basis of computer analysis that the manned RS-70 bomber would be outmoded by the time it could come into full production, and that it would be wiser to concentrate on missiles. . . .

The traditional services, and their chiefs, have reacted to all this with dismay. As a recent article in *Fortune* put it:

> It was at this point that the military professionals begin to exhibit real alarm. McNamara did not ignore them; they had their say, as usual, in defense of their service budgets. But his drive, his intense preoccupation with figures and facts, left the Chiefs and their staffs with the feeling that the computers were taking over.

And the *Fortune* article, reflecting the dismay of the service Chiefs, was also a veiled attack on McNamara's penchant for "quantification," for his failure to respect "the uncomputable that had made Curtis Le May (the head of the big bomber command) the world's finest operational airman," for his "inexperience" in military strategy and for his reliance on the technipols, "the inner group of lay experts who were dispersed through State, the White House, and Defense." The import of the article was clear: the traditional military professionals were being dispossessed. . . .

One can already see, in the behavior of retired officers, the rancor of an old guard that finds its knowledge outdated, its authority disputed or ignored, and that is beginning to argue, bitterly, that if only its advice had been followed, America would not be on the defensive. A surprising number of high-ranking officers on active duty, as well as high-ranking retired officers, have become active in extreme Right organizations. A few—Major General Walker is an example—may feel that all intellectuals are involved in a "plot" against the nation. No doubt most of the military men will be forced—a number have already plunged—into the more complex and bureaucratic game of recruiting particular groups of scientists for their own purposes (in part through the power of the purse) or attempting to make alliances. In the long run, the military profession may itself become transformed through new modes of training, and a new social type may arise.

The Southern Dispossessed

In his primer on "one-upmanship," Stephen Potter observed that one could destroy any political generalization by asking, "but what about the South?" The American South contains many of "the dispossessed," and partakes of the Radical Right, but, to be sure, the reasons for this evolution may be of a somewhat different order.

For many decades, there has not been one South but two Souths, that of myth and that of reality, and the fact is that for the past hundred years the South has lived more by its myth than its reality. . . .

At the heart of the myth is this idea of a community, of an organic way of life, which is morally superior to the deracinated, vulgarized, tinseled North. Mr. Davidson's words merely reiterate the note struck by George Fitzhugh, in his *Sociology for the South* (1854), when he attacked the North for instituting an industrial wage slavery which was worse than the direct master-slave relationship in the South. ("There can never be among slaves a class so degraded as is found about the wharves and suburbs of cities.") The pastoral society of the South ("quiet and contented . . . has suffered so little from crime or extreme poverty") was contrasted with the brutish system of industrial laissez-faire (which only promoted selfishness [and] indifference to community and to liberty itself).

But any "traditional" view of the Southern past usually ignores, in the most extraordinary way, not only the direct economic exploitation of the Negro slave, but the *unrestrained* way in which the Negro could be dehumanized—unrestrained as Stanley Elkins has pointed out in his book *Slavery,* because of the lack of any moral agency, such as existed in Catholic countries, which could impose a set of limits through a conception of the Negro as a human soul.

All this has left its mark. One rarely finds in other former slave-holding societies the fear of color and especially the sense of guilt (deriving in considerable measure from unconscious sexual fantasies and fears) over the treatment of the Negro as subhuman, a buffoon, or a child that one finds in the American South. To say to the post-Civil War South, as Mr. Davidson does, that its difficulty lies in having lived with Negroes as "technical citizens, endowed with their citizenship without Southern consent," is a nicety that begs the question whether the South is indeed a part of the larger American polity and its moral code (or only a "defeated union"), and to ignore altogether the exploitative economic and social nature of the "organic community."

If a huge portion—in some areas the majority—of a population has to be exempted from the Southern "community," so, too, must one subtract the large stratum of "poor whites." For a society that, in myth at least, describes itself as reproducing the "constitutional order of the early Republic," the existence of Southern populism, with its raw appeals to violence, with its rant and swagger, with its contempt for culture, must be most embarrassing. It is much too easy—and simply false—to ascribe Southern populism to "northern theories of egalitarianism." Tom Watson, Tom Heflin, Gene Talmadge, Cole Blease, James K. Vardaman, Theodore Bilbo, Huey Long, John Rankin, and Orval Faubus (Snopeses that they may be)—are as indigenous to the South as John C. Calhoun, George Fitzhugh, Thomas R. Dew, or any other genteel intellectual and political figures. . . .

The Revolt Against Modernity

In the broadest sense, the attitude of the Right in the United States is a revolt against modernity and the requirements of planned social change in the society. (By "planned social change" I mean the attempt to be aware of the ramified consequences of any social action and to plan accordingly; a modern corporation could not exist without planning its future; neither can a society.)

Often, as in the jibe of Senator Goldwater against the "whiz kids in the Pentagon" or the heavy-handed attack by former President Eisenhower against the "theorists" in government, these attitudes are part of an anti-intellectualism which is a defensive posture against the complexities of modern problems. But more is at stake for the Right. There is a deeper threat which they correctly perceive—the threat of displacement.

The new nature of decision-making, its increasing technicality, forces a displacement of the older elites. Within a business enterprise, the newer techniques of operations research and linear programming almost amount to the "automation" of middle management and its displacement by mathematicians and engineers, working either within the firm or as consultants. In the economy, the businessman finds himself subject to price, wage, and investment criteria laid down by the economists in gov-

ernment. In the polity, the old military elites find themselves challenged in the determination of strategy by scientists, who have the technical knowledge on nuclear capability—missile development and the like—or by the "military intellectuals" whose conceptions of weapon systems and political warfare seek to guide military allocations.

In the broadest sense, the spread of education, of research, of administration and government creates a new constituency, the technical and professional intelligentsia. While these are not bound by the common ethos that would constitute them a new class, nor even a cohesive social group, they are the products of a new system of recruitment for power (just as property and inheritance represented the old system) and those who are the products of the old system understandably feel a vague and apprehensive disquiet—the disquiet of the dispossessed.

10

The New Left

JACK NEWFIELD

There seems to be a general tendency on the part of unthinking people to lump all radicals together. How does Jack Newfield avoid this misconception? In what ways does the author distinguish between the New and the Old Left? Is there any danger in attempting to define a movement in its infancy? In view of subsequent developments since its publication, what comments, reservations, or criticisms would you make of Newfield's analysis of the New Left?

. . . There is now a deep disjunction between generations of American radicals.

From Jack Newfield, A Prophetic Minority (New York: World Publishing Company, 1970), pp. 15–17. Copyright © 1970 by Jack Newfield. Reprinted by permission of the publisher.

The older ideological Left—socialist and Communist—virtually withered away during the drought of the 1950's. A New Left then began slowly to take root, nourished by the pacifist and socialist British New Left of the Aldermaston Marches and the *New Left Review;* by the Beats' private disaffection from and rage at the Rat Race; by the Cuban revolution; and by the writings of such men as C. Wright Mills, Albert Camus, and Paul Goodman. This New Left blossomed dramatically in the spring of 1960 with the lunch-counter sit-ins, peace marches, capital-punishment protests, and a riot against the chief symbol of McCarthyism—the House Un-American Activities Committee.

Defining this New Radicalism at its current youthful stage is a little like defining the infant abolitionist movement in 1850. Nevertheless, it seems, at bottom, an ethical revolt against the visible devils of racism, poverty, and war, as well as the less tangible devils of centralized decision-making, manipulative, impersonal bureaucracies, and the hypocrisy that divides America's ideals from its actions from Watts to Saigon.

The New Radicalism appears to be an attempt to add a wholly new communitarian and existential dimension to American politics by a generation that grew up during the years of Warsaw, Auschwitz, Hiroshima, Nuremberg, Seoul, and Budapest. Such events convinced many of us that all the old, pat leftist formulas had failed, and a new ethical politics was desperately required.

The New Left expresses this new ethical-rooted politics in its affirmation of community, honesty, and freedom, and in its indifference to ideology, discipline, economics, and conventional political forms.

What is explicitly *new* about the New Left is its ecumenical mixture of political traditions that were once murderous rivals in Russia, Spain, France, and the United States. It contains within it, and often within individuals, elements of anarchism, socialism, pacifism, existentialism, humanism, transcendentalism, bohemianism, Populism, mysticism, and black nationalism.

I define the New Radicalism broadly to include organizations like Students for a Democratic Society (SDS) and the Student Nonviolent Coordinating Committee (SNCC); *ad hoc* decentralized movements like the Berkeley Free Speech Movement (FSM) and the movement against the war in Vietnam. It includes idealistic Peace Corps and VISTA (domestic Peace Corps) volunteers and nihilistic Berkeley bohemians; new institutions like the Institute for Policy Studies and the Mississippi Freedom Democratic Party; new publications like *Liberation* and the *Southern Courier;* individuals like Bob Parris, Tom Hayden, and Staughton Lynd; it even spills over into sociocultural movements represented by Bob Dylan, Phil Ochs, Dr. Timothy Leary, and Allen Ginsberg.

In addition to the organizational New Left of radical activists, there is also an invisible layer to what is called the movement. This consists of recent college graduates and young intellectuals now tucked away in government agencies, publishing houses, faculties, graduate schools, and editorial offices. Perhaps uncomfortable with the gritty militance of the full-time radicals, these career-oriented sympathizers nevertheless share the New Radicals' basic values and assumptions about a commercial, militaristic, bureaucratic, and exclusive society.

However, I carefully distinguish from the New Left a phenomenon I call the Hereditary Left, represented by the Progressive Labor Party, the W.E.B. Du Bois Clubs, and the recently dissolved May 2nd Movement. I contend that despite surface similarities with the New Left, the Hereditary Left is actually an ideological extension of the old 1930's Left, is ideologically Leninist in structure and outlook, and is oriented toward either China or the Soviet Union rather than toward forging a new vision of American society.

The New Left includes probably no more than 250,000 people, between the ages of fifteen and thirty. It is only a minute—but intellectually gifted—fraction of a generation that has 5.2 millions of its members in colleges, and several millions more just graduated or about to enter a university. But I think it will be the fragment to give my generation (I am twenty-eight) its historical character, just as a visionary fragment gave the Lost and Beat Generations their identities.

My criticisms of the New Left are serious ones, but they do not detract from the ultimate validity of the movement. My reservations are of three basic types. One is that the New Radicals, while justified in most of their assaults on the Great Society, have been weak on providing creative alternatives. Occasionally they have been negative to the edge of nihilism. Two, they are sometimes hopelessly romantic, especially about unromantic aberrations like violence and authoritarianism. Some of them don't quite understand what nondemocratic socialism has done to the lives of those who live under its yoke; they don't quite understand the equal duplicity of the phrases "free world" and "national liberation." My third qualification is that segments of the New Left are anti-intellectual, sometimes even anti-rational. . . .

8

VOTING BEHAVIOR, NOMINATIONS, AND ELECTIONS: GOVERNMENT BY THE CONSENT OF THE GOVERNED OR THE GOVERNING?

Without question the most recognizable and generally accepted hall-mark of popular government is the free election. Obviously a free society requires additional safeguards, but without regular, unshackled elections, popular rule as we understand it cannot exist. Not all countries with elections are free, but no country can be free without them. Indeed, our judgment of the democratic character of nations, states, and even local communities frequently hinges upon the integrity of the ballot box, contested elections, and public participation in the political process. Elections are a way in which power can be maintained or transferred in an orderly manner. In many respects, free societies achieve their finest hour when the governed elect their governors.

The choosing of elected officials involves several processes—selection, solicitation, and election. All are so basic and intermingled that it is difficult to tell where one stops and another begins. In running for the Presidency, a candidate's campaign for his party's nomination and his drive for ultimate victory are almost inseparably linked. Presidential candidates and their advisers devise campaign strategy months and even years before the official kickoff, and a candidate's "buildup" begins about the same time.

Campaigning is the high drama of American politics. Every Presidential candidate has an individual style and conducts a campaign based upon the times, the mood of the people, and the issues. Nevertheless, all candidates try to project a positive image in order to give the appearance of victory. Techniques vary greatly, but every major candidate attempts to identify the key voting blocs and to assess shifts and trends within these blocs and the emergence of new coalitions and voting alignments.

Two hurdles must be surmounted before a candidate can move into 1600 Pennsylvania Avenue. The first is the national nominating convention, and the second is the electoral college scoreboard. Both of these political institutions—the national nominating convention and the electoral college—have recently come under serious criticism. Since each of them has its supporters and its reformers, the probabilities are that some modifications (but not radical change) will be forthcoming.

Chapter 8 is divided into four problem areas. The first issue deals with the changing character of voting behavior. From this topic we move into the matter of the nominating convention. The third question deals with the electoral college, and the chapter ends with the major question, "What does an election mean?"

Voting Behavior: Old, New, or Slightly Revised Voting Blocs?

Analyzing changing voting patterns and forecasting the emergence of new minorities and majorities is a fascinating subject. The topic has intrigued numerous sophisticated political commentators who write with varying views and in the process often arrive at conflicting conclusions. During the last few years a number of books on voting behavior have had wide publicity. Kevin Phillips' *The Emerging Republican Majority* places special emphasis upon growing Republican strength in the South and in the Mountain States, and has frequently been cited as a guidebook for a Republican victory. Samuel Lubell's *The Hidden Crisis in American Politics* questions whether any majority coalition with unifying influence exists today. Richard M. Scammon and Ben J. Wattenberg, in *The Real Majority,* suggest that some of the old ethnic, social, and economic blocs are still there, and waiting for the right candidate and the right party to mobilize them into voting statistics. The thesis of *The Real Majority* is that success in American politics is achieved in the moderate middle, the vital center, and not in the extreme areas of the political spectrum.

In investigating this problem, we first focus on Scammon and Wattenberg's analysis, "The Real Majority." While noting that nothing is certain in love, war, or politics, the authors suggest that some potential new voters may not be as potent as their proponents insist, and are not the center of the political spectrum. Two differing views follow—Kate Millet, "Sexual Politics," and Alan L. Otten, "Hello, Young Voters."

The National Nominating Convention: Prefabricated Pageantry or Underrated Political Institution?

Foreign visitors are often amazed and sometimes offended by the manner in which Americans nominate their Chief Executive. They regard the national convention as something of a circus, "disgustingly wasteful of time, lacking in taste and seriousness." And almost everyone, both foreign and domestic observers alike, agrees that the campaigning before and after a national convention is an exhaustive physical and emotional marathon.

The national convention, however, is not without merit. As a political institution, it helps to build party morale, regenerates loyalty and allegiance, and brings the insignificant party worker in contact with party leaders. Since the advent of radio and television, the national convention has brought the candidates closer to the people, many of whom would not listen to political speeches at any other time. Thus the convention stimulates interest in the candidates and serves as a good method of advertising the party.

Clinton Rossiter notes, "We see our follies as a people in the follies of the convention, and unless we reform ourselves, which I know we will not and I suspect we dare not do, the convention will continue to disturb the reasonable, shock the fastidious, and fascinate all of us." Other authorities see both good and bad in the convention, and, like Dwight D. Eisenhower, urge reform.

The Electoral College: Anachronism or Vital Safeguard?

Perhaps no other major governmental institution has been discussed as widely or denounced as fully in recent years as the electoral college system. Undoubtedly the 1968 election gave the movement for reform a sense of urgency when George Wallace, running on a third party ticket, posed the possibility of preventing either of the two major candidates from receiving a majority of the electoral votes. Thoughtful observers speculated on what might happen if selection of the President were foisted on the House of Representatives. Fortunately, the threat never materialized, but the possibility of deadlock or even the defeat of the majority-backed candidate remains lurking in the background, and public concern justifiably continues.

The electoral system is characterized as archaic and undemocratic. Critics point out that the electoral college not only violates the one-man, one-vote concept, but is a complete traversy on its original purpose and remains a dangerous relic of the past in a modern age.

The most popular proposal for reform of the electoral college is a plan for direct popular election of the President. Reformers are articulate and persuasive; however, their views are countered by critics who charge that direct popular election would not be a panacea, and adoption of the direct election plan would raise as many problems as it would solve. Supporters of the electoral college system point out that even the proponents of change admit that there is probably no perfect method of electing a President. At this point the battlelines are drawn and debate continues on the merits of reform vs. modified change in the present system.

In the sixth article in this chapter, The American Bar Association's Commission on Electoral Reform presents a case for elimination of the

electoral college and substitution of a direct election plan. Professors
Wallace S. Sayre and Judith H. Parris oppose this view in "The Electoral
College Serves Its Purpose."

Elections: What Does an Election Mean?

Elections in this country are never absolute mandates. The United
States does not have party government as it exists in Great Britain, and
further, we do not vote for the President and all of the members of
Congress at one time. As a consequence, elections are general guidelines
rather than finished houseplans. Moving beyond these considerations,
however, there is still room for debate as to: (1) the significance of elections, and (2) the extent to which an election represents an individual's
decision on political issues.

In the last selections in this chapter, Bernard R. Berelson, Paul F.
Lazarsfeld, and William M. McPhee report part of their research on the
1948 campaign in the city of Elmira, New York. A somewhat different
point of view is suggested by Arthur Maass in "Voters Are Not Fools."

1

The Real Majority

RICHARD M. SCAMMON/BEN J. WATTENBERG

*Voting studies of the past indicate that the youth vote is a very small factor in
American politics. Other studies also indicate that voters tend to become somewhat
more conservative with the passage of time. Is it possible that the authors are pro-
jecting past patterns into future possibilities? Could it not be that current cultural
trends may be reversing these predictions? Might candidates be misled and fail to
campaign vigorously to activate traditionally passive voting groups?*

In 1966, it may be argued, Ronald Reagan's stand against the Berkeley demonstrators won him the governorship of California. Suppose Eugene McCarthy had
been nominated in 1968; suppose Robert

From *Richard M. Scammon and Ben J. Wattenberg*, The Real Majority (*New York: Coward-Mc-
Cann, Inc., 1970*), pp. 50–58, 70–71. Copyright ©
1970 by Richard M. Scammon and Ben J. Wattenberg. Reprinted by permission of the publisher.

Kennedy had not been murdered and had
been nominated in 1968. Would they have
been held indirectly accountable for any
unruliness of their supporters—and, more
critically, for *any* unruliness by *any* youth?
What would have happened if the
Weathermen and the Mad Dogs had gone
wild as they did a year later in Chicago
and Washington? Would a youth candidate
have been vulnerable to a slashing attack
precisely on the grounds of the Social
Issue? It is not hard to imagine Richard

Nixon and Spiro Agnew making political hay with any opponents identified with disruptive young activists.

There is a final thought about the so-called youth vote. Peter Pan is make-believe. People do get older. Advocates of the New Politics have used this fact to support the contention that in the years to come their influence and numbers will swell. This will happen as the young, highly educated activists of the 1960's mature to take on leadership positions and simultaneously become a larger fragment of the electorate due to reach voting age and to the increased voting participation that comes with age. Further, there will be newer youth cohorts, presumably equally radical, adding to the numbers of the New Left or the New Politics, or whatever the phrase may be next year.

There is probably some truth to this notion. When Socialist leader Michael Harrington writes of the large enthusiastic college audiences he speaks to around America, no one disputes him. A generation ago the late Norman Thomas spoke to similar enthusiastic audiences, and it may well be that some of his auditors are the parents of Harrington's listeners today. Surely, then, many of the articulate, politicized students of the 1960's will emerge as leadership cadre in the years to come. Surely, the current youth cohort will mature and vote in higher percentages. And there will no doubt be radicals in the new youth cohorts.

However, four thoughts partially mitigate this theory. First, it is not only the radical or activist youth who will be aging. The pro-Wallace youth, the Nixon youth, and the pro-Humphrey youth will be aging, too. The teenage hands that held the tire chains in Cicero will soon be hands that are pushing baby carriages, lawn mowers, and the starter button on the engines of powerboats. The young people that were hawks will be getting older at the same rate as the youth who were doves.

Second, the fact that youth today are more likely to be college-educated would not normally correlate to a more *Demo-*

cratic or more *liberal* electorate in the future. In the past, the more educated a voter, the more likely he has been to be affluent, and the more educated *and* affluent the voter, the more likely he has been to vote *Republican* and think *conservatively*. This happened even though the 1930's equivalent of the "kids" were radicals, agitators, Communists, or what have you. There would not seem to be any good reason for this pattern to change. Only a small percentage of the current college youth are categorized as "revolutionaries," 3.5 per cent in the Yankelovich/CBS survey. Another 9.5 per cent are categorized as "radical reformers." The balance, about 87 per cent, are "moderate reformers," "middle of the road," or "conservatives," and there are, incidentally, slightly more "conservatives" than "radical reformers." In short, the college experience may be regarded as liberalizing, but not revolting. And doctors who will be making $60,000 a year in the 1970's or 1980's would not seem to be good bets to be throwing rocks through hospital windows.

Third, even though the number of young Americans in college is greater today than it was in the past, in the decade of the seventies students will still have limited numerical power. . . . But by the decade's end a projection based on Census data reveals that only 10 per cent of the electorate will be "young college graduates" (*i.e.,* under age forty in 1980). Later on in the century, in the elections of 1984, 1988, 1992, 1996, the percentage of college-educated in the electorate will be rising substantially. But an interesting question arises: In the land of the one-eyed is the one-eyed king? When most people are college-educated, will the fact of college education mean much politically? Isn't it likely then that the elitist will not be the "college graduate," but perhaps the PhD, while the mere college graduates are relegated to the ranks of the unwashed?

Fourth, something funny happens to people as they get a little older—and it even happens to the avant-garde. From only a slightly earlier era here is poetic evidence from the pen of Judith Viorst, reporting on life-styles in Greenwich Village:

Alvin and Barbara are real Village people
They lived together before they were married,
And her father came to dinner.

She is a vegetarian and an ethical nihilist
He sings Gregorian chants.
They sleep on a mattress on the floor.

He would have loved her even if she were Negro.
She would have loved him even if he weren't Jewish.
They were made for each other.

Alvin and Barbara decided to marry
They said,
Because living together is square.

They have decided to have a baby,
They said,
Because being irresponsible is square.

They may even leave the Village,
They said,
Because the Village is getting square.

I hope they don't move to New Jersey.

There is demographic evidence that when the babies come, Alvin and Barbara do indeed move to suburban New Jersey. Once there, they do not turn conservative, but neither are they quite as ready to tear down the "corrupt middle-class society" that they have become a part of. The onset of orthodontistry for their children usually coincides with the making of two more deradicalized reformers. Beware, New Left; beware, New Politics—you'll become Old Liberals before you know it!

Summing up: Six of every seven Americans are over thirty, and the average voter is closer to fifty than he is to forty. Peter Pan rarely registers; people get older every four years; as they get older, they change.

If our electorate of the 1970's is to be unyoung, it will also be basically unpoor . . . and unrich, too.

It can be seen clearly that "poor people" as a group do not make up a major segment of the electorate, if one uses a line of $3,000 as "poor." And they are becoming an even smaller minority. In 1964 the percentage of under-$3,000 families was much greater: 13 compared to the 1968 figure of 9. Even if one draws the poverty line at $5,000, the projection for 1972 reveals that only no more than 15 per cent of the voters will be "poor." This is compared to the 22 per cent in 1968.

Even that is a considerable number, to be sure. But again, as with youth, poor Americans show only small tendencies toward bloc voting as a "poor bloc." In the big cities of the North most poor are Democrats, but actually, the "poor" may be best seen as *many* blocs, each going its own way. When one thinks of who "poor people" are in America, this lack of bloc voting becomes almost self-evident. Poor people are blacks in big-city slums, who tended to vote for Humphrey. Poor people are rural whites in the Midwest, who tended to vote for Nixon. Poor people are rural whites who live in the South, who voted for Wallace. Disproportionately, poor people are aged, with their own political interests that may cross partisan lines.

Clearly, an aged white New Hampshire farm couple of limited income will have a different political background and a different political attitude from, say, a poor young black man living in East St. Louis. Yet both are "poor." Accordingly, except during depression times, a cohesive poor

Voter Participation, by Income, 1968

FAMILY INCOME PER YEAR	% OF TOTAL VOTE	% OF ELIGIBLES WHO VOTED
Under $3,000	9%	54%
$3,000–$5,000	13%	58%
$5,000–$15,000	66%	72%
$15,000 and over	12%	84%

U.S. Census Bureau

people's bloc has never really emerged in America. And like the "formerly young," there is no real evidence that the "formerly poor" continue to vote on the basis of previous poverty. In fact, a common remark one hears from those who weathered the Depression or who got out of a ghetto is: "I made it on my own, I worked my way up, why can't they?"

Although the "poor" are properly considered Democratic on balance, it is interesting to note that of the poorest dozen states in the nation, six went for Nixon, five went for Wallace, and only one for Humphrey. The richest state, Connecticut, went Democratic.[1]

Summing up: Depending on where one draws the poverty line, either four in five or nine of ten voters are *not* poor. Those that are poor do not vote similarly. The emergence of a "poor people's bloc" at a time when there are and will be fewer poor people than ever is unrealistic.

Unyoung, unpoor, the American electorate can also be viewed as unblack. (As will be noted later, the electorate is also un-Jewish, un-Catholic, un-Eastern, un-Western, un-Southern, and sometimes unnerving.) Blacks constitute only about 11 per cent of the American population—about one in every nine.

Moreover, as in the case of young and poor, blacks in America are disproportionately less likely to vote.

Percentage and Number of Eligible Voters Who Voted, by Race, 1968

	PER CENT	PER CENT OF TOTAL VOTE
White	69%	91%
Non-White	56%	9%

U.S. Census Bureau

Thus, while nonwhites are 11 per cent of the population, they cast only about 9 per cent of the vote.

[1] The poorest dozen, ranked poorest first, by per capita income: Mississippi, Alabama, Arkansas, South Carolina, West Virginia, Tennessee, Kentucky, North Carolina, Louisiana, New Mexico, Idaho, Georgia.

But in one very crucial way, black voting behavior differs quite sharply from the behavior of the "young" and "poor" groups mentioned earlier. Blacks, having a more cohesive community of interest, *have* voted as a bloc:

Non-White [2] Vote 1964 and 1968

	REPUBLICAN	DEMOCRATIC	A.I.P.
1968	12%	85%	3%
1964	6%	94%	—

Gallup

Because the blacks who do not vote are largely potential Democratic voters, it is apparent why the leaders of all the "Get Out the Vote" drives and "Be a Good Citizen" drives are so frequently Democrats. The pool of nonvoting blacks constitutes an important potential plus for Democrats.

Just how important can be seen from a breakdown of the Presidential vote in 1964 and 1968:

Voter Participation Rates by Race and Region, 1964 and 1968

	1964	1968	DIFFERENCE 1964–1968
In the South			
White	60%	62%	+ 2%
Non-White	44%	51%	+ 7% (!)
Outside the South			
White	75%	72%	− 3%
Non-White	72%	61%	− 11% (!)

U.S. Census Bureau

Blacks in the South voted in far greater numbers than ever before in American history. This increase can be largely attributed to the implementation of the Voting Rights Act of 1965 and the energetic work of organizing and registering blacks in Southern states. This work paid off, even though in the Presidential race Democrats

[2] The data here are for "nonwhites," of whom roughly 90% are "Negro." Other sample data for purely black precincts show even higher percentages Democratic.

carried only Texas and Maryland of all states south of the Mason-Dixon Line. However, the number of *local* black office-holders in the South increased dramatically. By early 1970 there were 565 black officeholders. In 1960 there had been fewer than 200.

At the same time, however, blacks outside the South were far *less* likely to vote: a decrease from 72 per cent in 1964 to 61 per cent in 1968.

How important was this on a national canvas? Very, because the election was so close. Had nonwhites outside the South come to the polls in 1968 as they had in 1964, *Hubert Humphrey would have received a greater popular vote than Nixon.* In short, while the black vote did turn out solidly Democratic, it did not solidly turn out.

What happened to the non-Southern black nonvote? Several reasons can be put forth explaining the poor showing.

There are those who say the heart went out of the black electorate when Robert Kennedy was killed. To be sure, Senator Kennedy had immense popularity among the black electorate, and it is interesting to ponder two points: Had he lived and *won* the nomination from Humphrey, could he have brought out those extra black votes needed for a Democratic victory without alienating white votes? Had he lived and *lost* the nomination and then campaigned for Hubert Humphrey, could he have brought out the additional black votes?

Another reason for the low black participation is that the effective choice in 1968 was Humphrey or Nixon, not, as in 1964, Johnson or Goldwater. While Humphrey was clearly superior from the point of view of most blacks, Mr. Nixon did not represent the sort of disaster that Mr. Goldwater represented. In 1968, it can be argued, Mr. Wallace represented the Goldwater position, and he never had a serious chance of winning. Therefore, blacks felt less threatened and felt less need to go to the polls.

Finally, in 1968, the voter turnout was somewhat lower all across the board. The Census Bureau in 1964 reported a voter turnout of 69.3 per cent. In 1968 the Census figure was 67.8 per cent.[3]

Summing up: Blacks constitute a small segment of the national vote. In recent times they have voted largely Democratic. In a close election, this can help. In a close election, anything helps.

In all: unyoung, unpoor, unblack. Furthermore, the young and the poor are un-monolithic in their Presidential voting behavior. Six in seven voters are over thirty. Nine out of ten are unpoor. Nine out of ten are white. Because there is some duplication—a young poor black man, for example—a fair guess is to say that seven of ten American voters are neither young, nor poor, nor black.

Lesson: Talk about building a powerful "new political coalition" whose major components are all the young, all the poor, and all the blacks doesn't make much electoral sense.

Reprieve: That the electorate is unyoung, unpoor, and unblack does *not* mean they are antiyoung, antipoor, or antiblack. Remember that woman's suffrage was voted on by men. The electorate was unfemale. Not antifemale.

. . .

So there you have it: Middle Voter. A metropolitan Quadcalian [a resident of a geographic area devised by the authors which includes 16 states with approximately 300 electoral votes where the majority of voters live and where our Presidents are elected], middle-aged, middle-income, middle-educated, Protestant,[4] in a family whose working members work more likely with hands than abstractly with head.

Think about that picture when you consider the American power structure. Mid-

---

[3] Both these figures are a few percentage points too high. As the Census Bureau reports in its publication *Voting and Registration in the Election of November 1968,* "estimates of voter participation that are higher than the official counts have been the common experience of other survey organizations which have studied voting behavior."

[4] Quadcalians would tend to be more Catholic than the rest of the country, but still predominantly Protestant.

dle Voter is a forty-seven-year-old house-wife from the outskirts of Dayton, Ohio, whose husband is a machinist. She very likely has a somewhat different view of life and politics from that of a twenty-four-year-old instructor of political science at Yale. Now the young man from Yale may feel that he *knows* more about politics than the machinist's wife from suburban Dayton, and of course, in one sense he does. But he does not know much about politics, or psychology, unless he understands what is bothering that lady in Dayton and unless he understands that her circumstances in large measure dictate her concerns.

To know that the lady in Dayton is afraid to walk the streets alone at night, to know that she has a mixed view about blacks and civil rights because before moving to the suburbs she lived in a neighborhood that became all black, to know that her brother-in-law is a policeman, to know that she does not have the money to move if her new neighborhood deteriorates, to know that she is deeply distressed that her son is going to a community junior college where LSD was found on the campus—to know all this is the beginning of contemporary political wisdom.

2

Sexual Politics

KATE MILLETT

Would you agree with Kate Millett that we are living in a cultural revolution which must inevitably involve political and economic institutions? It is true student protest occurred almost simultaneously in virtually all of the major countries. Does it also follow that a women's movement will evolve equally rapidly into a radical coalition? Will women become the "real" majority in American politics in fact as well as numbers in the immediate future?

. . . [T]here is evidence in the last few years that the reactionary sexual ethic . . . has nearly spent itself.

Other progressive forces have recently asserted themselves, notably the revolt of youth against the masculine tradition of war and virility. Of course the most pertinent recent development is the emergence of a new feminist movement. Here again, it is difficult to explain just why such a

development occurred when it did.[1] The enormous social change involved in a sexual revolution is basically a matter of altered consciousness, the exposure and elimination of social and psychological realities underlining political and cultural structures. We are speaking, then, of a cultural revolution, which, while it must necessarily involve the political and economic reorgan-

From Kate Millett, Sexual Politics *(Garden City, N.Y.: Doubleday & Company, Inc., 1969) pp. 362–363. Copyright © 1969, 1970 by Kate Millett. Reprinted by permission of the publisher.*

[1] Civil Rights was undoubtedly a force, for second-generation feminists were, like their predecessors, inspired by the example of black protest. The disenchantment of women in the New Left with the sexist character of that movement provided considerable impetus as well.

ization traditionally implied by the term revolution, must go far beyond this as well. And here it would seem that the most profound changes implied are ones accomplished by human growth and true re-education, rather than those arrived at through the theatrics of armed struggle—even should the latter become inevitable. There is much reason to believe that the possession of numbers, dedication, and creative intelligence could even render unnecessary the usual self-destructive resort to violent tactics. Yet no lengthy evolutionary process need be implied here, rather the deliberate speed fostered by modern communication, in an age when groups such as students, for example, can become organized in a great number of countries in a matter of some two years.

When one surveys the spontaneous mass movements taking place all over the world, one is led to hope that human understanding itself has grown ripe for change. In America one may expect the new women's movement to ally itself on an equal basis with blacks and students in a growing radical coalition. It is also possible that women now represent a very crucial element capable of swinging the national mood, poised at this moment between the alternatives of progress or political repression, toward meaningful change. As the largest alienated element in our society, and because of their numbers, passion, and length of oppression, its largest revolutionary base, women might come to play a leadership part in social revolution, quite unknown before in history. The changes in fundamental values such a coalition of expropriated groups— blacks, youth, women, the poor—would seek are especially pertinent to realizing not only sexual revolution but a gathering impetus toward freedom from rank or prescriptive role, sexual or otherwise. For to actually change the quality of life is to transform personality, and this cannot be done without freeing humanity from the tyranny of sexual-social category and conformity to sexual stereotype—as well as abolishing racial caste and economic class.

It may be that a second wave of the sexual revolution might at last accomplish its aim of freeing half the race from its immemorial subordination—and in the process bring us all a great deal closer to humanity. It may be that we shall even be able to retire sex from the harsh realities of politics, but not until we have created a world we can bear out of the desert we inhabit.

3

Hello, Young Voters

ALAN L. OTTEN

What does the author mean by conventional wisdom? Summarize the conventional wisdom in regard to the impact of young voters in national elections. Cite several factors which could invalidate this supposition. In what ways will the eligibility of 18-year-old voters in national elections likely affect state and local elections? In your own judgment and experience, what will be the results of lowering the voting age?

Conventional wisdom holds that the new 18-to-21-year-old voters won't have very great impact on national elections.

The reasoning runs like this: Preoccupied with college, settling into a first job or military service, comparatively few actually will register and vote. Experience in those few states that already have permitted under-21 voting shows only one-third to one-fourth turnouts, far below the percentages for older voters.

Moreover, the argument continues, even when young voters do go to the polls, they vote pretty much as the rest of the electorate does. The younger the voter, in fact, the more likely he is to follow parental patterns; there is no monolithic "youth" allegiance to any party or personality.

Conventional wisdom isn't always right, however, and this may be one of the times it's wrong. The lowered voting age, particularly when counted with new, more liberal residency requirements, may have far more impact than most professional politicians and election-watchers currently predict.

President Nixon seems to be one pro, in

From Alan L. Otten, "Hello, Young Voters," The Wall Street Journal, January 7, 1971, p. 12. Reprinted by permission of the publishers.

fact, who recognizes this possibility. On his televised "conversation" Monday night, he conceded that younger voters appear to favor the Democrats, though he quickly added his belief that large numbers of young people are undecided, and that coming achievements would give the GOP a very good crack at this age group by 1972.

As a result of Congressional action and Supreme Court decisions, 18-to-21-year-olds will be able to vote in future national elections for President and Congress; there will be an estimated 11.5 million in this group in 1972, a little more than 8 per cent of the total electorate then. In addition, residency requirements for voting for President are lowered to 30 days for everyone, young or old, enfranchising another five million persons in states with longer residency rules.

The conventional reasoning could err on two counts: More of the 18-to-21-year-olds may vote than expected, and they may vote more monolithically, usually on the liberal side. In 1972, at least, widespread publicity about the first-time voters should swell their participation. Youth groups and civic organizations plan special drives to spur registration and voting by young people.

The war, the draft, student loan policy or other special impact issues could enlarge the youth turnout.

The new ground rules for national elections will pressure states to liberalize age and residency requirements for state and local elections as well; a broader range of candidates and issues could induce still heavier youth voting. Right now, only eight states permit under-21 voting—three at 18, three at 19, two at 20.

Older voters have been sufficiently anti-youth of late to defeat soundly most state referenda for lowered voting ages; last year, for instance, 11 of 16 such proposals were turned down. Now, however, youth advocates have a potent new argument: If the 18-year-old is qualified to vote for President, why not for governor or mayor? Many state officials, too, now have extra incentive to conform state law to national law, and thus avoid the headache and expense of separate registration books and separate ballots for the under-21 and over-21, for the long-time resident and the newcomer.

The new, young voters may well vote differently than predicted. Certainly liberals are too ready to think of all young people as far-out collegians; census figures say that of the 11.5 million in the 18-to-21 group in 1972, only four million will be in college, while 4.1 million will be at work and the rest will be housewives, in high school or on military duty. The young voter, as analyst Richard Scammon repeatedly notes, is just as likely to be a Polish-American short-order cook as a longhaired college protester. And even the college group is not solidly liberal but includes a wide range of political attitudes.

Nonetheless, most recent analyses of the "youth vote" have looked at the 21-to-30 or 21-to-25 groups, and the 18-to-21s could be importantly different from their immediate elders. They have been educated during a period of liberalization and even radicalization of the high school; they have come to political awareness during the great national agony over Vietnam.

Younger voters, college and non-college, are probably even less party-loyal and more personality-prone than their increasingly independent elders, but they do not seem to find Mr. Nixon a sympathetic personality. Two recent polls by Louis Harris, for instance, showed Sen. Edmund Muskie and other Democratic hopefuls running considerably better in the 18-to-21 group against Mr. Nixon than they did among older voters. Polls also tend to show the youngest voters, again regardless of education, highly critical of Vice President Agnew.

Even if the younger men and women vote in smaller percentages than their elders, they still could be crucial in close Presidential elections, and two of the last three have been exceedingly close indeed. Allowing for minimal registration and voting by the under-21s, Mr. Harris says, the present strong edge over Mr. Nixon in this age group converts into a two or three percentage point improvement in the Democratic showing in the total vote; obviously, such a gain could easily be decisive.

Younger voters may also affect the shape of the campaign. National, and state and local candidates as well will have to keep these 18-to-21-year-olds in mind in taking stands on military service, marijuana penalties, or any other issue on which the youth viewpoint may be special.

One final fascinating speculation: What might happen in college communities if large numbers of students manage to meet residency requirements to vote there rather than in their home towns? Many cities with large colleges or universities are now represented by quite conservative Congressmen—Columbus, Ohio, for instance, by Samuel Devine, and Chalmers Wylie; Champaign-Urbana, Illinois, by William Springer. Enlarged student voting at Ohio State or the University of Illinois could change Congressional results there radically.

Even without this somewhat far-out possibility, however, the younger voters may wind up packing more punch than currently counted.

4

Our National Nominating Conventions Are a Disgrace

DWIGHT D. EISENHOWER

Why does former President Dwight D. Eisenhower reject a national primary as a substitute for the national nominating convention? What activities in the convention especially contribute to disorder? How can the problems of the national nominating convention be solved?

In my opinion—and I think most Americans will agree—our Presidential nominating conventions have become a thoroughly disgraceful spectacle which can scarcely fail to appall our own voters and create a shockingly bad image of our country abroad. Now that we are midway between the conventions of 1964 and 1968, it seems time to discuss this matter frankly. We can view the events of two years ago with some perspective, and there is still time to adopt reforms before the summer of 1968 is upon us.

First, I want to make it clear that I am not among those who wish to abolish the nominating conventions in favor of a national primary. Over the years, the conventions have done a reasonably good job of choosing men of ability and honor. There are, moreover, compelling arguments against a national primary. In most Presidential years at least two primary elections would be necessary. With perhaps four or five men seeking the nomination in each party, it is unlikely that any one of them —except an incumbent President—could win

a majority vote on the first round. Unless we nominated by plurality, which certainly is not desirable, a runoff would be necessary. All this would prolong the selection of candidates almost unbearably and wear down the interest of voters long before the main event.

Furthermore, if we nominated by primary, only wealthy men could normally run for the Presidency. Any campaign which attempts to cover this big country is enormously expensive. Once a candidate is nominated, of course, he is backed by the resources of his party. But in a primary campaign the aspirant must find a way to pay his own expenses—and I certainly do not think we should close the door of the Presidency to any man of integrity and ability simply because he cannot afford to run. Therefore I feel that the nominating conventions must be retained.

Point of Disorder

There is, however, no reason under heaven why these conventions must be exercises in chaos and tumult—unmannerly, undignified, ridiculous. Here we have men and women meeting to perform a vital task. The same atmosphere of dignity should prevail that we find in Congress or in any other major deliberate body. Yet our conventions now resemble a rioting mob of juvenile delinquents.

The floor often becomes a scene of milling humanity, and the din is such that delegates frequently cannot hear what is said on the podium. The thumping of the chairman's gavel, as he futilely tries to restore order, is an endless refrain to television viewers, many of whom turn off their sets in frustration.

Press, radio and television reporters roam the aisles at will, and often work their way into the center of a delegation for an interview. Reporters and delegates alike chatter into walkie-talkies, thereby increasing the hubbub. The confusion becomes so frustrating that it is almost impossible for a delegation to hold a caucus on the floor.

The ultimate in mob scenes occurs, of course, after each candidate is placed in nomination. The band plays the candidate's theme song *ad infinitum,* and the parade of demonstrators begins. The doors at the rear of the halls are opened, and imported shouters—who have no official status whatsoever—swarm in with their banners and placards and noisemaking devices. The moment the uproar begins to diminish a bit, the candidate's managers whip up the frenzy of the faithful and prod the mercenaries into new feats of raucous clamor. The theory seems to be that the man who gets a 20-minute ovation would make twice as good a candidate as the 10-minute man.

Besmirched by Travesty

Sometimes the artificiality of these demonstrations is so ludicrous as to be acutely embarrassing. I recall one such instance some years ago. The hour was late, and most of the delegates had left the hall. But one more name remained to be placed in nomination—the name of a distinguished American who had served his country long and well. Finally, the speeches were ended, and the time had come for the joyous ovation. With few delegates left to participate, a motley assortment of characters from the city streets—obviously hired for the occasion—came in. Their performance, in a hall littered with wastepaper and debris, was lifeless and pathetic. Yet all this went out on television. As an American, I was embarrassed for my country. As a human being, I was outraged that the name of a prominent citizen should have been besmirched by such a travesty.

In times past, bad manners at our conventions—such as talking and visiting during a speech—have been largely due to thoughtlessness and the delegates' preoccupation with their own affairs. At the 1964 Republican convention in San Francisco, however, a new note of deliberate rudeness was injected. Booing and hissing were common, and insulting remarks were exchanged. The low point of the convention—perhaps of all conventions—came when New York's Gov. Nelson Rockefeller found it virtually impossible to deliver his speech. Chairman Thruston Morton furiously tried to quell the shocking display of bad manners, but without much success.

I suppose that this rudeness at San Francisco was the outgrowth of the sharp conflict between opposing camps. Whatever the reason, it was unpardonable—and a complete negation of the spirit of democracy. I was bitterly ashamed. I wish to add most emphatically that none of this was caused or condoned by the principal figures of the convention. It resulted from the lack of machinery for firm control of the unruly.

The Road to Reform

Until recent times, the spectacle of our nominating conventions was strictly for domestic consumption, and even in our own country few people ever *saw* a convention. Now, with television coverage, these riotous proceedings go into virtually every home. Worse, millions of TV viewers in foreign countries see the conventions, either live by satellite communication or from tapes flown across the oceans.

Now, I am all for television, radio and press coverage of the conventions. It is one way to bring home to our own people the issues and problems of government and to make them conscious of their duties as citizens. It is a way to show the workings of our brand of democracy—which is still the best form of government on earth—to our friends overseas. But certainly we should show all these people, at home and abroad, a dignified deliberative body at work, not "Operation Chaos."

I am happy to say that my own party is now making a determined start toward reform. Our national chairman, Ray Bliss, has appointed a committee of distinguished Republicans to study convention procedures and make recommendations. Somewhere along the way, I am told, the committee may ask for my suggestions, and I shall be most happy to coöperate.

My recommendations will be about as follows:

1. The permanent chairman should have better means for controlling convention procedure. If a violation of the rules occurs—a disturbance, an exhibition of rudeness—he should have the power to eject the disorderly or even to clear the hall and reconvene the convention at a later hour. If this were done even once, I think that people would soon get the idea that dignified and courteous deportment is obligatory.

2. No one except delegates and those with official convention business should be permitted on the floor. Even the alternate delegates should be seated in the gallery; when needed they could descend to the floor.

3. The above rule should apply to all reporters —television, press and radio. They could be provided with ample facilities *off the floor.* This recommendation may bring loud protest from some of our public media, but I think it is highly necessary. Congress wouldn't think of letting reporters come onto the floor of the House or Senate to interview members. The business of a convention is just as important as that of Congress, and the convention should have the same right to reach its decisions undisturbed. I have discussed this problem with one top network official, and I gather that at least some of the broadcasting people would be happy and relieved to operate under more orderly rules.

4. Walkie-talkies should be banned from the floor. Closed telephone circuits should be set up in the hall *for the delegates,* so that they could reach anyone in the hall quickly and easily, but these phones should not be connected with outside circuits. If a delegate wished to talk with someone outside the hall, he could go to a telephone elsewhere in the building.

5. All noisemaking devices should be banned from the hall, and any delegate or spectator using one of these abominations should be ejected. Moreover, there should be only one band inside the building—the official one. It could play some rousing music at the beginning and end of sessions, and play the theme song of each candidate during his demonstration—but at no other time.

6. Demonstrations should be restricted to ten minutes—ample time for a display of genuine enthusiasm. Participation in demonstrations should be limited to delegates and alternates —no hired hands from the streets, no pretty high-school girls in cheerleader costumes.

7. Any booing or hissing or other disorderly conduct from spectators in the galleries should be quelled instantly and firmly, and the culprits should be evicted from the hall.

8. Although the convention should in no way interfere with protest demonstrations by legitimate groups *outside the hall,* it should have the right to expect that its business will not be impeded by them. Demonstrators who try to prevent the entry or departure of delegates by lying down in streets or doorways should be removed by the police. Any city unwilling to give a firm guarantee of such protection should be avoided as a convention site.

These are my recommendations. If they were adopted and enforced, I am sure that they would make our conventions respectable exhibits of democracy at work. It may be objected that such rules would be so inhibiting as to take all the steam and enthusiasm out of party procedure. I believe that the opposite is true. I am aware that genuine emotion—loyalty to a candidate, deep conviction on issues, patriotism—is an essential ingredient of political gatherings. But I believe that, within the framework of these rules, there would still be full scope for honest emotion and the kind of enthusiasm that makes party wheels turn.

The Urgent Need

There is one other suggestion which I think merits careful consideration by both parties. Each of the two conventions now lasts four days. That is much too long. If the recommendations I have offered were adopted, and if speeches were reduced in number and duration, the entire business of a convention could easily be accomplished in two days. This would be highly desirable for virtually everyone concerned, including the long-suffering public.

In any case, the urgent job before us now is to reform convention procedures—so that the summer of 1968 will not find us once more presenting to the world an inept, inane interpretation of the democratic process. As a Republican, I am delighted that my party is diligently studying the problem. As an American, I ardently hope that *both* parties will take the proper steps as soon as humanly possible.

5

The Hiring of Presidents

CLINTON ROSSITER

What does Clinton Rossiter mean when he states that criticisms of the national nominating convention are really criticisms of our civilizations? Has any national nominating convention ever passed over a first-rate candidate or ignored the wishes of the people? What is meant by the statement that the convention is "part and parcel of the magic by which men rule"?

.   .   .

The case against the nominating convention is almost too familiar to bear repeating. I doubt that I need rehearse the cultural sins of which it is accused by sensitive observers. It should be enough to remind ourselves that this windy, vulgar circus is met to nominate a candidate for the most powerful office on earth, and to wonder if there could be any gathering of men that seems less in character with its high purpose, that seems more unhappily to express what Henry James called "the

From Clinton Rossiter, The American Presidency *(rev. ed.; New York: Harcourt Brace Jovanovich, 1960), pp. 191–194. Copyright © 1956, 1960 by Clinton Rossiter. Reprinted by permission of the publisher.*

triumph of the superficial and the apotheosis of the raw." The convention is certainly a gross distortion of that picture of intelligent men reasoning together which we carry in our heads as the image of free government. It was the sight of an American convention that led a famous European scholar (Ostrogorski) to observe, first, that "fifteen thousand people all attacked at once with Saint Vitus' dance" was not his idea of democracy; and, second, that God in His infinite wisdom watches benevolently over drunkards, little children, and the United States of America.

And yet the case against the convention as a cultural abomination is itself a distortion. It is, indeed, a barrage directed through clouded sights at the wrong target. For the plain truth is that most criticisms of this noisy, plebeian, commercial institution are really criticisms of the noisy, plebeian, commercial civilization within which it operates. We see our follies as a people in the follies of the convention, and unless we reform ourselves, which I know we will not and suspect we dare not do, the convention will continue to disturb the reasonable, shock the fastidious, and fascinate all of us. In any case, it is yet to be proved that men who act like deacons can make a better choice of candidates for the Presidency than men who act like clowns, and that—the kind of choice the convention makes—is the meaningful test of its value as an institution of American life.

The more technical charges against the nominating convention are that it is undemocratic, since it cuts the rank and file of the party out of the process of selecting a candidate; unreliable, since it ignores or distorts the real sentiment of the party in making the selection; and corrupts, since it puts a premium on the kind of horse trading in which men cannot expect to succeed unless they unlearn every rule of public and private morality. The convention, we are told, offers us a man we neither want nor deserve, and it offers him on a platter of corruption and cynicism. Those who make these charges usually go on to advocate some sort of nationwide presidential primary. The convention would become a pep rally to shout approval of the people's choice or quite possibly, would be abolished altogether.

These charges, it seems to me, are a caricature of reality. The first and third might just as easily be leveled at Congress as at the nominating convention, while the second, which is most often and earnestly advanced, simply cannot stand up under the scrutiny of history. When in the twentieth century, except perhaps in the Republican convention of 1912, has a majority of the voters of either great party been handed a candidate it did not want? When, except in the nomination of Harding in 1920, did a convention pass over several first-rate men to choose an acknowledged second-rater? Quite to the contrary of ac-

cepted legend, the convention has done a remarkable job over the years in giving the voters of each party the man whom they, too, would have selected had they been faced with the necessity of making a responsible choice. The convention is anxious to satisfy, not frustrate, the hopes of the members of the party; if the latter give an unmistakable sound, the former will echo it gladly and faithfully. If they speak in a babble of voices, if they cannot agree on a clear choice, the convention will choose their man for them, even if it takes a hundred ballots, and the choice, moreover, will be made finally with near or complete unanimity. One of the undeniable merits of the convention, as opposed to the primary, is that it heals most of the wounds that are inevitably laid open in the rough process of making so momentous a political decision.

There is something to be said, I suppose, for the efforts of Senator Douglas and his friends to encourage the growth of presidential-preference primaries. In more than one-third of the states of the Union the voters of each party are now given some chance to elect or instruct their delegation to the convention, and no one would argue that professional politicians should be protected against such expressions of the public mood or choice. Yet it would be a mistake to make these exercises in public opinion much more uniform in pattern or binding in effect than they are at present. Reformers should be careful not to upset the nice balance that history has struck between the hard responsibilities of the professionals at the convention and the vague wishes of the voters at home. The real question about our presidential primaries, it seems to me, is not whether they should take over completely the key role of the convention, which is an academic question at best, but whether they are worth all the fuss they cause in the minds of the public and all the strain they put upon even the most hard-shelled candidates. The active campaign for the Presidency becomes much too long drawn out a process; money becomes much too decisive a factor in the hopes and plans of any one candidate; some of the best candidates are torn between the responsibility of the important position they already fill and the lure of the one after which they hunger and thirst. Under the system as it now operates, even the most popular candidates are hostages to whim and accident, especially to the whim of the "favorite sons" who sprout quadrennially and to the accident of the timetable of the primaries. The Democrats of New Hampshire, where the first primary is usually held, are all fine people, I am sure, but neither so fine nor so wise that they should be able to make or break a presidential aspirant all by themselves. I am inclined to agree with Adlai Stevenson, who speaks to the point with matchless authority, that the presidential primaries are a "very, very questionable method of selecting presidential candidates." Rather than have a handful of primaries spread carelessly over the months between February and July, it might be the wiser and even more democratic thing to have none at all. I for one would be happy to see our strongest candidates take the advice of the publisher of the *Adirondack Daily Enterprise*, James Loeb, Jr., and join in boycotting the present system entirely. It is, by almost any standard, one of the failures of our political system.

The convention, to the contrary, is a clear if not brilliant success. It meets the one test to which we like to put all our institutions: it does the job it is asked to do, and does it remarkably well. Indeed, one can be more positive than this in defense of the convention, for it performs several tasks that no other institution or arrangement can perform at all. Not only does it serve as the major unifying influence in political parties that are decentralized to the point of anarchy; it is, as Professor V.O. Key has written, "part and parcel of the magic by which men rule." And Americans, I again insist, are far from that enlightened condition in which political magic has lost its usefulness. The nominating convention fills a constitutional void; it unites and inspires each of the parties; it arouses interest in the grand plebiscite through which we choose our President. We will have to hear more convincing charges than have hitherto been pressed against the convention before we tamper with this venerable instrument of American democracy.

6

The Electoral College Should Be Abolished

THE AMERICAN BAR ASSOCIATION

In your judgment, would the two-party system be strengthened or weakened by direct election of the American President? Would the suggested revision of the electoral system tend to produce more liberal or more conservative candidates, stronger or weaker parties? What is the significance of the statement, "There may be no perfect method of electing a President"?

It is the consensus of the commission that an amendment to the United States Constitution should be adopted to reform the method of electing a President and Vice President. The amendment should:

1. Provide for the election of the President and Vice President by direct, nation-wide popular vote;
2. Require a candidate to obtain at least 40 per cent of the popular vote in order to be elected;
3. Provide for a national runoff election between the two top candidates in the event no candidate receives at least 40 per cent of the popular vote;
4. Require the President and Vice President to be voted for jointly;
5. Empower Congress to determine the days on which the original election and the runoff election are to be held, which days shall be uniform throughout the United States.

The electoral-college method of electing a President of the United States is archaic, undemocratic, complex, ambiguous, indirect and dangerous.

The present system allows a person to

From "Direct Election of Presidents," St. Louis Post-Dispatch, *January 29, 1967.*

become President with fewer popular votes than his major opponent; grants all of a state's electoral votes to the winner of the most popular votes in the state, thereby canceling all minority votes cast in the state; makes it possible for presidential electors to vote against the national candidates of their party; awards all of a state's electoral votes to the popular winner in the state regardless of voter turnout in the state; assigns to each state at least three electoral votes regardless of its size; fails to take into account population changes in a state between censuses; allows for the possibility of a President and a Vice President from different political parties; and employs an unrepresentative system of voting for President and House of Representatives.

While there may be no perfect method of electing a President, we believe that direct, nationwide popular vote is the best of all possible methods.

Perhaps the most important objection that has been voiced to direct election is that it would lead to a proliferation of parties and weaken the American two-party system.

Authorities who have studied our party system in great depth attribute the dualism to both noninstitutional factors. There is

14 "Minority" Presidents

YEAR	ELECTED		OPPONENTS	
1824	J. Q. Adams 30.54	Jackson 43.13	Clay 13.24	Crawford 13.9
1844	Polk 49.56	Clay 48.13	Birney 2.30	
1848	Taylor 47.35	Cass 42.52	Van Buren 10.13	
1856	Buchanan 45.63	Fremont 33.27	Fillmore 21.08	Smith .01
1860	Lincoln 39.79	Douglas 29.40	Breckenridge 18.20	Bell 12.60
1876	Hayes 48.04	Tilden 50.99	Cooper .97	
1880	Garfield 48.32	Hancock 48.21	Weaver 3.35	Others .12
1884	Cleveland 48.53	Blaine 48.24	Butler 1.74	St. John 1.49
1888	Harrison 47.86	Cleveland 48.66	Fisk 2.19	Streeter 1.29
1892	Cleveland 46.04	Harrison 43.01	Weaver 8.53	Others 2.42
1912	Wilson 41.85	T. Roosevelt 27.42	Taft 23.15	Others 7.58
1916	Wilson 49.26	Hughes 46.12	Benson 3.16	Others 1.46
1948	Truman 49.51	Dewey 45.13	Thurmond 2.40	Wallace 2.38
1960 °	Kennedy 49.71	Nixon 49.55	Unpledged .92	Others .27

From The Christian Science Monitor.

general agreement that, institutionally, the selection of representatives by plurality vote from single-member districts has strongly encouraged and reinforced the two-party structure. Neither this factor nor other contributing factors would be changed by direct election of the President.

Moreover, our recommendations do include factors which, we think, would have a substantial tendency to support the two-party system. . . . [The] 40 per cent plurality requirement would encourage factions and splinter groups to operate, as now, within the framework of the major parties.

We further recommend that there be a national runoff popular election between the top two candidates in the event that no candidate receives at least 40 per cent of the popular vote. A runoff would [tend] to limit the number of minority party candidates in the original election, because it is improbable that a minor candidate would be one of the top two.

In addition . . . it is no easy matter for a group to become a national party.

It is also noted that direct election of the President would wipe out state lines or destroy our federal system.

The President is our highest nationally elected official. . . . The problems and the issues with which he deals are largely national in character. It is only fitting that he be elected directly by the people.

Under our recommendations, states would continue to have primary responsibility for regulating the places and manner of holding the presidential election, for establishing qualifications for voting in such elections, and for controlling political activity within their state boundaries. . . .

There is the view that direct election would never be proposed by Congress or ratified by state legislatures. It is interesting to note that members of Congress from both large and small states have been leading proponents of direct election. Moreover, 13 states, both large and small, recently attempted to strike down as unconstitutional the unit-vote feature of our system.

The present procedure of handling a contingent election is fraught with perils. Under it the House chooses the President from the top three candidates.

As the political alignment of the House . . . (following the 1948 election) demonstrated, an election there could well have resulted in a deadlock. Moreover, since the Senate selects the Vice President under present contingent-election procedure,

there could be a President from one party and a Vice President from another.

Realistically, an election in Congress is likely to involve political deals and pressures and to place the President in a position of indebtedness to those who voted for him. It could result, as history shows, in members casting their votes contrary to the popular vote.

We recommend that Congress be given the power to deal with a case where a state attempts to exclude the name of a major candidate from the ballot.

In 1860 the name of Abraham Lincoln was left off the ballot in 10 states. Similarly, in 1948 and again in 1964, the voters of one state were not afforded any opportunity to vote for the national candidates of the Democratic party because of the device of unpledged electors.

7

The Electoral College Serves the Purpose

WALLACE S. SAYRE/JUDITH H. PARRIS

Is the present Presidential electoral system a politically neutral institution? What interests or sections of the country are advanced by this system? What groups might gain from a revised program for direct election? Do you feel that the recommendations proposed by the authors provide sufficient safeguards?

This analysis leads us to make the following policy suggestions:

1. The electoral vote system with the general-ticket system should be retained. It is not perfect. But its defects are known,

From Wallace S. Sayre and Judith H. Parris, Voting for President: The Electoral College and the American Political System *(Washington, D.C.: The Brookings Institution, 1970), pp. 149–151. Reprinted by permission of the publisher.*

and they are relatively minor. The defects of the proposed alternatives are uncertain, and they appear to the authors to be major.

Most grievances against the existing system can be resolved through the political process without recourse to a constitutional amendment. It is preferable that desirable adaptations be brought about, as they have been in the past, by means other than the amendment procedure. If it is believed that some constitutional amendment must be passed, the most prudent choice would be the automatic plan, with a required electoral vote majority and the general-ticket system, and the provision that in a contingency election the President should be chosen (a) from the top two candidates by majority vote in either the House or a joint session of Congress, or (b) by designation as President and Vice President of the ticket winning the popular vote. In broad outline, this plan would continue the essential characteristics of the existing electoral college system.

2. Within the present electoral college system, national party leaders should take the steps necessary to ensure loyalty from state electors of their party. They can minimize the problem of the "faithless" elector by seeing that more care is taken in the selection of individual electors. They can call for loyalty resolutions at national party conventions. The sanctions of national patronage, campaign funds, and general support are at their disposal. In short, they have the opportunity to bargain for the election of responsible and loyal electors. In some instances, leaders have made such efforts, often with success. The failure to secure faithful electors has frequently been the result of insufficient attention on the part of national leaders. Their success in assuring loyal electors depends largely upon their own skill, but a continuing effort is required; frenetic, last-minute efforts every four years may be too little and too late. To this end, regular, routinized communications among national, state, and local party leaders would be desirable. National party leaders and staff members could work to assure that the names of their presidential and vice presidential candidates or full slates of electors loyal to their candidates are on the ballot in each state.

3. If, under the existing procedures, an election appears to be so close that a winner seems doubtful even in the House, there are opportunities for responsible negotiations and prior (even continuing) agreements. For example, House members could agree—as some did in 1968—to elect the popular winner if the electoral vote system failed to produce a President. The Senate could agree to do the same in choosing a Vice President.

4. An important procedural matter that should be resolved is the problem of what to do if a candidate dies or is otherwise incapacitated. The national party organizations should continue to take responsibility in this area by adopting a rule dealing with this possibility at each national convention. The parties have shown commendable foresight in adopting such resolutions in the past. Candidates for national office are political, rather than governmental, leaders; and the line of succession to their posts should accordingly be determined by the political party organizations.

5. Similarly, the states should deal with the possibility that an elector may be unable to carry out his function. Some states already have passed laws covering this possibility; and those that have not should do so.

We believe that with these improvements, the electoral college could continue and expand the benefits it has provided the American political system. Although imperfect, as Hamilton predicted, the electoral college system has at least been excellent. It has worked well. It has evolved along with the nation and has in every era produced Presidents accepted as legitimate and capable of governing effectively. It has been a salutary force in American politics, in ways of which Hamilton never dreamed. It has encouraged political leaders to wage their struggles within two great parties. It has provided a point of access for metropolitan interests that are often ignored elsewhere. It has promoted national stability in the battle for the presidency. We see no reason to abandon, and many reasons to support, an institution whose assets have been very tangible and whose liabilities have been largely conjectural.

8

Voting

BERNARD R. BERELSON/PAUL F. LAZARSFELD/
WILLIAM N. MCPHEE

The following selection is taken from a study of Elmira, New York, during the presidential campaign of 1948. What do the authors mean when they say, "His vote is formed in the midst of his fellows in a sort of a group decision"? Do you agree with the quotation, "the decisions of men, when they come to choose their governors, are influenced by considerations which escape all scientific analysis"? How do the authors relate traditional democratic theory to their findings in voting research?

The Social Group and the Political System

Underlying the influence of the social group is the ambiguity of political stimuli. The individualistic tradition of thinking about politics, as typically expressed in democratic theory, implies that it is possible and reasonably convenient for the voter to see clear-cut alternatives: to judge the differences between candidates, weigh the relevance of the issues to his own needs, and then rightly or wrongly "decide" what to do. The scheme implied in this tradition of thinking about politics requires a reasonably clear political choice that can be responded to directly by the individual, but this is not always, or even usually, the case.

Suppose we think of two polar types of modern elections. An unusual type of election (e.g., 1936) presents a clear-cut and easily understood program that had major

From Bernard R. Berelson, Paul F. Lazarsfeld, William N. McPhee, Voting (Chicago: University of Chicago Press, 1954), pp. 114–115, 320–323. Reprinted by permission of the publisher.

consequences for a large number of voters, that was highlighted by dramatic events, and that was symbolized by a magnetic candidate. At the opposite pole there is an election period (e.g., 1948) in which voters can find no clear programs, no simple picture of what is at stake, no visible consequences win or lose for the average citizen, no appealing and dramatic candidates —in short, a thoroughly ordinary period against the backdrop of reasonably stable times during which the citizen would prefer to be left undisturbed in the normal pursuit of job and family activities.

In situations of high ambiguity, according to the evidence of psychological experiments, two kinds of behavior occur that we have encountered in this political analysis. First, with no clear directives from stimuli outside themselves, people are likely to fall back on directive forces within themselves. This means that voters are likely to fall back on early allegiances, experiences, values, and norms—for example, those associated with being raised as a member of the working class or a minority group. Second, voters are likely to be especially vulnerable to less relevant influences than direct political stimuli. If voters cannot test the appropriateness of their decisions by reference to political consequences, then they are especially likely to be influenced by other, nonpolitical facts—for example, what trusted people around them are doing. As a result, old interests and traditions of class and minority blocs are brought to bear upon the determination of today's vote. In this process the principal agencies are not Machiavellian manipulators, as is commonly supposed when bloc votes are delivered at the polls, but the ordinary family, friends, co-workers, and fellow organization members with whom we are all surrounded. In short, the influences to which voters are most susceptible are opinions of trusted people expressed to one another. . . .

. . .

Lord Bryce pointed out the difficulties in a theory of democracy that assumes that each citizen must himself be capable of voting intelligently:

Orthodox democratic theory assumes that every citizen has, or ought to have, thought out for himself certain opinions, i.e., ought to have a definite view, defensible by argument, of what the country needs, of what principles ought to be applied in governing it, of the man to whose hands the government ought to be entrusted. There are persons who talk, though certainly very few who act, as if they believed this theory, which may be compared to the theory of some ultra-Protestants that every good Christian has or ought to have . . . worked out for himself from the Bible a system of theology.

In the first place, however, the information available to the individual voter is not limited to that directly possessed by him. True, the individual casts his own personal ballot. But, as we have tried to indicate throughout this volume, that is perhaps the most individualized action he takes in an election. His vote is formed in the midst of his fellows in a sort of group decision—if, indeed, it may be called a decision at all—and the total information and knowledge possessed in the group's present and past generations can be made available for the

group's choice. Here is where opinion-leading relationships, for example, play an active role.

Second, and probably more important, the individual voter may not have a great deal of detailed information, but he usually has picked up the crucial *general* information as part of his social learning itself. He may not know the parties' positions on the tariff, or who is for reciprocal trade treaties, or what are the differences on Asiatic policy, or how the parties split on civil rights, or how many security risks were exposed by whom. But he cannot live in an American community without knowing broadly where the parties stand. He has learned that the Republicans are more conservative and the Democrats more liberal—and he can locate his own sentiments and cast his vote accordingly. After all, he must vote for one or the other party, and, if he knows the big thing about the parties, he does not need to know all the little things. The basic role a party plays as an institution in American life is more important to his voting than a particular stand on a particular issue.

. . .

How can our analysis be reconciled with the classical theory of liberal political democracy? Is the theory "wrong"? Must it be discarded in favor of empirical political sociology? Must its ethical or normative content be dismissed as incompatible with the nature of modern man or of mass society? That is not our view. Rather, it seems to us that modern political theory of democracy stands in need of revision and not replacement by empirical sociology. The classical political philosophers were right in the direction of their assessment of the virtues of the citizen. But they demanded those virtues in too extreme or doctrinal a form. The voter does have some principles, he does have information and rationality, he does have interest—but he does not have them in the extreme, elaborate, comprehensive, or detailed form in which they were uniformly recommended by political philosophers. . . . [T]he typical citizen has other interests in life, and it is good, even for the political system, that he pursues them. The classical requirements are more appropriate for the opinion leaders in the society, but even they do not meet them directly. Happily for the system, voters distribute themselves along a continuum:

that normative theory about the proper health of a democracy has nothing to gain from analytic studies like ours; with those who believe that the whole political tradition from Mill to Locke is irrelevant to our realistic understanding and assessment of modern democracy; or with those like

SOCIABLE MAN
   (Indifferent to public affairs, nonpartisan, flexible . . .)

POLITICAL MAN

IDEOLOGICAL MAN
   (Absorbed in public affairs, highly partisan, rigid . . .)

And it turns out that this distribution itself, with its internal checks and balances, can perform the functions and incorporate the same values ascribed by some theorists to each individual in the system as well as to the constitutive political institutions!

Twentieth-century political theory—both analytic and normative—will arise only from hard and long observation of the actual world of politics, closely identified with the deeper problems of practical politics. Values and the behavior they are meant to guide are not distinctly separate or separable parts of life as it is lived; and how Elmirans choose their governors is not completely unrelated to the considerations of how they are *supposed* to choose them. We disagree equally with those who believe

Harold Laski who believe that "the decisions of men, when they come to choose their governors, are influenced by considerations which escape all scientific analysis."

We agree with Cobban: "For a century and a half the Western democracies have been living on the stock of basic political ideas that were last restated toward the end of the eighteenth century. That is a long time. . . . The gap thus formed between political facts and political ideas has steadily widened. It has taken a long time for the results to become evident; now that we have seen what politics devoid of a contemporary moral and political theory means, it is possible that something may be done about it."

9

Voters Are Not Fools

ARTHUR MAASS

Do the findings of V.O. Key, Jr., support the thesis that voting is a group experience rather than an individual decision? What does Key conclude about the Switch Voter? How much importance does Key attach to the cult of personality in presidential elections? How important are policy preferences in influencing vote decisions?

. . . "The perverse and unorthodox argument of this little book," says V.O. Key, Jr., "is that voters are not fools."

Such an argument is unorthodox because some social scientists, using data and analytical techniques similar to Key's, have for years been teaching us something different.

From his analysis of presidential campaign data of recent decades, Key finds that the American voter and electorate are neither "strait-jacketed by social determinants" nor "moved by subconscious urges triggered by devilishly skillful propagandists." The portrait that emerges is rather that of "an electorate moved by concern about central and relevant questions of public policy, or governmental performance, and of executive personality."

When V.O. Key in April 1963 was struck by an illness from which he was unable to recover, he was working with intense urgency on this manuscript, in part, as his close friends have testified, because he knew that these "perverse" findings were of

From Arthur Maass, Foreword to V.O. Key, Jr., The Responsible Electorate (Cambridge, Mass.: The Belknap Press of Harvard University Press, Copyright © 1966, by the President and Fellows of Harvard College), pp. vii-xv. Reprinted by permission of the publishers.

basic importance for both the theory and the practice of democracy in America.

Broadly, Key's method is to classify voters in presidential elections as standpatters (those who vote for the candidate of the same party in successive elections), switchers, and new voters, and to determine whether there are significant correlations between the presidential choice of these three types of voters and their opinions of the issues, events, and candidates of the campaigns.

From the data on the actions and attitudes of the shifting voters, Key concludes that they move from party to party in a manner that is broadly consistent with their policy preferences, and that switchers are far more numerous than is commonly supposed. The data on those voters who stand pat with their party from election to election do not lead to a very different conclusion, however. On the average, "the standpatters do not have to behave as mugwumps to keep their consciences clear; they are already where they ought to be in the light of their policy attitudes."

The major conclusions to be drawn from Key's findings are first, that political man is rational, and second, that the political institutions that he has developed, at least those for election of the president, are rational too.

In elaborating his argument Key shows certain characteristics that are familiar to those who have followed his work closely over the years. His deep commitment to democratic and human values and his optimism about the human race are combined with superb craftsmanship, a fine sensitivity to the relevance and irrelevance of political data and arguments, and a hardheadedness that ensures that moral purpose never passes as a cover for sloppy analysis. Thus Key is unsympathetic with, and distrustful of, political and behavioral theories that degrade the rationality of man and of the institutions that man creates freely; and with a great mastery and inventiveness of technique, he is able to prove that many such theories are false. I can illustrate this with several examples.

(1) It has been popular among political scientists and commentators to analyze election returns according to the voting behavior of large groups of persons with like attributes: occupation, religion, residence, education; and to imply that the imperatives of these economic and demographic factors guide the voting. Despite recent efforts of some political scientists to discourage this use of group imperatives, an astonishing number of people persist in doing so. Key is unsympathetic to the unflattering, deterministic implications of this analytic technique, and he shows that the technique is faulty. Gross characteristics of groups of individuals serve as an adequate indication of attitudes only when the issues of the campaign affect directly and clearly the members of the group. "The fact that a person is, say, a Negro serves as an index to what he believes and to why he votes as he does only when an election concerns Negroes as Negroes and when the members of the group are aware of the issue and see it as basic among their concerns of the moment." Where gross data indicate, for example, that 70 per cent of businessmen voted one way, Key invariably asks the question why 30 per cent did not vote their apparent economic interests; and the answer not infrequently is that the classification provided by the gross data is

irrelevant. Furthermore, he finds that even where group attitudes are present, voters' individual policy preferences are important. To understand elections, the investigator should examine directly the voters' attitudes about issues and other questions of the campaign. This is precisely what Key does in this book.

(2) Some political commentators have found a significant factor of irrationality in the way we elect the president. This they derive from the frequency of elections in which the same party retains power, and from their assumption that this is the consequence of simple repetitive voting. Key inquires, as most others have not, about the process by which a majority party maintains its dominance, and he finds that its apparently stable majority may be in fact highly changeful. The popular majority does not hold together like a ball of sticky popcorn; no sooner has it been constructed than it begins to crumble. "A series of maintaining elections occurs only in consequence of a complex process of interaction between government and populace in which old friends are sustained, old enemies are converted into new friends, old friends become even bitter opponents, and new voters are attracted to the cause." Electoral majorities, then, although they may have a stable base, are frequently majorities of the moment, *ad hoc* majorities created by the voters' responses to the actions and policies of government.

(3) Some voting studies have concluded that the standpat voter is on the average more interested and more intelligent than the switchers; that those who most readily change their party voting preferences are the least interested and the most inconsistent in their beliefs. Since switchers contribute the necessary flexibility to our political system, this means that the system's rationality depends on the "least admirable" voters. Confronted with this pessimistic conclusion for democratic government, Key is impelled to a careful re-examination and reinterpretation of the evidence. First he develops a different, and for his purposes more reliable, definition of a switching

voter as one who changes his party vote from one election to another, rather than one who changes his views during a campaign. He then finds that although the characteristics of the switchers can vary from election to election, they are not necessarily either less informed or less involved than the standpatters. In some elections, at least, they do not differ significantly from standpatters in their average level of education, in the frequency of their "don't know" or "no opinion" answers to public policy questions, or in their level of interest in politics. The major factors that distinguish switchers from standpatters are those of issues and opinions of presidential candidates' qualities. "Those who switch do so to support governmental policies or outlooks with which they agree, not because of subtle psychological or sociological peculiarities." Thus the political system is not held together by a buffer function of the uninterested voter.

(4) Some political writers have made much of an irrational cult of personality in presidential elections. While granting that personality plays a role in voting and that our data and analytical tools do not permit completely satisfactory appraisals of this role, Key rejects the cult of personality, with its disturbing implications about the motivation of voters and the rationality of the political system. With respect to the claim that personality cult accounts for Roosevelt's re-elections, he says poignantly that "it becomes ridiculous immediately if one contemplates what the fate of Franklin Delano Roosevelt would have been had he from 1933 to 1936 stood for those policies which were urged upon the country by the reactionaries of the day." And as for the pretended power of the father image of Eisenhower, Key doubts the necessity of resorting to such "dubious hypotheses" to explain the response of the electorate.

(5) Key's study confirms earlier findings that the electorate judges retrospectively. Voters respond most clearly to those events that they have experienced and observed; proposals for the future, being hazy and uncertain, neither engage the voter nor

govern his actions in the same degree. From this evidence some commentators conclude that voters are playing a largely irrelevant role, for their choices in a presidential election should be based on the candidates' positions on new issues and future polices and programs.

Key does not hesitate to draw attention to the limiting consequences of the evidence. He notes that the minority party cannot play the role of an imaginative advocate, for it is captive of the majority. It gains votes principally from among those who are disappointed by, or disapprove of, the Administration. "Thus, as a matter of practical politics, it must appear to be a common scold rather than a bold exponent of innovation." But Key is also quick to point out that a combination of the electorate's retrospective judgment and the custom of party accountability enables the electorate in fact to exercise a prospective influence; for governments, and parties, and candidates "must worry, not about the meaning of past elections, but about their fate at future elections." The most effective weapon of popular control in a democratic system is the capacity of the electorate to throw a party from power.

To uncover the true nature of American voting behavior and the functions that the electorate and elections perform in the system as a whole, Key wanted to study a series of presidential elections extending over a considerable period of time and including campaigns and results of considerable variety, as did those of 1936, 1948, 1952, and 1960. To do this he had to tap data sources (largely Gallup polls) that previously had been eschewed by many analysts of voting behavior, in part because the data were considered to be soft. (There were questions about the methods used to select the samples, construct and test the questions, conduct the interviews, test the reliability of a voter's recall of his vote four years earlier, etc.) To use these data, therefore, Key had to improvise techniques of analysis as well as apply tests of significance and reliability. At these tasks he was, of course, expert, but nonetheless he corresponded with several professional associates to get their reactions to what he was doing. After a careful examination of this correspondence, of Key's comments on it, of the dating of the correspondence in relation to that of successive drafts of the chapters, and above all of the text itself, Professor Cummings and I have no doubt that Key was satisfied that his data were of sufficient quality to support his analytical techniques and that the techniques were adequate to support his findings.

Key anticipated two possible objections to his attribution of significance to the parallelism of policy preferences and the direction of the vote. It might be claimed that when voters are interviewed they improvise policy views that seem to be consistent with the way they plan to vote for other reasons entirely. Key believed that although this doubtless occurs to some unknown extent, its importance should be discounted, for a voter must be fairly well informed if he is able to simulate a pattern of policy preferences that is consistent with his intended vote. A second objection might be that policy preferences are merely views that voters who are identified with a political party perceive as the orthodox party line. Key affirms that the doctrines of the party leadership can shape the policy preferences of many persons, but here too he discounts the significance of the phenomenon for his argument. Although this type of formation of policy attitudes may occur among standpatters, it is not even relevant for the millions of switching voters at each presidential election who can play a decisive role in the outcome. Finally, and with regard to both of these objections, Key points out that it is the parallelism of vote and policy that is significant, not its origin. However the opinions come into being,

their supportive function in the political system should be the same.

V.O. Key died a year before the 1964 election, and before most observers thought that Barry Goldwater had a real chance to become the Republican presidential nominee. The relationships between the voters' policy preferences and their votes in 1964 are still being studied by the analysts. Yet the broad pattern of the 1964 results appears to confirm Key's thesis that voters on the average base their vote decisions on the issue positions of the candidates and on their expectations concerning how the candidates would perform as president.

Compared with 1960, and with most other presidential elections in recent years, the candidates were poles apart in 1964. The oft-noted absence of a meaningful dialogue on issues in the campaign only masked the fact that there was a wide gap between the policy positions the two candidates espoused on such vital matters as civil rights, domestic welfare legislation, and, many voters thought, on the restraint the candidate would exercise as president on questions involving war or peace.

There is evidence that many Republicans voted for Barry Goldwater despite misgivings about many of his policy positions. But Goldwater's determination to give the voters "a choice, not an echo" seems also to have wrenched an extraordinarily large number of voters from their traditional party loyalties. An election in which the State of Mississippi votes 87 per cent Republican, while nationwide, one Republican in every five supports the Democratic presidential nominee points up the importance that policy considerations can assume when the choice given the voters on issues is sharply drawn.

9

THE PRESIDENCY: THE HARDEST JOB IN THE WORLD?

The American Presidency is a product of growth as much as creation. The office was "made" not only by the framers at the Constitutional Convention but by virtually every strong president who has occupied the White House. Today the Presidency is described as "the nerve center of the nation," "our main contribution to democratic government," and "the great glue factory that binds the party and the nation."

The dramatic increase in presidential power and responsibility has spotlighted certain institutional and operational problems. The office places enormous burdens upon one man. Unlike the British monarch, who merely reigns, while the British Prime Minister and his cabinet rule, the American president must both "reign and rule." Furthermore, the President has no strong party system to help him steer a program through an independent and sometimes hostile legislature. It is not at all curious that a number of scholars urge reform and regeneration of the office, at the same time that equally strong and more numerous voices caution, "Leave Your Presidency Alone."

First among the distinguishing characteristics of the American Presidency is the fact that the office is independent, in the sense that the President is separated from Congress physically, politically, and Constitutionally. Second, and perhaps equally important, the Presidency is a single office (some assert that it is a solitary office) rather than a collective one. The President has no "real" cabinet such as the cabinet which governs in the British parliamentary system. Third, the Presidency is the only office in American politics which is truly national in scope. The President is elected indirectly by all of the people from a national constituency every four years. It is this national character that caused Harry S. Truman to describe the President as "the lobbyist of the people," and Theodore Roosevelt to call the office a "bully pulpit." Fourth, changes in American politics and the influence of the electoral system put a premium upon victory in the large, urban states, which are "swing" states with highly competitive political parties. Hence, both parties nominate candidates of liberal persuasion. The Republicans (with the exception of Barry Goldwater) nominate a candidate more liberal than the rank and file, while the Democrats invariably nominate someone more liberal than the southern wing of the party. The reason is that a presidential candidate must identify with and appeal to the aspirations of ethnic and minority groups in large cities, so he must be an activist with a program. Since the urban vote is crucial to election (and urban problems are critical) the President has become an urban spokesman. Finally, the President speaks with one voice and speaks first. Thus the Presidency has become a focal point for the introduction of broad national legislation. Virtually all major bills flow from the Executive Office to Congress. As a consequence, the President spends a considerable amount of energy, time, and staff resources in guiding and/or attempting to guide major proposals through both houses of Congress. The President has become our fourth federal legislative representative and, in some respects, he is the most important of all four.

This chapter deals with two problems: the nature of the Presidency and its strengths and weaknesses as a political institution, and the relationship between the Presidency and the bureaucracy.

The Presidency: Transition or Major Transformation?

The problems of the Presidency are manifold. Woodrow Wilson, who knew the office during a stress period in American history, warned "Men of ordinary physique and discretion cannot be presidents and live, if the strain be not somehow relieved. We shall be obliged always to be picking our chief magistrates from among wise and prudent athletes—a small class."

The sprawling Executive Office still defies complete presidential direction and control. There is a wide gap between the President's responsibility and his authority to administer. At times the breech between President and Congress seems to grow larger rather than smaller. Since there is no strong party or cabinet system to give the President needed help, it appears as though intolerable burdens were being placed upon one man.

The question remains: Is the Presidency simply adjusting to contemporary events, or is it, as an institution, undergoing a major transformation? Harvey Wheeler urges collective leadership. George Reedy suggests improved communications and the creation of new institutions. Clinton Rossiter urges only minor adjustments.

Should or Can the President Control the Federal Bureaucracy?

There is a quotation from *Alice in Wonderland* which reflects the average person's thinking about bureaucracy: "We are getting into the woods and it is getting very dark." The truth is, however, that we cannot live without organization. Bureaucracy is the inevitable product of a large-scale complex society. It has its counterparts in business, government, large professional associations, and even education itself. The basis of bureaucracy is technical knowledge, specialized skills, and know-how. Certain jobs in a large organization require particular training and skills. The persons who occupy them must be able, on the basis of knowledge, to make certain decisions.

Many of the common assumptions regarding bureaucrats and bureaucracy are wrong. Most of the 2.5 million plus bureaucrats do not live in Washington. They are not a homogeneous group, but a cross section of the population. Over 50 per cent of them work for the army, navy, or air force. Only about 10 per cent are working in any activity connected with welfare. On the whole, bureaucracy is efficient, and it is doubtful whether the work of any large organization could be carried on without a type of bureaucratic organization.

In a sense, expertise (specialized knowledge and work based upon job analysis and specific skills) is basic to any modern industrialized country. Even the emerging countries need administrators and bureaucrats. The bureaucrat need not be a superfluous office employee. He may be the man at the control tower of a congested city airport, his colleague in the Weather Bureau, or the public health technician who tests our water supply. All of these people help keep the country going on a relatively smooth road.

On the other hand, bureaucratic structures and procedures may stunt initiative, discourage creativity, and bury decision-making in a mass of red tape and referrals.

The problem of the President's relation to the bureaucracy assumes that bureaucracy is here to stay and the only question worth discussing is how we can best organize and control it. Can greater control by the President make the federal bureaucracy more innovative, efficient, and responsive to the popular will? Arthur M. Schlesinger, Jr., writes on the problems which President John F. Kennedy faced in trying to get the country moving. Somehow the bureaucracy didn't get the message. Turning the bureaucracy over to the Executive completely would create other problems. Peter Woll, "The President Is Not In Fact Chief Administrator?" asserts that the logistics and the size of the federal service prevents the President from directly administering and controlling the federal bureaucracy. To be effective at all, the President has to limit his control to certain agencies and specific policies within those agencies.

1

Powers of the Presidency, a Report

HARVEY WHEELER

How does Harvey Wheeler's personal proposal for reform of the Presidency differ from other views advanced in his report? What are the primary themes considered in the conference? Why does Wheeler admire Dwight D. Eisenhower's administration? How would Wheeler reconcile his preference for a "weak Presidency" with the need for executive leadership in domestic affairs? Would collective leadership in the Presidency work as well as it does in business and in the corporate structure?

Two arguments have run through this conference on the powers of the American Presidency. One is that there is overweening strength in the Presidency today. The other is that at least in domestic affairs the Presidency is not strong enough.

What is the evidence to support the first argument? First, there is the sheer size of the Presidential bureaucracy. This means, among other things, that the President can go outside his own formal roster of governmental personnel and enlist enormous bureaucratic aid from nongovernmental agencies, organizations, and individuals who are eager to provide such help.

The President also has a monopoly on complete information. We have learned to be skeptical about the fullness and accuracy of his information, but it remains true that the Presidency is the only place in government where an overview is possible. This gives the President a commanding position over all other citizens, who can have only a partial grasp of the facts. The

From Harvey Wheeler, "The Powers of the Presidency: Report on a Conference," The Center Magazine, IV, No. 1 (January/February 1971), 7–11, a publication of the Center for the Study of Democratic Institutions in Santa Barbara, California.

increasing complexity and interrelatedness of the problems facing us make it impossible to touch any of the problems in a truly creative and comprehensive fashion on a level lower than the pinnacle itself, that is, the Presidency, where the problems mesh into some kind of concatenation.

Also, foreign affairs have become an overwhelming force in the domestic politics of all countries. An exclusively domestic problem is almost impossible today. Even something as domestic as the corn/hog ratio in Indiana or Illinois is bound up with international problems in the production and distribution of foods and the struggle of the developing countries to meet their needs.

There is also the power of the President as Commander-in-Chief of our armed forces. With that power, Presidents tend to solve problems by wielding a big stick. And whether they are conscious of it or not, military actions like the Korean and Vietnam wars have made it easier for Presidents to handle certain kinds of domestic problems.

Then, too, with the advent of mass communications, especially television, a President can claim the national spotlight any time he wants it. He is able not only to secure maximum exposure for himself and his policies but, by determining when and how he will use television, he can cast into the shadow any critic who may want to call attention to alternatives to them. The President on television becomes not so much a person as the producer of the image of himself he deems appropriate for the situation at hand. But the person behind this image need not have any real contact with the people. He makes contact, rather, with a poll-taking staff whose duty it is to assemble a public-opinion profile of the people. The result is not a President talking to the people but an image talking to a statistical profile.

Also, we have all heard about the ways in which Presidents can silence their critics by using the agencies of government—for example, the Central Intelligence Agency, Army Intelligence, the Justice Department, or the Internal Revenue Service. In a recent issue of the *New York Review of Books* Hans Morgenthau claimed that he was the object of a massive Presidential harassment a few years ago when he tried to change the White House policy on Vietnam.

Finally, there has been an organizational revolution in government bureaucracy, illustrated by the famous order from President Lyndon Johnson to institute a Planning, Programming, and Budgeting System throughout the executive and administrative agencies of government. Whether or not the efficiency promised by that particular order has been realized, there has been a radical change in the Washington bureaucracy, the effect of which has been to strengthen governmental centralization.

The evidence suggesting that the Presidency may be too weak is largely centered around the problems Presidents have always had in domestic politics. The American political system still has its Madisonian birthmarks. The assumption at the time of our founding was that the most compelling and important issues confronting the people would appear first on the local level (in what we now call congressional districts), that they would be resolved by regional power groups and political forces, and that the ultimate resolution by these competing and conflicting forces would take place in the halls of Congress. But as Congress becomes overwhelmed by the variety and magnitude of problems, such issues begin to find their way to the Presidency. However, the President's authority is sharply limited. The most he can do, rather than offer creative leadership, is orchestrate existing forces.

The President is not confronted with peer groups who are able to correct his misinformation and supply the information he does not have. George Reedy has informed us of the extent to which he is a prisoner in the White House and a captive of his own staff.

There are serious charges, too, about the extent to which society is manipulated by governmental agencies that are virtually without constraints or limitations. These agencies include the Federal Bureau of Investigation, the Department of Defense, the Central Intelligence Agency, and the Atomic Energy Commission. Such agencies are apparently out of control. It seems that the President is often at their mercy. Sometimes we have only conjecture and suspicion to go on, and the examples cited may be no more than food for the paranoia of political scientists, but it has been curious indeed how often, at precisely those times when there appeared to be a chance for rapprochement and international reconciliation, there was, for example, a new American bombing in North Vietnam while the Soviet Ambassador was there, or some other kind of escalation that would heat up the international atmosphere.

Another piece of evidence of the weakness of the Presidency is the breakdown of the party system. In the past, Presidents have often been opposed by their own party. However, at the beginning of their administrations, when patronage was copious, Presidents could rely on party affiliates to support their programs. With the disintegration of the parties, this source of Presidential strength has disappeared.

Still another piece of evidence is the

extent to which science and technology have become dominant political concerns even as we are beginning to recognize that we have no effective way to deal with science- and technology-related issues either in Congress or in the executive branch. The scientific and technological elite is still a tight little club able to distribute federal and nonfederal funds. Political tenure is for specific limited periods of time, but scientific-technological problems and issues require policies, planning, and investment whose effects may reach decades into the future. It is almost impossible for politicians to deal with these complex issues on their own terms because politicians look to the next election and judge everything in the light of it.

A variety of prescriptive suggestions, some of them conflicting, have been made in response to this conference's analysis of the Presidency.

One concerns the possibility of structural changes. Mr. Reedy, however, holds that structural changes, though necessary, are not sufficient, and that in the end there has to be some kind of high political invention.

Party reforms have been proposed. It seems clear enough that our traditional party system is distintegrating. In my view, it is still debatable whether a reformed system, if there is to be one, should retain the two-party tradition. I am not opposed in principle to some kind of one-party system. The political tradition in California prior to legislation prohibiting cross-filing some years ago did result in something like a one-party system. I think a large part of our national history has been marked by one-party politics. Certainly the founding fathers favored something like a one-party system. Some political scientists point out that, while there is a multi-party system nationally, inside some states there is essentially a one-party tradition. So, the idea of a one-party system should not be automatically associated with fascism or communism and therefore rejected out of hand. On the contrary, we may be heading into an era characterized by the absence of the multi-party systems which were a high point of liberal constitutionalism in the nineteenth century.

It has been suggested that a devil's advocate be created within the Presidency. Nobody, however, has been able to figure out how that might work. One idea is that the devil's advocate role should be coordinated with an ombudsman function on the federal level. A devil's advocate needs independence, authority, and full access to Presidential decision-making and policy-forming channels. With all that, a devil's advocate in the White House might be a salutary innovation.

Something must also be done to constitutionalize the "outlaw agencies" that seem at times to be beyond the control of either Congress or the Presidency.

In addition, science and technology must be put under law, constitutionalized.

And it may be valid and useful to set up a medical-pharmaceutical board on which an appropriate congressional or Presidential peer group could rely for information about the health of an incumbent President.

In my view, some of the most serious problems of the Presidency, problems that are in large part responsible for the way the Presidency has grown and developed, arise not from domestic matters but from international affairs. The Cold War, for example, has given the American Presidency a preëminence it might not otherwise have had. If this proposition is valid, then it is foolish to think that one is going to find a solution to the problem of excessive Presidential power simply by fiddling around with structural changes. If the Cold War is an inherent factor shaping the Presidency in undesirable ways, only the ending of the Cold War will resolve the Presidential-power problem.

. . . [W]e now have a situation that produces false crises and the appearance of the need for frequent and instant decision-making. It would be much healthier if we could simply slow down reactions, slow down decisions, get a do-nothing President as it were. (That was one of the reasons I liked Mr. Eisenhower. He wasn't on the job often enough to make many big decisions. As a result, things that might have been the occasion for precipitous action on the part of his predecessors or successors were allowed to simmer down because it was so hard to get a decision out of the White House.)

Direct institutional innovation, then, may be necessary for the muting of what now look like crises in international affairs—but need not be.

I think there is an overriding need to make the Presidency weaker rather than stronger. I would like to see a contemporary counterpart of the way in which the founding fathers hemmed in the Presidency in 1787 in order to produce, if not a weak President, at least a limited President.

Today in organization theory, information theory, and systems analysis there are four kinds of operating principles associated with decision-making techniques that might serve to limit the power of the Presidency. These principles could be programmed into an information system in any decision-making operation, including that of the Presidency and the White House. . . . The intricate machinery of the Constitution—separation of powers, checks and balances—was aimed at preventing the exercise of unchecked authority, a clear analogue of the four operating principles. The question is whether the constitutional devices which have become ineffective can be revived and once more made effective through the application of contemporary organization theory.

My own proposal is for a weak Presidency combined with a modernized set of limitations. I also think there is need for a plural executive, for a collective leadership. It seems strange to me that we still cling to the cult of personality in our national government. What we know of large-scale organizations in industrial and corporate life is that the plural-executive or collective-leadership approach has been effective. In contrast, the organization of the Presidency in our government is sadly out of date. Collective leadership would, of course, also be protection against the contingency of a Presidential illness. It would certainly also be an added protection against precipitous action by the military and other agencies.

2

The Twilight of the Presidency

GEORGE E. REEDY

George Reedy is quoted as saying, "the most important, and the least examined problem of the Presidency is that of maintaining contact with reality." How does Reedy support this contention in the following selection? Why does the presence of a "devil's advocate" not solve the problem of keeping the President in touch with reality through open debate? What recommendations would you make to improve communications between the President and the world outside the White House?

During the early days of a president's incumbency, the atmosphere of reverence which surrounds him acquires validity in his own eyes because of the ease with which he can get results. Congress is eager to approve his nominees and pass his bills. Business is anxious to provide him with "friends" and assistants. Labor is ready to oblige him with a climate of industrial peace. Foreign ambassadors scurry to locate suitable approaches.

It is a wonderful and heady feeling to be a president—at least for the first few months.

The environment of deference, approaching sycophancy, helps to foster another insidious factor. It is a belief that the president and a few of his most trusted advisers are possessed of a special knowledge which must be closely held within a small group lest the plans and the designs of the United States be anticipated and frustrated by enemies. It is a knowledge which is thought

to be endangered in geometrical proportion to the number of other men to whom it is passed. Therefore, the most vital national projects can be worked out only within a select coterie, or there will be a "leak" which will disadvantage the country's security.

Obviously, there *is* information which a nation must keep to itself if it is to survive in the present world climate. This means that the number of minds which can be brought to bear on any given problem is often in inverse proportion to the importance of the problem.

The steps that led to the bombing of North Vietnam were all discussed by a small group of men. They were intelligent men—men of keen perception and finely honed judgment. It is doubtful whether any higher degree of intelligence could have been brought to bear on the problem. But no matter how fine the intelligence or how thoroughgoing the information available, the fact remained that none of these men was put to the test of defending his position in public debate. And it is amazing what even the best of minds will discover when forced to answer critical questions. Unfortunately, in this as in many other instances, the need to comment publicly came after, and not before, irreversible commitment.

Of course, within these councils there was always at least one "devil's advocate." But an official dissenter always starts with half his battle lost. It is assumed that he is bringing up arguments solely because arguing is his official role. It is well understood that he is not going to press his points harshly or stridently. Therefore, his objections and cautions are discounted before they are delivered. They are actually welcomed because they prove for the record that decision was preceded by controversy.

As a general rule, the quality of judgment usually varies directly with the number of minds that are brought to bear upon an issue. No man is so wise as to play his own "devil's advocate," and workable wisdom is the distillation of many different viewpoints which have clashed heatedly and directly in an exchange of opinion. To maintain the necessary balance between assurances of security and assurances that enough factors have been taken into consideration is perhaps the most pressing problem of statecraft. The atmosphere of the White House, in which the president is treated constantly as an infallible and reverential object, is not the best in which to resolve this problem.

In retrospect, it seems little short of amazing that President Kennedy would ever have embarked upon the ill-fated Bay of Pigs venture. It was poorly conceived, poorly planned, poorly executed, and undertaken with grossly inadequate knowledge. But anyone who has ever sat in on a White House council can easily deduce what happened without knowing any facts other than those which appeared in the public press. White House councils are not debating matches in which ideas emerge from the heated exchanges of participants. The council centers around the president himself, to whom everyone addresses his observations.

The first strong observations to attract the favor of the president become subconsciously the thoughts of everyone in the room. The focus of attention shifts from a testing of all concepts to a groping for means of overcoming the difficulties. A thesis which could not survive an undergraduate seminar in a liberal-arts college becomes accepted doctrine, and the only question is not *whether* it should be done but *how* it should be done. A forceful public airing of the Bay of Pigs plan would have endangered the whole project, of course. But it might have prevented disaster.

On a different level can be cited the far less serious setback suffered by President Lyndon B. Johnson when he attempted to merge the Commerce and the Labor departments into one agency. Out of a desire for a "surprise" headline, this proposal was held in the utmost secrecy between the president and his speech writers until a few moments before his State of the Union message was scheduled for delivery. Quick calls were made to the secretaries of labor and commerce, who were pressed for a quick response and who reacted as any government official reacts to such a call from the White House. They said, "Yes."

In a matter of days, it was apparent that the project had as much chance of getting off the ground as a kiwi. To organized labor, still headed by men with long memories, the Labor Department was a sacrosanct institution for which they had fought and bled in their youth. They had no intention of acquiescing to the removal from the cabinet of what they regarded as "our spokesman." Business, while far less emotional, made it quite clear that industrialists did not relish the prospect of "our agency" being merged with what they regarded as the opposition. The president quietly buried the whole idea.

The truly baffling question, however, is how a man with the political sensitivity of Lyndon B. Johnson would ever embark on such a futile enterprise. The basis of his success as the Senate Democratic leader had been his insistence upon touching every base before launching a project. He was famous throughout the political community for "taking the temperature" of every affected group in advance and laying careful plans to meet any objections they might have before the objections were even raised. And yet here was an instance where even a perfunctory conversation with a few of his friends would have made clear that humiliation was the only conceivable outcome of his proposal.

The only conclusion that an observer can draw is that the atmosphere of the White House—the combination of sycophancy and a belief in the efficacy of closely held knowledge—had done its work. The man regarded as the outstanding politician of the mid-twentieth century had stepped into a buzzsaw which could have been foreseen by a wardheeler in any major city of America.

A reader of history will find innumerable and startling examples of political bloopers committed by men with a record of political sagacity. How is one to explain President Truman's inept handling of the Communist spy scare of the late 1940s—a mistake which opened up the era of Joe McCarthy? How is one to explain Franklin D. Roosevelt's futile effort to "pack" the Supreme Court? How is one to explain Woodrow Wilson's clumsy treatment of the Senate, which led directly to its refusal to permit United States participation in the League of Nations? None of these men had shown themselves politically inept on such a grand scale at any previous moment of their lives. It is only an inference but an inescapable one that the White House is an institution which dulls the sensitivity of political men and ultimately reduces them to bungling amateurs in their basic craft—the art of politics.

The real question every president must ask himself is what he can do to resist the temptations of a process compounded of idolatry and lofty patriotic respect for a national symbol. By all the standards of past performance, he should be well equipped to face it. As a general rule, he has fought his way up through the political ranks. He has flattered and been flattered —and the mere fact that he has survived to the threshold of the White House should indicate a psychological capacity to keep flattery in perspective. He has dealt with rich people, poor people, wise men, fools, patriots, knaves, scoundrels, and wardheelers. Had he not maintained his perspective on human beings generally, it is doubtful that he would ever have received his party's nomination.

But the atmosphere of the White House is a heady one. It is designed to bring to its occupant privileges that are commensurate in scope with the responsibilities that he must bear. A privilege is, by definition, a boon not accorded to other people. And to the extent that a man exercises his privileges, he removes himself from the company of lesser breeds who must stand in line and wait their turn on a share-and-share-alike basis for the comforts of life. To a president, all other humans are "lesser breeds."

Furthermore, a president would have to be a dull clod indeed to regard himself without a feeling of awe. The atmosphere of the White House is calculated to instill in any man a sense of destiny. He literally walks in the footsteps of hallowed figures —of Jefferson, of Jackson, of Lincoln. The almost sanctified relics of a distant, semi-mythical past surround him as ordinary household objects to be used by his family. From the moment he enters the halls he is made aware that he has become enshrined in a pantheon of semidivine mortals who have shaken the world, and that he has taken from their hands the heritage of American dreams and aspirations.

Unfortunately for him, divinity is a better basis for inspiration than it is for government. The world can be shaken from Mount Olympus but the gods were notoriously inefficient when it came to directing the affairs of mankind. The Greeks were wise about such matters. In their remarkable body of lore, human tragedy usually originated with divine intervention and their invocations to the deities were usually prayers of propitiation—by all that is holy, leave us alone!

A semidivinity is also a personification of a people, and presidents cannot escape the process. The trouble with personification is that it depends upon abstraction and, in the course of the exercise, individual living people somehow get lost. The president becomes the nation and when he is insulted, the nation is insulted; when he has a dream, the nation has a dream; when he has an antagonist, the nation has an antagonist.

The purpose . . . is to examine the effects of this environment upon the president of the United States. This has become a matter of great urgency. It is increasingly evident that the tasks of the presidency are more and more demanding. It is also increasingly evident that presidents spend more of their time swimming in boiling political waters. There is even a respectable body of thought which holds that the problems are out of control and that, in the present context, the nation must look forward to a series of one-term presidents, incapable of holding the office for more than four years.

As a general rule, efforts to remedy the deficiencies of the presidency center on proposals to bring a greater administrative efficiency to the White House itself. It is held that the problems would become manageable if the president had better tools at his command. In my mind there is a strong suspicion that the problems are no more unmanageable today than they have been in the past. They are, of course, bigger in terms of consequence. But they are still decision rather than management problems. Perhaps a more fruitful path lies in an exploration of the extent to which the atmosphere of the White House degrades a man's political instincts and abilities. Our thoughts should be centered not on electronic brains but on the forces that would foster the oldest, the noblest, and the most vital of all human arts—the art of politics.

3

Leave Your Presidency Alone

CLINTON ROSSITER

As a governmental institution, Clinton Rossiter finds the American Presidency to be not without fault. In fact, he urges reforms and corrections. In the main, however, he concludes that the office may be tinkered with for minor adjustments but should not be radically changed. As it now stands, the Presidency is "one of our chief bulwarks against decline and chaos."

. . . I detect a deep note of satisfaction, although hardly of complacency, with the

From Clinton Rossiter, The American Presidency (rev. ed.; New York: Harcourt Brace Jovanovich, 1960), pp. 258–261. Copyright © 1956, 1960 by Clinton Rossiter. Reprinted by permission of the publisher.

American Presidency as it stands today. A steady theme seems to have run all through this final review of its weaknesses and problems, a theme entitled (with apologies to the genius of Thurber) "Leave Your Presidency Alone!" This feeling of satisfaction springs, I am frank to admit, from a political outlook more concerned with the world as it is than as it is said to have been by reactionaries and is promised to be by radicals. Since this outlook is now shared by a staggering majority of Americans, I feel that I am expressing something more than a personal opinion. If we accept the facts of life in the 1960's, as we must, and if we shun the false counsels of perfection, as we do, then we are bound to conclude that we are richly blessed with a choice instrument of constitutional democracy. Judged in the light of memory and desire, the Presidency is in a state of sturdy health, and that is why we should not give way easily to despair over the defects men of too much zeal or too little courage claim to discover in it. Some of these are not defects at all; some are chronic in our system of government; some could be cured only by opening the way to others far more malign.

This does not mean that we should stand pat with the Presidency. Rather, we should confine ourselves to small readjustments— I have noted a dozen or more that might be worth a try—and leave the usual avenues open to prescriptive change. We should abolish the electoral college but leave the electoral system to pursue its illogical but hitherto effective way. We should plan carefully for mobilization in the event of war but take care that the inherent emergency power of the president—the power used by Lincoln to blockade the South, by Wilson to arm the merchantmen, and by Roosevelt to bring off the Destroyer Deal —be left intact and untrammeled. We should experiment with a joint executive-legislative council and the item veto but be on our guard against the urge to alter radically the pattern of competitive coexistence between Congress and President. We should give the president all the aides he can use but beware the deceptively simple solution of a second and even third vice-president for executive purposes. And we should tinker modestly with the president's machinery but wake from the false dream of perfect harmony in high places, especially in the highest place of all. For if the Presidency could speak, it would say with Whitman:

Do I contradict myself?
Very well then I contradict myself.
(I am large, I contain multitudes.)

"Leave Your Presidency Alone": that is the message of this chapter, and I trust I have made clear . . . why I transmit it so confidently. To put the final case for the American Presidency as forcefully as possible, let me point once again to its essential qualities:

It strikes a felicitous balance between power and limitations. In a world in which power is the price of freedom, the Presidency, as Professor Merriam and his colleagues wrote in 1937, "stands across the path of those who mistakenly assert that democracy must fail because it can neither decide promptly nor act vigorously." In a world in which power has been abused on a tragic scale, it presents a heartening lesson in the uses of constitutionalism. To repeat the moral of an earlier chapter, the power of the Presidency moves as a mighty host only with the grain of liberty and morality. The quest of constitutional government is for the right balance of authority and restraint, and Americans may take some pride in the balance they have built into the Presidency.

It provides a steady focus of leadership: of administration, Congress, and people. In a constitutional system compounded of diversity and antagonism, the Presidency looms up as the countervailing force of unity and harmony. In a society ridden by centrifugal forces, it is, as Sidney Hyman has written, the "common reference point for social effort." The relentless progress of this continental republic has made the Presidency our one truly national political institution. There are those who would reserve this role to Congress, but as the least aggressive of our presidents, Calvin Coolidge, once testified, "It is because in their hours of timidity the Congress becomes subservient to the importunities of organized minorities that the president comes more and more to stand as the champion of the rights of the whole country." The more Congress becomes, in Burke's phrase, "a confused and scuffling bustle of local agency," the more the Presidency must become a clear beacon of national purpose.

It is a priceless symbol of our continuity and destiny as a people. Few nations have solved so simply and yet grandly the problem of finding and maintaining an office of state that embodies their majesty and reflects their character. Only the Constitution overshadows the Presidency as an object of popular reverence, and the Constitution does not walk about smiling and shaking hands. "The simple fact is," a distinguished, disgruntled Briton wrote at the end of the "Royal Soap Opera" of 1955, "that the United States Presidency today is a far more dignified institution than the British monarchy." In all honesty and tact we must quickly demur, but we can be well satisfied with our "republican king."

4

Kennedy and the Problem of Presidential Control

ARTHUR M. SCHLESINGER, JR.

Is it possible or even desirable for the Presidency to control and to implement all activities of the administrative branch? Which of the following would do most to improve the federal administration: (a) reorganization; (b) recruitment of more able staff; or (c) higher payment of salaries to career personnel? Would you be in sympathy with a move to give the President more appointive power in staffing the federal bureaucracy in order to insure response to presidential direction?

In the thirties conservatives had bemoaned the expansion of the federal government as a threat to freedom. Instead they should have hailed the bureaucracy as a bulwark against change. The permanent government soon developed its own stubborn vested interests in policy and procedure, its own cozy alliances with committees of Congress, its own ties to the press, its own national constituencies. It began to exude the feeling that Presidents could come and Presidents go but it went on forever. The permanent government was, as such, politically neutral; its essential commitment was to doing things as they

From Arthur M. Schlesinger, Jr., A Thousand Days (Boston: Houghton Mifflin Company, 1965), pp. 680–686. Copyright © 1965 by Arthur M. Schlesinger, Jr. Reprinted by permission of the publisher.

had been done before. This frustrated the enthusiasts who came to Washington with Eisenhower in 1953 zealous to dismantle the New Deal, and it frustrated the enthusiasts who came to Washington with Kennedy in 1961 zealous to get the country moving again.

The Eisenhower administration in the end met the problem of the permanent government by accepting the trend toward routinization and extending it to the Presidency itself. This was congenial both to President Eisenhower, accustomed all his life to the military staff system, and to the needs of a regime more concerned with consolidation than with innovation. The result was an effort to institutionalize the Presidency, making it as nearly automatic in its operations and as little dependent on particular individuals as possible. It was a perfectly serious experiment; but in the end it was defeated, both by the inextinguishably personal character of the Presidency, which broke out from time to time even in the case of one so well disciplined to the staff system as Eisenhower, and also by the fact that even the Eisenhower administration was occasionally forced to do new things in order to meet new challenges.

Kennedy, who had been critical of the Eisenhower effort to institutionalize the Presidency, was determined to restore the personal character of the office and recover presidential control over the sprawling feudalism of government. This became a central theme of his administration and, in some respects, a central frustration. The presidential government, coming to Washington aglow with new ideas and a euphoric sense that it could not go wrong, promptly collided with the feudal barons of the permanent government, entrenched in their domains and fortified by their sense of proprietorship; and the permanent government, confronted by this invasion, began almost to function (with, of course, many notable individual exceptions) as a resistance movement, scattering to the *maquis* in order to pick off the intruders. This was especially true in foreign affairs.

The Bay of Pigs was a crucial episode in the struggle. This disaster was a clear consequence of the surrender of the presidential government to the permanent government. The inherited executive bureaucracy rallied in support of an undertaking which the new administration would never conceivably have designed for itself. The CIA had a heavy investment in this project; other barons, having heavy investments in their own pre-Kennedy projects, doubtless wished to show that the newcomers could not lightly reject whatever was bubbling up in the pipeline, however repugnant it might be to the preconceptions of the New Frontier. But the result, except for leading the President to an invaluable overhaul of his own operating methods, was ironically not to discredit the permanent government; instead, it became in certain ways more powerful than ever. The reason for this

was that, one risk having failed, all risks were regarded with suspicion; and, since the permanent government almost never wished to take risks (except for the CIA, where risks were the entrenched routine), this strengthened those who wanted to keep things as they were as against those who wanted to change things. The fiasco was also a shock to the President's hitherto supreme confidence in his own luck; and it had a sobering effect throughout the presidential government. No doubt this was in many ways to the good; but it also meant that we never quite recaptured again the youthful, adventurous spirit of the first days. "Because this bold initiative flopped," I noted in June 1961, "there is now a general predisposition against boldness in all fields." With one stroke the permanent government had dealt a savage blow to the élan of the newcomers—and it had the satisfaction of having done so by persuading the newcomers to depart from their own principles and accept the permanent government's plan.

The permanent government included men and women of marked devotion, quality and imagination. Kennedy knew this, seized many occasions to say so publicly and gave John Macy, the chairman of the Civil Service Commission, every support in improving the morale of the career services. Yet, though a valuable reservoir of intelligence and experience as well as a valuable guarantee against presidential government's going off the tracks, the permanent government remained in bulk a force against innovation with an inexhaustible capacity to dilute, delay and obstruct presidential purpose. Only so many fights were possible with the permanent government. The fighters—one saw this happen to Richard Goodwin when he went over to the State Department—were gradually weakened, cut off, surrounded and shot down, as if from ambush, by the bureaucracy and its anti-New Frontier allies in Congress and the press. At the start we had all felt free to "meddle" when we thought that we had a good idea or someone else a poor one. But, as the ice began to form again over the government, freewheeling became increasingly difficult and dangerous. At Wellfleet in the summer of 1962, I wrote that our real trouble was that we had "capitulated too much to the existing momentum of government as embodied and urged by the executive bureaucracy. Wherever we have gone wrong—from Cuba to fiscal policy—has been because we have not had sufficient confidence in the New Frontier approach to impose it on the government. Every important mistake has been the consequence of excessive deference to the permanent government. In too many areas we have behaved as the Eisenhower administration would have behaved." The problem of moving forward seemed in great part the problem of making the permanent government responsive to the policies of the presidential government.

Kennedy could not solve this problem as Roosevelt had by bypassing the bureaucracy. An emergency agency, after all, required an emergency. Kennedy had no depression or war; and in the days since the New Deal the traditional structure had moved to absorb into itself as much as it could of the new functions. It was no accident that the organization which best expressed the distinctive spirit of the New Frontier—the Peace Corps—was almost the only one established as an emergency agency and carefully preserved from the embrace of the bureaucracy.

In the long run, the problem of the permanent government could no doubt be solved by permeation and attrition. "Getting the bureaucracy to accept new ideas," as Chester Bowles once said, "is like carrying a double mattress up a very narrow and winding stairway. It is a terrible job, and you exhaust yourself when you try it. But once you get the mattress up it is awfully hard for anyone else to get it down." But it also required day-to-day direction and control. This was Kennedy's preferred method: hence his unceasing flow of suggestions, inquiries, phone calls directly to the operating desks and so on. This approach enabled him to imbue government with a sense of his own desires

and purposes. A Foreign Service officer once remarked on the feeling that "we were all reading the cables together"—the man at the desk, the Secretary of State and the White House. Nothing was more invigorating and inspiring, epecially for the imaginative official, than personal contact with the President.

Kennedy tried in a number of ways to encourage innovation in the permanent government. His call for "dissent and daring" in the first State of the Union message concluded: "Let the public service be a proud and lively career." He took particular pleasure in the rehabilitation of government servants who had been punished for independence of thought in the past. Early on, for example, Reed Harris, whom Senator McCarthy had driven from USIA a decade before, came back to work under Edward R. Murrow, who himself had been one of McCarthy's bravest critics. The President looked for an appropriate occasion to invite Robert Oppenheimer to the White House and soon found one. He was vigilant in his opposition to any revival of McCarthyism. One of his few moments of anger in press conferences came when a woman reporter asked him why "two well-known security risks" had been given assignments in the State Department. Kennedy remarked icily that she "should be prepared to substantiate" her charges and unconditionally defended the character and record of the officials involved.

But Kennedy's habit of reaching into the permanent government was disruptive as well as exciting for the bureaucracy. For the permanent government had its own set of requirements and expectations—continuity of policy, stability of procedure, everything within channels and according to the book. These were essential; without them government would collapse. Yet an active President, with his own requirements and expectations, was likely to chafe under the bureaucratic minuet.

Early in 1963 a group of communists hijacked a Venezuelan freighter. The President was vastly, if somewhat amusedly, annoyed by the incapacity of his government to help Caracas cope with the situation. One day he beckoned me into his office while he was phoning the Secretary of the Navy to find out why the Navy had been so slow to send out planes to locate the ship. The Secretary apparently was saying that this was not his responsibility; it was a matter for the Joint Chiefs of Staff; nothing had come down through channels. A few days later President Betancourt arrived for a visit. Preparations had been made for a splendid military reception. Then a terrific rainstorm came, and the show was canceled. An hour later Kennedy looked out of his window and saw a forlorn group of soldiers still in formation in the rain. He immediately called General Clifton, his military aide, and asked why, since the ceremony was off, the soldiers were still there. Clifton replied that they had not yet received their orders through channels. Kennedy instructed him to go out right away and tell them to go home. Then he said acidly, "You can see why the Navy has been unable to locate that Venezuelan freighter."

He considered results more important than routine. "My experience in government," he once said, "is that when things are noncontroversial, beautifully coordinated, and all the rest, it must be that not much is going on." He was not, like Roosevelt, a deliberate inciter of bureaucratic disorder; he found no pleasure in playing off one subordinate against another. But his total self-reliance, his confidence in his own priorities and his own memory, freed him from dependence on orderly administrative arrangements. In any case, the Constitution made it clear where the buck stopped. "The President," he once said, "bears the burden of the responsibility. . . . The advisers may move on to new advice." The White House, of course, could not do everything, but it could do something. "The President can't administer a department," he said drily on one occasion, "but at least he can be a stimulant." This Kennedy certainly was, but on occasion he almost administered departments too.

His determination was to pull issues out of the bureaucratic ruck in time to defend his own right to decision and his own freedom of innovation. One devoted student of his methods, Prime Minister Harold Wilson, later spoke of the importance of getting in on emerging questions "by holding meetings of all relevant ministers at an early stage before the problem gets out of hand. That's one of the techniques the world owes to Kennedy." In this and other respects he carried his intervention in the depths of government even further than Roosevelt.

At luncheon one day Ben Cohen and Tom Corcoran drew an interesting comparison. "One of F.D.R.'s great strengths," Cohen said, "was a certain detachment from the details of his administration. He did not try to run everything himself, but gave his people their head. Sometimes he was criticized for letting them go off too much on their own and squabble among themselves. But this was his way of trying people out." Corcoran interjected, "Also it reduced his responsibility for their mistakes. Since he wasn't directly involved, he could wash his hands of bad policies more easily." Ben went on: "Then, when it mattered, he was always ready to weigh in and settle things. We often wished at the time that he would get involved earlier; but in retrospect I think he was right. I am afraid that your man in contrast tries to run too many things himself. He has too tight a grip on his administration. He is too often involved in the process of shaping things which should be shaped by others before they are presented to a President. I doubt very much whether the Bay of Pigs decision would have been made if the President had not taken part in the preliminary discussions—if he had been confronted in an uncommitted way with the final recommendation. . . . Kennedy is really a President on the model not of Roosevelt but of Wilson. Wilson also tried to run too much himself."

Cohen had a point, though I think he underestimated the extent to which the hardening of the permanent government since Roosevelt's day required presidential intervention at an earlier stage, as well as the extent to which the irreversibility of decisions in the nuclear age compelled a President to make sure that small actions at a low level would not lead ineluctably to catastrophic consequences. In any case, every President must rule in his own fash-

ion. The President, Richard Neustadt had said, is "a decision-machine." Kennedy's purpose in his time of almost constant crisis was to control and stimulate a vast and unwieldy government in order to produce wise decision and efficient execution. He deisgned his methods to suit his purpose.

5

The President Is Not in Fact "Chief Administrator"

PETER WOLL

Why does the author assert that the President cannot be "Chief Administrator"? What would be the consequences of the President's attempting to "coordinate all of the activities of the administrative branch"? What specific areas can (and must) the President control? What activities would the President find it difficult to control even if he wished to do so?

. . . First, consider, a few fields in which the President usually does not have a defined policy. Most regulatory fields fall into this category. For example, the President does not have a program for air safety and the regulation of the airlines and airways generally. This he leaves to the primary agencies involved, the Civil Aeronautics Board and the Federal Aviation Agency. There is simply not enough time for either the President or his staff to master the numerous complex details that are involved in formulating a policy. Likewise, in other regulatory fields, such as communications, transportation, stock exchanges and securities regulation, public utilities, and sometimes anti-trust policy, there is usually no well-defined presidential policy. In addition to these and other regulatory fields

From Peter Woll, American Bureaucracy *(New York: W. W. Norton & Company, Inc., 1963), pp. 171–173. Reprinted by permission of the publisher.*

there are numerous areas of administrative activity with which the President is necessarily unconcerned. For example, much of the day-to-day work of such Departments as Health, Education, and Welfare, Interior, Commerce, and so forth, is not related to any particular presidential policy. And information concerning the judicial activities of the agencies is generally excluded from presidential purview.

On the other hand, definite presidential policies exist in such crucial areas as defense and foreign affairs. The strength of our ground forces, the kinds of weapons we will use, where they will be located, the circumstances under which they will be employed, and so forth, are matters on which all modern Presidents have policies. In case of national emergency the National Security Council will be called into session, chaired by the President, and although possible decisions will be discussed in such meetings the President makes the final choice. In areas such as these the President is solely responsible for what is done; thus, it is desirable that he be able to gain adequate information from the bureaucracy to formulate policies which will in turn be implemented.

The fact is that the Presidency as an institution cannot carry out its major responsibilities and at the same time control and coordinate all the activities of the administrative branch. Thus, information becomes one of the vital factors of presidential control, and its complexity produces a high degree of administrative independence that otherwise might still come from political, constitutional, and legal factors. This becomes abundantly clear when one realizes that an administrative agency may select a course contrary to definite presidential policy. An interesting current illustration is the Federal Reserve Board, which has threatened to carry out money policies in direct opposition to the wishes of the . . . administration. The Federal Reserve has done so in the past; it has both the legal authority and the political support to be successful, even in the face of a clear-cut presidential program.

. . .

The realities of the relationship between the President and the bureaucracy must be recognized. In terms of our Constitution and the nature of our political system today it is not possible, necessary, or desirable that every aspect of administrative activity be controlled by the White House. If the President were to concentrate on this task it would mean a virtual abdication of his more important responsibilities. Delegation of authority and power is an integral part of our government, and it must be recognized that within broad areas administrative agencies are the primary groups responsible for legislation and adjudication.

Critics of this position contend that if the President cannot control administrative activity it is up to his staff to step in and fill the gap. Here it should be noted that it is the President who is elected by the people, not his staff. Moreover, because his staff is detached from operating activities it can in some instances function secretly and without accountability except to the President himself. . . . [T]he bureaucracy is a highly representative branch of our government, in many respects more representative than Congress; it should be added that the bureaucracy may be more representative in some ways than the President, and certainly more than the presidential staff. Private groups will very likely get more knowledgeable and more direct representation in those agencies to which they have access, than in the Presidency. The democratic process must reflect group demands as well as the more nebulous demands of the public at large. The President is the best representative of the latter, but the agencies are often the more effective representatives of the former.

Finally, it should be noted that in our political system the President is not always motivated to control the bureaucracy—a key consideration raised before with respect to Congress. The President's political survival depends upon a nationwide electoral process in which his personality and a few key issues determine the outcome. He need not always know what policies the agencies are following, or what decisions they are making in their judicial spheres: they are the primary concerns of the agencies themselves, and their political survival may depend upon the policies and decisions they carry out.

The American Presidency is a great institution, but the President is not in fact "Chief Administrator." He cannot, nor does he wish to, control all the complex activities engaged in by the administrative branch. In many key areas of presidential responsibility he demands, and generally receives, loyalty from administrative agencies. But in other fields the agencies function with partial autonomy in the policy spheres that have been assigned to them by Congress.

CONGRESS: THE NEW,
OLD, OR LAST FRONTIER?

Since representative government has such a high place in our value system, it is curious that Congress should have such a poor public image. The droll story and the humorous anecdote frequently satirize the national legislature, while the Senators Phogbounds and Claghorns in the mass media tend to stereotype the average congressman.

Part of the problem stems from a failure to understand the critical function of Congress in compromising controversial issues and achieving a degree of consensus among disparate interest groups. At the same time, the substantial committee work in Congress is seldom seen. Instead the public eye falls upon a listless, half-empty chamber ignoring a prepared speech by an equally disinterested colleague, or a newspaper headline describing the circus-like performance of a reckless investigating committee.

Congress has its shortcomings—inertia and delay, conservatism, and a tendency, at times, to intervene in the province of the Executive. The system, nevertheless, does work, despite a congressman's lack of systematic information, his overburdening committee duties, and the endless demands of constituents who regard a congressman as something of a cross between a Capitol guide and a glorified bell boy. In a nation where 70 per cent of the people do not know the name of their senator or congressman, it is highly probable that the national legislators do a better job than most apathetic citizens realize or, perhaps, deserve.

This chapter explores two major issues relating to Congress as a political institution. The first of these, "Congress: Alteration or Adaptation?" deals with the response of Congress to the twentieth century. The second problem, "Power in Congress: Views from the 'Hill,'" relates to the problem of leadership, roles, and power in the national legislature.

Congress: Alteration or Adaptation?

Most suggestions which one hears for the reform of Congress involve procedural changes. Such proposals as joint committee hearings or the installation of electronic voting equipment in the House might save time, money, and energy, but these innovations would probably not drastically alter present patterns. On the other hand, there are possible changes which would affect the basic power structure of Congress. The question raised in this section is, "Which way should Congress move?" Should the changes be procedural or substantive, or should there be no changes? The various points of view are expressed here. Samuel P. Huntington suggests that unless Congress undertakes fundamental reform it will find it increasingly difficult to perform some of its historic functions. However, Congress could adapt itself to be current trends, modify traditional patterns, and expand other functions. David B. Truman points out ways in which many of the suggested reforms would alter or fail to alter the power structure.

Power in Congress: Views from the "Hill"

Fundamental to an understanding of Congress is awareness of the patterns of influence and of power within each house. It is important to know something of the leadership and followship, the concentration and distribution of power, and the role of the individual congressman in the legislative process. In fact, without this background it is impossible to understand or to evaluate Congress as a governmental institution.

Woodrow Wilson was one of the first political scientists to examine the internal operation of Congress. His *Congressional Government* remains a classic account of the power of the leadership in the House and Senate, and the influence of committees and committee chairmen. In recent years, other writers have analyzed the power of informal groupings, such as the inner club of the Senate, as well as the place of the "outsider" and other individuals who refuse to go along with the system but who, by force of character and personality, frequently become highly effective legislators.

The second section of this chapter presents some observations on the exercise of power in Congress. Joseph S. Clark discusses the congressional establishment. Nelson W. Polsby evaluates the "inner club" of the Senate and finds that it does not live up to its reputation.

1

Congressional Responses to the Twentieth Century

SAMUEL P. HUNTINGTON

Would you agree with the author that Congress has conceded both the initiative in lawmaking and the dominant influence in determining the final content of legislation? Does it follow that Congress has lost its future? What possible directions does Professor Huntington see for Congress?

. . . Eighty per cent of the bills enacted into law, one congressman has estimated, originate in the executive branch. Indeed, in most instances congressmen do not admit a responsibility to take legislative action except in response to executive requests. Congress, as one senator has complained, "has surrendered its rightful place in the leadership in the lawmaking process to the White House. No longer is Congress the source of major legislation. It now merely filters legislative proposals from the President, straining out some and reluctantly letting others pass through. These days no one expects Congress to devise the important bills." [1] The President now determines the legislative agenda of Congress almost as thoroughly as the British Cabinet sets the legislative agenda of Parliament. The institutionalization of this role was one of the more significant developments in presidential-congressional relations after World War II.[2]

Congress has conceded not only the initiative in originating legislation but—and perhaps inevitably as the result of losing the initiative—it has also lost the dominant influence it once had in shaping the final content of legislation. Between 1882 and 1909 Congress had a preponderant influence in shaping the content of sixteen (55 per cent) out of twenty-nine major laws enacted during those years. It had a preponderant influence over seventeen (46 per cent) of thirty-seven major laws passed between 1910 and 1932. During the constitutional revolution of the New Deal, however, its influence declined markedly: only two (8 per cent) of twenty-four major laws passed between 1933 and 1940 were primarily the work of Congress.[3] Certainly its record after World War II was little better. The loss of congressional control over the substance of policy is most marked, of course, in the area of national defense and foreign policy. At one time Congress

From Samuel P. Huntington, "Congressional Responses to the Twentieth Century," in The Congress and America's Future, ed. David B. Truman (Englewood Cliffs, N.J.: Prentice-Hall, Inc., 1965), pp. 23–24, 26–31. Copyright © 1965 by The American Assembly. Reprinted by permission of the publisher.

[1] Abraham Ribicoff, "Doesn't Congress Have Ideas of Its Own?" *The Saturday Evening Post,* 237 (March 21, 1964), 6.

[2] Richard E. Neustadt, "Presidency and Legislation: Planning the President's Program," *American Political Science Review,* 49 (December 1955), 980–1021.

[3] Lawrence H. Chamberlain, *The President, Congress, and Legislation* (New York: Columbia University Press, 1946), pp. 450–52.

did not hesitate to legislate the size and weapons of the armed forces. Now this power—to raise and support armies, to provide and maintain a navy—is firmly in the hands of the executive. Is Congress, one congressional committee asked plaintively in 1962, to play simply "the passive role of supine acquiescence" in executive programs or is it to be "an active participant in the determination of the direction of our defense policy?" The committee, however, already knew the answer:

To any student of government, it is eminently clear that the role of the Congress in determining national policy, defense or otherwise, has deteriorated over the years. More and more the role of Congress has come to be that of a sometimes querulous but essentially kindly uncle who complains while furiously puffing on his pipe but who finally, as everyone expects, gives in and hands over the allowance, grants the permission, or raises his hand in blessing, and then returns to the rocking chair for another year of somnolence broken only by an occasional anxious glance down the avenue and a muttered doubt as to whether he had done the right thing.[4]

In domestic legislation Congress's influence is undoubtedly greater, but even here its primary impact is on the timing and details of legislation, not on the subjects and content of legislation. . . .

Adaptation or Reform

Insulation has made Congress unwilling to initiate laws. Dispersion has made Congress unable to aggregate individual bills into a coherent legislative program. Constituent service and administrative overseeing have eaten into the time and energy which congressmen give legislative matters. Congress is thus left in its legislative dilemma where the assertion of power is almost equivalent to the obstruction of action. What then are the possibilities for institutional, adaptation or institutional reform?

[4] House Report 1406, Eighty-seventh Congress, Second Session (1962), p. 7.

Living with the Dilemma

Conceivably neither adaptation nor reform is necessary. The present distribution of power and functions could continue indefinitely. Instead of escaping from its dilemma, Congress could learn to live with it. In each of the four institutional crises mentioned earlier, the issue of institutional adaptation came to a head over one issue: the presidential election of 1824, the House of Commons Reform Bill of 1832, the Lloyd George budget of 1910, and the Supreme Court reorganization plan of 1937. The adaptation crisis of Congress differs in that to date a constitutional crisis between the executive branch and Congress has been avoided. Congress has procrastinated, obstructed, and watered down executive legislative proposals, but it has also come close to the point where it no longer dares openly to veto them. . . . If Congress uses its powers to delay and to amend with prudence and circumspection, there is no necessary reason why it should not retain them for the indefinite future. If Congress, however, did reject a major administration measure, like tax reduction or civil rights, the issue would be joined, the country would be thrown into a constitutional crisis, and the executive branch would mobilize its forces for a showdown over the authority of Congress to veto legislation.

Reform Versus Adaptation: Restructuring Power

The resumption by Congress of an active, positive role in the legislative process would require a drastic restructuring of power relationships, including reversal of the tendencies toward insulation, dispersion, and oversight. Fundamental "reforms" would thus be required. To date two general types of proposals have been advanced for the structural reform of Congress. Ironically, however, neither set of proposals is likely, if enacted, to achieve the results which its principal proponents desire. One set of reformers, "democratizers" like Senator Clark, attack the power of the Senate

"Establishment" or "Inner Club" and urge an equalizing of power among congressmen so that a majority of each house can work its will. These reformers stand four-square in the Norris tradition. Dissolution of the Senate "Establishment" and other measures of democratization, however, would disperse power among still more people, multiply the opportunities for minority veto (by extending them to more minorities), and thus make timely legislative action still more difficult. The "party reformers" such as Professor James M. Burns, on the other hand, place their reliance on presidential leadership and urge the strengthening of the party organization in Congress to insure support by his own party for the President's measures. In actuality, however, the centralization of power within Congress in party committees and leadership bodies would also increase the power of Congress. It would tend to reconstitute Congress as an effective legislative body, deprive the President of his monopoly of the "national interest," and force him to come to terms with the centralized congressional leadership, much as Theodore Roosevelt had to come to terms with Speaker Cannon. Instead of strengthening presidential leadership, the proposals of the party reformers would weaken it.

The dispersion of power in Congress has created a situation in which the internal problem of Congress is not dictatorship but oligarchy. The only effective alternative to oligarchy is centralized authority. Oligarchies, however, are unlikely to reform themselves. . . . Reform of Congress would depend upon the central leaders' breaking with the oligarchy, mobilizing majorities from younger and less influential congressmen, and employing these majorities to expand and to institutionalize their own power.

Centralization of power within Congress would also, in some measure, help solve the problem of insulation. Some of Congress's insulation has been defensive in nature, a compensation for its declining role in the legislative process as well as a cause of that decline. Seniority, which is largely responsible for the insulation, is a symptom of more basic institutional needs and fears. Greater authority for the central leaders of Congress would necessarily involve a modification of the seniority system. Conversely, in the absence of strong central leadership, recourse to seniority is virtually inevitable. Election of committee chairmen by the committees themselves, by party caucuses, or by each house would stimulate antagonisms among members and multiply the opportunities for outside forces from the executive branch or from interest groups to influence the proceedings. Selection by seniority is, in effect, selection by heredity: power goes not to the oldest son of the king but to the oldest child of the institution. It protects Congress against divisive and external influences. It does this, however, through a purely arbitrary method which offers no assurance that the distribution of authority in the Congress will bear any relation to the distribution of opinion in the country, in the rest of the government, or within Congress itself. It purchases institutional integrity at a high price in terms of institutional isolation. The nineteenth-century assignment of committee positions and chairmanships by the Speaker, on the other hand, permitted flexibility and a balancing of viewpoints from within and without the House. . . . The resumption of this power by the Speaker in the House and its acquisition by the majority leader in the Senate would restore to Congress a more positive role in the legislative process and strengthen it vis-à-vis the executive branch. Paradoxically, however, the most ardent congressional critics of executive power are also the most strenuous opponents of centralized power in Congress.

Congressional insulation may also be weakened in other ways. The decline in mobility between congressional leadership positions and administration leadership positions has been counterbalanced, in some measure, by the rise of the Senate as a source of Presidents. This is due to several causes. The almost insoluble problems confronting state governments tarnish the glamor and limit the tenure of their governors. The nationalization of communications has helped senators play a role in the news media which is exceeded only by the President. In addition, senators, unlike governors, can usually claim some familiarity with the overriding problems of domestic and foreign policy.

Senatorial insulation may also be weakened to the extent that individuals who have made their reputations on the national scene find it feasible and desirable to run for the Senate. . . .

. . . In 1964 Robert Kennedy would probably have been the strongest candidate in any one of a dozen northeastern industrial states.

Recruitment of senators from the national scene rather than from local politics would significantly narrow the gap between Congress and the other elements of national leadership. The "local politics" ladder to the Senate would be replaced or supplemented by a "national politics" line in which mobile individuals might move from the Establishment to the administration to the Senate. This would be one important step toward breaking congressional insulation. The end of insulation, however, would only occur if at a later date these same individuals could freely move back from the Senate to the administration. Mobility between Congress and the administration similar to that which now exists between the Establishment and the administration would bring about drastic changes in American politics, not the least of which would be a great increase in the attractiveness of running for Congress. Opening up this possibility, however, depends upon the modification of seniority and that, in turn, depends upon the centralization of power in Congress.

Adaptation and Reform: Redefining Function

A politically easier, although psychologically more difficult, way out of Congress's dilemma involves not the reversal but the intensification of the recent trends of congressional evolution. Congress is in a legislative dilemma because opinion conceives of it as a legislature. If it gave up the effort to play even a delaying role in the legislative process, it could, quite conceivably, play a much more positive and influential role in the political system as a whole. Representative assemblies have not always been legislatures. They had their origins in medieval times as courts and as councils. An assembly need not legislate to exist and to be important. Indeed, some would argue that assemblies should not legislate. "[A] numerous assembly," John Stuart Mill contended, "is as little fitted for the direct business of legislation as for that of administration." [5] Representative assemblies acquired their legislative functions in the 17th and 18th centuries; there is no necessary reason why liberty, democracy, or constitutional government depends upon their exercising those functions in the twentieth century. Legislation has become much too complex politically to be effectively handled by a representative assembly. The primary work of legislation must be done, and increasingly is being done, by the three "houses" of the executive branch: the bureaucracy, the administration, and the President.

Far more important than the preservation of Congress as a legislative institution is the preservation of Congress as an autonomous institution. When the performance of one function becomes "dysfunctional" to the workings of an institution, the sensible course is to abandon it for other functions. In the 1930s the Supreme Court was forced to surrender its function of disallowing national and state social legislation. Since then it has wielded its veto on federal legislation only rarely and with the greatest discretion. This loss of power, however, has been more than compensated for by its new role in protecting civil rights and civil liberties against state action. . . .

[5] John Stuart Mill, "On Representative Government," *Utilitarianism, Liberty, and Representative Government* (London: J. M. Dent), p. 235.

The redefinition of Congress's functions away from legislation would involve, in the first instance, a restriction of the power of Congress to delay indefinitely presidential legislative requests. Constitutionally, Congress would still retain its authority to approve legislation. Practically, Congress could, as Walter Lippmann and others have suggested, bind itself to approve or disapprove urgent presidential proposals within a time limit of, say, three or six months. If thus compelled to choose openly, Congress, it may be supposed, would almost invariably approve presidential requests. Its veto power would become a reserve power like that of the Supreme Court if not like that of the British Crown. On these "urgent" measures it would perform a legitimizing function rather than a legislative function. At the same time, the requirement that Congress pass or reject presidential requests would also presumably induce executive leaders to consult with congressional leaders in drafting such legislation. Congress would also, of course, continue to amend and to vote freely on "non-urgent" executive requests.

Explicit acceptance of the idea that legislation was not its primary function would, in large part, simply be recognition of the direction which change has already been taking. It would legitimize and expand the functions of constituent service and administrative oversight which, in practice, already constitute the principal work of most congressmen. Increasingly isolated as it is from the dominant social forces in society, Congress would capitalize on its position as the representative of the unorganized interests of individuals. It would become a proponent of popular demands against the bureaucracy rather than the opponent of popular demands for legislation. It would thus continue to play a major although different role in the constitutional system of checks and balances.

A recent survey of the functioning of legislative bodies in forty-one countries concludes that parliaments are in general losing their initiative and power in legislation. At the same time, however, they are gaining power in the "control of government activity." [6] Most legislatures, however, are much less autonomous and powerful than Congress. Congress has lost less power over legislation and gained more power over administration than other parliaments. It is precisely this fact which gives rise to its legislative dilemma. If Congress can generate the leadership and the will to make the drastic changes required to reverse the trends toward insulation, dispersion, and overseeing, it could still resume a positive role in the legislative process. If this is impossible, an alternative path is to abandon the legislative effort and to focus upon those functions of constituent service and bureaucratic control which insulation and dispersion do enable it to play in the national government.

[6] Inter-Parliamentary Union, *Parliaments: A Comparative Study on Structure and Functioning of Representative Institutions in Forty-One Countries* (New York: Frederick A. Praeger, 1963), p. 398.

2

The Prospects for Change

DAVID B. TRUMAN

What does the author mean when he states " 'waste' is after all a relative term . . ."?
Comment on the quotation, "The Congress and its power structure cannot profitably
be viewed as something separate and isolable from the remainder of the government
and the society."

. . .

The Congress today is more nearly a legislature in the strict sense than is the national assembly in any other major country of the world. One may, however, question whether it is in any realistic sense possible, under the technical conditions of an industrialized and interdependent society, for the Congress more fully to exercise the legislative function. The point is raised not in order to propose an answer but rather to introduce the third problem to be confronted in assessing proposals for change, the problem of feasibility: Can it be done?

Discussions of reform frequently are carried on with the unstated assumption that anything is possible, that the question of feasibility is essentially irrelevant. Yet proposals for change that would require major alterations in the Constitution almost certainly are beyond the bounds of feasibility. . . .

. . .

Many suggestions for revision, of course, would have no appreciable effect on dis-

From David B. Truman, "The Prospects for Change," in The Congress and America's Future, ed. David B. Truman (Englewood Cliffs, N.J.: Prentice-Hall, Inc., 1965), pp. 177–183. Copyright © 1965 by The American Assembly. Reprinted by permission of the publisher.

persion, whatever else they might accomplish. In turn, a number of these could be adopted without major difficulty simply because they do not significantly affect the power structure or the political risks of the individual members. In this category would fall most of the suggestions for altering the "workload" of the Congress, such as providing separate days for committee and floor work, delegating to some special tribunal the handling of additional private bills—since 1946 chiefly bills dealing with the immigration and naturalization problems of individuals—and adding to the personal staffs of representatives and senators. They might well lighten the burdens of members, but none of them would touch the power structure at all closely. Some of them would, of course, promote efficiency in the sense that they would save time, but "waste" is after all a relative term, to be measured by what might have been done with what was saved. What appears as a "waste" of time, moreover, may, in a chamber in which power is diffused, be a source of some control by leaders, as the adjournment rush in most legislatures demonstrates.

Also in the neutral category probably should be placed proposals that Congress divest itself of the somewhat anachronistic duty of being the legislature for the District of Columbia. The change would reduce the power and perquisites of two committees; and it would be at least a symbolic loss for those who fear self-government in a city in which white citizens are not a majority, but the effects on Congress would be slight. Equally nominal, for the Congress, would be a requirement of joint hearings by House and Senate committees. If the change could be made, which is doubtful, some time of administration witnesses would be saved, which would be a gain, but the congressional effects would be insubstantial. Unless it were given power over revenue and appropriations, the creation of a joint committee on fiscal policy would likely go the way of the 1946 reorganization's legislative budget or at best become a vehicle for instruction, such as the Joint Economic Committee. (If it were given such power, which is unlikely, it would become a formidable rival to any other points of control in the Congress.)

Finally, it seems likely that proposals in the realm of congressional "ethics"—chiefly conflict-of-interest and "moonlighting" activities—would have a neutral effect as long as they went no farther than disclosure. They might reduce the utility of some Congressmen to outside interests, and they would tend to increase public respect for the Congress—clearly an advantage, especially if they resulted in eliminating the double standard for the legislative and executive branches—but their power implications would otherwise be slight.

A considerable number of suggestions, especially some that are urged in the name of "democratizing" the House or Senate, would have the effect of further weakening the power of the central "elective" leadership, the Speaker and the floor leaders. Thus the suggestion, recurrent over the years, that the number of signatures required in the House to make effective a petition discharging a committee from further consideration of a bill be reduced from the present 218 to something like 150 would transfer control from one minority to another (and shifting) one equally inaccessible to control by the elective leaders. Similarly, as noted earlier, under a twenty-one-day rule for calling a bill out of the House Rules Committee in which authority so to act were granted to the standing committees, the effect would be to weaken the Speaker's control of the agenda if he "owned" the Rules Committee. In any case it would in this form enhance the powers of the chairmen of the legislative committees.

In both House and Senate several proposed modifications of the seniority rule, however unlikely of adoption, would tend toward further dispersion. For example, caucus election of committee chairmen by secret ballot or the choice of chairmen by majority vote of the committee members would at best give nothing additional to the central leadership and at worst would strengthen the autonomy of chairmen, especially if an incumbent were regularly reelected.

Further increasing the professional staffs of the standing committees, whatever its benefits in other respects, would tend to strengthen committee autonomy. Similarly, the elimination of remaining jurisdictional ambiguities among committees would, as did the "reforms" of 1946, reduce further the discretion of the elective leaders in both houses.

Finally, the introduction of electronic voting equipment, frequently recommended by outsiders as a timesaver, especially in the House, would strengthen minority control by facilitating snap votes. Further, it probably would take from the central leadership the time it now has during a long roll call to muster maximum support from the waverers or the negotiators.

A great many devices can be imagined that would directly increase central control from within the House and Senate or do so indirectly by reducing the opportunities for a minority to block or seriously to delay congressional action. These would in varying degrees assault the collective powers of the present oligarchy, and their prospects are therefore correspondingly limited. In a body where risks are individual and localized, decentralized authority is likely to have a broad base of support, especially among those who have been re-elected at least once. Such decentralization puts within a member's reach the means of helping himself politically—an entirely worthy motive—and it is the more attractive because he cannot clearly see the capacity of any central leadership, in or out of Congress, to do the equivalent for him. A successful assault, therefore, would require a crisis severe enough to isolate the members of the oligarchy and to solidify the rank and file around central leaders willing to spearhead a serious shakeup.

The most promising, though not necessarily feasible, means all would have one feature in common, namely, increased leadership control of the timetable, not only in the chambers, but also in the committees. In the Senate a simpler and more easily invoked rule for limiting debate than the present two-thirds of those present and voting would control the most serious and most notorious threat to the timetable in that chamber, the filibuster. In the House a reinstituted twenty-one-day rule, but one that placed the authority to call up a bill blockaded by the Rules Committee in the hands of the Speaker or the majority leader, would strengthen the position of at least the Democratic leaders in the chamber.

In both houses some alternatives to or modifications in the seniority rule would aid the leaders in relation to the committees and in the chambers generally. A return to the practice under which the Speaker designated committee chairmen in the House and a granting of comparable power to the majority leader in the Senate would of course contribute to centralized control. The circumstances that would have to exist in order to make such a change possible, moreover, would assure use of the power, at least for several years. The less drastic proposal for caucus election of chairman from among the three most senior members of a committee would have the same tendency only if the Speaker and majority leader were able and willing to make their preferences prevail. If they were not, the result would be a reinforcement of dispersion.

A striking fact about the Congress in this century is that most, if not all, of those developments that have tended toward reducing or restraining the dispersion of power in the separate houses and in the Congress as a whole have come from outside the legislature and chiefly from the White House. In some instances the Congress has been formally a partner in the changes, where legislation has provided the occasion for them, and in some instances not. But in either case, the anti-dispersion effects have been secondary, and largely unintended, consequences of lines of action taken by the President primarily to discharge his own responsibilities and to meet the needs of his role.

Thus the Budget and Accounting Act of 1921, which established the executive budget in pursuit of the goal of fiscal efficiency, created for the first time a government-wide fiscal program and gave the President responsibility for its formulation and, equally important, its public presentation. The act did not achieve quite the integration of the appropriating and revenue activities in the Congress that some sponsors hoped for, but it did lead to the setting of rational, if not inflexible, proportions in expenditure. In the course of time, moreover, it created something of a counterbalance to the agency-committee relation that could be useful in as well as outside the Congress. The Employment Act of 1946, though it created no comparable operating functions, placed on the President the responsibility for developing and pronouncing the requirements of the economy as a whole and the government's part in meeting them. Although little more than an agenda-setting device, it is at least that and as such is a check on complete committee freedom in setting the congressional program.

Alongside and reinforcing these formal and legislatively created activities, at least three less conspicuous practices have developed since the 1930s. In the first place, the President's legislative program, as Neustadt has demonstrated . . . developed from the needs of a succession of chief executives, but it acquired vigor and, in all probability, permanence because it also met the needs of others—the agencies and, more important, the Congress, including its committees. It has provided the latter with not merely a "laundry-list" but a set of priorities. Its priority-setting qualities, moreover, have been strengthened in consequence of the increased and continuing prominence of foreign policy-national security problems. Presidential priorities are not coincident with congressional ones, but in these areas limits have grown up around committee autonomy and hence around congressional disjunction.

In the second place, as a likely consequence of the President's stake in his program, the growth of a White House staff specialized in legislative liaison has introduced an element of coherence and coordination into congressional deliberations, especially at the committee stage. Again, although it has been little studied, one suspects that its viability depends not merely on presidential desire but also in its utility in *general,* and not necessarily for identical reasons, to committee chairmen, to elective leaders, and even to some agencies. It clearly is not and cannot be a legislative high command, but it seems to have acquired informational and secondary influence capabilities that are centripetal in tendency.

Thirdly, the now well-established practice of regular presidential consultation with his party's principal elective leaders in the Congress works in the same direction. Like the two developments already mentioned, it was initially an outgrowth of presidential needs, but apparently it also has utility for elective leaders, especially if they head a nominal majority in Congress. Particularly if these leaders in name see themselves potentially as leaders in fact —and they need not do so—their relations with the President seem useful. The President's program and priorities are not necessarily theirs, and they do not, if they are prudent, attempt to operate simply as his lieutenants. But they may share with him the handicaps of power dispersion in the

Congress, and their collaboration with him may—again if they see themselves as more than the servants of the congressional oligarchy—place limits on its effects, to their joint advantage.

A possible implication of these developments for the further restriction of dispersion is that they may offer something of a pattern for the future. Needs in the Presidency, if they are at least consistent with needs in Congress and among its central leaders, may lead to new practices whose consequence, in all likelihood unintended, could be some further limit on the dispersion of power. One such need, as yet not clearly felt, is suggested by Neustadt . . . in his discussion of the common stakes of elective politicians against career officials.

A next step, though it would be a long and difficult one, might be, as Walter Lippmann and Huntington . . . have suggested, toward a commitment in Congress to bring to a vote, at least by mid-session, any legislation carrying top priority from the administration. The prospect of such a commitment would require more care in the construction of the President's program, since some means would be needed explicitly to distinguish urgent needs from trial balloons, and the invidious judgments that this would require might be too costly politically. It also would require a collegial commitment from the congressional oligarchy that might prove impossible of achievement. But the attempt would at least follow logically from the trends of several decades.

Prospects of strengthening central leadership through jointly acceptable leverage from outside Congress have at least the semblance of feasibility, and not only because of the developments already identified. Evidence suggests that reforms that would rest largely on the initiative of the Congress itself do not command requisite majorities. For example, a random sample of the House in 1963 found a majority supporting only fourteen of thirty-two specific proposals of reform. Of the proposals enjoying such support, only two were ones likely to be of major consequence—reinstatement of the twenty-one-day rule and a four-year term for representatives (which senators certainly would not favor). The remainder . . . appealed only to a minority.[1]

Whether or not outside leverage leads to

[1] Michael O'Leary, ed., *Congressional Reorganization: Problems and Prospects* (Hanover, N.H., 1964), pp. 18–21, 58–63.

a reduction in dispersion, the examples discussed here underscore a central point: The Congress and its power structure cannot profitably be viewed as something separate and isolable from the remainder of the government and the society. They affect and are affected by needs and changes in the society, and in the government as a whole. They must, therefore, be looked at within this context.

3

Dissenting Word on Any Change in Congress' Set-Up

JAMES J. KILPATRICK

While most voices today seem to be crying for Congressional reform, James J. Kilpatrick takes an opposing view. On what grounds does he base his plea for leaving Congress pretty much as it is? Would you agree with his thesis that we must keep the check and balance system as a barrier to hasty action? What is the basis for his statement that the seniority system is "the worst possible system, except for all other systems ever tried"?

. . . I am minded, if I may, to murmur a few words of dissent to the underlying spirit of congressional reform. The object is to make things more efficient. The vigorous revisionists would speed things up. Their most familiar target is the seniority system, by which the committee member with the longest service automatically becomes the chairman. What about all this?

I venture the thought, for whatever it may be worth, that the "cumbersome" and "antiquated" rules of the House and Senate are in fact indispensable adjuncts of a

From James J. Kilpatrick, "Dissenting Word on Any Change in Congress' Set-Up," *Washington Star, December 29, 1970. Reprinted by permission of the Washington Star Syndicate, Inc.*

wise and prudent legislative process. They function as brakes upon a powerful machine. They operate as one more rein upon the wild beast of untamed democracy.

Our governmental system is filled with such checks and safety valves. Many of them are built into the Constitution: The Senate checks the House, and the House checks the Senate. The presidential veto is a restraint upon them both. At every vital point where the tyranny of a 51 per cent might have fateful consequence, the system demands something more than 51 per cent —two-thirds to impeach, two-thirds to ratify a treaty, three-fourths of the states to change the Constitution.

Beyond these familiar restraints upon unbridled power, the system has created additional barriers to hasty action. That much maligned rule of the Senate—the filibuster rule—is one such device. If the reformers have their way, the rule would be further weakened. Yet the rule is precious. It is the last barricade of strong men possessed of convictions they cannot compromise. Once the bastion of Southern conservatives, lately the rule has been put to use by Northern liberals. And it is a good rule.

The seniority system also drives my re-forming friends to frenzy. Everyone knows the catalogue of evils: The system puts into power a handful of old men, way behind the times; these aging virtuosos often are out of tune with current administrations; and the system denies authority to competent junior members who could run the committees as tight ships. True, all true.

Yet the seniority system is like democracy: It is the worst possible system, except for all other systems ever tried. The alternative to creating chairmen by reason of seniority is to let them be chosen by secret party caucus, or to have them named (in the House) by the speaker. Either of these alternatives would throw the Congress into unrelenting intraparty warfare. At this level of political fighting, we are talking of heavyweight battles for power—battles that scar and wound and rend a party into factional pieces. So long as seniority prevails, this feudal warfare is avoided.

This point also: Doubtless the rule of seniority does result, now and then, in the elevation of dotards or tyrants to a chairman's seat. Everyone could name his own examples. But equally as often, the system works happily: We get a John Stennis at the head of Senate Armed Services, a John McClellan leading Government Operations. With the steady decline of the one-party South, chairmanships increasingly are scattered among liberals, moderates and conservatives across the nation. Experience counts; and a chairman's encyclopedic recollection of what has gone before is no small asset.

The House took several sound and useful steps toward reform a few months ago. If members will stand by these procedural improvements, and give them a fair trial, the Ninety-second Congress will be less secret and more responsible than Congresses of the past. We ought to see how these changes work. Reform is 100 proof whisky; even the most experienced boozer should sip it with care.

4

Making Congress Work

COMMON CAUSE

Several students of the American Congress have argued that piecemeal reform of Congress is an illusion; only radical change could be effective. This selection suggests a series of reforms without radically restructuring the institution. Are these reforms realistic? Which of the suggested reforms are needed most? What chances are there of effectuating the suggested changes?

All organizations of society—government, business, labor unions, community groups— need vigorous leadership and adequate procedures to function effectively. The U.S. Congress has fallen behind in both respects. Consequently, the burdens of finding solutions to our national problems have fallen increasingly on other branches of government: the courts and the Executive Branch, principally the President. When Congress does assert itself, power too often rests in the hands of a small group of men, many of whom have a narrow and low vision of national needs. It is not surprising that many observers no longer regard the Congress as an equal part of our tripartite government.

The inability of Congress to play its full role is centered in these two problems: lack of strong leadership and obsolete procedures. The leadership issue includes the key problems of seniority, the role of committee chairmen and the length of service of elected representatives. The procedures issue includes committee jurisdiction, staffing and operation, lobbying regulation and election campaign financing.

From Making Congress Work, *Common Cause,* Washington, D.C., November 1970.

Leadership and New Blood

PROBLEM:

Seniority. Seniority is the principal method by which positions of power in Congress are determined. A Senator or Representative moves up the ladder on the committee to which he is assigned simply by being re-elected; the system rewards survival rather than merit. It generally has the effect of frustrating young and able members of Congress who see little hope of obtaining influence for the 20 or more years often required to build up some seniority.

SOLUTION:

Both the Republican and Democratic parties in the House are considering modifications of the system. Basically, these modifications would provide that the chairman of each committee (or the highest ranking member of the minority party) would be elected by his party colleagues with consideration for merit instead of automatically for length of service.

The best method would be to have the leaders of each party in the House nominate the person they consider best qualified for the top job. All members of each party then would vote on their party's nominee;

if the nomination were rejected, another person would be nominated and voted on. The most important benefit of the plan is the new leverage it would give party leaders in dealing with committee chairmen. Many committee chairmen can now safely ignore their party leaders and public opinion as well. As a result, national and Congressional party leaders often are unable to obtain passage (and sometimes even consideration) of the programs to which they are pledged. A first task of seniority reform is to circumscribe this absolute and irresponsible power of committee chairmen. . . .

PROBLEM:

Incumbency. The fact that Congressional leadership is made up chiefly of men who have served three or even four decades lends an inevitable quality of staleness to the institution. Men come to Washington from one-party areas and never leave. The Congressional process is denied the vitality that comes from a steady flow of new blood, new energy, and new ideas. Long incumbency increases the incumbents' ties to lobby groups and careerists in Executive Branch agencies. It contributes to continual over-representation of special interests from the one-party states and Congressional districts. It contributes to a less vigorous legislative process as a result of the diminished physical capacity of some of the more aged members of Congress.

SOLUTION:

The first step is to establish a mandatory retirement age for elected representatives. This limit could be 65, in line with common practice in many private organizations, but certainly should be no more than 70 years of age. A second step is to place a limit on the number of years a person could serve in the House or Senate, regardless of age. This would assure a continual turnover in Congress and the infusion of new members with new ideas and new energies. The maximum length of service might be set at 12 years, a period long enough to assure continuity but short enough to overcome

rigidity of habit and thought and to prevent domination of Congress by a handful of men who come from one-party areas.

Campaign Financing and Lobby Controls

The American political system is limping along with a campaign financing system that endangers the public interest. Campaigns are becoming shockingly expensive, particularly with expanded use of television. At the same time, many expenditures of lobbyists go unreported even though these individuals are major sources of funds for campaigns.

PROBLEM:

Congressional Campaign Aid. The principal problem facing candidates is how to finance their campaigns without becoming beholden to a few wealthy donors. Many candidates face the problem of getting adequate funds regardless of the source; some can do so only by going into deep personal debt. Existing law supposedly limits contributions from any one person to a candidate to a few thousand dollars. This is easily evaded by giving the maximum contribution to an endless number of separate committees (often consisting of one man —a treasurer), supporting the same candidate.

Moreover, existing laws do not require all campaign committees to report the source of their funds. Some states have good reporting laws but most do not. The District of Columbia, the home of well-heeled lobbyists and the common location of all members of Congress, has absolutely no reporting requirements for campaign committees. The public never knows where the money is coming from. Another major flaw is the absence of any federal requirements on financing of primary campaigns. The nation deserves a more open and honest system.

SOLUTION:

First, strict federal campaign finance reporting standards should be established covering all committees regardless of where they are established or where they operate.

Second, Congress should devise a system to limit campaign costs. Elective office should not be an exclusive franchise of the wealthy (or those who are willing to put themselves under obligation to the wealthy). Congress made an important start this year by passing a bill limiting the amount of money any candidate may spend on television advertising. President Nixon vetoed it even though the measure had considerable Republican support when it passed Congress. He said, among other things, that it did not attack all the problems of campaign financing. Although his statement was true, his reasoning was that of a man who decided not to undergo a much needed appendectomy because the doctor was not prepared to deal with his liver and back problems at the same time. The bill Mr. Nixon vetoed was at least a good start.

A third solution is to have Congress devise a system of public subsidies of campaign expenses that will assure that all candidates for Congress on major party tickets have access to adequate funds without going into personal debt or into the clutches of wealthy donors and lobbies.

PROBLEM:

Lobby Controls. Currently, laws are inadequate to regulate lobbying of federal officials by special interests. The Constitution guarantees the right of all citizens to lobby their government, but it does not say that anyone who decides to do so may operate under a shroud of secrecy. The public should at least know who is spending how much money on what issues. The present 24-year-old law is chock full of loopholes and nearly impossible to enforce.

SOLUTION:

First, the Government Accounting Office, a professional and well-staffed agency of the Federal Government, should be given the power to investigate lobby registrations and reports to assure that lobbyists are giving the public all the information the law requires. This job is now vested in patronage officials of Congress who are under political pressure to sit on their hands.

Second, the law should be strengthened to require complete information about a lobbyist's pay and purpose in Washington.

Third, the law should be strengthened to require all organizations which have a "substantial purpose" in influencing legislation to register and report financial information. The present wishy-washy law lets many groups avoid registering even though they influence legislation. Until recently, the powerful National Rifle Assn., which has blocked gun-registration bills for years, never had a registered lobbyist.

Fourth, the law should require detailed information from lobbyists about contingent fees they receive from their clients. These are fees based on the success of the lobbyists' activities. Thus, a lucrative contingent fee for the passage of a bill, for example, places enormous pressure on a lobbyist to do whatever may be necessary, regardless of how unethical or even illegal, to obtain passage. Congress might even consider outlawing contingent fees.

Senate Filibusters

PROBLEM:

The Filibuster. A long-established rule of the Senate, permitting unlimited debate, allows a minority of Senators to prevent action on a bill by talking it to death. The rule says that in order to end a filibuster two-thirds of the Senate must vote to put a time limit on debate. Historically, a two-thirds majority to invoke cloture (i.e., to halt debate) has been difficult to obtain.

Although Senate rules in theory may be changed by simple majority vote, in practice a two-thirds majority vote will be needed to change the cloture rule. That is because proponents of the filibuster will use that device to block a vote on changing the rule. Thus the cloture obstacle is self-perpetuating.

SOLUTION:

The self-perpetuating tradition must be overturned so that a simple majority vote of the Senate may change the cloture rule. This issue will be before the Senate early next January.

Many Senators, particularly those from the South or from sparsely populated states, want no change. A compromise proposal would allow cloture by a three-fifths majority rather than the current two-thirds. This might be more acceptable than a majority vote provision, particularly if the Senators who have perpetrated the filibuster find that their own constituents favor a change to prevent a willful minority from blocking action on important legislation. Basically at issue is whether the principle of majority rule will be allowed to operate in the Senate a little, some, or not at all.

The Committee System

The committee system is the central element in Congressional operations. It is the method by which Congress divides the enormous amount of work that must be done each year into manageable components. It is where the most essential work is done.

PROBLEM:

Committee Jurisdiction. Each of Congress' committees has specific responsibilities and subject-matter jurisdictions which continue from year to year. There is little or no review of these divisions of work to determine if they make sense in terms of the actual problems facing Congress. For example, at least 10 committees and subcommittees work on some aspect of environmental issues.

Some committees develop tunnel vision on subjects they handle; they act as advocates of their programs rather than as critical analysts. This is particularly true of agriculture, military and veterans committees. Other committees, for reasons buried in antiquity, have jurisdictions so broad, and often including matters so complex, that they cannot give adequate consideration to certain parts of the subjects. This is true of the tax-writing committees which handle the financial as well as the social aspects of welfare, Social Security and certain health programs.

Still other committees have no reason for existing at all. Examples here are Merchant Marine and Fisheries, Veterans' Affairs and District of Columbia. The subjects of the first two could be handled by committees with broader jurisdiction, while the latter should be handled by a popularly elected city council in Washington, D.C.

SOLUTION:

Congress should restudy and revise its committee structure at least once every 10 years just as it reapportions its seats in the House every 10 years according to population changes. Committee jurisdiction should be based more along broad functional lines than is now the case.

PROBLEM:

Committee Selection. A number of committees are dominated by members from one or another region of the nation. For example, the powerful House Ways and Means Committee, which considers tax, trade and Social Security bills, has seven Democratic members from Southern states but only eight Democratic members from the other three regions of the United States. The Agriculture Committees are dominated by Representatives and Senators from rural areas, thereby reinforcing the provincialism of those groups. Similarly, the Interior Committees are dominated by Westerners; the Senate Committee has only one member from the eastern half of the United States.

SOLUTION:

Each committee should, as nearly as possible, include members from all regions in roughly the same proportion that the region is represented in the total House or Senate membership.

Staffing and Administration. Because committees are the work-horses of Congress, it is important that they have adequate staffs and modern information systems. Some committees are very well staffed. In the area of tax legislation, staff quality rivals that of the Executive Branch. But more often, committees must rely on information and legislative assistance from outsiders, such as department bureaucrats and lobbyists, for even rudimentary data and analysis. This means that Congressional review of department operations and efficiency is often weak and uneven.

Congress should hire more and better personnel to match that of the Executive Branch. Committee staff members should be brought under the Civil Service system. There is also need to develop modern computer facilities. Although Congress this year took an initial step to upgrade the Library of Congress' research capabilities, it rejected a proposal to develop computer uses for Representatives, Senators and committees. It was rejected because of opposition from the chairman of a subcommittee that has been dragging its heels on the subject.

5

The Congressional Establishment

JOSEPH S. CLARK

What relationships does Senator Clark see between the American and Congressional Establishments? Who belongs to the Congressional Establishhment? Does the Congressional Establishment always win? Why or why not?

An intelligent reader's guide to the Congressional Establishment must begin with a definition of the ruling clique in both Houses. Richard Rovere, one of the ablest Washington correspondents, defines "The American Establishment" as "a more or less closed and self-sustaining institution that holds a preponderance of power in our more or less open society." [1] His definition,

applied to the more limited Congressional field, remains accurate.

The two Establishments, American and Congressional, have much in common. For example, the members of each constantly deny there is such a thing. In both cases experts disagree on exactly what the Establishment is and how it works; but, as Mr. Rovere points out, they disagree also about the Kingdom of God—which doesn't prove *it* doesn't exist. Within both Establishments there is a good deal of tolerance for doctrinal divergence so long as the members stand solidly together when the chips are down and the Establishment's power, prestige and prerogatives are under attack.

From Joseph S. Clark, Congress: The Sapless Branch *(rev. ed.; New York: Harper & Row, Publishers, 1965), pp. 111–115. Copyright © 1964 by Joseph S. Clark. Reprinted by permission of the publisher.*

[1] Richard H. Rovere, *The American Establishment* (New York: Harcourt, Brace & World, Inc., 1962).

John Kenneth Galbraith aptly defined members of any Establishment as "the pivotal people." Most writers on the subject, including the present one, exclude themselves when defining the Establishment and even consider themselves its victims. Douglas Dillon and John McCloy are the prototypes of Mr. Rovere's American Establishment; Richard Russell and Judge Howard Smith are patriarchs of the Congressional Establishment.

The Congressional Establishment is organized in the same easygoing way as its broader national big brother. There are no written bylaws, no conventions, no overt determination of a program. The essential difference is that the Congressional Establishment defends the status quo and views majority rule with distaste, while the American Establishment is content to abide by the principles of democracy along the more liberal lines suggested by the editorial page of its house organ, *The New York Times*.

Within broad limits and subject to some exceptions the Congressional Establishment consists of those Democratic chairmen and ranking Republican members of the important legislative committees who, through seniority and pressures exerted on junior colleagues, control the institutional machinery of Congress. They use this control to prevent a fair hearing and a vote on the merits of the President's program. The official "leadership" group of the Congress—Speaker of the House, Senate Majority Leader, et al.—are usually captives of the Establishment, although they can sometimes be found looking out over the walls of their prison, plotting escape.

The Establishment does not always win. It frequently does not use all the parliamentary tools which are available to it. In the Senate it has lost strength consistently since the election of 1958. Its members, almost without exception, are charming and amiable gentlemen, popular with their colleagues, who sincerely believe that the safety of the Republic depends on defeating the "dangerous innovations" in our social life and political economy which are constantly being proposed by the President of the United States.

It is important to note that the views of the Congressional Establishment are not shared by a majority of their own colleagues, who, left to their own devices, would be prepared to bring the Congress into line to cope with the necessities of our times.

In an earlier work I described the Senate Establishment as "almost the antithesis of democracy. It is not selected by any democratic process. It appears to be quite unresponsive to the caucuses of the two parties, be they Democratic or Republican. It is what might be called a self-perpetuating oligarchy with mild, but only mild, overtones of plutocracy." [2]

There are plenty of rich men in the Senate, but only a few of them are high in the ranks of the Establishment; and none of them would admit to a belief that the accumulation of great wealth is a principal object of life. This is another distinction between the American and the Congressional Establishments. The former has, despite its slightly liberal orientation, definite overtones of plutocracy, although its tolerance is much more for inherited than for recently acquired wealth.

The bonds which hold the Congressional Establishment together are: white supremacy; a stronger devotion to property than to human rights; support of the military establishment; belligerence in foreign affairs; and a determination to prevent Congressional reform. The high-water marks of the Senatorial Establishment in 1963 were the two votes on limiting debate in the Senate in order to change the filibuster rule. In response to a question posed by the Vice President, "Does the Senate have the right, notwithstanding its rules, to terminate debate at the beginning of a new Congress by majority vote in order to pass upon a change in its rules?" there were 44 ayes and 53 nays. The Establishment, know-

[2] Joseph S. Clark, *The Senate Establishment* (New York: Hill and Wang, 1963), p. 22.

ing it had finally rallied enough votes to assure a negative result, permitted a vote on January 21 after a desultory filibuster lasting nine days. On February 7 a cloture petition which would have cut off further debate on the proposed changes in Rule XXII and which required a favorable vote of two-thirds of those present was lost 54-42. Including the announced position of the four absentees, the Senate stood 56-44 in favor of limiting debate (and therefore almost certainly in favor of a more liberal rule of terminating debate), nine short of the necessary two-thirds. But the majority did not prevail.

A low-water mark of the Establishment was the Test Ban Treaty, which came to a vote on September 24, 1963, after more than a month of desultory debate. Under the Constitution two-thirds of those present and voting were required for ratification. The affirmative vote was 80-19. The hard core of the Establishment with the exception of Senator Mundt voted "no."

The most crushing defeat ever suffered by the Establishment was when cloture was applied to the Civil Rights Bill on June 10, 1964, by a vote of 71 to 29.

A typical Establishment line-up occurred on the Mundt bill to block the sale of wheat to Russia (by prohibiting the Export-Import Bank from guaranteeing loans to finance the sales) when all but two of the "anti-test ban" Senators supported Senator Mundt and opposed Presidents Kennedy and Johnson—the vote was on November 26, 1963—in their attempt to further relax the tensions of the Cold War. The Mundt proposal was tabled by a vote of 57 to 35.

Every member of the Senate, except one, Senator Lausche, who voted against the Test Ban Treaty, also voted in the negative on the question posed by the Vice President regarding the right of the Senate to change its rules, and on the motion for cloture on rules change. The eighteen Senators listed [in the table] represent the hard core of the Establishment and its loyal followers.

Note the absence on this list of several staunch card-carrying members of the Establishment: Ellender of Louisiana, Hay-

DEMOCRATS	RULES CHANGE AND CLOTURE THEREON	TEST BAN TREATY	WHEAT SALE TO RUSSIA	CLOTURE ON CIVIL RIGHTS	REAPPOR-TIONMENT
Russell of Georgia	no	no	no	no	no
Stennis of Mississippi	no	no	no	no	no
Eastland of Mississippi	no	no	no	no	no
Long of Louisiana	no	no	yes	no	no
Byrd of Virginia	no	no	no	no	no
Byrd of West Virginia	no	no	yes	no	no
Robertson of Virginia	no	no	no	no	no
Talmadge of Georgia	no	no	no	no	no
McClellan of Arkansas	no	no	no	no	no
Thurmond of South Carolina *	no	no	no	no	no
REPUBLICANS					
Curtis of Nebraska	no	no	no	yes	no
Goldwater of Arizona	no	no	no	no	no
Mundt of South Dakota	no	yes	no	yes	no
Simpson of Wyoming	no	no	no	no	no
Jordan of Idaho	no	no	no	yes	no
Smith of Maine	no	no	no	yes	yes
Bennett of Utah	no	no	no	no	no
Tower of Texas	no	no	no	no	no

* Senator Thurmond became a Republican in the fall of 1964.

den of Arizona, Holland of Florida, Johnston of South Carolina, Hill and Sparkman of Alabama, Cannon of Nevada; and on the Republican side Cotton of New Hampshire, Williams of Delaware, Mundt of South Dakota and Dirksen of Illinois. They all voted *against* cloture but *for* the Test Ban Treaty. Note also that, unlike Wilson's "twelve willful men" in 1917, the hard core of the Establishment did not utilize the filibuster to prevent a vote on the treaty or on the wheat deal. It seems clear that it is only in opposition to Congressional reform and civil rights that the Establishment will play all its cards. . . .

6

Goodbye to the Inner Club

NELSON W. POLSBY

Why was Lyndon Johnson such an admirer of William S. White's Citadel: The Story of the U.S. Senate? *Would Professor Polsby agree or disagree with the statement that the internal norms of the Senate have become less influential in the last twenty years? What evidence does Professor Polsby cite to discredit the idea that there is an all-powerful Inner Club operating in the United States Senate?*

. . .

To a generation of followers of the U.S. Senate, these were peculiar goings-on. Whoever heard of Senators leaving important committees to go on unimportant ones—voluntarily? Or committee chairmen worried about uprisings of the peasants? Or an agreeable young man of negligible accomplishments, one eye cocked on the Presidency, knocking off a senior Southern chairman running for a job tending the inner gears of the institution?

If this sort of thing can happen in broad daylight these days on Capitol Hill, there must be something seriously the matter with the ideas that have dominated conversation about the Senate for the last 15 years. For at least since the publication of William S. White's *Citadel: The Story of*

From Nelson W. Polsby, "Goodbye to the Inner Club," Washington Monthly, August 1969, pp. 31–33. Reprinted by permission of the publisher.

the U.S. Senate (1956), the common assumption has been that the Senate has been run by an "inner club" of "Senate types." "The Senate type," White wrote, "is, speaking broadly, a man for whom the Institution is a career in itself, a life in itself, and an end in itself." Although others might belong to the inner club, "At the core of the Inner Club stand the Southerners, who with rare exceptions automatically assume membership almost with the taking of the oath of office."

"The Senate type," White continued, "makes the Institution his home in an almost literal sense, and certainly in a deeply emotional sense. His head swims with its history, its lore. . . . To him, precedent has an almost mystical meaning. . . . His concern for the preservation of Senate tradition is so great that he distrusts anything out of the ordinary. . . . As the Southern members of the Inner Club make the ultimate decisions as to what is proper in point of manner—these decisions then infallibly pervading the Outer Club—so the whole generality of the Inner Club makes the decisions as to what *in general* is proper in the Institution and what *in general* its conclusions should be on high issues."

White conceded, of course, that the Senate had its "public men," who made their way by inflaming or instructing public opinion. But he argued that it was not these grasshoppers but rather the ants of the Inner Club who got their way in the decision-making of the Senate.

Since the publication of *Citadel*, commentators on Senate affairs have routinely alluded to the Inner Club as though to something as palpable as an office building. No senatorial biography—or obituary—is now complete without solemn consideration of whether the subject was in or out. Discussions of senatorial business can hardly compete with dissections of the Inner Club's informal rules, tapping ceremonies, secret handshakes, and other signs and stigmata by which members are recognized. One writer, Clayton Fritchey in *Harper's*, took the further step—in 1967— of actually naming names.

By far the most zealous promoter of the whole idea was someone whose opinion on the matter must be given some weight. This is the way Joseph S. Clark described a lunch that Majority Leader Lyndon B. Johnson gave for Clark's "class" of freshman Democrats in 1957:

As we sat down to our steaks at the long table in the office of Felton M. (Skeeter) Johnson, Secretary of the Senate, . . . we found at our places copies of *Citadel: The Story of the U.S. Senate,* autographed "with all good wishes" not only by its author William S. White . . . but by the Majority Leader as well. During the course of the lunch, which was attended by the other recently re-elected leaders, Senator Johnson encouraged us to consider Mr. White's book as a sort of *McGuffey's Reader* from which we could learn much about the "greatest deliberative body in the world" and how to mold ourselves into its way of life.

These days, somehow, the mold seems to have broken. Ten years after the John-son lunch, Clayton Fritchey's *Harper's* article named Russell Long as a "full-fledged member" of the Inner Club. Of Edward M. Kennedy, Fritchey said: "On his own, the amiable Teddy might some day have become at best a fringe member of the Club, but he is associated with Robert F., who like John F., is the archetype of the national kind of politician that the Club regards with suspicion. It believes (correctly) that the Kennedy family has always looked on the Senate as a means to an end, but not an end in itself." And yet, only two years later, Kennedy unseated Long.

Power in the Senate

Some time ago, in *Congress and the Presidency* (1964), I argued that the notion of an inner club misrepresented the distribution of power in the Senate in several ways. First, it vastly underplayed the extent to which *formal* position—committee chairmanships, great seniority, and official party leadership—conferred power and status on individual Senators almost regardless of their clubability. Second, it understated the extent to which power was spread by specialization and the need for cooperative effort. Fritchey's list bears this out; of the 92 nonfreshman Senators in 1967, he listed 53 as members or provisional members of the Inner Club. This suggests a third point: the existence of an inner club was no doubt in part incorrectly inferred from the existence of its opposite— a small number of mavericks and outsiders. The Senate has always had its share of these, going back at least as far as that superbly cranky diarist, Senator William Plumer of New Hampshire, who served from 1803 to 1807. But the undeniable existence of cranks and mavericks—uncooperative men with whom in a legislative body it is necessary (but impossible) to do business—does not an Inner Club make, except, of course, by simple subtraction.

To dispute that there is an all-powerful Inner Club is not, of course, to claim that no norms govern the behavior of Senators toward one another, or that this body of adults has no status system. Any group whose members interact frequently, and expect to continue to do so on into the indefinite future, usually develops norms. All groups having boundaries, a corporate history, a division of labor, and work to do may be expected to have folkways and an informal social organization. What was opened to question was whether, in the case of the U.S. Senate, the informal social organization was as restrictive or as unlike the formal organization as proponents of the Inner Club Theory believed.

To these observations I would now add a number of others, the most important of which would be to suggest that the role of the Senate in the political system has changed over the last 20 years in such a way as to decrease the impact of norms internal to the Senate on the behavior and the status of Senators.

One possible interpretation of what went on at the opening of the current Congress is that the Senate today is far less of a citadel than when William S. White first wrote. It is a less insular body, and the fortunes of Senators are less and less tied to the smiles and frowns of their elders within the institution.

Why Operations?

What is the great attraction, for example, of the Committee on Government Operations? It reports little legislation, has oversight over no specific part of the executive branch. Rather, it takes the operations of government in general as its bailiwick, splits into nearly autonomous sub-committees, and holds investigations. In short, it has the power to publicize—both issues and Senators. It takes less of a Senator's time away from the increasingly absorbing enterprise of cultivating national constituencies on substantive issues.

The claim that lack of ambition for the Presidency distinguishes members of the Inner Club could not have been correct even 20 years ago, considering the Presidential hankerings of such quintessentially old-style Senate types as Robert A. Taft of Ohio, Richard B. Russell of Georgia, and Robert Kerr of Oklahoma. Today, Presidential ambition seems to lurk everywhere in the Senate chamber.

Over the course of these last 20 years, the Senate has obviously improved as a base from which to launch a Presidential bid, while other bases—such as the governorships—have gone into decline. There has certainly, since World War II, been a general movement of political resources and of public attention toward Washington and away from local and regional arenas. Growth of national news media—especially television—has augmented this trend. The impact upon the Presidency of this nationalization of public awareness has been frequently noted. To a lesser extent, this public awareness has spread to all national political institutions. But of these, only the Senate has taken full advantage of its increased visibility. In the House, Sam Rayburn refused to allow televised coverage of any official House function, and Speaker John W. McCormack has continued this rule. The executive branch speaks through the President, or an occasional Cabinet member, and the Supreme Court remains aloof. Thus, only Senators have had little constraint placed on their availability for national publicity. Senate committee hearings are frequently televised. Senators turn up often on the televised Washington quiz shows on Sunday afternoons. House members, even the powerful committee chairmen, rarely do. National exposure does not seem to be as important a political resource for them.

As senatorial names—Kefauver, McCarthy, Kennedy, Goldwater—became household words, Governors slipped into relative obscurity. Where once the Governor's control of his state party organization was the single overwhelming resource in deciding who was Presidential timber at a national party convention, television and the nationalization of resources began to erode gubernatorial power. Early Presidential primaries, with their massive national press coverage, made it harder and harder for the leaders of state parties to wait until the national party conventions to bargain and make commitments in Presidential contests. Proliferating federal programs, financed by the lucrative federal income tax, were distributed to the states, in part as senatorial patronage. Governors were not always ignored in this process, but their influence was on the whole much reduced. Meanwhile, at the state level, services lagged and taxes were often inequitable and unproductive. Responsible Governors of both parties have often tried to do something about this problem, but it has led to donnybrooks with state legislatures, great unpopularity, and, on some occasions, electoral defeat.

. . .

11

THE SUPREME COURT:
SUPREME IN WHAT?

The United States Supreme Court puzzles not only foreigners but Americans as well. Its combination of powers and functions is one source of confusion, the limits of its power another. In one sense the Court can do so much, yet in another sense it can do very little. A clear picture of this situation is difficult even for lawyers to obtain because, as we shall see, the Court is a legal institution but not merely a legal body.

The Court can only hear cases—that is, issues must come before them in the form of arguments between two individuals or groups of individuals in which one party genuinely claims something from the other. The thing at issue may be, but doesn't have to be, monetarily valuable; one of the parties may want to imprison the other or interfere with what is claimed as the other one's freedom of religion, for example. (This limits the Court's functions, for it cannot create cases from whole cloth.)

Controversies may reach the Supreme Court on appeal from decisions of lower federal courts and (through these courts) from federal administrative decisions. The second great stream of cases comes directly from the highest state court having jurisdiction (not necessarily the state supreme court) in cases where a right is claimed under the federal Constitution, a federal law, or a treaty of the United States. This means that most state cases cannot be appealed to the Supreme Court, since only a very small number involve a federal right. It also means that very often the Supreme Court does not review the whole case involved but only that part of the controversy dealing with the federal right. There are a few cases that start right in the Supreme Court, such as cases involving ambassadors and suits between states, but these are comparatively unimportant most of the time.

The thing to remember in these cases that come up on appeal is that the Court can pretty well decide whether it wants to hear a case. Over three-quarters of the cases yearly come up by grant of the writ of *certiorari*, which means that the Court wants to hear the case and is ordering the lower court to send up the record. The judges must rule on a number of other cases, usually about 15 per cent of their total, when, for example, a state court rules a federal law unconstitutional or upholds its own law against a claim that it violates the federal Constitution. This is to keep the laws in the various states as uniform as possible. Even in these cases, however, the Court may reach a decision after a fairly cursory examination of the issue, and so keep a large measure of control over its docket.

What makes the United States Supreme Court the most important court in the world? (1) It has all of the powers that most high courts have to overrule the lower courts of the same judicial system; (2) it has many powers of review over federal administrative agencies; (3) it has power to interpret the words of Congress, subject, of course, to "correction" of this interpretation by Congress; (4) it has the power to interpret the Constitution subject only to correction by the very difficult method of amendment; (5) it has the power, exercised successfully at least since 1803 and *Marbury v. Madison,* to declare congressional and presidential actions out of bounds as having violated the Constitution; (6) it can declare state laws unconstitutional as violating rather vague provisions (particularly of the due process and equal protection clauses of the Fourteenth Amendment and the interstate commerce clause, which the Court in the absence of any words at all has held to be a limit on what states can do).

It is those last two powers that make the difference. Here the Court not only tries cases; in the course of hearing cases it can put on trial the very laws passed by the legislature or the acts of the Executive and the administration on the national level and all parts of the state governments. Within certain limits it is a censor of the actions of all other branches of government, and in many cases has the last say (short of amendment of the Constitution). Major laws and programs may and have been brought to a standstill as a result of lawsuits involving a corner chicken dealer or drugstore owner. Important issues may hinge on a legal technicality. The judge is caught between worrying about the technicalities and seeing the greater issues behind them. The power to discard laws as unconstitutional presents problems different in very real and obvious ways from a traffic court case or a divorce or a suit in an automobile collision.

There are some who claim that this power makes the Court the real ruler of America—one critic spoke of the United States as an example of "government by the judiciary." Others see in the Court a defense of free government. Some would like the Court to be tightly bound by the rules of the past; others call for a Court with statesmanlike vision to fashion the Constitution for the future.

In order to help you understand and choose from these positions, this chapter will focus on several questions. We will first take a quick look at the operations of the Court and attempt to get a vision of the Court's place in our governmental system—to see what kind of institution we have and how it is conceived of by different writers. Our second problem will be one of recruitment—where do the judges come from and where should they come from? What is the experience that qualifies them for their position of power? Our third problem is also a question of sources, but of the sources of the law. Is the law a "fixed" discoverable thing, as the laws of physics used to be thought, or is it the last guess of the fifth member of the Court or the prejudices of the majority of the Court? Finally, what is the place of the Court with regard to making policy? Can it lead the country, and should it try to? Running throughout these problems is an underlying issue which virtually all of the readings inevitably try to answer—how do you reconcile the power of these nine men with majority rule and democracy?

What Manner of Institution?

What does the Court do? This simple question has many different answers depending on how you want to view it. We will first look at what the Court does in the simplest way—the day-to-day routines of the Court. Then in a broader view we will consider its role in our political system. Finally, we will consider several different views of its basic meaning. By first understanding the operations of the Court and its position in the system, we can approach this deeper question. Does the Court represent the finest in American thought, a gyroscope keeping the system on an even keel, doing things no other institution can do? Or does it represent a strange and un-American oligarchy, more powerful than the men in the Kremlin?

Where Do the Judges and the Law Come From?

During the 1970 debate on the confirmation of Judge Carswell, Senator Roman Hruska suggested that objections to his mediocre record were beside the point, since mediocrity should be represented on the Court. That statement may well have cost Judge Carswell his chance to sit on the Court, as the other senators seemed to conclude there was a limit on Supreme Court representativeness. Still, President Nixon's quest for a southerner and a conservative is in keeping with a desire for diversity on the Court. Other presidents have followed much the same pattern. One thing they have been consistent in is choosing the vast majority from their own party. In this century, according to the American Bar Association, every president has chosen well over 80 per cent of all federal judges from his own political party.

Does this suggest that the Supreme Court is a political body? Is it perhaps wrong to choose judges to represent parts of the country, points of view, or political affiliation? In recent years there has been a cry for more judicial experience on the part of appointees to the Court. Some have suggested promotion from the lower courts, with previous experience being a prerequisite. Others call for a more radical approach—perhaps the replacement of our present system of appointment by the president and ratification by the Senate.

What is law anyway? Is it an expression of a great human need, the supremacy of rules and justice? Or is it merely the masking of privilege, another form of political control by the most powerful? Perhaps it may even partake of both qualities.

What Can the Court Do?

The ultimate test of a political institution is its ability to satisfy the people on whose behalf it acts. The Supreme Court is no exception to this rule. The Court must serve some useful function or go under. Another test of institutions is accountability; unchecked power is a source of danger both to the community and to the wielders of it. What is the function the Court serves? As we shall see, there are jobs in our system it alone does and which, some argue, it alone can do.

There are also definite limitations on the power of the Supreme Court. Some of these exist in law, others in fact. There is the power that other branches of government wield over the Court. There is also the simple fact that public acceptance is necessary to enforce Court decisions. As the desegregation controversy reflects so well, the arsenal of weapons of the judicial system is not unlimited in the face of popular hostility. This, in turn, raises questions: How far can the Court go in defying public opinion? When should it attempt to do so and when should it not?

Yet another problem exists in the field of civil liberties. Can the Court lead in requiring freedom of speech and other political freedoms? In so doing, will it serve democracy or weaken it by diluting majority rule and the responsibility of the community? The Supreme Court does not have tight self-defined limits to guide it in defining its total position in our government. For that reason the judges often disagree among themselves on this question. Ex-Justice Frankfurter argued that the Court should interfere almost never with laws of Congress. Black and Douglas represent a group that argues that where basic freedoms are concerned the Court should be less tolerant of majority rule. Because these freedoms are the heart of the political process of a democracy and are necessary to maintain political parties and the whole system of responsible scrutiny of policies, the judges argue that these require special protection. This argument has spilled over into popular discussion; it is one of the major problems now facing the Court and which will continue to face it in the years to come.

1

Powerful, Irresponsible, and Human

FRED RODELL

Not all people see the Court in an admiring way. Old-line Democrats and Progressives like Robert LaFollette and even Teddy Roosevelt were suspicious of the Court. These and others thought the power of the judges was a denial of majority rule. This point of view still persists, and has much logic behind it. Another example is Fred Rodell, a professor at Yale Law School and, incidentally, a close friend of Justice William Douglas. Whether any of the justices, including Douglas, would agree with the rather strong statements that follow seems doubtful.

At the top levels of the three branches of the civilian government of the United States sit the Congress, the President plus his Cabinet, and the Supreme Court. Of these three—in this unmilitary, unclerical nation—only one wears a uniform. Only one carries on its most important business in utter secret behind locked doors—and indeed never reports, even after death, what really went on there. Only one, its members holding office for life if they choose, is completely irresponsible to anyone or anything but themselves and their own consciences. Only one depends for much of its immense influence on its prestige as a semi-sacred institution and preserves that prestige with the trappings and show of superficial dignity rather than earning it, year after working year, by the dignity and wisdom of what it is and does. Under our otherwise democratic form of government, only one top ruling group uses ceremony and secrecy, robes and ritual, as instru-

ments of its *official* policy, as wellsprings of its power.

The nine men who are the Supreme Court of the United States are at once the most powerful and the most irresponsible of all the men in the world who govern other men. Not even the bosses of the Kremlin, each held back by fear of losing his head should he ever offend his fellows, wield such loose and long-ranging and ac-countable-to-no-one power as do the nine or five-out-of-nine justices who can give orders to any other governing official in the United States—from the members of a village school board who would force their young charges to salute the flag, to a president who would take over the steel industry to keep production going—and can make those orders stick. Ours may be, for puffing purposes, a "government of checks and balances," but there is no check at all on what the Supreme Court does—save only three that are as pretty in theory as they are pointless in practice. (These are the Senate's power to reject a newly named justice, used only once this century, and in the past usually unwisely; the power to impeach a justice, only once tried and never carried through; the power of the

From Fred Rodell, Nine Men: A Political History of the Supreme Court from 1790 to 1955 (New York: Random House, Inc., 1955), pp. 3–6. Copyright © 1955 by Fred Rodell. Reprinted by permission of the publisher.

people to reverse a Supreme Court decision by amending the Constitution, as they have done just three times in our whole history.) The nine justices sit secure and stand supreme over Congress, president, governors, state legislatures, commissions, administrators, lesser judges, mayors, city councils, and dog-catchers—with none to say them nay.

Lest these words sound like arrant overstatement, here are what three of the most thoughtful men who ever held high national office said about the Supreme Court's flat and final power of government. Thomas Jefferson, who was president when the Court first fully used this power, exploded, prophetically but futilely:

Our Constitution . . . intending to establish three departments, coordinate and independent, that they might check and balance one another . . . has given, according to this opinion, to one of them alone the right to prescribe rules for the government of the others, and to that one, too, which is unelected by and independent of the nation. . . . The Constitution, on this hypothesis, is a mere thing of wax in the hands of the judiciary which they may twist and shape into any form they please.

Jefferson was talking of the Court's then brand-newly wielded power to override Congress and the president. More than a century later, Justice Holmes revealingly in dissent, berated his brethren for freely using their judicial power to upset *state* laws:

As the decisions now stand I see hardly any limit but the sky to the invalidating of those rights ['*the constitutional rights of the states*'] if they happen to strike a majority of this Court as for any reason undesirable. I cannot believe that the [Fourteenth] Amendment was intended to give us carte blanche to embody our economic or moral beliefs in its prohibitions.

And a few years after, Justice Stone, he too in dissent, exclaimed: "The only check upon our own exercise of power is our own sense of self-restraint."

In Stone's same angry protest against the Court's six-to-three veto of the first Agricultural Adjustment Act—a protest that helped spark Franklin Roosevelt's "Court-packing" plan and later led FDR to reward its author with the Chief Justiceship—he also said: "Courts are not the only agency of government that must be assumed to have capacity to govern." This statement, while true on its face, is essentially and subtly—though of course not deliberately—misleading. No "agency of government" governs; no "court" governs; only the men who run the agency of government or the court or the Supreme Court do the governing. The power is theirs because the decisions are theirs; decisions are not made by abstractions like agencies or courts. Justice Stone, who knew what he meant, might a little better have said: "Five or six of the nine men who make up this Court are not the only men in our government who must be assumed to have the capacity to govern." And he might have added: "Nor are they necessarily the wisest in their judgements; I work with them and have reason to know."

2

Choosing Supreme Court Judges

HENRY STEELE COMMAGER

Are the judges merely expressing personal preferences when they act? What types of persons should they be? These are some of the questions discussed by a leading American historian looking back over the record of Supreme Court selection.

. . .

. . . The Constitution, which places some qualifications on other officeholders —the President, for example, must be thirty-five years of age and born in the United States, senators must be thirty years of age, and nine years a citizen of the United States, and so forth—is wholly silent about the qualifications of judges. As far as the Constitution is concerned a judge of the Supreme Court could be foreign born (he need not even be a citizen), twenty-five years old, and wholly without legal training or experience.

. . . President Eisenhower, in his *Memoirs—Mandate for Change: The White House Years*—submitted four principles, or criteria, which should be observed in appointments to the Supreme Court. First, every nominee under consideration should be thoroughly investigated by the FBI and given "security" clearance. Second, no one should be appointed who holds "extreme legal or philosophical views." Third, each appointee should be vetted by the American Bar Association, and fourth—and most important—appointees should be drawn

From Henry Steele Commager, "Choosing Supreme Court Judges," The New Republic, 162, No. 18 (May 2, 1970), 13–16. Reprinted by permission of The New Republic, © 1970, Harrison-Blaine of New Jersey, Inc.

from the inferior federal and state courts.

President Nixon has now explicitly endorsed two of these criteria and implicitly sanctioned the other two. He has asserted that he will make his choices from the inferior federal and the state benches; he has gone on record as opposing any person with "extreme" liberal views—whether he is prepared to extend his disapproval of extremism to conservatives is not clear. He has relied—not very successfully—on "security" and other clearances and he has —again by implication—approved of and endorsed the role of the American Bar Association in the process of selection.

Now what shall we say of these criteria, so suddenly emerging on the American constitutional scene? The first and obvious thing to say is that they are unknown to the Constitution and, until Eisenhower, to history. They are therefore a radical departure from American constitutional law and practice and, too, a radical abdication of the Presidential prerogative—something Mr. Eisenhower may have been prepared to accept, but whose acceptance by President Nixon is quite out of character. To permit the FBI to substitute its judgment of the character and qualifications of a candidate for the judgment and discretion of the President is astonishing; to permit a private, or semi-public, organization like the American Bar Association a kind of veto power over the Presidential decision is an aberration. Mr. Nixon, who . . . rebuked the Senate for exercising its constitutional right to advise and consent and who proclaimed (in his letter to Senator Saxbe) the principle that the Senate had a moral obligation to accept his appointees, is now prepared to concede to a minor government bureau with no experience or expertise in this arena, and to a private organization unknown to the Constitution or to law, a veto power on appointment to the highest bench. Are we now to anticipate an American Bankers Association veto on appointments to the Treasury Department, an American Legion veto on appointments to the Defense Department, or a Chamber of Commerce veto on appointments to the Commerce Department?

. . . What are "extreme philosophical views" deponent saith not, but we may assume that Mr. Eisenhower, who was not given to fine distinctions, meant by this esoteric phrase extreme radicals or extreme conservatives—terms which do not necessarily have anything to do with philosophy. But this, alas, does not get us very far. For extremeness is, after all, in the eye and the mind of the beholder. At one time or another Presidents have thought most of the great Justices "extreme." John Adams had the highest regard for John Marshall, but Jefferson thought him dangerously extreme and, after *Marbury v. Madison,* was prepared to entertain proposals of impeachment. Madison thought Joseph Story a moderate, but Jefferson warned that he was "unquestionably a tory." . . . Theodore Roosevelt, who wanted only ardent nationalists on the Court, concluded rather wildly (after Holmes's dissent in the Northern Securities case) that Holmes was a weakling; "I could carve out of a banana a justice with more backbone than that," he said. President Wilson did not think Louis Brandeis extreme, but a substantial segment of the American bench and bar did, and tried desperately to block his confirmation. . . .

Perhaps the simplest thing to say about this notion of the danger of extreme philosophical views is that to nonphilosophical minds any philosophical views will seem extreme, and that in the circumstances the country is pretty lucky to get a judge with any philosophical views at all.

More important than any of these criteria is the fourth qualification, one which Mr. Nixon has not only endorsed but (unlike President Eisenhower) adopted: that all appointees should be selected from the inferior federal or the state courts.

The first thing to note here is that the Constitution makers clearly did not contemplate any such limitation. . . .

. . .

Certainly the notion that Supreme Court judges should be selected from inferior federal tribunals was absent from the minds of members of the Convention, for they did not provide for such inferior tribunals, but left the creation of these entirely to the discretion of Congress. As for selection from the state courts, about all that can be said here is that when it came to appointing the original justices, Washington did in fact select a majority of his judges —ten in all—from the state courts.

. . . A qualification of previous judicial experience, had it been written into the Constitution, would have denied us the services of a majority of our Chief Justices (and, we should add, the best of them); neither Marshall nor Taney, Chase nor Waite, Fuller nor Hughes, Stone nor Warren, had any judicial experience before ascending to the Chief Justiceship. This generalization is valid, too, for many of the most distinguished associate justices of the Court: thus Joseph Story, John McLean, Benjamin Curtis, John Campbell, Joseph Bradley, the first John Harlan, Louis Brandeis, George Sutherland, and Hugo Black, while Lucius Q. C. Lamar, Charles E. Hughes, Felix Frankfurter, Harlan Stone and Wiley Rutledge—all without judicial experience—had taught at distinguished law schools. A qualification which would have denied us the services of these men does not commend itself to us at a time the need for judicial statesmanship is as acute as at any time in our past.

What should be the criteria for appointment to the Supreme Court?

Judges of the United States Supreme Court are required—the word is dictated even more by history than by the constitutional document—to fulfill responsibilities heavier and more far-ranging than are judges of any other country on the globe. Their task is neither strictly legal or political, in the accepted meaning of those terms; they are called upon not so much to expound the law, as to expound the Constitution; they are engaged, willy-nilly, not in politics but in statesmanship of the highest order. . . .

. . .

First, legal erudition is, of course, desirable, but there is little evidence that it is essential, and little correlation between legal erudition and judicial greatness. Justice Story was more erudite than John Marshall. Sutherland knew more law than Chief Justice Hughes. Frankfurter was more learned in the law than Chief Justice Warren, but Marshall, Hughes and Warren were all more effective on the Court than their more learned brethren.

Courage and independence are, of course essential, but should be taken for granted. After all judges enjoy the independence that is rooted in the principle of the separation of powers, and the security that is assured by tenure. . . .

The ideal judge needs other qualities besides learning and courage. Perhaps the most important, as the most elusive, quality is, quite simply, judiciousness—the ability to judge issues dispassionately and impersonally. This means that the judge is to represent neither party nor interest nor section, but the Constitution. President Washington, to be sure, began the practice of appointing judges to the Supreme Court from their own section. There were practical reasons for this: in the beginning (and until 1869) judges were required, quite literally, to "ride circuit," and it could scarcely be expected that a judge from New England could ride circuit in Virginia or the Carolinas, or—as the nation expanded, a judge from Georgia ride circuit in Indiana and Illinois. With the passing of this onerous requirement the rationale of geographical appointment disappeared. It can scarcely be argued that there is an eastern and a western and a Pacific Constitution, a southern and a northern Constitution. There is one national Constitution and there should be one national law. No judge should be appointed to the Supreme Court primarily because he comes from a particular section of the country. As Senator Borah said when the appointment of Benjamin Cardozo to the Supreme Court aroused opposition because New York already had two judges on that Court: "Cardozo belongs to Idaho as much as to New York." . . .

Nor is there any compelling reason why racial background, party affiliations, or presumed economic philosophy should play a decisive part in the appointment or the confirmation of judges to the highest court. Indeed if there is any one place in the broad arena of American politics where these considerations should be excluded, it is the Court. We do not want judges who confess a regional view, a partisan view, a racial view, or an economic view; we want judges who express a commonwealth view. This may be a counsel of perfection, but if we are allowed to strive for perfection anywhere, it is in the judiciary.

It is improbable that any judge can ever emancipate himself completely from what Justice Holmes called his can't-help-but-believes. Holmes himself, who argued that the Court should be "eternally vigilant against attempts to check the expression of opinions that we loathe and believe to be fraught with death," allowed his ardent nationalist sentiments to influence some of his most powerful opinions, and his natural elegance and fastidiousness to color some of his most famous. Yet the recognition that judges are human should not for a moment abate their zeal, or ours, for an ideal of reason and justice that is above and beyond the beguilements of private interest.

Judicial temperament is essential, but it is not enough. Equally important are broad and generous social sympathies, sensitive to and responding to the felt needs of society. . . .

The greatest of our judges have been deeply versed in the history, rather than in the technicalities, of the law, and have recognized that mastery of the history emancipates from slavery to the technicalities. . . .

This brings us to a fourth qualification

for the highest Court: resourcefulness and imagination—the resourcefulness to find in the elusive phrases of the Constitution authority for making it an instrument rather than a limitation, and the imagination to foresee the direction which the law and the Constitution must take if the Constitution, and the nation, are to "endure for ages to come." . . .

3

A Child's Garden of Law and Order

JUNE L. TAPP

Recent studies in the behavioral sciences have concerned themselves with how children learn to adapt themselves into society—or fail to do so. This study of children in several societies and their attitude toward laws raises a number of interesting questions. Is the quest for law a human need? What is the significance of the different responses in different societies?

Every country, whatever its political and economic philosophy, must produce individuals who are both independent and compliant: citizens who will conform to the socially prescribed rules of behavior and accept them as their own values. But neither the proliferation of programs nor a recitation of rules can assure these goals.

Legal theorists and psychologists have increasingly realized that the internalization of values, not the threat or risk of specific legal penalties, is responsible for compliance with the law and social rules. To understand what makes people obey these norms—or deviate from them—one

must begin from the perspective of the normal citizen, not from the perspective of the criminal.

Many researchers dislike the terms *obedience* and *compliance* because of their strong moral connotations. Stanley Milgram's experiment on conditions of disobedience, for example, made the point that blind obedience to an authority is destructive; he concluded that too few persons behave autonomously. But the study of legal socialization does not necessarily have as a premise that compliance itself is good or bad; the study is concerned with the ways in which individuals learn the rules and norms of their society.

Across

A good way to achieve this understanding is to observe children in different cultures, inquiring: 1) whether the same au-

From June L. Tapp, "A Child's Garden of Law and Order," Psychology Today, 4, No. 7 (December 1970), 29–31, 62, 64. Reprinted by permission of the publisher. Copyright © Communications/ Research/Machines/Inc.

thority figures are important across nations; 2) whether people throughout the world share notions about the legitimacy of rule-breaking and the nature and function of rules and laws; 3) whether children develop in similar ways in their attitudes toward legitimacy, morality and justice.

. . .

Questions

We gave a battery of tests to all of these children [almost 5,000 middle-school children in seven cultures in Greece, Denmark, India, Italy, Japan and the United States (black and white)] and then, for more intensive study, we interviewed a random sample of 406 children, roughly 60 in each culture. These included 20 from each of three grades (fourth, sixth and eighth), equally divided in turn by social class (professional or working) and sex.

In the interview we asked 79 open-ended questions, including these basic ones:

1. *What is a rule?*
2. *What is a law?*
3. *What is the difference between a rule and a law?*
4. *What would happen if there were no rules at all?*
5. *What is a fair rule?*
6. *Are there times when it might be right to break a rule?*
7. *Who can make you follow a rule?*

Norms

Before anyone can understand a system's legal order, he must have a concept of a rule and a law, and their differences. Cross-culturally, children believed that the nature and function of rules and laws were the same. When we asked: *What is a rule?* and *What is a law?*, children in all seven cultures defined both, using the same three functional categories:

1. *Prescriptive*—a general guideline, a neutral regulation. "It's a guideline to follow," said a U.S. white eighth-grade girl. "Just—well, you just follow it."

2. *Prohibitive*—a guideline that forbids behavior. An American white sixth-grade boy explained: "A rule, to me, it's more like a restriction that tells you what you can do and what you can't do . . . well, like a rule at school is that you can't chew gum or you'll get in trouble."

3. *Beneficial*—a guideline with a rational social or personal reason for existing. "It is what is necessary for the group life," reported a Japanese sixth-grade girl, "and—if it is kept by all—the group activity goes in order."

Although there was some variation between cultures in the frequency with which these three functions were cited, in five of seven cultures children's characterizations of rules and laws were parallel. We found that the *prescriptive* quality was the most widely recognized. In all seven cultures it was a typical answer (defined here as at least 20 per cent). Older children were more inclined to stress prescription; they gave fewer *don't know* responses, reflecting their newly increased knowledge and social awareness. In five of seven cultures, *prohibitive* was the second most typical answer for rules; this was true in six of seven for laws.

Most children, then, saw the *functions* of laws and rules as the same: they regarded both as special norms that guide behavior and require obedience. A key finding was that the concept of coercion was noticeably absent from their answers. The children focused on the content and purpose of rules, not on punishment and authority. This reluctance to recognize coercion suggests, as many legal scholars and social scientists maintain, that coercion and force do not insure obedience to the law, and that they are not the defining quality of all things legal or rulelike.

Although children thought that rules and laws perform in the same way, they saw differences between them when they were asked. Not surprisingly, in six out of seven cultures they saw rules as more specific and laws as more general. This distinction, however, was more a matter of sphere, scope, or jurisdiction than function. For example, the children's answers reflected the popular notion that *laws* had a government or state implication, whereas *rules* were nongovernmental in nature. This suggests that understanding the function of state law is part of a larger enterprise of understanding the function of rules and laws in other institutions.

We found marked developmental similarities across cultures. Regardless of country, the older a child was, the more likely he was to impute specificity to rules and generality to laws. With experience and age children learn that it is permissible to use the terms *laws* and *the law* in speaking of the rules that are more comprehensive and general.

Shadow

What if there were no rules at all? Children in all countries predicted the same result: without rules there would be chaos, disorder and anarchy. In addition, children in five cultures foresaw violence, crime and personal gain as outcomes.

As children saw it, the essential purpose of rules was to order man's relationships in the world: to facilitate human interaction. The children also seemed to have a fearful, distrusting view of mankind. Without rules, they said, man's natural evil would take over—anarchy, violence and greed would win out. One fourth-grade, white American boy represented the view taken by most of the children: "Well, it would be a lot of disorganizing in the world. You know, people would go around killing each other. It wouldn't be organized, and there wouldn't be any school or anything like that." Said one Danish boy: "The whole world would be under chaos."

Age and experience apparently darken a child's view of human nature. Older children in all but two of the countries studied were more likely than younger ones to say that disorder and personal gain would prevail if rule and law failed. "Everyone would do what he wanted," said an Italian sixth-grader. A more sophisticated Italian eighth-grader explained: "Life would not have a logical direction."

Because socialization aims to produce individuals who will want to comply, children may be learning explicitly—from parents and other authorities—that chaos and conflict would ensue if we had no rules. In any case few children can imagine a world without laws and few dare suggest that good might survive without them. Rules and laws control and deter man's irrational, aggressive and egoistic motives.

Justice

Given this acceptance of rules how do children distinguish among them? Are all rules fair, or are some more fair than others? To ascertain the essence of justice, we asked: *What is a fair rule?*

In six out of seven cultures, children could separate the concept of rule from that of a fair rule. Only in one country—India—was *All rules are fair* the typical response. Interestingly, in all seven cultures fewer than 5 per cent defined a fair rule as one created by an authority; the fact that a rule was made by the powers-that-be did not necessarily mean that it was just.

Although there was some variation across countries in definitions of rule fairness, two components stood out in the children's responses:

1. *Consensus.* A primary response in five cultures was that a fair rule is one with which everyone agrees. American children gave us some good examples of this answer: "Everybody likes it," said a white fourth-grade girl, and, "When somebody suggests a rule and everybody thinks it's right, then it's fair," said a black eighth-grade boy.

2. *Equality.* A typical answer in four cultures was that a fair rule is one everyone must obey, one that affects everyone without favoritism. As one U.S. white fourth-grade girl observed: "We should both get yelled at for talking, but it's not fair for one person to get yelled at." A U.S. black eighth-grade boy defined a fair rule as: "a rule that would apply to everyone fairly and it wouldn't put one person out and another person in."

Among U.S. children a third answer was

WHAT THE CHILDREN SAY	GREECE	INDIA	ITALY	JAPAN	DEN-MARK	U.S. WHITES	U.S. BLACKS
What is a rule?	Percentages						
Prescriptive	35	32	45	27	40	44	54
Prohibitive	25	7	13	43	57	34	38
Beneficial	27	10	17	45	2	18	6
What is a law?							
Prescriptive	33	52	20	39	40	41	38
Prohibitive	42	3	32	27	38	49	46
Beneficial	7	10	25	30	—	6	6
What is the difference between a rule and a law?							
Rules specific, laws comprehensive	51	30	37	52	15	33	29
Rules nongovernmental, laws governmental	17	32	8	63	3	57	25
No difference	15	23	15	23	12	16	46
Differences unspecified	25	20	15	11	50	21	19
What would happen if there were no rules?							
Personal gain	53	15	33	25	16	23	33
Violence and crime	42	5	7	50	22	61	57
Anarchy, disorder and chaos	40	65	22	57	24	39	40
What is a fair rule?							
Equality	33	12	7	50	29	48	19
Rational/beneficial	5	2	12	—	10	33	35
Consensus	42	3	18	9	24	25	24
Absolute, all rules are fair	15	50	13	16	12	—	5

In the above tables children were allowed to give as many answers as they wanted; therefore percentages may total more than 100. Where answers were too idiosyncratic or uncodeable the categories have been dropped.

Are there times when it might be right to break a rule?							
No, unspecified (no rule is breakable)	35	42	17	20	19	15	25
Yes, unspecified	17	5	5	9	24	3	3
Yes, morality of circumstance	18	30	17	36	43	64	54
Yes, morality of rule	18	22	38	20	9	15	8

characteristic: both blacks and whites emphasized the *rational-beneficial* dimension of fairness. A fair rule, they said, is one that is reasonable and useful. In the words of a fourth-grade black boy: "Because it is a good thing and it is helping you from getting hurt."

Demands

In five cultures, as children grew older they were less likely to believe that all rules are fair; and in six cultures were more likely to think that equality is basic to the concept of fairness. With age, they also question adults more and make increased demands for respect and reciprocity.

There are important implications for legal systems in the fact that children see a fair system as one that embraces participatory and cooperative efforts among equals. Justice requires consensual participation, impersonal distribution, and shared power.

Violation

We further probed attitudes about the function and fairness of rules by asking: *Are there times when it might be right to break a rule?* Only in two cultures were children most likely to reply that *no* rule was breakable; in five, children readily accepted the possibility of rule-breaking. Although in all cultures their reasons varied, in five cultures children thought that rule-breaking was permissible for higher moral reasons—that is, if the rule were less important than the situation or reason for breaking it. This answer, based on the *morality of circumstances*, was well expressed by a U.S. white eighth-grader: "Well, it depends on what's going on. If it's a matter of life and death or you know something pretty important, then it's all right. But the rule should be followed as much as possible." Or, as a more imaginative child expounded: "When you're hungry and you go in the store and steal something. When you need money, like for someone kidnapped someone in your family and he stole it from the bank, paid the ransom and you try to pay the money back to the bank. Money and food could be replaced but the person in life couldn't."

Only in one country, Italy, was the *morality of the rule* itself the dominant response; that is, children felt freer to break a rule they thought was intrinsically unfair.

Substantial numbers of children, then, recognized that rules and laws are not infallible or absolute. They accepted just and legitimate reasons for transgressions. As they grew older, children in at least five countries increasingly accepted the legitimacy of breaking rules with moral cause, findings consistent with work on moral development by Jean Piaget and Lawrence Kohlberg.

Authority

Finally, to determine what authority figures were important in socializing children into compliance, we asked: *Who can make you follow a rule?* Father, mother, teacher and policeman emerged as the major authorities for children.

In six of the seven cultures, parents were most able to make children follow rules; there was variation as to which parent came first, reflecting different norms about who does the punishing in the home. In only one country, Japan, the teacher ranked higher than parents; everywhere else, the teacher generally followed parents in ranking of effective rule enforcers. The number of children who said policemen made them follow rules was comparatively lower, but substantial percentages nominated this symbol of law enforcement. The police ranked at least fourth in all cultures except in India, where children mentioned government officials instead.

Parents, being closest to children and most familiar to them, were, as we would expect, most able to make them obey; the distant policeman and official were not as effective in gaining compliance. This finding suggests, along with other research in psychology and law, that affiliative, nurturant strategies—rather than punitive ones —are most effective in inducing compliance and assuring the stability of systems. Persuasion, not coercion, is more likely to be linked with compliance and independence.

Hope

Considering the range of countries and the diversity of political, religious and economic styles represented in our survey, it is remarkable that there should be such similarities across the seven cultures. The children see rules and laws as performing equivalent functions in the ordering of human conduct. They recognize the need for order in human affairs, and the role that rules and laws play in providing that order. They want a fair system—one that emphasizes equality and consensus. And they agree that with good reason or moral justification, rules could legitimately be violated.

Such striking convergences across such divergent nations are, I like to think, a good sign. The common trends of child development and the socialization goals that transcend nationality suggest that the shared values throughout our world are more compelling than diverse ideologies would imply. If these children's wisdom could be maintained into adulthood, there might be a better chance for freedom and justice within a world society, which after all is the message of law.

4

On the Limits of Litigation

SIDNEY E. ZION

Is law all that objective and necessarily fair? Zion suggests political power always limits the radiating effect of a principle. Is this a chicken and egg question or a meaningful one—"which is more effective, a principle or power?"

On the Poverty Suits Lately Being Brought

There's an interesting combination of legal shrewdness and naïveté involved in what has really been a revolution in the law in the area of poverty. The poverty lawyers are employing a kind of Mother Goose device to deal with terrible problems that the courts have in the past not tackled seriously.

Not because the courts couldn't tackle these issues. The architecture was always there, the theories were always around and about. The limits, as usual, were in the minds of the actors. This time including the clients' minds.

The poor, being taught by the relatively comfortable, were hardly endowed with *chutzpah* concerning their station in life. They were taught to respect the middle class not only for the handout but for the example of success provided by middle-class achievement. If you're busted out,

then try to break out. If you can't we'll make sure you don's starve. Getting uppity was always out of the question.

Charity requires gratitude, and that is not to be taken lightly; it seems to be part of the human instinct. In the old blues number you can have a "hand full of gimme" but you damn well better have a "mouth full of much oblige."

Now into this ago-old milieu recently came a bunch of young poverty lawyers. And together with the social workers they managed in an amazingly short period of time to convince both the poor and the courts that rights beget rights. Thus the welfare protests, where the poor were saying, in traditional common-law language, that no bureaucat could deprive them by regulation of what the legislature had given them by statute.

That was very shrewd of the poverty lawyers. They tied a guilt complex to solid legal principles and they got somewhere. For example, the welfare system can no longer police the bedrooms of the poor. And that is major, very major. For the first time, the Supreme Court held that the com-

From Sidney E. Zion, "On the Limits of Litigation," The Antioch Review, XXX, No. 2 (Summer 1970), 185–194. Reprinted by permission of the publisher.

fortable class has no inherent right to define the happiness of the poor. Until that recent ruling it was understood that one of the strings attached to welfare payments was also attached to the boudoir. We were simply not going to pay mothers to bed down with unwed fathers.

If it took so long to legitimize relief sex, how long will it take to establish the poor as a middle economic class? That, I take it, is at least the unconscious goal of the poverty Bar, to create a quasi-socialism through litigation. I'm afraid that here they are slightly naive. Because their success depends on *really* blowing minds, the minds of the judges and the minds of the Bar and the minds, ultimately, of the public.

Scratch the sophistication off any specific opposition to welfare rights and you will generally find a basic disbelief that the poor have *any* rights. Privileges, yes, but not rights. There is this basic instransigence against accepting the *fait accompli*. We have, after all, decided long ago the major issue: that the poor are not going to starve. From that fundamental determination flowed many small successes all adding up to a *fait accompli*: the poor are a class, they are here and they hold a pretty good mortgage on our comfort.

Should they, then, be represented by their own in Congress? Should a guy on welfare go to Congress? Why not? Why should Nelson Rockefeller be Governor? He never had to work. His money was produced by a robber baron. Why should a man who can't work be different from one who doesn't have to work?

These are going to be very painful questions to answer. And the deeper the questions probe the more likely it is that people will fall back on the instinct which dictates against letting the poor demand *anything*.

On the Outs Against the Ins

Legally, the outs of the society are limited by their ability to con the establishment into thinking that they (the establishment) are not doing anything different from what they did in 1890. Sound enough

like a St. John's Law School textbook and you can sell the average judge anything. In the law, there are words to justify anything. . . .

. . .

Very smooth, very sharp, these judges and law professors. But the kind I'm talking about are as bad as the people who run South Africa. Worse in some ways, for they give to racism and cant and lying a wonderful legitimacy. Felix Frankfurter produced far greater damage to civil liberties than Joe McCarthy. McCarthy was so gross and rotten—what the Jews call a *grubbe yung*—that finally even Eisenhower recognized it. But no such luck with a "gentleman" like Frankfurter.

Felix would pound his chest and say "ooh, bubba, bubba, how could I do this to you," and then he'd go right ahead and do it. And get away with it. Because he was a scholar, a civilized man, a gentleman. In such silks he managed to give to people like Joe McCarthy a patina of legitimacy that they never could have achieved alone.

The same thing happened, in a much starker way, when the Junkers of Germany wrote books justifying anti-Semitism. That made it possible for Hitler to carry it to the outer limits. Once you concede that a little violation of the First Amendment is all right, once you don't spit in the eye of the guy who proposes that, right then and there you are on the road out. Let them diddle a bit with the Bill of Rights and the next thing you read is a decision on how the Japanese concentration camps are constitutional. They did that, the Supreme Court did that. And of all guys, Hugo Black wrote the decision. And that great humanitarian, Franklin Roosevelt, wrote the law. And Earl Warren was the chief prosecutor.

You know, you could get paranoic reading American history. I don't get that way because I consider it no different from the history of man's soul. It is a very sad and sick history of seeking to get along with whoever appears to be in power. Even the men in power are afflicted: they want to get along with themselves. A very funny thing happens to the mind when it becomes "responsible."

Since—to cite Mencken again—America has no institutions but only fashions, this "flexibility" can occasionally be conned into goodness. But goodness, with a nod to Mae West, has nothing to do with it.

. . .

. . . [C]onsider Legal Aid. If the Legal Aid leadership had a panoramic vision, would they not see that their clientele was collective, not individual, but a class? They can see it as a class when they bring class actions, as say in opposition to mass prostitution arrests or bail pogroms. But what if you say to Legal Aid that it can best serve its "class" by pleading them all not guilty? Do you know what that would mean in most big cities? It would mean that the criminal courts would virtually collapse. The system could not take it. There is no room for so many trials. No chance. As it is, the system is cracking though more than 90 per cent of the defendants plead guilty.

Now, since so many plead guilty, and thus get criminal records if not jail, why should not Legal Aid plea them all *not* guilty? Then they wouldn't be tried and therefore no jail and no records. A system that could try no one could hardly justify money bail. They would simply have to let the blokers go.

But Legal Aid lawyers would never seriously consider such a thing. Why not? Because nobody would like them. People want to be liked. Nobody in the legal fraternity would respect them. People want to be respected. Judges would shun them, prosecutors would bawl them out daily in the press and would stop saying nice things to them in the halls. The people who pay them would be upset and would stop going to the Legal Aid Ball and soon the money would dry up as well as the prestige. Governments would surely not keep picking up part of the tab for a group dedicated to helping its own clients.

Of course, if you ask Legal Aid lawyers why they don't plead everybody "not guilty," they will not tell you that it is because they want to be liked or need the money. They will say that they owe it to each individual client to handle him in the best way appropriate to his needs. If they defend Mr. X at trial for robbery, they say, rather than plead him guilty to "breaking and entering," then Mr. X might get a very long prison sentence. And that is true, since plea bargaining is what it sounds like, a bargain wherein one side gets a short sentence in return for saving the other side the bother of a trial. The trouble is that Legal Aid is in a buyer's market and is acting as though it is at the mercy of a seller's market.

That is the logical trouble. The real trouble is that Legal Aid lawyers are still lawyers, and as such they believe in the very system they must attack to be loyal to their clients. To attack it properly they should not hesitate to destroy it. But they cannot even consciously think of it in this manner. If they did, they might do something terrible. They might become unpopular.

Now of course it is possible that someday a new breed of Legal Aid lawyers will find that they cannot be invited to parties because they are viewed by their friends as an integral part of the system. This depends on having different kinds of friends than at present. But it could happen. And if it does, we may really find out just what are the limits of litigation.

5

A Political Approach to the Courts

MARTIN SHAPIRO

In recent years political scientists and other social scientists, as well as legal theorists, have examined more closely the relationship between law and politics. Reflecting the trends in political science, this has taken two broadly conceived modes of analysis. In the first instance, attention has been given to theoretical ways of conceptualizing legal action. In the second, a quantitative or statistical approach has become more dominant. Both, but especially the second, have proven to be controversial, particularly among traditional legalistic writers.

. . . [A] new approach to the study of courts is in the making. . . .

Professor David Truman has been a catalyst for this new jurisprudence. It may be argued that his brief section on the judiciary in *The Governmental Process* is little more than an assertion that courts can be just as conveniently handled within his system of analysis as other government bodies can. Truman attempts to analyze all government in terms of the influence and interactions of interest groups measuring influence largely in terms of "access." He admits that there is little of the kind of direct access to the courts that pressure groups have to legislative bodies. The Supreme Court is after all not subject to the same types of pressure as the Congress. He emphasizes indirect access through such means as influencing the selection of judges. . . .

. . .

. . . Truman does mention that organized groups do gain direct access to the courts by engaging in litigation and he emphasizes that litigation, like war, is the conduct of politics by other means.

Furthermore, Truman's rather general suggestions about group access to the courts have been followed up in terms of both pressure-group lobbying and the "constituency" of the Court. Lobbying techniques like the *amicus* brief, the test case, and the writing of law-review articles favorable to certain causes have been described, and the long-range judicial campaigns of such groups as the N.A.A.C.P. have been analyzed. . . .

. . .

. . . This approach leads us away from broad generalizations about the role of Congress or the Presidency or the Supreme Court in American government and into the problem of exactly what parts certain agencies of government, including the Supreme Court in the hierarchy of courts has also begun to receive some attention in terms of the political relationships between superior and subordinate in a highly bureaucratized governmental structure.

. . .

From Martin Shapiro, "Political Jurisprudence," in Law and Politics in the Supreme Court (New York: The Free Press, 1964), pp. 8–14. Copyright © by The Free Press of Glencoe, a Division of The Macmillan Company, 1964. Reprinted by permission of the publisher.

Particular attention has been paid to the bar as a group that has constant access to the Court through the arguments and briefs of its members, their academic and polemic writing, and their recruitment as justices. Lawyers are no longer viewed simply as contestants before an impartial referee or as officers of the Court. They form a constellation of political forces that play upon a political agency.

Indeed the whole discussion of lobbying and constituency inevitably leads to the question of whether or not the Court is a "clientele" agency. This expression is usually associated with those regulatory agencies that have become spokesmen for the interests they were established to regulate. It has often been argued that the I.C.C. has served as a clientele agency for the railroads. The Court has, of course, always been viewed as a spokesman for upholding "The Constitution" against the hostile sentiments of the moment. If, however, the Court is visualized as caught in reciprocal relations of service and support with various special interests or constituencies, then the concept of clientele agency may be applicable to the Supreme Court, as well as to the I.C.C.

. . .

. . . The "political" attacks on the Court in the late '30s and early '50s have inspired considerable commentary, much of which inevitably, and some deliberately, describes and evaluates the political power of the Court in terms of its ability to protect itself in the clinches.

. . .

Supreme Court justices, of course, vote, and their individual votes determine the general outcomes of the cases. Their votes, or more precisely the internal alignments or arrangements of their votes, shift from case to case. The opinions of the justices in individual cases also add up to a kind of over-all record for the term, in the way that the sum of a given Congress's legislative decisions allows us to generalize about its legislative behavior. It is not surprising therefore that the same voting analysis

techniques that have been used to describe how legislatures and electorates arrive at decisions have now been applied to the Supreme Court. Much of this statistical analysis is strictly descriptive, an attempt to show the relation of one Justice's votes to another's, the presence of blocs, the possibility that certain Justices vacillate, or the direction in which the Court is moving on particular issues.

Behind the gross description of voting patterns, however, lies an attempt to understand the motivation of judges. The foundation of behavioral psychology is the proposition that we may discover the way men think by observing how they behave. One, perhaps the crucial, aspect of a justice's behavior is how he votes. The study of his voting may therefore tell us how he thinks. Two basic techniques have been used in this approach. In the first, the level of agreement between each possible pair of Justices is recorded, and those Justices with the highest level of agreement, in terms of voting the same way in the same cases, are grouped. Justices belonging to the same bloc, that is, voting together in a relatively large number of cases, are assumed to share a common attitude around which the bloc clusters. A group of Justices who constantly vote for the individual and against the government in civil-rights cases may be described as having a procivil-rights attitude. The other basic method is scalogram analysis, which also measures behavior on the basis of votes with or against the majority. If certain cases "scale," that is, show symmetrical voting patterns among the Justices, then it is assumed that voting on those cases was determined by a single attitude dimension, for instance, sentiment toward labor unions or business.

The general assumption of both group and scale analysis has been that attitudes toward the various socioeconomic and political interests presented by the cases are an important factor in determining at least some of the decisions of some of the Justices. Attitudinal-statistical research has not only sought to isolate and measure attitudes toward social values like freedom of speech or free enterprise, but it has also sought to measure the Justices' attitudes toward other government agencies and toward the Court itself, that is, toward judicial self-restraint, spheres of competence, and so forth.

. . .

Parallel to attitudinal research and using much of the same data is an approach that treats the Court as a small group and subjects it to the general modes of analysis and measurement that psychologists and sociologists have devised for examining such groups. The nine Justices then become the subject of studies in small-group psychology, which aim at discovering patterns of leadership, deference, and so forth. The role of the Chief Justice as political leader has been described and attempts have been made to assess the relative power and influence of the Justices *vis-à-vis* one another. While much of bloc analysis is aimed at identifying operative political attitudes, it can also be employed to chart the group politics of the court itself. The existence of relatively firm blocs may ensure the power of "swing Justices" and the need for compromise in order to gain a majority. Conversely, it may explain the intransigent and absolutist opinions of Justices caught in a minority bloc that has no hope of gaining a majority and therefore no motivation to compromise.

Also closely related to attitudinal studies are some research results that may be labeled crudely "behavioral." Although statistics may demonstrate that Justice X always votes probusiness, they offer no proof that he does so because he allows strongly probusiness sentiments to shape his decisions. Indeed, there is a kind of basic circularity in statistical approaches to the problem of judicial attitudes. Consistency in voting behavior is used to infer the attitude, and then the attitude is used to explain the consistency. This circularity can be at least partially broken by seeking for information on attitudes in materials other than voting records or by manipulating the case samples to reduce the possibility of incursions by stray variables. Even with their circularity, however, statistical studies are useful to political jurisprudence. If we find that Justice X or, more important, Justices X, Y, Z, A, and B always vote prolabor, we may still not have learned why, but we have discovered something about the impact of the Supreme Court on labor policy and the nature of its relations with other labor policy-makers. A simple description of what happened, that is, who won, may be quite useful in assessing the political role of the Supreme Court. . . .

6

The High Court's Role in Policy

The news clipping reprinted below summarizes a study by Robert Dahl of Yale University attempting to assess the political conditions under which the Court may flourish. The point of view here is an interesting supplement to the idea that a political conflict determines the question of Court influence.

Washington, Sept. 30—Two questions that have arisen in the minds of many Americans, particularly in the South, about the Supreme Court these past few years are:

1. Can the court really make new national policy, and make it stick even if it is widely disapproved?
2. What can a disapproving citizenry do to reverse or modify new policies set by the court? And with what chance of success?

Question number 1 has been studied of late by an expert, and his findings have been published in the *Journal of Public Law,* issued by the Emory University Law School in Atlanta.

In this study, Dr. Robert A. Dahl, a Yale University Professor of Political Science, analyzed what had happened in the seventy-eight cases in which the high tribunal, in its history up to 1957, had struck down as unconstitutional eight-seven (*sic*) provisions of federal law.

There were instances in which the court was changing policy fixed by Congress and, in nearly every case, approved by the President.

From "High Court's Role in Policy Studied: Bench and Congress Never Split Permanently on an Issue, Survey Finds," The New York Times, October 5, 1958. Copyright © 1958 by The New York Times Company. Reprinted by permission of the publisher.

Decisions Modified

No fewer than twenty-six times Congress passed new legislation that had the effect of reversing the court. In other instances the situation itself changed, and the new court policy was unimportant. Or, several times, the court modified its own earlier decisions.

This led Dr. Dahl to the conclusion that the policy views of the court never remain for long out of line with the policy views of the lawmaking majority. And he noted that to have a strong lawmaking majority, Congress and the White House must be controlled by the same party.

He found that, on rare occasion, the court could "delay the application" of policy up to twenty-five years. But, he said, it is most likely to be successful when faced with a "weak" lawmaking majority. And, he added, "by itself the court is about powerless to effect the course of national policy."

Dr. Dahl said he felt the court had got by so far with its school segregation decision of 1954 because of an unusual situation in political leadership. He said, in effect, that advocates of school integration while "not strong enough to get what they wanted enacted by Congress, still were and are powerful enough to prevent any successful attack on the legislative powers of the court."

This leads to the second question: What can be done?

If Dr. Dahl is right about pro-integration strength, present attempts to limit the appellate jurisdiction of the court are doomed to failure.

In certain limited areas—such as spelling out that Congress must specify that a new federal law is to supersede state laws on the same subject before the High Court can rule that Congress intended to do so—Congress may well curb the court.

History shows that presidents over a period of years have exerted powerful influence over the court. This is due, obviously, to their power of nomination (which usually amounts to appointments) of new High Court justices.

7

Interview with Chief Justice Warren E. Burger

The Supreme Court has institutional problems, and plays roles in the U.S. Courts system, the governmental structure generally, and American society. Here Chief Justice Burger presents his views of some of those interrelationships.

Q. Mr. Chief Justice, a recent Gallup Poll shows that the federal judiciary generally and particularly the Supreme Court have fallen in public esteem. How do you account for that?

A. I would have to say that it is difficult to explain the rise or fall of public acceptance of any institution at any time, including the courts. All the institutions of our society are under attack, and the courts are not excepted. There are many causes.

Some of the attitude, of course, is related to the understanding that people have of what the courts have been doing—for example, in the area of criminal justice. People who don't like what they understand the Court has been doing will have a lowered opinion of the Court, just as other people who may have a different understanding will have a higher opinion of the Court.

Q. Are you saying the public is misinformed about what courts do?

A. No—not quite that. But the public is not well-informed—fully informed—and much of that is probably unavoidable.

Some of it is due to misunderstanding because of the tradition that the Court does not explain its function and its decisions to the public. Unlike other governmental agencies, courts do not undertake to explain through regular news conferences and press releases.

I think probably the public doesn't have a much better understanding of courts at the State level, or the federal courts generally, than it does of the Supreme Court. The Supreme Court's work is simply more in the news. We are at the hub of a great news center, and we deal with newsworthy cases. With rare exceptions, all our decisions are news.

Q. Within two months after you took office in 1969, you made some proposals to the American Bar Association at its convention in Dallas and followed that up this year with a series of proposals and a message on the "state of the federal judiciary" at St. Louis. What were the proposals and what response did you get?

A. I made three very specific proposals to the 1969 ABA meeting in Dallas:

The first, I thought, was the most urgent —namely, the need for introducing more modern methods into the courts in terms of the techniques, machinery and the administration.

. . .

The second proposal I made related to the desperate need for a re-examination of our penal systems. I proposed that the American bar do that at every level.

. . .

Q. Can you point to the principal problems you see?

A. The great shortcoming has been—at the State level particularly—a lack of any meaningful educational system for inmates, many of whom can't even read or write, and then the lack of vocational training and the lack of what we vaguely call "rehabilitation," in terms of psychological testing and counseling to get them ready to make a living on an honest basis.

Two thirds of the people in prisons, roughly—in all penal institutions—are people who have been there before and who will be back again. We simply can't permit this to run that way any more. No other public business is run as badly as our prisons.

. . .

Q. What was your third proposal?

A. The third proposal was that, particularly with respect to the administration of criminal justice, the law schools were doing an inadequate job of training people for the realities of litigation. This has a relationship to civil litigation as well.

There has long been a debate between law-school faculties and lawyers and judges on this subject. Many professors in the past took the position generally that they were not running trade schools; they're teaching people to think, they're teaching legal theory. That is good, but it is not enough. They must also be trained as to how they should act.

I think most lawyers and most judges who've had to preside over trials have long felt that there were terrible gaps in the training of these recently graduated lawyers in terms of how to conduct themselves in the courtroom and in terms of their attitude toward professional responsibility. And this can best be taught when these students are learning their profession. It is really more important than pure legal learning.

This is essentially what is done in England in the training of a lawyer for litigation under their bifurcated system. It is done in the four Inns of Court. And that's the only place you can become a trial lawyer—a barrister—in England. The colleges of these Inns are managed and run by lawyers and judges, just as medical education in this country is almost entirely in the hands of practicing physicians and surgeons.

. . .

Q. Do they have the volume of criminal cases that exists in this country?

A. They do not—either in relative volume or otherwise—but the difference in population is not enough to explain the difference in the way cases are handled. In the way they dispose of them, there's a great disparity.

Ninety-five to 97 per cent of all criminal cases in England are disposed of—and with finality—in justice-of-the-peace courts and county courts. There is nothing comparable to our long-drawn-out appeals and reviews after the conviction is final. And when there are appeals they are decided within a matter of months, and that is the end of the case.

Q. But in this country can't someone accused of a crime hire a clever lawyer and find a way to prolong appeals that go clear to the Supreme Court?

A. He can certainly keep the litigation going for a very great length of time—years, in many cases. Our system permits this; some critics think our system encourages it.

. . .

Limiting the Right to Appeal

Q. Does this imply a limitation on the right to appeal?

A. I suppose, when you talk about finality, that must carry with it a limit somewhere—that there is a point at which proceedings of all kinds are terminated. We haven't found that point in our system. We are fumbling and groping because every judge in America knows we must make some changes.

Q. You wouldn't limit a defendant to one appeal, say—

A. No, you can't have rigidity of that kind. The point is to be sure that the accused has a meaningful review or appeal that explores all of the claims that he could possibly have. And when he's had that, then we should be very near the end of it —unless, of course, there is the discovery of some significant new evidence.

Q. In this country, can a defendant appeal on one point, lose that appeal and then appeal on another point?

A. Not quite. The direct-appeal process requires the defendant to raise all his claims at that time. But we have vastly enlarged what are called the "postconviction remedies." The petitions for writs of habeas corpus, which are collateral attacks on the conviction, are an example. They are not yet under reasonable control.

Q. Does all this legal maneuvering contribute to the congestion of criminal cases in the courts?

A. It contributes very heavily. Let me illustrate that with just one example:

Twenty years or so ago, there were virtually no petitions from prisoners in State prisons to the federal courts. An opinion of the Supreme Court in recent years gave the State prisoners that right—the right to habeas corpus review in federal courts. Petitions in that category have grown from less than 100 annually 20 years ago to approximately 12,000 this year—quite a load on the federal courts.

Q. To do that, doesn't the defendant have to raise a constitutional issue?

A. Yes—but we can't always know whether he has raised a valid constitutional issue until it is reviewed by a federal judge. Now, only a fraction of these people ever get relief, but the proceeding is in the court, thereby using the time of the federal court and the whole machinery of the court.

Q. Do you feel that certain types of criminal cases should not get to the federal courts?

A. Well, it would be difficult to say how you would eliminate certain criminal jurisdiction in the federal courts: Those for violation of federal statutes belong in federal jurisdiction.

In the broad sense—and this goes beyond your question—I have a strong feeling that a great many matters traditionally handled in the court systems, both State and federal, should be diverted away from the courts entirely.

Q. In what way?

A. Now I'm going out of my field of responsibility in my present position, but there is a broad and serious social question —I think you would have to call it—whether such things as divorce, child custody, adoptions, receiverships, various other matters of that kind belong in the courts at all.

There is a curious paradox relating back to your opening question: In spite of what seems to be a lessening of esteem for the courts, there is an attitude that the courts should resolve all problems.

But that is not realistic; courts can serve only a limited function, and it should not be broadened any more than is absolutely necessary.

. . .

The question of dealing with the chronic alcoholic, the narcotic addict, the serious mental patient—there's a serious question whether they should be dealt with in the judicial framework at all.

Q. How would such things be handled?

A. Well, this is what some very competent people should study carefully. It would be some administrative treatment necessarily, but with limited judicial review. Here we will encounter some constitutional problems.

. . .

Q. A recent development has been what one could call "antic lawyers" in courtrooms, who turn trials into circuses. Are these lawyers within their legal rights?

A. . . . Again, a comparison with the English system is useful. Under their system, with the trial lawyers being trained in the importance of professional responsibility, personal conduct and decorum—manners, if you will—are recognized as the indispensable lubricants to what is essentially a contentious and abrasive process.

The British have no such thing as antics in the courtroom. It simply never happens, because a lawyer—a barrister in England—knows that certain kinds of conduct which are widely practiced and tolerated in this country would lead to swift and severe discipline and possibly disbarment under the British system.

. . .

Q. What about antics on the part of accused persons?

A. In the ultimate sense, the opinion of the Court last year in Illinois against Allen, in which the Court spoke through Mr. Justice Black, has settled the extremes of that problem, vesting very broad power in trial judges, both State and federal, to remove any offending person, any person interfering with the process—remove him from the courtroom even though it be the defendant. . . .

Q. Earlier you seemed to reject the notion that the Supreme Court was by its decisions in any way responsible for the rise in crime and violence—

A. I don't think I said "in any way." It's a factor which enters the total stream of causation.

Q. Well, the court system in general has been accused of contributing to the rise through lack of speedy trials, lack of significant punishment. Do you agree with this?

A. I do, in part. It's the lack of certainty, and the promptness of the judicial process, and the punishment. Swift and sure trials and reasonable finality would cure a great many evils.

. . .

Q. We've had a great growth in the last few years of legal-aid societies, public-defender systems, tax-exempt public-service law firms and things like that. Do you think that that adds to litigation? Is this in the public interest?

A. I would not want to suggest for one moment that anything which adds to litigation is automatically against the public interest or for the public interest. There is more to it than that.

The legal-aid systems began on a private, volunteer basis half a century ago and have been slowly growing. The public-defender system for criminal cases began soon after that time and has had a slower growth, but it has flowered in recent years. And I must confess a conflict in a way, because I have a bias in favor of some of these programs, provided they are conforming to high professional standards.

Neighborhood Legal Services under the Office of Economic Opportunity has 57 million dollars in the federal budget this year for the OEO legal staffs alone. That's almost half of the total amount being spent on all operations of the federal courts. It is not a correct assumption that all of the cases of these Neighborhood Legal Services are going to get into the federal courts—or indeed into any courts.

. . .

I said at the ABA meeting in St. Louis in August that a sense of confidence in the courts is essential to maintain the fabric of ordered liberty for a free people, and there are three things that could destroy it:

One is that people come to believe that inefficiency and delay will drain even a just judgment of its value. Four, five or six years after you've broken your leg or damaged your automobile is too long a time to wait for a recovery.

Second, if people who have been exploited in the smaller transactions of daily life—home appliances, repairs, finance charges, and the like—come to believe that courts cannot vindicate their legal rights from fraud and overreaching on the part of others.

The third thing I spoke of was a feeling that the system isn't protecting the public from criminal matters.

Let me go back to the second point—and this is important because it enters into the feeling on the part of some people that there is one code of justice for the rich and another one for the poor.

The private practitioner with rent to pay, books to buy and secretaries to hire simply could not afford to take the small case for the man whose wife has been high-pressured into signing a contract for an encyclopedia, the other door-to-door things, or a shingle job on the house—often with unconscionable conditions in the fine print. All of these affairs were too small to engage the attention of a practitioner. He simply couldn't afford to take that case.

This is really, basically, no different from a man who has a ruptured appendix or tuberculosis and can't hire a doctor.

Q. Then the Neighborhood Legal Services program is not really new—

A. It is new as a federally financed program, but not in fundamentals. We've now come to accept the idea that society is going to take care of these problems.

. . .

Problems in Legal-Aid Programs

Q. Why are these programs under so much criticism?

A. Now we're in the transition stage—from the individual lawyer doing this as a service to the society and to his profession, to putting it on a more efficient and highly organized basis, really. . . .

In modern terms, it is a matter of delivery of legal assistance. We're in the transition period, and, like any tooling-up for a new process, whether in a factory or in public administration, it isn't very efficient in the beginning. This program attracts young, idealistic lawyers, and sometimes they have more zeal and adrenalin than judgment and skill. This naturally creates tensions and friction. But that will pass. The program needs idealistic young people, but it needs seasoned and experienced lawyers in the management.

What we as a society have said now is that the "poor"—people who can't afford lawyers—can go to the Neighborhood Legal Services. And if there is some law about

his medical aid or his Social Security or whatever and he thinks this is discriminating against his particular problem in some way, legal assistance is now furnished to him to settle his problem and, if necessary, test that out in the courts. And if a court decides that he's right, I have difficulty seeing how we can quarrel with that result.

There is nothing new or revolutionary about testing laws and rights in the courts. Surely it is a more sensible solution than the picket line, a demonstration or a riot.

. . .

Q. What does the Judicial Conference do?

A. That body functions somewhat as a board of directors for the entire federal judicial system—a "general staff" might be another term for it, except that it's a part-time function of all the members.

I might say parenthetically it is becoming an increasing burden for these judges to carry.

In addition, the Chief Justice, by law, is chairman of the Federal Judicial Center, recently set up by Congress primarily as a research arm to study problems of the kind we're discussing here today, and also to carry on training programs for court personnel—judges, court clerks, probation officers, magistrates and others.

The Judicial Conference and the Judicial Center have more than 25 committees dealing with our problems, and I must try to keep informed as to what they are doing and what they ought to be doing.

So I am involved in all of these activities —and increasingly so, I find. These matters take approximately one third of my working hours.

Q. When did you begin to see your function in this light?

A. I decided immediately on taking office that the time to begin was then and there, and the means was co-operation with the legal profession.

The American Bar Association now has about 150,000 members in, I think, 1,700 State and local bar associations around the country. It is a grass-roots organization in every sense. The association has done monumental work in improving criminal justice and in other fields.

Q. What percentage of the legal professions is that?

A. I don't know, but it has increased so rapidly that I would say it must be in the neighborhood of half of all the actively practicing lawyers in the country.

The American Bar Association is not the ultraconservative, dormant, ceremonial organization that it perhaps was 35 or 40 years ago. It is a very dynamic organization, and if it puts its will and its force and its influence behind any particular activity, the odds are it will get done.

Witness the court-administrator program: Have you ever seen lawyers or judges move that fast before?

I made the speech on August 10. I drew a rough blueprint for the program while I was on a vacation in September. We had the first meetings in October, and on Dec. 7, 1969, the final meeting approving the structure, selecting a director and setting up the plan of operations was completed. In May of 1970 the classes of a six months' course opened at the University of Denver.

Q. Are you saying that could not have been done without the American Bar Association?

A. That couldn't have been done—there wasn't a chance of getting that done—without the prestige and the power of the American Bar Association, the American Judicature Society and the Institute of Judicial Administration, as cosponsors. They selected a board of directors, and Herbert Brownell, former Attorney General, was selected chairman of the board. James Webb, former NASA Administration; John Macy, former Civil Service Chairman, and some other very distinguished lawyers and judges are on the board.

This is the best illustration of how I can be helpful in getting these things done. If I ask the American Bar Association to take on a responsibility, I find that if it is reasonable, if it makes sense to them, they will get the task done. And the ABA can draw many organizations into a collective program, partly because most of the leaders of other lawyer organizations are also leaders of the ABA.

Q. A lot of people are going to be surprised to learn that the Chief Justice is as active as he is in all these other functions. Is this a proper role?

A. I've had a few letters questioning—but, very, very few.

Q. How do you answer?

A. Well, usually I answer them and ask: "Who do you suggest will do it? If I don't do it, who will?" Some people have written back and said, in essence, "I now see this, and I was wrong. Thank you very much and keep on going." However, the overwhelming volume of mail is warmly favorable and very encouraging.

Q. When the federal courts have a financial problem—a budgetary problem—do you have direct access to Congress?

A. Not really—except to do it in a formal way in a budget request, which isn't a very eloquent way of arguing your case. It seems to be against tradition for me to appear before the Appropriations Committee to support my requests, and this is probably sound. I doubt the need for a personal appearance in the conventional sense. If we make out a good case in writing, I am confident Congress will co-operate. They are as much interested in justice as judges—and they are much closer to the people.

Q. Do you think, from a technological standpoint, that the Supreme Court machinery has fallen behind the times?

A. Yes, in certain respects, although I would not put it in quite those terms. The equipment—the machinery in the broader sense than hardware—just isn't there. And some of our methods are not adequate for the present volume of cases. We have a need for the kind of modern equipment most government agencies and all successful businesses use.

We have almost nothing but the most primitive basic equipment. At least 25 employees still use manual, nonelectric typewriters. We had no efficient, modern copying machine until recently. Justices read thousands of pages of carbon copies of legal memos each year—typed with 10 copies on very thin paper. These memos were called "flimsies" and, of course, were terribly difficulty to read. We now have two modern copiers, and no Justice reads a seventh, eighth or ninth carbon copy.

These are small details, but they are important in our daily work. We are working on other improvements.

Q. How much has the work of the Supreme Court changed in recent years?

A. It has changed in volume, chiefly. Just consider these figures: In 1940, in the Supreme Court, there were approximately 1,000 cases filed, and in 1970—30 years later —4,400. The projection for 1975 is 5,629.

We now project 7,182 cases in 1980. Before that—long before that—the work of the Supreme Court of the United States will either break down or it will deteriorate in quality so that its historic role will not be performed adequately.

Q. Do you mean the Court by 1975 will be so inundated by work that the whole system will just stop at the top?

A. No, it won't stop. I think what will happen is we'll keep on going but the quality of the work will progressively deteriorate.

Q. What do you think should be done?

A. The entire jurisdiction of the Supreme Court should be carefully studied.

One example is the volume of three-judge district courts which deal with constitutional claims. Those courts are specially convened and are a mixture of three trial and appellate judges. Direct appeal to the Supreme Court is allowed. These cases are an enormous burden in some circuits and a burden on the Supreme Court. Few cases, except in limited emergencies, should ever go directly to the Supreme Court from federal district court. Cases should go through the courts of appeal. This is just one example.

The Supreme Court of the United States cannot perform its constitutional and historic function if it must review over 4,000 cases a year and hear arguments in 150 to 160. Some screening process must take this crushing burden off nine men and spread it over a greater number in other courts.

We can expand and enlarge the other federal courts. We have more than doubled the number of district and circuit judges in recent years, but the Supreme Court probably cannot effectively operate if we increase it to 12 or 18 or 24. So the only solution is to limit the volume of cases.

Q. What about other courts?

A. This matter of modernizing equipment and methodology is the sort of overhaul that's needed all up and down the line. It's true in most of the Senate systems, too.

Q. Should there be an intermediate review court?

A. I'm not sure what the solution is, but we must do something—and do it very, very soon.

For example, when I tried to find out in the last year how many automobile cases there were in all the State courts in the country, there was no reliable place where that information is gathered. I wanted to find out how many jurors were used in all the State court systems and what the cost was, but there was no place I could find that information.

Q. Do you need a central agency to serve all the States?

A. Yes, definitely—a clearinghouse of information—very important information, available to all courts. We need some kind of national judicial center.

There's no great reason, for example, why there should be an enormous disparity in the salaries of judges of various States, nor in the method of selection and the tenure. And here again, the legal profession can do something about that.

But if we had this central establishment —and I think the American bar will do something on this before too long—we could make many improvements. The Institute of Judicial Administration at New York University has tried to do this task, but it is underfinanced and understaffed and cannot meet all the demands.

State Judges: Underpaid

Q. Are most State judges still elected?

A. Most of them are. And you can't expect to get first-class supreme-court judges in the States at $16,500 or $20,000 a year except by great personal sacrifice by these men. State judicial salaries range from $16,500 to $40,000. That is an unfair situation.

Q. It sounds as though you agree that some critics are on the right track when they compain that the judicial system in this country is out of date—

A. It's very much out of date. It is literally true that, as to procedure, if you could get John Adams, Alexander Hamilton and Thomas Jefferson and bring them back— you wouldn't even have to give them a haircut—all they would need would be about a two-day briefing over at the Federal Judicial Center, and they could walk into court in Washington, D.C., or St. Paul or San Francisco and try a case.

There is value to continuity, but that's carrying continuity and stability a little bit far. Can you think of where we'd be if hospitals and doctors were still using techniques, drugs and equipment of 30 years ago?

Q. Mr. Chief Justice, do you envision a big expansion in the number of federal courts?

A. I hope not. I would rather see a contraction of jurisdiction.

Some people seemed to think that at St. Louis I believed that pollution cases and consumer cases should be kept out of the federal courts. That isn't what I said at all.

I said if Congress is going to pass new statutes relating to pollution control and new statutes about consumer actions, it had better at the same time think of the impact on the federal courts, try to put some calipers on it and say, "Well, this will take x number of additional judges over the period of the next five years" and start feeding them in, plus additional court reporters—who are harder to find than judges. You don't have much trouble finding judges, but court reporters are almost impossible to find.

What I was pointing to was the relationship: that if you're going to do one, you've

got to do the other. We must give the workman his tools.

Beyond that there is indeed a question. Some people glibly assume that all pollution cases and class actions belong in federal courts. That is a simplistic notion on a very complex problem. Some of those cases will involve federal questions properly for federal courts, but many can better be treated in State courts.

Generalizations are not very constructive.

Electronic Recording of Trials

Q. That raises still another question— the use of electronic recording of trial proceedings as a supplement or substitute for traditional court reporting. What about that?

A. There has been much research and experimentation in that field. But to rely entirely on voice recording dealing with testimony in which every word and nuance may be crucial presents problems: First, the equipment must be improved; second, the operator probably must be a trained court reporter; and, third, lawyers and judges must change their habits of courtroom performance.

For example, the judge, witnesses and lawyers must become microphone-conscious, and the starting point will be to put each lawyer in something like the witness box so that he cannot move out of range of the microphone, wandering about the courtroom. These are a few of the problems, but they are all open to solution.

Q. Will it be possible to get lawyers and judges to make these changes?

A. It will take some monumental efforts, but it must be done.

Q. What happens if we just drag along as we have?

A. Well, as with all archaic methods and procedures, it's somewhat like a car that you keep on running and don't repair or put any oil in it and don't buy new tires: Finally, that car just stops. And that's what will happen.

We're breaking down in spots. In New

York City, the recent outbreaks of violence in the jails really resulted in part from the fact that the city had a great pile-up of people confined and couldn't get them to trial.

Q. Haven't they had repeated increases in the number of judges in New York?

A. I believe so. This is why the organization-and-system aspect has got to be emphasized. Judges without system and organization—and expert staffs—are a bit like an army with no leaders and no discipline.

Here we have a completely new space science, new in the highest twentieth-century sense—we've trained 58 astronauts in less than 10 years—and yet we think we're doing well because for the first time in our history we're just getting the first formally trained court administrators in this country on Dec. 12, 1970.

I don't mean to say there aren't any good court administrators now. There are, but I think it would be fair to say there are no more than a dozen or so—and they have trained themselves.

Q. Many complaints about the conduct of the Supreme Court have hinged on the extensive summer recesses of the Court. Is that a valid complaint?

A. This is really part of the American folklore. The other day I called the Clerk of the Court and asked him to take a typical week of last summer—any week—and let me see the briefs and petitions filed so that I could see what was assigned to each Justice in any week from the time we recessed on June 30 until the first week of October.

I had made my own guess that it would be the equivalent of a stack of ordinary paperback books about two feet high. I was off the mark. It was nearly three feet high. This is what is sent to every Justice every week. I had estimated the summer filings at 80 cases a week. It turned out to be precisely 99 cases each week.

Q. Just during the so-called vacation?

A. Yes. And those cases must be processed in the sense that, one way or another, each Justice must familiarize himself with each case so that at the conference the

first week in October each Justice is ready to vote.

During those summer months, 1,186 cases came in after we stopped hearings—after we went on that "vacation" we read about. Of course, that term "vacation" is used in the legal sense, but now people have come to think of it as playing golf or lying on a beach somewhere.

Q. On what do you base your view that these extra burdens are part of the function of a Chief Justice?

A. It is really as much necessity as it is a matter of choice. Realistically, if the Chief Justice of the United States doesn't try to bring about progress on these things I've been talking about, they aren't going to be done very fast.

An Attorney General of the United States could get attention, but these are not his problems. He is not the minister of justice; he's an advocate for the Government. Probably, if an Attorney General undertook to deal with these problems, judges might resist his efforts.

The absence of some official who is the counterpart of the Lord Chancellor in England is very sharply in focus for me. The Lord Chancellor in England is the highest judicial officer, but he devotes only a limited time to purely judicial duties. He is also Speaker of the House of Lords and a member of the Prime Minister's Cabinet. Thus, he has access and constant communication with all three branches of government and can keep the executive and legislative branches fully informed on almost a day-to-day basis.

Such an officer is not possible under our concept of separation of powers, and that is why I proposed in St. Louis that Congress create a permanent Federal Judiciary Council appointed one third by Congress, one third by the President and one third by the Judicial Conference of the U.S. This Council, with a small staff, could establish the three-way communication now absent on all problems of the courts on which Congress and the President share responsibility.

One more thing: The office of the Chief Justice desperately needs a high-level administrative deputy or assistant. I devote four to six hours a day on administrative matters apart from my judicial work, and it is not possible—not physically possible—to continue this schedule very long.

Q. Can you give a concrete example of what this Council and this administrative deputy would do?

A. The Council staff would review existing federal jurisdiction, co-operating with congressional staffs, the Attorney General and the Federal Judicial Center, and recommend changes to divert some direct appeals away from the Supreme Court and to the courts of appeal. It would examine all new legislation to make sure resort to federal courts was sound, as a matter of policy. When federal jurisdiction was significantly enlarged, it would measure the projected need for more judges and staffs.

The administrative deputy to the Chief Justice would work closely with this Council, with the Federal Judicial Center and its committees and the Judicial Conference of the U.S. and its committees and with the Administrative Office of the United States Courts. In short, he would do what the Chief Justice would do if he had no cases to hear and decide. There are more than 20 standing and special committees the Chief Justice should keep up with. He cannot do it adequately in a 24-hour day, but a highly qualified assistant could do so and keep the Chief Justice informed and take important policy questions to him for decision.

Today, as we sit here in this discussion, a crisis approaching a breakdown is in sight in the Fifth Circuit that embraces all the Gulf States from Texas to Key West, Fla., plus Georgia and South Carolina. Their case load increases 10 per cent to 20 per cent each year, and they simply cannot continue to cope with it. A Federal Judiciary Council of the kind I advocate would have moved on this years ago.

I have been in the courts of almost every country of Europe except Spain, Portugal and the Iron Curtain countries. I've seen something of how they work and how, even though we may think that our system is very much better in many areas, there is much we can learn from some of them.

In England, a patent case, for example, is not tried with a jury. They have not tried civil cases with a jury in England for 35 years, except libel and slander cases.

When they try a patent case, the judge has a great flexibility, and if the case involves new spacecraft problems or chemical engineering or airplanes, the judge will get a physicist or a chemical engineer or an aeronautical expert, and they sit on either side of him and they decide the case together. They probably finish the trial in a fraction of the time we would require.

Q. Do the men at the judge's side decide the facts and he decides the law?

A. Essentially that is about the way it works. We don't have that kind of flexibility.

Q. Should a recidivist—a man who is convicted time after time—be automatically sentenced to life imprisonment with no opportunity for parole?

A. This raises two points: the mandatory-sentence problem and the permanent incarceration of the chronic repeater or incurable recidivist—the three or four-time loser, for example.

First, the mandatory sentence is no solution for anything. The mandatory sentences that are written into the statutes are one of the impediments, not one of the assets, to the administration of criminal justice.

The indeterminate sentence is much the better system, and yet the public response to rising crime is often: "Double the sentence." What it does is make it harder sometimes to get a conviction and harder to get the conviction affirmed by an appellate court. So that solution doesn't do it.

We may have to come to something similar to the system used in some Northern European countries where courts decide that a chronic offender is a hazard and he is confined until they think he is safe to rejoin society. This can be a long, long time. Of course, that's easier in a small country operating under a central government.

Q. What kinds of institutions are the incurable offenders confined in?

A. Generally speaking, they have no high-security institutions. They use open prisons, penal farms in which all inmates keep busy. It would be fairly easy to escape, but it isn't very useful to escape from a prison in Holland or Denmark, for example, because the prisoner has almost nowhere to go. With all the stringent passport and travel limitations, he can be picked up very easily. As a result, they have no prisons in the sense that we do.

Q. What about prison personnel?

A. The prison guards in our country pretty generally are poorly trained and poorly paid. They're very often patronage jobs, but almost at the bottom rung of the political ladder. In Northern Europe, men in these jobs are carefully screened, substantially trained and paid well—perhaps proportionately one and a half or two times as well paid as is a guard in a State prison in this country.

Q. Does the European system rehabilitate a convict?

A. It does a much better job than ours does, but it isn't perfect. There is no perfect solution in this business. Anybody who ever thinks there is is deceiving himself. In these older societies they are more philosophical —less impatient than we are. But they are firm with the so-called incurable or incorrigible offenders. They have many centuries of experience; we have only two.

I have visited many prisons here and abroad. If you want a depressing experience, visit a State prison on a Saturday, particularly, when the prisoners' work is over for the week. There are exceptions as to some States.

If any one of you were running the institution, you would see to it that the inmates—mostly young men—had a ball field and volley-ball courts and other exercise facilities. Absolutely nothing in most of these places. These young fellows are just lounging around, sitting, vegetating. Many of them are confined two to a tiny cell that was built to hold one man before the time of the Civil War.

If we set out on a deliberate program to brutalize and dehumanize people and produce more criminals, this would be the way to do it.

Q. Do you think that's typical of our penal institutions?

A. Unfortunately, yes. There are exceptions.

California is an example. When Earl Warren was Governor, he completely reformed the whole penal system. But even there the growth of the State and increase in crime are giving them many new problems.

Wisconsin has an excellent system.

Q. Is one of the problems that people will not vote the tax money for prison reform?

A. Yes, but they're paying more without it and don't realize it. It's a hidden tax that is enormous, and the public must be made aware of it. Look, for example, at the growth of private police forces. Financial journals report that costs have now reached a figure of over 2 billion dollars a year for private policing, plant protection, neighborhood patrols and office buildings. This is an indirect cost every person helps pay— and there are many other indirect costs of inadequate correction systems.

Q. Mr. Chief Justice, to return for a moment to the matter of being labeled an "activist" in your nonjudicial affairs, is there a danger that in the public mind this will be associated with your attitude on the bench?

A. That is possible, but as with a pudding the final test will be the taste. Someone must make these problems of the courts known to the public so that intelligent choices can be made. This, to me, is one of the functions of those who carry the responsibility.

I expect—on the basis of many letters— that State chief justices will become more articulate on these problems. Perhaps Governors and the Congress, even though overwhelmed with other problems, will give more thought to the needs of the judicial systems. I am optimistic enough to believe so.

8

Is the Supreme Court Attempting Too Much?

ROBERT G. McCLOSKEY

The Warren Court was a most active one, with many accomplishments to its credit in the field of civil rights and civil liberties. Some, indeed, think it took on more than a court should. There are two sides to this question. What is proper in a democracy for such a body to attempt? Another is the problem of what is practical for an agency that has no troops or finances available to effectuate its decisions. This provocative study by Robert McCloskey attempts to analyze the potential assets and liabilities of the Court, and ways of viewing legal power.

. . .

Historical generalizations are almost always either contestable or obvious. The first one offered here may strike some readers as open to doubt and others as self-evident. It is that the Court of the past dozen years has developed "judicial activism" to a degree that at least matches the record of the "Old Court" of the 1920's and 1930's and that certainly exceeds the record of any other Court in our constitutional history. When we reflect that the American Supreme Court has, since Marshall, been by long odds the most potent court in the world, this statement about modern judicial tendencies can be seen in all its implications. We might say, paraphrasing Mr. Churchill, that only once before in history has a judicial tribunal tried to influence so many so much.

. . . [T]he Warren Court appears to have succeeded impressively in freeing itself from the self-doubts that deterred constitutional development during the 1940–1953 period. With a zeal that seemed to increase as the years went by, the Justices have advanced boldly along the civil rights front. A variety of new subjects—e.g., libel

From Robert McCloskey, "Reflections on the Warren Court," Virginia Law Review, 1965, pp. 1233, 1247, 1249, 1263. Reprinted by permission of the publisher.

and censorship laws, the right to travel, the postal power—have been brought within their purview. Old doctrines that offered a pretext for judicial inaction, like the doctrine of "political questions" or the "privilege doctrine," have been jettisoned or greatly eroded. . . . The 1920–1936 Court invalidated nearly 200 state acts: its batting average is distinctly the higher, although the Warren Court's performance in this category has improved—if that is the word—in very recent years. . . .

Yet it is arguable that the role of the Warren Court is in some ways still more imposing, that it has attempted even more than its famous predecessor. . . . No Court ever challenged the national will as boldly as did the "Old Court" when it struck at the New Deal, but no Court ever so sharply and hastily backed down as that same tribunal did in 1937. A sequence in which a throne is audaciously claimed in one moment and abdicated in the next can hardly be viewed on the whole as an example of judicial intrepidity. . . .

Beyond that, there is another difference between the nature of the Warren Court's undertakings and those of any Court of the past; and the difference may be crucial to our comparison. Traditionally the Supreme Court has been chiefly concerned with preserving the cake of custom, with telling the people of the nation that they must continue to operate as they were already used to operating. The modern Court has assumed the more affirmative task of breaking old habits, of telling the nation that it must stop doing what it was accustomed to and must start doing something else. It has been trying, that is, not only to forbid certain kinds of governmental and social action, but to bring a different state of affairs, and even a different state of mind, into being.

. . . [W]hat are its prospects for maintaining that claim successfully? This is not, be it noted, the question whether the Court has the *right* so to command America, that is, whether constitutional text and tradition can warrant such regality. Nor is it the somewhat different question whether in terms of democratic theory the judiciary *ought* to be entrusted with such an important part in the moulding of public policy. The issue is a narrower one. . . . Does the Supreme Court have enough such power to play its modern self-assigned role as a major initiative-supplying agency of modern government?

There are in the current sense some legitimate grounds for doubt about the Court's power to play the momentous part it has chosen, and there have been some danger signals. For one thing it may be that "judicial realism" has eroded the traditional mystique that often lent support to Court authority in other days. For more than half a century scholars and judges have been repudiating the mythology that the Court is merely the impersonal voice of indisputable constitutional verities, and have been emphasizing that the judicial process involves an element of free choice based on policy judgments. . . . [T]he modern Court is bereft of another kind of backing which historically sustained it: the active support of the business community and related elements such as commercial lawyers and the conservative press. . . . [F]or the past twenty-five years the Justices have been making it abundantly plain that the Constitution is no longer a refuge for disgruntled property holders, and have turned their sympathy to other objects—to Negroes

and other disadvantaged minorities, to religious and political dissenters, to persons accused of crime. However morally justifiable this shift may be, it has meant that the business community no longer rises to the Court's defense with its old enthusiasm, and this loss of a powerful traditional ally is not a small matter in an assessment of the present Court's capabilities.

. . . [T]he Court, like other governing bodies, must maintain a favorable balance between the forces that bolster its authority and those that oppose it—between friends and enemies, to put the matter bluntly. No doubt its capital of public support, deriving from the American tradition of respect for the judiciary, is sufficient to counterbalance the disaffection evoked by a certain number of commands that vex those who are commanded. Though the Justices drew very heavily on that capital in the desegregation decisions, this alone was not too heavy a withdrawal for the Court's prestige to stand. But since then the Warren Court has gathered in a whole series of further commitments in fields like criminal procedure, school religious practices, censorship and the rest; and it is arguable that each commitment has strained the capital a little further. Each one, that is, has augmented the accumulating mass of judicial enforcement problems, has created a new and additional body of critics and adversaries.

. . .

Yet there is an argument to be made on the other side: there are considerations lending some support to a belief that the modern Court's power is equal to its aspirations. In the first place it is of course possible that the balance between friends and adversaries has been redressed on both sides. . . . Perhaps the losses are partially compensated by an increase of amicability among those who approve recent judicial policies—that is, Negroes and Northern liberals of various types. . . .

Ironically enough, their ranks seem to have been strengthened at least temporarily by the 1964 election. Not for many years has a presidential candidate criticized the Court as sharply as Mr. Goldwater did. He chose to make the judiciary a secondary but significant campaign issue, and Mr. Johnson's overwhelming victory could thus be interpreted, rightly or wrongly, as an implied vindication of the Court. . . . Sometimes the right enemy is as valuable as a friend.

In still another way the march of recent political events may have improved the Court's position. In the analysis above I have emphasized the scope and the cumulative weight of the tasks which the Warren Court has assumed. . . . [T]he heaviest load the Court has borne throughout most of this time was the responsibility for coping with the issue of racial discrimination. For almost ten years this arduous matter, surely the most formidable of modern domestic problems, was left virtually untouched by presidents and congresses; insofar as a national governmental policy was developing, it was being fashioned by the judiciary alone. But in very recent years, the other two branches have at length bestirred themselves to take the problem in hand, and the result has been a lightening of the Court's total burden. . . .

These considerations favoring an optimistic prognosis bring to mind another, more general speculation about the nature of current American political opinion and the relationship of the Court to American public attitudes. In reviewing the factors that might give pause to judicial activists, I have assumed *arguendo* that the Court's power to command America is in the nature of a capital fund which is diminished by each expenditure of power; and further that the potential alignment of supporters and opponents for a given judicial policy is relatively fixed. But this reckons without the possibility that the Court's political environment is more dynamic than static. It may not be true that power is automatically depleted in proportion to its exertion. Not only is it likely, as already mentioned, that a policy judgment will make friends as well as enemies in the short run. There is also the possibility that the analogy of a capital fund is faulty, that in the long run the assertion of power will to some extent augment power. Perhaps a sweeping judicial claim of authority helps generate a disposition to accept that authority; perhaps the habit of command tends to produce a habit of obedience.

9

The New Activism Under Fire

ALPHEUS T. MASON

Another legal scholar finds McCloskey too pessimistic and negative, and thinks the Warren Court's achievements representative of the best tradition of American democracy. How much can the Court do, as suggested by these discussions? Would Mason advocate the Court undertake all creativity in the system? Where would he find limits on judicial power?

The New Activism Under Fire

. . . [T]he Warren Court's brand of judicial activism has impressive title

From Alpheus T. Mason, "Judicial Activism," Virginia Law Review, 55, No. 3 (April 1969), 385–426. Reprinted by permission of the publisher.

deeds. Nevertheless, a highly articulate minority, led by Justices Harlan and Black, is convinced that the majority is headed toward the same precipice from which the Hughes Court, under pressure from Congress, the President and the country, narrowly saved itself in 1937.[1]

The current attack indeed recalls F.D.R.'s bombardment. But surely the interests and values involved and the Court's responsibility toward them differ significantly. In 1935–36 a narrow, headstrong majority, flounting persistent pleas for judicial self-restraint voiced by a highly esteemed minority, blocked government regulation of the economy. In the hands of an obtuse majority, the Constitution became a straitjacket rather than what Woodrow Wilson said it should be—"a vehicle of the nation's life." The Warren Court, on the other hand, is expanding the limits of freedom, buttressing the moral foundations of society, keeping open peaceful alternatives to violent change.

Reflecting on the judicial activism of the 1920's, Professor Frankfurter noted:

That a majority of the Court which frequently disallowed restraints upon economic power should so consistently have sanctioned restraints of the mind is perhaps only a surface paradox. There is an underlying unity between fear of ample experimentation in economics and fear of expression of heretical ideas.[2]

It seems odd that this remarkable insight into the subtleties of judicial activism should not have always enlightened Justice Frankfurter's opinions.

Thanks to the Warren Court the plea implicit in Frankfurter's words has been answered. Ideas, good, bad and indifferent, have a chance to make their influence felt. The Supreme Court provides disgruntled

individuals and minorities a peaceful forum in which to air their grievances and perhaps win vindication. Madison and Hamilton did not deny the moral right of revolution, but they argued strenuously that under the proposed constitution the occasions for resort to violence would be reduced to a minimum.[3] John F. Kennedy sensed the Framers' underlying thought: "[T]hose who make peaceful revolution impossible will make violent revolution inevitable."[4]

Through judicial review, "revolution" has, in some measure, been domesticated.[5] Change can be and indeed has been accomplished within the four corners of the Con-

---

[1] In his dissent in the *Tinker* case . . . Justice Black stated: There was at one time a line of cases holding "reasonableness" as the court saw it to be the test of a "due process" violation. Two cases upon which the Court today heavily relies for striking down these school orders used this test of reasonableness, *Meyers* [sic] *v. Nebraska,* 262 U.S. 390 (1923) and *Bartells v. Iowa,* 262 U.S. 404 (1923). . . . This constitutional test of reasonableness prevailed in this Court for a season. It was this test that brought on President Franklin Roosevelt's well-known Court fight. Tinker v. Des Moines School Dist., 89 S. Ct. 733, 743 (1969) (Black, J., dissenting).

[2] F. Frankfurter, *Mr. Justice Holmes and the Supreme Court* 62 (1938).

[3] See A. Mason, *The Supreme Court: Palladium of Freedom,* 41–45 (1962).

[4] Quoted in T. Sorensen, *Kennedy,* 535 (1965). In his separate opinion in Bell v. Maryland, 378 U.S. 226, 242–45 (1964), Justice Douglas put the late President's thought in a judicial context:

The people should know that when filibusters occupy other forums, when oppressions are great, when the clash of authority between the individual and the State is severe, they can still get justice in the courts. When we default, as we do today, the prestige of the law in the life of the Nation is weakened.

The increase, especially during the 1967–68 term, of cases in which the Court has refused to face up to the problems of cities, race, poverty and Vietnam, appears strange in an activist Court. See Henkin, *Foreword: The Supreme Court, 1967 Term,* 82 HARV. L. REV. 63, 88–89 (1968) for a list of cases relating to Vietnam. In the most notable instance, Mora v. McNamara, 389 U.S. 934 (1967), Justices Douglas and Stewart protested the majority's denial of certiorari in a case that would have tested the President's power to wage an undeclared war. Three soldiers had rejected duty in Vietnam, contending that the war was illegal and immoral. Said Justice Stewart:

These are large and deeply troubling questions. . . . We cannot make these problems go away simply by refusing to hear the case of three obscure Army privates. I intimate not even tentative views upon any of these matters, but I think the Court should squarely face them by granting certiorari and setting this case for oral argument.

[5] Jefferson, in later years a bitter critic of the Court, advocated "[binding] up the several branches of government by certain laws, which, when they transgress, their acts become nullities. . . ." Such a system, he suggested, would "render unnecessary an appeal to the people, or in

stitution. Adolf Berle calls his books on the Warren Court "a report on a revolution." "The unique fact is," Berle writes, "that the revolutionary committee is the Supreme Court of the United States." Far from condemning the Court's exercise of "senior legislative power . . . particularly in the field of education and local government," he believes "it could not have acted otherwise," and maintains that history will probably record that "the Supreme Court's action saved the country from a far more dangerous and disorderly change." [6]

In a free society, majorities—and this is the key point of democratic theory—are in flux. Tomorrow's majority may have a different composition as well as different goals. Defense of the political rights of minorities thus becomes not the antithesis of majority rule but its very foundation. The majority must leave open the political channels by which it can be replaced when it is no longer able to command popular support. The alternative is violent overthrow—revolution. By protecting the integrity and unimpeded operation of the entire process by which majorities are formed, "a bevy of Platonic Guardians" [7] becomes a surrogate for revolution, contributing positively to the preservation of a free society.

New-style judicial activism casts doubt on the accuracy of Justice Frankfurter's dictum that courts are not "a good reflex of a democratic society." More sensitive to recognized wrongs than either the executive or legislative branches of government, the Warren Court "has spearheaded the progress in civil rights, administration of criminal justice, protection of individual liberty, and the strengthening and extension of political democracy." [8] In the ab-

stract, it would have been better if encroachments on individual freedom such as Connecticut's anti-contraceptive statute, Virginia's poll tax and the police-state methods used in law enforcement, could have been remedied by the state legislatures. But remedies had not been forthcoming and the prospects for their appearance were dim. As in the areas of school desegregation, reapportionment and administration of criminal justice, failure of the states to protect individual liberties or undertake corrective measures drove the Court, sometimes in the face of delimiting precedents, into untrodden fields.

. . .

Thus the issue becomes whether modern America is willing to run the risks to which the Constitution's Framers committed us— dangers inescapable in a free society. Are Americans willing to take the risk that in enforcing the precautions set out in the Bill of Rights to prevent punishment of the innocent, some criminals will escape? [9] Are we willing to take the chance that dissenters will exceed the bounds of reason? Are we willing, in short, to risk radical change in the organization and structure of government itself? In a simpler agrarian age, Jefferson was willing to take that chance.

. . .

In the face of this background, certain commentators and Supreme Court Justices resist the positive, creative approach. Carl Swisher insists that "[l]eadership in constitutional development must come through the legislative and executive branches." [10] For him the judicial duty is merely to "refine, restrain, and harmonize. . . . [The Court] cannot safely take over the task of leadership without threat of disaster both for itself and for the country. . . ." [11] Jus-

---

other words a rebellion, on every infraction of their rights. . . ." *Notes on Virginia,* 2 *The Writings of Thomas Jefferson,* 178 (Memorial ed. 1903) (Jefferson was speaking of the government of Virginia).

[6] A. Berle, *The Three Faces of Power,* vii, viii (1967).

[7] L. Hand, *The Bill of Rights,* 73 (1958).

[8] A. Cox, *The Warren Court: Constitutional Decision As An Instrument of Reform* 4 (1968).

[9] During his CBS television interview, December 3, 1968, Justice Black was asked whether recent Supreme Court decisions had made it more difficult for police to combat crime. "Certainly," the Justice replied firmly. "Why shouldn't they? That is what the Bill of Rights was intended to do." *N.Y. Times,* Dec. 4, 1968, at 30, col. 3.

[10] Swisher, *"Dred Scott One Hundred Years After,"* 19 *Journal of Politics,* 167, 183 (1957).

[11] *Ibid.*

tice Frankfurter declared that the Judiciary is not the place for " 'originators of transforming thought'. . . ." [12] His ideological successor, Justice Harlan, mirrored this declaration in his recent expression of shock at the Court's application of the "one man, one vote" principle to malapportioned local governments:

I am frankly astonished at the ease with which the Court has proceeded to fasten upon the entire country at its lowest political levels the strong arm of the federal judiciary, let alone a particular political ideology which has been the subject of wide debate and differences from the beginnings of our Nation.[13]

The Paradox of Activism

Whatever the values involved, judicial activism results in a paradox at the heart of constitutional interpretation. While wearing the magical habiliments of the law, the Justices take sides on controversial issues. The Court must face up to the political implications of judicial review and at the same time keep alive the mystery that it is merely declaring the law.

The occult and power aspects of governing are both essential,[14] but mingling them leads to confusing complexities. The Court is both temple and forum, both symbol and instrument of government. The High Bench is the American counterpart of the British Crown, but unlike a queen on the throne, the court has real power. It can bring Congress, President, state governors and legislators to heel.

To render more palatable this oligarchic, occult element in our politics, Supreme Court Justices, including John Marshall, fostered the notion that judges exercise only judgment, not will. "The thrill is irresistible," Judge Cardozo, tongue-in-cheek, commented on Marshall's famous rationalization; "[w]e feel the mystery and awe of inspired revelation." [15] So the mystery was born and consecrated. It has been exposed again and again by the Court's own actions, and yet it survives.

The dilemma judicial activism poses bothers lawyers more than it does political scientists.[16] It has been suggested that Herbert Wechsler's famous lecture, *Toward Neutral Principles of Constitutional Law*,[17] reflects the lawyer's nostalgia for legalism, underscores his reluctance to recognize the political nature of the Court's function. "The dilemma is insoluble," Archibald Cox observes. It may be eased, Cox suggests, "by preserving the power of judge-made law to command consent while at the same time changing it to serve the new and newly felt needs of the community and the demands of individual justice." [18]

The difficulty of fusing myth and reality in Supreme Court decisions is measured

[12] Frankfurter, *"John Marshall and the Judicial Function,"* in *Of Law and Men,* 6 (P. Elman, ed., 1956).

[13] Avery v. Midland County, 390 U.S. 474, 490 (1968) (Harlan, J., dissenting).

[14] Walter Bagehot classifies the institutions of the British government as "efficient" and "dignified," the former being the Cabinet and Parliament, the latter the King or Queen. Those elements in the governing process which "excite most easy reverence," Bagehot writes, "[are] the *theatrical* elements . . . [t]hat which is mystic in its claims; that which is occult in its mode of action." W. Bagehot, *The English Constitution,* 76 (rev. ed. 1872). To regard the Court merely as an instrument of power might limit its effectiveness. "Without a constant and sincere pursuit of the shining but never completely attainable ideal of the rule of law above men," Thurman Arnold writes, "we would not have a civilized government. If that ideal be an illusion, to dispel it would cause men to lose themselves in an even greater illusion, the illusion that personal power can be benevolently exercised." Arnold, *"Professor Hart's Theology,"* 73, *Harv. L. Rev.* 1298, 1311 (1960).

[15] B. Cardozo, *Law and Literature,* 11 (1931). Cardozo's remark was in reaction to Marshall's incredible observation: "Judicial power is never exercised for the purpose of giving effect to the will of the Judge; always for the purpose of giving effect to the will of the . . . law." Osborn v. Bank of the United States, 22 U.S. (9 Wheat.) 738, 866 (1824).

[16] M. Shapiro, *Law and Politics in the Supreme Court* 14 (1964). See Mason, *"Myth and Reality in Supreme Court Decisions,"* 48, *Va. L. Rev.* 1385 (1962); Deutsch, *"Neutrality, Legitimacy and the Supreme Court: Some Interactions between Law and Political Science,"* 20 *Stan. L. Rev.* 169 (1968).

[17] 73, *Harv. L. Rev.* 1 (1959).

[18] A. Cox, *The Warren Court: Constitutional Decision As An Instrument of Reform* 22–23 (1968).

by the fact that for ammunition against judicial activism, whatever its orientation, the most resourceful arsenal is the dissenting opinion. "Every Justice," the late Justice Jackson observed, "has been accused of legislating and every one has joined in that accusation of others. . . ."[19] In 1937, F.D.R. drew his most telling weapons from the opinions of Brandeis and Stone. And in the 1960's one need not descend to the blunderbuss of George Wallace or Strom Thurmond for criticism of the Court; one need only read the dissenting opinions, particularly those of Justices Black and Harlan.

However, not all the dissenters from the Court's activist opinions are cut from the same mold. The process of constitutional adjudication is a continuous search for the appropriate balance between "reason" and "fiat," between the oft-conflicting imperatives of deciding "according to law" and of acknowledging compelling social needs. The two activist majorities have struck the balance in certain identifiable ways. But the dissenters, past and present, although objecting with equal vigor to what they deemed majorities functioning as naked power organs, have not advocated the same alternatives. The grounds of dissent—by Holmes, Brandeis and Stone on the one hand, and by Black and Harlan on the other—offer yet another distinction between judicial activism, old and new.

· · ·

A Plea for Judicial Self-Awareness

In a period of unbridled activism Holmes and Brandeis advocated judicial self-restraint. It is well to remember, however, that their advocacy was based upon well-articulated reasons. The judiciary was busily invalidating progressive economic legislation on excessively visceral grounds. Holmes and Brandeis felt compelled to reply to such action. They suggested that the Court should recognize its role as a

partner in the political process[20] and consequently take notice of the social factors necessitating government action. Judicial evaluation of legislation is complex and imprecise; overly simple standards lead to error and self-delusion.

Any statement that Holmes and Brandeis would object to positive judicial action in all seasons is therefore incorrect. It is noteworthy, for example, that citations from their opinions are prominent in Justice Stone's assertion that the Court is obligated to exercise more exacting scrutiny in reviewing statutes affecting human rights than in examining economic legislation.[21] Holmes, Brandeis, Stone and Hand urged judicial self-restraint not because they believed that a judge's preference should not enter law, but because it inevitably did. The sharp barbs of their thought, Justice Stone's in particular, were intended for the flesh of judges, Right and Left, who without taking the trouble to weigh social values, *prematurely* enforced personal conviction as law. Awareness of the subjective element, inescapable in the judging process, must end in curbing it. Preference and prejudice can be tamed but not eliminated.

[20] The notion that when judges upset "desirable" legislation, the blame rests squarely on the Constitution of 1789, not upon the Justices who at the moment are its interpreters, still has respectable adherents. On this patent self-deception Cardozo commented:

> Judges march at times to pitiless conclusions under the prod of a remorseless logic which is supposed to leave them no alternative. They deplore the sacrificial rite. They perform it, none the less, with averted gaze, convinced as they plunge the knife that they obey the bidding of their office.

B. Cardozo, *The Growth of the Law,* 66 (1924). Before he was himself anointed, Felix Frankfurter was similarly realistic. "[C]onstitutional law," he declared, "is not at all a science, but applied politics." Frankfurter, *"The Zeitgeist and the Judiciary,"* in *Law and Politics,* 6 (1939).

[21] In United States v. Carolene Prods., 304 U.S. 144, 152–53 (1938), Stone cited the following opinions by Holmes or Brandeis: Nixon v. Herndon, 273 U.S. 536 (1927) (Holmes); Whitney v. California, 274 U.S. 357, 372 (1927) (Brandeis, J., concurring); Gitlow v. New York, 268 U.S. 652, 672 (1925) (Holmes, J., dissenting).

[19] R. Jackson, *The Supreme Court in the American System of Government,* 80 (Harper Torchbook ed. 1963).

Awareness of self is the first step toward proper exercise of the judicial role.

Such a description of Holmes' constitutional jurisprudence belies placing it in the tradition of James Bradley Thayer, whose 1893 essay [22] was for Justice Frankfurter the most important single piece of writing on American constitutional law. Thayer's essay appeared at the beginning of a period of unparalleled judicial activism in defense of property and contract rights. Judges were determined, he observed, to enlarge their part "in the political conduct of government." [23] In opposition, Thayer argued that judges "can only disregard [an act] when those who have the right to make laws have not merely made a mistake, but have made a very clear one—so clear that it is not open to rational question. . . . [W]hatever [legislative] choice is rational, is constitutional." [24] One might refuse to endorse a proposed bill on constitutional grounds as a legislator but be compelled to uphold the same measure as a judge. Thayer concluded:

If what I have been saying is true, the safe and permanent road towards reform is that of impressing upon our people a far stronger sense than they have of the great range of possible harm and evil that our system leaves open, and must leave open, to the legislatures, and of the clear limits of judicial power; so that responsibility may be brought sharply home where it belongs. The checking and cutting down of legislative power, by numerous detailed prohibitions in the constitution, cannot be accomplished without making the government petty and incompetent. This process has already been carried much too far in some of our States. Under no system can the power of courts go far to save a people from ruin; our chief protection lies elsewhere.[25]

[22] Thayer, "The Origin and Scope of the American Doctrine of Constitutional Law," 7, Harv. L. Rev. 129 (1893).

[23] Ibid. at 152.

[24] Ibid. at 144.

[25] Ibid. at 155–56. Other lawyers, contemporaries of Thayer, took up the cudgels in support of judicial self-restraint during this crucial period. See, e.g., McMurtrie, "The Jurisdiction to Declare Void Acts of Legislation—When Is It Legitimate and When Mere Usurpation of Sovereignty?," 32, Am. L. Reg. 1093 (1893); Reno, "Arbitration and

To Thayer the tendency of judicial activism was to dwarf the political capacity of the people, and to deaden its sense of moral responsibility.[26] But the political process on which his remedy presumably depends may itself become impeded and corrupted, delaying or defeating the relief he assumed would be forthcoming. Similarly, Justice Frankfurter's cure for the inequities of representation was an "informed, civically militant electorate." [27] Like Thayer, he had lost sight of "the auxiliary precautions" which, on the basis of "experience," the Founding Fathers had felt duty bound to provide.

. . .

Under Chief Justice Warren's leadership, the Supreme Court presents a remarkable paradox. In structure and organization the Court is the most oligarchical branch of our government, yet the Justices, by precept and example, provide the primary impetus in bringing us closer to the ideals embodied in the Declaration of Independence. While maintaining the golden mean Chief Justice Marshall thought he had attained,[28] the Supreme Court has become a major creative force in American life.

the Wage Contract," 26, Am. L. Rev. 837 (1892). See generally A. Paul, Conservative Crisis and the Rule of Law (1960).

[26] See Thayer, supra note 22. . . .

[27] Baker v. Carr, 369 U.S. 186, 270 (1962) (Frankfurter, J., dissenting).

[28] In his appraisal Archibald Cox writes:

[T]here will be few who, if they could relive recent history, would choose to exchange closer attention to conventional legal doctrines for the great strides taken under the leadership of the Warren Court in civil rights, the strengthening of democratic self-government, and the administration of criminal justice.

A. Cox, The Warren Court: Constitutional Decision As An Instrument of Reform 23 (1968). "I am confident," Cox concludes, "that historians will write that the trend of decisions during the 1950's and 1960's was in keeping with the mainstream of American history—a bit progressive but also moderate, a bit humane but not sentimental, a bit idealistic but seldom doctrinaire, and in the long run essentially pragmatic—in short, in keeping with the true genius of our institutions." A. Cox, The Warren Court As An Instrument of Reform 133–34 (1968).

UNITED STATES FOREIGN POLICY

This book has thus far treated the United States as a nation living in isolation. We have considered the philosophical assumptions around which American government is organized; we have examined its structure and institutions; we have looked at its informal government devices. But however effective this approach may be for classroom purposes, true perspective is greatly distorted by such a treatment.

The United States is only one nation among many. We live in a world which has over 150 sovereign nations and only fragments of international government. In such a chaotic international scene, national survival itself is at stake. Furthermore, the possibility of withdrawing from the turbulence of world affairs diminishes steadily because of intercontinental ballistic missiles, TV programs, scheduled supersonic flights, and competing probes into outer space. Over 10 per cent of our gross national product is spent each year for national defense.

In the international arena the United States has an uneven balance sheet: in terms of population we have less than 6 per cent of the world's people; in terms of wealth and power we loom as the world's leading nation. Our standard of living is the world's highest, our productive plant is the world's largest, and our military strength, thanks to an advanced technology, is the greatest single force in world affairs.

With such power goes responsibility. Obviously, if our diplomats are committed to preservation of American interests in the contemporary world, those interests need definition. Also, the fate of many other nations is tied to American policy. It has been said that "when the United States sneezes, Europe gets a cold." What is true of Europe is also true for Asia, Africa, and islands of the sea.

America and The World: Which Approach To Foreign Policy?

Prior to World War II, the "Great Debate" over American foreign policy centered around *isolation* or *intervention*. That issue was resolved by the march of events in favor of intervention. Having rejected isolation, the United States moved toward a policy of involvement in every aspect of world affairs. Spurred by the threat of Soviet domination, we were equally concerned with the economic restoration of Western Europe, the politics of the Middle East, and revolutions against the existing order in Asia, Africa, and Latin America. There appeared to be no limits to our intervention on this planet or in outer space.

Today this policy is being called into question. How realistic is it for any nation to assume responsibility as the world's father image? Does the United States have either the power or the wisdom to play such a role? Is there some sort of middle position between isolation and total intervention? Where is the true self-interest of the United States located? How can we, if we wish, gracefully retreat from total involvement? These questions are among those to which Americans address themselves as they forge a foreign policy for the 1970's.

In their search for solutions, some foreign policy spokesmen have become hard-liners, often called "hawks"; others are soft-liners, otherwise known as "doves." Some Americans believe that the United States' moral mission is to spread the doctrine of individual worth and integrity throughout the world. Others dismiss this as gross sentimentality, and insist that the chief role of foreign policy is to protect us from predatory neighbors. Some spokesmen plead for a clear-eyed realism, divorced from ideology, while others insist that the basic United States commitment should be to treaties, alliances, and the growing body of international law.

Such a sample does not exhaust the conflicting philosophies. But the spokesmen and viewpoints presented here are in the mainstream of present United States debates over foreign policy.

The United States and The Communist Bloc: Permanent Hostility or Decreasing Tensions?

One approach to the Communist bloc rests heavily on ideology and the historical record. Advocates of this approach point out that Marx, Lenin, and Stalin agreed that there could be nothing except a strategic truce with world capitalism. Communism is dedicated to the overthrow of other economic-political systems, and is only temporarily diverted from such long-range goals. The foreign policy records of the USSR and Red China confirm this ideological analysis.

Another approach denies the preceding thesis, asserting that the Communist world is not a single massive entity with a single true faith. Rifts and dissension are apparent everywhere. Many third-generation Russian Communists seem eager to grasp the good life of the present, rather than to pursue world revolution.

The conflict between these schools of thought is direct and sharp. Who is right? Can we or should we negotiate with Soviet leaders? Are the American hard-liners actually creating the situation they most fear by refusing to negotiate? Is the Soviet Union an unstable, scheming conspiracy, or do Russian leaders simply work for the best interests of the Soviet Union as they define them?

What position should we take toward the Soviet satellites of Eastern Europe? Was the visit of President Nixon to Peking a shrewd move? Should we open trade negotiations with Poland, Bulgaria, Yugoslavia, and Czechoslovakia? Is there any point to cultural exchange programs with the Soviet Union? Should we negotiate disarmament treaties with Russia? What about Red China? Should her admission to the U.N. be regarded as a U.S. defeat? How far should we go in relaxing trade barriers? Should we "play off" Russia and China against each other? Should we modify our "all out" support of Nationalist China? Which of the above positions are in keeping with a foreign policy for the 1970's?

The Third World: An American Responsibility?

The "Third World" is a convenient term used to describe those countries struggling to become nations in their own right. For the most part they are a segment of neither the permanent Soviet nor United States bloc, although Latin America, which has traditionally been aligned with the United States, is often included in the Third World.

By and large, Third World nations are new and underdeveloped. Over fifty countries are former European colonies that have won their independence since 1945. Most of them share several prominent characteristics of underdevelopment: low level of technology; high birth rate; unstable political institutions; very low gross national product; an economy often centered on one or two natural resources (Kuwait—oil; Congo—copper; Cuba—sugar); endemic disease and poverty; and the concentration of land and wealth in few hands.

What should the relationship of the United States be with this world? One longstanding tradition would have us become responsible for the modernization of these countries so that eventually they will take on the characteristics of Western society. Another theory would deny this responsibility and emphasize economic relationships based on self-interest. Still another theory regards these nations as pawns in an international struggle between the Soviet Union and the United States.

Even if we accept the idea that we are responsible for the modernization of these nations, other questions immediately arise. How do nations modernize? Are there ways of eliminating steps in the historical pattern? Can any outsider speed up the process? Can the institutions of the United States be transplanted into another culture? How does our experience with the Marshall Plan and the Alliance For Progress differ? How has American experience of the past twenty years forced us to rethink our original approach?

1

Old Myths and New Realities

J. W. Fulbright

Senator Fulbright has played a questioning, critical role as Chairman of the Senate Foreign Relations Committee. His great concern, expressed in the following selection, has been that the United States would adopt a moralistic, unswerving course in world affairs. According to Fulbright, what are some "old myths" and "new realities"? What are some "unthinkable thoughts"? Can a nation survive when it is cut loose from moral commitments?

There is an inevitable divergence, attributable to the imperfections of the human mind, between the world as it is and the world as men perceive it. As long as our perceptions are reasonably close to objective reality, it is possible for us to act upon our problems in a rational and appropriate manner. But when our perceptions fail to keep pace with events, when we refuse to believe something because it displeases or frightens us, or is simply startlingly unfamiliar, then the gap between fact and perception becomes a chasm, and action becomes irrelevant and irrational.

There has always—and inevitably—been some divergence between the realities of foreign policy and our ideas about it. This divergence has in certain respects been growing rather than narrowing, and we are handicapped, accordingly, by policies based on old myths rather than current realities. The divergence is dangerous and unnecessary—dangerous because it can re-

duce foreign policy to a fraudulent game of imagery and appearances, unnecessary because it can be overcome by the determination of men in high office to dispel prevailing misconceptions through the candid dissemination of unpleasant but inescapable facts.

. . .

These astonishing changes in the configuration of the postwar world have had an unsettling effect on both public and official opinion in the United States. One reason for this, I believe, lies in the fact that we are a people used to looking at the world, and indeed at ourselves, in moralistic rather than empirical terms. We are predisposed to regard any conflict as a clash between good and evil rather than as simply a clash between conflicting interests. We are inclined to confuse freedom and democracy, which we regard as moral principles, with the way in which they are practiced in America—with capitalism, federalism, and the two-party system, which are not moral principles but simply the preferred and accepted practices of the American people. There is much cant in American moralism and not a little inconsistency. It resembles in some ways the religious faith of the many respectable people who, in Samuel

Butler's words, "would be equally horrified to hear the Christian religion doubted or to see it practiced."

Our national vocabulary is full of "self-evident truths," not only about "life, liberty, and happiness," but about a vast number of personal and public issues, including the cold war. It has become one of the "self-evident truths" of the postwar era that, just as the President resides in Washington and the Pope in Rome, the Devil resides immutably in Moscow. We have come to regard the Kremlin as the permanent seat of his power and we have grown almost comfortable with a menace which, though unspeakably evil, has had the redeeming virtues of constancy, predictability, and familiarity. Now the Devil has betrayed us by traveling abroad and, worse still, by dispersing himself, turning up now here, now there, and in many places at once, with a devilish disregard for the laboriously constructed frontiers of ideology.

We are confronted with a complex and fluid world situation, and we are not adapting ourselves to it. We are clinging to old myths in the face of new realities, and we are seeking to escape the contradictions by narrowing the permissible bounds of public discussion, by relegating an increasing number of ideas and viewpoints to a growing category of "unthinkable thoughts." I believe that this tendency can and should be reversed, that it is within our ability, and unquestionably in our interests, to cut loose from established myths and to start thinking some "unthinkable thoughts"—about the cold war and East-West relations, about the underdeveloped countries and particularly those in Latin America, about the changing nature of the Chinese Communist threat in Asia, and about the festering war in Vietnam.

. . .

When all is said and done, when the abstractions and subtleties of political science have been exhausted, there remain the most basic unanswered questions about war and peace and why we contest the issues we contest and why we even care

about them. As Aldous Huxley has written: "There may be arguments about the best way of raising wheat in a cold climate or of re-afforesting a denuded mountain. But such arguments never lead to organized slaughter. Organized slaughter is the result of arguments about such questions as the following: Which is the best nation? The best religion? The best political theory? The best form of government? Why are other people so stupid and wicked? Why can't they see how good and intelligent we are? Why do they resist our beneficent efforts to bring them under our control and make them like ourselves?" [1]

In our search for answers to the complex questions of war and peace, we come ultimately to the paradox of man himself, which I have never heard better expressed than in a one-page essay called "Man," written by an American hill-country philosopher whose writings suggest strongly the style and thought of Mark Twain. It reads as follows:

Man is a queer animal, like the beasts of the fields, the fowls of the air, and the fishes of the sea, he came into this world without his consent and is going out the same way.

At birth he is one of the most helpless creatures in all existence. He can neither walk, talk, swim nor crawl, and has but two legs while most other animals have four legs. Unlike other animals he has no covering for his body to protect it against the bite or sting of poisonous insects, tooth or claw of ferocious beasts save a little hair which appears about his body only in patches.

With all his limitations he yet has one advantage over animals—the power of reason, but history shows that he often discards that for superstition. Of all the animals on earth, man has shown himself to be the most cruel and brutal. He is the only animal that will create instruments of death for his own destruction.

Man is the only animal on all the earth that has ever been known to burn its young as a sacrifice to appease the wrath of some imaginary deity. He is the only one that will build homes, towns

[1] Aldous Huxley, "The Politics of Ecology" (pamphlet, published by The Center for the Study of Democratic Institutions, Santa Barbara, California, 1963), p. 6.

and cities at such a cost in sacrifice and suffering and turn around and destroy them in war.

He is the only animal that will gather his fellows together in creeds, clans, and nations, line them up in companies, regiments, armies, and get glory out of their slaughter. Just because some king or politician told him to.

Man is the only creature in all existence that is not satisfied with the punishment he can inflict on his fellows while here, but had to invent a hell of fire and brimstone in which to burn them after they are dead.

Where he came from, or when, or how, or where he is going after death he does not know, but he hopes to live again in ease and idleness where he can worship his gods and enjoy himself, watching his fellow creatures wriggle and writhe in eternal flames down in hell.

The root question, for which I must confess I have no answer, is how and why it is that so much of the energy and intelligence that men could use to make life better for themselves is used instead to make life difficult and painful for other men. When the subtleties of strategy and power and diplomatic method have all been explained, we are still left with the seemingly unanswerable question of how and why it is that we *care* about such things, which are so remote from the personal satisfactions that bring pleasure and grace and fulfillment into our lives.

The paradoxes of human nature are eternal and perhaps unanswerable, but I do think we know enough about elemental human needs to be able to apply certain psychological principles in our efforts to alleviate the tensions of the cold war.

. . .

We must bring to bear all the resources of human knowledge and invention to build viable foundations of security in the nuclear age—the resources of political science and history, of economics and sociology, of psychology and literature and the arts. It is not enough to seek security through armaments or even through ingenious schemes of disarmament; nor is it enough to seek security through schemes for the transfer of territories or for the deployment and redeployment of forces. Security is a state of mind rather than a set of devices and arrangements. The latter are important because they contribute, but only to the extent that they contribute, to generating a *psychological process* in which peoples and statesmen come increasingly to think of war as undesirable and unfeasible.

It is this *process* that has critical importance for our security. Whether we advance it by seeking a settlement on Berlin or a new disarmament agreement, by the opening of consulates or by a joint enterprise in space, is less important than that the process be advanced. Our emphasis at any one time should be on those issues which seem most likely to be tractable and soluble. As long as we are by one means or another cultivating a world-wide state of mind in which peace is favored over war, we are doing the most effective possible thing to strengthen the foundations of our security. And only when such a state of mind is widely prevalent in the world will the kind of unprecedented political creativity on a global scale which has been made necessary by the invention of nuclear weapons become possible as well.

2

A Foreign Policy for the 1970's

RICHARD M. NIXON

American foreign policy in the post-World War II period was based on several assumptions, the foremost being that we faced a monolithic Communist world with an ideology that precluded change. The United States, it was believed, possessed permanent military and economic superiority. As one of the two superpowers, we created satellites that included Western Europe, Latin America, and newly emerging nations. That era has ended. What are the basic components of a peaceful world, according to President Nixon? What is the "Nixon Doctrine"? How must postwar American policy be modified to fit this new format? What basic relationship should exist between American commitments and American interest? Can we live in isolation?

The postwar period in international relations has ended.

Then, we were the only great power whose society and economy had escaped World War II's massive destruction. Today, the ravages of that war have been overcome. Western Europe and Japan have recovered their economic strength, their political vitality, and their national self-confidence. Once the recipients of American aid, they have now begun to share their growing resources with the developing world. Once almost totally dependent on American military power, our European allies now play a greater role in our common policies, commensurate with their growing strength.

Then, new nations were being born, often in turmoil and uncertainty. Today, these nations have a new spirit and a growing strength of independence. Once, many feared that they would become simply a battleground of cold-war rivalry and fertile ground for Communist penetration. But

From Richard M. Nixon, Presidential Documents *(Washington, D.C.: U.S. Government Printing Office, 1970), February 23, 1970, pp. 195–198.*

this fear misjudged their pride in their national identities and their determination to preserve their newly won sovereignty.

Then, we were confronted by a monolithic Communist world. Today, the nature of that world has changed—the power of individual Communist nations has grown, but international Communist unity has been shattered. Once a unified bloc, its solidarity has been broken by the powerful forces of nationalism. The Soviet Union and Communist China, once bound by an alliance of friendship, had become bitter adversaries by the mid-1960's. The only times the Soviet Union has used the Red Army since World War II have been against its own allies—in East Germany in 1953, in Hungary in 1956, and in Czechoslovakia in 1968. The Marxist dream of international Communist unity has disintegrated.

Then, the United States had a monopoly or overwhelming superiority of nuclear weapons. Today, a revolution in the technology of war has altered the nature of the military balance of power. New types of weapons present new dangers. Communist China has acquired thermonuclear weapons. Both the Soviet Union and the United States have acquired the ability to inflict unacceptable damage on the other, no matter which strikes first. There can be no gain and certainly no victory for the power that provokes a thermonuclear exchange. Thus, both sides have recognized a vital mutual interest in halting the dangerous momentum of the nuclear arms race.

Then, the slogans formed in the past century were the ideological accessories of the intellectual debate. Today, the "isms" have lost their vitality—indeed the restlessness of youth on both sides of the dividing line testifies to the need for a new idealism and deeper purposes.

This is the challenge and the opportunity before America as it enters the 1970's.

The Framework for a Durable Peace

In the first postwar decades, American energies were absorbed in coping with a cycle of recurrent crises, whose fundamental origins lay in the destruction of World War II and the tensions attending the emergence of scores of new nations. Our opportunity today—and challenge—is to get at the causes of crises, to take a longer view, and to help build the international relationships that will provide the framework of a durable peace.

I have often reflected on the meaning of "peace," and have reached one certain conclusion: Peace must be far more than the absence of war. Peace must provide a durable structure of international relationships which inhibits or removes the causes of war. Building a lasting peace requires a foreign policy guided by three basic principles:

—Peace requires *partnership*. Its obligations, like its benefits, must be shared. This concept of partnership guides our relations with all friendly nations.
—Peace requires *strength*. So long as there are those who would threaten our vital interests and those of our allies with military force, we must be strong. American weakness could tempt would-be aggressors to make dangerous miscalculations. At the same time, our own strength is important only in relation to the strength of others. We—like others—must place high priority on enhancing our security through cooperative arms control.
—Peace requires a *willingness to negotiate*. All nations—and we are no exception—have important national interests to protect. But the most fundamental interest of all nations lies in building the structure of peace. In partnership with our allies, secure in our own strength, we will seek those areas in which we can agree among ourselves and with others to accommodate conflicts and overcome rivalries. We are working toward the day when *all* nations will have a stake in peace, and will therefore be partners in its maintenance.

Within such a structure, international disputes can be settled and clashes contained. The insecurity of nations, out of which so much conflict arises, will be eased, and the habits of moderation and compromise will be nurtured. Most important, a durable peace will give full opportunity to the powerful forces driving toward economic change and social justice.

This vision of a peace built on partnership, strength and willingness to negotiate is the unifying theme of this report. In the sections that follow, the first steps we have taken during this past year—the policies we have devised and the programs we have initiated to realize this vision—are placed in the context of these three principles.

Peace Through Partnership— The Nixon Doctrine

As I said in my address of November 3, "We Americans are a do-it-yourself people —an impatient people. Instead of teaching someone else to do a job, we like to do it ourselves. This trait has been carried over into our foreign policy."

The postwar era of American foreign policy began in this vein in 1947 with the proclamation of the Truman Doctrine and the Marshall Plan, offering American economic and military assistance to countries threatened by aggression. Our policy held that democracy and prosperity, buttressed by American military strength and organized in a worldwide network of American-led alliances, would insure stability and peace. In the formative years of the postwar period, this great effort of international political and economic reconstruction was a triumph of American leadership and imagination, especially in Europe.

For two decades after the end of the Second World War, our foreign policy was guided by such a vision and inspired by its success. The vision was based on the fact that the United States was the richest and most stable country, without whose initiative and resources little security or progress was possible.

This impulse carried us through into the 1960's. The United States conceived programs and ran them. We devised strategies, and proposed them to our allies. We discerned dangers, and acted directly to combat them.

The world has dramatically changed since the days of the Marshall Plan. We deal now with a world of stronger allies, a community of independent developing nations, and a Communist world still hostile but now divided.

Others now have the ability and responsibility to deal with local disputes which once might have required our intervention. Our contribution and success will depend not on the frequency of our involvement in the affairs of others, but on the stamina of our policies. This is the approach which will best encourage other nations to do their part, and will most genuinely enlist the support of the American people.

This is the message of the doctrine I announced at Guam—the "Nixon Doctrine." Its central thesis is that the United States will participate in the defense and development of allies and friends, but that America cannot—and will not—conceive *all* the plans, design *all* the programs, execute *all* the decisions and undertake *all* the defense of the free nations of the world. We will help

where it makes a real difference and is considered in our interest.

America cannot live in isolation if it expects to live in peace. We have no intention of withdrawing from the world. The only issue before us is how we can be most effective in meeting our responsibilities, protecting our interests, and thereby building peace.

A more responsible participation by our foreign friends in their own defense and progress means a more effective common effort toward the goals we all seek. Peace in the world will continue to require us to maintain our commitments—and we will. As I said at the United Nations, "It is not my belief that the way to peace is by giving up our friends or letting down our allies." But a more balanced and realistic American role in the world is essential if American commitments are to be sustained over the long pull. In my State of the Union Address, I affirmed that "to insist that other nations play a role is not a retreat from responsibility; it is a sharing of responsibility." This is not a way for America to withdraw from its indispensable role in the world. It is a way—the only way—we can carry out our responsibilities.

It is misleading, moreover, to pose the fundamental question so largely in terms of commitments. Our objective, in the first instance, is to support our *interests* over the long run with a sound foreign policy. The more that policy is based on a realistic assessment of our and others' interests, the more effective our role in the world can be. We are not involved in the world because we have commitments; we have commitments because we are involved. Our interests must shape our commitments, rather than the other way around.

We will view new commitments in the light of a careful assessment of our own national interests and those of other countries, of the specific threats to those interests, and of our capacity to counter those threats at an acceptable risk and cost.

3

The Limits of American Foreign Policy

WALTER LIPPMANN

The failure of American military intervention in Vietnam has had a traumatic effect on our foreign policy. In the article that follows, widely respected commentator and philosopher Walter Lippmann offers his evaluation of the meaning of this ill-fated adventure. Why does he contend that we were not defeated in Vietnam? What proof does he offer that our vital interests were not involved there? Why was our great military power ineffective in Vietnam? What long-standing U.S. military policy did we violate by sending troops there? Was the Korean War also a violation of that policy? How did we arrive at an exaggerated idea of our ability to police the world?

When the war in Indochina ends, it will matter a great deal how we understand what happened, and why. For this country can tear itself apart if it falls into bitter quarrels about what happened. There will be those who say that we have been defeated although we could have won. There will be others who say that we should not have intervened but that we were deceived and seduced. "There are two things that will always be very difficult for a democratic nation," said Alexis de Tocqueville, "to start a war and to end it." The heavy losses of the dead and wounded and the enormous costs and frustrations of the war will be tolerable only if we can come to some common understanding as to what went wrong, and why it happened.

I must begin by insisting on a point that President Johnson and President Nixon have needlessly obscured and confused. It is the difference between a mistake and a failure on the one hand and a defeat on the other. The United States has not been and

From Walter Lippmann, "The Limits of American Foreign Policy," Newsweek, Vol. 76:32–33, December 14, 1970. Reprinted by permission of the publisher.

cannot be defeated in Indochina even though we withdraw our armed forces and realize that in the longer run the South Vietnamese Government is not likely to be able to stay on a course that is independent of North Vietnam. For the United States this will have been a large and costly failure to do what we said we were going to do. But the United States will not have been defeated. For defeat is what happened to Nazi Germany and to Japan: to surrender, to have the armed forces lay down their arms, to have the country occupied and governed by the enemy. No such thing can happen to us in Indochina, *which is proof that it is not a vital area to the United States.* And therefore President Nixon would do the country a service if he would cease to confuse a mistaken war with the downfall of being defeated.

We need at the same time to explain to ourselves what at first seems to be absurd. Here we are, some 200 million of us, with the greatest armaments that any country has ever possessed and there are the North Vietnamese, some 20 million of them, with a primitive industrial system. Yet we have been unable to make them do what we want them to do. Why not? Because armed peasants who are willing to die are a match for the mightiest power. Elephants cannot clear the mosquitoes from a swamp. The United States has been unable to conquer the armed guerrillas of the vast Asian continent.

Why, we are asked, have we not used *all* our weapons and bombed them back into the Stone Age? The answer is that the United States had compelling reasons to believe that China and the Soviet Union would not stand idly by if we did, and that nothing that was at stake in Indochina was worth another world war.

Thus, our failure in Vietnam sprang from a great mistake. We asked the armed forces to do what it was not possible for them to do. Our senior military leaders, the men who were the commanders before and during the second world war, knew better. They had always believed that the United States' military power was on the ocean and that Asian land wars were to be avoided studiously. The men who did commit the United States to a land war in South Vietnam had to ignore the precedents and override the advice of men like Dwight D. Eisenhower, Douglas MacArthur and Matthew B. Ridgway.

If we are pacifists and doves about Vietnam, it is because of the old American view of a land war in Asia. The opposition to intervention on the Asian continent begins with the teachings of our senior commanders in the second world war, long before Senator Fulbright and his colleagues in the Senate began to dissent. The question is why the United States ever violated its own military doctrine.

The reason for the mistake which led to the failure was certainly not the villainy or the ambition or the profit-seeking of anyone. The reason was the global confusion which existed when the second world war came to an end. The two principal enemies of the United States, Germany and Japan, were utterly defeated and all the principal allies and friends, the Soviet Union, China, France and Britain, were prostrated. Only the United States was uninvaded, powerful and rich, unhurt and invulnerable.

The recovery of our allies and of our enemies was greatly helped by wise and beneficent measures like the Marshall plan and NATO, and for a few years it looked as if we could do anything anywhere in the world. The whole world seemed to depend on the United States for protection and for recovery and reconstruction, even for food. Never, it seemed, was there such a total victory, and never before, therefore, was it so difficult to judge with any accuracy what needed to and what could be done. In these circumstances there flourished the illusion of American omnipotence, the fantastic notion that one nation could act as global policeman.

It was not, I think, the United States which yearned to police the world, though there were a few intoxicated imperialists among us. Events and the pleading of our friends abroad nourished the illusory role of world policeman and world benefactor.

While that illusion flourished during the late '40s, it became exceedingly difficult to measure wisely the extent of our power and of our responsibilities. Although the postwar distribution of power in the world was proved to be short-lived, the postwar situation was complicated by the first appearance of nuclear weapons. They were unbelievably destructive and for a time the United States had a monopoly of them. It was difficult to understand the limitations of nuclear weapons, and to realize that though those weapons would destroy anything, they could not do anything in particular. We have learned gradually the limitations of nuclear power, but it has been difficult for most people to understand why, if we are so powerful, we do not succeed in anything we attempt to do.

And then, last but not least, there was a third novelty in the postwar world which made it difficult to judge foreign policy accurately. This was the emergence of the Russian empire as the citadel of a world revolution against established order everywhere. Americans had never before confronted such a state of affairs. The consequence was the cold war to contain Communism, to roll it back and to insist that the confrontation with Communism would have to precede not only stable recovery, not only peace and harmony in the world, but the recognition of the balance of power.

It is very easy in retrospect to see that the war in Vietnam was a great failure owing to a great mistake. It is also easy to see that this great mistake was made by a new generation of men who were faced with the unique conditions of the postwar world—the total victory of the United States, the unmeasured nuclear weapons, and the Soviet Communist crusade which, for living Americans, was unprecedented.

When the Vietnamese war ends—we pray without a catastrophe—there will be only one salve for our wounds, for our pride, for our honor and for our dignity. Honesty and no pretenses. It is to recognize the mistake as being a mistake, to refrain from pretending that it was not a mistake, and to find the remedy in the universal human knowledge that to err is human.

4

The United States Must Not Negotiate with the Soviet Union

SLOBODAN M. DRASKOVICH

One position with respect to United States–Communist relations is clear-cut. It advocates regarding Communism as a world-wide conspiracy, undeviatingly committed to our destruction. Any negotiation is futile. Any hope that the passage of time will soften orthodox Marxism only reveals American muddleheadedness. A vigorous summary of that position appears below.

If this concept is accepted, certain questions regarding United States foreign policy follow. Faced with an implacable enemy, should we not wage preventive war? Is there any chance that the Communist world will eventually fall because of its own inner contradictions? Can any segments of the Communist bloc be split off through adroit diplomacy?

Implementing the various points of our non-political approach to the problem of our foreign policy, as I suggested last month, America has spent all its energy in attempts to attain non-political goals. The purpose of this article will be to briefly examine some of these goals:

THE RELAXATION OR LESSENING OF TENSION. Here is a Soviet propaganda device

From Slobodan M. Draskovich, "American Foreign Policy," American Opinion, *December 1962, pp. 37–42. Reprinted by permission of the publisher.*

which means that anybody who resists the Communist conquest of the world is, obviously, a warmonger, who is creating tension. Tensions, as everybody knows, lead to war. Thus this slogan makes sense only from the Communist point of view and within the framework of Communist political warfare. It does not make any sense from our viewpoint. Our efforts for lessening tensions can be judged honest, sincere, and efficient by the USSR only if, and in the degree to which, we surrender.

. . .

NEGOTIATION has been a basic ingredient of our foreign policy. But negotiations make no sense under the circumstances. What can antipodes—when one is waging total political war with the aim of destroying the other, while the other is imploring the one for a little understanding of her peaceful soul, to "give us a fair shake"—negotiate about? About ways and means to avoid war? But that is precisely the Communist aim. Why should they negotiate about that? And their atom-rattling is no threat of war, since Communists do not threaten to take action when they are ready. They take it, without warning. If the Communists indulge in negotiations, and very long and wearisome ones, it is because negotiations have an important place in their strategy and arsenal. They serve to blackmail us, expose us to the world as unyielding warmongers, to ridicule us, and to force us to retreat and prepare further retreats. Negotiations pave the way for the Communist conquest of the world, without war. That is why the Communists negotiate. But what have we ever won from our negotiations with the Communists?!?

WORKING TO REACH AGREEMENTS. The Communists have a unique record of disregarding obligations and violating agreements. To them such things are scraps of paper, or pie crusts whose only function is to be broken, in the witty explanation of Nikita Khrushchev. Where is the agreement that the Communists have respected!?!

DISARMAMENT. From the Communist point of view, this is of supreme importance. They know their superiority in political warfare, just as they are fully aware of their irremediable inferiority in military strength and capacity. Therefore the Communists are interested in seeing the United States disarm, as much as possible, as soon as possible, and as unilaterally as possible. We have gone a long way to accommodate them. We have imposed on ourselves a three-year moratorium in nuclear testing, which made it possible for the Soviets to gain a little on us in the meantime. They then put more pressure behind their prop-

aganda that the United States was threatening the health of mankind and the sanity of future generations.

. . .

CULTURAL CONTACTS WITH THE COMMUNISTS' WORLD. Great importance is attributed to cultural contacts with the Communists. These are supposed to show how erudite we are and to establish strong links in the non-controversial fields of art, literature, theater, and ballet. However, the theoreticians of the cultural exchange programs regret that Communist "culture" is permitted to exist only to serve the political sphere. Every Communist ballet ensemble or troupe has its political commissar, who does not come to dance but to accomplish those subversive missions assigned to him. Even the artistic performance of the *Bolshoi* or *Moyseyev* accomplishes the important political task of compelling our naive eyes to look the other way—away from the Communist reality of terror, subversion, subhuman treatment of citizens, ruthless fomenting of civil war throughout the globe, and hunger riots in the land of the victorious proletariat.

And, finally, we have strong doubts regarding the importance, for the fate of mankind, of establishing whether Jasha Heifetz is a better violinist than David Oistrakh, or Van Cliburn has a more elegant touch on the piano than Emil Gilels, or whether Danny Kaye can crack funnier jokes than his Soviet counterparts. As a newspaperwoman aptly remarked after a review of the travels of a group of American entertainers, "the world will not be impressed and attracted to our country if we prove that we are the most entertaining nation on earth, they want to know if we are the strongest and most determined to defend freedom."

TRADE AND ECONOMIC AID. If the Communists simply held different views on economic problems, without any imperialist ambitions and criminal notions about men and nations, it would be conceivable to trade with them and teach them modern methods in agriculture, or industry, or communications. But—once more—the Communists want to conquer the world and use everything, especially economics, to that end. A rather well-known Communist, Vladimir Ulyanov-Lenin reportedly stated that "When the capitalist world starts trade with us, on that day it will begin to finance its own destruction." The Communists force their people to produce under slave labor conditions, which makes the production costs much lower. They are interested in buying only what is useful for the purposes of strengthening their total revolutionary strength. Finally, . . . they are squeezing all of the knowledge and profit from us which they possibly can. At the same time they are working at the realization of their mammoth plan of capturing all former Western colonies, so as to deprive the economy of the Free World of vital raw materials (uranium in Katanga, for instance), and markets.

By trading with the Communist countries, we are strengthening them economically, we are saving the most irresponsible and incapable clique ever to wield power anywhere, at any time, to escape certain and deserved doom. And, we are financing our own destruction.

ANTI-COLONIALISM. In the view of our foreign policy makers and planners, the main problem today is not Communism: It is poverty and the new emerging nations of the world (which are poor because—so runs the explicit or implicit theory—the nations of the Free World have exploited them for centuries). And, it is only natural and right that the free nations, and above all the United States, go about feeding and freeing. First, and before anything else, we must give to the Watusi his political independence, because such is the "irresistible force" of history, the "rising expectation," the "Wind," the "trend."

The problem has many aspects. Most of these so-called nations are centuries or millennia away from possessing the requirements for nationhood and independence. The favorite theme about the alleged analogy between the "winds of freedom" in Africa and the same winds in America in 1776 betray either abysmal ignorance and lack of judgment or—much worse—deliberate distortion. It is true that in these days the techniques of governing masses have been perfected to such an extent that anybody, any group of ambitious men can, provided that they have enough international support or political influence, diplomatic and financial pressure, and brute force, rule anywhere. For, on the world market, human lives are cheaper than ever. So, you do not need to have a nation, meaning national identity, to proclaim "national independence." But then the revolutionary forces behind the movement are not those of nationalism. The best proof of this shameless fraud is the fact that everything has been done by the Communists to enslave 100 million Europeans and 500 million Chinese with old traditions of nationhood and independence. Yet not one of the great readers of the tea leaves of history detects any sign or need for restoring national independence to *those* nations. To grant "national independence" to Uganda or Tanganyika is the sacred duty of mankind. But where is the sacred duty to restore the independence of Poland, or Latvia, or Rumania, or China?!

· · ·

ACTIVE AID TO COMMUNISTS. But the real core of the thinking of our foreign policy experts is probably best exemplified in the case of Communist Yugoslavia and Joseph Broz-Tito. There is no example where the facts of the matter have been so clear and unequivocal, and where the supporters of a Communist dictator and his regime have been bolder in defiance of the most elementary truth, logic, and decency. A well-known Washington columnist has called this the law of "investment in error."

. . . The harm which the Tito "defection" has done to world Communism can be taken seriously only by those who entertain a superstitious fear and awe of Communism, so that the slightest sign of internal Communist difficulties is taken as a valid substitute for the non-existent struggle of the

Free World to destroy Communism by creating real trouble for the Communists.

While it is nonsense to speak of Tito breaking up the Communist monolith, the Tito phenomenon has been used to revolutionize American political thinking. And, it has split American unity regarding Communism. Until 1948 the prevalent idea among Americans was that Communism was bad, that it was irreconcilably opposed to everything America represents and stands for. Titoism put forth and promoted the idea of "good," and therefore acceptable, Communism. The most important consequence is that it has permitted the most sinister maneuvers against freedom to pass as "anti-Communism." For if Tito is an enemy of Moscow and Communist Internationalism (which he is not and never has been) then, logically, helping Tito is hurting Moscow. Yes, only anti-Communists aid good old Tito.

. . .

Space does not permit me to go into the pertinent and thoroughly misrepresented cases of Communist "anti-Communism": Milovan Djilas (*The New Class and Conversations with Stalin*), Imre Nagy, the Communist "martyr for freedom," Boris Pasternak, the great Communist champion of "humanism," and their ilk. Nor do we have space to go into the cases of United States participation in bringing Castro to power, or American aid to Communist Chedi Jagan, or Communist Wladyslaw Gomulka, or Communist Ben Bella. What must be emphasized is that the United States policy, supposed to defend the national interests of the United States and defeat the maneuvers of its enemies, has actively helped known and avowed Communists, in spite of their overwhelmingly documented work against our interests and in favor of World Communism.

And last, there is the fact that, as we have worked for our enemies, we have rejected our allies and worked against them.

The conviction, that if you want to get American help you must be against America, started as a cautious joke. But in the course of years it has become a matter of undisputable fact.

5

A Fresh Look at the Communist Bloc

J. W. FULBRIGHT

Senator Fulbright insists that the Communist bloc is not a monolithic unit unless we make it so by our policies. He foresees the possibility of gradually lessening tensions and believes that the United States should be constantly on the alert to exploit such possibilities. If the Fulbright thesis were adopted, what attitude should we take toward developing trade with East Europe? Toward disarmament proposals? Toward suggestions for cooperation in the exploration of space?

. . .

The master myth of the cold war is that the Communist bloc is a monolith composed of governments which are not really governments at all, but organized conspiracies, divided among themselves perhaps in certain matters of tactics, but all equally resolute and implacable in their determination to destroy the free world.

I believe that the Communist world is indeed hostile to the free world in its general and long-term intentions, but that the existence of this animosity in principle is far less important for our foreign policy than the great variations in its intensity and character both in time and among the individual members of the Communist bloc. Only if we recognize these variations, ranging from China, which poses immediate threats to the free world, to Poland and Yugoslavia, which pose none, can we hope to act effectively upon the bloc and to turn its internal differences to our own advan-

tage and to the advantage of those bloc countries which wish to maximize their independence. It is the responsibility of our national leaders, both in the executive branch and in Congress, to acknowledge and act upon these realities, even at the cost of saying things which will not win immediate widespread enthusiasm.

For a start, we can acknowledge the fact that the Soviet Union, though still a most formidable adversary, has ceased to be totally and implacably hostile to the West. It has shown a new willingness to enter mutually advantageous arrangements with the West and, thus far at least, to honor them. It has therefore become possible to divert some of our energies from the prosecution of the cold war to the relaxation of the cold war and to deal with the Soviet Union, for certain purposes, as a normal state with normal and traditional interests.

If we are to do these things effectively, we must distinguish between communism as an ideology and the power and policy of the Soviet state. It is not communism as a doctrine, or communism as it is practiced *within* the Soviet Union or *within* any other country, that threatens us. How the Soviet Union organizes its internal life, the gods and doctrines that it worships, are

From J. W. Fulbright, Old Myths and New Realities *(New York: Random House, Inc., 1964), pp. 8–14, 77–78. Copyright © 1964 by J. W. Fulbright. Reprinted by permission of Random House, Inc.*

matters for the Soviet Union to determine. It is not Communist dogma as espoused within Russia but Communist imperialism that threatens us and other peoples of the non-Communist world. Insofar as a great nation mobilizes its power and resources for aggressive purposes, that nation, regardless of ideology, makes itself our enemy. Insofar as a nation is content to practice its doctrines within its own frontiers, that nation—except under certain extreme circumstances—is one with which we have no proper quarrel. We must deal with the Soviet Union as a great power, quite apart from differences of ideology. To the extent that the Soviet leaders abandon the global ambitions of Marxist ideology, in fact if not in words, it becomes possible for us to engage in normal relations with them, relations which probably cannot be close or trusting for many years to come but which can be gradually freed of the terror and the tensions of the cold war.

In our relations with the Russians, and indeed in our relations with all nations, we would do well to remember, and to act upon, the words of Pope John in the great Encyclical *Pacem in Terris:* "It must be borne in mind," said Pope John, "that to proceed gradually is the law of life in all its expressions; therefore, in human institutions, too, it is not possible to renovate for the better except by working from within them, gradually . . . Violence has always achieved only destruction, not construction, the kindling of passions, not their pacification, the accumulation of hate and ruin, not the reconciliation of the contending parties. And it has reduced men and parties to the difficult task of rebuilding, after sad experience, on the ruins of discord. . . ."

Important opportunities have been created for Western policy by the development of "polycentrism" in the Communist bloc. The Communist nations, as George Kennan has pointed out, are, like the Western nations, currently caught up in a crisis of indecision about their relations with countries outside their own ideological bloc. The choices open to the satellite states are limited but by no means insignificant. They

can adhere slavishly to Soviet preferences or they can strike out on their own, within limits, to enter into mutually advantageous relations with the West.

Whether they do so, and to what extent, is to some degree within the power of the West to determine. If we persist in the view that all Communist regimes are equally hostile and equally threatening to the West, and that we can have no policy toward the "captive nations" except the eventual overthrow of their Communist regimes, then the West may enforce upon the Communist bloc a degree of unity which the Soviet Union has shown itself to be quite incapable of imposing—just as Stalin in the early postwar years frightened the West into a degree of unity that it almost certainly could not have attained by its own unaided efforts. If, on the other hand, we are willing to re-examine the view that all Communist regimes are alike in the threat which they pose for the West—a view which had a certain validity in Stalin's time—then we may be able to exert an important influence on the course of events within a divided Communist world.

We are to a great extent the victims, and the Soviets the beneficiaries, of our own ideological convictions and of the curious contradictions which they involve. We consider it a form of subversion of the free world, for example, when the Russians enter trade relations or conclude a consular convention or establish airline connections with a free country in Asia, Africa, or Latin America—and to a certain extent we are right. On the other hand, when it is proposed that we adopt the same strategy in reverse—by extending commercial credits to Poland or Yugoslavia, or by exchanging ambassadors with a Hungarian regime which has changed considerably in character since the revolution of 1956—then the same patriots who are so alarmed by Soviet activities in the free world charge our policy-makers with "giving aid and comfort to the enemy," and with innumerable other categories of idiocy and immorality.

It is time that we resolved this contradiction and separated myth from reality. The myth is that every Communist state is an unmitigated evil and a relentless enemy of the free world; the reality is that some Communist regimes pose a threat to the free world while others pose little or none, and that if we will recognize these distinctions, we ourselves will be able to influence events in the Communist bloc in a way favorable to the security of the free world. "It could well be argued," writes George Kennan, ". . . that if the major Western powers had full freedom of movement in devising their own policies, it would be within their power to determine whether the Chinese view, or the Soviet view, or perhaps a view more liberal than either would ultimately prevail within the Communist camp." [1]

There are numerous areas in which we can seek to reduce the tensions of the cold war and to bring a degree of normalcy into our relations with the Soviet Union and other Communist countries—once we have resolved that it is safe and wise to do so. We have already taken important steps in this direction: the Antarctic and Austrian treaties and the nuclear test ban treaty, the broadening of East-West cultural and educational relations, and the expansion of trade.

On the basis of recent experience and present economic needs, there seems little likelihood of a spectacular increase in trade between Communist and Western countries, even if existing restrictions were to be relaxed. Free-world trade with Communist countries has been increasing at a steady but unspectacular rate, and it seems unlikely to be greatly accelerated because of the limited ability of the Communist countries to pay for increased imports. A modest increase in East-West trade may nonetheless serve as a modest instrument of East-West détente—provided that we are able to overcome the myth that trade with Communist countries is a compact with the Devil, and to recognize that, on the contrary, trade in nonstrategic goods can serve

as an effective and honorable means of advancing both peace and human welfare.

. . .

The cold war and all the other national rivalries of our time are not likely to evaporate in our lifetimes. The major question of our time is not how to end these conflicts but whether we can find some way to conduct them without resorting to weapons that will resolve them once and for all by wiping out the contestants. A generation ago we were speaking of "making the world safe for democracy." Having failed of this in two World Wars, we must now seek ways of making the world reasonably safe for the continuing contest between those who favor democracy and those who oppose it. It is a modest aspiration, but it is a sane and realistic one for a generation which, having failed of grander things, must now look to its own survival.

Extreme nationalism and dogmatic ideology are luxuries that the human race can no longer afford. It must turn its energies now to the politics of survival. If we do so, we may find in time that we can do better than just survive. We may find that the simple human preference for life and peace has an inspirational force of its own, less intoxicating perhaps than the sacred abstractions of nation and ideology, but far more relevant to the requirements of human life and human happiness.

There are, to be sure, risks in such an approach. There is an element of trust in it, and we can be betrayed. But human life is fraught with risks, and the behavior of the sane man is not the avoidance of all possible danger but the weighing of greater against lesser risks and of risks against opportunities.

We have an opportunity at present to try to build stronger foundations for our national security than armaments alone can ever provide. That opportunity lies in a policy of encouraging the development of a habit of peaceful and civilized contacts between ourselves and the Communist bloc. I believe that this opportunity must be pursued, with reason and restraint, with due regard for the pitfalls involved and for

---

[1] George Kennan, "Polycentrism and Western Policy," *Foreign Affairs*, January, 1964, p. 178.

the possibility that our efforts may fail, but with no less regard for the promise of a safer and more civilized world. In the course of this pursuit, both we and our adversaries may find it possible one day to break through the barriers of nationalism and ideology and to approach each other in something of the spirit of Pope John's words to Khrushchev's son-in-law: "They tell me you are an atheist. But you will not refuse an old man's blessing for your children."

6

Beginning Anew in Latin America

EDWARD M. KENNEDY

The Alliance for Progress was launched over a decade ago by President John F. Kennedy as a program to bring social justice, political freedom, and democratic government to Latin America. Ten years later, little progress had been made toward any of these goals. In the speech that follows, Senator Edward Kennedy calls for renewed efforts to make his brother's dream come true.

Why did the original Alliance fail? Have we actually supported wholesale social and political change in Latin America? Can outside forces ever bring about significant change in an area with 270,000,000 people? Why does Kennedy believe that we should end military assistance programs? How could economic aid be used to produce social justice? What should our policy be toward Cuba? How would Kennedy respond to the question raised elsewhere in this chapter by Bernard Nossiter: "Does foreign aid really aid?"

We began the Sixties by joining with Latin American nations in a call to hemispheric action, a call to promote a better life for millions of Latin Americans who are forced to endure both poverty and oppression. They had been deprived of hope, of faith in political institutions, of a share in the economic and social progress of most of the Western Hemisphere, and of the most basic right that the hemisphere promised the world—the dignity of the individual. In recognition of these deprivations, in March of 1961, the sound of a revolutionary trumpet echoed to the governments and to the people of Latin America, calling on them to join with us in a new alliance: la Alianza para el Progreso.

Yet, barely a month later, on April 17, 1961, we launched the Bay of Pigs invasion, an embarrassing reminder of our history of gunboat diplomacy toward the hemisphere. It showed we had not yet learned the lesson that we have no divine right to intervene, forcibly or otherwise, in the internal affairs of Latin American nations.

Rarely in our history have two events, coming so close together, so clearly symbolized the best and worst in American foreign policy. Time and again over the past decade we have seen the noble goals of the Alliance for Progress perverted by the cold war philosophy symbolized by the Bay of Pigs.

From *Edward M. Kennedy, "Beginning Anew in Latin America," Saturday Review, October 17, 1970, pp. 18–21. Copyright © 1970 by Saturday Review, Inc. Reprinted by permission of the publisher and the author.*

For decades, the Pentagon, the State Department, and our intelligence agencies have urged the United States to intervene on the side of stability in Latin America out of fear that an end to the hegemony of the oligarchs would throw open the door to communist revolution. Our policy was not just a policy for Latin America. It was the same policy that led us to support Chiang Kai-shek against every force for change in China in the 1940s.

It is the same policy that leads us to support the Thieu regime in Vietnam today. In 1965, this rigid cold war philosophy prompted the landing of Marines in the Dominican Republic. The U.S. intervention, clothed once again in anti-communist rhetoric, was intended to bring order and democratic rule. It produced neither, and we have not yet realized the final cost of that action.

The Alliance for Progress was our first great effort to alter our anachronistic policies. President Kennedy and many others tried to bring our policies into line with the winds of social revolution sweeping across the continent. The alliance was not meant merely to repeat the narrowly conceived economic assistance programs of the 1950s. It was a basic attack on the exploitation of man that for too long has characterized the institutions of the hemisphere. The alliance embraced the goals of social justice, political freedom, and democratic government, as well as economic progress. It embodied a spirit of change that dared to challenge the traditions of the hemisphere. The alliance produced schools, roads, and bridges. More important, it spurred the development of an institutionalized planning process that was nonexistent a decade ago. On a regional level, the Inter-American Committee for the Alliance for Progress has become a creative and highly competent mechanism for evaluation and planning.

But today, the alliance—that bold attempt, that new initiative—is slowly dying. Each year its spirit has grown weaker. Our own commitment now has vanished. For the vast majority of Latin Americans, the better life has remained a fragment of a broken dream. There has been no outcry from the American public at our abandonment of the ideals of the Alliance for Progress. There is a fundamental lack of concern here at home for what happens in Latin America. Few know that there is a new Charter of the Organization of American States or that the first OAS General Assembly meeting was held last summer. All too often news of Latin America attracts our attention only when a government is overthrown, a plane is hijacked, or an ambassador is kidnaped. The American public still does not realize that twenty-five republics share our hemisphere. Nor does it realize that more than ten million of our own citizens trace their heritage to the blood of Spanish, Portuguese, and Indian cultures that make up Latin America, or that millions of our black citizens have historical ties to the citizens of Jamaica, Trinidad, and Barbados.

It is a personal tragedy that I can repeat nearly the same somber statistics about Latin America that President Kennedy cited in 1960 and that Robert Kennedy cited in 1966. For the vast majority of Latin Americans, the alliance has failed. Nearly 30 per cent of the population still die before their fortieth birthdays. Poverty, malnutrition, and disease continue to deny strength and incentive to the majority of the people in Latin America. Family processions bearing miniature coffins offer testimony to one of the world's highest infant mortality rates. There still is a 55 per cent dropout rate in primary schools, and for every 100 students who enter the first grade more than seventy-five will have dropped out by the time they finish high school.

The alliance has been a major economic disappointment. The rate of economic growth per capita has averaged 1.8 per cent for the decade, lower than it was in Latin America in the years when there was no alliance. Part of the reason was that American economic assistance has averaged half of what we promised for the alliance in actual development funds. We cheapened our aid by demanding that our dollars be used to buy U.S. products, goods that in many instances could be bought more cheaply on the world market. We still demand that 50 per cent of the goods be transported in U.S. ships. These shackles on our foreign aid have reduced its value by 40 per cent. In too many countries, the only difference between the alliance and the previous U.S. foreign assistance outpost has been the nameplate on the door.

The alliance has been a social failure despite the well-intentioned efforts of many AID officials and Latin American leaders. Land remains in the hands of a minute percentage of the population. In some countries, less than 10 per cent of the people own 90 per cent of the land. One-third of the rural labor force is unemployed. The increase in the total population means that rural unemployment will grow higher, creating disorder and increasing the flow of unskilled persons in cities. And we know that the cities have not yet demonstrated the capacity to absorb their present labor force.

The alliance has been a political failure. It was intended to write a new page of political history in Latin America, to end the depressing chapter of family dictatorships and military coups. Instead, thirteen constitutional governments have been overthrown in nine years. Today, in eleven Latin American republics, military governments rule, supported by hundreds of millions of dollars in American military assistance. In some of those nations, basic human rights are violated and the democratic ideals of the alliance have vanished.

And the spirit of the alliance has failed here at home. Despite our strong traditions of democracy, the United States continues to support regimes in Latin America that deny basic human rights. We stand silent while political prisoners are tortured in Brazil. In some instances, their only crime was advocating change.

. . .

Much of the $673-million in military aid granted in the past nine years has gone to those governments that displayed their contempt for democratic principles. The premise has been that anti-Americanism, subversion, and communist insurgency will end if police and military forces are better trained and equipped. In fact, we have seen an even more virulent form of anti-Americanism expressed by some of the leaders of recent military coups. The experience of the past decade has shown that the people of Latin America are not vulnerable to foreign ideologies. It was not the efficiency or the power of the U.S.-equipped Bolivian army that brought defeat and death to Che Guevara, but the sea of Bolivian peasants who resented foreign intrusion.

Subversion remains in Latin America not because the police forces are untrained but because human misery is omnipresent. The answer to the threat of unrest produced by hunger, poverty, disease, and injustice is not to import arms against the insurgents who exploit them, but to eradicate these ancient evils. It is time to recognize that fundamental social change is inevitable in the world. Stability for its own sake is a sterile policy destined to produce confrontation with the revolution of rising expectations in Latin America. We cannot prevent that change. The only rational policy for American assistance to Latin America is to direct our efforts to responsive, representative governments, reflective of the needs of their people.

The destiny of Latin America is for Latin Americans to decide, not the United States. But we can make it clear that, although we will not intervene, neither will we be party to any form of repression of the people and their aspirations.

A test of the political maturity of all nations in the Western Hemisphere is now at hand in Chile. The past six years of Eduardo Frei's Presidency represent a positive and progressive epoch in Chilean political history. Nevertheless, a self-described Marxist polled the most votes in the recent Presidential election. The action of the Congress will form the final step in the electoral process. The history of respect for the political process in Chile has been long and distinguished. Regardless of the final outcome, the U.S. and other nations must display equal respect for the right of the Chilean people to choose their own leaders.

What is now clear is that the Alliance for Progress of the 1970s must return to the spirit that launched a wave of enthusiasm in Latin America nine years ago. That spirit called for political freedom and social justice, not just economic development. The basic failure of the Alliance for Progress is that it was never tried. For a decade, we have emphasized the need for alliance and we have forgotten the need for progress.

If we are to end poverty and injustice for the vast majority of the continent's people, the second decade of development must produce fundamental changes in the distribution of power and wealth in Latin America. The real question is not whether the change will come. The question is whether with intelligence and compassion we can accelerate peaceful change and avoid a more violent and destructive transformation. The vital decision for the United States in the 1970s must be how to reform our own efforts so that they complement the Latin Americans' struggle to modernize But if we are to reaffirm the ideals of the alliance, strong steps must be taken.

First, the United States should reassert the political goals of the alliance. We must match our actions to our rhetoric. Contrary to the report produced by Governor Rockefeller after his trip to Latin America, the United States should not consent to the overthrow of democratic governments on the belief that a "new type of military man has come to the fore."

Second, I urge the immediate withdrawal of all of our military missions. I believe that we must begin now to demonstrate our opposition to military intrusion in the political arena by our attitudes, speech, and actions. . . .

We also should lose no time in phasing out our military assistance programs and halting sales of arms on credit to Latin America. The futility of our military policy was demonstrated in the war last year between El Salvador and Honduras. Both armies and their officers were equipped and trained by the United States.

Third, the United States should reserve its economic assistance for development programs designed to produce social justice and not solely those projects aimed at economic growth. The agenda for reform of the alliance in the 1970s must be based on acceptance of fundamental change. We must reject the claims of those who would cling blindly to the status quo. The alliance must reassert the priorities of assuring the people of Latin America an adequate education, health care, and the opportunity to participate in the process of development.

. . .

Land reform is perhaps the single most critical area where we must demonstrate our commitment. Agricultural production per capita declined in ten countries during the past nine years. Since 1961, the number of landless families plunged into rural poverty has outstripped the number resettled. We are falling further and further behind. There are now nine to eleven million Latin American rural families without land. The present land tenure system reflects the archaic and unjust social structure that took form after the Spanish conquest. To free the *campesino* and permit productive utilization of the land, the large estates, which spread for thousands of acres, must be divided into economically self-sustaining farms with individual or cooperative ownership. Nothing less than a thorough reformation of rural society is required.

. . .

Fourth, the United States must ensure that American private investment in Latin America plays a much more positive role in the development process. In the past eight years, American business has repatriated $8.3-billion in private profits from past investments, more than three times the total of new investments. Equally serious, the repatriation of U.S. profits has been matched by a slowdown in U.S. private investment. Part of the explanation is that there are more attractive investment opportunities in the United States and other developed nations. However, the impact of rising nationalism has affected investment decisions. Expropriation of foreign businesses has become accepted policy for regimes anxious for popular approval. It is in the interest of the United States and Latin America to find a means to avoid the political trauma that accompanies such actions. . . .

The fall of the Belaúnde government in Peru was particularly unfortunate because of the promise it held for progressive democratic change. Like the governments of Mexico, Chile, Costa Rica, Colombia, and Venezuela, it was pledged to carry out social and economic change. For nearly his entire term in office, President Belaúnde sought a negotiated settlement with the International Petroleum Company, despite strong pressure to nationalize the oil fields. Yet, our State Department decided to put pressure on Peru and withheld funds for social and economic programs. That action weakened Belaúnde and was a crucial element that led to his overthrow. The effect of our policy was to undermine a government that had been responsive to the democratic ideals of the alliance.

. . .

Fifth, we must look more closely at our relationship with Cuba. In 1962, Cuba was ousted from active membership in the Organization of American States. That action was based on two indictments against the regime of Fidel Castro: Castro's call for subversion and revolution against legitimate governments of Latin America and the introduction of Soviet military influence into the Western Hemisphere.

Castro's past attempts to export his revolution have been defeated. Since the failure of the guerrilla movement in Bolivia, there has been no direct Cuban intervention reported by any Latin American nation. And the decisive actions of President Kennedy in the Cuban missile crisis removed the Soviet threat at that time.

. . .

I suggest only that we explore taking the first step with Cuba, a review of our trade and travel restrictions. The process may be long and the response from Cuba may be unenthusiastic, but we must begin. By geography, history, and culture, Cuba is a part of the Western Hemisphere. As long as the Cuban government respects the OAS Charter's prohibition against interference in the internal affairs of other nations and does not introduce a new Soviet strategic threat, we should join our Latin American allies in exploring the quiet steps leading to Cuba's reintegration into the inter-American system.

We are starting a new decade; let us discard cold war concepts and look to the future. It is time to seek a recommitment to the spirit of the Alliance for Progress—to political freedom, social justice, and economic progress. If that spirit does not infuse our programs, we will fail no matter how much money and assistance flow across the border, or how intelligently our programs are conceived. We have the capacity, talent, and technology to help bring about the transformation of Latin America without violent and bloody disorder. But to do that, we must return to the spirit that began the decade. Nine years ago, John Kennedy challenged us to "transform the American continent into a vast crucible of revolutionary ideas and efforts—a tribute to the power of the creative energies of free men and women, an example to all the world that liberty and progress walk hand in hand." Difficult as it may be, it is time to start anew; it is time again to meet that challenge.

7

Does Foreign Aid Really Aid?

BERNARD NOSSITER

Economic aid has become almost an article of faith in American foreign policy. Our undisputed success with the Marshall Plan in Western Europe led us to believe that we had a formula that would bring American prosperity to the underdeveloped world. Despite the Pearson Report, which urged that wealthy nations redouble their efforts, that assumption is now being challenged.

Can the world be viewed as a global village? Are cultural differences a massive barrier against economic expansion? Can any meaningful relationship be established between the amount of aid and economic growth? How effective have such widely touted inventions as the "Green Revolution" and intrauterine devices been in India? How has aid sometimes delayed necessary decisions?

In May of 1968, the hot season was on us in full force at New Delhi, and I had been a correspondent in that troubled capital for eight months. Late one afternoon, I sought relief over tea in the home of a wise and skilled Indian journalist. My host led me to a high-ranking official in the Ministry of Food and Agriculture, a shrewd career official. I told him I brought some unpleasant news: the ticker had just reported from Washington that a House committee had further reduced the President's modest request for foreign aid.

"Good," he said, to my surprise. "I am only sorry they didn't cut it off entirely. Then perhaps we might do some of the things that need doing."

I am reminded of that tea party by the October release of "Partners in Development." This is the portentous report of the

From Bernard Nossiter, "Does Foreign Aid Really Aid?" The Atlantic Monthly, February 1970, pp. 61–63. Copyright © 1970 by the Atlantic Monthly Company, Boston, Mass., 02116. Reprinted by permission of the publisher.

Pearson Commission, enjoining the rich nations to do more for the poor. It asserts that the world is a global village in which none can be indifferent to the fate of others, and that the security of the affluent in Neuilly and Grosse Pointe is somehow tied to the kutcha hovels of Calcutta. It deplores the declining course of foreign aid, particularly in the United States, and urges a sharp reversal of this trend. More specifically, it calls on the rich to double their transfer of resources, public and private, to the poor, from $12.8 billion in 1968 to $23 billion by 1975. For the same period, the report proposes nearly a tripling in official aid, from $6.4 billion to $16.2 billion. Achievement of these levels, the document proclaims, would launch the poor on something called "self-sustaining growth."

Well Meaning

Predictably, right-thinking persons have solemnly applauded the Pearson report, and it is almost certain to become a measure of how badly the rich are failing the poor. The New York *Times* described it as a "persuasive picture of what can be accomplished by foreign aid—and how."

Certainly the report was issued with all the proper credentials. Its origin lies in a deep concern of George Woods, the former World Bank president. He saw that rich governments were becoming increasingly disenchanted with development aid, that political support could be found only for funds that subsidized the exports of the wealthy or gained them a substantial measure of political influence over the poor. Woods called for a "grand assize" on the question and charged Lester Pearson, the Nobel laureate and former Canadian Prime Minister, with the task.

Pearson chose fellow commissioners whose reputations for sobriety and calculated vision matched his own. Among them were Roberto Campos, the brilliant Brazilian economist who had labored heroically to impose a measure of respectability on the inflation-ridden economy run by his country's military dictators; Robert Marjolin, the cool Parisian economist and administrator, who had vainly attempted to bring the same degree of coherence to the plans of the six nations in the Common Market that he had achieved among the European recipients of Marshall Plan aid; and C. Douglas Dillon, a rare American finance minister because he had a feel for policy beyond an accountant's ledger and the bond market.

Their professional staff was of the same impeccable caliber, and the Commission produced 399 pages of unlovely committee prose, the hallmark of any serious international document. Reading through this high-minded effort, however, I was increasingly struck by nagging doubts and contradictions, some in my own mind and some that were evidently in the minds of the commissioners.

On page 78, for example, the report declares that "the interests of both rich and poor require that developing countries advance at the most rapid feasible rate, but, in fact, many of them face the prospect of cutting back on their planned rates of growth because they must now assume

significant reductions in aid." This, of course, is the Commission theme writ large, that there is a direct relation between the volume of aid and the pace of development. But back in the appendix on page 235 the Commission observes: "Oversimplifications led both industrial and low-income countries to overemphasize aid flows and per capita GNP growth, a habit which is only slowly giving way to the realization that the impact of aid flows on GNP depends largely on the efficiency with which the recipient uses domestic resources and on the over-all economic and social policies which he pursues." Or, more plainly, there is no simple link between aid and growth. This notion, of course, puts in question the recommendations for a big increase in aid and was properly buried in the appendix. To be sure, the main body of the report does note that "the correlation between the amounts of aid received in the past decades and the growth performance is very weak." But this is explained away on the grounds that slow growers got the wrong kind of aid and fast growers received lots of private capital.

The Commission was understandably anxious to overcome the belief that aid is money down a rathole, that the larger poor countries in particular are making a botch of things. Thus, it asserts that "the growth record has been good" and calculates that the rate of output between 1960 and 1967 was a round 5 per cent, precisely the target set by the United Nations for the sixties, the so-called "Development Decade."

I was at once reminded of another ponderous report that had turned up in Delhi, one prepared by the secretariat of UNCTAD, the United Nations Conference on Trade and Development. This organ, created by the poor to air their grievances against the rich, shares many of the Pearson Commission goals, but its clientele requires a different tactic. In season and out, UNCTAD is obliged to emphasize how badly the poor are faring (due, of course, to the selfishness of the rich). Thus, its report began: "Growth achievements by the developing countries in the early years of the

Development Decade have been disappointing, and the likelihood is very slight that the minimum 5 per cent growth target . . . will be reached." For that 1960–1967 period, UNCTAD computes the growth of the poor at about 4.6 per cent.

Getting by on Faith

The answer, of course, is that neither and both, UNCTAD and Pearson, are right and wrong. The computation of a single growth figure for wildly different economies is a game that can be played to yield almost any result the players want. For one thing, the underlying statistics that compose gross product in poor nations are not worth very much. A block development officer in a remote district of Uttar Pradesh is not likely to make a close count of the millet crop in his region; he will probably send in a report that best satisfies the peculiar needs of his immediate superiors. For another, economists who translate the domestic market value of a given nation's output at the official exchange rate for dollars—which appears to be what the Pearson Commission has done—engage in a large measure of poetic license. (Officially, the rupee is 13.3 cents, yielding an income per person of about $60 at the official rate. If Indians or anyone else tried to live on the purchasing-power equivalent of little more than one American dollar a week, they would all be dead. Obviously, the rupee goes further than its 13.3 cent official rate suggests.)

Apart from these difficulties, there is the fearsome problem of weighting. In calculating a comprehensive growth rate for a group of nations—the poor in this case—what portion of the whole should be attributed to each country? Should its weight reflect its population, its output, or what? Indeed, the "disappointing" figure UNCTAD announced at its New Delhi meeting improved in the next two years. This does not mean that growth among the poor suddenly took off but that the UNCTAD aggregate heavily weights India's performance. The fact is that after two years of drought, India enjoyed two years of rains.

As a sometime India Hand, I was particularly interested in how the Commission would square the circle for the World Bank's biggest client. How would it attempt to reassure the fainthearted and still make the case for heavier doses of aid to Delhi? The report, of course, hailed what is now called the "Green Revolution," the introduction in Asia of high-yielding wheat and rice seeds. The document triumphantly observed that India's food output in the year ending June 30 was 97 million tons, 8 million more than the record four years earlier. It carfully did not note that this amounts to an annual gain of about 2 per cent, or substantially less than the yearly increase in mouths to feed.

It is true that in a few districts, notably in the Punjab and Tamilnad, some farmers have achieved some remarkable yields and rupee millionaires are being created. But again, one has to turn to the appendix and page 290 to discover that "the new technology affects only a small percentage of the rural population, those with adequate holdings and access to water." Less diplomatic observers might have said that the Green Revolution is largely a matter for celebration among the happy few with the political clout or cash to bribe officials controlling the new seeds and all-important chemical fertilizer.

The Pearson document also praises India's economic planning. However, the report does not mention the fact that India has been operating without a plan for three years because the Planning Commission was faced with the Hobson's choice of proclaiming targets that were wildly unrealistic or painfully depressing. In fact, the Plan, like so many other paper schemes, bears only a marginal relationship to the way farmers, businessmen, and even the government conduct their affairs. At best, it is a guide to budget-makers in the Finance Ministry, and it is not clear how much attention they pay to it.

Perhaps the most triumphant note in the Pearson report is its announcement about birth control. "The development of intra-uterine contraceptive devices (IUD's) and of oral pills has amounted to a major breakthrough in family planning techniques." This statement is separated from the report's special discussion of India and for good reason. An effort of sorts was mounted to distribute IUD's in India; for a variety of reasons, the rate of rejections has probably been as high as the insertions. Indian women just won't have them. As for the pill, apart from its expense, it requires a degree of numerical sophistication that is still beyond most villagers—and it is in villages that the bulk of India's population lives. Family planning authorities in Delhi, with a very imperfect grasp of what happens to their schemes in the field, are now quietly waiting for a miracle injection to solve their problem. The explosive birthrate remains virtually unchanged.

Most telling of all is the discussion (in the appendix) of the negative consequences of food aid. The gifts and near-gifts, donated partly for humanitarian reasons and partly to work down American surpluses, became what the Pearson report accurately describes as a "crutch." Thanks to this grain, the Indian government was able to postpone politically difficult policies to spur domestic farm output. It is too bad that this discussion is buried in the section after the report. For it raises a question that should trouble all right-minded persons. If food aid tended to impede domestic agricultural development, what of aid in general? Is there something in the argument usually ascribed to the illiberal and narrow-minded? Or, in the jargon of the bureaucrats, is aid counterproductive?

Heresy

All of which brings us back to my Indian official at the Food and Agriculture Ministry and his paradoxical delight in the aid cut. The Pearson report notwithstanding, he and some other heretics suspect that aid has spared the Indian government from making the harsh decisions that would do most to further economic development. For example, many development theorists agree that investment—the plowing of resources into the means of production for future income—is the single most important ingredient for growth. Investment requires savings; someone with money income must refrain from spending it on consumption so that resources can be employed to produce investment goods.

This seems like a fearful burden to impose on impoverished nations. But there is a substantial source of income in India that goes untapped: the incomes of the new rupee millionaires and other successful farmers. Because farmers are politically powerful, the Indian government places no income tax on their earnings. Thus, India is unique among poor countries, for in India, industry subsidizes agriculture rather than vice versa. Without foreign aid, this odd state of affairs might not last.

Again, India has embraced a peculiar system of food zones. Under this arrangement, one or several of its seventeen states together prohibit the sale of food grains outside their borders. States that lack food must buy what they need from the central government. Delhi, in turn, tried to build up a stock by purchases from states with a surplus. In fact, the central government picked up very little and fed the deficit states largely with grains brought in through aid. In other words, under political pressure from the states, it created separate, balkanized markets with all the inefficiencies that this implies. Without food aid, the pressure to reverse this course might have been irresistible.

Again, the Congress Party in New Delhi and the state political parties attempt to woo vocal and articulate city voters by keeping down the price of food. Thus, the national government is reluctant to raise farm price supports to a level that would encourage more output. A price-support program that spurred farm output might, in time, turn India into a food exporter, actually earning the foreign exchange with which to buy machines and parts needed for industrial development. But aid provides foreign exchange and removes some of the pressure for a higher and more productive support policy.

The examples could be multiplied, but the point remains the same. Aid is not necessarily an engine of development, at least in India. The biggest obstacle to growth is probably what Gunnar Myrdal has called the "soft state," a concept to which the Pearson report pays only glancing attention. Development in India is frustrated by a government unwilling to make hard choices or impose its will. At the crudest level, it is a Hindu police force looking the other way in Gujarat while Muslim shops and people are set upon by mobs. It is the great paper plans for birth control at New Delhi and the lack of disciplined cadres in the villages. It is the ability of the powerful and politically connected to grab off the credit, fertilizer, and seed required for a real leap in farm output.

To be sure, I have based this critique exclusively on India, the poor country I know best. But India contains more than a fifth of the population of what is optimistically called the developing world, and as the Pearson report says, "India is a major test of whether development can be significantly accelerated through external assistance."

The authors of the Pearson report are decent and able beyond question. They did note in passing that the effectiveness of aid depends in large measure on how well it is used. But this ritual bow does not interfere with their clarion call for more aid. My tour in India, however, has left me wobbling in the ranks of the right-thinking and profoundly impressed with Myrdal's notion of the "soft state." I suggest that it is no longer clear that a massive increase in aid, without a concomitant hardening of soft states, will yield any great consequences for the economic development of the poor. Indeed, the one might very well frustrate the other.

13

GOVERNMENT AND THE ECONOMY: DIRECTION WITHOUT DOMINATION?

In an earlier age Americans believed that politics and economics were distinct and separate activities. The business cycle moved through its various phases—prosperity, recession, depression, recovery—without attracting more than passing attention from political spokesmen. Business leaders created vast industrial empires without any government intervention. The impact of new machines on the labor force was largely ignored by governors and presidents.

Today, domestic economic issues automatically become political questions. The earlier sharp distinction separating government and the economy have been replaced by active government intervention in economic affairs.

Overall Direction: Can Government Curb the Business Cycle?

The United States experienced major economic crises during the administrations of Martin Van Buren, James Buchanan, U. S. Grant, and Grover Cleveland without government showing any great concern for falling prices, unemployment, and breadlines. When President Cleveland vetoed a bill that would have given federal funds for farm relief, he firmly declared that the people should support the government, but that government should never support the people. This philosophy was discarded during the Great Depression of the 1930's. In the face of wholesale disaster, a demand arose that government become a team captain who would organize the economy's players (business, labor, farmers, consumers) into a winning combination called prosperity. If depression or inflation threatens today, we assume that it is the responsibility of government to take action that will restore relative price stability. The big question today is no longer "should we" but "can we?" It is an article of faith among world Communists that a "boom-bust" cycle is part of the very nature of capitalism. Max Lerner, a famous American commentator on the current scene, has written that "It is on the test of stability that American capitalism is most vulnerable."

Recently the government's "new economists" have asserted that they can eliminate the frightening extremes that have marred our history. In the Kennedy-Johnson era they claimed credit for the booming economy that produced nearly full employment and a soaring gross national product. But this prosperity went hand-in-hand with an unchecked inflationary thrust. Alarmed by this trend, Nixon economists attempted to cool the economy through a tight monetary policy, high interest rates, restricted credit, and cuts in government spending. Inflationary trends continued, although to the distress of the administration these policies produced the highest interest rates in a century, a general slowdown of business activity, widespread unemployment, and numerous bankruptcies. At the moment, the ability of economists to control the business cycle is in question.

Where does this experience leave us? Would alternate policies have achieved the desired ends? Perhaps the economists can produce prosperity, but only with an inflationary price tag. To achieve their ends, will they need government regulation so vast as to threaten personal freedom? From what direction do we face the greater threat—the unchecked business cycle or the "new economics"?

Big Business and Government: Logical Partners or Natural Enemies?

The relationship between business and government is a matter of much concern to Americans. At one extreme are those who argue that the country should be governed by those who own it, that since businessmen have a great financial stake in the country they have the greatest concern that government policies do not thwart that interest—or more positively, that government must become an active agent to preserve national prosperity. This policy can be reduced to the simple formula, "What's good for United States Steel is good for the United States." Expressed in another way, a comparison between business and government operations is made, with the conclusion that "we need more business in government."

At the other extreme in this debate are those who view with alarm the role played by business leaders in political affairs. To buttress their argument these spokesmen advance evidence of political control through campaign contributions, the staffing of regulatory agencies, and the attempt of corporate leaders to speak for their stockholders and employees. At a more basic level, C. Wright Mills has described a ruling class in the United States composed of business, military, and political leaders, many of whom are subject to no democratic controls.

Questions of policy are debated within the foregoing framework. Do we need more business in government? Do we already have too much? Should rigid restriction be placed on business campaign contributions and other avenues of influence? Should unions be similarly restricted? Should business and labor groups be encouraged to compete for voter favor? Finally, how can we dispose of the concern (expressed in the following pages by former President Eisenhower) that we face a constant danger from the dual alliance between business and the military establishment?

1

The "New Economists" Take Over

NEIL W. CHAMBERLAIN

During the past 20 years a number of sophisticated theories and policies have been developed to stabilize the business cycle and stimulate economic growth. Put forward by the so-called "new economists," these policies require bold, decisive action on the part of the national government. Contemporary debate over government action is unintelligible without an understanding of the assumptions upon which such action is based.

In the article that follows the economic thinking that has governed our historical development is categorized in three periods. Several questions should be answered by the careful reader. Why did Keynesian economists reject the "housekeeping" concept of the budget? How did they propose to achieve a balanced budget? How do the "new economists" differ from the Keynesians in their attitude toward balanced budgets?

The history of [government taxation and spending policy] can be traced most simply in three stages of thought concerning the government's budget and when it should be balanced. We commit only slight violence to the facts by treating these as three neat and successive intellectual epochs, as future historians will doubtless do anyway.

The first period lasted longest, from the earliest conception of a nation's governmental budget almost to World War II. During it, the federal budget was regarded as an instrument of governmental housekeeping, performing the same function as a

From Neil W. Chamberlain, "The Art of Unbalancing the Budget," The Atlantic Monthly, January 1966, pp. 58–61. Copyright © 1966 by the Atlantic Monthly Company, Boston, Mass. 02116. Reprinted by permission of the author and publisher.

family's budget. The government had certain functions to perform, which had been assigned to it by society: keeping order, carrying the mails, running the courts, providing a monetary system, regulating interstate and foreign commerce, manning the army and navy. A well-administered government would see to it that in carrying out these functions it lived within its means, a feat of good housekeeping comparable with that of the prudent household. Taxes were levied only to provide the revenue needed for the performance of the services which society required. If special circumstances—most commonly a war—obliged the government to borrow funds, this was to be viewed as an unfortunate but temporary expedient. The sooner the debt was extinguished, the better. To produce a surplus at the end of the fiscal year, which could be applied against the national indebtedness, won for a government a crown of glory.

. . .

It conceived the government's economic role in the same terms as it would any other economic unit, private or public: private business performed certain economic functions, such as providing goods; households performed other economic functions, such as providing labor services; and similarly, the federal government performed still other economic functions. The federal budget was the largest of all budgets, to be sure, even though not by the same margin as today, but this was a difference in degree and not in kind.

Or was it? Was there something about the government's budget that distinguished it from that of the Jones family and of U.S. Steel? Was there some special function connected with it which gave it a purpose other than the economical provision of particular services? There was indeed, said a school of economists, whose minority voice failed to attract much notice until the late 1930's, when John Maynard Keynes became its spokesman. Their view gained ascendancy largely as a consequence of the Great Depression, which lingered on until finally dispelled by wartime activity, and memories of which provided the emotional undertow on which full employment policies rode to legislative approvals in post-war Western Europe and North America. The second stage of our budgetary history was thereby ushered in.

Managed Prosperity

This second-stage school of economic theorists looked on the budget as performing not just one function—proper federal housekeeping—but two. The second function was to preserve the economic health of the nation as a whole. It was the government's duty, said this group, to see that the nation remained prosperous, a duty no less important than preserving law and order and maintaining courts and other such time-honored governmental services.

The nation's economic health was the business of the government because no other agent or institution could serve as doctor.

The doctor's implements were not only monetary policy—making money cheaper to use in depressions so that business and households would use more of it, hopefully returning the nation to prosperity; the instrument kit of the federal government as economic doctor included its budget as well. In times of depression, it could spend more than it took in, thereby directly putting people and plants to productive use. It did not have to wait for businesses and households to become optimistic enough to borrow money at lower rates of interest. It could put money in their pockets directly by cutting its tax take, or it could itself spend on a variety of projects, or it could increase the amount of money it transferred to people who could be counted on to spend it. All these ways would put the government budget in the red, but it would increase the nation's economic activity. It would put people and plants to work whose services would otherwise be irretrievably lost.

All very well, said more traditional economists, but how long could this go on? How many times could the medicine be repeated? If the government persisted in deficit spending, its debt would double, its credit would crumble, and it would find no buyers for its bonds. Fiscal responsibility could not be evaded. The balanced budget was not a luxury to be dispensed with under pressure but a necessity of a solvent government.

Cyclical Balancing

The economic freethinkers had an answer. It might be true that the government could not afford to go on piling up new debt on old every time there was a downturn of business activity. But it would not have to; the fear that government credit would sooner or later go under, in a persistently rising sea of debt, was unwarranted. The alarmists were ignoring the existence of the business cycle, with its alternating phases of boom and depression.

If the economy was depressed at times, experience showed that this was followed by periods of excessive—inflationary—activity. The government as doctor was no less needed in the one case than in the other, but the remedy for one was the opposite of the remedy for the other. In depressions it would spend more than it took in and use budget deficits to bring the economy back to normal. In inflations it would take in more than it spent, and use budget surpluses to restore economic normality. And the surpluses of the inflation end of the business cycle could be used to pay off the deficits of the depression phase of the cycle.

Was it necessary to balance the budget? Yes, but only over the period of a business cycle. Annual balancing was an error, since it ignored the cyclical rhythm of the nation's health. Outgo and income could be matched over an appropriate span of years, in which the minuses of some were wiped out by the pluses of others.

. . .

Planned Deficits

A more daring set of economists began to feel their way toward a different answer. The nation could not count on regular budgetary surpluses to wipe out regular deficits. There was no reason to expect that such cyclical balancing would ever occur. But if the budget were balanced in the good years, then one could afford to run deficits in those years when the economy slowed down. This would mean that the national debt would steadily rise over the years, but this need not cause alarm, since the nation's assets and income were also growing. Not annual budget balancing, not even cyclical balancing, but balancing only in the years of plenty was looked on as the appropriate policy.

. . .

This was the general line of reasoning behind the income tax cut of 1965 and the excise tax cuts projected for the next few years. By reducing taxes to a level which at full employment *would* produce only as much revenue as *would* be needed to cover expenditures, the government necessarily collects less *now*. It leaves more money in the business and household sectors; if they spend it, as they will in large proportion, this augments economic activity and brings us nearer the full-employment goal.

Tax-Cutting: New Fiscal Toy

It is this phenomenon that has given rise to the colorful description of the new fiscal policy as "spending our way to prosperity." In effect, we can buy more and be better off for doing so.

Skeptical politicians have wondered whether such a policy courts inflation. They are uneasy with a policy which appears to reward profligacy. An amusing instance of this attitude occurred during Senate hearings over the proposed income tax reduction. A New England lawmaker asked Walter Heller, then chairman of the President's Council of Economic Advisers, why so many people resisted the new fiscal philosophy if, in effect, it promised reward for self-indulgence. Heller said he supposed any public disapproval stemmed from a residual Puritanism—to which the New England senator, still dubious but not doleful, replied that he himself was more of a puritan than a Heller.

But any earlier doubts now seem largely to have been dispelled as a result of the success of the 1965 tax reduction, and an increasing number of legislators appear to embrace the new approach with enthusiasm. What politician can for long resist the appeal of voting for tax reductions? Is there, then, danger that the new fiscal toy will be overused with inflationary consequences?

Any policy is of course subject to abuse, but as long as the size of budgetary deficits is geared to the full-employment surplus, there is a built-in monitor. In the final analysis, the new fiscal policy is based less on deficit budgeting than on budget balancing. When the potential GNP is reached, the government's outlay will be in line with its income, since that is the point at which the government's budget is *planned* to be in balance.

Balance the budget? Of course, but what budget? The answer which is now being given is the full-employment budget. At levels short of full employment this means balancing not an actual but a hypothetical budget, the budget as it would be if we were operating at potential GNP. This is not a matter of running in the red in a vague hope that this will do the economy some good, as the bloodletting of earlier days was expected to restore a patient's health. It is the incurring of deficits in an amount which is guided by calculations of potential GNP, which in turn is based on computations of the level of acceptable compromise between unemployment and price increases.

National Debt No Mortgage

. . . There is of course no basis for believing that economic "truth" about budget balancing has now, finally, been divulged. We can be sure that a fourth stage in our thinking lies somewhere over the horizon. We might even surmise that it has something to do with relative advantages of tax cuts versus government expenditures, a matter which so far has been more the subject of vocal inflection than cerebral reflection.

But of one other thing we can also be sure. Our present stage-three thinking represents a vast improvement over its predecessor stages. And whether it appears excessively simplistic to some or dubiously synthetic to others, it is a product of contemporary social science no different in its fundamental importance from current innovations in the physical sciences.

2

The End of the Economist's Dream

ROBERT LEKACHMAN

The simple yet highly successful economic theories described in the preceding Chamberlain article had lost their glamour and certainty by the early 1970's. Unemployment was high and rising; the stock market had plunged, with the Dow-Jones averages at ten year lows; industrial production and corporate profits were falling; and interest rates hit hundred year highs. In the face of these disasters, inflation continued unabated.

    What went wrong? What happened to the brave new economic world of the mid-1960's? The following article suggests that blame must be widely distributed among recent Presidents and their economic advisers. What errors did President Nixon allegedly make on tax policy? On federal spending? What was the result of Federal Reserve monetary policy? Why did Nixon resist economic guidelines? What version of Kennedy's economic policy do his admirers recite? What conflicting version does the author give? What economic myths do Americans believe? How does the author rate the following Presidents as economic managers: Eisenhower, Kennedy, Johnson, Nixon?

I

    By any rational political or intellectual standard, Republican economic policy has dismally failed. When the Dow-Jones index of industrials cracked the 700 barrier in the middle of May the investment community gave public utterance to its flagging private confidence in the Nixon Administration. This was no crisis of nerves. All the news of real economic events had been bad. Unemployment had indeed risen and this by the peculiar inverted logic of economists was good news since the profession grimly believes in an inevitable trade-off between unemployment and the pace of price inflation. The only trouble was that prices

From Robert Lekachman, "Money in America," Harper's Magazine, *August 1970, pp. 29–34. Copyright © 1970, by Minneapolis Star and Tribune, Inc. Reprinted from the August, 1970 issue of* Harper's Magazine *by permission of the author.*

continued their merry ascent quite as though a million men and women were not out of work who a year ago had jobs and quite as though other signs of a cooling economy were not plentiful—among them a drop in corporate profits to the lowest level since late 1967, a resumption in the slippage of industrial production, slumping auto sales, continued calamity in construction, and murderously high interest rates.

    Economic management falls far short of an exact science. Nevertheless, the Republican failures are very substantially those of ineptitude, political cowardice, and ideological prejudice rather than those of poor economic theory or inadequate tools of control. Justification of this harsh judgment demands a little preliminary exegesis of contemporary doctrine. These days economists are locked in one of their periodic controversies over the relative importance of monetary and fiscal policy. At Chicago Milton Friedman and the monetary school which he leads are persuaded that what affects most this year's Gross National Product is the rate at which the Federal Reserve Board allowed the nation's monetary supply to grow *last* year. It is the lag between monetary and other economic changes which led the monetarists to predict a sharp recession in 1970 on the basis of the monetary policies of 1969.

As the monetarists see the world, the way to control an inflation is to clamp down upon the money supply by the Federal Reserve's traditional techniques, higher rediscount rates, severer reserve requirements, or sale of Treasury securities on the open market. Each technique has the effect of tightening credit and raising interest rates. To have its promised impact upon prices, monetary policy must be determined and it must be applied long enough to hurt. The pain manifests itself in drooping sales, falling output, and spreading layoffs. Even the more bellicose unions will bargain with caution in such a climate and even monopolistic sellers will pause before trying to raise prices.

So testify the monetarists. The opposing camp of fiscal economists, led by Walter Heller and Paul Samuelson, will freely concede that money and credit are important, but they are convinced that still more important is the stream of personal incomes out of which businessmen make their investment decisions and consumers their buying choices. This flow of personal incomes can be widened or narrowed by the budgetary decisions taken by the federal government. Such fiscal interventions assume the shape either of tax variations or expenditure changes. Tax cuts and rising expenditures increase consumer spending, improve investment prospects, and enlarge the Gross National Product by some multiple of the original tax or public-expenditure change. Of course rising taxes and falling budgetary outlays have the reverse impact. As a matter of the sheer fiscal hydraulics, it doesn't really make a great deal of difference whether Congress and the President tinker with taxes or expenditures. From the standpoint of social justice or the equi-

ties of urban and black necessities, the choice may be crucial. Either policy adequately implemented will repress inflation.

There's the rub. Since January 1969, the Nixon Administration has demonstrated its unwillingness or inability to pursue sufficiently severe and sufficiently consistent policies of either variety. The reasons for the failure are various. During the 1968 campaign, Nixon pledged the phasing out of the hated 10 per cent Johnson surtax, apparently regardless of the inflationary condition of the country, and evidently on the standard conservative premise that all taxes are bad and Democratic taxes worst of all. Although once in office Mr. Nixon hedged by seeking extension of the tax at a halved rate until July 1, 1970, he evaded the necessities of the situation which called for an indefinite extension at least of the original 10 per cent surcharge and probably for an increase in the rate at which it was levied.

Nor did the President do much better in controlling federal spending, his fiscal alternative. A sharp reduction in military, space, and agricultural appropriations would have dampened the economy as surely as a tax increase. The President has instead pressed for the second stage of the ABM, recommended more funds for the supersonic transport, and reaffirmed his commitments to the space boondoggle. At this writing the budgetary consequences of the Cambodian misadventure are conjectural, but it is difficult to see them as doing other than casting further out of balance a federal budget somewhat fancifully in balance to start with. Pleased enough to economize on health, education, housing, and research, the President has been unwilling to place his favorite clients on short rations and still less eager to inform his constituency of silent, middle Americans that if they truly favor peace with "honor" in Southeast Asia and if they really are as appalled as their President at the prospect of losing a war to a minor Communist power, they must pay higher taxes to control the inflation which past pursuit of "honorable" peace has generated.

Since his fiscal policy is something of a shambles, Mr. Nixon has been compelled to rely upon Federal Reserve control of credit availability and interest rates. At the outset there are two things to be said about monetary policy. The Federal Reserve is in law and quite frequently in fact an independent agency, subject to Presidential influence but not to Presidential direction. More important, monetary policy is a tough, unpopular way to control inflation, unlikely to enhance the electoral prospects of the party which embraces it. When credit gets scarce, General Motors and General Electric do not go short, but school districts, city governments, small businessmen, and prospective buyers of inexpensive houses (where they exist) feel the pinch almost instantly. All the same, an Administration sufficiently cold-blooded about repressing inflation through credit stringency will have its way, at the expense as usual of the weak and the unprotected. From the middle of 1969 to the early months of the current year, the Federal Reserve kept the money supply practically constant.

Why, in the light of what I have claimed for monetary policy, did the inflation persist? One reason was general skepticism of the durability of the Federal Reserve's intentions and the dependability of Presidential support, once unemployment began to rise, industrial output sag, and profits shrink. A second explanation is a testimonial to the ingenuity of the major New York banks in defeating Federal Reserve efforts by borrowing Eurodollars from Western Europe and selling commercial paper in this country. These loopholes are now plugged. But the doubts of Presidential firmness have been validated by heavy public suggestions by Mr. Nixon and some of his advisers that perhaps the time has come to relax the credit squeeze and allow a resumption of moderate monetary growth. The current Chairman of the Federal Reserve, Dr. Arthur F. Burns, testified to the Joint Economic Committee in these terms: "The Board cannot overlook the possibility that the present slowdown in economic activity, which is a healthy development, may yet be followed by a recession. . . . There is also the possibility, however, that the inflationary processes with which we are dealing may prove more stubborn than we realize. . . . For some time this year, our monetary and credit policies are therefore likely to tread a narrow path between too much restraint and too much ease." All of which, if it means anything, implies that the Federal Reserve's course is now as unpredictable as the President's foreign policy.

As Raymond J. Saulnier, former Chairman of an Eisenhower Council of Economic Advisers, put it, comparing Nixon's policies with the successful deflation over which he himself presided between 1958 and 1960, "For twice as bad a disease, it's using half as much medicine." A consistent conservative, Saulnier was willing in both the 1950s and the 1970s to pay the unemployment price required to still the demon of inflation.

But as a man who blames his 1960 defeat on an election-year recession, President Nixon has set out quite deliberately to control inflation without paying the price of unemployment. Although his motives are more likely electoral than compassionate, a reluctance to increase unemployment can only be applauded, even by the President's critics. The trouble appears to be that half-hearted budgetary and monetary policy on the evidence does increase unemployment, but it does not check inflation. The key Administration failure is to grapple with the implications of its unwillingness to accept a recession in order to cure an inflation. There is only one way to reconcile the President's apparently inconsistent policy preferences: this is to impose some form of effective control over the key price and wage decisions which giant corporations and major unions make. One of the reasons why effective monetary policy almost demands recession to work is to be found in the power of a few important people at the key controls in a small number of major industries to force wages up even if, as in the construction trades, employment falls as a consequence, and to advance prices even if, as repeatedly in steel, sales are lost to imports or substitutes. Called cost-push inflation by economists, the phenomenon is almost entirely the effect of the extreme concentration of economic power.

Not at all to their credit, many economists tend to minimize the extent of monopoly power and exaggerate the competitiveness of the economy, possibly because economists explain competition a good deal more elegantly than they do the monopoly, oligopoly, and hybrid mixtures of competition and control which actually pervade American business. For a conservative Administration, served by conservative advisers, it is of course exceedingly convenient to deny that out there in the Republican heartland thrive men of power whose fiat is able to defeat the best-laid plans of the Federal Reserve.

Thus it was that at his first press conference as President, Mr. Nixon delivered himself of these sentiments: "I do not go along with the suggestion that inflation can be effectively controlled by exhorting labor and management and industry to follow certain guidelines." The words foreshadowed complete abandonment of the timid wage-price guideposts with which the Kennedy and the Johnson Administrations had experimented. Weak as these were, they had at least the merit of defining criteria for noninflationary wage and price changes in the private economy. They allowed an activist President, affronted by some especially outrageous wage or price gouge, to intervene within the context of a coherent intellectual rationale and a stated national policy. Lacking statutory authorization, the wage-price guideposts depended for their influence upon a President's capacity to mobilize public sentiment against corporate or union offenders, or in the last resort upon the implicit threat of shifted defense contracts, tax inquiries, and grand-jury probes into possible violations of the antitrust laws. To this day the experts argue over impact of the guideposts. Almost certainly, they were better than nothing.

By junking them, the Nixon Administra-

tion explicitly declared its intention of refraining from intervention in major union negotiations and major corporate pricing decisions. Wages and prices, it seemed to say, were the consequences of the operations of impersonal, competitive markets, not the outcome of the concentration of economic power and the political decisions which corporate and union leaders make.

In 1970 what is required is a good deal more than guideposts. If present monetary and fiscal policies are to work without severe recession, what is urgently needed is a set of effective controls over wages, profits, prices, and credit. This is neither politically nor administratively a simple proposition. Yet what else is there to do? As usual John Kenneth Galbraith, a World War II price controller, put it best in urging "a tailored system of wage and price controls as the only feasible alternative to inflation." Speaking of himself and other price controllers, he remarked, "Better than any others we know the difficulties. We have also faced the sad fact that there is no alternative." Galbraith is right but the Nixon Administration is unmoved. It has presented us with a depressing combination of recession and inflation and no sign that it knows what to do next.

II

We are all living in the ruins of Republican policies. I do not believe it unduly charitable to this Administration if I leave the scene of the disaster, temporarily at least, and turn to more interesting matters than the unimaginative mismanagement of a complex economy by an ungifted politician. The key question is this one: how did we ever get ourselves into a situation where so little that is essential to the health of the polity is politically feasible? The answer is to be found in the apparent successes as well as the manifest failures of two Democratic Presidents.

I shall begin with a bit of New Frontier hagiography. As the story is told to this day by Kennedy admirers, it goes like this. In economic as in political and social affairs, the key New Frontier commitment was a promise to get the country moving again after eight years of Republican stagnation, punctuated by three recessions. This was achieved, largely because of successful management of taxes and public spending by an intelligent President who absorbed the teachings of the New Economics. In the first Kennedy year the investment tax credit (in effect a 7 per cent cut in the price of new machines) stimulated business investment, and, just as the President's Keynesian advisers predicted, had an even greater multiplier impact upon employment and income. No doubt the rewards flowed initially to executives and stockholders, but humbler folk soon reaped enjoyable benefits in the shape of more employment and higher wages. It was not that Mr. Kennedy wished to be soft on the rich. As a former student and present patron of the author of *The Affluent Society,* he was better aware than most politicians of the needs of the public sector. The President, however, was an even more devoted student of the art of the possible in politics than he was of the works of John Kenneth Galbraith. And his study told him that Congress was in no mood to enact such staples of the liberal agenda as Medicare, general aid to education, or other programs of rescue for urban America.

As the President analyzed his situation, the route to social expenditure was indirect. In fact, a preliminary necessity was general tax reduction. In late 1962 when the President decided to follow Walter Heller's advice and seek tax legislation from Congress, he did so not because he disputed Galbraith's famous diagnosis of public squalor and private affluence, but because he judged that Congress might be persuaded to cut taxes $10 billion or so but could not be coaxed or coerced into spending an additional $10 billion for social purposes. Yet if tax cuts worked their anticipated magic, the economy would expand so vigorously that total tax collections would actually rise each year. Out of this annual growth bonanza, Congress, its heart softened by prosperity, might just possibly do something for the poor, the urban, and the black.

The tax cut worked better than most economic nostrums. Aided by a generous helping of good luck, the $10 billion tax cut (finally enacted in February 1964) did lead to the $30 billion enlargement of Gross National Product that the Council of Economic Advisers prayerfully forecast. Best of all, unemployment finally began to shrink toward the Administration's stated "interim" target of 4 per cent. Although Mr. Kennedy did not live to see Congress endorse his policy, his successor enjoyed the harvest of social legislation which New Frontier political strategy had at length made Congressionally feasible.

Circa 1964–65, those *anni mirabiles* of the Great Society, everything came up roses. An obedient Congress delivered to Lyndon Johnson Medicare, a variety of educational programs, regional health centers, Model Cities, rent supplements, and even, in the shape of the Office of Economic Opportunity, ratification of the President's "unconditional" war upon poverty. All this, and in 1965, a second tax cut into the bargain. During all this legislative turmoil, the economy seemed as responsive to the will of the Texas autocrat as Congressmen and Senators were. Prices were quiescent. Few wage settlements disobeyed the guideposts. The New Economics, the New Frontier, and the Great Society had produced full employment without inflation, social progress, and lower taxes, a painless march to justice and prosperity for all.

It's a pity, but the fault neither of the New Economists nor their assassinated patron, that this grand story had such an unhappy ending. The familiar villain of course was Lyndon Johnson, who forgot that he had won his 1964 landslide as a peace candidate. The wickedness of Vietnam escalation destroyed the sweet harmonies of economic progress. Roses were superseded by thorns. The President soon stooped to deceit and evasion. If he had wanted both his Vietnam hobby and continued price stability, he should have heeded his advisers and raised taxes early in 1966. Instead, intent on early victory, sedulous to conceal the scale of the Asian nightmare, he preferred to underestimate by some $10 billion the next year's Vietnam costs. The economy took off, inflation began to accelerate, and we still suffer the consequences.

The architect of disaster was Lyndon Johnson. Disaster's eager heir appears to be Richard Nixon.

I find a rather different version of these same events considerably more plausible. It begins with the underestimated Presidency of Dwight Eisenhower. Mr. Eisenhower presided over an Administration notably skeptical of Pentagon claims. It may be that only a former general possesses both the knowledge and the self-assurance to say no to his former colleagues when they come crying for more of their deadly playthings. In retrospect, it is plain that President Eisenhower deserves gratitude not only for his famous warning against the undue influence of the military-industrial complex, but even more for his refusal to excuse the military from the normal controls of the Bureau of the Budget and the reasonable constraints of overall economic policy. In those days there were frustrated generals in the land, among them such notables as Maxwell Taylor and James Gavin, who were sincerely convinced that Eisenhower parsimony was in a fair way to endangering the security of the nation.

Reflecting and speaking the language of liberal imperialism and American interventionism, the Kennedy circle quite early embraced a global activism which it contrasted with the inertia of Eisenhower foreign policy, constrained as it had been by the starvation of conventional ground forces. The campaign rhetoric of missile gaps and alleged softness on Castro was implemented by the new Administration initially at the Bay of Pigs. This disaster was followed in June by an unpleasant Vienna confrontation between the President and Khrushchev which convinced Mr. Kennedy that the only way to make American determination credible to the Russians was by a posture of strength. From this esti-

mate flowed partial reserve mobilizations and a sharp increase in requests for military appropriations, notably in support of counterinsurgency forces. A still more fateful result was the sending of more advisers to Vietnam, as a sign to the Russians rather than as a response to any special emergency in Southeast Asia. It is far from reassuring, one might add parenthetically, that one of the justifications advanced for 1970's Cambodian invasion was just this same alleged need to impress the Russians and this time, no doubt, the Chinese as well.

In November 1963 the 900 Americans in Vietnam at the end of the Eisenhower years had been joined by more than 25,000 reinforcements. No doubt Lyndon Johnson could still have liquidated the war, but at a political cost much higher than Mr. Kennedy would have had to pay early in 1961. That the roots of present calamities are to be found in Kennedy policy is of course ancient history. The point to be made here is related but slightly different. As Mr. Kennedy defined American foreign policy, large increases in military spending were essential. This central evaluation had important budgetary consequences. To the general reluctance of Americans to pay higher taxes for social purposes was added the beginnings of that military preemption of available funds from present taxes which has reached fruition in Richard Nixon's Washington.

There is a further point. Any President has a limited stock of political capital and a limited access to the ear of his constituents. If he asks for some things, he cannot feasibly ask for others. In his three years, what John Kennedy asked for had rather little to do with social improvement. The better part of a year was devoted to passage of the Trade Expansion Act, a much oversold piece of legislation fueled as much by the calculations of NATO strategists as by economic evaluations of American commercial interest. And then there was the moon race, the mobilization of American technology and science in the interests of winning the big game with the Russians. In short, President Kennedy, motivated by the successful politician's blend of personal preference and electoral calculation, took the easier of the available courses. He appealed to American pride, competitiveness, distrust of Communists, and affection for technology.

In 1970 a great deal of what President Nixon says and does grotesquely parodies the man who a decade earlier elbowed him aside. It is the burden of these remarks that President Kennedy's choices were often wrong. Nevertheless, they were made with a certain grace, consideration for friends, and compassion for opponents. And there was always the hope that so quick a man would benefit from harsh experience. At his death there were signs that the hope was justified. If today's President seems to be repeating the errors, there are few signs that he is learning from them.

Nevertheless, what John Kennedy did prepared the way for the deterioration that followed him. It is harsh but unavoidable to say that like such less appealing political leaders as Leonid Brezhnev, Mao Tse-tung, and Gamal Abdel Nasser, President Kennedy directed his people's attention away from the complex and intricate issues which divided them toward the enemies who appeared to threaten their interests. For us, Cubans and North Vietnamese served much the same domestic functions as Israelis for Arabs and Chinese for Russians. The foreign policies of 1961-63 foreshadowed later Vietnam policy and limited the resources available for domestic improvement.

It is important to emphasize the nature of this limitation. What the military took was naturally not open to alternative civilian purposes. On the New Frontier the military fared financially considerably better than did civilian social-service programs, which had to await the Johnson years for very much in the way of funding. But it is a second sort of limitation which is still more important. What the times cried for was a national debate over American priorities. There was even a manifesto available, for in the late 1950s *The Affluent Society* was a best-seller, one of the most

influential volumes of its day. If the President had so chosen, Galbraith, that premature enemy of mindless growth, trivial private consumption, urban neglect, and environmental decay, could have served a role more central than his position as Ambassador to India permitted.

The opportunity was lost. In 1962 when President Kennedy accepted his Council of Economic Advisers' recommendation to seek tax cuts in preference to expenditure expansion, he no longer had a real political alternative. Thus the New Frontier's major domestic failure was the direct consequence of its emphasis upon foreign intervention, races in space, and armaments buildups. The three years that an exceptionally appealing and extraordinarily gifted President might have devoted to educating his people to the point of action in meeting their real needs, he expended and largely wasted on purposes which if not actually mistaken were of lower orders of priority.

As a result the great society was an exceedingly fragile construction, tolerated by Congress just so long as most of its benefits flowed to the affluent and the middle class, its costs were kept low, and further tax reductions accompanied new social programs. Because the Great Society rested upon such limited national understanding of social priorities, it has been possible for a conservative Administration to chip away at its moderate achievements with amazingly little difficulty.

And thus it is also that the myths which Americans find it pleasant to believe, and their political leaders accordingly profitable to indulge, linger on. It seems a part of the national credo that Americans are heavily taxed. In truth most citizens in the advanced industrial nations pay more. Congress and President collaborate in such cynical exercises as the 1969 Tax Reform Act which, starting as a fairly serious attempt to rectify some of the more glaring of tax inequities, ended as a tax-reduction measure which probably opened as many new loopholes as it closed old ones. Yet the demands alike of anti-inflationary policy and the revenue-starved cities dictate tax increases not tax slashes. Members of both parties scramble for precedence in the sponsorship of revenue-sharing with the states. The policy guarantees continued discrimination against the cities and confers responsibilities upon the states which they have shown few signs of wishing to discharge.

So badly has the public education of Americans proceeded that most voters define taxes as diversions from superior private expenditures, and public spending as invariably less important than private consumption. The legacy of the New Economics to the 1970s is an enlargement of the American appetite for tax reduction, a taste already much too ravenous for the national good. The great failure of the New Economics was its sunny confidence in growth as the universal solvent of social ills. It is, of course, true that political choices are easier when they concentrate upon redistribution of increments to national income rather than upon a *static* national income itself. It is easier to divide something new than to take something away from one group and give it to another. And it is only fair to add that the New Economics accomplished something of value in shoving the economy to higher levels of employment than had been customary during the 1950s. Unhappily, although wise decision was made somewhat easier, the terms of the discussion during the early 1960s did not convert opportunity very frequently into adequate policy. When economic growth occurs in the context of military and space programs and tax reductions, all that the exercise of creating the growth may do is enlarge the taste for more tax cuts and increase general indulgence for military and space spending.

Unless one believes in devil theories of politics, the dismantling of the modest gains of the 1960s, now well under way, is not the handiwork of any single man, nor even of Nixon, Agnew, and Mitchell all put together. Reaction is possible because so little understanding of past progress and present needs was advanced by the two Administrations which preceded Mr. Nixon.

III

The economy is in its present slough of despond because the 1960s produced a situation and a President inhospitable to consistent conservative or liberal strategies. It is worth recalling the contents of these strategies. Of monetary policy it can again be said that a sufficiently brutal credit squeeze, long enough protracted to convince businessmen that the central bankers are out for their blood, will kill any inflation. Of course it will also idle a good many workers and bankrupt a good many merchants. The policy is politically too dangerous for any President to follow. If no other event served, the impending midterm election would be enough to deter Mr. Nixon from encouraging the Federal Reserve to persevere in its financial brutalities. It is one thing to make blacks and Democratic unionists pay the anti-inflation freight. It is quite another to injure those middle Americans vital for 1970 and 1972.

Beginning with the Kennedy Administration, both parties have pandered to the tax-cut mania. His own campaign promises, and probably his own participation in the tax-cut neurosis, limit the President's opportunities to raise taxes. Unless he attacks some of his favorite programs, military, space, or supersonic, he cannot very sharply reduce federal outlays. Indeed the postal workers and other government workers have done their bit to raise them. Unless the Vietnam war is rapidly phased out and the military are not allowed to grab the resultant savings for themselves, it is hard to see how federal spending can be significantly reduced.

Prudently administered, addressed with sophistication to the power centers of the economy, and complemented with sensible fiscal and monetary restraints, wage-price controls can do a great deal to curb inflationary fevers without pushing an economy into a recession. For reasons already sufficiently discussed, this Administration has turned its face against all such proposals.

Faithful to the temperament of its master, the Nixon Administration in all likelihood will fluctuate in the coming year between attacking unemployment as it mounts and damages Republican electoral prospects, and reverting to anti-inflationary monetary policies when prices continue to rise. The erratic design of the policy mixture and the weakness of the tools employed render it probable that the present recession will be quite severe, nearer the 1957–58 episode than its milder 1960–61 brother.

There are of course radical ways to combat inflation just as there are radical methods of treating social maladies. The focus must be upon the related phenomena of power and wealth. Inflation raises in a peculiarly painful form the crucial importance of the wage and price decisions taken by corporate and union oligarchs. But their activities demand public supervision at all times. The New Economists' growth preoccupations left little room for analysis of the inequities of the distribution of income and wealth. At an inflationary time like this one, it would make excellent sense to raise higher-bracket tax rates, impose punitive inheritance levies, and really plug the tax loopholes. An awful lot of money would be collected, enough both to repress inflation and to do something for the cities, the poor, and the unemployed. Even in a time of inflation, one could imagine guaranteed public employment, a decently liberal guaranteed annual income, a major program of low-income housing.

The very implausibility of such a scenario, the paucity of politically feasible policy alternatives, and the general retrogression the nation is undergoing are the sour fruit of the large hopes and the exuberant language of John F. Kennedy and Lyndon B. Johnson. In these bad times justice should be done even to dislikable men. On his present showing, Richard Nixon is a failure as an economic manager. But he had much help from better men.

3

Monopoly and Inflation

HOBART ROWEN

Most government policy directed toward curbing inflation has stressed money supply, government spending, and tax policy. Behind such action is the assumption that prices and wages can be controlled in this indirect fashion. In one sense this belief flies in the face of investigations that have shown that prices in near-monopoly industries are not determined by supply and demand. What is "target pricing"? How has it been used by General Motors? What has happened in target pricing industries during hard times? Does a parallel situation exist with labor unions? Can any government price policy work that ignores monopoly labor and monopoly industry?

The seeming paradox of persistent inflation at a time of rising unemployment troubles many thoughtful people; somehow, the idea of rising prices seems inconsistent with recession. This is the specter of "the worst of both worlds" that the Nixon administration had desperately hoped to avoid.

Yet, in this community and in others throughout the nation, scientists and teachers are driving taxis or working behind sales counters—and others aren't that lucky. The unemployment rate is a matter of serious concern at 5.8 per cent nationally; 10.6 per cent in Seattle; 6.4 per cent in Detroit; and 6.2 per cent in Los Angeles.

If the price thus paid had at least cut down the high cost of living, Mr. Nixon's policy could be said to be working, in part. But the record on prices has been a shocking disappointment: the rate of the increase had diminished, but only slightly. As Paul Samuelson has said, the improvement is only in the eye of the expert.

But why do prices continue to rise while more people struggle for jobs? There is a relatively simple answer: many prices and wages do not respond to changes in supply and demand.

There is an important area of our industrial economy, which is unresponsive to slack or recession. But industry and big labor can tell and have told Mr. Nixon and his "game plan" to go hang.

The distinguished economist, Gardiner C. Means, has pointed out over the years that some industries (where a monopoly or near-monopoly exists) can "administer" prices regardless of so-called "free" market factors.

In a forthcoming book, "Economic Concentration" to be published early next year by Harcourt Brace Jovanovich, John M. Blair goes far to explain the "paradox" of economic slack and rising prices.

Blair, chief economist for the landmark Kefauver Committee studies of price-fixing in the steel, drug, oil and other industries, makes a strong case that during a recession —even a mild one—prices in concentrated industries not only fail to come down—they actually tend to rise. Thus, efforts to stop

From Hobart Rowen, " 'Target Pricing' and Inflation," Washington Post, December 16, 1970. Reprinted by permission of the publisher.

inflation "by contracting the economy will not merely be ineffective; they will have an opposite effect to that intended."

Blair's explanation rests on the manner in which the price leaders in key industries set their prices. The price for, say, a Chevrolet is not determined by supply and demand factors, but by General Motors' "target return pricing." The company makes a judgment on the likely sales volume; then it calculates its cost per unit, and sets a price that will yield a percentage or "target" on the net worth (stockholders' investment).

General Motors seeks to price its cars in relation to costs (including taxes, which means they are passed on to the consumer) in such a way as to yield a fat 20 per cent annually on net worth.

What Blair shows in his new book is that General Motors and other price leaders, in a demonstration of brilliant corporate management, have been able to make the target consistently. This is great for the stockholders, but it doesn't do much to combat inflation. It's the key to the recession-inflation paradox: in years when the volume falls off, prices are pushed up to cover higher per-unit costs.

Most of the leaders made their targets most years. When they missed, there usually was an explanation. Thus, in 1958, voluntary import quotas on oil broke down and Jersey Standard missed its target. But when mandatory quotas were slapped on the next year, Jersey Standard's profits again were on the beam.

To show how successful the "administered" price industries are in keeping prices high enough in leaner years to make their "targets," here is a table derived from Blair's study comparing pricing goals with actual results over an extended period.

The record thus shows that whether or not people are out of work, or times are "poor," prices can be managed by key industries to maintain an established target. U.S. Steel compensated for a production loss of about 20 per cent in each of the 1953–54 and 1957–58 recessions by substantial price increase (4.7 per cent and 3.5

Target Return Pricing

	% RATE OF RETURN ON NET WORTH AFTER TAXES	% ACTUALLY AVERAGED 1953–68
General Motors	20.0	20.2
U.S. Steel	8.0	8.4
Alcoa	10.0	9.5
Standard Oil (N.J.)	12.0	12.6
DuPont	20.0	22.2
Average of all 5	14.6	15.1

per cent respectively). That produced the established return (and since other companies in the industry are more efficient than Big Steel, they did even better when they followed Steel's price leadership).

Blair reinforces his argument with an analysis of 16 pairs of products—one of which tends to be concentrated, and the other more responsive to classic demand-supply pressures. Thus, he compares the price actions of competitive items such as steel building materials vs. lumber; and pig iron vs. steel scrap. In every case, the unconcentrated products had price decreases during the two recessions of the 1950s; but 13 of the 16 concentrated products actually increased. No one has done a comparable study on the power of major unions. But it's clear from recent events that the fact of growing unemployment hasn't diminished the belief of labor leaders that they must "catch up" both with recent large settlements and the continuing pace of inflation.

The Nixon administration, to be sure, does not accept the Blair analysis. Yet, its second inflation alert points out that "intermediate," non-ferrous and scrap materials are the "kind" that react best "to the cooling off of an overheated economy," while prices for such things as fuel, machinery and equipment were still advancing.

Because there is a difference in the response which relates to concentrated power, the President has been urged to establish an "incomes policy." This point was laid out in a courageous speech last month by Assistant Treasury Secretary Murray L. Weidenbaum and echoed by Federal Reserve Chairman Arthur Burns a few days ago.

The administration's temptation, so far, has been to level its fire on the labor unions, effectively losing the good will of George Meany that it had earlier cultivated. What Mr. Nixon needs to do now is to develop a specific policy incorporating a specific guidepost to deal with wage-price inflation. And if it isn't even-handed, it would be worse than no policy at all.

The administered-price explanation for inflation-cum-recession does not deal, of course, with excessive doctors' fees, hospital costs, and other service prices. And no one can deny that inflation in services is one of today's most pressing problems. On the other hand, there is little evidence that the economic crunch created by traditional monetary and fiscal restraints has an impact on the cost of services, either.

What Blair's study suggests is that direct government pressure of some kind should be able to diminish that part of the inflation problem that stems from monopoly or oligopoly power. Target pricing, Blair notes, is not the product of "antisocial irrationality but the logical consequence of a . . . highly successful method of pricing." The government needs an equally logical, rational, and successful counter move.

4

The Power of Big Business

Robert L. Heilbroner

The power of any major institution, such as the giant corporation, is hard to measure out. Some contemporary analysts view modern American big business with alarm, while others hail it as a benign force. Still others regard it as an aging Sampson, shorn of its earlier strength. Although the Sherman Anti-Trust Act was enacted over three-quarters of a century ago, on the surface, at least, the multimillion dollar corporation expands and thrives in the shadow of this fundamental law. Should Americans fear this expansion? Are political leaders dwarfed by the power of their corporate counterparts? Or has big government made the modern corporation a pale, housebroken imitation of its nineteenth century counterpart?

The power of big business is an apparition that has haunted almost as many men as has the specter of Communism. Like the cartoon of the bearded Bolshevik with his bomb, the picture of the big businessman is familiar to all of us, with his top hat and frock coat, a dollar sign across his bulging vest, one foot trampling the scenery of America and the other crushing its workmen, the fingers of one gloved hand picking the pockets of the ordinary citizen while those of the other manipulate legislators and even Presidents.

It is a caricature, of course—but how much of a caricature? How much significance should we accord to the fact that six hundred businesses produce goods worth-half the entire gross national output, or that an average one of these supercorporations handles as much revenue in a year

From Robert L. Heilbroner, "The Power of Big Business," The Atlantic Monthly, September 1965, pp. 89–93. Copyright © 1965 by The Atlantic Monthly Company. Reprinted by permission of William Morris Agency, Inc.

as an average state? How alarmed should we be that the national defense and offense of the United States has become the chief source of profit of some of its large corporations, and that the heads of these corporations enjoy easy access to the corridors of the White House and the Pentagon? What attention should we pay to the opinion of Professor A. A. Berle, one of the most informed and least hysterical students of big business power, who has said, "Some of these corporations can be thought of only in somewhat the way we have heretofore thought of nations"?

These are the kinds of awkward but all-important questions to which a consideration of business power leads us. Perhaps we should realize at the outset that the questions cannot be answered altogether objectively—wish, suspicion, and apology crowd in irresistibly along with the facts. Nevertheless, they are questions with which we must try to come to grips if we are to understand our society. So let us begin by examining one aspect of the problem of business power where the facts are pretty clear. This is the question of what is happening to the sheer size of big business within the economy.

The answer may come as something of a surprise to those who are familiar with the trend of corporate amalgamation in the past. Thirty years ago, when Professors Berle and Means made the first brilliant study of the two hundred biggest nonfinancial corporations, they came up with the half-fanciful prognostication that if the observed rate of expansion of the big corporations relative to the smaller ones were maintained for another 360 years, all the nation's corporations would have disappeared into one mammoth concern, which would then have a life expectancy roughly equivalent to that of the Roman Empire. Long before that day, however—in fact, by 1950—Berle and Means warned, the two hundred largest corporations would already have absorbed 70 per cent of all corporate wealth.

Well, 1950 has come and gone, and it appears that these worst fears have not been realized. We do not have statistics exactly comparable with the Berle and Means estimates, but a study published by A.D.H. Kaplan of the Brookings Institution is close enough. It shows that the top one hundred industrial corporations in 1960 had amassed 31 per cent of all industrial corporate assets, compared with 25 per cent in 1929. This is evidence of continuing concentration, but at nothing like the rate envisaged in the Berle and Means projection.

Why? One main reason is simply that the great corporations, for all their enormous mass, are not totally invulnerable to attack, to erosion by technology, or to suicide by incompetent management.

A complementary reason for the standstill in the trend toward concentration lies in a change that has affected the big corporation from within rather than from without. This is the growing reluctance of the big companies to ram home the economic advantage that is theirs by running their competitors out of business. General Motors, for example, makes three times as much profit as the entire asset value of American Motors, but no one expects GM to "compete" by eliminating its rival from the field.

Do these standard explanations promise a continuance of the relative stability of big business size within the economy? We do not know. There is some evidence that the vulnerability of the topmost corporations is decreasing, lessening the chances that they will be displaced by other firms; between 1948 and 1960 only twenty-four of the top hundred had their places usurped, whereas between 1909 and 1919, forty-one leaders were displaced. Then, too, large areas of the economy—construction, for instance, or the service industries—are still characterized by small or medium-sized business, and it would be in line with past experience if largescale enterprise eventually "rationalized" these fields. Finally, the new technology of administration and control, automation, may provide the techniques and the impetus to further concentration.

Thus the relative quiescence of the "monopoly" problem today does not guarantee as much for tomorrow. It is at least possible that the economic pressures toward agglutination will again rise. In that case much will depend on the attitude of the top corporation officialdom and on the counterpressures exerted by other groups in society.

The Men at the Top

Fifty or sixty years ago it would have been a much easier task to form an opinion about the attitudes of big businessmen, for the supercorporations were then still dominated to a considerable extent by the supermen who started them. Not alone the names but also the personalities of Rockefeller, Carnegie, Morgan, Harriman, Frick were familiar to every reader, albeit often in romanticized versions. Today it is not so simple to identify or to dissect the business elite. We are confronted with a largely faceless group known as "the management." How many well-informed people can name or describe in any way even one of the chief executive officers (except Henry Ford, Jr.) in the ten biggest industrial firms: GM, Standard Oil of New Jersey, Ford, General Electric, Socony, U.S. Steel, Chrysler, Texaco, Gulf, Western Electric? . . . [I]t seems clear to me, comparing the big businessman of today with those of a few decades back, that the contemporary executive represents a generation of administration rather than of acquisition. This is not merely a matter of the statistics of concentration we have already examined. It refers as well to a style of business leadership in which "good public relations" have come to play an extraordinarily important role. Here perhaps is where the increased educational exposure, the lengthened training, the so-called "professionalization" of the executive, should be given its due.

One result of this new style, particularly noticeable among the executives of the biggest firms, is a certain caution in utterance and action quite untypical of their prede-cessors a generation back. In the main, the approved managerial tactics are now those of long-run security rather than short-run risk, of staying out of trouble rather than of taking a chance, of bucking for the title of "business statesman" rather than "tycoon." Among the smaller firms, we still see something of the uninhibited drive of the past, but at the top, inhibition itself begins to appear as a managerial virtue.

Another characteristic of the business elite is its essentially reluctant relationship to political power. Noise, oratory, and table-thumping to the contrary notwithstanding, I think that what is noticeable about the great majority of big businessmen in America is a striking absence of real political involvement. What is visible instead is a profound unwillingness to get embroiled in anything that might take them away from their jobs, or that might not look good in the newspapers, or that might incur the displeasure of their main customers or their boards. There is in the big business world a great deal of political rhetoric but not much political commitment—what could be more significant than the fact that for all the endless business talk of freedom, not a single major corporate executive found the Alabama Freedom March important enough to warrant leaving his desk, although educators, government officials, housewives, trade unionists, students, and scientists felt the need to go to Selma, despite the nuisance, the call of other duties, or the danger to which it exposed them.

The New Elites

All this discussion of the structure of big business and the sociological attributes of big businessmen circles around our main subject—the power of big business—and yet fails to engage it squarely. What is big business power? What does it look like in ordinary life?

The oldest and purest exercise of business power has always been the market exploitation of the weak. We think of labor, the historic victim of the big corporation, working a twelve-hour day and a seven-day week (with a twenty-four-hour shift every two weeks) as late as 1919 in the dangerous mills of the United States Steel Corporation. We think of little business, undersold and outbought and forced to pay additional freight charges to the railroads, who then turned the money over to the Standard Oil combine. We think of the consumer, pictured by a commentator of the 1890s as "born to the profit of the Milk Trust and dead to the profit of the Coffin Trust."

To recall these instances from the past does more than give reality to one meaning of the words "business power." It also serves to give some historical perspective on the trend of that power. Surely the strength of labor vis-à-vis big business has been enormously enhanced since the days when labor unions were literally afraid of the big company. So, too, although less noticed, has the position of little business improved. We often forget that it was the political pressure of little business and not of the public that brought about the passage of most anti-big-business legislation, including the antitrust acts. But this animus of the past seems largely to have evaporated. Now and again there is some anti-big-corporation talk, as when the auto dealers rose up against General Motors or when small business complains that big companies get all the defense contracts. But the complaints, however true, quickly subside. From the peace that prevails, it is hard not to conclude that little business no longer feels the brunt of big business power as it did in the past.

It is less easy to make an unambiguous determination in the case of the third historic target of business power in the marketplace, the consumer. Certainly he is more ardently wooed than in the public-be-damned days, but the wooing is sometimes accompanied by breach of promise; not too long ago, for instance, the Federal Trade Commission found that General Foods was charging more per unit of weight for its "economy-sized" packages than for its regular packages. Nor does leafing through Consumer Reports overwhelm one with a sense of corporate solicitude for the consumer. Still more important, perhaps, although the trusts have gone, there is no evidence that profit margins have declined over the past fifty years or so. General Motors, for example, makes almost as much in profits before taxes per car as it pays out for wages on that car.

But even if we leave the case of the consumer undecided, it seems fair enough to conclude that the power of big business to throw its weight around in the marketplace has been considerably restricted in the past three or four decades. Yet that does not fully satisfy our inquiry. For everyone knows that market exploitation, however bad, is not all of what we mean by "big business power." In fact, what usually comes to mind when we say the words is not so much these instances of market abuse, but larger and subtler kinds of influence—for instance, the use of the national government to create new domains of private profit such as the enormous land-grabs of the railroads era, or the insinuation of business goals into foreign policy such as the banana-republic diplomacy that once made the world safe for United Fruit, or the blind deference accorded to business views just because they were business views, as in the general adulation of the businessman during the 1920s.

It is difficult to assay the trend of this hugely varied exercise of power with much accuracy. Certainly, we cannot airily dismiss the influence of big business on the nation's affairs as being a thing of the past. Nonetheless, I would still hazard the opinion that its ability to manipulate public affairs or to have its way in the formation of national policy is declining.

I base this opinion not so much on the static size of big business within the economy or on the quieter bearing of its executives as on another development that strikes me as being of signal importance. This is the rise within our society of new elites, whose competence for government is rapidly becoming of greater importance for national survival or even well-being than that of business leaders. One such new elite consists of the military professionals. A second is composed of advisers from the fields of science, economics, sociology, and the academic world in general. A third includes the civil servants and the career administrators of public programs.

These new elites play increasingly central roles in the elaboration and exercise of government policies in the crucial areas that now confront us: education, civil rights, poverty, urban renewal, foreign aid, the scale of the military establishment, the determination of fiscal and monetary policy, and the conduct of foreign affairs. At the same time, it seems undeniable that the voice of big business in the delineation of these specific programs is much smaller than in comparable programs of the past.

Further, it seems to me that this swing of power toward the new elites is likely to become intensified. I expect to see fewer big businessmen in positions of power in Washington and more soldiers, scientists, educators, and government administrators; to see fewer big businessmen as trustees of universities and more of the new men of power there; to hear less about the sanctity of private investments abroad and more about international government-to-government programs; to find less attention paid to the aging rhetoric of laissez-faire and more to the academic language of neo-Keynesianism and input-output tables. To be sure, we still live in a civilization in which the accumulation of individual wealth is believed to be the most admirable objective of human life, and in such a civilization great centers of wealth must perforce be great centers of influence. Nonetheless, I think the exercise of business power in the direction of national affairs is on the wane and that the power of new non-business groups is sharply on the rise.

Managed Capitalism

As for the new elites that now contest with businessmen for the control of the levers of the nation's working programs, they are certainly not anti-big business. The new elites have no thoughts of nationalization, of extensive decommercialization, of far-reaching changes in the enjoyment of property incomes. At most, their programs imply a kind of managed capitalism in which the great corporations, largely maintained intact, would be coordinated within the national effort by some form of permissive planning. But it is in itself indicative of the total acquiescence in the ideology of business that even the formulation of such mild goals comes as something of a shock, and that most of the elites would plead that they have no goal other than a day-to-day "pragmatic" approach.

If this is true, what does it portend for the future? There are, it seems to me, important possibilities for social evolution still unexplored within the business system, and I would hope that in the hands of a new guard, uncommitted to the ideological fundamentalism of the old guard, a liberal capitalism might develop greater stability, less poverty, more public concern. At the same time there is also a less pleasant possibility. The prospect of a business society no longer made uncomfortable by the presence of alternative social formulations presents the threat of a human community arrested at a still primitive level of striving and quieted by an intellectual asphyxiation and a moral dullness. But this brings us far beyond the bounds of permissible speculation. Perhaps at the moment we can say no more than that we seem to stand at the threshold of a new era of contained capitalism, in which the power of big business is more constrained—and yet less contested—than in the past. What may be the horizons and what the limitations of such a society we must now begin to find out.

5

Big Business, Militarism, and Democracy

DWIGHT D. EISENHOWER

During the past decade the relationship between government and the economy has changed most dractically in the field of military expenditures. More than 10 per cent of the American gross national product is now spent each year for defense purposes. A single military contract can be worth five or six billion dollars. Cancellation of a contract can mean economic disaster for an entire area. A multimillion dollar award means boom times. With so much at stake it is not surprising that an uneasy business-military power axis has arisen. President Eisenhower voiced his concern over this new facet of American life in the article that follows. Why did he believe that "The potential for the disastrous rise of misplaced power exists and will persist"? What is the basis for his contention that the independence of the universities is threatened?

My fellow Americans: Three days from now, after half a century in the service of our country, I shall lay down the responsibilities of office as, in traditional and solemn ceremony, the authorty of the Presidency is vested in my successor.

This evening I come to you with a message of leavetaking and farewell and to share a few final thoughts with you, my countrymen.

Like every other citizen, I wish the new President and all who will labor with him Godspeed. I pray that the coming years will be blessed with peace and prosperity for all.

II

We now stand ten years past the midpoint of a century that has witnessed four major wars among great nations. Three of these involved our own country. Despite

these holocausts, America is today the strongest, the most influential, and most productive nation in the world. Understandably proud of this preeminence, we yet realize that America's leadership and prestige depend not merely upon our unmatched material progress, riches, and military strength but on how we use our power in the interests of world peace and human betterment.

III

Throughout America's adventure in free government our basic purposes have been to keep the peace, to foster progress in human achievement, and to enhance liberty, dignity, and integrity among people and among nations. To strive for less would be unworthy of a free and religious people. Any failure traceable to arrogance or our lack of comprehension or readiness to sacrifice would inflict upon us grievous hurt both at home and abroad.

Progress toward these noble goals is persistently threatened by the conflict now en-

From the "Farewell to the Nation" speech delivered by President Dwight D. Eisenhower over radio and television on January 17, 1961.

gulfing the world. It commands our whole attention, absorbs our very beings. We face a hostile ideology—global in scope, atheistic in character, ruthless in purpose, and insidious in method. Unhappily the danger it poses promises to be of indefinite duration. To meet it successfully there is called for not so much the emotional and transitory sacrifices of crisis but rather those which enable us to carry forward steadily, surely, and without complaint the burdens of a prolonged and complex struggle—with liberty the stake. Only thus shall we remain, despite every provocation, on our charted course toward permanent peace and human betterment.

Crises there will continue to be. In meeting them, whether foreign or domestic, great or small, there is a recurring temptation to feel that some spectacular and costly action could become the miraculous solution to all current difficulties. A huge increase in newer elements of our defense, development of unrealistic programs to cure every ill in agriculture, a dramatic expansion in basic and applied research— these and many other possibilities, each possibly promising in itself, may be suggested as the only way to the road we wish to travel.

But each proposal must be weighed in the light of a broader consideration: The need to maintain balance in and among national programs—balance between the private and the public economy, balance between cost and hoped-for advantage, balance between the clearly necessary and the comfortably desirable, balance between our essential requirements as a nation and the duties imposed by the nation upon the individual, balance between actions of the moment and the national welfare of the future. Good judgment seeks balance and progress; lack of it eventually finds imbalance and frustration.

The record of many decades stands as proof that our people and their government have, in the main, understood these truths and have responded to them well in the face of stress and threat. But threats, new in kind or degree, constantly arise. I mention two only.

IV

A vital element in keeping the peace is our military establishment. Our arms must be mighty, ready for instant action, so that no potential aggressor may be tempted to risk his own destruction.

Our military organization today bears little relation to that known by any of my predecessors in peacetime, or indeed by the fighting men of World War II or Korea.

Until the latest of our world conflicts, the United States had no armaments industry. American makers of plowshares could, with time and as required, make swords as well. But now we can no longer risk emergency improvisation of national defense; we have been compelled to create a permanent armaments industry of vast proportions. Added to this, 3½ million men and women are directly engaged in the defense establishment. We annually spend on military security more than the net income of all United States corporations.

This conjunction of an immense military establishment and a large arms industry is new in the American experience. The total influence—economic, political, even spiritual—is felt in every city, every statehouse, every office of the federal government. We recognize the imperative need for this development. Yet we must not fail to comprehend its grave implications. Our toil, resources, and livelihood are all involved; so is the very structure of our society.

In the councils of government we must guard against the acquisition of unwarranted influence, whether sought or unsought, by the military-industrial complex. The potential for the disastrous rise of misplaced power exists and will persist.

We must never let the weight of this combination endanger our liberties or democratic processes. We should take nothing for granted. Only an alert and knowledgeable citizenry can compel the proper meshing of the huge industrial and military machinery of defense with our peaceful methods and goals so that security and liberty may prosper together.

Akin to and largely responsible for the sweeping changes in our industrial-military posture has been the technological revolution during recent decades. In this revolution research has become central; it also becomes more formalized, complex and costly. A steadily increasing share is conducted for, by, or at the direction of the federal government.

Today the solitary inventor, tinkering in his shop, has been overshadowed by task forces of scientists in laboratories and testing fields. In the same fashion the free university, historically the fountainhead of free ideas and scientific discovery, has experienced a revolution in the conduct of research. Partly because of the huge costs involved, a government contract becomes virtually a substitute for intellectual curiosity. For every old blackboard there are now hundreds of new electronic computers.

The prospect of domination of the nation's scholars by federal employment, project allocations, and the power of money is ever present and is gravely to be regarded.

Yet, in holding scientific research and discovery in respect, as we should, we must also be alert to the equal and opposite danger that public policy could itself become the captive of a scientific-technological elite.

It is the task of statesmanship to mold, to balance, and to integrate these and other forces, new and old, within the principles of our democratic system—ever aiming toward the supreme goals of our free society.

14

THE POLITICS OF WELFARE:
ALLEVIATION OR ELIMINATION?

Government in modern America engages in a wide range of activities designed to protect the individual from economic disaster. Minimum wages, old age pensions, unemployment insurance, Medicare, aid for the physically and mentally handicapped, and public housing are all facets of the government welfare system. The controversy over welfare centers around two basic problems:

1. Who are the impoverished and why are they poor?
2. Is present government welfare legislation designed to cure the poverty problem, or are we using Band-Aids when the prognosis calls for surgery?

Most welfare policies have been designed to help middle class Americans who have difficulties inside the system, such as unemployment, old age, or catastrophic illness. Largely untouched by these insurance-type arrangements is the poverty subculture of semi-literate whites and black families headed by women, both of whom have been uprooted from a rural setting and dropped into our urban, industrial society. Present welfare policies are extremely expensive, yet they do not reach many people of this subculture. If all those eligible were to participate in existing programs, the cost would be astronomical.

In any event, welfare rolls seem to grow, good times or bad. We have little evidence that such widely criticized programs as aid to dependent children spend much time or effort in moving people from the impoverished subculture toward the economic mainstream. Nearly everyone agrees that new proposals costing billions more are needed if we are to eliminate poverty rather then alleviate it.

American Poverty: Who and Why?

To deal effectively with welfare issues demands an analysis of the scope of American poverty. Who are the poor? What causes poverty? Why does poverty appear to be concentrated in certain groups (case poverty)? If poverty is either inherited or environmentally transmitted within the poor family, can the cycle be broken best by birth control, sterilization, or placing the children in foster homes? Do the poor tend to reproduce themselves? If so, why? Is poverty the result of a lack of opportunity? Mental incapacity? Physical handicaps? Illness? Broken homes? Racial prejudice? Lack of education? Unproductive work? Or are the causes more sophisticated, perhaps a combination of moral, physical, and mental decadence? Are the poor an inevitable by-product of our industrial society, a kind of national slag pile that is the hallmark of a productive nation? Or should they be viewed as a kind of silent reproach and rebuke to those millions of Americans who bask in the greatest affluence the world has ever known?

What Role for Government: Alleviation or Elimination?

Should poverty be regarded as evil and un-American, a virus in our economic bloodstream that should be pursued and eliminated? Or should it be seen somewhat complacently as an individual challenge, a necessary handicap that spurs men to action? Is the eradication of poverty an individual problem, or is it more properly the concern of government?

If the elimination of poverty is accepted as a concern of government, other problems remain. Should our major effort be directed toward raising general productivity and living standards? If we raise the national standard of living, will the impoverished be benefited automatically? Or does this group represent a peculiar, isolated segment of our people whose life is outside the mainstream of the American economy? Perhaps the impoverished should be regarded as charity cases, and tax dollars should be diverted to them as a salve to the national conscience. Or is the welfare of these people a basic component of our national prosperity? By aiding the physically and mentally handicapped, the unemployed, and the aged, are we not actually taking out an economic insurance policy for the nation? In other words, are the charity aspects of the case secondary to our concern for general welfare and prosperity?

A final set of questions centers around the issue "How?" Assuming that the welfare of all is accepted as a national goal, how can it be achieved? What role should be assigned to education? Medicine? Housing? What about a government-guaranteed annual wage? How should these various conditioning factors be blended? How can static acceptance of poverty ("The poor ye have always with ye") be replaced by an aggressive, positive policy? The Johnson administration began a host of new programs (Job Corps, Operation Head Start, Vista, Appalachia Program, federal school aid) with a great deal of fanfare under the general banner of a "War on Poverty." President Johnson's critics soon complained that the War on Poverty, however noble in concept, was badly managed, too expensive, and lacking in results.

President Nixon tried a different tack. He proposed a comprehensive welfare program that centered on the family. Each working family unit would be guaranteed a minimum yearly income. The unemployed would enlist in job training programs, and day care centers would be provided for working mothers. These proposals encountered rough going in Congress, where they were buffeted by critics of both the Right and the Left. The best hope of ultimate change and improvement lay in the fact that few Congressmen defended the existing system either in whole or in part. Elimination of poverty will certainly cost more than a holding pattern, but few Americans are willing to accept national poverty as a permanent condition.

1

Poverty Amid Plenty

PRESIDENT'S COMMISSION

For most Americans the past decade has been a golden age, with a fallout of goods and services beyond their wildest dreams. Two-car garages, European holidays, and snowmobiles became the norm in middle class suburbia. Largely forgotten in this affluent society was the poverty remnant—25 million poor people. Nevertheless, the poor remained as an enduring fact of American life. How can poverty be defined in modern America? Why are food plans for the poor unrealistic? Can the poor be expected to "make ends meet"? Do the poor have different hopes and aspirations? Are most of the poor "locked in" to their existing plight? Will increased national prosperity eventually bring them into the prosperous mainstream?

The Poor

The postwar period has witnessed a remarkable improvement in the material welfare of most Americans. Even with the effect of inflation taken into account median family income grew by 76 per cent between 1947 and 1967. The proportion of families enjoying a total income of $10,000 or more increased from 22 to 34 per cent during the same period. And, in recent years, we have taken justifiable satisfaction in the reduction of poverty from 22 per cent of the population in 1959 to 13 per cent in 1968. But the

From *President's Commission on Income Maintenance Programs,* Poverty Amid Plenty *(Washington, D.C.: U.S. Government Printing Office, 1969), pp. 13–16, 21.*

fact remains that 25 million persons are still poor.

Thousands of pages of statistics about the poor have been tabulated and published. The poor have been measured, surveyed, and sorted into numerous categories. . . . But in the end, the diversity of the poor overwhelms any simple attempt to describe them with statistics. What may be said simply is that millions of our fellow citizens are living in severe poverty, with few prospects for a better life, and often with little hope for the future.

To the poor, poverty is no statistical or sociological matter. Their condition exists as a daily fight for survival. This Commission has found their deprivation to be real, not a trick of rhetoric or statistics. And for many of the poor, their poverty is not a temporary situation, but an enduring fact of life.

The Poverty Living Standard

Any discussion of the poor must begin by defining those who are poor and those who are not. But it is obvious that any single standard or definition of poverty is arbitrary, and clearly subject to disagreement. The standard which this Commission has employed is the widely used poverty index, developed by the Social Security Administration. This index is based on the Department of Agriculture's measure of the cost of a temporary low-budget, nutritious diet for households of various sizes. The poverty index is simply this food budget multiplied by three to reflect the fact that food typically represents one-third of the expenses of a low-income family. The resulting figure is the minimum income needed to buy a subsistence level of goods and services; the 25 million people whose incomes fall below the index are poor, while those above it are, officially at least, nonpoor. According to this poverty index, in 1968 a nonfarm family of four required a minimum income of $3,553 per year, or $2.43 per person per day to meet its basic expenses.

Clearly, the poor family must do without many of the things that families with an average income consider to be "necessities" —a car, an occasional dessert after meals, rugs, a bed for each family member, school supplies, or an occasional movie. Nothing can be budgeted for medical care or insurance.

This food budget requires more than a third of the poor family's income, but still allows only $1.00 a day for food per person. A family can buy a nutritionally adequate diet for this amount, using the Department of Agriculture's food plan, but it must eat considerably more beans, potatoes, flour and cereal products, and considerably less meat, eggs, fruits, and vegetables than the average family. Each member of the poor family may consume less than one-quarter pound of meat a day.

Unfortunately, the Department's food plan, the basis of the poverty index, is not very realistic. It is estimated that only about one-fourth of the families who spend that much for food actually have a nutritionally adequate diet. The plan calls for skills in meal-planning and buying that are rare at any income level, and it requires extensive efforts by poor families to make the varied and appetizing meals which are ostensibly possible under the plan. Many of the poor lack common kitchen appliances. Moreover, the Department's plan assumes the shopper will buy in economical quantities and take advantage of special bargains, but this is particularly difficult for a poor family with inadequate storage and refrigeration facilities.

The poor family's budget has no provision for eating outside of the home. Any lunches bought by working members or school children will reduce funds available for eating at home, since few outside meals can be bought for the 33 cents per meal allotted to each family member. Many schools charge more than this for a Federally-subsidized lunch.

The poor family's budget provides only $91 a month for all housing costs—including rent, utilities, and household operation —for four persons. No allowance is included for the poor family to purchase household furnishings. In Head Start programs, for example, teachers found that many children never had eaten at a table. Thirty per cent of families on welfare live in homes where each family member does not have a bed.

The money allotted to transportation for a poor family would not cover even daily transportation for a worker. The moderate-income family not only has more money to spend on recreation, but its automobile permits it to take the children on inexpensive outings, while poor children rarely have access to any form of transportation. Thus, many poor children have never left their own neighborhoods.

Clothing school children is a major problem in poor families. Many poor children wear hand-me-down clothes which they receive from relatives, neighbors, and even teachers. Some clothing may be purchased at second-hand stores. But many poor children have to go to school on rainy days with no boots or raincoats—or stay home.

The poor family has $108 annually—about $9 a month—to spend on "luxuries": reading matter, recreation, education, gifts and contributions, tobacco, alcohol. But it is likely that this money will be spent on necessities, supplementing the meager food, clothing, and housing allowances. There is no room in the budget for luxuries—or emergencies.

Technically, an income at the poverty level should enable families to purchase the bare necessities of life. Yet an itemized budget drawn at that level clearly falls short of adequacy. There are many items for which no money is budgeted, although those items may be needed. Funds for them can only come out of sums already allotted to the basic necessities of life. As one witness told the Commission, "I either eat good and smell bad, or smell good and don't eat." When another witness was asked how he made ends meet, he simply replied, "They don't meet."

. . .

Conclusion

The poor inhabit a different world than the affluent, primarily because they lack money. Often they live an isolated existence in rural and urban pockets of poverty. But most of the poor do not live apart from the larger society in terms of their hopes and aspirations. Through television, magazines, and newspapers, they become aware of what others have. Their aspirations for education and achievement often differ from those of the middle class only in the possibility for realization:

And I want to say someone ought to start doing something to show that there is emotion in disadvantaged people. They bleed like anybody else. It is not distant and strange. They do bleed. They might not get enough to eat and might not get enough sleep but they do these things. They think that you are born distant, you have no feelings, that you were born to tear up, burn up, corrupt and whatever. You have to stop telling him, gee, I know you feel bad, look at your house, look at the holes in your shoes, and things of this sort. Showing a man how really down he is, is not going to help him.

You know when you have a bunch of kids out here and don't have a steady job, just part-time, you think about them. You look around at yourself when the bills start coming in and the children want to eat and need clothes to wear to go to school. You can imagine how you feel.

The poor are living poorly and are aware of it. They are generally unhappy with their circumstances and would like to be unpoor. Many Americans wonder why the poor do not escape from poverty. The answer to this question is clear to us: They usually cannot, because most are already doing as much as can reasonably be expected of them to change their conditions.

2

Poverty on the Land

JOHN STANLEY

Rural America is a study in economic contrasts and extremes—from shiny Cadillacs and sleek cattle to corn bread, grits, and subsistence farming. The following description is an accurate portrait of impoverished rural America—the 30 per cent of farmers who produce only 3 per cent of agricultural sales. For this group such issues as parity payments and the soil bank are remote. Unless they have part-time jobs, these people are almost completely outside our present money economy. Why does Stanley conclude that the rural poor "have a culture so different from the bulk of their middle-class compatriots that 'foreigner' is not a completely illegitimate term to use on them"?

The shower of snow mutes the ragged outlines of a farm that embarrasses the hopeful, willing country in New York and Kentucky and Maine and the rest of the states. The snow is both a promise of suffering and its alleviation; at least there will be water now after the long summer that has dried up the shallow spring up the hill; but with snow will come the cold wind that cuts its way through the thin boards. The family will huddle around the kitchen range, and the children will whine and the parents will scold—it will be a situation that is beyond homework and no one will want to go to the wintry cold bedrooms. Everyone will be longing for rest; there will be the dry fatigue that always comes from a constant diet of thin food, unsatisfying clothes and a steadily deteriorating situation.

Every decade millions leave this sort of thing and move into town. They are as worn out as the land they leave behind them. They realize that they are not re-

ceiving their share of what this country has to offer. They feel like an out-group, they're not as smooth and shiny as everyone else, and everything else, is getting to be. It takes cash to get into the national rhythm and shape, and the place to do this is in town. So, at a certain point in the complex pattern of endurance and desire, and urged by the sharp pricking of abrupt personal dissatisfaction, the farmer decides to go and share the things the city can provide, even though this may, will, mean the loss of an increasingly dubious "independence," fresh air and the shredded remnants of an inherited tradition.

.   .   .

Picture this: a frame house of skimpy proportions, two stories high with a shaky, narrow porch along one side, built of second-hand lumber and covered with tar shingles pressed to look like yellow brick. It's on a dirt road pocked with ruts and stones—dust in August, a slough in March and a mad toboggan-slide in December; two cars cannot pass. It's more than a mile to the nearest paved road, and three miles more to the nearest general store and post office and school. The view is magnificent:

From John Stanley, "Poverty on the Land," The Commonweal, November 18, 1955, pp. 161–63. Reprinted by permission of the publisher.

a thousand feet below and miles away is a winding river lined with rich black farms where the land is as carefully utilized as it is in France. In the distance there are lavender hills, and in the winter moonlight, blue snow and black trees. Inside the kitchen door hangs the only light bulb in the whole house. Last year there was electricity for the first time in the area but there was only enough credit to wire the one room. You go to the "bathroom" and up to bed by candlelight, which makes for an atmosphere not of romance but of melancholy, and the mother of small children is ever on the alert for disaster. There is neither radio nor telephone. In the summertime the cooking is done on a kerosene stove that smokes and stinks if it is not carefully tended and expertly used; in the winter there is a kitchen range. If cash and credit are relatively adequate there is the luxury of coal, usually bought by the hundred-weight, which is more expensive than by the ton. And when things get really difficult the derelict barn gives a few more boards, and these are sawed up by hand.

The poor, both rural and urban, are forced to live constantly in extravagant debt: they must buy cheap shoes that wear out quickly, cheap foods that do not keep the body in top form, cheap tools that break and are inefficient, second-hand, broken down, wasteful cars that bad roads soon tear up completely. The result is exhaustion that permits no rest, no growth, and little joy at the bright vistas in the fertile valleys below. There is only weary dragging on from day to day, almost a guilt-sense of failure at such poverty in the midst of the nation's storied progress recorded in much expensive color in the shiny magazines each week.

Here there is no fieldstone pumphouse with cedar shingles snugly housing a plump tank of cold and sweet artesian water; there is only the shallow spring that drools the water through for half the year; when the trickle stops, water must be fetched in buckets down the road, starting in the summertime when all the fields in the val-

ley below are being worked by men who cannot spend their time carting water in a bucket; they're out producing. Here the fields are full of wild flowers, with only patches cultivated for the sake of quaint, small fruit that makes one say, "Well, it's not worth it, cheaper to buy it in town."

At one time this land was cleared of trees and made to yield some fruit, support some families. Up the road there is still the heaped-up wreckage of a one-room schoolhouse that served a score of families until sometime between 1918 and 1939. Now the trees are growing back, along with untidy brambles and black-eyed Susans, thistles and grape vines that run wild. Little foxes scoot across the road, and the dog barks on the leash. The children stand in the mud near the postbox in their thin clothes waiting for the school bus moving carefully in the November weather. They do not come home again until it is almost dark.

There is no hot water in the house except for what can be heated on the stove in a bucket so, except in warm weather, there are mostly sponge baths in the kitchen. There is an outhouse, frigid in winter and alive with flies and stench and foraging rats in the summer, a sweatbox under the slow-moving sun. In winter the house is a cave of draughts because everything is fitted poorly.

Discouragement and fatigue and loss of vision line the face of rural poverty. It is difficult to see beyond the muddy dooryard in the grey morning, and the mood lasts all day. No one comes and no one goes. A longing sets in for a little escape from the water-stained walls and unmended furniture, the cracked saucer and the wrinkled housedress. The supreme objective becomes the capture of a moment of spice, covered with spangles and filled with bubbles; a jukebox, a movie, a glass of lemon and lime or a comic book for the children, a permanent wave—which are wasteful as the thrifty and virtuous know. And there is always alcohol.

It is quite something to pass through a

West Virginia town that looks like a movie set for a Wild West film circa 1903. There are only timber houses and covered wooden sidewalks, and a big raw sign that yells *whiskey*. There seems to be a lot of fierce-looking dark-eyed young men squatting on their haunches in the open in the middle of a weekday morning. Their eyes seem to follow strangers, and they roll cigarettes and seem silent. The report is that they don't do much of anything, many of them; they hunt and fish and from time to time cut down a tree and sell it; they make their own liquor and sell some of it. They are the men one wrote letters for in the army. They have a culture so different from the bulk of their middle-class compatriots that "foreigner" is not a completely illegitimate term to use on them.

Rural poverty is lived in isolation, in the imprisonment of broken fences and un-pruned fruit trees that bear small, hard, wormy fruit. Rural poverty is as various as the terrain of the country. It is the lot, in God's mysterious justice, of millions of human beings, including the "single-men-in-barracks" types, the dark-skinned pickers in the "factories-in-the-fields," and the blue-eyed "crackers," some of whom have their huts dug into the sides of the red hills planted with stunted corn, and whose principal passion is a transference of all their resentment and frustration to a hatred of the Negro—a fellow prisoner. The rural poor are weighted down with chains of poor health and lassitude and ignorance. Their final humiliation is their removal—in one light it looks like a deliverance—from their wasted properties, rented or mortgaged, to the great institution of the industrial slum or housing project. Thomas Jefferson died a long time ago.

3

Welfare Reform

RICHARD M. NIXON

The national government first became deeply involved in welfare programs during the Great Depression of the 1930's. It was assumed these emergency measures would become unnecessary with the adoption of Social Security and the return of prosperity. Instead, program was piled upon program; welfarism became a way of life rather than a stopgap measure; costs rose steadily year after year despite record prosperity. President Johnson recognized these defects and declared a war on poverty to bring welfare clients into the mainstream of American life. President Nixon, early in his administration, proposed a wholesale reordering of the welfare approach, with an emphasis on family renewal.

How did the existing system break up families? How did the system encourage migration to large cities? How would the Nixon proposals benefit the working poor? What distinctions did the President draw between his program and a guaranteed income? What incentives would be offered to welfare clients who took jobs or entered job training programs? How would the new program be financed?

. . .

Nowhere has the failure of government been more tragically apparent than in its efforts to help the poor, and especially in its system of public welfare. Since taking office, one of my first priorities has been to repair the machiney of government, to put it in shape for the 1970s. I have made many changes designed to improve the functioning of the executive branch, and I've asked Congress for a number of im-

From Richard M. Nixon, Presidential Documents (Washington, D.C.: U.S. Government Printing Office, 1969), August 11, 1969 (speech delivered on national television, August 8, 1969), pp. 1103–1112.

portant structural reforms: among others, a wide-ranging postal reform, a comprehensive reform of the draft, a reform of unemployment insurance, a reform of our hunger programs, a reform of the present confusing hodge-podge of Federal grants-in-aid.

Last April 21st I sent Congress a message asking for a package of major tax reforms, including both the closing of loopholes and the removal of more than 2 million low-income families from the tax rolls altogether. I am glad that Congress is now acting on tax reform, and hope the Congress will begin to act on the other reforms that I have requested.

The purpose of all these reforms is to eliminate unfairness, to make government more effective as well as more efficient; and to bring an end to its chronic failure to deliver the service that it promises.

My purpose tonight, however, is not to review the past record, but to present a new set of reforms—a new set of proposals—a new and drastically different approach to the way in which Government cares for those in need, and to the way the responsibilities are shared between the state and Federal Governments.

I have chosen to do so in a direct report to the people because these proposals call for public decisions of the first importance; because they represent a fundamental change in the nation's approach to one of its most pressing social problems; and because, quite deliberately, they also represent the first major reversal of the trend toward ever more centralization of government in Washington, D.C.

After a third of a century of power flowing from the people and the states to Washington it is time for a new federalism in which power, funds and responsibility will flow from Washington to the states and to the people.

During last year's election campaign, I often made a point that touched a responsive chord wherever I traveled. I said that this nation became great not because of what government did for people, but because of what people did for themselves.

This new approach aims at helping the American people do more for themselves.

It aims at getting everyone able to work off welfare rolls and onto payrolls.

It aims at ending the unfairness in a system that has become unfair to the welfare recipient, unfair to the working poor and unfair to the taxpayer.

This new approach aims to make it possible for people—wherever in America they live—to receive their fair share of opportunity. It aims to ensure that people receiving aid, and who are able to work, contribute their fair share of productivity.

This new approach is embodied in a package of four measures: first, a complete replacement of the present welfare system; second, a comprehensive new job training and placement program; third, a revamping of the Office of Economic Opportunity; and fourth, a start on the sharing of the Federal tax revenues with the states.

Next week—in three messages to the Congress and one statement—I will spell out in detail what these measures contain. Tonight I want to explain what they mean, what they are intended to achieve, and how they are related.

Whether measured by the anguish of the poor themselves, or by the drastically mounting burden on the taxpayer, the present welfare system has to be judged a colossal failure.

Our states and cities find themselves sinking in a Federal welfare quagmire, as caseloads increase, as costs escalate, and as the welfare system stagnates enterprise and perpetuates dependency. What began on a small scale in the Depression thirties and has become a monster in the prosperous sixties. And the tragedy is not only that it is bringing states and cities to the brink of financial disaster, but also that it is failing to meet the elementary human, social and financial needs of the poor.

It breaks up homes. It often penalizes work. It robs recipients of dignity. And it grows.

Benefit levels are grossly unequal—for a mother with three children, they range from an average of $263 a month in one state, down to an average of only $39 in another state. Now such an inequality as this is wrong; no child is "worth" more in one state than in another state. One result of this inequality is to lure thousands more into already overcrowded inner cities, as unprepared for city life as they are for city jobs.

The present system creates an incentive for desertion. In most states, a family is denied welfare payments if a father is present—even though he is unable to support his family. Now in practice, this is what often happens: a father is unable to find a job at all, or one that will support his children. And so to make the children eligible for welfare, he leaves home—and the children are denied the authority, the discipline and the love that come with having a father in the home. This is wrong.

The present system often makes it possible to receive more money on welfare than on a low-paying job. This creates an incentive not to work; and it also is unfair to the working poor: It is morally wrong for a family that is working to try to make ends meet to receive less than the family across the street on welfare.

This has been bitterly resented by the man who works, and rightly so—the rewards are just the opposite of what they should be. Its effect is to draw people off payrolls and onto welfare rolls—just the opposite of what government should be doing. To put it bluntly and simply—any system which makes it more profitable for man not to work than to work, or which encourages a man to desert his family rather than stay with his family, is wrong and indefensible.

We cannot simply ignore the failures of welfare, or expect them to go away. In the past eight years, three million more people have been added to the welfare rolls—and this in a period of low unemployment. If the present trend continues, another 4 million will join the welfare rolls by 1975. The financial cost will be crushing; and the human cost will be suffocating.

And that is why tonight I therefore propose that we abolish the present welfare system and that we adopt in its place a new family assistance system. Initially, this new system will cost more than welfare. But unlike welfare, it is designed to correct the condition it deals with and thus to lessen the long-range burden and cost.

Under this plan, the so-called "adult categories" of aid—aid to the aged, to the blind, the disabled—would be continued, and a national minimum standard for benefits would be set, with the Federal Government contributing to its cost and also sharing the cost of additional state payments above that amount.

But the program now called "aid to families with dependent children"—the program we all normally think of when we think of "welfare"—would be done away with completely. The new family assistance system I propose in its place rests essentially on these three principles: equality of treatment across the nation, a work requirement and a work incentive.

Its benefits would go to the working poor, as well as the nonworking; to families with dependent children headed by a father, as well as to those headed by a mother; and a basic Federal minimum would be provided, the same in every state.

What I am proposing is that the Federal Government build a foundation under the income of every American family with dependent children that cannot care for itself—and wherever in America that family may live.

For a family of four now on welfare, with no outside income, the basic Federal payment would be $1,600 a year. States could add to that amount and most states would add to it. In no case would anyone's present level of benefits be lowered.

At the same time, this foundation would be one on which the family itself could build. Outside earnings would be encouraged, not discouraged. The new worker could keep the first $60 a month of outside earnings with no reduction in his benefits, and beyond that his benefits would be reduced by only 50 cents for each dollar earned.

By the same token, a family head already

employed at low wages could get a family assistance supplement; those who work would no longer be discriminated against. For example, a family of five in which the father earns $2,000 a year—which is the hard fact of life for many families in America today—would get family assistance payments of $1,260 so that they would have a total income of $3,260. A family of seven earning $3,000 a year would have its income raised to $4,360.

Thus, for the first time, the Government would recognize that it has no less an obligation to the working poor than to the nonworking poor; and for the first time, benefits would be scaled in such a way that it would always pay to work.

With such incentives, most recipients who can work will want to work. This is part of the American character.

But what of the others—those who can work but choose not to? Well, the answer is very simple.

Under this proposal, everyone who accepts benefits must also accept work or training provided suitable jobs are available either locally or at some distance if transportation is provided. The only exceptions would be those unable to work, and mothers of pre-school children.

Even mothers of pre-school children, however, would have the opportunity to work—because I am also proposing along with this a major expansion of day-care centers to make it possible for mothers to take jobs by which they can support themselves and their children.

This national floor under incomes for working or dependent families is not a "guaranteed income." Under the guaranteed income proposal, everyone would be assured a minimum income, regardless of how much he was capable of earning, regardless of what his need was, regardless of whether or not he was willing to work.

No, during the Presidential campaign last year I opposed such a plan. I oppose it now, and I will continue to oppose it. And this is the reason. A guaranteed income would undermine the incentive to work; the family assistance plan that I propose increases the incentive to work. A guaranteed income establishes a right without any responsibilities; family assistance recognizes a need and establishes a responsibility. It provides help to those in need, and in turn requires that those who receive help work to the extent of their capabilities. There is no reason why one person should be taxed so that another can choose to live idly.

In states that now have benefit levels above the Federal floor, family assistance would help ease the states' financial burdens. But in 20 states—those in which poverty is most widespread—the new Federal floor would be above present average benefits and would mean a leap upward for many thousands of families that cannot care for themselves.

Now I would like to turn to the job training proposals that are part of our full opportunity concept. America prides itself on being a "land of opportunity." I deeply believe in this ideal, as I am sure everyone listening to me also believes in this ideal.

Full opportunity means the chance for upward mobility on every rung of the economic ladder—and for every American, no matter what the handicaps of birth.

The cold, hard truth is that a child born to a poor family has far less chance to make a good living than a child born to a middle-income family.

He is born poor, he is fed poorly, and if his family is on welfare, he starts life in an atmosphere of handout and dependency; often he receives little preparation for work and less inspiration. And the wonder of the American character is that so many have the spark and the drive to fight their way up. But for millions of others, the burdens of poverty in early life snuff out that spark.

The new family assistance would provide aid for needy families; it would establish a work requirement, and a work incentive; but these in turn require effective programs of job training and job placement—including a chance to qualify not just for any jobs, but for good jobs, that provide both additional self-respect and full self-support.

Therefore, I am also sending a message to Congress calling for a complete overhaul of the nation's manpower-training services.

The Federal Government's job-training programs have been a terrible tangle of confusion and waste.

To remedy the confusion, arbitrariness and rigidity of the present system, the new manpower-training act would basically do three things:

It would pull together the jumble of programs that presently exist, and equalize standards of eligibility.

It would provide flexible funding—so that Federal money would follow the demands of labor and industry, and flow into those programs that people most want and most need.

It would decentralize administration, gradually moving it away from the Washington bureaucracy and turning it over to states and localities.

In terms of its symbolic importance, I can hardly overemphasize this last point. For the first time, applying the principles of the New Federalism, administration of a major established Federal program would be turned over to the states and local governments, recognizing that they are in a position to do the job better.

For years, thoughtful Americans have talked of the need to decentralize government. The time has come to begin.

Federal job training programs have grown to vast proportions, costing more than a billion dollars a year. And yet they are essentially local in character. As long as the Federal Government continues to bear the cost, they can perfectly well be run by states and local governments, and that way they can be better adapted to specific state and local needs.

The Manpower Training Act will have other provisions specifically designed to help move people off welfare rolls and onto payrolls:

A computerized job bank would be es-tablished to match jobseekers with job vacancies.

For those on welfare, a $30 a month bonus would be offered as an incentive to go into job training.

For heads of families now on welfare, 150,000 new training slots would be opened.

And as I mentioned previously, greatly expanded day-care center facilities would be provided for the children of welfare mothers who choose to work. However, these would be day-care centers with a difference. There is no single ideal to which this Administration is more firmly committed than to the enriching of a child's first five years of life, and thus helping lift the poor out of misery at a time when a lift can help the most. Therefore, these day-care centers would offer more than custodial care; they would also be devoted to the development of vigorous young minds and bodies. And as a further dividend, the day-care centers would offer employment to many welfare mothers themselves.

One common theme running through my proposals tonight is that of providing full opportunity for every American. A second theme is that of trying to equip every American to play a productive role. And a third is the need to make government itself workable—which means reshaping, reforming, innovating.

The Office of Economic Opportunity is basically an innovative agency—and, thus, it has a vital place in our efforts to develop new programs and apply new knowledge. But in order to do so effectively what it can do best, the O.E.O. itself needs reorganization.

. . .

We come now to a proposal which I consider profoundly important to the future of our Federal system of shared responsibilities.

When we speak of poverty or jobs or opportunity, or making government more effective or getting it closer to the people, it brings us directly to the financial plight of our states and cities.

We can no longer have effective government at any level unless we have it at all levels. There is too much to be done for the cities to do it alone, for Washington to do it alone, or for the states to do it alone.

For a third of a century, power and responsibility have flowed toward Washington—and Washington has taken for its own the best sources of revenue.

We intend to reverse this tide, and to turn back to the states a greater measure of responsibility—not as a way of avoiding problems, but as a better way of solving problems. Along with this should go a share of Federal revenues. I shall propose to the Congress next week that a set portion of the revenues from Federal income taxes be remitted directly to the states—with a minimum of Federal restrictions on how those dollars are to be used, and with a requirement that a percentage of them be channeled through for the use of local governments.

The funds provided under this program will not be great in the first year. But the principle will have been established, and the amounts will increase as our budgetary situation improves.

This start on revenue sharing is a step toward what I call the new federalism. It is a gesture of faith in America's states and local governments, and in the principle of democratic self-government.

.   .   .

The investment in these proposals is a human investment; it also is a "start-up cost" in turning around our dangerous decline into welfarism in America. We cannot produce productive people with the antiquated, wheezing, overloaded machine we now call the welfare system.

If we fail to make this investment in work incentives now, if we merely try to patch up the system here and there, we will only be pouring good money after bad in ever-increasing amounts.

If we do invest in his modernization, the heavily burdened taxpayer at least will have the chance to see the end of the tunnel. And the man who now looks ahead only to a lifetime of dependency will see hope—

hope for a life of work and pride and dignity.

In the final analysis, we cannot talk our way out of poverty; we cannot legislate our way out of poverty; but this nation can work its way out of poverty. What America needs now is not more welfare but more "workfare."

The task of this Government, the great task of our people, is to provide the training for work, the incentive to work, the opportunity to work, the reward for work. Together, these measures are a first long step in that direction.

For those in the welfare system today, or struggling to fight their way out of poverty, these measures offer a way to independence through the dignity of work.

For those able to work, these measures provide new opportunities to learn work, to find work.

And for the working poor—the forgotten poor—these measures offer a fair share in the assistance given to the poor.

This new system establishes a direct link between the Government's willingness to help the needy, and the willingness of the needy to help themselves.

It removes the present incentive not to work, and substitutes an incentive to work; it removes the present incentive for families to break apart, and substitutes an incentive for families to stay together.

It removes the blatant inequities and injustices and indignities of the welfare system.

It establishes a basic Federal floor, so that children in any state can have at least the minimum essentials of life.

Together, these measures cushion the impact of welfare costs on states and localities, many of which have found themselves in fiscal crisis as costs have escalated.

They bring reason, order and purpose into a tangle of overlapping programs, and show that government can be made to work.

Poverty will not be defeated by a stroke of a pen signing a check; and it will not be reduced to nothing overnight with slogans or ringing exhortations.

Poverty is not only a state of income. It is also a state of mind, a state of health. Poverty must be conquered without sacrificing the will to work, for if we take the route of the permanent handout, the American character will itself be impoverished.

. . .

. . . We can resolve to make this the year, not that we reached the goal, but that we turned the corner—turned the corner from a dismal cycle of dependency toward a new birth of independence; from despair toward hope; from an ominously mounting impotence of Government toward a new effectiveness of Government—and toward a full opportunity for every American to share the bounty of this rich land.

4

Government Can't Eliminate Poverty

EDWARD C. BANFIELD

Most Americans believe that, with enough time, effort, and money, all problems can be solved. Such a philosophy sets no limits on the ability of government to cope with a social problem such as poverty. Professor Banfield raises a dissenting voice, suggesting that government has had and will have limited success in eliminating poverty.

Why do the poor resent their poverty so keenly today? Are they actually searching for income or status? Do many of the poor represent a subculture (lower class) with different values? Can higher incomes or government payments cure "internally" caused poverty? What similarity exists between the Victorian "friendly visitor" and today's Vista worker? How do community action programs resemble the old settlement house? What major problem have modern community leaders encountered in achieving "maximum feasible participation"? Which group does Banfield believe will respond to poverty programs? Can American poverty be eliminated?

. . . The poor today are not "objectively" any more deprived relative to the non-poor than they were a decade ago. Few will doubt, however, that they *feel* more deprived—that they perceive the gap to be wider and that, this being the case, it *is* wider in the sense that matters most. By constantly calling attention to income differences, the war on poverty has probably engendered and strengthened feelings of relative deprivation. This subjective effect may have more than offset whatever objective reduction occurred in income inequality.

Finally, it may be that poverty in the sense of relative deprivation is only incidentally related to a lack of material things, and that therefore even "equality" of income (whatever that may mean) would leave as many people "poor"—i.e., feeling deprived—as before. This conclusion is implied by some of David Caplovitz's comments on the behavior of the low-income consumers he studied. They bought console phonographs, color television sets, and so on, he says, in order to "embellish" their

From Edward C. Banfield, The Unheavenly City (Boston, Mass.: Little, Brown and Company, 1970), pp. 124–131. Copyright © 1968, 1970 by Edward C. Banfield. Reprinted by permission of the publisher.

social status; having failed to move up the social ladder, they "compensated" by climbing symbolically through consumption of such things. If he is right, no amount of income redistribution can reduce, much less eliminate, their poverty: it consists not of lack of income, but of lack of *status*. Indeed, the more far-reaching the income redistribution, the more painfully apparent it may become that such symbols as color television sets cannot provide "real" status. If what the poor really want is a reduction of the extremes of status inequality, then income redistribution, however comprehensive, cannot help much. If they want the elimination of *all* status differences, then nothing can help.

There is another kind of poverty, however. Robert Hunter described it in 1904:

They lived in God only knows what misery. They ate when there were things to eat; they starved when there was lack of food. But, on the whole, although they swore and beat each other and got drunk, they were more contented than any other class I have happened to know. It took a long time to understand them. Our Committees were busy from morning until night in giving them opportunities to take up the fight again, and to become independent of relief. They always took what we gave them; they always promised to try; but as soon as we expected them to fulfill any promises, they gave up in despair, and either wept or looked ashamed, and took to misery and drink again,—almost, so it seemed to me at times, with a sense of relief.

In Hunter's day these were the "undeserving," "unworthy," "depraved," "debased," or "disreputable" poor; today, they are the "troubled," "culturally deprived," "hard to reach," or "multiproblem." In the opinion of anthropologist Oscar Lewis, their kind of poverty "is a way of life, remarkably stable and persistent, passed down from generation to generation along family lines." This "culture of poverty," as he calls it, exists in city slums in many parts of the world, and is, he says, an adaptation made by the poor in order to defend themselves against the harsh realities of slum life.

The view to be taken here . . . is that there is indeed such a culture, but that poverty is its effect rather than its cause. (There are societies even poorer than the ones Lewis has described—primitive ones, for example—in which nothing remotely resembling the pattern of behavior here under discussion exists.) Extreme present-orientedness, not lack of income or wealth, is the principal cause of poverty in the sense of "the culture of poverty." Most of those caught up in this culture are unable or unwilling to plan for the future, to sacrifice immediate gratifications in favor of future ones, or to accept the disciplines that are required in order to get and to spend. Their inabilities are probably culturally given in most cases—"multiproblem" families being normal representatives of a class culture that is itself abnormal. No doubt there are also people whose present-orientedness is rationally adaptive rather than cultural, but these probably comprise only a small part of the "hard-core" poor. . . .

Outside the lower class, poverty (in the sense of hardship, want, or destitution) is today almost always the result of external circumstances—involuntary unemployment, prolonged illness, the death of a breadwinner, or some other misfortune. Even when severe, such poverty is not squalid or degrading. Moreover, it ends quickly once the (external) cause of it no longer exists. Public or private assistance can sometimes remove or alleviate the cause—for example, by job retraining or remedial surgery. Even when the cause cannot be removed, simply providing the nonlower-class poor with sufficient income is enough to enable them to live "decently."

Lower-class poverty, by contrast, is "inwardly" caused (by psychological inability to provide for the future, and all that this inability implies). Improvements in external circumstances can affect this poverty only superficially: one problem of a "multiproblem" family is no sooner solved than another arises. In principle, it is possible to eliminate the poverty (material lack) of such a family, but only at great expense, since the capacity of the radically improvident to waste money is almost unlimited. Raising such a family's income would not necessarily improve its way of life, moreover, and could conceivably even make things worse. Consider, for example, the H. family:

Mrs. H. seemed overwhelmed with the simple mechanics of dressing her six children and washing their clothes. The younger ones were running around in their underwear; the older ones were unaccounted for, but presumably were around the neighborhood. Mrs. H. had not been out of the house for several months; evidently her husband did the shopping. The apartment was filthy and it smelled. Mrs. H. was dressed in a bathrobe, although it was mid-afternoon. She seemed to have no plan or expectations with regard to the children; she did not know the names of their teachers and she did not seem to worry about their school work, although one child had been retained one year and another two years. Mrs. H. did seem to be somewhat concerned about her husband's lack of activity over the weekend—his continuous drinking and watching baseball on television. Apparently he and she never went out socially together nor did the family ever go anywhere as a unit.

If this family had a very high income—say $50,000 a year—it would not be considered a "culture of poverty" case. Mrs. H. would hire maids to look after the small children, send the others to boarding schools, and spend her time at fashion shows while her husband drank and watched TV at his club. But with an income of only moderate size—say 100 per cent above the poverty line—they would probably be about as badly off as they are now. They might be even worse off, for Mrs. H. would be able to go to the dog races, leaving the children alone, and Mr. H. could devote more time to his bottle and TV set.

Such families constitute a small proportion both of all families in the city (perhaps 5 per cent at most) and of those with incomes below the poverty line (perhaps 10 to 20 per cent). The problems that they present are out of proportion to their numbers, however; in St. Paul, Minnesota, for example, a survey showed that 6 per cent of the city's families absorbed 77 per cent of its public assistance, 51 per cent of its health services, and 56 per cent of its men-

tal health and correction casework services. Moreover, their misery is (or at least seems) far greater than that of the other poor—the garbage-strewn, rat-infested hovels with toilets out of order are now almost exclusively theirs. Giving them income, even in rather large amounts, is unlikely to reduce and may even increase their poverty.

Welfare agencies, recognizing the difference between "internally" and "externally" caused poverty, have long been trying first by one means and then another to improve the characters or, as it is now put, to "bring about personal adjustment" of the poor. In the nineteenth century, the view was widely held that what the lower-class individual needed was to be brought into a right relation with God or (the secular version of the same thing) with the respectable (that is, middle- and upper-class) elements of the community. The missionary who distributed tracts door to door in the slums was the first caseworker; his—more often, her—task was to minister to what today would be called "feelings of alienation."

The stranger, coming on a stranger's errand, becomes a friend, discharging the offices and exerting the influence of a friend. . . .

Secularized, this approach became the "friendly visitor" system under which "certain persons, under the direction of a central board, pledge themselves to take one or more families who need counsel, if not material help, on their visiting list, and maintain personal friendly relations with them." The system did not work; middle- and upper-class people might be "friendly," but they could not sympathize, let alone communicate, with the lower class. By the beginning of the twentieth century the friendly visitor had been replaced by the "expert." The idea now was that the authority of "the facts" would bring about desired changes of attitude, motive, and habit. As it happened, however, the lower class did not recognize the authority of the facts. The expert then became a supervisor, using his (or her) power to confer or withhold material benefits in order to force the poor to do the things that were supposed to lead to "rehabilitation" (that is, to a middle-class style of life). This method did not work either; the lower class could always find ways to defeat and exploit the system. They seldom changed their ways very much and they never changed them for long. Besides, there was really no body of expertise to tell caseworkers how to produce the changes desired. As one caseworker remarked recently in a book addressed to fellow social service professionals:

Despite years of experience in providing public aid to poor families precious little is yet known about how to help truly inadequate parents make long term improvements in child care, personal maturity, social relations, or work stability.

Some people understood that if the individual's style of life was to be changed at all, it would be necessary to change that of the group that produced, motivated, and constrained him. Thus, the settlement house. As Robert A. Woods explained:

The settlements are able to take neighborhoods in cities, and by patience bring back to them much of the healthy village life, so that the people shall again know and care for one another. . . .

When it became clear that settlement houses would not change the culture of slum neighborhoods, the group approach was broadened into what is called "community action." In one type of community action ("community development"), a community organizer tries to persuade a neighborhood's informal leader to support measures (for instance, measures of delinquency control) that he advances. In another form of it ("community organization"), the organizer tries to promote self-confidence, self-respect, and attachment to the group (and, hopefully, to normal society) among lower-class people. He attempts to do this by encouraging them in efforts at joint action, or by showing them how to conduct meetings, carry on discussions, pass resolutions, present requests to politicians, and the like. In still another form ("community mobilization"), the organizer endeavors to arouse the anger of lower-class persons against the local "power structure," to teach them the techniques of mass action—strikes, sit-ins, picketing, and so on—and to show them how they may capture power. The theory of community organization attributes the malaise of the poor to their lack of self-confidence (which is held to derive largely from their "inexperience"); community mobilization theory, by contrast, attributes it to their feelings of "powerlessness." According to this doctrine, the best cure for poverty is to give the poor power. But since power is not "given," it must be seized.

The success of the group approach has been no greater than that of the caseworker approach. Reviewing five years of effort on the part of various community action programs, Marris and Rein conclude:

. . . the reforms had not evolved any reliable solutions to the intractable problems with which they struggled. They had not discovered how in general to override the intransigent autonomy of public and private agencies, at any level of government; nor how to use the social sciences practically to formulate and evaluate policy; nor how, under the sponsorship of government, to raise the power of the poor. Given the talent and money they had brought to bear, they had not even reopened very many opportunities.

If the war on poverty is judged by its ability "to generate major, meaningful and lasting social and economic reforms in conformity with the expressed wishes of poor people," writes Thomas Gladwin, ". . . it is extremely difficult to find even scattered evidence of success." The Economic Opportunity Act of 1965 might require "maximum feasible participation" in the planning and conduct of programs financed under it, but the poor rarely cared to participate even to the extent of voting. In Philadelphia, for example, there was a polling place in each of the twelve "poverty areas," and the Gas Works contributed twelve trucks and drivers to carry additional voting machines from block to block; the turnout, however, was only 5.5 per cent of those eligible in 1966.

Although city agencies have sent community organizers by the score into slum neighborhoods, the lower-class poor cannot be organized. In East Harlem in 1948, five social workers were assigned to organize a five-block area and to initiate a program of social action based on housing, recreation, and other neighborhood needs. After three years of effort, the organizers had failed to attract a significant number of participants, and those they did attract were upwardly mobile persons who were unrepresentative of the neighborhood. In Boston a "total community" delinquency control project was found to have had "negligible impact," an outcome strikingly like that of the Cambridge-Somerville experiment—a "total caseworker" project—a decade earlier. Even community mobilization, despite the advantages of a rhetoric of hate and an emphasis on "action," failed to involve lower-class persons to a significant extent. Gangsters and leaders of youth gangs were coopted on occasion, but they did not suffer from feelings of powerlessness and were not representative of the class for which

mobilization was to provide therapy. No matter how hard they have tried to appeal to people at the very bottom of the scale, community organizers have rarely succeeded. Where they have appeared to succeed, as, for example, in the National Rights Organization, it has been by recruiting people who had some of the *outward* attributes of the lower class—poverty, for example—but whose outlook and values were not lower class; the lower-class person (as defined here) is incapable of being organized. Although it tried strenuously to avoid it, what the Mobilization for Youth described as the general experience proved to be its own experience as well:

Most efforts to organize lower-class people attract individuals on their way up the social-class ladder. Persons who are relatively responsible about participation, articulate and successful at managing organizational "forms" are identified as lower-class leaders, rather than individuals who actually reflect the values of lower-class groups. Ordinarily the slum's network of informal group associations is not reached.

Caution: Cities May Be Hazardous To Your Health

15

THE CRISIS IN URBAN GOVERNMENT: WILL CITIES REMAIN HABITABLE?

Long-range population trends in the United States indicate a steady shift toward a new suburban majority. Farm population has declined by one-third since 1960. In the same period, thirteen of the twenty-five largest cities have also lost population as the affluent flocked to the suburbs. Today suburbanites outnumber those living in central cities. The term to describe population patterns is not rural-urban, but urban-suburban (metropolitan areas). The most dramatic trend is the creation of megalopolises—groups of metropolitan areas stretching across state lines in an almost unbroken pattern. For example, one-sixth of the nation's people now live in a 450 mile strip running from Boston to Washington (BoWash) along the Atlantic Ocean and stretching 150 miles inland. Other megalopolises run from Chicago to Pittsburgh (ChiPitts) and from San Francisco to San Diego (SanSan). These population patterns indirectly spell out the political economic-social problems of the 1970's—a nation troubled by central city decay and suburban sprawl.

Does a Crisis Exist?

How serious are the problems that confront American cities? Is the total situation properly described as a crisis, a term that in its medical sense implies a choice between recovery and death? Or are the present problems, however difficult, only the growing pains of a new world? In recent years the prophets of disaster have spoken without many challengers. It is commonly said that American cities are becoming uninhabitable. The catalogue of particulars is long and grim. What is more, according to the critics, the situation becomes worse every year. Implicit in this analysis is a suggestion that American cities may die, unable to cope with their increasingly complex problems.

Other observers are more optimistic. Although they recognize the present plight of most metropolitan areas, they believe that the very pressure of events will generate solutions. In effect, they believe that once the crisis is widely recognized, it will receive the scientific, financial, and political attention it deserves. Also, say the optimists, American cities in their present state have much to recommend them. Most migration to them has been voluntary; the older rural America was not the Arcadia pictured by some urban critics.

What Are the Major Problems?

The major problems of American cities are rather easily identified, although satisfactory solutions are apt to require massive scientific and financial efforts and a complete reshuffling of the present governmental structure.

Consider, for a moment, the shifting population patterns within metropolitan areas. Nearly every central city has lost population during the past 20 years to its satellite suburbs, while the racial-ethnic composition of the remaining residents has changed radically. As older immigrant groups head for the suburbs they have been replaced by the modern "underdogs" of contemporary America—Southern Negroes, Puerto Ricans, Mexican Americans. Many core cities are well on their way toward becoming superghettos, filled with impoverished slum dwellers. A result of this process is a shrinking tax base as financial needs increase. Another by-product appears to be a rising threat to personal safety—"crime in the streets."

Meanwhile, a large percentage of suburban residents daily enter and leave the central city, most of them by private automobile. The number of such vehicles has nearly tripled in the past 20 years, with no end to the growth rate in sight. Within the core cities they jam expressways as quickly as they are built and create gigantic parking problems. They also contribute to air pollution.

Pollution of water and air are a direct result of our booming economy. Most water pollution is caused by industrial wastes; air pollution comes from factories, power plants, and automobiles. Both types of pollution are now a universal metropolitan problem. Clean water is in short supply; clean air is being replaced by smog.

Inevitably, the problems outlined above become political problems, but our present political structure is ill-suited to deal with such issues. Most metropolitan areas are fragmented into dozens of political units. The Pittsburgh metropolitan area, for instance, has nearly 200 political subdivisions, each largely independent of the others. The relationship among cities, states, and the national government is also being subjected to reappraisal in the face of these issues. The cry of "states rights vs. central control" appears somewhat shopworn in this context. What governmental unit can best deal with pollution and transportation problems? How do we check slums? Perhaps there are no clear-cut answers. Is a solution to be found in some new kind of cooperative effort? Cooperative federalism between central cities and suburbs? Cooperative federalism among cities, states, and the national government? Or should we conclude that most of these issues are beyond the range of effective government action?

What Is the City's Future?

For most of us the future of American cities is closely bound up with our own future. Faced with a multitude of immediate problems, it is easy to conclude that the pessimists are right—that the outlook for American cities is bleak indeed. As an antidote to this depressing conclusion we present a rather optimistic description of American urban life in the year 2000. Although life in the twenty-first century will not be without problems, according to the author we will have surmounted many dilemmas.

1

The American City in Travail

PETER F. DRUCKER

Two facts concerning American metropolitan areas are almost immediately apparent: (1) they are growing at a fantastic rate, as they absorb rural immigrants and their own birth rate soars; (2) this growth is creating a host of problems that overwhelm our antiquated city governments. Regarding the trend of population growth there appears to be no turning back. Regarding the escalation of problems and the need for governmental reorganization to cope with them there seems to be little disagreement among those who face the issues. The chief issue appears to be one of political education. What are the problems of metropolitan America? How can they be solved? Who will give direction? Who will foot the bill? How can we design governments that match the scope of the problems?

That our big cities are hell-bent on committing suicide is hardly news. They are rapidly becoming unlivable. Attempts to assuage the disease seem to aggravate it. New freeways create more traffic jams and more air pollution; urban renewal dispossesses the poor or moves them from the jungle of the slum into the desert of the housing development; zoning for "racial balance" ends up by creating another Black Belt or Bronzeville.

From Peter F. Drucker, "American Directions: A Forecast." Copyright © 1965 by Peter F. Drucker. Originally appeared in Harper's Magazine and reprinted by permission of Harper & Row, Publishers. From the forthcoming book American Directions by Peter F. Drucker.

A real solution, if one can be found, will have to be primarily aesthetic (or if you prefer the word, moral). At stake is the environment of modern man, rather than administration. We need a city that enriches and ennobles rather than degrades the individual, and not one that most efficiently fits him into well-planned public services. But long before we can hope to come to grips with the city as a human environment we will have to come to grips with the city as a government.

And the need is desperate. Within a few years three-quarters of the American people will live in a fairly small number of metropolitan areas, fewer than 200. Nearly two-fifths of the population will live in or close by the three monster supercities—one spreading from Boston to Norfolk, another from Milwaukee to Detroit (if not to Cleveland), and a third from San Francisco to San Diego. We will have to be able to supply people in the metropolis with water, sewers, and clean air. We will have to provide decent housing and schools for them, plus easy mobility for people, things, and ideas—which is the very reason for the existence of a city.

And for all this we shall need governmental institutions that will, of necessity, cut across or replace a whole host of local governments in existence today.

The Government We Lack

The metropolis is the decisive community today. But it does not exist as a government at all. Instead our system is built on the old preindustrial units of town, county, and state. No attack on the problems of the metropolis is possible without attacking at the same time these most deeply entrenched political bodies of our tradition and laws.

The tax issue alone will make sure of that. Within the next five years, local government expenses will double—from fifty billions to one hundred billions, very largely for education. But most of the big cities have already drained their tax reservoirs. We might tackle the financial problem of the big city by bringing the suburbs into the metropolitan tax system; by using the taxing powers of the states to finance the cities; or through large-scale grants from the federal government. My guess is that we will use all three methods. And each of them is sure to touch off a major political fight.

Similarly the "war on poverty" will raise the issue of metropolitan government. For the hard core of present-day poverty consists of city people who dwell outside our affluent, high-education society. Compared to them, the unemployed coal miners in the hollows of West Virginia or the submarginal farmers of Appalachia are a mopping-up operation.

The battle over the city's place in American government has already been joined. The Supreme Court decision last spring on reapportionment decreed that state legislatures must give equal representation to all voters regardless of their residence. It was fully as revolutionary as was that other Supreme Court decision, ten years ago, that decreed racial integration for the public schools. And like the school decision, reapportionment clearly was just the first skirmish in what will be a long and bitter fight. Lieutenant Governor Malcolm Wilson of New York was not exaggerating when he warned (in a speech to the County Officers Association of New York last September 22) that reapportionment eventually might lead to the end of counties as units of government. Connecticut has already abolished them. And when New Jersey celebrated its Tercentenary in 1964, quite a few of its inhabitants must have wondered whether their state now serves any real purpose—with a population divided between residents of Metropolitan New York and residents of Metropolitan Philadelphia, separated rather than held together by Princeton Junction.

Of course, the issue will be fought out on specifics. It will be fought out as an issue of power balances within the nation, over tax sources and their division, and over the by-passing of states and counties by a federal government which increasingly works directly in cooperation with the cities.

Mass transportation in and out of our big cities is, for instance, likely to be entrusted to a new federal agency before very long.* In our largest cities (New York, Philadelphia, and Chicago) it requires planning beyond the boundaries of one state, and money beyond the capacity of any local government.

But such specifics are only symptoms of a great constitutional crisis of our political institutions and structure.

---

* Mr. Drucker's forecast has been confirmed. A new cabinet-level Department of Transportation was created by Congress in 1966.

2

A Second Look at the Urban Crisis

IRVING KRISTOL

Today there is general agreement that ours is an urban society. It is also generally agreed that this urban society is faced with problems that bid fair to be insoluble. At this point there is value in reviewing all of the evidence for some ray of hope. Are we being urbanized in an inexorable fashion? Or do the population statistics actually show something else? Will the urban ghetto spread without check? Are traffic conditions growing steadily worse? Are slums spreading? If we manage to survive these challenges, are we doomed to polluted water, smog, and crime in the streets? Mr. Kristol challenges the assumptions that most Americans accept without much thought or reflection.

Do we, in fact, have an urban crisis? Most people by now are conditioned to believe so. But would we believe any of the following propositions?

1. Since 1920, the percentage of the American population living in cities of over 250,000 has remained just about stationary. We have not become a nation of big cities—only 10 per cent of Americans live in cities of over 1,000,000, not significantly more than in 1910. And only 29 per cent today live in cities of over 100,000. We have become to a greater extent than before, a nation of suburban and exurban towns and villages and of "cities" with less than 50,000 population.

2. Since World War II, there has been a steady decline in the proportion of substandard urban housing units. In 1960, according to the Census Bureau, less than 3 per cent of dwelling units in cities of 50,000 or more were substandard.

From Irving Kristol, "Not A Bad Crisis To Live In," The New York Times Magazine, *(January 22, 1967). As condensed in the* St. Louis Post-Dispatch, *February 8, 1967. Copyright © 1967 by The New York Times Company. Reprinted by permission of the author and publisher.*

3. Since World War II, it has been estimated the proportion of our urban population living below the poverty line has been approximately halved.

4. Only 22 per cent of the American people—according to Gallup—want to live in cities, even small ones, whereas fully half prefer towns or rural areas. Put another way: There are many more people interested in leaving our larger cities than in inhabiting them.

5. The overwhelming majority of Negroes and Puerto Ricans on New York's Upper West Side, when polled, report that they like living in the area, and that their squalid housing represents a clear improvement over their previous living conditions.

6. In Philadelphia (population 2,000,000), 70 per cent of the homes are owner-occupied. That particular urban "behavioral sink" contains three trees per inhabitant.

7. While it is true that traffic in a half-dozen or so of our largest cities is worse today than it was in 1940, such evidence as we have suggests strongly that it is no worse than in 1900, or perhaps even 1850. (There were fewer people and vehicles then, of course; but there were also fewer

thoroughfares and traffic was slower-moving.) In any case, most "city dwellers" live outside our big cities and have no intolerable traffic problem.

8. By any objective, statistical index, our slum areas today appear positively benign in comparison with the teeming, filthy slums of yesteryear. They are certainly less densely populated than they used to be.

If anything is certain about the direction in which American society is moving, it is this: more and more people are going to be living in suburbs. (More and more are going to be working there, too: perhaps 70 per cent do so already.) Even now, it is probable that the total suburban population is greater than the total central city population of the nation.

And I should say that it is equally certain that the new suburbs of today are not going to permit themselves to be swallowed up by their nearest big city. Why should they? It used to be the case that the big city had vital services to offer its outlying townships—sewage, road-building, electricity. This is no longer so.

It seems safe to say that, for most Americans today, the central city serves as a point of entry—a vast staging ground—for the suburbs they will end up in. To these Americans, the "urban problem" consists of saving enough money to get out of the city. All sorts of people regard this as deplorable. But that's the way it is.

It is indisputable that our central cities have some very serious problems—problems which everyone is aware of, though confusedly.

The first problem, of course, is money. City income, though increasing, just cannot keep up with the increase in city expenditures.

Then, there is "the revolution of rising expectations" among the urban poor. These people will not be satisfied with a very slow, modest improvement of their conditions, but insist that the improvement be substantial and swift. The only real way out of this dilemma is economic growth which would create jobs.

To create the jobs that are needed, one would have to entice businesses to establish themselves in the central city. But, for historical reasons, trade unions are extremely powerful in the central city, and their high wage rates and restrictive practices are not inviting to new business.

Moreover, the political administrations of most of our large cities are "liberal" in complexion, and it is very difficult for them to do anything that might be construed as giving "Handouts" to business men. Smaller towns, either in the suburbs or beyond, are not so handicapped; and that's where the business men go.

The greatest single disaster in the history of American big city government, during these past decades, has been the decline of the "machine" and of the political boss. Yes, the machine and the boss were more often than not corrupt. Unfortunately, our new breed of incorruptible and progressive mayors is deficient in one not unimportant respect; they seem unable to govern.

The old-time boss could use his power to "get things done." He could, for instance, expel several thousand squatters from an underdeveloped area of the city in order to create Central Park, as we know it. Can anyone imagine John Lindsay expelling—or even relocating—several thousand people from a rural section of Staten Island in order to create a park? The real-estate developers, the merchants, the construction unions, and CORE would rise up in wrath and indignation. It wouldn't be done.

But our urban poor will doubtless survive the economic mismanagement of our cities. They will make it on their own—to the suburbs: what is now a trickle of Negroes and Puerto Ricans will become a stream and then a flood.

By the time some of the fancier new programs for "rehabilitating" the "local community" begin to have an appreciable effect, many of the people who constitute this "community" will have been largely dispersed and the area itself will be—who can say what it will be then? At that point, we shall be living in a very different world, and coping with some very different "urban crisis."

3

The Commuting Motorist: Urban Enemy Number One

C. W. GRIFFIN, JR.

Each year our major cities expend millions of dollars in a losing battle to solve the transportation crisis created by suburban motorists. Each year the traffic jams grow longer. Each year the metropolitan areas become more thickly populated with automobiles and people.

This pattern is familiar to all Americans. Our instinctive solution is to do more of what we have traditionally done—to add more parking lots, more expressways, more bridges, tunnels, and skyways. The author of the following article is a professional engineer and city planner. After describing the American transportation crisis, he makes specific recommendations for reform. In capsule form, he would wage war against the motorist who uses downtown streets and divert tax dollars from highway building to mass transit.

Having examined the evidence, the reader may have unanswered questions. Are desirability and feasibility always matched in a society governed on the principle "one man, one vote"? In other words, will voters who are also motorists agree that the commuting motorists be regarded as "a public nuisance"? How can the present image of mass transit be made more appealing? Still more basically, how can our metropolitan areas, with their dozens of independent political units, develop a unified transportation policy?

Sam Jepson is an intrepid knight of the highway who lives in northern New Jersey and works in Manhattan. At half past seven on a typical weekday morning, he lights a cigar, pulls out of his driveway in Lake Hontapocus, and starts the thirty-mile trek to New York.

After a short spell of easy driving, Sam is in stop-and-go traffic as cars, trucks, and buses converge on the main highway. Now he draws upon his long experience as a commuting motorist. Negotiating each bottleneck is a test of skill, brains, and daring. Tense and eager at every impending showdown, he questions and admonishes his unresponding enemies aloud while cunningly gauging their speed and intentions —and above all, their determination. Occasionally, Sam discreetly chickens out when an undaunted rival stubbornly holds his lane as the highways merge. A sudden swerve of the Lake Hontapocus bus nearly forces Sam into the guard rail. He jams on the brakes, mutters un-Christian sentiments

From C. W. Griffin, Jr., "Car Snobs, Commuters, and Chaos," Harper's Magazine, *July 1962, pp. 53–58. Copyright © 1962 by Harper's Magazine, Inc. Reprinted by permission of the author.*

about the bus driver, but, hardened by years of such irritations, quickly regains his grim composure.

Approaching the Lincoln Tunnel, traffic slows to the speed of chilled molasses. Sam's tactics now become more aggressive —and so do his adversaries'. At this crawling pace, you can usually count on the other fellow's brakes if you cut in front of him.

As traffic oozes through the tunnel, Sam dourly puffs his cigar, inhales the exhaust fumes perfuming the tunnel, and mumbles about "too damned many cars on the roads." Finally—an hour and twenty-minutes after his departure—he pulls into his midtown Manhattan garage, slightly jaded and cheered by the thought that driving home will be worse than driving in.

Even in summer, on those horrible Monday mornings and Friday evenings when his trip may take two hours or more, Sam's faith remains unshaken. Never will he yield the sacred right of the commuting American to jam streets and highways; never will he submit to the ignominy of riding the train or bus.

Sam Jepson is a life member of the brotherhood of commuting motorists who cause so much of our transportation mess. Their cars crawling in and out of our cities are as costly as they are inefficient. Even the most rabid automaniac knows that rapid transit is a far faster and cheaper way to move masses of people into densely built downtown areas. (A single rapid-transit track can carry as many people as sixteen to twenty freeway lanes occupying ten times as much land.) But the automobile manufacturers, the automobile clubs, and the bridge and tunnel authorities whose revenues swell with traffic congestion defend motorized commuting as a basic American Freedom. "Freedom of Automobility," a slogan of the National Highway Users Conference, is the citizen's inalienable right to drive his car wherever and whenever he damned well pleases. . . .

Big Wheels on Wheels

. . . The national bias favoring highway transportation is supported by a durable myth—long cultivated by automobile manufacturers—that highway users pay for their facilities. This premise is false, especially in the big cities. A Chicago study in the mid-fifties revealed an average annual city subsidy of $84.54 for each motor vehicle using the city streets; a similar study in Milwaukee showed an annual average subsidy of $90. Bureau of Public Roads statistics indicate that in 1960 the nation spent about $1.5 billion more for building, maintaining, and policing streets and highways than was received by federal, state, and local governments from highway users.

Commuting motorists also receive other less direct subsidies. Real-estate-tax assessment policies in most states reward owners for using valuable land for parking lots. According to the general manager of the Chicago Transit Authority, the city loses an estimated $6.3 million in tax receipts a year because some thirty-five acres of privately owned land in the Loop are devoted to parking automobiles and are hence assessed far below the potential value. Expressways are even more parasitical devourers of land than parking lots. The vast acreages they carved out of cities are removed from the tax rolls to become a permanent financial liability. In short, the city's property owners subsidize the street and highway users.

Because of the bias favoring automobile travel, federal highway spending is not balanced by any comparable program for mass transit. Since Washington finances 90 per cent of the cost of urban freeways under the interstate program, the highway solution to surface-transportation problems is almost irresistible, for a city must bear the full burden of financing a mass-transit system. Thus a rapid-transit network that costs only one-fifth as much as a federally aided expressway system would actually cost the local government twice as much. . . .

People vs. Automobiles

. . . One of the most radical proposals to date calls for permanent weekday banning of private automobiles from Manhattan, except in the downtown financial district and the midtown shopping and theatre district. The architect-writer team of Percival and Paul Goodman proposes a basic pattern of traffic arteries forming grid squares roughly 400 yards on a side. This would mean closing to general traffic about four out of five crosstown streets and alternate avenues. With its 25 per cent gain in usable space, each block could add recreation areas and trees. The closed streets would become pedestrian walks, as well as roads for service vehicles. An occasional tennis court, ice-skating rink, or softball diamond might bloom in the largest traffic-free intersections. Buses and small electric taxis could shuttle people around at speeds far greater than today's congestion permits. . . .

Less utopian but more likely is a car-banning scheme designed for downtown Fort Worth by architect-planner Victor Gruen, who has long been a champion of the pedestrian. Although his plan has been stymied for the past six years by lack of funds, it is still very much alive. Gruen proposes converting the present downtown core—about one square mile—into a pedestrian island. Electrically powered shuttle cars would transport the lame, the lazy, and the package-laden, and tunnels would admit trucks and taxis. Six huge garages along the belt roadway encircling the core would project into the island, as would bus loops, so that the longest walk would be about two hundred yards. . . .

On the other side of the continent, the undistinguished core of Los Angeles' smog-polluted, traffic-harassed metropolis is well on its way to becoming a vast complex of intersections bordered by parking garages and a few buildings standing as nostalgic reminders that once upon a time the downtown had a purpose. Less dismal but similar prospects menace just about every metropolitan area in the US.

The Right Track

Many measures, well this side of utopia, can help counter the threat. An obvious first step is to institute rush-hour tolls on all congested highways, bridges, and tunnels in and around a city. Adjusted to limit traffic to manageable volume, these tolls would not only put the charge where it belongs, they would also make the motorist aware of expenses other than operating costs. They might even convert him to mass transit.

. . . Repeal of the 10 per cent federal transportation tax on interstate rail and bus fares, which tends to encourage automobile commuting.

. . . Amendment of federal highway legislation to include financing of rapid-transit track construction on the rights-of-way of urban expressways. . . .

Along with policies discouraging automobile commuting, cities would, of course, have to expand and improve public transportation. Reserving street or freeway lanes for rush-hour buses speeds commuters' trips in several cities—notably Chicago, Baltimore, and Nashville. Express buses are four times as efficient as cars; in bumper-to-bumper traffic, probably fifteen times as efficient. Park-ride service between strategically located parking lots and downtown cores, with buses speeding along a reserved lane while cars fight with trucks for the remaining lanes, should win friends for public transportation.

The stale arguments against public transportation disintegrate in the light of a few facts. Contrary to anti-transit propaganda, many commuters who don't use the antiquated mass-transit facilities generally available today will patronize a modern system. Within three years, Philadelphia's subsidized rail program, with its improved schedules and faster trains, has increased patronage of commuter railroads by 44 per cent— and at a bare fraction of the public cost of building freeways for the added riders. In the San Francisco area, according to consulting engineers Parsons, Brinkerhoff, Quade & Douglas, 77 per cent of the commuters patronize mass transit if it's as quick as car travel. And 2,600 commuting drivers in three major cities questioned by *Fortune* magazine in the mid fifties overwhelmingly favored mass transit if it could match their driving time. For a saving of ten minutes or more a day, five out of six said they would desert their cars. . . .

The propagandists urging ever-increasing hordes of automobiles in the cities have neither economics nor civilized values on their side. They understand little of the need for dense, pedestrian-oriented development to preserve the cities as thriving centers of commerce and culture, and they care even less.

Like the freedom to pollute air and water, the unrestricted right to jam city and suburban highways can't be tolerated as we crowd ever more densely around our great urban centers. We must stop treating the commuting motorist as an aristocrat whose whims must not only be indulged, but subsidized. We should treat the commuting motorist as a public nuisance. He hogs a disproportionate share of public space; he robs pedestrians and bus riders of time, lost in the traffic jams he creates; he endangers public health as his idling engine pollutes the air with poisonous exhausts. As Lewis Mumford counseled the American Institute of Architects:

"Forget the damned motor cars; design the cities for friends and lovers."

"So *that's* where it goes! Well, I'd like to thank you fellows for bringing this to my attention."

4

Urbanitis: The Sick Environment

Nicholas Gage

Top billing among city problems may well go to pollution—sewage, garbage, water, noise, air. New York City residents confront the mayor with 38,000,000 pounds of solid waste each day. Upstream cities dump their partially treated sewage into the rivers from which downstream cities get their drinking water. The noise level creates a universal state of hypertension. Enveloping the entire fetid scene is a blanket of foul air that the inhabitants must breathe.

Why is it sometimes said of the air that "if you can see it, it won't hurt you"? What are the dangerous components of city air? Where do they come from? What harm can they cause? How do residents try to adjust to pollution? How do apartment buildings, industry, and automobiles contribute to the dirty air? What has New York City done to stave off disaster?

In Central Park, on a knoll just behind the Metropolitan Museum of Art, stands an unintended monument to the effects of air pollution.

The monument is a 224-ton granite obelisk known as Cleopatra's Needle, carved in 1600 B.C. and presented to the city in 1882 by the khedive of Egypt. The obelisk's makers cut hieroglyphic characters into all four of its sides, and the ancient writing was still plainly visible when it was brought here.

Today, however, there are markings only on two sides. Those on the south and west sides, which face prevailing winds and concentrations of air pollution, have been entirely obliterated. "Several inches of granite have been literally eaten off the obelisk by the chemicals in the air," says an official of the city parks department. "Ninety years in New York have done more damage to it than 3,500 years in Egypt."

Obviously, if New York's polluted air can

From Nicholas Gage, "Danger in the Air," The Wall Street Journal, May 26, 1970. Reprinted by permission of the publisher.

eat away rock, it can hurt people. Doctors know it contributes to respiratory ailments, and they suspect it may cause cancer and even brain damage.

Just Somewhat Dirtier

What's particularly frightening about all this is that New York's air is not much different from the air of many other U.S. cities —just somewhat dirtier because the city is bigger. Even traditional pure-air havens like Arizona, Colorado and Vermont increasingly are finding their air fouled with the same corrosive pollutants that, in sufficient volume, can damage monuments and threaten human health.

But because of the concentration of population and pollution here, New York City provides a model of sorts for those seeking to identify pollutants, trace their sources and sort out their effects.

The most obvious pollutants—though generally among the least dangerous to health—are tiny particles of dust from the streets and soot from incinerators, residential furnaces and industrial smokestacks.

Scientists say most of these particles are too large to work their way into lung tissues, so they are more an aesthetic nuisance than a health menace.

There are a number of smaller particles, however, that are less visible but more menacing to health. They include asbestos fibers, which have been linked to chronic lung disease and cancer, and lead, which may cause brain damage in children and injure the nervous systems of adults.

A Higher Death Rate

Lead comes chiefly from auto exhaust. Asbestos is released constantly into the air from disintegration of automobile brake linings and from the construction of the city's massive buildings, where asbestos is sprayed on as a sheathing for steel girders. Dr. Cuyler Hammond, a former director of the American Cancer Society, has found that smokers working where they are also exposed to asbestos dust have a rate of lung cancer eight times that of the general population.

Altogether, the U.S. Public Health Service says, New Yorkers were bombarded last year by 70,000 tons of "particulate matter."

At the same time, however, the city's air was invaded by 400,000 tons of sulphur dioxide and 1.6 million tons of carbon monoxide—gaseous compounds that in Manhattan regularly exceed the levels scientists consider harmful to health.

Sulphur dioxide comes from the combustion of fossil fuel (coal and oil) for energy and heating. Last year New Yorkers burned 2.5 billion gallons of fuel oil and 700,000 tons of coal. These fuels contain varying amounts of sulphur that are converted, on combustion, into sulphur dioxide and sulphuric acid.

Caused Chemical Changes

Beyond such effects as causing nylon fabrics to disintegrate mysteriously, these compounds can be breathed deep into the lungs, injuring sensitive tissues. Prolonged exposure to even low levels of sulphur dioxide has been linked to heart attacks, mutations and cancer.

"We know that sulphur dioxide causes certain chemical changes," says Robert Shapiro, associate professor of chemistry at New York University. "If these same changes occur in human sperm cells, they could lead to mutations that would pose great threats to future generations. And if these changes occur in other cells, such as in the lungs, then sulphur dioxide might even be a cause of cancer."

In Manhattan sulphur dioxide in the air is often as high as .12 parts per million (ppm)—three times the .04 ppm mark established by the Federal Government as an acceptable level. In the city as a whole sulphur dioxide concentrations average .06 ppm.

The main pollutant in New York—as in most other areas—is carbon monoxide, chiefly from motor vehicles. Carbon monoxide is dangerous because it hampers the delivery of oxygen to the body's tissues. "At high concentrations it kills quickly," says the Public Health Service. "At lower concentrations it brings on headaches and a slowing of physical and mental activity."

As might be expected, carbon monoxide is most harmful to people who are exposed to high levels of it for long periods. And many people in New York breathe high concentrations of carbon monoxide over the entire day. New York state guidelines warn that levels should not exceed 15 ppm more than 15 per cent of the time during an eight-hour period. But after four months of measurements in midtown Manhattan it was determined that carbon monoxide levels remained above that level all day every day.

During daytime hours when traffic is heaviest, the carbon monoxide level in Manhattan often soars to between 25 and 30 ppm, having an impact on the lungs equivalent to that of two packs of cigarettes a day. In some areas of the city, such as the Lincoln Tunnel and the approaches to the George Washington Bridge, the carbon monoxide level reaches an astronomical

100 ppm—nearly seven times the "safe" level.

According to medical studies, exposure to this much carbon monoxide, even for short periods, can cause headaches, nausea and dizziness. After 90 minutes of exposure to only 50 ppm, the ability to make certain visual discriminations and time judgments is impaired—indicating that high carbon monoxide levels on streets and highways may be a factor in traffic accidents. Even exposure to levels as low as 15 ppm may have an effect on mental and sensory responses, researchers say.

The celebrated surliness of some New York City taxi drivers and policemen may actually be a symptom of carbon monoxide exposure, according to some authorities. Cab drivers and traffic policemen must be in the streets constantly, often in areas where concentrations of the gas are highest. "Every time I work days I wind up with a headache," says one cab driver, Robert Uzak. "So I've asked to be put on nights permanently. I've been held up twice while on night shifts, but I would rather risk getting shot or stabbed than dying slowly from all the poison in the air."

Like a Coal Bin

Dirty air has caused other New Yorkers to make adjustments in their living habits, too. Few Manhattan residents, for instance, risk keeping their apartment windows open long. "I once went away for a day without shutting a window in my kitchen, and when I came back the room looked like the inside of a coal bin," says Phillip Rosenberg, who lives on Manhattan's upper West Side.

Some people say the city's dirty air has contributed to decisions to move away from New York. Joseph Wicherski, a public relations man for the Chase Manhattan Bank, says air pollution is a major reason he decided recently to give up his job and move to the West Coast. "I never had a cold in my life until I moved here," he says. "But in the past year I've missed six weeks of work because of colds. It's this damned air pollution. Sometimes I take a breath and I can feel the dirt going down my throat."

The pervasiveness of air pollution in Manhattan is apparent to anyone who spends time here, and the sources are not hard to find.

The single biggest industrial polluter of the city's air is Consolidated Edison Co., which supplies electricity throughout the city and in suburban Westchester County. Con Edison says it burns 1.18 billion gallons of fuel oil, 3.7 million tons of coal and 79.2 billion cubic feet of natural gas a year to produce electricity. As a result, its 11 fossil fuel plants throughout the city hurl into the atmosphere each year 156,000 tons of sulphur dioxide, 6,400 tons of fly ash and other particulates and 113,300 tons of nitrogen oxides.

(Con Edison says that its emissions of sulphur dioxide have dropped 55 per cent and its emissions of particles have dropped 53 per cent in the past three years due to a switch to low-sulphur fuels and a $150 million investment in pollution-control equipment. Con Edison also says it plans to eliminate the burning of coal almost entirely by the end of 1972 and is negotiating with suppliers to switch from its present low-sulphur fuel oil, which contains 1 per cent sulphur, to a "low-low" sulphur oil containing one-third of 1 per cent sulphur.)

The air near Con Edison's plants is usually the most polluted in the city. A long walk near the East River and 14th Street, where the company has a plant, can leave the stroller's neck begrimed with a layer of soot thick enough to scrape off with a finger.

Another major industrial polluter is the Phelps Dodge Corp. copper refinery in Queens, one of the five boroughs that make up the city. In its manufacturing process the plant belches out 100 tons of solid copper, copper oxides, fly ash and other particulates each year, city officials say.

A Phelps-Dodge spokesman says, however, that "there is no particular pollution at all" from the refinery.

Most New Yorkers needn't look beyond their own homes or offices, however, for a source of pollution. Most of the aerial garbage that floats over the city every day actually comes from incinerators and heating units in apartment and office buildings, particularly older buildings that lack pollution control devices.

The city's Air Resources Administration cites a structure at 40 Fifth Avenue, just north of Greenwich Village, as a typical example of how apartment buildings contribute to pollution. The building is not large by New York standards—16 stories, 78 apartments with 400 rooms. But the amount of smoke, soot and dirt it sprays into the air is sizable.

The oil burner in the building, which uses 235,000 gallons of oil a year, pours 18 tons of sulphur dioxide and 140 pounds of particulates into the atmosphere annually, the Air Resources Administration says. The incinerator, in which 575 pounds of refuse are burned daily, produces 200 pounds of sulphur dioxide and 400 pounds of dirt particles a year. Most of the particles are too heavy to be carried away by the wind, and they fall within the immediate area of the building.

New Yorkers are apt to suffer most from air pollution during the months from October to February, when freakish temperature inversions are most likely to occur. A temperature inversion takes place when a layer of cool air is held under a layer of unseasonably warm air, trapping pollutants over the city and sometimes allowing them to build up to lethal proportions.

New York's worst temperature inversions in recent years occurred in late 1953, early 1963 and over the Thanksgiving weekend in 1966. Dr. Leonard Greenberg, former air pollution control commissioner for the city and now a professor at Albert Einstein College of Medicine, has studied all three incidents for the number of deaths recorded compared with normal periods. He has concluded that air pollution caused the deaths of 220 persons during the first inversion, 300 to 350 during the second and 168 during the third. (The worst disaster attributed to air pollution occurred in London in 1952, when some 4,000 "excess" deaths were recorded during a three-day temperature inversion in early December.)

City officials say that smog disasters like those of 1953, 1963 and 1966 will not happen again. Under an emergency plan adopted in 1967, the mayor has the power to restrict the operation of incinerators, the use of electric power, business operations and even city traffic to reduce pollution during a prolonged temperature inversion. A 38-station air monitoring network and a pollution alert system have been set up to warn of impending danger.

The warning system is part of an extensive program to curb air pollution launched in 1966. City laws now require the use of low-sulphur fuel for heat and power and require that all incinerators used in the city be fitted with equipment to curb the fumes and fly ash that otherwise spew into the air. The use of low-sulphur coal and oil has reduced the amount of sulphur dioxide in the air by more than 50 per cent from the pre-crackdown era, though the level is still higher than the .04 ppm maximum recommended by the Federal Government.

But the installation of control devices on incinerators has been slowed by court challenges brought by real estate owners who contend the antipollution law has an unnecessarily hasty timetable. "Real estate people in this city want clean air as much as anybody," says Harold J. Traynor, lawyer for the Real Estate Board of New York, "but they want sufficient time to upgrade their equipment." It costs about $10,000 to install pollution-control gear on an incinerator, and building owners complain they need time to make such an outlay.

Widely Divergent Views

Meantime, of course, the city's air continues to be polluted by automobiles and by various other sources such as the city government's own refuse incinerators, and there are widely divergent views on how bleak the outlook is.

"The city has scored very substantial gains against air pollution," says Norman Cousins, the editor of the *Saturday Review* and Mayor John Lindsay's adviser on pollution control. "There is no doubt that New York's air is much more breathable now."

But many New Yorkers share the view of Mrs. Linda Fosburg, executive director of a private group known as Citizens for Clean Air, who says that air pollution in the city "is worse now than it ever was." In a sense, both views are right, says Kenneth L. Johnson, New York regional director of the Federal Air Pollution Control Administration. While sulphur dioxide and particulates have been reduced, he says, the amounts of carbon monoxide and lead are actually increasing.

5

Urbanitis: Crime and Violence

"If the environment doesn't get you, the muggers will," says one cynical Chicago resident. Increasingly, city dwellers huddle indoors after dark, behind barricades of alarms, electric eyes, and hand weapons. In too many American cities the thin veneer of civilization disappears with the setting sun, and a modern law of the jungle takes over. Is there any real reason for the fear of most city people? How have their fears changed their life style? Where is crime concentrated? What kind of defensive weapons are popular? Will an increased police force reverse current trends? What are the causes of rising crime and violence?

City people can get used to almost anything, but it takes a long time to learn to live with fear—and fear is the scourge of the cities these days. With each new rise in the crime rate, with each neighborhood burglary or mugging or rape, more city dwellers come to the alarming realization that somebody out there may be out to get them. And with this discovery, the quality of city life subtly changes. "You learn to survive like a rabbit in the bushes," says a State Department official in Washington. "Even without thinking, I'm more wary now."

Many women, and quite a few men, avoid walking at night anywhere on the big-city streets of America. City dwellers fortify their homes with an incredible array

From Newsweek, *March 24, 1969, "Learning to Live with Fear," pp. 62–63. Copyright © 1969 by Newsweek, Inc. Reprinted by permission of the publisher.*

of burglar alarms, electric eyes, lights that switch on and off automatically, guns, chemical sprays, watchdogs trained to attack. Night life dwindles for lack of trade. Tales of parking-lot muggings cut down the attendance at sports events. In quest of a sense of security, many people take judo lessons—at least for awhile. "Women come to my classes because they think judo will protect them," says George Mattson, owner of a Boston karate academy. "They stay for a few weeks, then quit when they realize I haven't got a magic wand. Even a few lessons, though, makes them feel better." In Atlanta, banker H. C. Tuggle's new burglar alarm isn't making him popular with the neighbors—it tends to ring loudly whenever somebody knocks on the door at night—but Tuggle insists he sleeps better knowing it is there.

Is there real reason for fear? Unquestionably the crime rate is rising—it jumped 17 per cent last year alone—but sociologists haggle over just what the figures mean. Working from official crime reports, a Presidential commission calculated that in a given year an American has one chance in 550 of serious personal attack, one chance in 3,000 of being mauled badly enough to need hospital care, one chance in 20,000 of being murdered. The odds seem reassuring enough—although surveys show that government figures probably include only half the violent crime that takes place; the rest goes unreported to the police.

Whatever the actual blood count, the psychological reality is that crime is rising —and a sour pall of fear pervades the cities. "You wait until your number is up," says a Washington working girl. Her number has come up four times in eighteen months: a wallet theft, a purse-snatching, a burglary and a street holdup during which "people sat on their front porches, watching." The enemy seems to own entire sections of town. "I have a mental map of where not to go," says another Washington girl. Suburbanites feel themselves under the gun, too. In the posh Corrales suburb of Albuquerque, an old Western town where residents formerly disdained to lock their doors, homeowners are installing buzzers under their rugs, sirens on their roofs, floodlights and heavy deadfalls over their doors. There are electric-eye devices that automatically summon police when an intruder breaks the beam, strongboxes that buzz loudly when opened, aerosol sirens to be carried in purses, inflatable plastic dummies to simulate a passenger in an empty auto seat.

A Man's Castle

Even the most elaborate precautions, of course, can fail. Earlier this year, a Dallas millionaire was sequestered in his "safe room"—an interior chamber that is all but impregnable—when burglars invaded the house. Using a ruse, they lured him out of his sanctuary, took away his shotgun, tied him up and decamped with $31,000. For the next month, the millionaire and his wife spent their nights with relatives, occupying their home only in daylight hours, while workmen installed window alarms, rug pressure pads and a closed-circuit television surveillance system.

San Francisco architect Peter C. Witmer went to extraordinary lengths to fortify his renovated Victorian house fronting Alamo Square with triple-locked windows of tempered glass that will stop a brick and a 12-foot-high gate with curved prongs on top blocking the side alleyway. Even so, a thief climbed the gate two weeks ago, pried open a side window and rifled the house. Witmer now has a huge Plexiglas shield above the gate to make the climbing even harder. But, he says, "unless you have somebody at home all day the odds are you'll be broken into."

Mail Race

Poor people have fewer options for defense—and crime is worst in the slums. In Brooklyn's Bedford-Stuyvesant ghetto, Mrs. Sylvia Burton and her eight children race the thieves for the $569 in welfare checks that keeps them going through the month. When a check arrives in the mailbox, it has to be retrieved before the thugs simply yank the mailbox off the wall and take it away to be opened at leisure. Mrs. Burton says she has bought four new mailboxes in the past year. In Harlem, says a black policeman who lives there, "it's so bad that when I go home at night I carry my pistol in my coat pocket, with my hand on it. Getting it out of the holster might take too long."

Defensive weapons proliferate. "I used to have a tear-gas gun," says red-headed Liz Dickerson, a Checker cab driver in Atlanta, "but I took pity on a passenger from New York and gave it to her for protection." But Liz kept her pearl-handled .32-caliber pistol.

The lady from New York could easily have found her own weapons. The novelty stores around Times Square bristle with legal and illegal knives and do a thriving trade in Mace-like chemical sprays. Will the stuff deter attackers? "You bet," says a clerk. "It'll blind 'em." Other big sellers: sword-canes, blackjack-canes, an ebony walking stick loaded with a 2-pound steel ball that could brain an elephant.

As disturbing as the arms race is the growing white distrust of Negroes, who tend to be blamed indiscriminately for the rise in street crime. "I go on the bus and people look at me scared," says Maynard Johnson, who lives in Boston's Roxbury. "Just because I'm a Negro doesn't mean I'm going to mug them." Increasingly, whites are reluctant to give any black the benefit of the doubt. On riot-torn Fourteenth Street in Washington—a city that counted its 57th murder of the year last week—a liquor dealer waits for the next invasion with an arsenal of seven pistols, a rifle and a Browning automatic rifle. He has an electric gate—"20,000 volts"—at front and rear. He has offered a standing bounty of $500 to anyone who kills a robber fleeing his store. "I know all these people," he says of his customers. "Most of the people walking through that door have been charged with murder or armed robbery."

Bad Business

Guns may be easy for shopkeepers to come by, but insurance—against riot damage or everyday pilferage—is another question. Brazen shoplifting is common all across the country. "These guys steal openly," says a Phoenix police captain, "then spit in your eye." Some New York boutiques have had so many minis filched that they have taken the doors off the dressing rooms. Holdups of bus drivers have become so frequent that Chicago and New York are taking a cue from Detroit, Milwaukee and Washington and switching to exact-fare systems with the fare boxes bolted to the bus, and no change available.

For businessmen, as for residents, the situation is worst in decayed parts of the cities. In East St. Louis, Ill., where some schoolteachers carry guns to class and at least three persons have been killed by sniper fire downtown, a jeweler says crime isn't the problem any more: "We have nothing downtown—no crime, no people and no business."

Everywhere, man's eye is on his neighbor: from Harlem to Los Angeles, citizens are banding together to demand better street lighting and more police protection. Some verge on vigilantism, forming crime councils to patrol their own streets. And the unwinking gaze of the closed-circuit TV camera sees more every day—in supermarkets, banks, department stores and apartment elevators, even in the Baltimore Zoo. The scrutiny is already Orwellian, but nearly anything goes in the name of security: Robert Short, new owner of the Washington Senators, now wants to put TV cameras in the lavatories at Kennedy Stadium.

A good part of living in the culture of fear is simply learning not to think too much about it. "We've lost a lot of innocence," says Mrs. Alexandria Rodriguez of New York's Harlem. "It's like living under the atomic bomb. It's just too much to think about all the time." But occasionally people do take stock; and when they do, it is with a distinct sense of shock. In San Francisco, Mrs. Robert Hurwich has curtailed her social life, stopped taking buses, triple-locked every window in the house and installed a barbed-wire fence on the roof. "It's a funny thing," she mused last week. "We go out the front door, and then we always pause and look up and down the hill before we set forth." Mrs. Hurwich chuckled, a little uncertainly. "And then we really go fast. It's certainly an odd way of living."

6

What Can Be Done?

EDWARD C. BANFIELD

Most authors who discuss urban problems offer pat answers for their solution. Professor Banfield's answer to his question, "What can be done?" is "very little." Feasible answers are politically unacceptable; acceptable answers are unfeasible.

Why are proposals that we change the culture or the "hearts and minds of men" unworkable? Why will higher welfare payments probably fail to end poverty? Why would Banfield discount President Nixon's sweeping proposals for manpower retraining programs? Will school lunch programs prevent riots? What stands in the way of eliminating problem families by involuntary sterilization? Why does Banfield believe that his twelve point program for improving city life would be blocked? Why does he believe that "doing good" is a growth industry?

Often travelers, technical advisers, or "old hands" from a given country return with tales of how disorganized, dishonest, or untrustworthy the people are; but once the tales have been told, everyone settles down to a theoretical description of, or plan for, the economy of that country which does not take into account in any formal way the psychological characteristics of the people just described.

—David McClelland

. . .

This chapter tries to show, first, that the range of feasible measures for dealing with the serious problems of the cities is much narrower than one might think, and second, that within this range hardly any of the measures are acceptable. If what is, in general, feasible is not acceptable, the reverse is also true: what is acceptable is not, in general, feasible. Government seems to

have a perverse tendency to choose measures that are the very opposites of those which would be recommended on the basis of the analysis in the preceding chapters. The reasons for this perversity may be found in the nature of American political institutions and, especially, in the influence on public opinion of the upper-class cultural ideal of "service" and "responsibility to the community."

Clearly, a measure is infeasible if aimed at the simultaneous attainment of mutually exclusive ends. Two persons cannot both be satisfied if one's satisfaction is *constituted* of the other's nonsatisfaction. Insofar as the poverty problem, for example, has this relational character (that is, insofar as it is one of "relative deprivation"), it is insoluble. In Hollywood, Leo C. Rosten writes, "it is natural for the actress who earns $20,000 a year to envy the actress who earns $50,000 who envies the actress making $100,000. In a community where one can make $350,000 a year, $75,000 a year is not especially impressive—either to

From Edward C. Banfield, The Unheavenly City (Boston, Mass.: Little, Brown and Company, 1970), pp. 239–247, 249–251, 253–254. Copyright © 1970 by Little, Brown and Company. Reprinted by permission of the publisher.

the group or the self." [1] The same problem arises, of course, even in the least glamorous places and with people of very ordinary income. That objective differences in income can be reduced to almost nothing does not necessarily mean that the problem of relative deprivation can be solved, for the smaller objective difference in income may come to have a greater subjective importance. The same problem arises with the distribution of things other than income. It is in the nature of deference, for example, that some persons receive more than others. There is really no way to prevent those who receive relatively little from perceiving that fact and being made unhappy or suffering a loss of self-respect because of it. As Frank H. Knight has written, "The real scarcity which seriously afflicts individualistic civilization is the scarcity of such things as distinction, spectacular achievements, honor, victory, and power." [2] Since there can never be enough of these things to go around, the problem of poverty with respect to them is logically insoluble.

Another class of "solutions" must be considered infeasible because in the absence of an adequate specification of the means by which they are to be brought about it must be presumed that no one knows how and that they represent mere wishful thinking. Doubtless a "change in the heart and minds of men" would solve a great many problems. But how is such a change to be brought about? Until the means are specified, this "solution" must be dismissed as utopian.

Those who use the terminology of social science may talk of changing "culture," rather than "hearts and minds." The fact is, however, that no one knows how to change the culture of any part of the population—the lower class or the upper, whites or Negroes, pupils or teachers, policemen or criminals. Moreover, even if

one *did* know how, there is good reason to suppose that doing so would be infeasible on other grounds; for example, it might require unconstitutional methods, such as taking infants from their parents at birth, or entail other disadvantages that more than offset its advantages.

Some "solutions" are infeasible because (1) there is no reason to expect people to do the things that would constitute a solution unless government motivates them to do them, and (2) government for one reason or another cannot so motivate them. If, as Lee Rainwater asserts, "only effective protest can change endemic patterns of police harassment and brutality, or teachers' indifference and insults, or butchers' heavy thumbs, or indifferent street cleaning and garbage disposal," [3] then (assuming that effective protest must be carried on from *outside* the government) measures to correct these abuses lie beyond the bounds of feasibility. In other words, if there are solutions to these problems they are not *governmental* ones, which is to say that one cannot implement them by calling into play the state's ultimate monopoly on the use of force.

Repeal of the minimum-wage laws is certainly feasible, but elimination of the *informal* minimum wage, which would reduce unemployment among the low-skilled even more, is not. Government cannot prevent the formation of a social definition of what is a "decent" wage, and (what amount to the same thing) it cannot prevent workers from feeling some loss of self-respect in working for "peanuts." From the standpoint of the policymaker, then, the informal minimum wage presents an insoluble problem.

. . .

There is much to be said for the idea of giving small sums at any hour of day or night to persons, mostly youths, who might otherwise steal or kill to get the price of a

---

[1] Leo C. Rosten, *Hollywood; the Movie Colony, the Movie Makers* (New York: Harcourt Brace, 1941), p. 40.

[2] Frank H. Knight, *Freedom and Reform* (New York: Harper, 1947), pp. 41–42.

[3] Lee Rainwater, "Crucible of Identity: The Negro Lower-Class Family," in Talcott Parsons and Kenneth B. Clark, eds., *The Negro American* (Boston: Houghton Mifflin, 1966), p. 199.

few drinks or a "fix" of heroin. It would not be feasible to do this, however, because of the adaptive behavior that it would evoke. Once it became known that money was being given away (and of course the scheme would not work unless it *was* known), the demand would become too great to satisfy.

Essentially the same problem will exist with any welfare program that offers generous support to all who can be considered poor. Such a program will encourage people to adapt either by reducing their incomes (the wife leaving her job, for example) or by lying, thus increasing the number of the "poor" and, if the inducement is strong enough, eventually swamping the system.[4]

Some "solutions" are infeasible because the very feature(s) of social reality that constitute the problem make them impracticable. Training programs do not as a rule offer any solution to the problem of hardcore unemployment because the same qualities that make a worker hard-core also make him unable or unwilling to accept training. More generally, giving lowerclass persons "really good" jobs is not a feasible way of inducing them to change their style of life, because that very style of life makes it impossible to give them "really good" jobs.

"Solutions" that deal with minor, as opposed to key or strategic, factors in a situation are also infeasible. To put the matter in another way, it does not help to create a necessary condition when there is no way of creating the sufficient conditions; similarly, in situations of multiple causation, it is of little use to set in motion a cause that contributes a trivial amount to the total effect desired when there is no way to set in motion those that would contribute a significant amount to it. It is less than likely that the McCone Commission, in its report on the background of the Watts riot, was correct in asserting that "an adequate midday meal is essential to a meaningful edu-

cational experience"[5] (it may be a contributing factor, but it is certainly not *essential*). Even assuming for the sake of argument that the Commission *was* correct, the conclusion does not follow that a school lunch program would have an appreciable effect on the problem of preventing riots of the sort that occurred in Watts. The school lunch program "solution," however desirable it might be on other grounds, would not touch a great many much more important causes that would make riots just as likely as ever.

The assumption of the McCone Commission that an improvement in material welfare is bound to make a major contribution to the solution of almost any social problem is a pervasive one: better nutrition, better housing, better transportation, better street cleaning and refuse removal—all such things are commonly seen as ways of reducing crime, of preventing the break-up of the family, of encouraging upward social mobility, and so on. Although one cannot demonstrate it rigorously, such measures probably do have some effects of this kind.[6] However, even if this is the case, the policymaker needs to ask the same question about them as about adequate mid-day meals: Is the contribution that this one cause makes to the total effect that is desired (i.e., what would constitute the solution of the problem) more than trivial?

Even if it is feasible in all other respects, a measure lies outside the bounds of feasibility if its implementation would entail costs that more than offset its benefits. The proponents of a particular measure are usually blessed with tunnel vision: they can see only their objective; all peripheral and background values are invisible. The policymaker, however, should take *all* relevant values into account, and however great the gain in terms of his objective, he

---

[4] E. C. Banfield, "Welfare: A Crisis Without 'Solutions,'" *The Public Interest*, Summer, 1969: 89–101.

[5] Governor's Commission On The Los Angeles Riots, *Violence In The City—An End or A Beginning?*, Los Angeles, December 2, 1965, p. 55.

[6] Nathan Glazer, "Housing Problems and Housing Policies," *The Public Interest*, Spring, 1967: 21–60.

must discard a measure as infeasible if the losses in terms of peripheral and background values would be even greater. Stopping immigration of the unskilled from present-oriented cultures would reduce the size of the lower class from what it would otherwise be, and involuntary sterilization of chronic delinquents and heads of "problem families" would before long eliminate it entirely. To make invidious distinctions among cultures on the basis of their orientation toward the future would create ill will for the United States abroad, however, and the violation of human rights involved in involuntary sterilization would be an intolerably high price to pay even for the many benefits that would follow from the elimination of the lower class. A generous welfare program would put an immediate end to poverty (defined otherwise than as relative deprivation), but by causing the break-up of a great many families, by reducing motivation to work and to save and in general to take some account of the future, and by discouraging migration from areas of poor opportunity to areas of good opportunity it might in the long run do more harm than good on the whole. Making heroin and other addictive drugs readily available on prescription would reduce violent crime in New York and some other large cities by relieving the addict of the necessity of stealing —and therefore of sometimes killing—in order to support his habit. But the effect would also be to increase the number of addicts (unless the demand for a commodity is inelastic, the amount sold tends to increase as the price goes down), and it is likely that the resulting harm would be greater than the benefit from the reduction in violent crime.

There follows a list of measures that might well be regarded as feasible. . . . It will be seen that the list is rather short; that many of the items on it are not "constructive"—that is, they call for *not* doing something; and that far from being a comprehensive program for making the city into what one would like, it hardly begins

to solve any of the problems that have been under discussion. Even if all the recommendations were carried out to the full, the urban situation would not be fundamentally improved. Feasible measures are few and unsatisfactory as compared to what it would be nice to have happen or what one would do if one were dictator. What is more to the present point, however, *hardly any of the feasible measures are acceptable.* The list is as follows:

1. Avoid rhetoric tending to raise expectations to unreasonable and unrealizable levels, to encourage the individual to think that "society" (e.g. "white racism"), not he, is responsible for his ills, and to exaggerate both the seriousness of social problems and the possibility of finding solutions.

2. If it is feasible to do so (the disagreement among economists has been noted earlier), use fiscal policy to keep the general unemployment level below 3 per cent. In any case, remove impediments to the employment of the unskilled, the unschooled, the young, Negroes, women, and others by (a) repealing the minimum-wage and occupational licensure laws and laws that enable labor unions to exercise monopolistic powers, (b) ceasing to overpay for low-skilled public employment, and (c) ceasing to harass private employers who offer low wages and unattractive (but not unsafe) working conditions to workers whose alternative is unemployment.

3. Revise elementary and secondary school curricula so as to cover in nine grades what is now covered in twelve. Reduce the school-leaving age to fourteen (grade 9), and encourage (or perhaps even require) boys and girls who are unable or unwilling to go to college to take a full-time job or else enter military service or a civilian youth corps. Guarantee loans for higher education to all who require them. Assure the availability of serious on-the-job training for all boys and girls who choose to go to work rather than to go to college.

4. Define poverty in terms of the nearly fixed standard of "hardship," rather than in terms of the elastic one of "relative deprivation," and bring all incomes above the poverty line. Distinguish categorically between those of the poor who are competent to

manage their affairs and those of them who are not, the latter category consisting of the insane, the severely retarded, the senile, the lower class (inveterate "problem families"), and unprotected children. Make cash income transfers to the first category by means of a negative income tax, the rate structure of which gives the recipient a strong incentive to work. Whenever possible, assist the incompetent poor with goods and services rather than with cash; depending upon the degree of their incompetence, encourage (or require) them to reside in an institution or semi-institution (for example, a closely supervised public housing project).

5. Give intensive birth-control guidance to the incompetent poor.

6. Pay "problem families" to send infants and children to day nurseries and preschools, the programs of which are designed to bring the children into normal culture.

7. Regulate insurance and police practices so as to give potential victims of crime greater incentive to take reasonable precautions to prevent it.

8. Intensify police patrol in high-crime areas; permit the police to "stop and frisk" and to make misdemeanor arrests on probable cause; institute a system of "negative bail" —that is, an arrangement whereby a suspect who is held in jail and is later found innocent is paid compensation for each day of confinement.

9. Reduce drastically the time elapsing between arrest, trial, and imposition of punishment.

10. Abridge to an appropriate degree the freedom of those who in the opinion of a court are extremely likely to commit violent crimes. Confine and treat drug addicts.

11. Make it clear in advance that those who incite to riot will be severely punished.

12. Prohibit "live" television coverage of riots and of incidents likely to provoke them.

There can be little doubt that with one or two possible exceptions these recommendations are unacceptable. A politician with a heterogeneous constituency would strenuously oppose almost all of them. In most matters, the actual course of policy is likely to be the very opposite of the one recommended, whichever party is in power.

Government is likely to raise expectations rather than to lower them; to emphasize "white racism" as *the* continuing cause of the Negro's handicaps rather than to deemphasize it; to increase the minimum wage rather than to decrease or repeal it; to keep children who cannot or will not learn in school a longer rather than a shorter time; to define poverty in terms of relative deprivation rather than in terms of hardship; to deny the existence of class-cultural differences rather than to try to distinguish the competent from the incompetent poor on this basis; to reduce the potential victim's incentives to take precautions against crime rather than to increase them; to give the police less discretionary authority rather than more; to increase the time between arrest, trial, and punishment rather than to decrease it; and to enlarge the freedom of those who have shown themselves to be very likely to commit violent crimes rather than to restrict it.

One reason why these recommendations are politically out of the question is that there exist well-armed and strategically placed veto groups (as David Riesman calls them in *The Lonely Crowd*) which can prevent them from being seriously discussed, much less adopted. The recommendation of the Moynihan Report, that government try to strengthen the Negro family, is a case in point: official consideration of this idea had to stop abruptly when the civil rights organizations and their allies objected.[7] What these organizations did with this proposal organized labor could do with one to free up the labor market, organized teachers could do with one to reduce the school-leaving age, organized social workers could do with one to define poverty in terms of hardship, and so on.

That interest groups have such power does not represent a malfunctioning of the political system. When they designed the system, the Founding Fathers took great

---

[7] *See* Lee Rainwater and William L. Yancey, *The Moynihan Report and The Politics of Controversy* (Cambridge, Mass.: MIT Press, 1967).

pains to distribute power widely so that "factions" would check one another, thus preventing the rise of any sort of tyranny. The arrangement has worked remarkably well, but there is no denying that it has the defects of its virtues. One of these defects is that a small minority can often veto meaures that would benefit a large majority.

. . .

The American political style was formed largely in the upper classes and, within those classes, mainly by people of dissenting-Protestant and Jewish traditions. Accordingly, it is oriented toward the future and toward moral and material progress, for the individual and for the society as a whole. The American is confident that with a sufficient effort all difficulties can be overcome and all problems solved, and he feels a strong obligation to try to improve not only himself but everything else: his community, his society, the whole world. Ever since the days of Cotton Mather, whose *Bonifacius* was a how-to-do-it book on the doing of good, service has been the American motto. To be sure, practice has seldom entirely corresponded to principles. The principles, however, have always been influential and they have sometimes been decisive. They can be summarized in two very simple rules: first, DON'T JUST SIT THERE. DO SOMETHING! and second, DO GOOD!

These two rules contribute to the perversity that characterizes the choice of meaures for dealing with the urban "crisis." Believing that any problem can be solved if only we try hard enough, we do not hesitate to attempt what we do not have the least idea of how to do and what, in some instances, reason and experience both tell us cannot be done. Not recognizing any bounds to what is feasible, we are not reconciled to—indeed, we do not even perceive—the necessity, so frequently arising, of choosing the least objectionable among courses of action that are all very unsatisfactory. That some children simply cannot be taught much in school is one example

of a fact that the American mind will not entertain. Our cultural ideal requires that we give every child a good education whether he wants it or not and whether he is capable of receiving it or not. If at first we don't succeed, we must try, try again. And if in the end we don't succeed, we must feel guilty for our failure. To lower the school-leaving age would be, in the terms of this secular religion, a shirking of the task for which we were chosen.

The recommendations listed earlier are mostly unacceptable, even repellent, to public opinion because what they call for does not appear to be and (although this is beside the point) may in fact not be morally improving either to the doer or to the object of his doing. It does not appear to be improving to a youth to send him to work rather than to school, especially as this is what it is in one's interest as a taxpayer to do. It does not appear to be improving to a recidivist to keep him in jail pending trial, especially as this is what accords with one's feelings of hostility toward him. It does not appear to be improving to a slum dweller to say that if he has an adequate income but prefers to spend it for things other than housing he must not expect the public to intervene, especially as it is in one's "selfish" interest that the public not intervene. In reality, the doing of good is not so much for the benefit of those to whom the good is done as it is for that of the *doers,* whose moral faculties are activated and invigorated by the doing of it, and for that of the community, the shared values of which are ritually asserted and vindicated by the doing of it. For this reason, good done otherwise than by intention, especially good done in pursuance of ends that are selfish or even "nontuistic" is not really "good" at all. For this reason, too, actions taken from good motives count as good even when in fact they do harm. By far the most effective way of helping the poor is to keep profit-seekers competing vigorously for their trade as consumers and for their services as workers; this, however, is not a way of helping that affords members of the upper classes the chance to flex their moral muscles or the community the chance to dramatize its commitment to the values that hold it together. The way to do these things is with a War on Poverty; even if the War should turn out to have precious little effect on the incomes of the poor—indeed, even if it should *lower* their incomes—the undertaking would nevertheless represent a sort of secular religious revival that affords the altruistic classes opportunities to bear witness to the cultural ideal and, by doing so, to strengthen society's adherence to it. One recalls Macaulay's remark about the attitude of the English Puritans toward bear-baiting: that they opposed it not for the suffering that it caused the bear but for the pleasure that it gave the spectators. Perhaps it is not far-fetched to say that the present-day outlook is similar: the reformer wants to improve the situation of the poor, the black, the slum dweller, and so on, not so much to make them better off materially as to make himself and the whole society better off morally.

. . .

Looking toward the future, it is impossible not to be apprehensive. The frightening fact is that large numbers of persons are being rapidly assimilated to the upper classes and are coming to have incomes—time as well as money—that permit them to indulge their taste for "service" and doing good in political action. Television, even more than the newspapers, tends to turn the discussion of public policy issues into a branch of the mass entertainment industry. Doing good is becoming—has already become—a growth industry, like the other forms of mass entertainment, while righteous indignation and uncompromising allegiance to principle are becoming *the* motives of political commitment. This is the way it is in the affluent, middle-class society. How will it be in the super-affluent, upper-middle-class one?

7

Urban America in the Year 2000

Mitchell Gordon

In modern America the gap between science fiction and cold, sober reality has constantly narrowed. The article that follows originally appeared in a newspaper dedicated to the interests of the business community. The editors noted that their reporters had "talked to experts in many fields to get the best-informed opinions on probable developments between now and the year 2000."

If this is indeed the shape of the future, with what problems will government be compelled to wrestle during the next quarter century? Is centralized direction of urban growth a necessity, or should it be regarded as a threat? What justification can be offered for "New Towns" and malls? How and by whom can transportation problems be solved? What changes can we anticipate in the structure of major cities? Why do some experts believe that the racial ghetto will have disappeared by the year 2000?

If you don't like urban life, start running.

Houses and concrete and businesses and schools will spill over more of the countryside in coming decades. In the central sections of cities buildings will soar higher and the atmosphere will grow still more impersonal. The noise level will climb as new types of short-haul intercity aircraft capable of operating from tiny downtown landing strips begin adding their jet roar to the present din.

But the citified society of the future may not be quite as grim as some pessimists would have you believe. Though urban "sprawl" is expected to continue, most planners are confident their campaigns for land-use projects that leave green spaces for recreation will start to pay off soon. Transit experts predict that dramatic progress in their field will ease commuting for people

From Mitchell Gordon, "Urban America in the Year 2000," The Wall Street Journal, January 30, 1967, pp. 1, 16. Reprinted by permission of the publisher.

who work in the central city but live in new suburbs 100 miles or more distant; "air-cushion" vehicles that shoot through tubes at speeds up to 600 miles an hour or more are one of the proposed new modes of commuter transportation.

In the core areas of cities, slums will largely disappear, though some aging, ill-planned suburban subdivisions will take on a slum-like aspect. The crime rate will drop in cities, partly because television and other surveillance devices will improve police efficiency. Racial tensions also will decline sharply, in the view of some sociologists.

Another urban problem, downtown congestion, will be alleviated by turning many crowded streets into pedestrian malls and by barring private cars from some areas. Restrictions on the use of autos—or at least on those powered by internal-combustion engines—may also help combat air pollution. And some researchers go so far as to predict that a number of urban communities will solve the pollution problem completely by enveloping themselves in vast air-conditioned plastic canopies where residents will breathe filtered air—and bask in an ideal climate year round.

Planners balk at setting precise timetables for many of the changes they foresee in urban areas between now and the year 2000. True, marvels like domed cities or jet-speed commuting face enough technological and other problems so their advent probably can be safely assigned to the closing years of the century, if then.

Politics and Progress

But in some fields, such as pollution and land-use planning, the pace of change hinges to a considerable extent on the ability of local and regional administrative units to cooperate. Otherwise, confused, overlapping jurisdictions will frustrate efforts to carry out rational solutions to the problems of growing urban areas. With a few exceptions, urban planners note, past attempts to achieve metropolitan and regional cooperation have met dogged resistance, and the experts can't predict when problems will become serious enough to break down such opposition.

The role of the Federal Government is another imponderable in the future of cities. Rightly or wrongly, cities look to Washington for massive help in attacking slums and crime and in improving mass transit. So the rate of progress in these fields will depend to a high degree on the money and impetus from Washington—which, in turn, may depend on how preoccupied the U.S. remains with overseas problems, such as Vietnam.

Nevertheless, certain urban trends are clear. The most unmistakable one is that more and more people will live in urban areas.

At present some 70 per cent—or 139 million—of the total U.S. population of 198 million are classed as city dwellers under Census Bureau standards. By 2000 a minimum of 83 per cent—or 281 million—of a total population of 338 million are expected to be living in urban areas. Some analysts regard the 83 per cent projection as far too

low, contending the proportion of city residents will top 90 per cent by the end of the century.

Experts agree that almost all these new urban dwellers will settle in the suburbs, at least through the next couple of decades or so. Typically, Robert C. Wood, Under Secretary of the Department of Housing and Urban Development, says that what he terms the "spread city of the 1940s-60s era" will remain "the dominant form for some time to come."

Urban and suburban sprawl will produce immense metropolitan areas—"megalopolises"—in some parts of the U.S. By 2000, some experts say, unbroken stretches of urban civilization will run from just above Boston to below Washington, D.C., some 450 miles; from Chicago to Detroit, over 250 miles; from Cleveland to Buffalo; and from Santa Barbara (100 miles north of Los Angeles) to the Mexican border.

. . .

The "New Town" movement offers another approach to the problem of urban sprawl. It envisions the creation in open countryside of new communities that would have their own employment opportunities, stores and recreational facilities, so residents would not have to travel long distances daily.

. . .

The expectation that governments will encourage the construction of New Towns is based on the assumption that the need for some sort of planning to insure ordered urban growth eventually will be recognized by almost everyone. As Edward J. Logue, boss of Boston's redevelopment agency, puts it: "By the year 2000 some kind of green belt or open space policy will be effectively in force as the discovery is more generally made that sprawl just doesn't make sense."

But not all forecasters are this optimistic. Daniel Bell, a Columbia University professor of sociology and chairman of the Commission on the Year 2000, which was established in 1965 by the American Academy of Arts and Sciences to examine a variety of future problems, fears many large metropolitan areas won't take the ambitious planning measures needed to make their growth rational. Consequently, he expects smaller cities, particularly well-situated ones in the 50,000 to 100,000 category, to grow fastest in the future, simply because they will be more livable and therefore more attractive to job-generating industries.

Programs for rebuilding the old central cities of metropolitan areas could well prove easier to carry out than plans to guide suburban growth. One reason is that in core-area planning only one local government is involved, eliminating the need to reconcile the views of several jurisdictions.

Strong political pressures also are likely to speed the renaissance of metropolitan cores. Says Edward C. Banfield, professor of government at Harvard: "There's too much political power in our central cities for the Federal Government to let the cities go under and too much power in central business districts for central cities to let their downtowns go under."

As a result of such factors, authorities expect most city centers to undergo drastic transformations in the years ahead. Some aspects of these transformations will have their detractors. A number of critics complain, for example, that rebuilding programs break up close-knit neighborhoods. But the majority of urban planners obviously think the benefits far outweigh the drawbacks.

Rebutting the criticism of the disruption of old neighborhoods, they note that many of these are Negro ghettos. Dispersion of the residents into formerly all-white neighborhoods, while it may produce frictions initially, could contribute significantly to improved race relations in the long run. "By 2000 we'll be wondering what all the shouting was about," says sociologist Daniel P. Moynihan, newly appointed director of the Joint Center for Urban Studies at Massachusetts Institute of Technology and Harvard.

Some of the decaying structures due for destruction will be replaced by vertical cities within the city. These immense complexes may achieve heights of 200 or more stories, compared with 102 for the Empire State Building. They will contain apartments for tens of thousands of families, along with offices, shops, and recreational areas. In theory, residents would hardly ever have to step outside.

. . .

Greatly improved mass transit will be essential to link tomorrow's central cities and the ever more distant fringes of metropolitan areas, urban planners stress. Though many jobs will move to the suburbs along with families, armies of commuters will still pour into the metropolitan cores daily. As these trips become longer and expressway traffic becomes more congested, swift new transit will be the only recourse.

How quickly transit needs are met is particularly dependent on developments in the political field. In major metropolitan areas transit lines must cross municipal, county and even state lines, making cooperation among several governmental units vital. The trials faced by the San Fancisco area in its efforts to build a new $1 billion-plus rapid transit system illustrate some of the problems; routes have had to be redrawn time after time in keeping with the demands of the communities the system will serve.

Help From Washington

Though San Francisco is managing with little help from Washington, experts think many metropolitan areas will be unable to create new transit systems without Federal funds.

Some methods for improving transit—such as the reservation of expressway lanes for the exclusive use of buses—are relatively simple. But in most places the provision of adequate transit service will be an enormously expensive undertaking, and local governments and private firms are likely to lack the resources to tackle it.

. . .

Transit specialists are exploring many

ideas. New or expanded subway systems will serve at least as short-term solutions to transit problems in some cities. Monorail is still considered a good possibility for single-leg transit service, such as the new monorail line linking Tokyo's airport and downtown. But difficulties with switching may rule out monorail for complex systems.

Far swifter than subway train or monorail, however, would be the 600-mile-an-hour air-cushion vehicles now under development. Laboratory models of such vehicles have been built at the University of Manchester in Britain and at MIT. Garrett Corp., a Los Angeles subsidiary of Signal Oil Co. that makes components for space vehicles and electric power systems, last year received a Federal contract to study the feasibility of the concept.

Electromagnetic energy from a power source embedded in a concrete roadbed would pull the wheelless vehicles along. When at rest or slowing down they would settle onto the roadbed, but at other times they would travel inches above the surface.

They would blast jets of air against the walls of the tube enclosing the system in order to keep centered over the roadbed and on course. The tube would muffle noise from the vehicles that might otherwise disturb areas along the right-of-way.

The high-speed air-cushion vehicles, which researchers think are 20 to 30 years off, could supplement air transport on heavily intercity routes. But they would also be suitable for the long-distance commutes of the future.

A West Coast executive could live on a hilltop overlooking the Pacific Ocean at Carmel, Calif., for example, and commute the 300 miles to Los Angeles with ease. He might board his reserved-seat air-cushion coach at Carmel at 8:15 A.M. It would lift off the roadbed, whirl around an acceleration loop and plunge into the main tube running from Seattle to San Diego. Little more than half an hour later the car would peel off into the deceleration loop in downtown Los Angeles. By 9 A.M. the executive would be at his desk.

16

AMERICAN CIVILIZATION:
THE QUEST FOR A GREAT SOCIETY

The United States is frequently described as a materialistic nation. Certainly there is much evidence of our preoccupation with the production and consumption of material goods. In fact, when Americans compare their country with others they often cite comparative national statistics on the number of telephones, automobiles, bathtubs, TV sets, and electric razors. Both American conservatives and liberals have been caught up in this thought pattern, and the full platform of American liberalism for many years seems to have concentrated on higher living standards (more goods) for the underprivileged.

Perhaps every civilization eventually achieves what it believes to be important. At any rate, Americans seem to be on the edge of achieving a surfeit of goods for most U.S. citizens. It is no longer only the dreamer who believes that we can provide abundance for all. Our engineers and factory managers have the blueprints at hand.

This development promises to provoke a great deal of soul searching during the next decade. In its simplest form, the new problem can be phrased thus: Is material abundance enough? Can any society be numbered among the great simply because its citizens are all steam heated in winter, air conditioned in summer, and have full bellies from cradle to grave? Are material goods enough, or are they only the threshold to a Great Society? Furthermore, is the quest for a Great Society a proper function of the government, or is it best left to the individual or informal groups?

A Great Society: Can Political Leaders Point the Way?

In the first selections in this chapter you are asked to examine two conflicting interpretations of the role of government in providing a "good life" for modern man. One analysis finds that modern man is alienated from his world, that under both Capitalism and Communism men are becoming well-fed, well-clad automatons headed toward insanity. The solution proposed is the reorganization of the modern world into small groups and deemphasis of the large nation-state.

The other analysis visualizes the nation-state as playing a major role in evolution toward a Great Society. First the remnants of poverty will be mopped up; then government will open new doors that lead toward beauty, knowledge, and rewarding leisure. President Nixon has proposed, for instance, that government take leadership in improving the total environment, which would also involve a rebirth of spiritual idealism and a rekindling of a belief in our destiny. Although the President concedes that "never has a nation seemed to have had more and enjoyed it less," he asserts that elected leaders should "inspire young Americans with a sense of excitement, a sense of destiny, a sense of involvement in meeting the challenges we face in this great period of our history."

In one version of the good life, then, government itself is part of the problem. In the other, government becomes the chief instrument for achieving quality. An example of such a role for government is to be found in the proposal that tax funds be used to expand the arts.

Domestic Disillusionment: Is Utopia Obsolete?

Americans have traditionally been an optimistic people, believing without much question that the future would be better than either the past or present. Each year we would have more and more; the path to the future would be strewn with mounting piles of goods and services. In the early 1970's this vision of Utopia was rejected by millions of Americans, young and old, who listened as President Nixon declared, "We can be the best clothed, best fed, best housed people in the world, enjoying clean air, clean water, beautiful parks, but we could still be the unhappiest people in the world without an indefinable spirit—the lift of a driving dream which has made America from its beginning the hope of the world."

In this chapter a great deal of attention is paid to the nature and scope of the current disillusionment. Because the young are normally among our more optimistic citizens, their disenchantment is given particular emphasis with an extract from the SDS "Port Huron Statement" and an interview with three young radicals. The disillusionment and misgivings of the middle aged is set forth by former President of Columbia University Grayson Kirk, who was later driven from office by student radicals. These selections are largely dedicated to pessimism and the concept that, despite our great material successes, we have lost a sense of purpose and community. They should not be read as the final judgment on American society, but as an indictment filed by the prosecution which should be studied with great care by the defense.

What Are the Grounds for Studied Optimism?

For many Americans the United States has been a unique society, still in its formative years. The ultimate destiny of the nation seemed so remote that it received little attention. Other nations had grown, matured, and declined, but somehow this historical pattern did not apply to us. America was outside history.

Suddenly, in the early 1970's many thoughtful Americans saw in the turmoil of the moment an end to the American dream. Had we, unnoticed, reached our apogee and begun our rapid descent to oblivion? This question would have struck earlier generations as a philosophical exercise, but noted scholars (here represented by Professor Andrew Hacker of Cornell University) argued that we had indeed begun that descent. Others (such as author James Michener) regarded the question as relevant, but thought the answer was still an open one dependent on our ability to solve our problems.

1

Towards a Sane Society

Erich Fromm

German-born psychoanalyst Eric Fromm has been commenting on the contemporary world for more than a quarter of a century. In the selection that follows he presents a penetrating critique of modern industrial society and offers his proposals for reform. Why, according to Fromm, does increased economic well-being fail to satisfy modern man? What do Capitalism and Communism have in common with respect to goals and organization? Other than atomic war, what great danger does modern man face? Why is he alienated? What is Fromm's solution? How does it differ from proposals by President Nixon?

. . . [I]n the middle of the twentieth century, a drastic change is occurring, a change as great as ever occurred in the past. The new techniques replace the use of the physical energy of animals and men by that of steam, oil and electricity; they create means of communication which transform the earth into the size of one continent, and the human race into one society where the fate of one group is the

From Eric Fromm, The Sane Society (New York: Fawcett Publications, Inc., 1965), pp. 308–315. Copyright © 1955 by Eric Fromm. Reprinted by permission of Holt, Rinehart and Winston, Inc.

fate of all; they create marvels of devices which permit the best of art, literature and music to be brought to every member of society; they create productive forces which will permit everybody to have a dignified material existence, and reduces work to such dimensions that it will fill only a fraction of man's day.

Yet today, when man seems to have reached the beginning of a new, richer, happier human era, his existence and that of the generations to follow is more threatened than ever. How is this possible?

Man had won his freedom from clerical and secular authorities, he stood alone with his reason and his conscience as his only judges, but he was afraid of the newly won freedom; he had achieved "freedom from"—without yet having achieved "freedom to"—to be himself, to be productive, to be fully awake. Thus he tried to escape from freedom. His very achievement, the mastery over nature, opened up the avenues for his escape.

In building the new industrial machine, man became so absorbed in the new task that it became the paramount goal of his life. His energies, which once were devoted to the search for God and salvation, were now directed toward the domination of nature and ever-increasing material comfort. He ceased to use production as a means for a better life, but hypostatized it instead to an end in itself, an end to which life was subordinated. In the process of an ever-increasing division of labor, ever-increasing mechanization of work, and an ever-increasing size of social agglomerations, man himself became a part of the machine, rather than its master. He experienced himself as a commodity, as an investment; his aim became to be a success, that is, to sell himself as profitably as possible on the market. His value as a person lies in his salability, not in his human qualities of love, reason, or in his artistic capacities. Happiness becomes identical with consumption of newer and better commodities, the drinking in of music, screen plays, fun, sex, liquor and cigarettes. Not having a sense of self except the one which conformity with the majority can give, he is insecure, anxious, depending on approval. He is alienated from himself, worships the product of his own hands, the leaders of his own making, as if they were above him, rather than made by him. He is in a sense back where he was before the great human evolution began in the second millennium B.C.

He is incapable to love and to use his reason, to make decisions, in fact incapable to appreciate life and thus ready and even willing to destroy everything. The world is again fragmentalized, has lost its unity; he is again worshiping diversified things, with the only exception that now they are man-made, rather than part of nature.

The new era started with the idea of individual initiative. Indeed, the discoverers of new worlds and sea lanes in the sixteenth and seventeenth centuries, the pioneers of science, and the founders of new philosophies, the statesmen and philosophers of the great English, French and American revolutions, and eventually, the industrial pioneers, and even the robber barons showed marvelous individual initiative. But with the bureaucratization and managerialization of Capitalism, it is exactly the individual initiative that is disappearing. Bureaucracy has little initiative, that is its nature; nor have automatons. The cry for individual initiative as an argument for Capitalism is at best a nostalgic yearning, and at worst a deceitful slogan used against those plans for reform which are based on the idea of truly human individual initiative. Modern society has started out with the vision of creating a culture which would fulfill man's needs; it has as its ideal the harmony between the individual and social needs, the end of the conflict between human nature and the social order. One believed one would arrive at this goal in two ways; by the increased productive technique which permitted feeding everybody satisfactorily, and by a rational, objective picture of man and of his real needs. Putting it differently, the aim of the efforts of modern man was to create a sane society. More specifically, this meant a society whose members have developed their reason to that point of objectivity which permits them to see themselves, others, nature, in their true reality, and not distorted by infantile omniscience or paranoid hate. It meant a society, whose members have developed to a point of independence where they know the difference between good and evil, where they make their own choices, where they have convictions rather than opinions, faith rather than superstitions or nebulous hopes. It meant a society whose members have developed the capacity to love their children, their neighbors, all men, themselves, all of nature; who can feel one with all, yet retain their sense of individuality and integrity; who transcend nature by creating, not by destroying.

So far, we have failed. We have not bridged the gap between a minority which realized these goals and tried to live according to them, and the majority whose mentality is far back, in the Stone Age, in totemism, in idol worship, in feudalism. Will the majority be converted to sanity—or will it use the greatest discoveries of human reason for its own purposes of unreason and insanity? Will we be able to create a vision of the good, sane life, which will stir the life forces of those afraid of marching forward? This time, mankind is at one crossroad where the wrong step could be the last step.

In the middle of the twentieth century, two great social colossi have developed which, being afraid of each other, seek security in ever-increasing military rearmament. The United States and her allies are wealthier; their standard of living is higher, their interest in comfort and pleasure is greater than that of their rivals, the Soviet Union and her satellites, and China. Both rivals claim that their system promises final salvation for man, guarantees the paradise of the future. Both claim that the opponent represents the exact opposite to himself, and that his system must be eradicated—in the short or long run—if mankind is to be saved. Both rivals speak in terms of nineteenth-century ideals. The West in the name of the ideas of the French Revolution, of liberty, reason, individualism. The East in the name of the socialist ideas of solidarity, equality. They both succeed in capturing the imagination and the fanatical allegiance of hundreds of millions of people.

There is today a decisive difference between the two systems. In the Western world there is freedom to express ideas critical of the existing system. In the Soviet world criticism and expression of different ideas are suppressed by brutal force. Hence, the Western world carries within itself the possibility for peaceful progressive transformation, while in the Soviet world such possibilities are almost non-existent; in the Western world the life of the individual is free from the terror of imprisonment, torture or death, which confront any member of the Soviet society who has not become a well-functioning automaton. Indeed, life in the Western world has been, and is even now sometimes as rich and joyous as it has ever been anywhere in human history; life in the Soviet system can never be joyous, as indeed it can never be where the executioner watches behind the door.

But without ignoring the tremendous differences between free Capitalism and authoritarian Communism today, it is shortsighted not to see the similarities, especially as they will develop in the future. Both systems are based on industrialization, their goal is ever-increasing economic efficiency and wealth. They are societies run by a managerial class, and by professional politicians. They both are thoroughly materialistic in their outlook, regardless of Christian ideology in the West and secular messianism in the East. They organize man in a centralized system, in large factories, political mass parties. Everybody is a cog in the machine, and has to function smoothly. In the West, this is achieved by a method of psychological conditioning, mass suggestion, monetary rewards. In the East by all this, plus the use of terror. It is to be assumed that the more the Soviet system develops economically, the less severely will it have to exploit the majority of the population, hence the more can terror be replaced by methods of psychological manipulation. The West develops rapidly in the direction of Huxley's *Brave New World*, the East *is* today Orwell's *1984*. But both systems tend to converge.

What, then, are the prospects for the future? The first, and perhaps most likely possibility, is that of atomic war. The most likely outcome of such a war is the destruction of industrial civilization, and the regression of the world to a primitive agrarian level. Or, if the destruction should not prove to be as thorough as many specialists in the field believe, the result will be the necessity for the victor to organize and dominate the whole world. This could only happen in a centralized state based on force—and it would make little difference whether Moscow or Washington were the seat of government. But, unfortunately, even the avoidance of war alone does not promise a bright future. In the development of both Capitalism and Communism as we can visualize them in the next fifty or a hundred years, the process of automatization and alienation will proceed. Both systems are developing into managerial societies, their inhabitants well fed, well clad, having their wishes satisfied, and not having wishes which cannot be satisfied; automatons, who follow without force, who are guided without leaders, who make machines which act like men and produce men who act like machines; men, whose reason deteriorates while their intelligence rises, thus creating the dangerous situation of equipping man with the greatest material power without the wisdom to use it.

This alienation and automatization leads to an ever-increasing insanity. Life has no meaning, there is no joy, no faith, no reality. Everybody is "happy"—except that he does not feel, does not reason, does not love.

In the nineteenth century the problem was that *God is dead;* in the twentieth century the problem is that *man is dead.* In the nineteenth century inhumanity meant cruelty; in the twentieth century it means schizoid self-alienation. The danger of the past was that men became slaves. The danger of the future is that men may become robots. True enough, robots do not rebel. But given man's nature, robots cannot live and remain sane, they become "Golems," they will destroy their world and themselves because they cannot stand any longer the boredom of a meaningless life.

Our dangers are war and robotism. What is the alternative? To get out of the rut in which we are moving, and to take the next step in the birth and self-realization of humanity. The first condition is the abolishment of the war threat hanging over all of us now and paralyzing faith and initiative. We must take the responsibility for the life of all men, and develop on an international scale what all great countries have developed internally, a relative sharing of wealth and a new and more just division of economic resources. This must lead eventually to forms of international economic co-operation and planning, to forms of world government and to complete disarmament. We must retain the industrial method. But we must decentralize work and state so as to give it *human proportions,* and permit centralization only to an optimal point which is necessary because of the requirements of industry. In the economic sphere we need co-management of all who work in an enterprise, to permit their active and responsible participation. The new forms for such participation can be found. In the political sphere, return to the town meetings, by creating thousands of small face-to-face groups, which are well informed, which discuss, and whose decisions are integrated in a new "lower house." A cultural renaissance must combine work education for the young, adult education and a new system of popular art and secular ritual throughout the whole nation.

Our only alternative to the danger of robotism is humanistic communitarianism. The problem is not primarily the legal problem of property ownership, nor that of sharing *profits;* it is that of sharing *work,* sharing *experience.* Changes in ownership must be made to the extent to which they are necessary to create a community of work, and to prevent the profit motive from directing production into socially harmful directions. Income must be equalized to the extent of giving everybody the material basis for a dignified life, and thus preventing the economic differences from creating a fundamentally different experience of life for various social classes. Man must be restored to his supreme place in society, never being a means, never a thing to be used by others or by himself. Man's use by man must end, and economy must become the servant for the development of man.

Capital must serve labor, things must serve life. Instead of the exploitative and hoarding orientation, dominant in the nineteenth century, and the receptive and marketing orientation dominant today, the *productive orientation* must be the end which all social arrangements serve.

. . .

Man today is confronted with the most fundamental choice; not that between Capitalism or Communism, but that between *robotism* (of both the capitalist and the communist variety), or Humanistic Communitarian Socialism. Most facts seem to indicate that he is choosing robotism, and that means, in the long run, insanity and

destruction. But all these facts are not strong enough to destroy faith in man's reason, good will and sanity. As long as we can think of other alternatives, we are not lost; as long as we can consult together and plan together, we can hope. But, indeed, the shadows are lengthening; the voices of insanity are becoming louder. We are in reach of achieving a state of humanity which corresponds to the vision of our great teachers; yet we are in danger of the destruction of all civilization, or of robotization. A small tribe was told thousands of years ago: "I put before you life and death, blessing and curse—and you chose life." This is our choice too.

2

On the State of the Arts

AGNES DeMILLE

The American tradition does not recognize support of the arts as a government function. Recent administrations have hesitantly toyed with the idea of Advisory Councils and grants for the arts. Early in the 1970's noted choreographer Agnes DeMille appeared before a Congressional committee to plead for an expansion of government aid.

How have Americans regarded the arts, according to Miss DeMille? What contributions can the arts make to American life? How does our policy differ from that of Russia, Scandinavia, West Germany, Austria, and Great Britain? Does the United States have artists of comparable stature? Is ours an attractive society for artists? What does the National Advisory Council on the Arts do? Could a budding Sibelius develop his full potential in the United States today? Should we invest tax funds "in the talents of the truly gifted"?

. . . [W]e are a romantic people, if violent, and we like to persuade ourselves always, I think, that we love art and cherish it, and we go to the most extraordinary

From Hearings Before the Select Subcommittee on Education and Labor, *House of Representatives, 91st Congress, 2nd Session, pp. 391–394.*

lengths to persuade the rest of the world of that, but it is not true. We have not loved art. It is a historic fact that we have despised it, and if that were not so, these hearings would not be necessary. They would not be necessary in any other country.

We have considered it a frivolity—a plaything, but less desirable than other playthings like, for instance, competitive sport which we have come to realize is good for our health and our character. We concede no such virtues to art. Because of the years of hardship and deprivation in our beginnings, we have learned to place ultimate value on what is useful, and because we have eschewed all vestiges of aristocracy, we have built up an overwhelming admiration for material wealth. The art experience has been sidetracked.

But art, being magic, is a part of religion and vital to human experience. We must have release for our emotions, and if we do not find proper catharsis in acceptable channels, we will find it in improper and uncontrollable ways, and that is just what our youth is doing.

The Puritans turned to witchcraft, you remember, and bear in mind it was the children started the accusations. Our children are turning to the happy pills, in an agony of disappointment and distrust and for want of any better means of using their energies and exercising their emotions. The ventilated and busy spirit does not need drugs or general naughtiness and I would like to cite as an example of this the Harlem School of the Arts in New York, which has been founded and maintained by Dorothy Maynor, a very great soprano. She has been cited by the Governor and the Mayor for doing more for the children of Harlem than any other person.

The effort is placed in a small school, not particularly well endowed, but of very high quality. I have seen these children in Gracie Mansion so small that cushions had to be put on the pedals—playing Bach like mad. You think what it does to a small black boy in the dreadful conditions and situations of the ghetto up there to give him a violin, not just as a toy, but as an instrument of power.

Let him play superbly well, let him see what happens to other people's faces when he plays, give him that sense of power and glorious domination. He is not going out into the street and throw a rock through a window. It is bad for the hands, for one thing.

Art is the best therapy. Men all through the ages have known this. Scientists are admitting this now. Art is the best means of education—the church has always known this. Our colleges and civic bodies are learning it. Art is the best means of communication. The church has known this, too. The State Department is learning it. To quote Bernard Shaw, "Next to torture, art persuades fastest." We have watched this happen in the last few years.

Nothing we have sent abroad has done us as much good as our art exhibits and our performers. When our artists take the stage, even the most hostile and critical people stop and wonder if a nation that can produce such radiance can be totally hypocritical and predatory.

Indeed, there is no field in which so little goes so far, and yet this is the first field to be cut back as superfluous because, there being no profits involved except happiness and general well-being, there are no power lobbies.

Europe has always recognized the value of delight and supported its arts with substantial portions of the national treasuries. This has been said again and again in these hearings, but it can't be said too often. You can't guess what Russia gives. I don't know. But it is their glory and pride, and they will give anything to it. Scandinavia gives large amounts.

West Germany spends $50 million annually for music alone. Stuttgart gets $3 million with additional expenses when necessary, West Berlin $10 million for opera, $15 million for other theaters and art museums, Austria 11 per cent of its total budget for arts, $20 million for theater. British Arts Council gives two pounds for every one pound taken in at the Covent Garden box office, and, of course, it has the theater and royal support.

Does this sound like big money? Let me put you in a frame of reference. It costs $700,000 to pull up the curtain on a Broadway musical, $50,000 to fire all the guns on one destroyer once. The figures for larger activities you can supply better than I can.

We have had roughly between $3.5 and

$5 million for 50 states in all the arts, and we are the richest country in the world.

But while our Government is prepared to buy a war, or a trip to Mars, or to support one-fifth of the population on charity drawn from the working wages of another fifth, it is not prepared to give more than a pittance for our spiritual and emotional well-being. And this notwithstanding that we have among us by far the greatest, most varied, most creative and daring artists in the world, among them certainly the best choreographers, and dancers without match.

That sounds arrogant. I stand by that statement. I have been around the world. There is nobody that can top Jerome Robbins in his own field. There is no nation in the world that has produced anything like Martha Graham's theater, except Japan, with the Kabuki, and it took them 200 years to do it.

But let me tell you what an American soloist earns. A dancing star's life involves ten years of apprenticeship and only fifteen years of performing life. Soloists known around the world, our jewels, earn between $6,000 and $7,000 annually. They have no pension and because of taxes, no savings. There are dancers I know of repute and who are waiting on tables in third-rate restaurants.

A choreographer outside of Broadway will earn outside of the commercial media —and I'm speaking of the best choreographers in the world, artists equivalent to Stravinsky, Picasso or Eugene O'Neill— $10,000 or $12,000—not more. Our choreographers and dancers are leaving the country. They're being driven away and, believe me, they're in demand elsewhere. They would prefer to stay here. This is their home. Does anyone care?

There was considerable discussion in Miss Hanks' inclusive and brilliantly organized statement about opening new fields of art, reaching new and larger audiences. Let me say simply and emphatically that all great art is new and that great art always reaches an enormous audience. The operative word is "quality," but quality cannot easily be purchased. Quality requires time. It requires dedication and passion. These things cannot be bought with money, but money can provide the circumstances under which they can develop.

This is precisely what the National Advisory Council on the Arts has tried to furnish. I don't think in the history of government greater results accrued from so little and, contrary to dire predictions, I don't think any gross mistakes were made. There was one proposal to found a new orchestra, but musicians and managers rose up roaring and the plan was scotched before a penny was spent.

I was appointed by President Johnson to that first Advisory Council. Never I think did a similar group of people sit down at a table in this country since the 18th Century. Every one of us was a dedicated and proven expert in our field, with considerable achievement behind us and some world renowned. There were 24 of us, and only two political appointees among the group. One was rotated off in the natural course of events; the other was converted.

We knew there was no precedent to guide us. We also knew we would not be forgiven a single mistake and while other governmental committees have from time to time been forgiven lapses even going into several thousand dollars, we would not be, and so we tried, not to get what we wanted for our own particular profession, but what was best for the United States, and although we were a bunch of roaring egomaniacs, we tabled our special enthusiasm and thought in generous and embracing terms. We were able to do this because of the leadership of Roger Stevens.

Each specialist was served by a committee of advisors. I had sixteen, from all over the States, none an active critic and none with an ax to grind. I was outvoted several times. It was the committee's decision I laid before the Council, and although I was pretty mad to be flouted, I was nevertheless impressed by the way democracy works, and when I recommended something, the Board knew it had the complete backing of my advisors—or the majority of them—and I swear to you there was no special lobbying. Of course, the sums involved were pitiful, but dancers are used to pitiful sums. For us it was continuance or cessation. Just that.

We felt it was important to continue, and as a plain citizen, I feel now we were right. Artists are leaders and teachers, the best and most potent teachers.

Henry Adams said, "A teacher cannot know how far his influence will extend, a teacher reflects eternity."

And William James added, "Where quality is the thing sought after, the thing of supreme quality is cheap whatever the price one has to pay for it."

We take this for granted in all other fields. Why not in human well-being and spiritual growth?

What better investment can a country make than in the talents of its truly gifted?

Do you remember that when Sibelius was a young man his government took note of the fact that he had gifts, and decided to endow him for life so that he would never have to stoop to anything mundane or cheap? That was a big investment, how bold, how risky.

I remember in 1958, I was at the World's Fair in Brussels, and I am happy to report to you that our building was the most popular in the whole fairgrounds, not because it was the most beautiful building—and it was—but because it had two advantages: It had a big pool outside with a wide lip, on which people could sit and put their feet in the water when they got tired, and it had the only free toilets on the grounds.

The Russian building was interesting because it was stuffed with everything. There was eight of everything that the Russians owned except sables, of which there were twelve. But it was the Finnish building that I remember. It was small, beautifully designed. They had marvelous exhibitions of their kitchenware, weaving, furniture. But these were away, in side rooms. When one entered the big hall, it was very large, but very simple. It smelled of pine, with long, thin columns.

There was one object. The first pages of the score of "Finlandia" and on those pages rested a cast of the master's hand.

What is our going to be? What is our imprimature? What is our image? What footsteps do we leave behind? The unchanging marks on a dead satellite? My Lai?

Gentlemen, we deserve better.

3

The Port Huron Statement

STUDENTS FOR A DEMOCRATIC SOCIETY

Much of the protest over the quality of American life originated with university students. The Port Huron Statement, issued by the Students For A Democratic Society in 1962, is a sort of landmark statement of this discontent. How widespread is American anxiety over the state of our present society? In what sense have the universities allegedly failed? Why are the old slogans invalid? What is the basic human value that the SDS identifies? How do they feel that man is dehumanized today? Are the concerns expressed here exclusively the property of the SDS? Do they advance specific proposals for altering conditions?

We are people of this generation, bred in at least modest comfort, housed in universities, looking uncomfortably to the world we inherit.

. . .

Our work is guided by the sense that we may be the last generation in the experiment with living. But we are a minority —the vast majority of our people regard the temporary equilibriums of our society and the world as eternally-functional parts. In this is perhaps the outstanding paradox: We ourselves are imbued with urgency, yet the message of our society is that there is no viable alternative to the present. Beneath the reassuring tones of the politicians, beneath the common opinion that America will "muddle through," beneath the stagnation of those who have closed their minds to the future, is the pervading feeling that there simply are no alternatives, that our times have witnessed the exhaustion not only of Utopias, but of any new departures as well. Feeling the press of complexity

From Mitchell Cohen and Dennis Hale, The New Student Left *(Boston, Mass.: Beacon Press, 1966), pp. 9–13. Reprinted by permission of the publisher.*

upon the emptiness of life, people are fearful of the thought that at any moment things might thrust out of control. They fear change itself, since change might smash whatever invisible framework seems to hold back chaos for them now. For most Americans, all crusades are suspect, threatening. The fact that each individual *sees* apathy in his fellows perpetuates the common reluctance to organize for changes. The dominant institutions are complex enough to blunt the minds of their potential critics, and entrenched enough to swiftly dissipate or entirely repel the energies of protest and reform, thus limiting human expectancies. Then, too, we are a materially improved society, and by our own improvements we seem to have weakened the case for change.

Some would have us believe that Americans feel contentment amidst prosperity— but might it not better be called a glaze above deeply-felt anxieties about their role in the new world? And if these anxieties produce a developed indifference to human affairs, do they not as well produce a yearning to believe there *is* an alternative to the present, that something *can* be done to change circumstances in the school, the workplaces, the bureaucracies, the government? It is to this latter yearning, at once the spark and engine of change, that we direct our present appeal. The search for truly democratic alternatives to the present, and a commitment to social experimentation with them, is a worthy and fulfilling human enterprise, one which moves us and, we hope, others today. . . .

Values

Making values explicit—an initial task in establishing alternatives—is an activity that has been devalued and corrupted. The conventional moral terms of the age, the politician moralities ("free world," "peoples democracies") reflect realities poorly, if at all, and seem to function more as ruling myths than as descriptive principles. But neither has our experience in the universities brought us moral enlightenment. Our professors and administrators sacrifice controversy to public relations; their curriculums change more slowly than the living events of the world; their skills and silence are purchased by investors in the arms race; passion is called unscholastic. The questions we might want raised—what is really important? can we live in a different and better way? if we wanted to change society, how would we do it?—are not thought to be questions of a "fruitful, empirical nature," and thus are brushed aside.

Unlike youth in other countries we are used to moral leadership being exercised and moral dimensions being clarified by our elders. But today, for us, not even the liberal and socialist preachments of the past seem adequate to the forms of the present. Consider the old slogans: Capitalism Cannot Reform Itself, United Front Against Fascism, General Strike, All Out on May Day. Or, more recently, No Cooperation with Commies and Fellow Travelers, Ideologies Are Exhausted, Bipartisanship, No Utopias. These are incomplete, and there are few new prophets. It has been said that our liberal and socialist predecessors were plagued by vision without

program, while our own generation is plagued by program without vision. All around us there is astute grasp of method, technique—the committee, the *ad hoc* group, the lobbyist, the hard and soft sell, the make, the projected image—but, if pressed critically, such expertise is incompetent to explain its implicit ideals. It is highly fashionable to identify oneself by old categories, or by naming a respected political figure, or by explaining "how we would vote" on various issues.

Theoretic chaos has replaced the idealistic thinking of old—and, unable to reconstitute theoretic order, men have condemned idealism itself. Doubt has replaced hopefulness, and men act out a defeatism that is labelled realistic. The decline of utopia and hope is in fact one of the defining features of social life today. The reasons are various: The dreams of the older left were perverted by Stalinism and never recreated; the congressional stalemate makes men narrow their view of the possible; the specialization of human activity leaves little room for sweeping thought; the horrors of the twentieth century, symbolized in the gas ovens and concentration camps and atom bombs, have blasted hopefulness. To be idealistic is to be considered apocalyptic, deluded. To have no serious aspirations, on the contrary, is to be "tough-minded."

In suggesting social goals and values, therefore, we are aware of entering a sphere of some disrepute. Perhaps matured by the past, we have no sure formulas, no closed theories—but that does not mean values are beyond discussion and tentative determination. A first task of any social movement is to convince people that the search for orienting theories and the creation of human values is complex but worthwhile. We are aware that to avoid platitudes we must analyze the concrete conditions of social order. But to direct such an analysis we must use the guideposts of basic principles. Our own social values involve conceptions of human beings, human relationships, and social systems.

We regard *men* as infinitely precious and

possessed of unfulfilled capacities for reason, freedom, and love. In affirming these principles we are aware of countering perhaps the dominant conceptions of man in the twentieth century: that he is a thing to be manipulated, and that he is inherently incapable of directing his own affairs. We oppose the depersonalization that reduces human beings to the status of things. If anything, the brutalities of the twentieth century teach that means and ends are intimately related, that vague appeals to "posterity" cannot justify the mutilations of the present. We oppose, too, the doctrine of human incompetence because it rests essentially on the modern fact that men have been "competently" manipulated into incompetence. We see little reason why men cannot meet with increasing skill the complexities and responsibilities of their situation, if society is organized not for minority participation but for majority participation in decision-making.

Men have unrealized potential for self-cultivation, self-direction, self-understanding, and creativity. It is this potential that we regard as crucial and to which we appeal—not to the human potentiality for violence, unreason, and submission to authority. The goal of man and society should be human independence: a concern not with image or popularity but with finding a meaning in life that is personally authentic; a quality of mind not compulsively driven by a sense of powerlessness, nor one which unthinkingly adopts status values, nor one which represses all threats to its habits, but one which has full, spontaneous access to present and past experiences, one which easily unites the fragmented parts of personal history, one which openly faces problems which are troubling and unresolved—one with an intuitive awareness of possibilities, an active sense of curiosity, an ability and willingness to learn.

This kind of independence does not mean egoistic individualism; the object is not to have one's way so much as it is to have a way that is one's own. Nor do we deify man—we merely have faith in his potential. *Human relationships* should involve fra-

ternity and honesty. Human interdependence is contemporary fact; human brotherhood must be willed, however, as a condition of future survival and as the most appropriate form of social relations. Personal links between man and man are needed, especially to go beyond the partial and fragmentary bonds of function that bind men only as worker to worker, employer to employee, teacher to student, American to Russian.

Loneliness, estrangement, isolation describe the vast distance between man and man today. These dominant tendencies cannot be overcome by better personnel management, nor by improved gadgets, but only when a love of man overcomes the idolatrous worship of things by man.

As the individualism we affirm is not egoism, the selflessness we affirm is not self-elimination. On the contrary, we believe in generosity of a kind that imprints one's unique individual qualities in the relation to other men, and to all human activity. Further, to dislike isolation is not to favor the abolition of privacy; the latter differs from isolation in that it occurs or is abolished according to individual will.

. . .

In the last few years, thousands of American students demonstrated that they at least felt the urgency of the times. They moved actively and directly against racial injustices, the threat of war, violations of individual rights of conscience and, less frequently, against economic manipulation. They succeeded in restoring a small measure of controversy to the campuses after the stillness of the McCarthy period. They succeeded, too, in gaining some concessions from the people and institutions they opposed, especially in the fight against racial bigotry.

The significance of these scattered movements lies not in their success or failure in gaining objectives—at least not yet. Nor does the significance lie in the intellectual "competence" or "maturity" of the students involved—as some pedantic elders allege. The significance is in the fact that the students are breaking the crust of apathy and overcoming the inner alienation—facts that remain the defining characteristics of American college life.

If student movements for change are rarities still on the campus scene, what is commonplace there? The real campus, the familiar campus, is a place of private people, engaged in their notorious "inner emigration." It is a place of commitment to business-as-usual, getting ahead, playing it cool. It is a place of mass affirmation of the Twist, but mass reluctance toward the controversial public stance. Rules are accepted as "inevitable," bureaucracy as "just circumstances," irrelevance as "scholarship," selflessness as "martyrdom," politics as "just another way to make people, and an unprofitable one, too."

Almost no students value activity as a citizen. Passive in public, they are hardly more idealistic in arranging their private lives; Gallup concludes they will settle for "low success, and won't risk high failures." There is not much willingness to take risks (not even in business), no setting of dangerous goals, no real conception of personal identity except one manufactured in the image of others, no real urge for personal fulfillment except to be almost as successful as the very successful people. Attention is being paid to social status (the quality of shirt collars, meeting people, getting wives or husbands, making solid contacts for later on); much, too, is paid to academic status (grades, honors, the med school rat-race). But neglected generally is real intellectual status, the personal cultivation of the mind.

. . .

4

The End of Utopia

GRAYSON KIRK

The Great American Dream was once described as a nation where: ". . . the glory of the Present is to make the Future free,—/We love our land for what she is, and what she is to be" (Henry VanDyke, "America For Me"). In this older version of Utopia, troublesome political, social, and economic problems had vanished. The future lay before us, bright and alluring. That dream is today tarnished and discredited. Why are we now so unsure of ourselves? What doubts do we have about our form of government? How has our contact with non-Western people sapped our confidence? What have we learned about the limits of our physical power? How have our domestic problems subtracted from our early optimism?

. . .

Our country has rounded a corner in its history and the road which led to that corner no longer beckons us on ahead with

From commencement address delivered at Columbia University June 3, 1964. Reprinted by permission of the author.

the same legible signposts that guided our fathers. In one sense the American Dream is over. Many of the cherished beliefs of our national youth no longer seem to fit the conditions of life in our time. In consequence, it is fair to say that our people appear to be in a greater state of national confusion than at any time in their peacetime history. The future once seemed to be so sure, so certain and so alluring. Now we appear to be unsure of ourselves, of our course, and of our prospects.

Once we were busy with the physical building of our country. A vast and virgin land had to be peopled, tamed and developed. Because we were safe from the threat of external menace, and because we were proud of the speed with which we had subdued the forces of nature about us, we could be free to indulge ourselves in romantic dreams of our future. Our political system, obviously the best that man had yet devised, was destined to spread throughout the world, to topple monarchs from their thrones and tyrants from their seats of arbitrary power. Our free economic system would bring us affluence, and affluence would bring us happiness and the leisure that would enable us to cultivate all the gentler arts of civilized society. It was to be our destiny, through precept and example, to lead the world into a new and a golden age. And if precept and example did not suffice, there were among us those who were prepared on occasion to contemplate even the use of force to help pull the world after us into Utopia.

But now the glow of this youthful enthusiasm has faded. We have discovered that our form of government is not in every respect ideally suited even to our own present day needs, and that it is not generally regarded as a panacea for other countries in various stages of national political and economic development. We have discovered that the non-Western world is not filled with simple heathen peoples awaiting the Midas touch of our grace, but that, on the contrary, it is a complex of ancient and sophisticated civilizations whose leaders judge us freely, unsparingly and unsentimentally. Further, we have come to realize that our physical power, though the greatest ever possessed by any state in history, cannot in our time assure either our safety at home or the automatic implementation of our national will abroad. And, finally, we have become uncomfortably conscious of the fact that, though our

history is, on balance, a success-story without parallel, we continue to have a multitude of ugly and difficult domestic problems that cause much of the world to look upon us with a judgment that is far from that which we would wish them to have.

In this time of reassessment, and for the sake of perspective if not for comfort, we must be mindful of the fact that we are not alone in our current feeling of national uncertainty. In some countries the process of readjustment to a suddenly diminished international status has been painful and traumatic. In others, where old dreams of independence now have become reality, a host of unplanned problems, responsibilities and dangers have begun to pour out of Pandora's opened box. And even in other states where an avowed fidelity to a romantic dream of world mastery is still unrelinquished, there are signs of the coming of the gray dawn of reality even if there is as yet no assurance that the long day ahead will be sunny and bright. Throughout the earth ours is indeed a new world. It is our task, not only that it shall be brave, but also that it shall be successful.

In this time of confusion and readjustment to a changed world, what is our own national path to the future we need? As always, it is easier to point out the courses we should not take than to determine those we are prepared to adopt. . . .

Where, then, may we turn for hope and promise? How may we find our way out of our time of troubles? It is my judgment that first we must make a renewed and more serious effort to think more about the basic values of our whole society, and to relate to those values the specific problems arising from these changing circumstances of our national life.

Let there be no argument about the need for such a search. All men need ideals by which to live, and a society that is not bound together by widely-shared beliefs and aspirations is a society doomed to destruction. And we now know that mere affluence is no substitute because it is always relative and because once a minimum level of physical comfort is achieved, the further pursuit of material things is not a sufficiently rewarding goal either for the individual or for his society.

This is particularly important if we are to catch the imagination and hold the loyalties of youth, because youth, and particularly youth that has been reared in comparative physical comfort, simply will not settle for such a limited social goal. In one of the most brilliant and perceptive books of the year—and, incidentally, one written by a distinguished United States Foreign Service Officer—the author has one of his characters say, ". . . we've failed to give our young people what they need most. They have all the vitamin B_{12} they can swallow but they're starved for the bread of life. We've put the Holy Grail in the attic with the other Victorian antiques. Our grasp exceeds our reach. . . . Our ideals, wonderful and fundamental as they are, are two hundred, or two thousand, years old and we haven't been able to revive them in a way to stir the blood of our own young people, not to mention young people in the new impatient nations." [1]

The search for common social values must begin in our own back-yard. The age of the thermo-nuclear stale-mate is not conducive either to empire-building or international crusading. Happily enough, it is not possible in a free society to distract popular attention from domestic troubles by directing it to foreign threats or even opportunities. Therefore, as we begin to look at home for the ideals for our society, we must start with a renewed determination to shape and perfect a national community based on the practice as well as the profession of social justice. This does

not, and should not, mean that we should have, in any aspect of our life, an artificial levelling downward merely in order to have a proper norm. It means merely that no artificially imposed barriers should be allowed to restrict the opportunity of each individual to achieve in life the most that his aspirations and his abilities, fully developed and encouraged, lead him to desire. We will not march toward any Utopia if the men in the vanguard are restrained for the fear that they are too far ahead of those struggling in the rear ranks, and we will not march forward unless those in the rear can move up toward the front as freely as they are able.

Next, we must be prepared to adopt a priority of values that will enable us to make better choices in the use of our national income, choices directed not merely toward the more rapid advancement of those in the rear ranks of our march, but choices based on the concentration of effort upon those elements in our national life that will help us to achieve the future civilization that we must have. In the long record of history a nation is remembered, not by its material achievements so much as by its contribution to the flowering and emancipation of the human mind and spirit. The vision of a wealthy society deliberately devoting its life to such goals, once it is making progress toward the achievement of social justice, is one that will catch and hold the imagination of our youth. Thus, by way of illustration the United States must be prepared in the future, as never before in the past, to devote immensely increased portions of its national income to the advancement of education at all levels. Therefrom will flow the attainment of what is genuinely the "Good Society."

. . .

[1] Charles Yost, *The Age of Triumph and Frustration; Modern Dialogues*, New York, 1964, p. 34.

5

Lunch with Three Prospective Bombers

AMITAI ETZIONI

The existing American system is despised most by some young activists who talk casually about "trashing" skyscrapers, bridges, and banks. No clear goals are apparent. Alleged "evils of the system" are used to justify acts of terror and violence, and dynamiting becomes a variant form of finger painting. How do these young radicals differ from the Old Left? What relative emphasis do they give to reason and emotion? How deep is their concern for the welfare of others? Do they have any moral values? What response should people in authority make to such critics and protesters?

Last Sunday I met three would-be bombers, two young men and a young woman whom I'll call Jim, Dick, and Sally. As far as I could tell, they have not participated in any terrorist act nor do they really intend to. Nevertheless, they were full of "hip" talk about "blowing things up," and they professed admiration for the Weathermen's actions.

"If I had my way, I would blow up the bridges and stifle Manhattan," Dick maintained.

Jim showed his expertise: "It would be easy to blow a hole into the T-Z (Tappan Zee Bridge), but it would not stop the traffic for long. On the other hand, it is more difficult to get to the cables of the George Washington Bridge. But if you got to those—you'd bring down the whole thing."

"It's not that difficult," Dick protested, "just four or five feet above the ground."

"Yes," Jim demurred, "but you could work *under* the T-Z and have as much time

as you want, while everyone would see you working on the cable."

I interjected at this point. "What about the people on those bridges?"

"They will be called," Jim explained. "We will tell them they have 15 minutes to get off. We are after the property system, not the people."

"Well," I wondered aloud, "what about the janitor who was overlooked in the Queens Court House, and the young Ph.D. in the lab in Madison?"

Dick countered, in what seemed a compete non sequitur: "And what about all the death in Vietnam?"

Sally thought "that anyhow the bank will be first to be hit, I was afraid to go cash a check on Friday."

The conversation took place on a suburban lawn. The three young people were all under 30 but close to it. Dick is the son of a top executive of a middle-sized Manhattan firm. Jim is the son of a neighbor, a retired commodity broker. Sally is Dick's girlfriend.

A Shared Hatred

Both Dick and Jim come from families that are obviously well off but lead quite

From Amitai Etzioni, "Lunch with 3 Prospective Bombers," The Wall Street Journal, October 27, 1970, p. 10. Reprinted by permission of the publisher.

simple, almost hippie lives. The parents openly share their sons' hatred for "the system" and respond admiringly to most things "the children" come up with. Our hosts, Dick's father and mother, were matching their sons' extremist jargon. "The system is rotten at the core," explained the father in passing.

The youth rebellion is encompassing; it moves beyond politics and fashions in an entire life style. Dick is making films, in the Village, to promote "the cause," an activity that produces little income. Thus, at 28, he is living off his parents, sleeping late, hanging around the house most of the day and staying out late with one girl or another. Jim went to France to avoid the draft after flunking out of two law schools in the United States. He finally received a law degree from some little-known school, and is now studying law in New York City. He, too, lives at home, getting up at noon and studying at night. All three are surprisingly relaxed human beings. Sally's talk is almost slow. Dick and Jim seem as if they have all the time in the world. Sunday's lunch, which started at 2 P.M., stretched into the early evening hours. Large amounts of Sangria, Edam cheese and Spanish sausages with French bread were consumed. I saw no drugs. The youths wore their hair not much longer than Mayor Lindsay has of late. They were clean and sported no love beads. Without their faded jeans they could easily go unnoticed among any bank's clientele.

They may best be characterized as sympathizers, who far outnumber the actual bomb throwers in each revolutionary movement. They *can* be drawn into violent action, especially if they believe that the movement has a fair chance of succeeding in the struggle against the Government. On the other hand, as long as bombers are arrested fairly frequently and receive severe punishments, these sympathizers will stay on their lawns. They will still provide the hard-core terrorists with money, information, occasionally shelter and always with sympathy. They constitute the ocean in which the urban guerrillas swim.

"Doing Your Own Thing"

"What would you achieve by blowing up some banks or bridges?" I asked when coffee was served.

"*Achieve?*" Jim was indignant. "Man, this is an old generation hang-up. Doing your own thing is what counts."

"Yeah," Dick concurred. "Shake it up. Show it up."

Sally surmised, "If people's washing machines would cease to work—power failures, you know—they could not take it, and they would finally rebel."

Here I almost erupted. "What nonsense. Let's forget for the moment the question of whether this country is ripe for, or is in need of, a revolution. What kind of strategy is this? What if you do blow up a few places? What will this amount to, what will it accomplish?"

"You can't tell," Dick replied. "You cannot plan a revolution. Do you think Stalin knew, when he robbed a bank, that it would lead to a revolution? When Lenin studied, did he visualize himself a revolutionary leader? You try things. You blow things up. If this won't work, we will try something else. Anyhow—now it is time to act. We are mad. . . ."

Sally spoke softly, describing her vision. "You get to the banks, which is where their money is. And to the Federal buildings and to the armories and to the bridges. . . . You blow it all up. . . . The people's confidence in their Government will be shaken and its legitimacy will be undermined."

"Oh, come off it," I said, "Blowing up a few windows, ceilings, and floors will have no such consequence."

This response, all three agreed, was mere rationalization—an excuse for passivity.

Upon leaving, it was clear to me that these youngsters, brought up in an ultra-permissive home, were rather different from the disciplined die-hards in the Old Left who spouted Marxist dogma in response to any or all questions. These youths in the New Left were apparently without a systematic ideology and lacked an overall strategy. They responded emotionally and instinctively to a few "cue" words, rhetoric that has more psychoanalytic connotations than political ones.

A Selfish Philosophy

To the extent that their philosophy emerged from this encounter, it appeared to be a selfish, indulgent one. There seems to be a willingness to approve of, if not to actually engage in, acts of violence without a clear sense of social purpose or consequence. All as if terror were a mere act of self-expression and spontaneity; planting dynamite, a form of finger painting. Societal processes go unrecognized in what is surely the most individualistic revolutionary talk since anarchism. Ultra-progressive education, hip talk and the use of mind-expanding drugs seem to have left these three unable to carry an argument to its logical conclusion. Moral considerations are brushed aside by pointing to the "evils of the system."

I wish I could conclude by saying that this or that course of action—changing our curricula in schools, subscribing to the latest edition of Spock (which is much less permissive than the earlier ones), hiring more policemen—would help these infantile would-be terrorists to grow up and face the social and moral consequences of the "ego-trips" they endorse so willingly. Granted, our educational system, child rearing practices, and social system and crime prevention techniques all are in need of extensive reform, but this will take time.

Meanwhile, many thousands of youngsters like Jim, Dick and Sally will be with us. One day their parents will cease to finance their games, and responsibility will set in. Then, perhaps, they will tire of playing revolutionaries. For the time being, however, the most we can do, I am afraid, is to make it as clear as possible to these would-be bombers that dynamite theatrics are utterly unimpressive modes of self expression and are of no societal consequence.

6

The Malaise of the American Spirit

Andrew Hacker

It has been said that no person is concerned with his health until he is seriously ill. In parallel fashion, so goes the argument, our current concern with the quality of American life is the strongest evidence that we are in deep trouble. While we talk bravely of national purpose, the subordination of material to spiritual goals, and a forthcoming American Utopia, we have actually become hedonistic people, preoccupied with personal pleasures. This, at least, is the conclusion of distinguished political philosopher Andrew Hacker.

Why does Hacker call our time "the end of the American era?" What does he believe is the basic characteristic of good citizenship? What evidence does he present to show that we have lost it? Why does he believe that we will regard each other as enemies, rather than as fellow citizens? Does he see any hope for reversal of present trends?

The malaise of the American spirit cannot be blamed on wrongheaded policies, inept administrations, or even an inability to understand the dimensions of our current discontents. The reasons are more fundamental—I would say historical—arising from the kind of people we have become. I have called our time "the end of the American era" because as individuals we no longer possess the qualities upon which citizenship depends. To be specific: we cannot bring ourselves to make the personal sacrifices required to sustain domestic order or international authority.

We have, in short, become a loose aggregation of private persons who give higher priority to our personal pleasures than to collective endeavors. Americans no longer display that spirit which transforms a people into a citizenry and turns territory into

From Andrew Hacker, "We Will Meet as Enemies," Newsweek, July 6, 1970, pp. 24–25. Copyright © 1970 by Newsweek, Inc. Reprinted by permission of the publisher.

a nation. There eventually arrives a time when a preoccupation with self-centered concerns deflects a population from public obligations, when a willingness to be governed stands less in evidence. We have reached that time.

Current anxieties over our Asian involvement are only symptomatic. Even so, they reveal a good deal about our character. Let me remark upon a few aspects of our behavior connected with this venture.

While it may not be a role many of us desire, most nations have achieved greatness through their military conquests. But such success calls for citizens who are willing to die without questioning the mission in which they are enlisted. However, only a diminishing minority of Americans —and particularly young Americans—still possess the purblind patriotism which induces soldiers to take the risks which produce battlefield results. To be sure, Vietnam has witnessed instances of American valor. Yet my reading of the rosters of medal winners shows them most usually to be small-town boys—again a dwindling segment of our total population. It should be clear by now that the average Viet Cong is a braver fighting man, readier to battle to the end for a purpose he holds dear. And the Viet Cong, or others like them, will be our enemies for many years to come.

Whole classes of Americans have taken every opportunity to avoid active service, not excluding campus conservatives who stretch out their deferrals and non-college youths who join the National Guard. While in some part this avoidance may stem from disapproval of the war, it also derives from a widespread unwillingness to forgo the comforts of civilian life. In short, more and more Americans are turning too sybaritic to be good soldiers. Nor is it realistic to suppose that at some future time they will suspend their sophistication and rally to the recruiting stations. (How many Americans would actually volunteer to fight for Israel's survival or South Africa's blacks, let alone for Thailand and the Philippines?)

But even if we pull out of Southeast Asia—an unlikely eventuality—I see no prospect of our mobilizing resources for domestic reconstruction. We will continue to maintain an expensive military establishment, if only to gird ourselves for future Vietnams. (We may well be sending troops into Northeast Brazil before this decade is over.) So long as we feel we have a responsibility to police the world, or believe that every foreign flare-up endangers our security, further overseas expeditions cannot be ruled out.

Moreover, were we to reduce military outlays, the traditional American antipathy to taxes would create pressure for cutting public expenditures—so we can catch up with our purchases of snowmobiles, swimming pools, second homes and similar artifacts of indulgence. As John Kenneth Galbraith pointed out long ago, we measure prosperity by the expansiveness of our private purchases. I may *know* that the several hundred dollars I spent on eating out ought to be levied for social rehabilitation. But neither I nor anyone I know

has written his congressman asking that his taxes be raised by an appreciable margin.

For my own part, I am wary of historical analogies. The last time I read Oswald Spengler was twenty years ago, and I was never able to get all the way through Arnold Toynbee. The image of civilizations as cyclical may make sense to Europeans, but my mentality is too American to see history so schematically. Nevertheless I do believe that every nation has a history, a process most vividly reflected in the character of its inhabitants at any point in time.

Some writers have replied that Great Britain lost most of America in a colonial war and then went on to a century of industrial and international splendor: or that Russia suffered ignoble defeat from Japan and then Germany, yet proceeded to raise itself as a new society. But despite those setbacks, the British and Russian populations at that time consisted chiefly of peasants and proletarians willing to enlist themselves in a national endeavor. Americans are past that point. Thus when I speak of the decline of America's spirit, I refer principally to the changes which have occurred in us as individuals. My life is far more pleasant and much more interesting than that my grandparents knew. But these opportunities for enjoyment have undermined my ability to be the kind of citizen my grandfather could be.

James Reston recently remarked, "I have never known a time when we have faced the basic problems of the human condition so frontally." To this I would add that an awareness of problems need not lead to their solution. Indeed, too much comprehension can have the opposite effect. More and more of us are now part-time sociologists: we have no difficulty in dilating on all manner of crises ranging from poverty and civil liberties to pollution and violent crime. Whether in conferences, committee meetings, or cocktail parties, we talk endlessly about fatherless families, generation gaps, sexual inadequacy, bad architecture, racial intolerance, subjugated women, bureaucratic bungling, the need for community and the demise of the American spirit. We are literate, knowledgeable, and as correct as any society has ever been in its assessment of its dislocations.

Yet as one who might have contributed to this understanding—I have taught college students for fifteen years—I realize that sociological sophistication seldom prompts individuals to eschew personal pleasures so as to make society a better place. I am not unaware of the young law graduates working in poverty storefronts instead of Wall Street. They have my total respect, and I only wish that more young people would take jobs as prison guards or nurses in mental or municipal hospitals. Yet I am not persuaded that these terms of altruistic enlistment add up to a new trend. I wonder what this new generation will be doing ten years from now. Will the enthusiasts currently teaching in Bedford-Stuyvesant send their own children into those classrooms?

I foresee the rest of this century as a dangerous time, during which we will continue in our accustomed ways. We will claim to want new styles of leadership, overlooking our own inability to serve as followers in any but the most marginal of ways. I expect that I will enjoy myself as a consumer and a private person. But once we walk out of our own doors we will suffer increasing discomforts. In part these will consist of physical inconveniences such as congested highways and airports, silent telephones and absence of electricity, a polluted atmosphere and a brutalized landscape. But the greater irritant will be from fellow citizens of classes, races, ages and sexes different from our own, whose demands for new rights and expanded recognition will threaten our own security and self-esteem.

We can no longer be a single nation, possessed of a common spirit. Neither "class struggle" nor "civil war" entirely describes the contours of this discord. Suffice it to say that increasingly we will encounter one another as enemies, that as individuals we stand more vulnerable to the abrasions we effect on each other. Some of us will flee, to further suburbs and hoped-for havens. Others will literally fight, in the streets or through subterranean subversion. And many more will see their morale shattered, their confidence destroyed, their anxieties deepening.

Still, I do not regard this as a "gloomy" assessment, or a "pessimistic" prognosis—labels most reviewers have affixed to my ideas. Terms such as these only obscure the issues. I write as a student of America's history, of its people, of its contemporary condition. The only service I can provide is to indicate how we have arrived at our current perplexities, and why the options open to us are so narrowly limited.

7

Can We Preserve the American Spirit?

JAMES A. MICHENER

In a volume largely dedicated to America's problems, it is perhaps appropriate to end on a note of hope. James Michener is no blind optimist, but he does find that the world still sees us as a symbol of opportunity. How do you explain the strange mixture of criticism and faith that America evokes from foreign observers? How have we blended change and stability? Does he believe that we have solved the problem of national decline? What does Michener believe that our central problem will be in the next thirty years?

It is appropriate in the opening weeks of this decade which will witness the two hundredth birthday of our nation for us to take stock of where we are and where we are likely to go. It is especially fit that those who live in the Philadelphia area do this, because it was in our city that the foundations of the nation were cast into permanent form.

I am not sure that I am the man best suited to attempt this task. I have thought a good deal about our society, but I am not a philosopher. I have written a good deal of history, but I am not an historian. In the past I taught sociology, but I am not a sociologist, and although I love politics, I cannot be considered a political theorist.

But I have had one set of experiences which do partly qualify me for this task: I have worked abroad and have thus had an opportunity to see the United States from a distance, to see it whole, to see it through the eyes of others, to judge its true position in the world today. In looking at my homeland from abroad I have been struck by

two contradictory facts. First, foreigners have kept me well informed on every facet of our life that is wrong. Envious critics in Europe and Asia overlook no chance to denigrate America. Newspapers eager to sell a few more copies delight in parading our weaknesses and our follies, while the intellectual leaders of all foreign nations find joy in lambasting us. Live in London, Tokyo, Rome and Madrid if you want to know everything that is wrong with the United States.

However, in spite of this constant adverse barrage, if our nation were suddenly to drop all immigration barriers, we would see from those countries which criticize us most severely an exodus of people hungry for a new life in the United States. I have never worked in any foreign nation without being approached by some of its citizens who were trying to get to America. They have told me their reasons for wanting to come.

"In your country a man has a chance to get ahead. Children get a free education. With the same amount of work you live better." And always, voiced in a dozen different ways, there is the hope, "In America I could be free." Among the intellectuals there is an added reason, which has become increasingly important: "In America you're trying to do new things. A man with ideas has laboratories to work in and superiors who will listen."

As a result of this whiplash between criticism and love I have concluded that America is a nation with many flaws which only the stupid would deny, but with hopes so vast that only the cowardly would refuse to acknowledge them. We are not much different, therefore, from the great nations of the past; we have enormous opportunities to accomplish good, yet we contain within ourselves the seeds of our own destruction.

I am impressed by one fact as our nation ends its first two hundred years. We now have the oldest continuing form of government on earth. In the last two centuries every other nation has had to revise its form of government, most of them radically. China, oldest among the continuing nations, has experienced change of the most violent sort. Russia, one of the most powerful, has undergone total upheaval. Spain, France, Turkey . . . all the others have tried one form of government after another, seeking the stability which we miraculously attained.

The four nations which might seem exceptions to this theory are Great Britain, Switzerland, Sweden and Thailand, but upon inspection they are not. Since we started our history as a constitutional democracy in 1789, Switzerland has been forced to change its basic law several times, often to a radical degree. Sweden and Thailand have shifted enormously in their attitudes toward their kings, and even stolid, stable Britain has changed from strong kingly privileges to weak, and from a powerful House of Lords to one which serves principally as a cautionary figurehead.

Therefore, when I look at my country, I see the oldest continuing system of government and I take pride in the fact that we have founded a stable system while so many other nations did not. I think of the United States as a rather old nation, experienced, tested, so I tend to be preoccu-pied with the problems that overtake successful and established nations. I find no sense in theories which refer to us as a young nation, for among the family of nations we are the oldest brother.

. . .

. . . [W]e have struggled along like most nations, enduring the tragedy of civil war, experiencing a great depression and surrendering many of our illusions. We have also had periods of notable vitality and accomplishment. I suppose we will continue in that alternating pattern for the next two or even three hundred years, after which we will slow down and quietly break up into new patterns, as every major nation on earth before us has done. I find this prospect no more disturbing than a typhoon in the Western Pacific; no sailor in his right mind would seek out a typhoon, but nature does produce them and the gallant seaman does his best if caught up in one. No nation would willingly repeat the paths of Greece and Rome and Spain and the British Empire, but those are the paths that nature provides for nations, and escape is probably impossible.

We are immediately concerned, however, with what the quality of American life is likely to be in the remaining years of this century. In making our educated guesses, two constants must be kept in mind. They lie at the base of everything I have to say. They limit our choice, make decisions imperative and determine to a large extent the kind of life we shall enjoy.

The first is change. Practically everything we know today will change. Points of reference will fluctuate; values will alter; capacities will be modified and opportunities will be so magnified as to terrify the cautious and delight the adventurous. It is obvious that science stands at the threshold of fantastic accomplishments, each of which will require new mental adjustments; but almost all other aspects of life also stand at the edge of change. In religion the changes in the last decade are probably greater than any made in a comparable space of time since the Reformation.

Changes in morals have stupefied us and will continue to do so. Changes in the things we eat and wear and take to cure our illnesses will speed up rather than diminish. The ways we do business will alter so rapidly that those who do not grow with them will simply stop functioning, as several businesses which dominated the Philadelphia scene when I was a boy have already vanished.

Of course, amidst this accelerated change, the fundamentals of human living will continue. People will experience hunger, they will be stormily attracted to the opposite sex, they will have ambitions and fears, and in the end they will die of the same causes that men have always died of. These permanent things are always in the mind of the novelist, but I shall not comment upon them further.

The second limiting constant is the steady increase in population. More people will crowd into our cities than did so in the past, and everything we try to do will be dominated by this one compelling fact. In the body of this essay I shall mention six areas of concern . . . the city, race, education, youth, communications, and the environment . . . and in each our options will be limited by the huge numbers of people who will be involved.

Our problem is this: how can a vastly increased population, with no more living space than we had seventy years ago, find a satisfactory pattern of life in a society dominated by accelerating change?